Financial Institutions, Investments, and Management

An Introduction

SEVENTH EDITION

FINANCIAL INSTITUTIONS, INVESTMENTS, AND MANAGEMENT

An Introduction

SEVENTH EDITION

Herbert B. Mayo
The College of New Jersey

HARCOURT COLLEGE PUBLISHERS

Fort Worth Philadelphia San Diego New York Orlando Austin San Antonio
Toronto Montreal London Sydney Tokyo

Publisher	Mike Roche
Executive Editor	Mike Reynolds
Market Strategist	Charlie Watson
Developmental Editor	Kim Bartman
Project Editor	Jim Patterson
Art Director	Susan Journey
Production Manager	James McDonald

ISBN: 0-03-031298-1
Library of Congress Catalog Card Number: 00-100123

Address for Domestic Orders
Harcourt, Inc., 6277 Sea Harbor Drive, Orlando, FL 32887-6777
800-782-4479

Address for International Orders
International Customer Service
Harcourt, Inc., 6277 Sea Harbor Drive, Orlando, FL 32887-6777
407-345-3800
(fax) 407-345-4060
(e-mail) hbintl@harcourtbrace.com

Address for Editorial Correspondence
Harcourt College Publishers, 301 Commerce Street, Suite 3700, Fort Worth, TX 76102

Web Site Address
http://www.harcourtcollege.com

Printed in the United States of America

0 1 2 3 4 5 6 7 8 9 039 9 8 7 6 5 4 3 2

Harcourt College Publishers

For special friends:

C.E.M.N.R.S.S.T.T. and T.

The Harcourt Series in Finance

Amling and Droms
Investment Fundamentals

Berry and Young
Managing Investments: A Case Approach

Besley and Brigham
Essentials of Managerial Finance
Twelfth Edition

Besley and Brigham
Principles of Finance

Boone, Kurtz, and Hearth
Planning Your Financial Future
Second Edition

Brigham
Financial Management: Case & Models

Brigham, Gapenski, and Ehrhardt
Financial Management: Theory and Practice
Ninth Edition

Brigham, Gapenski, and Daves
Intermediate Financial Management
Sixth Edition

Brigham and Houston
Fundamentals of Financial Management
Ninth Edition

Brigham and Klein
2001 Cases in Financial Management: Dryden Request

Brigham and Houston
Fundamentals of Financial Management: Concise Second Edition

Chance
An Introduction to Derivatives and Risk Management
Fifth Edition

Clark, Gerlach, and Olson
Restructuring Corporate America

Conroy
Finance Interactive

Cooley
Advances in Business Financial Management: A Collection of Readings
Second Edition

Dickerson, Campsey, and Brigham
Introduction to Financial Management
Fourth Edition

Eaker, Fabozzi, and Grant
International Corporate Finance

Gardner, Mills, and Cooperman
Managing Financial Institutions: An Asset/Liability Approach
Fourth Edition

Gitman and Joehnk
Personal Financial Planning
Eighth Edition

Greenbaum and Thakor
Contemporary Financial Intermediation

Hall
Effective Use of a Financial Calculator

Hayes and Meerschwam
Financial Institutions: Contemporary Cases in the Financial Services Industry

Hearth and Zaima
Contemporary Investments: Security and Portfolio Analysis
Third Edition

Hirschey
Investment Analysis and Management

Johnson
Issues and Readings in Managerial Finance
Fourth Edition

Kidwell, Peterson, and Blackwell
Financial Institutions, Markets, and Money
Seventh Edition

Koch and MacDonald
Bank Management
Fourth Edition

Leahigh
Pocket Guide to Finance

Maness and Zietlow
Short-Term Financial Management

Mayes and Shank
Financial Analysis with Lotus 1-2-3 for Windows

Mayes and Shank
Financial Analysis with Microsoft Excel
Second Edition

Mayo
Financial Institutions, Investments, and Management: An Introduction
Seventh Edition

Mayo
Investments: An Introduction
Sixth Edition

Osteryoung, Newman, and Davies
Small Firm Finance: An Entrepreneurial Analysis

Reilly and Brown
Investment Analysis and Portfolio Management
Sixth Edition

Reilly and Norton
Investments
Fifth Edition

Sandburg
Discovering Your Finance Career

Seitz and Ellison
Capital Budgeting and Long-Term Financing Decisions
Third Edition

Siegel and Siegel
Futures Markets

Smith and Spudeck
Interest Rates: Principles and Applications

Stickney and Brown
Financial Reporting and Statement Analysis: A Strategic Perspective
Fourth Edition

PREFACE

When I was an undergraduate, I had no real conception of how I might spend my life. I sampled a variety of subjects that provided me with breadth (if not depth) of knowledge along with a better understanding of my likes and dislikes and my strengths and abilities.

Many students follow a similar pattern. Introductory courses and textbooks thus play an important role in the development of students by introducing them to disciplines about which they may have virtually no awareness.

Even within a specific area of study such as business administration, many students receive only a brief exposure to particular fields. An accounting or finance major may take just one course in marketing. Conversely, a marketing major may take only one course in finance. It is for these students that this textbook is written as it introduces the three important facets of finance: financial institutions, investments, and corporate finance. Since many students will have only this exposure to the subject, this textbook gives them a working knowledge of the terms, environment, and mechanics of finance and financial decision making.

Besides introducing the finance student to the broad field of finance, a secondary purpose is to encourage the non-finance major to do more work in the field. Survey and intro courses offer the instructor an excellent opportunity to encourage students to continue studying in that area. To facilitate this advanced study, students need sufficient background in the field, and by exposing students to all major facets of finance, this textbook lays that foundation.

Changes from the Previous Edition

Over the various editions, this text grew as reviewers and users suggested additions but virtually never subtractions. In the previous edition, the publisher suggested I address the increasing length of the book. The result was to delete some topics, streamline other material, and reorganize the order. One suggestion that virtually every reviewer thought was a good idea was to place three chapters devoted to specific tools of finance (time value of money, analysis of financial statements, and risk and its measurement) at the beginning of the text. Under this strategy, the tools could be taught independently of the order in which the instructor covered the subsequent chapters.

While this order seemed good in theory, some instructors found that it did not work well in practice. This finding led me to return to the original order in which the chapters that cover specific financial tools are placed close to where they will be used. Thus, the analysis of financial statements immediately follows the material on common stock valuation, and time value and risk immediately precede the chapters on bonds and stocks.

As a result of the reorganization, this edition has three divisions while the previous edition had four. Part I (Chapters 2 through 6) is devoted to financial institutions and covers the creation of financial assets, their subsequent trading in secondary markets, and the impact of monetary and fiscal policy on financial markets. Part II (Chapters 7 through 14) covers investments and encompasses the time value of money, risk, stocks, bonds, and derivatives. Part II ends with investment companies. Part III (Chapters 15 through 22) is devoted to managerial finance and covers the management of short- and long-term investments, their financing, forecasting, bankruptcy, mergers, and divestitures.

Other changes to this edition include topic coverage, content, and pedagogy. Perhaps the most obvious change is the addition of Internet addresses that are provided as sources of information. The inclusion of these sources has led me to delete the selected readings at the end of each chapter. To the extent that these readings are retained, they appear in applicable footnotes.

The Web addresses include government agencies (e.g., the IRS), financial institutions (e.g., the New York Stock Exchange), advisory and data services, and publicly held stocks. While addresses have been checked for accuracy, they do change. Some of the advisory services are fee based, but many offer complimentary information. In some cases, the information was initially free, but after a "teaser" period, the providers now charge for their information. Since I cannot know which information will continue to be complimentary, no attempt was made to differentiate sources on the basis of cost.

Changes to Individual Chapters

Chapter 1 (Introduction to Finance) includes a more comprehensive introduction to specific concepts (such as sources of funds, risk, return, and valuation) that permeate the entire text. A section that relates finance to other business disciplines has been added.

Chapters 2 and 3 (The Creation of Financial Assets and Financial Intermediaries) have been tightened and the material on different money market instruments has been clarified. Chapter 4 (The Federal Reserve and the Supply and Cost of Credit) has new material on the federal funds rate as a guide for monetary policy, and on the federal government's surplus and its possible impact on the financial system.

In Chapters 5 and 6 (International Finance and The Role of Security Markets), two sections (managing exchange rate risk and the impact of the margin requirement) have been simplified. New material on stock indexes and efficient markets has been added. The differences among brokers, dealers, and specialists have been clarified.

Chapter 7 (The Time Value of Money) and Chapter 8 (Risk and Its Measurement) have problems that may be solved with the Investment Analysis software. As is explained later in this Preface, this software may be accessed through Harcourt College Publishers' Web pages and used to solve problems in this text. How this software may be applied is illustrated in these chapters on the time value of money and the measurement of risk.

Chapter 11 (Valuation of Stock) covers one of the most vexing topics in finance. The dividend-growth model, which is presented in most finance and investment textbooks, is difficult to apply. In an effort to make valuation more consistent with industry practice, new material on the ratios—price-to-book and price-to-sales—has been added.

In the previous edition, Chapter 12 (Analysis of Financial Statements) employed a hypothetical firm to illustrate ratio analysis. This material has been recast using the financial statements of Pier 1 Imports. Pier 1's financial statements are straightforward, which facilitates the illustrations. The financial statements, however, also illustrate some possible problems with the application of ratios to analyze a firm's financial statements.

Many individuals ultimately delegate investment decisions to the managers of investment companies. Chapter 14 (Investment Companies) has been expanded to include material on investment styles, families of funds, mutual fund returns, factors to consider when selecting a mutual fund, and index funds.

Part III, Corporate Finance, has been reorganized with capital budgeting now being placed before working capital management. The material on break-even analysis has been trimmed and combined in Chapter 16 (Leverage and the Cost of Capital). Since breakeven analysis does not answer the question "Should an investment be made?" and since the cost of capital is necessary to answer that question, placing these topics together leads into capital budgeting. Capital budgeting is split into two chapters. Chapter 17 (Capital Budgeting) covers the basic techniques while Chapter 18 (Capital Budgeting: Extensions and Applications) expands the material by adding the analysis of risk and illustrating the application of capital budgeting techniques.

Chapter 19 (Planning: Forecasting and Budgeting) is devoted to the cash budget and predicting the level of assets and liabilities. The discussion of forecasting techniques, especially regression analysis, has been expanded. After forecasting the firm's need for short-term assets, Chapter 20 (Management of Short-Term Assets) and Chapter 21 (Sources of Short- and Intermediate-Term Funds) cover the management of short-term assets and their financing. The last chapter (Chapter 22: Mergers, Divestitures, and Overview of Finance) has new material on both mergers and divestitures. The text ends with a reiteration of the overview of finance and how it differs from the other functional areas of business.

Pedagogical Features

This textbook is constructed for the beginning student. First, no attempt is made to pad the book with theoretical subtleties and exceptions. Students will have plenty of opportunity to build on this base if they choose to do so in the future. Second, the examples in the textbook are relatively simple, for complex examples are not needed to clarify the points being discussed. The numerical examples employ simple arithmetic, and small numbers are used in these examples. Of course, in the real world a firm will not have sales of $100 or expenses of $80, but this textbook is seeking not to illustrate the complexity of the real word but to clarify a point in finance.

Finance employs many tools and concepts taught in introductory courses in accounting and economics. Knowledge of certain aspects of economics and accounting is desirable if the student is to have a good grasp of basic finance. Even though the student may have had a course or courses in either or both subjects, this textbook reviews material pertinent to finance. Thus, this book may also be used by the student who wants an introduction to finance but who lacks any formal coursework in economics or accounting.

Besides the text material, each chapter has additional aids for the student. Each chapter begins with a set of **learning objectives,** which identify topics to look for and learn as the chapter develops. Each objective is stated using an action verb such as "differentiate" or "define" or "describe." The choice of the verb gives the student an indication as to how the material may be learned. For example, the objective "differentiate systematic and unsystematic risk" directs the student to learn how these sources of risk differ. Without such knowledge, it is difficult to understand why systematic risk is more important from an aggregate view of risk management.

Each chapter includes **review questions** and, where appropriate, **problems.** The questions and problems are straightforward and are designed primarily to review the material. The instructor's manual includes points to consider when answering the questions, as well as solutions to the problems. Similar problems are also provided in the instructor's manual.

Time value of money illustrations and problems permeate this text. The use of interest tables is an excellent means to teach and illustrate time value problems, but many students have financial calculators that perform the calculations. While time value illustrations in the text employ interest tables, financial calculator solutions are placed in the margin. This placement of **Calculator Solutions** avoids breaking the flow of the text material.

There are also interesting points in finance that may not fit neatly into a particular chapter. To include these, I have added boxed **Financial Facts** in the chapters. These boxes may amplify the text material or present new material to supplement the coverage. The tone of the Financial Facts is often lighter than the text and is designed to increase reader interest.

An *Instructor's Manual and Test Bank* is available to instructors who adopt the book. The manual contains teaching guides for questions and problems in the text, as well as true/false and multiple-choice test questions and answers. A set of additional problems and questions can be used for homework assignments or as extra test items. The *Test Bank* is also available in computerized form for IBM PC and Macintosh.

A *Study Guide and Workbook,* which includes chapter outlines and summaries, problem illustrations, and fill-in-the-blank, multiple-choice, and true/false questions, is available for the student.

Computer Solutions: the *Investment Analysis Calculator*

As previously mentioned, time value of money problems are solved in the body of the text using interest tables and in the margin using a financial calculator.

These problems may also be solved using computer programs. (For example, performing time value calculations is part of Microsoft's Excel® package.) You may also use the *Investment Analysis Calculator* to solve time value problems. *Investment Analysis Calculator* is a set of programs designed for my companion text, *Investments: An Introduction*, Sixth Edition, (The Dryden Press, 2000). The software may be accessed through the Harcourt College Publishers Web page: **www.harcourtcollege.com/finance/mayo.**

To access the software, click on Investment Analysis Calculator on the home page, which takes you to the title screen. Clicking on the title screen brings up the main menu, which gives the following table of contents:

Financial Calculator
Statistical Calculator
Portfolio Standard Deviation
Common Stock Valuation
Capital Asset Pricing Model
Rate of Return (Dollar-Weighted)
Rate of Return (Time-Weighted)
Financial Statement Analysis
Bond Valuation and Duration
Yields
Convertible Bond Calculations
Option Valuation
Portfolio Evaluation

The section titled "Financial Calculator" can be used to solve the time value problems.

Several of the sections of the software have subsections (or submenus). (A listing of the table of contents and the submenus is provided in Exhibit 7.4 in the text). Many of the programs in this software can be used to solve financial problems that are illustrated in this text. Where appropriate, the text refers you to the section in the *Investment Analysis Calculator* that applies to the problems in the particular chapter you are reading. The software also permits you to print answers and to export the results to another document. To print, use the print command. To export, highlight what you wish to copy as you would in a Word® document and paste it into your Excel® or Word® document.

Possible Organizations of an Introductory Finance Course

Financial Institutions, Investments, and Management: An Introduction has 22 chapters. Few, if any, instructors will complete all of the chapters during one semester. One major advantage offered by this text is its adaptability to several approaches. If the course is a survey of the field, the instructor can use the material from Part I on financial institutions followed by selected chapters on investments. The investment component may include Chapter 7 on the time value of money; Chapters 10 through 12 on stocks, bonds, and the analysis of financial statements; and Chapter 14 on investment companies. Depending on the amount of available time, the course could end with selected chapters on corporate finance such as capital budgeting and working capital.

An alternative strategy is to approach finance through investments. Since many students have a natural interest in investments, the course may be built around this topic. Additional work on corporate finance can come later in the student's academic career and can build upon the foundation laid by the initial course. This approach would stress all the material in Part II and material from Part I, especially initial public offerings and the Federal Reserve. Selected material from corporate finance such as the management of cash, financial leverage, mergers, or divestitures could be included in a course that stresses investments.

If the course is primarily a corporate finance course, the emphasis will be on Part III with additional chapters (time value, measurement of risk, the different corporate securities, initial public offerings, and the subsequent trading of securities) from Parts I and II. This approach permits the book to be used in a traditional business finance course.

Acknowledgements

A textbook requires the input and assistance of many individuals in addition to its author. Over the years, The Dryden Press has provided thoughtful reviews from individuals who sincerely offer suggestions for improvement. Unfortunately suggestions sometimes are contradictory. Since an author cannot please all of the reviewers at the same time, I trust that individuals who offered advice that was not taken will not be offended.

The following individuals provided valuable suggestions for improving the seventh edition: Don Cox, Appalachian State University; David Durst, University of Akron; Lawrence F. Johnston, University of Colorado–Denver; Amir Tavakkol, Kansas State University; Cathy Ann Tully, Kean University; and Howard Whitney, Franklin University.

At this point in the Preface, it is traditional for the author to thank members of the editorial and production staff for their help in bringing the book to fruition. Over the years I have been spoiled by the staff at Harcourt College Publishers and The Dryden Press. The crew that worked on this edition is no exception. I wish to thank Mike Reynolds, executive editor; Kim Bartman, developmental editor; Charlie Watson, market strategist; James McDonald, production manager; Susan Journey, art director; and Linda Blundell, art and literary rights editor for their efforts and guidance. Jim Patterson, who once again served as project editor, deserves a special thanks for his continued help, support, and efficiency with which he took the manuscript through production to the final book.

I was once asked if I seriously consider comments from readers and reviewers. The answer is unequivocally "Yes!" Individuals reading the text know what is not clear, so I invite all readers to send me your comments, both complimentary and critical. All comments will be appreciated. I may be reached at 85 Linvale Rd, Ringoes, NJ 08551, or mayoher@tcnj.edu.

BRIEF CONTENTS

CONTENTS

Financial Institutions, Investments, and Management

An Introduction

SEVENTH EDITION

CHAPTER 1
Introduction to Finance

"Nothing endures but change."

"Times change and we change with them."

"Princes come and princes go."

These three quotes from Heraclitus, Lothair, and the musical *Kismet* are exceptionally apropos to finance. Yesterday's major success stories may be today's failures. Major financial personalities in the 1980s fell from grace during the 1990s, as was illustrated by Michael Milken. Leading retailers like Federated Department Stores declared bankruptcy. During the 1980s, Leslie Wexler led The Limited from a small operation to one of the most successful and largest retailers, but in the 1990s, The Limited's growth stalled, and the firm lost market share. Other firms and their managers maintained their success. Warren Buffett of Berkshire Hathaway achieved star status for his ability to identify superior stock investments. The result of his investment decisions was to convert a small investment in his company's stock into over $1 million. However, unlike The Limited, Mr. Buffett maintained success and the value of Berkshire Hathaway continued to appreciate.

As these examples suggest, finance studies money and its management, and, like economics, it explores the allocation of resources. The process of money management and resource allocation occurs over time. Firms invest in plant and equipment but the returns are earned in the future. Inventory is purchased in the present and then sold. If the sales are for credit, the accounts receivable are collected over a period of time. An individual investor acquires stocks or bonds and, like the firm's investment in plant and equipment, earns a return in the future. A financial institution, such as a bank, grants a loan in anticipation of earning interest and being repaid the principal. All firms, individual investors, and financial institutions make financial decisions in the present, but the returns from these decisions occur over time—that is, in the future.

Because the future is not known, finance studies the allocation of resources in a world of uncertainty. Of course, future events are anticipated, and these expectations are included in the current analysis that produces financial decisions. Anticipated returns must be sufficient to compensate investors for expected events. But not every possibility that affects returns can be anticipated, and these unexpected events infuse financial decisions with uncertainty and the potential for loss.

THE DIVISIONS OF FINANCE

Finance as a discipline is generally divided into three areas: financial institutions, investments, and business finance. The divisions are somewhat arbitrary, and they certainly overlap. Although any one of the three may be studied alone (and many colleges and universities offer courses devoted to each specific area), they should be viewed as interdependent. Investment decisions and corporate financing decisions are made within the current financial environment and its institutions. And business finance is not independent of investments. For a firm to be able to issue and sell new securities, there must be individuals who are willing to invest in and buy the new securities.

The study of financial institutions, as the name implies, is concerned with the institutional aspects of the discipline, which encompass the creation of financial assets, the markets for trading securities (for example, the New York Stock Exchange), and the regulation of financial markets. Financial assets are created through investment bankers and financial intermediaries, such as commercial banks, savings and loan associations, and life insurance companies. Each of these financial firms transfers the savings of individuals to firms needing funds, and this transfer produces financial assets. Once these financial assets are created, many may subsequently be bought and sold in the secondary markets. These security markets transfer billions of dollars of financial assets among investors ranging from individuals with small amounts to invest to large mutual funds and trust departments in commercial banks and insurance companies.

The study of investments is primarily concerned with the analysis of individual assets and the construction of well-diversified portfolios. Such portfolios will earn the highest return for a given amount of risk. The study of investments encompasses financial planning, specifying the investor's financial goals, analyzing various securities that the individual may acquire, and constructing diversified portfolios. Of course, investment decisions are not made in a vacuum, and the financial environment plays a role in the investment decision process. Certainly taxation, the monetary policy of the Federal Reserve, and the flow of information that publicly held firms are required to provide stockholders can and do affect the decision to buy or sell specific assets.

The study of corporate or business finance emphasizes the role of the financial manager. The financial manager must make certain that the firm can meet its obligations as they come due, determine which are the best sources of financing for the firm, and allocate the firm's resources among competing investment alternatives. The financial manager has a large and demanding job; in a large corporation, this job is performed by a staff that reports to a vice-president of finance. Of course, the management of a small business must also make many of the same decisions, but these individuals have fewer resources to devote to financial management.

Financial managers and investors make similar decisions, although on a different scale. While the individual may have a few thousand dollars to invest, the corporate treasurer may have millions to allocate among competing assets. The financial manager may also make more decisions involving real assets (plant and equipment) than the individual investor, who is primarily concerned with financial assets. Both, however, are affected by the financial environment. The Federal Reserve's monetary policy, the federal government's fiscal policy, the legal requirements for the dissemination of information, and fiduciary responsibilities to creditors and stockholders affect financial decision making. Neither the firm's financial manager nor the individual investor can ignore the potential impact of the financial and legal environment.

While individual investors may work alone for their personal benefit, a firm's financial manager must work within the framework of the business. Marketing and managing decisions can have important implications for the firm's financial well-being. Virtually every business decision has a financial implication, and financial resources are often a major constraint on the firm's nonfinancial personnel. It is certainly desirable for individuals in marketing, human resources, information systems, and planning to understand the basic concepts of finance and the role of the financial manager. Such understanding may lead to better communication, the creation of better data for decision making, and better integration of the various components of the business.

KEY FINANCIAL CONCEPTS

Three crucial concepts appear throughout this text. Although they cannot be fully developed in this introductory chapter, they should be introduced so you are aware of them. The first is the source of finance used by a firm. Firms can acquire assets only if someone puts up the funds. For every dollar that the firm invests, someone must invest that dollar in the firm.

The second concept centers around risk and return. Individuals and firms make investments in order to earn a return, but that return is not certain. All financial decisions involve risk. The third concept is valuation, or what an asset is worth. Because the return earned by an asset occurs in the future, the anticipated cash flow to be generated by the asset must be expressed in the present. That is, the asset must be valued in today's dollars in order to determine whether to make the investment. Because the goal of financial management is usually specified as the maximization of the value of the firm, the valuation of assets is probably individually the most crucial concept covered in this text.

Sources of Finance

Finance is concerned with the management of assets, especially financial assets, and the sources of finance used to acquire the assets. These sources and the assets that a firm owns are often summarized in a financial statement called a **balance sheet.**[1] A balance sheet enumerates at a moment in time what an economic unit, such as a firm, owns, its **assets;** what it owes, its **liabilities;** and the owners' contributions to the firm, the **equity.**

Other economic units, such as a household or a government, may also have a balance sheet that lists what is owned (assets) and what is owed (liabilities). However, since there are no owners, the equity section may be given in a different

BALANCE SHEET
Financial statement that enumerates (as of a point in time) what an economic unit owns and owes and its net worth

ASSETS
Item or property owned by a firm, household, or government and valued in monetary terms

LIABILITIES
What an economic unit owes expressed in monetary terms

EQUITY
Owners' investment in a firm; a firm's book value or net worth

[1] Notice that important terms are in **boldface** and the definitions appear in the margin to facilitate learning. The seven terms and their definitions that appear in this chapter illustrate the presentation. Each reappears in its proper place in the text.

name. For example, the difference between the assets and the liabilities might be referred to as the individual's "net worth," or estate.

Although the construction of financial statements is explained more fully in Chapter 12, the following balance sheet provides an introduction.

Corporation X Balance Sheet as of December 31, 20XX			
ASSETS		**LIABILITIES AND EQUITY**	
Total assets	$100	Liabilities	$40
		Equity	60
	$100		$100

Notice that the economic unit, Corporation X, has $100 in assets. It could not have acquired these assets unless someone (or some other firm) put up the funds. In this example, $40 was lent to the corporation, and the lenders have a legal claim. The equity ($60) represents the funds invested by the owners, who also have a claim on the corporation. The nature of the owners' claim, however, is different because the corporation does not owe them anything. Instead, the owners receive the benefits and bear the risks associated with controlling the corporation.

Both the creditors who have lent funds and the individuals who own the corporation are investors. Both groups are sources of the capital that will subsequently be invested in the corporation's assets. It is important to realize that creditors as well as owners are investors; the difference lies in the nature of their respective claims. The creditors have a legal claim that the borrower must meet; the owners do not have such a claim. The creditors and the owners, however, are both willing to make their respective investments in anticipation of earning a return, and both bear the risk associated with their investments.

A large part of this text is devoted to the sources of finance and their subsequent investment by the firm's financial managers. For example, Chapters 17, 18, and 20 are devoted to the management of current and long-term assets, while Chapters 9, 10, and 21 consider various sources of finance. It is important to understand the interdependence between the firm that uses the funds and the investors who supply the funds. Bonds, for example, are a major source of long-term funds for many corporations, but it should be remembered that individuals buy the bonds that a corporation (or government) issues. The sale of the bonds is a source of finance to the corporation, while the purchase of the bonds is a use of investors' funds. The basic feature of the bonds, however, are the same for both the issuer and the buyer.

Risk and Return

RETURN
What is earned on an investment; the sum of income and capital gains generated by an investment

All investments are made because the individual or management anticipates earning a **return.** Without the expectation of a return, an asset would not be acquired. While assets may generate this return in different ways, the sources of return are the income generated and/or price appreciation. For example, one individual may buy stock in anticipation of dividend income and/or capital gains (price appreciation). Another individual may place funds in a savings account because he or she expects to earn interest income. The financial manager of a firm may invest in equipment in anticipation that the equipment will generate cash flow and profits. A real estate investor may acquire land to develop it and sell the properties at an anticipated higher price. And the financial manager of a nonprofit institution may acquire short-term securities issued by the federal government in anticipation of the interest earned.

In each case, the investment is made in anticipation of a return in the future. However, the expected return may not be attained. That is the element of risk. **Risk** is the *uncertainty that an expected return may not be achieved.* All investments involve some element of risk. Even the funds deposited in a federally insured savings account are at risk if the rate of inflation exceeds the interest rate earned. In that case, the investor sustains a loss of purchasing power. The individual certainly would not have made that investment if such a loss had been anticipated; instead, an alternative course of action would have been selected.

RISK
Possibility of loss; the uncertainty that the anticipated return will not be achieved

Although the word *risk* generally has a negative connotation, it should be noted that the uncertainty of achieving the expected return may be positive. The asset may earn a return that exceeds the expected return. For example, a person who purchased the stock of Premark when the stock was selling for less than $35 a share, earned a large return when the stock sold for over $51 a share in response to Illinois Tool Works merger offer. A price increase from $35 to $51 (43 percent) must have exceeded most investors' anticipated return.

Because financial decisions are made in the present but the results occur in the future, risk permeates financial decision making. The future is not certain; it is only expected. However, possible sources of risk can be identified, and, to some extent, risk can be managed. One way to manage risk is to construct a portfolio consisting of a variety of assets. When the portfolio is diversified, events that reduce the return on a particular asset increase the return on another. For example, higher oil prices may benefit oil drilling operations but may hurt users of petroleum products. By combining both in the portfolio, the investor reduces the risk associated with investing in either the oil producer or the oil consumer.

Because risk is an integral part of financial decision making, it appears throughout this text. Of course, all investors and financial managers want to earn a return that is commensurate with the amount of risk taken. The relationship between risk and return is illustrated in Figure 1.1, which plots risk on the horizontal axis and return on the vertical axis. While the return is measured as a percent, the figure presents risk on an intuitive basis. Units for the measurement of risk are discussed in Chapter 8.

Figure 1.1 indicates that at a very low level of risk, the expected return is modest. An investor may even be able to achieve a modest return and bear virtually no risk. A federally insured savings account that earns 4 percent annually during a period of stable prices would be an example of a risk-free investment. Such low-risk, low-return assets will be referred to in subsequent chapters as risk-free investments. To earn a higher return, the individual investor or the firm's management

FIGURE 1.1

Relationship between Risk and Return

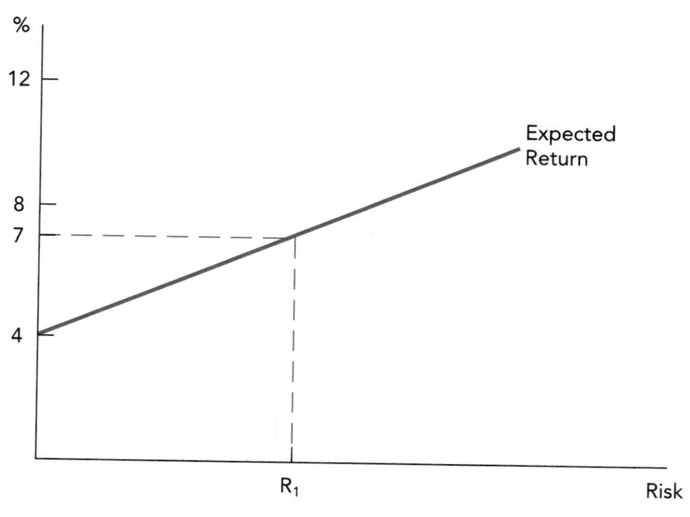

will have to bear additional risk, as indicated by the positively sloped curve showing the trade-off between risk and return in Figure 1.1. Correspondingly, to induce financial managers to bear more risk, such as R_1 units of risk, a higher return must be expected (such as the 7 percent in Figure 1.1).

Valuation

VALUATION
Process of determining what an asset is currently worth

Assets are acquired in the present, but their returns accrue in the future. No individual or firm would purchase an asset unless there was an expected return to compensate for the risk. Since the return is earned in the uncertain future, there has to be a way to express the future in terms of the present. The process of determining what an asset is currently worth is called **valuation.** An asset's value is the present value of the future benefits. For example, the current value of an AT&T bond is the sum of the present value of the expected interest payments and the expected repayment of the principal. The current value of a piece of equipment is the present value of the expected cash flows it will generate. And the current value of a stock is the present value of expected future dividends and the expected sale price.

The determination of present value is one of the most important topics developed in this text. It requires estimates of future cash flows and measurements of what the funds invested in the asset could earn in alternative, competitive investments. The mechanics of determining present value (as well as determining future value) are covered in Chapter 7. Understanding this material is crucial to understanding much of the material covered in this text.

A firm is a combination of many assets and, therefore, its value must be related to the value of the assets it owns. The value of these assets, in turn, depends on the returns they will generate in the future. In finance, the goal of the financial manager is to *maximize the value of the firm.* Schering-Plough even titled one of its annual reports "Maximizing Shareholder Value." All financial decisions are judged by their impact on the value of the firm. These decisions are made in the present, but their results occur in the future. Because the future is uncertain, the financial manager's decisions affect both the profitability of and the risk associated with the firm. The ultimate judgment of those decisions is their impact on the value of the firm. Did the decision increase or reduce the present value of the firm?

This value may be readily measured if the firm has shares of ownership (stock) held by the general public. The market price of the stock is indicative of the value of the company. Because the value of the firm is the sum of the value of its shares, the market value of a share of stock times the number of shares gives the value of the company. For example, as of July 30, 1999, CBS had 711,900,000 shares outstanding. At a price of $43 a share, that made the value of the firm's equity to be $30,611,700.

Although security prices are subject to fluctuations, firms that have consistently grown and prospered have seen the price of the stock, and hence the value of the company, increase. At the beginning of 1986 CBS had 23,440,000 shares outstanding. At the then current price of $115.875, the value of CBS was $2,716,110,000; the value of CBS thus rose over $27 billion from 1986 to 1999. This suggests that management made decisions that increased the value of the company. Over time, the price of a company's stock is indicative of management performance.

Smaller firms or firms whose stock is not owned by the general public—by far the largest number of firms in existence—do not have market prices for their stock. Hence, owners and managers may not be able to ascertain the value of the firm. In these cases, the value is determined only when the firm is liquidated or sold (at that time, the value of the firm is the liquidation value or sale price). Since such liquidation or sale generally occurs only once, the owners and managers do not know the true value of the firm. They may use the value of the firm's equity as shown on the accounting statements as some indication of the firm's worth, but management cannot be certain of the firm's true value.

FINANCE AND OTHER BUSINESS DISCIPLINES

Although finance is a separate academic discipline, its roots are in accounting and economics. Several years ago, the first finance courses tended to emphasize the analysis of financial statements and legal topics, such as the order of claims. Although this emphasis has diminished, accounting principles and financial statements continue to be a major source of information, and the analysis of financial statements is an integral component in the value approach to the selection of securities.

With the development of theories of portfolio behavior and asset valuation, economics began to play a more important role in finance courses. Theories based on economic principles encompassing corporate financial structure, the importance (or unimportance) of dividends, and option valuation became the backbone of finance and, in many cases, supplanted accounting's role. The development of empirical tools further augmented financial analysis, as statistics became a means to verify economic theory as it applies to finance. The ability to test economic and financial hypotheses further enriched the field of finance.

Although finance uses economic theory and accounting principles and financial statements, it has developed its own body of material. Finance courses, however, are generally offered as part of a program in business. Other academic disciplines within business may include information systems, human resource management, and marketing as well as accounting and economics. Finance, however, differs from these areas in one exceedingly important way. It can be studied from two perspectives: that of the users or that of the suppliers of funds.

This ability to approach finance from more than one perspective is important. Consider human resource management or marketing. In both of these disciplines (and in accounting or information systems or strategic planning), the emphasis is on the business. The individual area may have many subdivisions, but the emphasis is how each division fits into the business and its operations. The emphasis is not from an individual's perspective.

Finance may also be studied from a business perspective, which is exactly what occurs in corporate finance or financial management courses. Finance, however, may be studied from the investor's perspective. While corporate finance emphasizes raising funds and their subsequent allocation, investments emphasizes the construction of diversified portfolios and the allocation of wealth among competing securities. Of course, these two perspectives are often opposite sides of the same coin. The firm issues securities (for example, bonds or stock) to raise funds. Investors buy these securities to earn a return and diversify their portfolios. In either case, it is the same security.

The tools of analysis used in corporate finance and investments are also the same. A firm's financial statements are employed by both management and investors to analyze the firm's financial condition. Methods used to value and evaluate an investment in plant and equipment are conceptually the same as those used to value stocks and bonds. The calculations of returns on investments in stocks and bonds are the same as the calculations used to determine the returns on investments in plant, equipment, and other real (tangible) assets. The tax and legal environments and the financial institutions in which securities are initially sold and subsequently traded apply both to businesses and to individuals.

Although finance can have more than one perspective, the material as presented in an introductory finance course often emphasizes one side. Many traditional introductory finance courses stress corporate finance or financial management with a corporate emphasis. This approach makes the course more consistent with other classes taught in a business program. It also facilitates tying together marketing, human resource management, information management, and the various other areas of a business education.

PLAN OF THE TEXT

This text considers both perspectives: investments and business finance. Because both investment and financial management decisions are made within the financial environment, the text also includes the third area of the discipline: financial institutions. Thus the text encompasses the three major divisions of finance: financial institutions, investments, and corporate (or business) finance.

Part 1 is devoted to financial institutions and the environment in which financial decisions are made. Chapter 2 considers the transfer of funds from savers seeking to invest the money to firms in need of external financing. This chapter develops the direct transfer of these savings through investment bankers. Chapter 3 considers the indirect transfer of savings through financial intermediaries, such as commercial banks. The chapter also covers the changing regulatory environment and the blurring of distinctions among the various financial intermediaries. Chapter 4 discusses the multiple expansion in the supply of money and credit with emphasis on the Federal Reserve and monetary and fiscal policy. Chapter 5 covers the international financial system. Part 1 ends with a discussion in Chapter 6 on secondary financial markets, such as the New York Stock Exchange. These security markets transfer previously issued securities between investors seeking to liquidate their positions and other individuals seeking to add to their portfolios. This chapter also covers the mechanics of buying and selling securities and the role of brokerage firms.

Part 2 is devoted to investments and is primarily concerned with the financial assets an individual may include in his or her portfolio. The first two chapters in this section cover two of the most important topics in finance—the time value of money (Chapter 7) and the sources and measurement of risk (Chapter 8).

Most financial decisions involve time. An investment is made today but the return is earned in the future. Standardizing for time is done by expressing the present in terms of the future or the future in terms of the present. This is one of the most difficult financial concepts to grasp, but it is also one of the most crucial. Each student using this text needs to read carefully and understand the material in Chapter 7. Without an understanding of the time value of money, much of what is subsequently covered will have little meaning.

Chapter 8 is devoted to risk and return. Although risk can be understood on an intuitive basis, this chapter examines the sources of risk, the measurement of risk, and the means to manage it. As with the time value of money, the measurement of risk can be a difficult and involved topic. However, Chapter 8 is general and descriptive; there will be plenty of time for you to develop this topic at more depth in advanced courses.

Chapters 9 through 14 are devoted to specific financial assets. Chapters 9 through 11 cover the traditional financial assets that individuals acquire—bonds and stock. Chapter 9 discusses the features and valuation of bonds. Chapter 10 covers equity: preferred stock and common stock. This chapter includes dividends, stock splits, and the rights of stockholders. Chapter 11 is devoted to another crucial concept in finance: the valuation of stock. Chapter 12 considers the analysis of a firm's financial statements. Chapters 13 and 14 discuss several alternatives to investing in stocks and bonds. These alternatives include convertible bonds, futures and options (Chapter 13), and shares in investment companies, including mutual funds (Chapter 14).

Part 3 is devoted to corporate finance from the perspective of the financial manager. Unlike the preceding section in which the emphasis is on the valuation of financial assets and the transfer of existing wealth, corporate finance is concerned with the creation of wealth. Investments in new plant and equipment are made to generate new output (new wealth). However, without financial markets to transfer existing securities, few individuals would acquire stocks and bonds. They would not commit their savings to investments in plant, equipment, or inventory, and the economy would stagnate.

Part 3 begins with a discussion of the corporate form of business, taxation, and depreciation (Chapter 15). Chapter 16 considers leverage and its impact on the firm's cost of capital. Chapters 17 and 18 cover long-term investment decisions in plant and equipment. Chapter 19 discusses techniques used to forecast a firm's financial needs, while Chapters 20 and 21 cover the management of working capital (the firm's short-term assets and liabilities). Chapter 22 covers mergers and divestitures, and the text ends with a brief overview of finance.

THE INTERNET

Many of the questions and problems at the end of the chapters direct you to web pages to obtain information. These assignments and other Internet sources of information are spread throughout this text. (You should, of course, realize that these addresses may change.) While a substantial amount of information can be obtained through the Internet free of charge, some vendors do charge a fee for the material. The websites used in this text generally provide free information. Some fee sites are included because they offer complementary materials. However, there can be no assurance that a free site will not institute a fee in the future.

With the existence of the Internet, you face several problems. First, too much information may be available. A topic such as mutual funds will generate more facts and data than you could possible assimilate. The information problem is compounded because mutual funds are tied to other areas of investments, such as taxation or financial planning. Sorting through the information and putting it into a useful form takes time and patience.

The second problem concerning information received through the Internet is its accuracy. You may not know the provider's motivation! If you access a company's or government agency's web page, the information should be accurate. If you make a general search for information on a company, the data, analysis, and recommendations you find may be inaccurate or even purposefully misleading. There is probably little you (or anyone else) can do to stop the dissemination of inaccurate information through the Internet, but you do not have to act on it. If you limit your search to reliable sources, then the Internet (or any other source of data or advice) can help you make financial decisions.

STOCKS
THE WALL STREET

PART I

FINANCIAL INSTITUTIONS

My bank has assets in excess of $10 billion. My checking account may have $1,000 in it. I account for about 0.0001 percent of my bank's sources of funds. Just think how many depositors my bank must have in order to generate the money it has lent.

I own 500 shares of Textron. At $90 a share, that is $45,000. Although $45,000 is sufficient to buy any of a number of consumer goods, it is a very small fraction of the total value of all Textron shares. The firm has 163,612,000 shares outstanding for a total value of $14,725,080,000. My holdings are obviously a minute portion of the total.

Last year, my family vacationed in Canada. We spent over $3,000 outside the United States, which added to the nation's deficit in its merchandise balance of trade. The amount we spent was small, however, when compared to the federal government's foreign aid programs or military spending abroad, which also contributed to the deficit in the balance of trade.

Hardly a day goes by that I do not have contact with a financial institution. The same is true for most individuals. They write and receive checks, make deposits and withdrawals from depository institutions, buy and sell shares of stock in corporations and mutual funds, make contributions to pension plans, pay taxes, buy imported goods, and borrow funds from a variety of sources. Each of these acts involves contact with a financial institution.

The first part of this text discusses the financial environment and institutions with which we have so much contact. Some of these financial institutions facilitate the transfer of funds from lenders to borrowers (such as commercial banks), while others facilitate the exchange of securities from sellers to buyers (for example, the stock exchanges). Other financial institutions affect the level of income and the stability of consumer prices (such as the Federal Reserve), and yet another financial institution, the market for foreign currency, makes possible the exchange of foreign goods and services. The participants in these markets for financial products and services range from the large corporate giants and the federal government to the small corner store and the individual saver. Everyone reading this text is touched by these financial institutions, and increasing your knowledge of them by learning the material in the next five chapters can help you to better function in today's financial environment.

CHAPTER 2 The Creation of Financial Assets

Learning Objectives

1. Define money, enumerate its functions, and identify the composition of the money supply.
2. Differentiate the roles of money and interest rates.
3. Identify the general relationship between yields and the term of a debt instrument.
4. Illustrate the direct and indirect transfer of funds to business.
5. Distinguish between a financial intermediary and an investment banker.
6. Describe the components of a public sale of new securities.
7. Examine the price volatility of initial public stock offerings.

Polonius, in Shakespeare's *Hamlet*, gives the advice, "Neither a borrower nor a lender be." Fortunately, few individuals follow that advice, for borrowing and lending are crucial components of an advanced economy's financial system. Such an economy could not exist without them. Through borrowing and lending, resources are channeled into productive investments. Consider how firms would be constrained if they could not borrow funds to purchase plant or equipment, or how individuals would be prevented from purchasing homes without borrowing money through mortgage loans.

A sophisticated financial system has evolved to facilitate the transfer of funds from those with money to invest to those in need of funds. Each component plays an important and, in some cases, an indispensable role. These components include a variety of financial intermediaries that stand between the suppliers and users of funds, a mechanism for issuing and selling new securities (for instance, stocks and bonds), and a market for the subsequent sales of existing securities.

Since the deregulation of the banking system and the increase in competition among the various depository institutions, the clear distinction among commercial banks, savings institutions, brokerage firms, insurance companies, and other firms providing customer financial services has diminished. Many firms now offer savers a wide spectrum of choices ranging from traditional saving vehicles to new and sophisticated financial instruments. What has emerged is a type of financial supermarket that offers the customer (both the saver and the borrower) a variety of financial services and instruments.

Deregulation, increased competition, and technological change are also altering the way in which individuals make contact with financial institutions. Many banks offer services to individuals with access to personal computers. You may transfer money from your checking account to your savings account, apply for a loan, and make your mortgage, car, or credit card payments. You can shop for consumer goods, have the goods shipped, and immediately have the payment for the goods debited from your bank account. If this trend continues, you may never have to visit a bank again and many banks will have closed several of their branches and replaced them with automatic teller machines located in various retail establishments.

Although differences among financial firms have diminished, some remain, and the primary role of financial intermediaries and financial markets remains the same. Financial markets transfer funds from individuals, firms, and governments with money to invest to individuals, firms, and governments in need of funds. Explaining this transfer and differentiating among the various firms is the primary thrust of this and the following chapter. This chapter begins with a discussion of the roles of money and interest rates. Next is a discussion of the indirect transfer of funds to businesses through financial intermediaries. The balance of the chapter is devoted to the mechanics of the sale of new securities through investment bankers. The next chapter considers the variety of financial intermediaries, such as commercial banks, and differentiates them from investment banking.

THE ROLE OF MONEY

MONEY
Anything that is generally accepted as a means of payment

Money is anything that is generally accepted in payment for goods and services or for the retirement of debt. This definition has several important words, especially *anything* and *generally accepted.* Anything may perform the role of money, and many different items, including shells, stones, and metals, have served as money. During the history of this country, a variety of coins and paper moneys have been used. In the past, gold coins served as money in the United States, but today this is no longer the case.[1] Coins are presently made of cheaper metals, such as copper. The value of the metallic content of these coins is less than the value of the coin. For example, the value of copper contained in a penny is less than the value of the penny. If the copper in a penny were worth more in other uses than as money, people would melt pennies and remove the copper. Copper pennies would cease to exist as money, and the U.S. Treasury would have to alter the metallic content of the penny.

Because the value of the metal is less than the value of the coin, coins are only "token" money. The extreme case of such token money is paper money, which has virtually no physical value and is convenient to use. Perhaps the most convenient form of money is demand deposits (that is, checking accounts) in depository institutions. These deposits are readily transferred by check and are generally accepted as a means of payment. Actually, the form of money is not important, for the role of money is not determined by its physical content. As long as an item is generally accepted as payment for goods, services, or the retirement of debt, it is money.

[1] The U.S. Treasury still mints limited-edition gold coins for sale to collectors.

The other important words in this definition of money are *generally accepted.* What serves as money in one place may not be money elsewhere. This fact is readily understood by anyone who travels abroad and must convert one currency to another. The paper that serves as money in Great Britain, called pounds, is not used as money in Paris, where European euros are used. A traveler must convert pounds into euros to buy goods in Paris.[2]

Money performs a variety of important roles. It is (1) a medium of exchange and (2) a store of value. It is also (3) a unit of account and (4) a standard of deferred payment. Without money, there would be considerably fewer transactions of goods and services, for such transactions would occur only if two parties could agree on terms for a mutual exchange. Such direct transfer of goods and services is called **barter.** Barter is an inefficient means of transferring goods, and it should be no surprise that money developed as a substitute for bartering. Instead of trading one good for another, individuals sell goods and services for money and then use the money to purchase other goods and services. Money thus facilitates the flow of goods and services. An advanced economy could not exist without something functioning as a medium of exchange, and even less economically developed nations have a form of money to aid in the exchange of goods.

BARTER
Transfer of goods and services without the use of money; the trading of one good for another

Money may also be used to transfer purchasing power to the future. In this second role, money acts as a store of value from one time period to another. Money, however, is only one of many assets that may be used as a store of value. Stocks, bonds, savings accounts, savings bonds, real estate, gold, and collectibles are some of the various assets that savers may use to store value.

All these nonmonetary assets must be converted into money for the saver to exercise the purchasing power that has been stored. The ease with which an asset may be converted into money with little loss of value is called **liquidity.** Money is, of course, the most liquid of all assets. Some assets may not be readily converted into cash, and investing in them may cause the saver to lose a substantial amount of liquidity. For example, antiques may inflate in value but converting them into money may be a time-consuming and costly process. Hence this type of asset may be very illiquid.

LIQUIDITY
Ease of converting an asset into cash without loss

With the exception of interest-bearing checking accounts, money earns nothing for its owner.[3] Other assets provide their owners a flow of income or services. Bonds and savings accounts pay interest; stocks may pay dividends and grow in value; and physical goods, such as an Oriental rug or a painting, provide enjoyment and may appreciate. For money to be attractive as a store of value, its liquidity must offset the advantages offered by other assets.

Money also performs two other functions. It is a unit of account and a standard of deferred payment. The prices of goods are determined in terms of money instead of in terms of each other. For example, an apple costs $0.50 and a bottle

[2] The development of euros and their substitution for local currencies, such as French francs, is discussed in Chapter 5 on international finance.

[3] There is an exception to this general statement. If prices were to fall, money would purchase more goods, in which case holding money generates a positive return, but interest-bearing savings accounts would earn a higher return.

of beer costs $1.00. The price of the apple is not expressed as the price of half a bottle of beer. Both the price of the apple and the price of the beer are expressed in terms of money. Money is also the standard for expressing payments over time. For example, loans that are repaid in the future are defined in terms of money. A mortgage loan may be repaid at the rate of $750 per month for 20 years.

The power to create money is given by the Constitution to the federal government. Congress established a central bank, the Federal Reserve System, and gave it power to control the supply of money and to oversee the commercial banking system. Initially it was not the intent of Congress to create a central bank, for in the Federal Reserve Act of 1913, twelve district banks were established. The Federal Reserve was reorganized by the Banking Acts of 1933 and 1935 to become the central bank known today. The organization of the Federal Reserve and how it controls the supply of money are discussed in Chapter 4. Although the Federal Reserve has control over the supply of money, most of the money supply is produced through the creation of loans by the banking system. (This process of loan creation is explained in Chapter 4.)

Measures of the Supply of Money

MONEY SUPPLY
Total amount of money in circulation

M-1
Sum of coins, currency, and demand deposits

M-2
Sum of coins, currency, demand deposits, savings accounts, and small certificates of deposit

There are several measures of the composition of the **money supply.** The traditional measure (commonly referred to as **M-1**) is the sum of coins and currency in circulation outside of banks plus demand deposits (including NOW accounts and travelers' checks) held by the general public in all depository institutions. A broader definition of the supply of money (commonly referred to as **M-2**) includes not only demand deposits, coins, and currency but also regular savings accounts and small certificates of deposit (less than $100,000).[4] The actual amount of money outstanding depends on which definition is used. In 1999, the Federal Reserve reported that M-1 and M-2 were:

	M-1	M-2
Coin and currency	$ 490.9	$ 490.9
Demand deposits	363.4	363.4
Other checkable deposits (i.e., NOW accounts)*	240.9	240.9
Travelers' checks	8.7	8.7
Savings accounts and time deposits	—	2,557.0
	$1,103.9	$3,660.9

*NOW stands for "negotiable order of withdrawal."

Source: *Summary monetary statistics are available in the* Federal Reserve Bulletin. *Detailed data is available at the Federal Reserve's website* **www.bog.frb.fed.us** *under the section on Research and Data. The above data is "current" as of August 9, 1999, and derived from the website as of October 21, 1999. ("Current" data is often revised as additional information becomes available.)*

[4] Certificates of deposit are discussed in more detail in Chapter 3.

As may be seen in the above data, savings accounts constitute more than 70 percent of the money supply when the broader definition (M-2) is used. This broader definition of the money supply is preferred by those economists and financial analysts who stress the ease with which individuals may transfer funds among the components of M-2. There is virtually no monetary cost or effort for the individual to transfer funds from a savings account or time deposit into a checking account. Such a movement increases M-1, because demand deposits have risen, but the transaction has no impact on M-2, because the increase in demand deposits is offset by the decline in the other account.

Economists study the supply of money because of its impact on the level of national income and employment. These studies emphasize the relationship between the money supply and how changes in the supply of money alter spending (that is, the demand for goods and services). There is, however, disagreement among economists as to which definition, M-1 or M-2, is the better predictor of economic activity.

In summary, money is crucial to an advanced economy, for it facilitates the transfer of goods and resources. An advanced economy could not exist without something to perform the role of money. Since a large proportion of the money supply consists of deposits in various depository institutions, the student of finance should understand the banking system and its regulation. This is a large topic and is covered in detail in the next two chapters. The remainder of this chapter is devoted to a discussion of interest rates and the transfer of funds to business with special emphasis on investment banking.

THE ROLE OF INTEREST RATES

The words *money* and *interest* are often used together, but their meanings differ, and money and interest perform different roles. Money is used as a medium of exchange: its value is related to what it will purchase. The more dollars necessary to purchase something, the less each dollar is worth.

While the value of money depends on what it will purchase, an interest rate is the price of credit. Interest is the price paid for the use of someone else's money, that is, the cost of credit. The use of credit permits the borrower to defer payment until the loan is repaid.

The role of interest rates is to allocate scarce credit. Higher interest rates make credit more expensive and should discourage borrowing. Only those willing and able to pay the higher rate will obtain the funds. Thus, higher interest rates allocate the existing (and scarce) supply of credit among the competing users wanting to borrow the funds.

As is discussed throughout this text, there are many types of loans (such as mortgage loans, consumer credit, and bonds). A list of various types of debt instruments and where they are covered in this text appears in Exhibit 2.1. In addition to many debt instruments, there are also many interest rates that reflect the amount borrowed, the length of time the borrower will have the use of the funds, and the creditworthiness of the borrower. Generally, the longer the term of the

EXHIBIT 2.1

The Variety of Debt Instruments

Debt Instrument	Where Covered
Certificates of deposit (CDs)	Chapter 3
Commercial bank loans	Chapter 21
Commercial paper	Chapter 21
Convertible bonds	Chapter 13
Debentures	Chapter 9
Eurobonds	Chapter 5
Intermediate-term loans	Chapter 21
Leases	Chapter 21
Mortgage loans	Chapter 7
Repurchase agreement (REPO)	Chapter 3
Revolving credit agreement	Chapter 21
Series EE bonds	Chapter 9
Tax-exempt (municipal) bonds	Chapter 9
Trade credit	Chapter 21
Treasury bills	Chapter 3
Variable rate bonds	Chapter 9
Zero coupon bonds	Chapter 9

debt and the riskier (or less creditworthy) the debt instrument, the higher will be the rate of interest.

Debt, and hence interest rates, is often classified as short- or long-term. The time period is arbitrarily established at one year. *Short-term* refers to a year or less. *Long-term* refers to greater than a year. (Debt that matures in one to ten years is sometimes referred to as intermediate term.) Of course, with the passage of time, long-term debt instruments become short-term when they mature within a year.[5]

Financial markets have an analogous classification. The "money market" refers to the market for low-risk, large-denomination debt instruments that mature within a year. The "capital market" refers to securities with a longer term horizon. In the case of a bond or mortgage loan, the term may be 10, 20, or more years. In some cases, such as common stock, the time dimension is indefinite. A corporation may exist for centuries. Many of the nation's banks, such as Citicorp, were started in the 1700s or early 1800s. Industrial firms, such as AT&T, Coca-Cola, and Exxon, commenced operations in the 1800s. These three corporations have been paying cash dividends for over 100 years.

[5] Firms with bonds approaching maturity classify debt maturing within a year as a current liability and separate this debt on their balance sheets from bonds that mature after a year. The latter are classified as long-term liabilities.

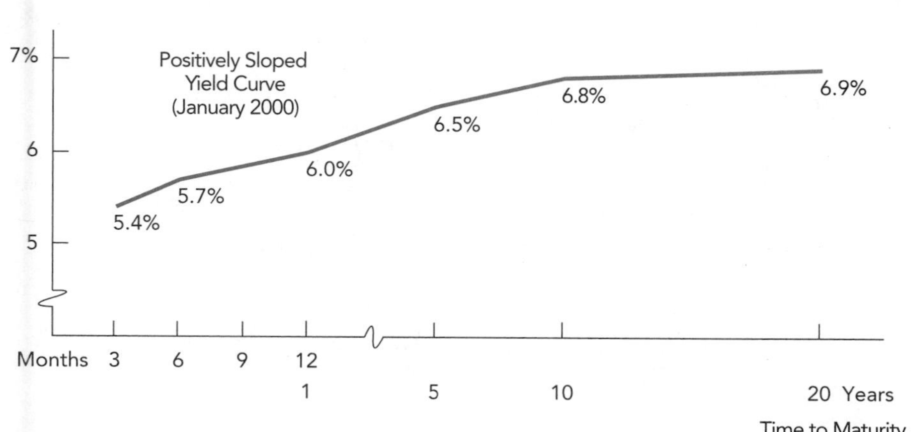

FIGURE 2.1

Positively Sloped Yield Curve

The Term Structure of Interest Rates

The relationship between interest rates (the cost of credit) and the length of time to maturity (the term) for debt in a given risk class is referred to as the **term structure of interest rates.** This structure is illustrated by a **yield curve,** which relates the yield on debt instruments with different terms to maturity. Such a yield curve is illustrated in Figure 2.1, which plots the yield on various United States government securities as of January 2000. This figure shows that the bonds with the longest term to maturity have the highest interest rates. For example, short-term securities with three months to maturity had yields of 5.4 percent, one-year bonds paid 6.0 percent, and bonds that matured after 10 years paid 6.8 percent.

TERM STRUCTURE OF INTEREST RATES
Relationship between yields and the time to maturity for debt with a given level of risk

YIELD CURVE
Graph relating interest rates and the term to maturity

One would expect such a relationship between interest rates and the term to maturity. To induce investors to lend their money for lengthier periods, it is usually necessary to pay them more interest. In addition, the fortunes of the issuer are more difficult to assess for longer time periods. This suggests that long-term investments are riskier, and investors will require additional compensation for bearing the additional risk associated with long-term debt instruments.

Although the positive relationship between time and interest rates illustrated in Figure 2.1 does usually exist, there have been periods when the opposite occurred. During 1981, short-term rates exceeded long-term rates; the yield curve became inverted and had a negative slope. This is illustrated in Figure 2.2. Securities maturing in less than a year had yields exceeding 14 percent, while long-term debt that matured after 10 years yielded 13 percent.

FIGURE 2.2

Yield Curves (Yields on Federal Government Securities)

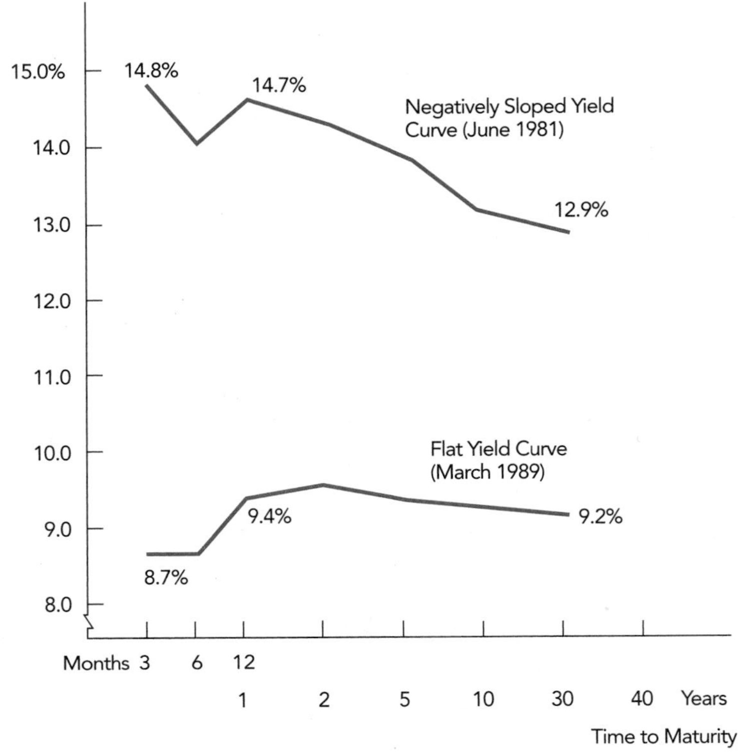

Such a yield curve can be explained by inflation and the action of the Federal Reserve to curb rising prices. As is explained in Chapter 4, the Federal Reserve fights inflation by selling short-term federal government debt securities. Such sales absorb credit by reducing the supply of money and the capacity of banks to lend because paying the Federal Reserve for the securities pulls money out of the banking system.

The sales depress security prices and increase their yields. While the yields on all debt instruments respond to changes in the supply of credit, the Federal Reserve's selling of short-term securities has the most impact on short-term rates. In the illustration in Figure 2.2, short term yields rose above long-term rates, resulting in an inverted yield curve. When the rate of inflation abated, the yield curve returned to the positive slope that it has maintained during most periods.

There have also been periods when the yield curve was relatively flat. Such a structure is also illustrated in Figure 2.2 by the yield curve for March 1989. The yield on short-term debt with three to six months to maturity was approximately 8.7 percent, and the rate on 30-year bonds was 9.2 percent. While the long-term rate did exceed the short-term rate, the small difference produced a gently rising, almost flat, yield curve.

THE TRANSFER OF FUNDS TO BUSINESS

The role of money is to serve as a medium of exchange to simplify the purchase and sale of goods and services. Interest rates help allocate credit among the different potential users of the credit. The role of financial markets is to facilitate the transfer of funds from lenders to borrowers and to ease the exchange of securities among investors. The process of transferring funds from lenders to borrowers creates a spectrum of financial assets. These securities expedite the transfer of savings from those with funds to those who need funds. Savers may include individuals, firms, or governments. Savings represent a command of resources that are currently not being used. Thus a government that has collected tax receipts but has not spent the funds has saved. So has a firm that has earned profits but has not distributed the earnings as dividends. Until the earnings are distributed, the firm has savings.

Those in need of funds may include individuals, firms, and governments. An individual may need funds to purchase a house. The local school board may need funds to build a school, or AT&T may require funds to purchase new equipment. The individual cannot obtain a mortgage to purchase a house, the school board cannot build the school, and AT&T cannot purchase the equipment unless some individual, firm, or government puts up the funds.

All financial assets (such as stocks, bonds, bank deposits, and government bonds) are created to facilitate this transfer. The creation of financial assets and the transfer of funds are crucial for the well-being of every economy. The individual could not obtain the resources to acquire the house, the local government could not build the school, and AT&T could not obtain the new equipment without the transfer of resources. And this transfer could not occur without the creation of financial assets.

The Direct and Indirect Transfers of Funds

Basically, two methods exist for transferring funds to businesses. One is the direct investment of money into businesses by the general public. This occurs when firms issue new securities that are purchased by investors or when individuals invest in partnerships or sole proprietorships. This initial market for securities is referred to as the **primary market** to differentiate it from the secondary market. The **secondary market** refers to subsequent sales of the securities in which one investor transfers the security to another. As is explained in detail later in this chapter and in Chapter 6, secondary markets permit investors to buy and sell *existing* securities. None of the funds transferred by these sales and purchases goes to the firm that issued the securities. The firm receives funds only once when the securities are initially issued and sold in the primary market.

PRIMARY MARKET
Market for the initial sale of securities

SECONDARY MARKET
Market for buying and selling previously issued securities

When a corporation issues a new security (a bond, for example) in the primary market and sells it to the general public, the following transaction occurs:

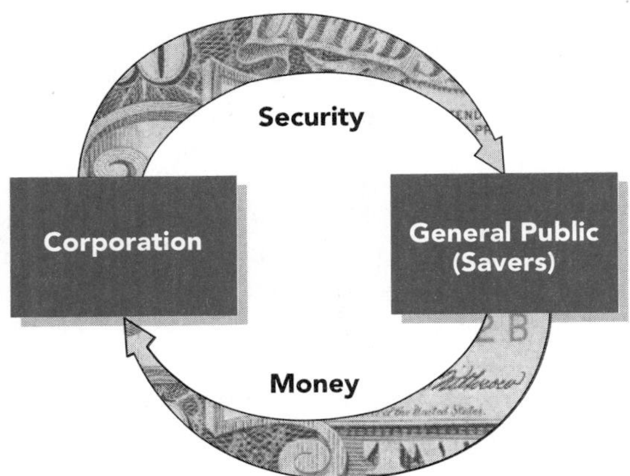

The saver purchases the security with money, thereby trading one asset for another. The firm acquires the funds by issuing the security; there is a direct transfer of money from the saver to the firm.

FINANCIAL INTERMEDIARY
Firm that transfers savings to borrowers by creating claims on itself

The second method for transferring savings to businesses is the indirect transfer through a **financial intermediary.** A financial intermediary transfers funds to firms and other borrowers from savers who currently are not using the money. The intermediary acquires the funds from savers by *issuing a claim on itself,* such as a savings account. The intermediary then lends the funds or buys new securities issued by the economic unit in need of the money. The financial intermediary stands between the ultimate supplier and the ultimate user of the funds. It facilitates the flow of money and credit between the suppliers and the users.

The flow of funds to the financial intermediary is illustrated by the following chart:

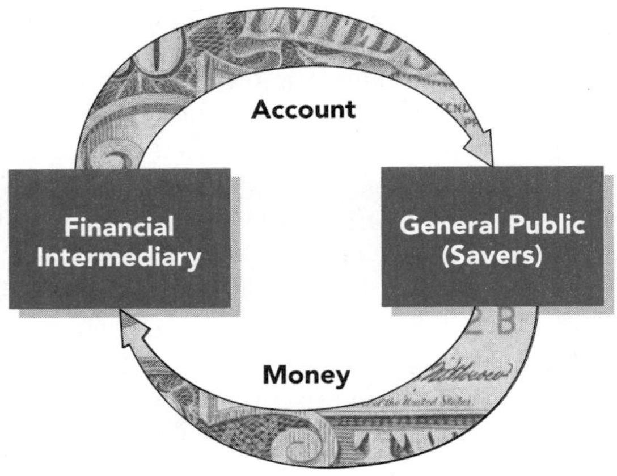

The saver trades one asset (the money) for another (the claim on the financial intermediary), and the financial intermediary acquires the funds by issuing a claim on itself.

The financial intermediary then lends the funds to an entity, such as a firm, government, or household, in need of the funds. That is, the financial intermediary buys a security such as a bond or makes a new loan, and the following transaction occurs:

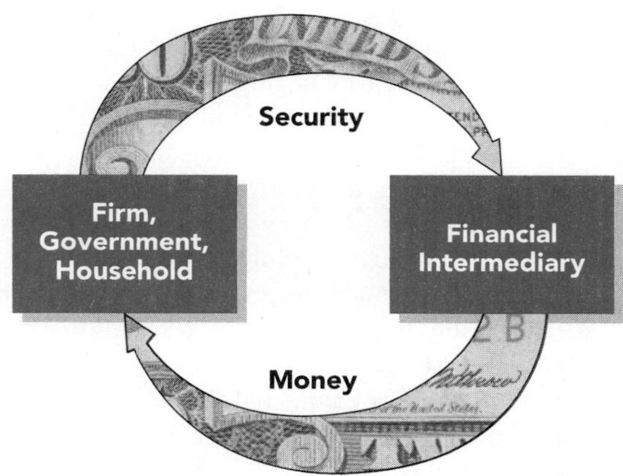

The financial intermediary gives up one asset, the money, to acquire another asset, the claim on the borrower. The borrower acquires the funds by promising to return them in the future and to pay interest while the loan is outstanding.

The preceding charts may be combined to illustrate the process of transferring funds from the ultimate lender (the saver) to the ultimate borrower.

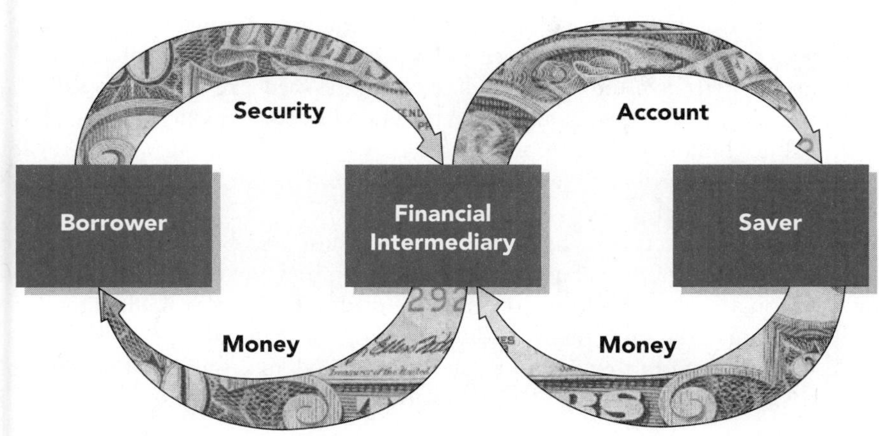

The savers's funds are transferred to the borrower through the financial intermediary. Through this process the borrower is able to acquire the funds because the financial intermediary was able to issue a claim on itself (the account) that the saver would accept.

THE ISSUING AND SELLING OF NEW SECURITIES

As was previously discussed, users of capital obtain funds directly by selling securities to the suppliers of the money or indirectly through the use of financial intermediaries. From the viewpoint of the aggregate economy, the indirect transfer of money from savers to firms through financial intermediaries is more important than the sale of new securities. Most individual households do not invest their savings directly in business. In addition, many firms sell new securities only on an intermittent basis, and many years may elapse between issues. Instead, funds are transferred through the system of financial intermediaries.

There is a large variety of financial intermediaries ranging from local commercial banks to insurance companies to money market mutual funds. The variety of financial intermediaries and their relative importance will be discussed in the next chapter. The remainder of this chapter is devoted to the direct transfer of funds through the issuing and sale of new securities. While the total amount raised by the sale of securities to the general public may be small when compared to the funds raised through financial intermediaries, this direct transfer of funds is important because the securities traded on the stock exchanges came into existence through this process.

It is important to realize that most purchases of securities by households do not transfer savings to businesses. Such transfers occur only once, in the primary market when the securities are issued. Any ensuing sales are between investors (that is, from the seller to the buyer) and not between investors and the issuing firm. These sales are made in secondary markets like the New York Stock Exchange. Secondary markets are an important component of the financial structure and their primary purpose is to transfer securities among investors. Secondary markets permit investors to hold securities for varying amounts of time. An investor does not have to hold the stock of IBM until the firm is liquidated in order to obtain the funds invested in the stock. Instead, the owner of IBM stock sells the stock and transfers the ownership to the buyer. Without secondary markets, individuals would be less willing to purchase securities, and it would be difficult for firms to sell new securities to raise funds directly from investors instead of through financial intermediaries.

Secondary markets, like financial intermediaries, are obviously important to the financial health of the economy. However, the discussion of these markets and how individuals buy and sell securities is deferred until Chapter 6, after the coverage of the material on the initial security sales, the material on financial intermediaries, and factors that affect these financial markets, such as the Federal Reserve System and the flow of funds to and from foreign countries.

The Role of Investment Bankers

A corporation can market its securities directly to the public. For example, Dominion Resources has a dividend reinvestment plan in which cash dividends are used to purchase additional stock. At one time, the company had a stock purchase plan for customers in which they made cash contributions to buy stock with their electricity payments. Dominion Resources has now developed an even more general plan (Dominion Direct Investment) in which anyone may participate to acquire the company's stock.[6] If a firm directly sells shares to the general public, the formal offer to sell these securities must be made by a prospectus, and the securities must be registered with the Securities and Exchange Commission—the SEC. This process of registering the securities and their subsequent sale to the general public is discussed below.

Selling securities directly to the general public involves expenses, so many firms employ **investment bankers** to market new securities. In effect, an investment banker serves as a middleman to channel money from investors to firms that need the capital. If the sale is the first sale of stock to the general public, it is referred to as an **initial public offering,** or **IPO.**

INVESTMENT BANKER
Middleman who brings together investors and firms (and governments) issuing new securities

INITIAL PUBLIC OFFERING (IPO)
First sale of common stock to the general public

Investment banking is an important financial institution, but confusion exists concerning it, part of which may be attributable to the misnomer *investment banker.* An investment banker is not a banker and does not generally invest. Instead, the investment banker is usually a division of a brokerage firm like Merrill Lynch. Although these brokerage firms own securities, they do not necessarily buy and hold the newly issued securities for investment purposes.

Investment bankers perform a middleman function that brings together individuals who have money to invest and firms that need financing. Since brokerage firms have many customers, they are able to sell new securities without the costly search that the individual firm may have to make to sell its own securities. Thus, although the firm in need of financing must pay for the services, it is able to raise external capital at less expense through the investment banker than it could by selling the securities itself.

THE MECHANICS OF UNDERWRITING If a firm needs funds from an external source, it can approach an investment banker to discuss an **underwriting,** which is a guaranteed sale of securities. In an underwriting, the firm that is selling the securities, and not the firm that is issuing the shares, bears the risk associated with the sale. When an investment banker agrees to underwrite a sale of securities, it is agreeing to buy the securities and thus supply the firm with a specified amount of money (that is, it *guarantees* the sale of the securities). If the investment banker is unable to sell the securities to the general public, it must still pay the agreed-on sum to the firm. Failure to sell the securities imposes losses on the underwriter, who must remit funds for securities that have not been sold to the general public.

UNDERWRITING
Purchase of an issue of new securities for subsequent sale by investment bankers; the guaranteeing of the sale of a new issue of securities

[6] Information on the plan may be found at Dominion Resources' website: www.domres.com.

The firm that is in need of financing and the investment banker discuss the amount of funds needed, the type of security to be issued, the price and any special features of the security, and the cost to the firm of issuing the securities. All these factors are negotiated by the firm that is seeking capital and the investment banker. If mutually acceptable terms are reached, the investment banker will be the middleman through which the securities are sold by the firm to the general public.

ORIGINATING HOUSE
Investment banker who makes an agreement to sell a new issue and forms a syndicate to sell the securities

Because an underwriting starts with a particular brokerage firm, which manages the underwriting, that firm is called the **originating house.** The originating house need not be a single firm if the negotiation involves several investment bankers. In this case, several firms can join together to manage the underwriting and the selling of securities to the general public.

SYNDICATE
Selling group formed to market a new issue of securities

The originating house does not usually sell all the securities by itself but forms a **syndicate.** The syndicate is a group of brokerage houses that join together to market a specific sale of securities. Each member of the syndicate is allotted a specified number of the securities and is responsible for their sale.

The use of a syndicate has several advantages. The syndicate has access to more potential buyers for the securities. Also, using a syndicate reduces the number of securities that each brokerage firm must sell. This increase in the number of potential customers and the decrease in the amount that each broker must sell increase the probability that the entire issue of securities will be sold. Thus, syndication makes possible both the sale of a large offering of securities and a reduction in the risk borne by each member of the selling group.

BEST EFFORTS AGREEMENT
Contract with an investment banker for the sale of securities in which the investment banker does not guarantee the sale but does agree to make the best effort to sell the securities

BEST EFFORTS SALE OF SECURITIES The investment bankers may agree to purchase (to underwrite) the entire issue of securities, which guarantees a specified amount of money to the firm that is issuing the securities. The alternative is a **best efforts agreement,** in which the investment bankers make their best efforts to sell the securities but do not guarantee that a specified amount of money will be raised. The risk of the sale is borne by the issuing firm. If the sale fails, the firm does not receive the funds. In an underwriting, the risk of selling the securities is borne by the investment bankers, and most sales of new securities are of this type. The underwriters purchase all the securities, pay the expenses, and bear the risk of selling the securities, with the anticipation of recouping the expenses through the sale. Since they have agreed to purchase the entire issue, the underwriters must pay the firm for all the securities even if the syndicate is unable to sell them.

PRICING A NEW ISSUE Because most sales of new securities are underwritings, the pricing of securities is crucial. If the initial offer price is too high, the syndicate will be unable to sell the securities. When this occurs, the investment bankers have two choices: (1) to maintain the offer price and to hold the securities in inventory until they are sold, or (2) to let the market find a lower price level that will induce investors to purchase the securities. Neither choice benefits the investment bankers.

If the underwriters purchase the securities and hold them in inventory, they either must tie up their own funds, which could be earning a return elsewhere, or must borrow funds to pay for the securities. The investment bankers must pay interest on these borrowed funds. Thus, the decision to support the offer price of the securities prevents the investment bankers from investing their own capital elsewhere or (and this case is the more likely) requires that they borrow the funds. In either case, the profit margin on the underwriting is decreased, and the investment bankers may even experience a loss on the underwriting.

Instead of supporting the price, the underwriters may choose to let the price of the securities fall. The inventory of unsold securities can then be sold at the lower price. The underwriters will not tie up capital or have to borrow money from their sources of credit. If the underwriters make this choice, they force losses on themselves when they sell the securities at less than cost. But they also cause the customers who bought the securities at the initial offer price to lose. The underwriters certainly do not want to inflict losses on these customers, because the underwriters' market for future new security issues will vanish. Therefore, the investment bankers try not to overprice a new issue of securities, for overpricing will ultimately result in their suffering losses.

There is also an incentive to avoid underpricing new securities. If the issue is underpriced, all the securities will readily be sold, and their price will rise because demand will have exceeded supply. The buyers of the securities will be satisfied, for the price of the securities will have increased as a result of the underpricing. The initial purchasers of the securities reap windfall profits, but these profits are really at the expense of the company whose securities were underpriced. If the underwriters had assigned a higher price to the securities, the company would have raised more capital.

Although there are reasons for the underwriters to avoid either underpricing or overpricing, there appears to be a greater incentive to underprice the securities. Studies have found that initial purchases earned higher returns as the buyers were given a price incentive to buy the new offering.[7] Subsequent buyers, however, did not fare as well and any initial underpricing appears to disappear after the original offering. In addition, many initial public offerings subsequently underperform the market during the first years after the original sale.

MARKETING NEW SECURITIES Once the terms of the sale have been agreed on, the managing house issues a preliminary **prospectus** that describes a proposed new issue of securities to be sold to the general public. This information is registered with the **Securities and Exchange Commission (SEC),** which, as is explained in more detail in Chapter 6, is the agency that enforces the federal security laws. **Registration** refers to the disclosure of information concerning the firm, the securities being offered for sale, and the use of the proceeds from the sale.

After the SEC accepts the firm's registration statement, a final prospectus is published. Except for changes that are required by the SEC, the final prospectus is virtually identical to the preliminary prospectus. The information regarding the price of the security, the underwriting fees (or **flotation costs**), and the proceeds

PROSPECTUS
Document filed with the SEC describing a proposed new issue of securities to be sold to the general public

SECURITIES AND EXCHANGE COMMISSION (SEC)
Federal agency that enforces the federal security laws

REGISTRATION
Process by which information concerning an issue of securities to be sold to the public is filed with the SEC

FLOTATION COSTS
Costs associated with an issue of securities

[7] See Seth Anderson, *Initial Public Offerings* (Boston: Kluwer Academic Publishers, 1995).

EXHIBIT 2.2

Title Page of a Prospectus for the IPO of Yahoo! Inc.

2,600,000 Shares

Yahoo! Inc.

Common Stock
(par value $0.001 per share)

All of the shares of Common Stock offered hereby are being offered by Yahoo! Inc. Prior to this offering, there has been no public market for the Common Stock of the Company. For factors considered in determining the initial public offering price, see "Underwriting".

In connection with this offering, the Underwriters have reserved approximately 200,000 shares of Common Stock for sale at the initial public offering price to persons associated with the Company.

See "Risk Factors" commencing on page 6 for certain considerations relevant to an investment in the Common Stock.

The Common Stock has been approved for quotation on the Nasdaq National Market under the symbol "YHOO".

THESE SECURITIES HAVE NOT BEEN APPROVED OR DISAPPROVED BY THE SECURITIES AND EXCHANGE COMMISSION OR ANY STATE SECURITIES COMMISSION NOR HAS THE SECURITIES AND EXCHANGE COMMISSION OR ANY STATE SECURITIES COMMISSION PASSED UPON THE ACCURACY OR ADEQUACY OF THIS PROSPECTUS. ANY REPRESENTATION TO THE CONTRARY IS A CRIMINAL OFFENSE.

	Initial Public Offering Price	Underwriting Discount(1)	Proceeds to Company(2)
Per Share	$13.00	$0.91	$12.09
Total(3)	$33,800,000	$2,366,000	$31,434,000

(1) The Company has agreed to indemnify the Underwriters against certain liabilities, including liabilities under the Securities Act of 1933. See "Underwriting".
(2) Before deducting estimated offering expenses of $700,000 payable by the Company.
(3) The Company has granted the Underwriters an option for 30 days to purchase up to an additional 390,000 shares at the initial public offering price per share, less the underwriting discount, solely to cover over-allotments. If such option is exercised in full, the total initial public offering price, underwriting discount and proceeds to the Company will be $38,870,000, $2,720,900 and $36,149,100, respectively. See "Underwriting".

The shares offered hereby are offered severally by the Underwriters, as specified herein, subject to receipt and acceptance by them and subject to their right to reject any order in whole or in part. It is expected that certificates for the shares will be ready for delivery in New York, New York, on or about April 17, 1996, against payment therefor in immediately available funds.

Goldman, Sachs & Co.

Donaldson, Lufkin & Jenrette
Securities Corporation

Montgomery Securities

The date of this Prospectus is April 12, 1996.

to the company, along with any more recent financial data, are added. Exhibit 2.2 illustrates the title page for the final prospectus for an issue of 2,600,000 shares of Yahoo!. The names of the managing underwriters are in large print at the bottom of the page. These managing underwriters formed the syndicate that sold the shares to the general public. In this example, 17 firms participated in the selling group.

The cost of underwriting, which is the difference between the price of the securities to the public and the proceeds to the firm, is also given in the prospectus shown in Exhibit 2.2. In this example, the cost is $0.91 per share, which is 7 percent of the proceeds received by the firm for each share. The total cost is $2,366,000 for the sale of these shares. Underwriting fees tend to vary with the dollar value of the securities being underwritten and the type of securities being sold. Since some of the expenses are fixed (such as the preparation of the prospectus), the unit cost for a large underwriting is smaller. Also, it may be more difficult to sell speculative securities than quality securities. Thus, underwriting fees for speculative issues tend to be higher.

In addition to the fee, the underwriter may receive indirect compensation, which may be in the form of the right (or option) to buy additional securities. If the price of the stock does rise, this right to buy more shares becomes valuable. Such indirect compensation may be as important as the monetary fee because it unites the underwriter and the firm. After the initial sale, the underwriter often becomes a market maker for the securities, which is particularly important to the investing public. Without a secondary market in which to sell the security, investors would be less interested in buying the securities initially. By maintaining a market in the security, the brokerage firm eases the task of selling the securities.

VOLATILITY OF THE MARKET FOR INITIAL PUBLIC OFFERINGS The new issue market (especially for initial public offerings of common stock, or IPOs) can be extremely volatile. Periods have occurred when the investing public seemed willing to purchase virtually any security that was being sold. There have also been periods during which new companies were simply unable to raise money, and large companies did so only under onerous terms.

The new issue market is not only volatile regarding the number of securities that are offered but also regarding the price changes of the new issues. When the new issue market is "hot," it is not unusual for the prices to rise dramatically. Yahoo!'s stock was initially offered at $13 and closed at $33 after reaching a high of $43 during the first day of trading.

Few new issues perform as well as Yahoo!, and many that initially do well subsequently fall on hard times. Boston Chicken went public in 1993 at $20 a share and rose to $48½ by the end of the first day of trading. By 1999, the company's rapid expansion overextended the firm's ability to sustain profitable operations. Boston Chicken filed for bankruptcy, and the stock traded for a few pennies a share. (One of the questions facing the holders of any IPO whose stock price rises dramatically is whether the initial performance can be continued, or at least sufficiently maintained so that the price does not fall.)

All firms, of course, were small at one time, and each one had to go public to have a market for its shares. Someone bought the shares of IBM, Xerox, and Johnson & Johnson when these firms initially sold shares to the general public. The new issue market offers the opportunity to invest in emerging firms, some of which may achieve substantial returns for those investors or speculators who are willing to accept the risk. It is the possibility of large rewards that makes the new issue market so exciting. However, if the past is an indicator of the future, many firms that go public will fail and will inflict losses on those investors who have accepted this risk by purchasing securities issued by the small, emerging firms.

SHELF-REGISTRATIONS The previous discussion was cast in terms of firms initially selling their stock to the general public (that is, the "initial public offering" or "going public"). Firms that have previously issued securities and are currently public also raise funds by selling new securities. If the sales are to the general public, the same basic procedure applies. The new securities must be registered with and approved by the SEC before they may be sold to the public, and the firm often uses the services of an investment banker to facilitate the sale.

There are, however, differences between an initial public offering and the sale of additional securities by a publicly held firm. The first major difference concerns the price of the securities. Because a market already exists for the firm's stock, the problem of an appropriate price for the additional shares is virtually eliminated. This price will approximate the going market price on the date of issue. Second, because the firm must periodically publish information (for instance, the annual report) and file documents with the SEC, there is less need for a detailed prospectus. Many publicly held firms construct a prospectus describing a proposed issue of new securities and file it with the SEC. This document is called a "shelf-registration." After the shelf-registration has been accepted, the firm may sell the securities whenever the need for funds arises. Such shelf-registrations offer the issuing firm considerable flexibility because the securities do not have to be issued but can be quickly sold if the firm deems that the conditions are optimal for the sale.

PRIVATE PLACEMENT
Nonpublic sale of securities to a financial institution

In addition to public sales of securities, firms may raise funds through **private placements,** which are nonpublic sales of securities. Such sales are made to venture capital firms or mutual funds that specialize in emerging firms. Small firms are often unable to raise capital through traditional sources. The size of the issue may be too small or the firm perceived as too risky for an underwriting through an investment banker. Venture capitalists thus fill a void by acquiring securities issued by small firms with exceptional growth potential.

Of course, not all small firms with exceptional growth potential realize that potential. Venture capitalists often sustain large losses on these investments, but their successes can generate large returns. If a venture capitalist invests $1,000,000 in five firms and four fail but one grows into a successful business, the one large gain can more than offset the investments in the four losers.

The venture capitalist's success depends on the ability to identify quality management and new products with market potential. While venture capitalists must negotiate terms that will reward their risk taking, they must not stifle the entrepreneurial spirit necessary to successfully manage an emerging business.

Once the firm does grow and achieve success, the securities purchased by the venture capitalist may be sold to the general public as part of the initial public offering. Many public offerings of securities combine a sale of new securities to raise funds for the firm and a sale of securities by existing stockholders. These holdings are often composed of shares originally purchased by the venture capitalists who are using the initial public sale as a means to realize their profits on their investments in the successful firm.

SUMMARY

Money is anything that is generally accepted for the exchange of goods and services. The supply of money depends on the amount of coins and currency in circulation and the demand deposits in banks. The value of money depends on what it may purchase. This value is different from an interest rate, which is the price of credit. While the role of money is to facilitate transactions, the role of interest rates is to allocate the nation's scarce supply of credit. During most periods, the longer the term of the loan, the greater is the interest rate.

The flow of capital to business is exceedingly important to an advanced economy, as the nation's supply of goods and services would be reduced if the funds available for investment were not transferred to firms, individuals, and governments in need of the funds. This transfer has led to the development of a sophisticated financial system that includes the issuing of new securities, the creation of financial intermediaries, and the development of secondary markets for transferring existing securities among investors.

The transfer of funds from individuals, firms, or governments with excess funds to those economic units needing the funds may occur either directly or indirectly. The direct transfer occurs when individuals invest in their own businesses or buy newly issued securities. The indirect transfer occurs through financial intermediaries that stand between the ultimate suppliers and ultimate users of the funds. A financial intermediary creates a claim on itself, such as a savings account, when it obtains the money from savers. When the intermediary lends the money, it creates a claim on the borrower. Thus, a financial intermediary in effect takes on the claim against the borrower and converts it into a claim on itself that the saver is willing to accept.

Firms may also obtain capital directly by selling new securities to savers. These sales are facilitated by investment bankers who act as middlemen between the issuing firm and the savers. In many cases the investment bankers guarantee the issuing firm a specified amount of money. That is, the investment bankers underwrite the securities and bear the risk of the sale. Investment bankers, however, do not create claims on themselves, such as the savings account issued by financial intermediaries. The savers who purchase new securities own claims on the firms that issued the securities. These savers do not own claims on the investment bankers.

Firms may also sell a block of securities to one buyer, such as an insurance company. Such a sale is a private placement, and it avoids the costs associated with an underwriting. There are also specialized venture capital firms that provide funds to small, emerging firms that offer exceptional potential for growth.

Review Questions

1. What is the role of money? How is the supply of money measured? How does the role of money differ from the role of interest rates?
2. What is a yield curve? Generally, what is the relationship between the term of a loan and the rate of interest?
3. How do financial intermediaries differ from investment bankers? What role does the creation of claims have on the transfer of funds from savers to firms and governments? How does this role differ for financial intermediaries and investment bankers?
4. What role does each of the following play in an underwriting?
   a. the originating house
   b. the syndicate
   c. the prospectus and the SEC
   d. the underwriting discount
5. If a company went public at $50 a share and the price of the stock immediately rose to $60, who receives the windfall gain? From the viewpoint of the underwriter, was this a successful underwriting? Why would an underwriter not want to overprice a new issue?
6. Risk is an unavoidable part of selling a new issue of securities. Who bears the risk in a best efforts sale, and how does such a sale differ from an underwriting? How does the SEC reduce the risk to investors?
7. Figure 2.1 provided the yields on Federal Government securities as of the beginning of year 2000. Compare those yields with the comparable yields as of the time you are reading this text. One possible source is *The Wall Street Journal,* which provides the yields on federal government securities. Yields may also be obtained through the Federal Reserve at **www.bog.frb.fed.us** under the section "Selected Interest Rates."

8. Go to the SEC's website (**www.sec.gov**) and determine the SEC's role and what laws it enforces.

9. Initial public offerings occur virtually every day. Go to a calendar of new offerings, select a company that has just issued stock, and track the price for a week after the initial public offering. Did the price increase by more than ten percent after the initial public offering? Possible web sites concerning IPOs include Hoovers' IPO Central (**www.ipocentral.com**) and **www.ipopro.com**, a site co-developed by R.R. Donnelley Financial and IPO Crossroads and includes a searchable database of current and historical IPOs.
10. In October 1999, Martha Stewart Living Omnimedia went public at $18 a share. The price rose to over $37 a share during the first day of trading. What is the current price of the stock?

CHAPTER 3

Financial Intermediaries

Learning Objectives

1 Explain the advantages associated with financial intermediaries.
2 Enumerate the assets and liabilities of a commercial bank.
3 Explain the source of a commercial bank's earnings and the importance of regulation of commercial banks.
4 Differentiate the portfolios of the various financial intermediaries.
5 Explain the popularity and pattern of growth in money market mutual funds.

Robert Frost noted that "a bank is a place where they lend you an umbrella in fine weather and ask for it back when it begins to rain." Banks and their managers are often viewed with more than a bit of cynicism. Perhaps this cynicism is the result of the visibility of commercial banks and other depository institutions. Virtually everyone has contact with a bank. The public is bombarded with advertisements ranging from types of deposits being offered to a variety of loans available to potential borrowers. In addition, the failure of a large thrift institution or bank and the resulting losses inflicted upon taxpayers are part of the news reported by the financial press.

Of course, a bank or any financial intermediary can only lend what is lent to it. All depository institutions and the various financial intermediaries compete intensely for those funds. The loans that banks make also compete with other sources of credit available to borrowers. Thus, an individual financial intermediary competes with other intermediaries for both funds and loans. To be successful, a financial intermediary must attract money and subsequently lend it for a profit. Profit margins are usually small, and a few bad loans can significantly reduce the intermediary's earnings.

This chapter is concerned with financial intermediaries—the assets they own, the liabilities they owe, the differences among them, and the failures of a large number of savings institutions. Since commercial banks constitute such an important intermediary, special emphasis is devoted to their assets, liabilities, and earnings. After this coverage of commercial banks, other depository institutions, such as savings and loan associations, life insurance companies, and money market mutual funds, are discussed. The chapter ends with descriptions of money market instruments and the competition for funds.

THE VARIETY OF FINANCIAL INTERMEDIARIES

As was explained in the previous chapter, a financial intermediary transfers command over resources (savings) from those with funds to lend to those who need funds. This process is achieved through the intermediary's creating a claim on itself. This process of creation of claims is crucial to the definition of a financial intermediary. A brokerage firm that buys and sells stock for its clients does not create a claim on itself; thus, it is not a financial intermediary but a middleman that facilitates the buying and selling of securities.

When a saver deposits funds in a financial intermediary, that individual has a claim on the intermediary, not on the person to whom the intermediary lends the funds. If the saver had directly lent the money to the ultimate user and the user subsequently failed, the saver would sustain a loss. This may not happen if the saver lends the money to a financial intermediary. If a financial intermediary makes a bad loan that fails, the saver does not sustain the loss unless the financial intermediary fails. Even then the saver may not sustain a loss if the deposits are insured. The combination of a claim on the intermediary (and not on the ultimate user of the funds) and the insuring of deposits have made these financial institutions a primary haven for the savings of many risk-averse investors.

To tap these sources of savings, a variety of institutions have evolved. Commercial banks, thrift institutions, credit unions, and life insurance companies are all financial intermediaries that channel the funds of savers to borrowers. Many savers, however, are not aware of differences among commercial banks, savings and loan associations, and mutual savings banks. These institutions offer similar services and pay virtually the same rate of interest on deposits. In addition, the portfolio of assets acquired by each depository institution is more similar than in the past. Although previously the savings banks made primarily mortgage loans, their portfolios have been broadened to include a more varied mix of assets.

This blurring of the distinctions among the various financial intermediaries is the result of changes in the regulatory environment. Under the Depository Institutions Deregulation and Monetary Control Act of 1980 (referred to hereafter as the Monetary Control Act of 1980), all depository institutions (commercial banks, savings and loan associations, mutual savings banks, and credit unions) became subject to the regulation of the Federal Reserve. The Federal Reserve's powers extend to the types of accounts these institutions may offer and the amount that the various depository institutions must hold in reserve against their deposits.

Although the Federal Reserve has supervisory power over depository institutions' portfolios, the Monetary Control Act of 1980 gave the managements of various financial institutions more flexibility to vary their loan portfolios. In addition, each depository institution was granted the right to borrow funds from the Federal Reserve. This reform legislation also phased out Regulation Q, which placed ceilings on the interest rates banks could pay depositors. Banks may now offer whatever yields they deem desirable to attract deposits. The net effect of these reforms has been to reduce the differentiation among the various types of financial intermediaries. Thus, for most individuals the difference between the local commercial bank and the local savings and loan association is slight.

Advantages of Financial Intermediaries

What are the advantages of a system of financial intermediaries? For such a system to exit there have to be advantages to all concerned—borrower, lender, and the financial intermediary. One of the major advantages to the borrower is that the intermediary is able to pool the funds of many savers and make loans of substantial size. A corporation like General Motors would have a major problem if it had to approach individual savers to borrow money. Commercial banks, however, can lend General Motors a large amount of funds.

For the saver, financial intermediaries offer the advantages of income, convenience, and risk reduction. Savings accounts pay interest, and checking accounts may pay interest and are a convenient means to make payments. These accounts also permit the savers to deposit and withdraw small amounts of money. Other securities, like stocks and bonds, may not be divisible into such small quantities, and if small quantities are available, there is a substantial commission cost for dealing with such small amounts of securities. Hence, these securities may not be as convenient as savings and checking accounts.

In addition, these accounts provide ways to earn modest returns with very little risk of loss. If an individual with a modest sum to invest (for example, $5,000 to $10,000) were to lend the funds directly to a firm, the entire amount could be lost. Even if the borrower were not to default on the loan, the saver may be unable to sell the debt instrument in case the individual needs the funds before the loan matures. A secondary market for many types of individual loans simply does not exist. Even if a secondary market does exist, there still is no assurance the seller will receive the amount invested in the debt instruments.

One of the most important advantages offered individual savers by banking institutions is the virtual elimination of these sources of risk. Such safety of principal cannot be achieved by savers who directly lend to other individuals and firms. However, there is virtually no risk of loss of funds deposited in a savings or a checking account. This has been true since the advent of deposit insurance from the **Federal Deposit Insurance Corporation (FDIC).** If a saver places $1,000 in a federally insured savings account, the $1,000 principal is safe and may be withdrawn at the saver's option.

FEDERAL DEPOSIT INSURANCE CORPORATION (FDIC)
Agency of the federal government that insures bank deposits

While federal insurance ensures this safety of principal, the very nature of the intermediary's portfolio reduces the risk of loss to the saver. The financial intermediary pools the funds of many savers and acquires a diversified portfolio of loans, which spreads the risk.[1] Even if the value of some of the intermediary's assets were to decline, such declines may not endanger the financial position of the intermediary. In the case in which the financial intermediary does experience financial difficulty, federal deposit insurance protects the depositors.

While many financial intermediaries do offer federal deposit insurance, it is important to realize that *not all offer such insurance.* For example, there is no federal insurance program for life insurance companies. A saver's policy is only as strong as the company and the assets it owns. If the company were to fail, the saver would stand to lose the funds that have been invested in the life insurance. Hence,

[1] Risk reduction through the construction of diversified portfolios is discussed in Chapter 8.

it is incorrect to assume that savings invested in a financial intermediary are necessarily free from the risk of loss.

Besides advantages to borrowers and lenders, there must also be an advantage to the financial intermediary. It must receive compensation for the service it is providing the lenders and the borrowers. This compensation is the potential for profit. The source of this profit is the difference between what the intermediaries pay depositors and what they charge borrowers. Of course, the lenders and the borrowers could deal directly with each other and share these profits (which they do when stocks and bonds are issued and sold to households). But the advantages offered by financial intermediaries, such as convenience and reduced risk to savers and the availability of large sources of funds for corporate borrowers, may not exist when the borrowers and lenders deal directly with each other.

Financial intermediaries also offer an important advantage to the aggregate economy. Since they facilitate the transfer of funds from savers to firms and households that need funds, financial intermediaries increase the aggregate level of income and employment. Because firms are able to acquire funds through the intermediaries, they are able to employ additional labor. These workers would not have been employed if firms had been unable to acquire the necessary funds from the financial intermediaries. Thus, all members of the society benefit from the existence of the financial intermediaries. The nation's level of output would be lower if financial intermediaries did not make possible the transfer of funds from savers to borrowers.

COMMERCIAL BANKS

In terms of size, commercial banks are the most important depository institution. The total amount of deposits and loans made by commercial banks is given in Exhibit 3.1. Commercial banks' importance to business is evident, as loans to firms exceeded $959 billion and accounted for 18.1 percent of commercial banks' total assets. Commercial banks are also a prime source of funds to consumers, with consumer loans accounting for 9.1 percent of banks' total assets. Most of the loans to firms and households are for a relatively short term (for instance, less than one to five years to maturity). Commercial banks tend to stress loans that must be paid off ("mature") quickly. This emphasis on short maturities is the result of the rapid turnover of bank deposits (especially demand deposits) and the need for banks to coordinate their portfolios with changes in the economic environment and the level of interest rates.

A Commercial Bank's Balance Sheet

Sovereign Bancorp's balance sheet is given in Exhibit 3.2. It is similar to the balance sheet of the aggregation of all commercial banks in Exhibit 3.1. The largest asset is the bank's loan portfolio, which constitutes over half its total assets. These loans include commercial loans, consumer loans including credit cards, real estate construction and mortgage loans, and commercial construction loans.

EXHIBIT 3.1

Assets and Liabilities of Commercial Banks as of July 1999 (in billions)

Assets			
Reserves			
Cash (currency and coins), cash items in process, and deposits with the Federal Reserve		$ 256.3	4.8%
U.S. government securities		814.7	15.4
Other securities		406.4	7.7
Loans			
Commercial and industrial	$ 959.9		18.1
Real estate	1,353.5		25.5
Loans to individuals	483.4		9.1
Interbank loans	239.6		4.5
Other loans	508.7		9.6
		$3,545.1	
Other assets		281.1	5.3
		$5,303.6	100.0%
Liabilities			
Demand deposits	$ 667.8		12.6
Savings accounts and CDs	2,001.9		37.7
Large time deposits	714.2		13.5
		$3,383.9	
Other borrowings and liabilities		1,488.3	28.1
Equity (net worth)		431.4	8.1
		$5,303.6	100.0%

Source: *Derived from the* Federal Reserve Bulletin, *October 1999, p. A15.*

Besides the loan portfolio, commercial banks hold a variety of investment debt securities. While the loans are individually negotiated between the bank and the borrower, these securities are bought (and sold) in the securities markets. The assets of the bank include the debt of state and local governments and U.S. government securities. The remaining assets are cash and reserves and various miscellaneous assets.

The debts of state and local governments are purchased by the bank in order for the bank to receive tax-free income.[2] For a particular bank these bonds may include the issues of local governments served by the bank. Many local governments have working relationships with local banks; they keep their accounts in these banks and borrow from them. Such working relationships between local

[2] The interest paid on debt issued by state and local governments is exempt from federal income taxation. These securities are discussed in Chapter 9 on bonds.

EXHIBIT 3.2

Simplified Balance Sheet for Sovereign Bancorp as of December 31, 1998 (in thousands)

Assets		
Reserves and cash	$ 471	2.1%
Securities	8,475	38.7
Loans	11,286	51.5
Miscellaneous assets	1,682	7.7
	$21,914	100.0%
Liabilities		
Deposits		
Demand deposits	1,104	5.0
NOW accounts	1,282	5.8
Savings accounts	2,295	10.5
Money market accounts	1,546	7.1
Certificates of deposit	6,095	27.8
Borrowings		
Short-term	3,922	17.9
Long-term	3,979	18.2
Other liabilities	485	2.2
Stockholders' equity	1,204	5.5
Liabilities and stockholders' equity	$21,914	100.0%

governments and local banks are often important for small communities, for these communities may have difficulty borrowing outside their geographic region.

Reserves (cash and deposits with the Federal Reserve) are assets that the bank is required to hold against its deposit liabilities. These assets do not earn interest, so a bank seeks to minimize the amount of funds tied up in these assets. (The reserve requirement is set by the Federal Reserve and is discussed in more detail in the following chapter.) The miscellaneous assets include such items as the building, plant, and equipment.

The primary liabilities of the commercial bank are its deposits: checking accounts (demand deposits and NOW accounts) and various types of savings and time deposits.[3] These deposits constitute 10.8 percent and 45.4 percent, respectively, of the bank's sources of finance. Demand deposits and NOW accounts are payable on demand, for the owner of a checking account may demand immediate cash, and funds in the account may be readily transferred by check.

Savings accounts, money market accounts, and certificates of deposit are interest-bearing accounts. Funds deposited in a regular savings account may be withdrawn at will. Time deposits, which are referred to as **certificates of deposit**

[3] NOW stands for "negotiable order of withdrawal" and is a type of checking account that pays interest.

(or **CDs,** as they are commonly called), are issued for a fixed term, such as six months or two years. The saver may redeem the CD prior to maturity but must pay a penalty, such as the loss of interest for one quarter. For CDs issued in denominations greater than $100,000, the rate of interest and the length of time to maturity are mutually agreed upon by the bank and the saver with the funds. These "jumbo CDs" may be subsequently sold, as there is a secondary market in CDs with denominations exceeding $100,000. Since large-denomination CDs may be bought and sold, they are often referred to as **negotiable CDs** to differentiate them from smaller denomination CDs, which cannot be sold but may be redeemed prior to maturity (usually with a penalty).

CERTIFICATE OF DEPOSIT (CD)
Time deposit issued by a bank with a specified interest rate and maturity

NEGOTIABLE CD
Certificate of deposit issued in amounts of $100,000 or more whose terms are individually negotiated between the bank and the saver and for which there exists a secondary market.

For denominations of less than $100,000, the bank establishes the terms and offers the CD to the general public. If the public finds the terms unattractive (perhaps the rate of interest is less than that offered by competing banks), the bank does not receive deposits. Thus, it is not surprising that the terms offered by one bank are similar to the terms offered by competing banks; differences tend to be small or very subtle, such as the frequency with which interest is added to the principal. (The more frequently the interest is added, or compounded, the more interest the depositor earns, as interest earns additional interest.)

The remaining liabilities of the commercial bank include other borrowings from a variety of sources. For example, commercial banks borrow from each other and borrow from the Federal Reserve.[4] The last entry on the commercial bank's balance sheet in Exhibit 3.2 is stockholders' equity, which represents the stockholders' investment in the firm.

While this balance sheet shows the various sources of funds available to the bank, it also illustrates that the various types of deposits are the most important. For this bank, checking and savings accounts and time deposits constitute 56.2 percent of the firm's sources of finance. The balance sheet also indicates that total deposits greatly exceed stockholders' equity. The bank has a large amount of debt outstanding when it is realized that the deposits are loans to the bank by households, firms, and governments.

Since the bank has only a small amount of equity and a large amount of debt, a small decrease in the value of the assets could eliminate the bank's equity. In this case, a 5.5 percent decline in the value of the assets will erase the equity. Bankers are aware of this potential risk, and it is one reason why they tend to be defensive. A bank must be cautious when making loans and investments, because a small amount of loss may cause the bank to fail.

A Commercial Bank's Earnings

A commercial bank's earnings are generated by the assets that it owns relative to the liabilities that it owes. The assets generate revenues that cover the bank's costs. If the bank generates sufficient revenues, it will operate profitably. Exhibit 3.3, a simplified income statement for Sovereign Bankcorp, lists the bank's revenues and

[4] Both of these sources of funds are covered in the next chapter.

EXHIBIT 3.3

Simplified Income Statement for Sovereign Bancorp for the Year Ended December 31, 1998 (in thousands)

Revenues	
Interest and fees on loans	$881.1
Interest on securities	466.9
Fees and miscellaneous income	82.9
Expenses	
Interest on deposits	440.3
Interest on other borrowings	421.5
Administrative expenses	277.4
Other operating expenses	80.5
Income before income taxes	211.2
Income taxes	74.8
Net earnings	$136.4
Earnings per share	$0.88

expenses. The prime source of the commercial bank's revenues is the interest earned by its loans, which accounted for 61.6 percent of the bank's total revenues. Service charges, such as credit card and ATM fees, and income produced by the other assets contributed 6.5 percent.[5] The cash in the vault and the reserves produced no revenue for the commercial bank; hence, it is no surprise that banks seek to minimize the amount of cash and reserves they hold.

The commercial bank's expenses include everyday running expenses, such as wages, salaries, and various employee benefits. These accounted for 22.7 percent of its expenses. The bank pays interest to its creditors, who include the holders of time and savings deposits and the various other sources from which the bank has borrowed funds. These interest expenses accounted for 70.7 percent of the bank's total costs. Miscellaneous expenses include insurance, maintenance, and advertising and accounted for 6.6 percent of the total cost of operations.

Operations for this bank were profitable, for it earned $136.4 million in profits. While the bank's operations were profitable, it took the bank $22,914 million in assets to earn the 136.4 million. Thus, the bank's return on total assets was only 0.595 percent ($136.4/$22,914), which appears to be a meager return. Unless it were able to increase the return on its assets, this return implies that the bank would have to increase its assets by $1,680 to earn an additional $10.00 ($1,680 × 0.00595 = $10). Although this profit margin is small, such a profit margin on total assets is typical of the banking industry. A bank must have a large amount of

[5] One important trend in commercial banking is the charging of more fees for such services as credit cards and automatic teller machines or accounts with low balances. This trend has two implications: (1) fees as a percentage of a bank's total revenues will increase and (2) banks' total revenues will become less sensitive to changes in interest rates.

assets (and, correspondingly, a large amount of deposits) to generate any significant amount of profit.

While the profit margin on total assets is modest, the profits earned for the stockholders can be substantial. As may be seen from the balance sheet in Exhibit 3.2, equity is $1,204 million, which is only 5.5 percent of the firm's sources of funds. Debt obligations, such as deposits, account for the remaining 94.5 percent. The bank is highly financially leveraged, which increases the return earned for the owners. In this case, the return on equity is 11.3 percent ($136.4/$1,204), which is considerably higher than the 0.595 percent the bank earned on its total assets.

Why are these percentages so different? How is the bank able to earn only 0.595 percent on its assets but earn 11.3 percent on its equity? The answer lies in the fact that the bank pays less interest for the funds it borrows and earns more interest on its portfolio of assets. The average return on its portfolio exceeds the cost of funds, so the bank magnified the return on its stockholders' investment. Thus, even though the bank nets only $0.595 on every $100 in assets, the stockholders earn 11.3 percent on their funds invested in the firm.

Regulation of Commercial Banks

Commercial banks and other savings banks are subject to government regulation, the purpose of which is to protect the banks' creditors, especially their depositors. The very nature of banking implies that when a commercial bank fails, substantial losses could be sustained by the bank's depositors. This is exactly what occurred during the Great Depression of the 1930s, when the failure of many commercial banks imposed substantial losses on depositors. These losses led to increased regulation of commercial banks and the establishment of federal deposit insurance, both of which are designed to protect depositors. Such protection promotes a viable banking system and eases the flow of savings into investment.

The regulation of banks comes from both state and federal banking authorities and the Federal Deposit Insurance Corporation. Banks that have national charters must join the Federal Reserve and are subjected to its regulation as well as to examination by the Comptroller of the Currency, which is the federal agency that grants national bank charters. Banks with state charters are regulated by the individual state banking commissions and, under the Monetary Control Act of 1980, are subject to regulation by the Federal Reserve. These various authorities regulate and supervise such facets of a bank's operations as its geographic location, the number of banks and branches in an area, and the types of loans and investments the bank may make.

RESERVES Commercial banks and all other depository institutions (savings and loan associations, mutual savings banks, and credit unions) must keep funds in reserve against their deposit liabilities (that is, **required reserves**). Under the Monetary Control Act of 1980, the minimum amount that all banks must maintain as a reserve is determined by the Federal Reserve. While holding reserves against deposit liabilities may increase the safety of the deposits, such safety is not the prime reason for having reserve requirements. As will be explained in Chapter 4, the reserve requirement is one of the major tools of monetary control. This

REQUIRED RESERVES
Funds that banks must hold against deposit liabilities

EXHIBIT 3.4

Reserve Requirements as of January 2000

Checking accounts, NOW accounts, and automatic transfer accounts	
First $46.5 million in deposits	3%
Total deposits exceeding $46.5 million	10%
Time deposits	
Maturity of less than 1½ years	0%
Maturity of 1½ years or more	0%

Source: Federal Reserve Bulletin, *January 2000, p. A8.*

element of control, not safety, is the reason for having a reserve requirement against the deposit liabilities of banks.

The amount of the reserve requirement varies with the type of account. For example, as of January 1, 2000, checking accounts had a reserve requirement of 10 percent. (The first $46.5 million in checking accounts, NOW accounts, and automatic transfer accounts have a reserve requirement of 3 percent.) Time deposits have no reserve requirements. These various reserve requirements are given in Exhibit 3.4.

EXCESS RESERVES
Reserves held by a bank in excess of those it must hold to meet its reserve requirement

Commercial banks may hold their reserves in two forms: (1) cash in the vault or (2) deposits with another bank, especially the Federal Reserve. If the bank's reserve requirement is 10 percent for demand deposits and the bank receives $100 cash in a checking account, it must hold $10 in reserve against the new demand deposit. The entire $100 in cash is considered part of the bank's total reserves, but the bank must hold only $10 against the deposit liability. The bank may choose to hold $1 of the required reserves in cash in the vault (to meet cash withdrawals) and $9 in the Federal Reserve. The remaining $90 are funds that the bank does not have to hold in reserve. In this example, these **excess reserves** (the difference between the bank's total reserves and its required reserves) total $100 − $10 = $90. A commercial bank's excess reserves may be lent to borrowers or used for some other purpose, such as purchasing government securities. If a commercial bank does not have any excess reserves, it is said to be "fully loaned up." To acquire additional income-earning assets, such as a government security or a business loan, the bank would have to acquire additional excess reserves.

CORRESPONDENT BANK
Major bank with which a smaller bank has a relationship to facilitate check clearing and to serve as a depository for reserves

Commercial banks (and other depository institutions) may deposit their reserves in a Federal Reserve bank, or they may deposit their reserves in other banks called **correspondent banks.** Correspondent banks in many cases are large, metropolitan commercial banks. These large correspondent banks frequently provide additional services. For example, they have efficient mechanisms for clearing checks that facilitate check clearing for smaller banks. The correspondent banks also have research staffs and give management advice and investment counsel. Thus, they are important to the well-being of the small, local banks. Of course, the correspondent banks are willing to provide these services because a small bank's deposits are like any other deposits: They are a source of funds that the larger banks may use. Thus, the large commercial banks use the funds deposited in them by small banks to purchase income-earning assets.

In addition to the required reserves, commercial banks also hold **secondary reserves.** These are high-quality, short-term marketable securities. While reserves on deposit at the Federal Reserve earn nothing, the market securities earn interest. These assets, such as U.S. government securities (Treasury bills), are also liquid. Thus, short-term marketable securities offer a bank both a source of interest income and a means to obtain funds to cover a shortage in its reserves.

SECONDARY RESERVES
Short-term securities, especially Treasury bills, held by banks to increase their liquidity

The importance of reserves and reserve requirements cannot be exaggerated. As is explained in the next chapter, the commercial banking system, through the process of loan creation, can expand or contract the nation's supply of money. The ability of commercial banks and other depository institutions to lend depends on their excess reserves. Thus anything that affects their reserves alters their ability to lend and create money and credit. Many financial transactions affect commercial banks' reserves, including the federal government's methods of financing a deficit or the open market operations of the Federal Reserve. The next chapter will discuss several of these financial transactions and their potential impact on commercial bank reserves.

DEPOSIT INSURANCE Federal government deposit insurance is one of the positive results of the Great Depression of the 1930s. The large losses sustained by commercial banks' depositors led to the establishment of the Federal Deposit Insurance Corporation. The establishment of FDIC has significantly increased the general public's confidence in the banking system. As of this writing, FDIC insures deposits to $100,000. Thus, if a commercial bank should fail, FDIC will reimburse depositors up to the $100,000 limit. Since most individuals do not have that much on deposit, these individuals know that their funds are safe. (If an individual has more than $100,000, the same degree of safety can be achieved by placing amounts up to $100,000 in different banks.) The $100,000 limit does mean that large depositors, including many corporations, are not fully insured and do stand to take losses should a bank fail.

All commercial banks that are members of the Federal Reserve System must purchase insurance from FDIC, and many state banking authorities also require that FDIC insurance be carried by their state nonmember banks. However, some state banking authorities do not require federal deposit insurance. Also foreign banks, such as Bank Leumi (Israel's largest commercial bank), that are licensed to operate in the United States do not have to carry FDIC insurance.

Besides offering deposit insurance, FDIC has further increased public confidence in the banking system through its powers of bank examination. By exercising this power to examine banks, FDIC, along with other regulatory agencies, has improved bank practices. The improved bank practices plus the deposit insurance have improved the quality of banking. However, the establishment of FDIC and other regulatory agencies has not eliminated bank failures, for banks do fail. Most of these are small banks, and losses are not sustained by the many individuals who deposit modest sums with these commercial banks. If necessary, such deposits are reimbursed in full by FDIC up to the $100,000 legal limit. Thus, for most individuals, depositing funds in a commercial bank does not subject the funds to risk of loss.[6]

When a commercial bank does fail, FDIC generally seeks to merge that bank into a stronger bank. This transfer of the deposits to the strong bank saves FDIC from having to reimburse the depositors. If such a merger cannot be arranged, the failed bank may be liquidated, in which case the depositors are reimbursed up to the legal limit, or the failed bank may be reorganized. Perhaps the most famous reorganizations occurred when FDIC assumed control of Continental Illinois National Bank and Trust Company and the Bank of New England in an effort to stop the banks from failing. Since both were among the nation's largest banks, failure to bail them out may have reduced the public's confidence in the banking system.

TRENDS IN COMMERCIAL BANK REGULATION Since the passage of deregulation legislation (the Monetary Control Act of 1980), the banking industry has been undergoing swift change. The industry is very fluid as banking practices and strategies are altered to meet the current legal and competitive environment. Certainly the blurring of the distinctions among various financial intermediaries is a direct result of the deregulation of the banking system. This trend will continue until it may be impossible for the depositor to differentiate between what used to be referred to as a commercial bank and what was referred to as a savings bank.

Even within the group referred to as commercial banks, there will continue to be important changes. Bank holding companies have non-banking operations. Thus, a company such as Citicorp, the parent of New York's Citibank, has national credit card operations (Diner's Club and Carte Blanche) and an international investment banking operation. Bank holding companies also have acquired smaller banks, combining them under the umbrella of the holding company and, in some cases, integrating their operations. For example, Virginia National Bankshares and First and Merchants combined to form Sovran Financial Corporation, which at that time was the largest banking operation in the state of Virginia. The Citizens and Southern, a large Georgia bank, merged with Sovran to form C&S Sovran. This firm then merged with NCNB, a bank headquartered in North Carolina, to create NationsBank Corporation, which, in turn, merged with BankAmerica to create the nation's largest bank: Bank of America.

THRIFT INSTITUTIONS

As the name implies, thrift institutions are a place for savers, especially individuals with modest sums, to deposit funds. The money is then loaned by the financial

[6] When the privately owned Exchange Bank of Bloomfield, Iowa, failed, the bank did not have FDIC insurance. Thus, the failure meant the depositors stood to lose a substantial proportion of their funds unless the bank's assets were sufficient to reimburse the depositors.

intermediary to borrowers in need of the funds. There are essentially two types of thrifts: mutual savings banks and savings and loan associations (S&Ls). Mutual savings banks developed in the early 1800s, primarily in the northeast, to encourage savings by working people. Many have colorful names (for example, Merchant Seaman's Bank) that indicate their origins. A mutual savings bank is owned by its depositors, but the bank itself is managed by a board of trustees. While a mutual savings bank may view its depositors as owners and not creditors, the owners may readily withdraw their funds. Thus, mutual savings banks must have sufficient liquidity to meet withdrawals.

Savings and loan associations developed later, primarily as a source of mortgage loans. Initially, savings and loan members pooled their money to build housing. Members borrowed the funds and when all borrowed funds were repaid, the association was dissolved. Since these initial savings and loans were self-liquidating, they could not grow. During the Great Depression, over 1,700 failed, which led to the passage of the Federal National Housing Act. This legislation established the Federal Savings and Loan Insurance Corporation (FSLIC) to insure deposits in federally chartered S&Ls. (As is discussed later in this chapter, S&Ls sustained major losses during the 1980s. FSLIC had insufficient funds to cover depositors' losses and was replaced by the Savings Association Insurance Fund (SAIF), which is a subsidiary of the FDIC.) While the establishment of deposit insurance enhanced the safety and attractiveness of S&L deposits, the real growth in S&Ls occurred after World War II when housing became a national goal and restrictions on commercial banks and favorable tax treatment encouraged the growth of S&Ls.

To attract deposits, thrifts tend to pay a rate of interest that is slightly higher than the rate paid by commercial banks (usually 1/8 to 1/4 percent higher). Like commercial banks, thrifts must hold reserves against their deposit liabilities. The reserve requirements for the thrifts are set by the Federal Reserve and are the same for all depository institutions. Thus, the capacity of thrifts to grant loans is no different than that of the commercial banks.

Although commercial banks grant a variety of loans, thrifts primarily invest their funds in mortgage loans, especially loans to finance personal homes. For example, West Corp., a California savings and loan reported in 1998 that mortgages accounted for 73.6 percent of its loan portfolio. This thrift (and others like it) is obviously borrowing from savers and passing the funds to households who need mortgage funds to finance the purchase of a home.

If additional savings were deposited into thrifts (a process called **intermediation**), their ability to make additional mortgage loans would be increased. If funds were to flow out of these savings accounts (a process called **disintermediation**), a thrift's ability to grant mortgage loans would be reduced. Since thrifts hold such a large proportion of their funds in mortgages, flows of savings into or out of these savings banks have considerable impact on the building sector of the economy. The ability to obtain mortgage money influences the demand for construction (especially residential housing). Since the flow of savings into thrifts alters the ability of potential homeowners to obtain mortgage money, this flow of savings has an important influence on the construction industry.

INTERMEDIATION
Process of lending funds to a financial intermediary which in turn lends the funds to the ultimate user of the money

DISINTERMEDIATION
Process of withdrawing funds from financial intermediaries and investing the funds in other securities

FINANCIAL FACTS

Taxpayers and the Savings and Loan Debacle

The 1980s were an exceptionally momentous decade for financial intermediaries. It began with the deregulation of commercial banks and the placing of all depository institutions under the control of the Federal Reserve. It ended with the failure of many savings and loan associations, the collapse of the FSLIC, which insured S&L deposits, and the creation of the Office of Thrift Supervision to oversee the assets of the failed thrifts and to provide the orderly liquidation of their assets. Depositors in federally insured S&Ls, however, did not sustain losses (up to the legal limit). While stockholders and uninsured creditors experienced losses, most of the losses were sustained by the insuring agent, the federal government. Hence, it was the nation's taxpayers who ultimately sustained the losses (which by 1994 exceeded $150 billion), as tax money had to be used to pay the interest and redeem the deposits. ¶ Where did the lost money go? What were the causes of the massive losses sustained by some thrifts, and why did some thrifts manage to avoid the losses? These are hard questions to answer because the money did not go to one beneficiary nor was there a single cause of the failures. ¶ The S&L business itself is inherently risky because depository institutions use a large amount of financial leverage. The small equity relative to the large amount of deposits means that a small decline in the value of an S&L's assets wipes out its equity. Thus, only a few problem loans destroy the profitability and equity of a savings and loan association. ¶ In addition, S&Ls tend to violate a major financial principle. They borrow short-term and lend long-term. The term of their deposits may be for one, two, or three years, and, in the case of a savings account, the depositor may withdraw the money on demand. While an S&L's source of money is short- to intermediate-term, its primary assets tend to have a longer term (such as 25-year mortgages). These can be a major problem if interest rates rise. The S&Ls have to pay higher interest on their deposits but have made long-term loans with lower rates of interest. ¶ The S&L debacle led to the Financial Reform, Recovery, and Enforcement Act (FIRRE) of 1989. Under this legislation, failed thrifts were seized, and their assets were sold to repay creditors. If the sales raised insufficient funds, insured depositors were paid by the federal government. Unfortunately, many of the savings and loans' assets were foreclosed properties or loans in default (that is, loans on which interest was not being paid or loans whose principal had not been repaid). These assets were sold at distress prices, which further contributed to the losses that had to be covered by taxpayers. ¶

LIFE INSURANCE COMPANIES

Life insurance companies also perform the role of a financial intermediary because they receive the funds of savers, create a claim on themselves, and lend the funds to borrowers. Since other types of insurance companies do not perform this financial intermediary role, a distinction has to be made between them and life insurance companies. Other types of insurance, such as property and liability insurance, are exclusively services that the individual buys. The price of the insurance is related to the cost of the product, just as the cost of any service, such as a movie or an electrician, is related to the cost of producing the service. Of course, the property and liability insurance companies invest the funds they receive from policyholders. However, suppliers of other services will also use the funds they receive. In neither case is there a transfer of savings to borrowers.

The feature that differentiates life insurance from other forms of insurance and makes life insurance companies financial intermediaries is that life insurance may provide more than insurance against premature death. Ordinary and universal life insurance policies and endowments contain two elements, the insurance and a savings plan. The policy's premiums cover both the cost of the insurance and the savings program. As long as the policy is in force, the policy accumulates cash value, which is the savings component of the policy. Many savers find such policies attractive because the periodic payments assure them of insurance plus a savings program. Others find them unattractive because the interest rate paid on the savings may be less than can be earned on alternative investments.

Life insurance companies use the proceeds of the policies to acquire income-earning assets. Exhibit 3.5, which presents the total assets of all life insurance companies, indicates that these companies purchase a varied mix of financial assets. Holdings of corporate debt and stock account for 40.5 percent and 17.3 percent, respectively, of the total assets, while mortgages account for 9.9 percent. The remaining assets include government securities, real estate, loans to policyholders, and various miscellaneous assets. As the table indicates, life insurance companies are a major source of financing for corporations because many companies are able to sell a substantial amount of stock and debt to life insurance companies. Therefore, life insurance companies are a major alternative to commercial banks for corporations.

Although life insurance companies do compete with commercial banks for corporate loans, they serve different financial markets. First, commercial banks stress liquidity and, hence, are a primary source of short-term finance. Life insurance companies, however, do not need to stress liquidity. Mortality tables are scientifically constructed and can predict with accuracy the volume of death benefits the life insurance company will have to pay. The company can forecast with a high degree of accuracy the amount of benefits it will have to pay during the year. Thus, it is able to construct a portfolio of assets that permits the company to have not only sufficient liquidity but also long-term investments. Since the long-term investments tend to have higher interest rates, a life insurance company will seek to have a substantial amount of its funds in these more profitable assets. The very nature of its financial obligations permits a life insurance company to own more long-term debt than a commercial bank would find prudent to hold.

Second, life insurance companies may hold the stock of corporations, while commercial banks may not.[7] Thus, life insurance companies participate in a

[7] Although commercial banks do not hold stock, bank holding companies may own stock. For example, Sovereign Bancorp, the bank holding company for Sovereign Bank, has brokerage services and can own stock as part of its brokerage operations.

EXHIBIT 3.5

Assets of Life Insurance Companies (in millions)

Assets		
Government securities	$ 409,304	19.1%
Corporate bonds	869,112	40.5
Corporate stock	371,867	17.3
Mortgage loans	211,815	9.9
Real estate	52,437	2.4
Policy loans	95,939	4.5
Other assets	133,070	6.2
Total assets	$2,143,544	100.0%

Source: Life Insurance Fact Book. *See the American Council of Life Insurers Web site at* **www.acli.com**.

market that is closed to commercial banks. (Commercial banks do manage other people's money in trust accounts and can purchase stock for these accounts.) There are also special tax laws that encourage corporations, including life insurance companies, to make investments in the stock of other corporations. For corporations, 70 percent of the dividends received from these investments is exempt from federal income taxation. Therefore, life insurance companies have an added incentive to purchase the stock of corporations and supply corporations with additional equity financing.

PENSION PLANS

The role of a pension plan is to accumulate assets for workers so that they will have funds for retirement. Funds are periodically put in the pension plan by the saver, the employer, or both. The money deposited with the fund then is used to purchase an income-earning asset. The saver's funds grow over time as additional contributions are paid into the pension plan, and the funds already in the plan earn income and appreciate in value.

Many pension plans exist, but not all of them really perform the function of financial intermediaries. Not all pension plans in turn invest or lend the money directly to borrowers. Instead they may purchase *existing* securities, such as the stock of General Motors; that is, the pension plan participates in the secondary, not the primary, market for securities. For a pension plan to serve as a financial intermediary, it must pass the funds directly to a borrower or invest them directly in a firm.

This distinction between pension plans may be illustrated by the pension plans used by many colleges and universities for their employees. Funds may be contributed by both the employer and the employee to the Teachers Insurance and Annuity Association (TIAA) or to the College Retirement Equity Fund

(CREF). The actual dollar amount of the contribution varies with the school and the employee's salary. The funds may be contributed to either plan or may be split between the two plans.

CREF primarily purchases existing corporate stock. Money that flows into CREF does not go to the companies that issued the stock. Instead, the money goes to the seller of the stock, who may have purchased the shares many years ago. As was explained in Chapter 2, the only time a company receives the proceeds of a stock sale occurs when the shares are first issued in the primary market. All subsequent sales are secondhand transactions, with the proceeds flowing from the individual buying the security to the individual selling the security. Funds are not being transferred to the firm. By purchasing the secondhand security, CREF is not performing the role of a financial intermediary.

TIAA purchases an entirely different type of portfolio that stresses debt, especially mortgages. In this case funds are transferred from savers to borrowers, and the pension plan is acting as a financial intermediary. It creates a claim on itself when it receives the savers' funds, and it receives a claim from borrowers when the funds are lent to finance purchases. The transfer of purchasing power from saver to borrower by an intermediary that creates claims on itself is the role of a financial intermediary. Hence, TIAA is an example of a pension plan that does serve the role of a financial intermediary.

MONEY MARKET MUTUAL FUNDS AND MONEY MARKET INSTRUMENTS

One of the most important financial institutions is the mutual fund that invests on behalf of individuals.[8] However, most of these funds are not financial intermediaries in the sense that they borrow from savers and lend the funds to the ultimate uses. It is true that they do create claims on themselves, since investors own shares in the funds (in other words, the investors own equity claims). Whether the fund is a financial intermediary depends on what it does with the money raised by selling the shares: Does it acquire newly issued securities or buy previously issued securities?

If the fund buys securities in the secondary markets, it is not serving as a financial intermediary. No money is transferred to a firm, government, or individual seeking to borrow funds. Instead, the money is transferred to another investor who is seeking to liquidate a position in the particular security.

Of course, a mutual fund could buy newly issued securities. Some funds specialize in purchasing shares of emerging and new firms, and to the extent that these funds participate in the primary market, they are operating as financial intermediaries. Other mutual funds specialize in government securities, which are purchased when the bonds are issued. Such funds also serve as financial intermediaries, transferring the money of savers to the ultimate users of the money. Most

[8] This section considers mutual funds only as financial intermediaries. The general discussion of these investment companies is deferred until Chapter 14.

mutual funds, however, do not serve as financial intermediaries, as they primarily buy and sell existing securities.

MONEY MARKET MUTUAL FUND
Investment company that invests solely in short-term money market instruments

Even though most mutual funds are not financial intermediaries, there is one major exception—the **money market mutual fund** that acquires short-term securities. While these are secondary markets in some money market instruments, money market mutual funds tend to acquire newly issued short-term debt instruments. These securities are then held until they are redeemed at maturity, at which time the process is repeated.

The development of these funds and their explosive growth was one of the most important developments in the financial markets during the 1980s. This growth is illustrated in Figure 3.1, which presents the value of money market mutual fund assets from 1980 through October 1999.

The initial growth was nothing short of phenomenal, as total assets rose from less than $10 billion in 1975 to over $1.1 trillion in 1998. This immediate popularity may be explained by three factors: safety of principal, liquidity, and high interest rates. The shares are safe since the money funds acquire short-term debt obligations whose values are subject to minimal price fluctuations. In addition, these debt obligations tend to have high credit ratings, so there is minimal risk of default.

Individuals may withdraw money invested in the money funds (that is, redeem shares) at will. This ease of converting to cash with minimal chance of loss means these shares are among the most liquid assets available to savers. The shares of money market mutual funds also offer savers competitive short-term yields. In many cases, these yields are higher than those offered by commercial and savings banks.

The money funds invest in a variety of short-term securities that include the negotiable CDs discussed earlier. Other money market instruments include the short-term debt of the federal government (Treasury bills), commercial paper issued by corporations, repurchase agreements (commonly referred to as repos), banker's acceptances, and tax anticipation notes. Of course, the individual investor may also directly acquire these securities, but the large denomination of some short-term securities (for example, the minimum denomination of negotiable CDs is $100,000) excludes most investors.

U.S. TREASURY BILL (T-BILL)
Short-term debt instrument issued by the federal government

The safest short-term security is the **U.S. Treasury bill** (commonly referred to as a **T-bill**), which is issued by the federal government. Before the political confrontation over the federal budget in 1995, there was no question that the federal government would retire the principal and pay the interest on its obligations. (The pricing of T-bills and the calculation of yields earned on the bills and other discounted short-term securities are covered in Chapter 20.) The short term of the bills also implies that if interest rates were to rise, the increase would have minimum impact on the bills, and the quick maturity means that investors could reinvest the proceeds in the higher-yielding securities.[9]

[9] Investors may buy Treasury bills through banks, brokerage firms, or the Federal Reserve. One-year bills are auctioned once a month; three- and six-month bills are auctioned every Monday. If the buyer purchases the bills directly from the Federal Reserve, the investor avoids paying any fees or brokerage commissions.

FIGURE 3.1

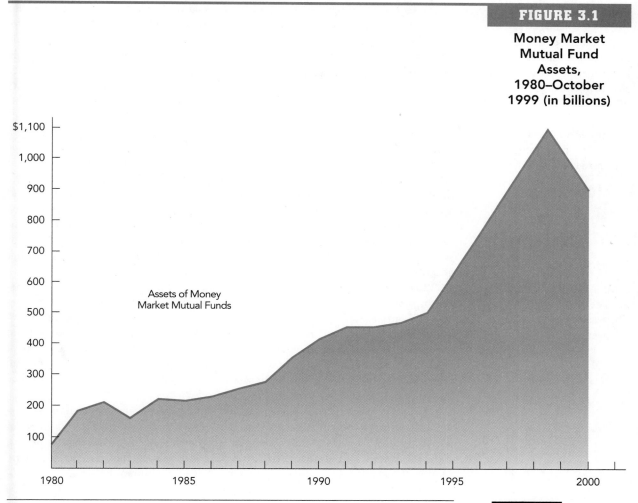

Money Market Mutual Fund Assets, 1980–October 1999 (in billions)

$1,100
1,000
900
800
700
600
500
400
300
200
100

Assets of Money Market Mutual Funds

1980 1985 1990 1995 2000

Source: *Derived from the* Investment Institute Mutual Fund Fact Book, *various issues and available at the Investment Company Web site:* **www.ici.org**.

COMMERCIAL PAPER
Unsecured short-term promissory notes issued by the most creditworthy corporations

Commercial paper is an unsecured promissory note issued by a corporation as an alternative to borrowing funds from commercial banks. Since the paper is unsecured, only firms with excellent credit ratings are able to sell it; hence, the risk of default is small, and the repayment of principal is virtually assured. Once again the term is short, so there is little risk from an investment in commercial paper.

REPURCHASE AGREEMENT (REPO)
Sales of a short-term security in which the seller agrees to buy back the security at a specified price

A **repurchase agreement (repo)** is a sale of a security in which the seller agrees to buy back (repurchase) the security at a specified price at a specified date. Repos are usually executed using federal government securities, and the repurchase price is higher than the initial sale price. The difference between the sale price and the repurchase price is the source of the return to the holder of the security. By entering into the repurchase agreement, the investor (the buyer) knows exactly how much will be made on the investment and when the funds will be returned.

BANKER'S ACCEPTANCE
Short-term promissory note guaranteed by a bank

Banker's acceptances are short-term promissory notes guaranteed by a bank. These acceptances arise through international trade. Suppose a firm ships goods abroad and receives a draft drawn on a specific bank that promises payment after two months. If the firm does not want to wait for payment, it can take the draft to a commercial bank for acceptance. Once the bank accepts the draft (and stamps it "accepted"), the draft may be sold. The buyer purchases the draft for a discount, which becomes the source of the return to the holder. Bankers' acceptances are considered to be good short-term investments because they are supported by two parties: the firm on which the draft is drawn and the bank that accepts the draft.

TAX ANTICIPATION NOTE
Short-term government security secured by expected tax revenues

Tax anticipation notes are issued by states or municipalities to finance current operations before tax revenues are received. As the taxes are collected, the proceeds are used to retire the debt. Similar notes are issued in anticipation of revenues from future bond issues and other sources, such as revenue sharing from the federal government. While these anticipation notes do not offer the safety of Treasury bills, the interest is exempt from federal income taxation.[10] Commercial banks and security dealers maintain secondary markets in them, so the notes may be liquidated should the firm need cash.

Money market mutual funds can invest in any of the preceding money market instruments (negotiable certificates of deposit, Treasury bills, commercial paper, repurchase agreements, banker's acceptances, and tax anticipation notes). Exhibit 3.6 shows aggregate distribution of money market fund assets. As may be seen in the exhibit, U.S. government securities and commercial paper constitute over half of these funds' assets, so the money funds are a major source of finance to the government and corporations.

Although the money funds as a whole own a wide spectrum of money market instruments, some of the funds do specialize. Schwab U.S. Treasury Money Fund, for example, invests solely in U.S. government securities or securities that are collateralized by obligations of the federal government. Other Schwab money funds invest in a wider spectrum of short-term debt obligations. For example, as of June 30, 1998, Schwab Money Fund had 0 percent of its assets in Treasury obligations, 12.4 percent in negotiable CDs, 78.7 percent in commercial paper, and the remaining percentage in various other short-term assets, such as repurchase agreements.

In addition to domestic short-term securities, money market mutual funds invest in Eurodollar certificates of deposit (Eurodollar CDs). These are similar to

[10] See footnote 2.

EXHIBIT 3.6

Distribution of Money Market Mutual Funds' Assets as of January 1999 (in billions)

Commercial paper	$ 420.9	36.2%
U.S. government securities	286.1	24.6
Repurchase agreements	141.7	12.2
Eurodollar certificates of deposit	30.7	2.6
Negotiable certificates of deposit	111.9	9.6
Banker's acceptances	2.9	0.2
Other	168.9	14.6
	$1,163.1	100.0%

Source: *Derived from* Investment Institute 1999 Mutual Fund Fact Book, *available at the Investment Institute Web site:* **www.ici.org**.

domestic negotiable CDs except they are issued either by branches of domestic banks located abroad or by foreign banks. Like domestic negotiable CDs, Eurodollar CDs are *denominated in U.S. dollars*, and they may be bought and sold because a secondary market exists. Eurodollar CDs offer a small yield advantage because they are not quite as liquid as domestic negotiable CDs and because they carry the additional risk of being issued in a foreign country.

COMPETITION FOR FUNDS

A commercial bank or any financial intermediary can only lend what has been lent to it. Unless the bank is able to induce individuals, firms, and governments to make deposits, that bank will be unable to grant loans and make investments. This general statement, of course, holds for all financial intermediaries. None can make investments without a source of funds. Whether these claims on the intermediaries are called life insurance policies or savings accounts or shares in money market mutual funds, the essential point remains the same. No financial intermediary can exist without its sources of funds.

Conversely, if funds flow out of financial intermediaries (if disintermediation occurs), all intermediaries will be able to hold fewer assets (that is, make fewer loans). Unless the outflow is reversed, it will tend to increase the cost of credit as the intermediaries raise the rates of interest they charge in order to ration their remaining lending capacity.

In addition to the aggregate flows into and out of all financial intermediaries, credit markets may feel the impact of flows among financial intermediaries. Funds deposited in one particular bank are not deposited in another competitive bank. If an individual saver has funds to invest and chooses a money market mutual fund instead of the local savings and loan association, it is the mutual fund that can lend the funds and not the savings and loan association. From the standpoint of the borrowers, it would not matter which intermediary makes the loans if all financial intermediaries had similar portfolios. But the portfolios of various financial intermediaries vary, as was illustrated in Exhibits 3.1, 3.5, and 3.6. As these exhibits showed, the holdings of the various intermediaries do differ.

These differences can have an important implication. A transfer of funds from one intermediary (for example, a savings and loan association) to another (such as a money market mutual fund) can have an important impact on the supply of credit available to a particular sector of the economy. Although the total supply of credit is unaffected (because the money market fund can lend only what the savings and loan association loses), there will be a redistribution of credit from those who borrow from savings and loan associations to those who borrow from the money funds. The money market mutual fund now has more funds to acquire income-earning assets, such as short-term securities. Simultaneously, the flow of funds out of the savings and loan association reduces its capacity to grant mortgage loans. Such a redistribution of funds from savings and loan associations to money market mutual funds will be felt by the construction industry and home buyers as the supply of mortgage money declines.

As this discussion implies, financial intermediaries compete with each other for funds. This competition occurs through yields and services offered. If a particular intermediary did not offer competitive rates, funds would flow from it to those intermediaries offering higher yields. Thus, differentiation among the intermediaries on the basis of yields tends to be small.

Historically, financial intermediaries have been categorized on the basis of services or products offered. Today, however, this is only partially true. In the past, savers bought life insurance through insurance agents, bought stocks through securities brokers, and invested funds in a savings account in a bank. Those days of specialization are disappearing. Insurance agents, stockbrokers, and bankers today offer a wide spectrum of services and financial products. For example, many commercial banks offer savers not only the traditional services of savings and checking accounts but other products as well, such as discount brokerage services to compete with stockbrokers), money market accounts (to compete with money market mutual funds), and pension plans (to compete with insurance companies and mutual funds). Such product competition also applies to savings banks. Savings and loan associations offer a variety of savings accounts as well as checking accounts that compete with commercial banks. Some S&Ls even sell life insurance and offer discount brokerage services.

Brokerage firms have also encroached on the domain of the banks through the creation of cash management accounts. For example, Merrill Lynch's pioneering Cash Management Account, which is known by the registered trademark CMA, combines the traditional brokerage custodial services with checking privileges, a credit card (VISA), and money market yields on funds in the account. Other brokerage firms either have instituted similar accounts or have correspondent relationships with money market mutual funds that offer checking privileges, credit cards, and rates comparable to other money market yields.

While the distinctions among financial institutions have become blurred, the Glass-Steagall Act of 1933 forbids banks from underwriting corporate securities. Commercial banks are permitted to serve as investment bankers for government securities, but they cannot serve in this capacity for corporate clients. Thus, the distinction still exists between brokerage firms that have investment banking divisions for the underwriting of corporate securities and commercial banks that do not. Whether this distinction will continue to exist is questionable. In many European countries, commercial banks are permitted to serve as investment bankers for corporate clients; legislation has been proposed that would permit U.S. banks to do the same. As might be expected, the large commercial banks support repeal of the Glass-Steagall Act, but brokerage firms do not want the additional competition that would result.

If commercial banks are permitted to underwrite corporate securities, the distinctions between brokerage firms and commercial banks will be blurred further. However, some distinctions will still remain. Commercial banks will continue to be the primary depository for checking accounts as well as a major source of short-term financing for corporations. Savings and loan associations will remain a major source of mortgage loans. Insurance companies will still provide their primary products: life, health, and casualty insurance.

SUMMARY

The flow of funds through financial intermediaries to those in need of funds is exceedingly important for an advanced economy. The benefits accrue to (1) savers, who have a place to invest their funds, (2) borrowers in need of funds, (3) the financial intermediaries themselves through the opportunity to earn a profit, and (4) the economy as a whole, since the level of economic activity would be lower without financial intermediaries.

Financial intermediaries include commercial banks, thrift institutions, life insurance companies, pension plans, and money market mutual funds. All financial intermediaries compete for funds, since an individual intermediary can only acquire a portfolio of assets if it can obtain funds. The deregulation of the banking system has increased competition among the various intermediaries and blurred the distinctions among them, allowing them to offer products and services that previously were the exclusive domain of a particular intermediary.

In terms of size, commercial banks are the most important financial intermediary. These banks make a variety of loans but tend to stress loans that are quickly repaid. Other financial intermediaries, such as savings and loan associations and life insurance companies, make longer-term loans.

The profit margins of a commercial bank are the result of the difference between what it pays depositors and what it charges borrowers. These margins tend to be small. Also, commercial banks and other financial intermediaries raise a substantial amount of money through the creation of claims on themselves. They are highly financially leveraged, which increases the risk associated with the operation.

Recent developments in financial intermediaries include the large growth in money market mutual funds. Money market mutual funds compete directly with banks; they offer the advantages of somewhat higher yields and almost comparable safety. While the shares are not federally insured as are the deposits in banks, the short-term nature of their portfolios affords the saver safety of principal.

Review Questions

1. What are a commercial bank's sources of funds and profits? What effect will a change in interest rates have on a bank's earnings?
2. What are the differences among a bank's total reserves, required reserves, and excess reserves?

3. What are the primary assets of a savings and loan association? If an individual deposits money in a savings account with a savings and loan, is that deposit safe? What is the role of the FDIC?
4. What differentiates the portfolios of a money market mutual fund, a commercial bank, a savings and loan association, and a life insurance company?
5. What explained the initial growth in money market mutual funds? Are the shares of these funds insured by the federal government? Are investments in the shares of money market mutual funds more risky than an investment in a commercial bank's certificate of deposit?
6. What proportions of a financial intermediary's assets are financed by debt and by equity? What effect does this financing have on the risk associated with a financial intermediary?

CHAPTER 4

The Federal Reserve and the Supply and Cost of Credit

Learning Objectives

1. List the goals of fiscal and monetary policy.
2. Enumerate the assets and liabilities of the Federal Reserve and describe its structure.
3. Explain how cash deposits may lead to a multiple expansion in the money supply.
4. Illustrate how the tools of monetary policy affect the supply of money and credit.
5. Identify the impact a federal government deficit or surplus may have on the supply of credit and the supply of money.
6. Explain how inflation may affect the cost of credit, and differentiate between the nominal and real rates of interest.

According to Will Rogers, "There have been three great inventions since the beginning of time: fire, the wheel, and central banking." While greatness may be disputed, there can be no denying the potential impact the nation's central bank, the Federal Reserve, has on credit markets, the supply of money, and the economy. By using its tools of monetary policy, the Federal Reserve may expand or contract the supply of money and credit and thereby have significant impact on the financial health of the economy.

In addition to the potential impact of the Federal Reserve, the fiscal policy of the federal government can also affect credit markets and the well-being of firms. When the federal government runs a deficit, that deficit must be financed. In 1992, the annual deficit had grown to $290,400,000,000, from a surplus of $3,236,000,000 in 1969.[1] Someone had to put up over $290 billion to cover the deficit. When the federal government borrows from the general public or the banking system, it competes with firms and individuals for the existing supply of credit. This competition affects interest rates and the capacity of the banking system to lend to firms.

During the late 1990s the federal government began to run a surplus as receipts exceeded disbursements. While a deficit has to be financed, the surplus raises the opposite question: what to do with the surplus? One possibility is to retire some of the federal government debt that was issued to finance the deficits.

[1] See the *Economic Report to the President* available at www.access.gpo.gov/eop.

This chapter is concerned with the Federal Reserve and its impact on the supply of money and the cost of credit. Initially, the roles and composition of the Federal Reserve are described. The second section discusses how changes in banks' reserves lead to a multiple expansion or contraction of the money supply. The third section considers the Federal Reserve's tools of monetary policy and their impact on the lending capacity of banks. The next section is devoted to the federal government's fiscal policy and how deficits and surpluses may affect the supply of money and credit. The last sections consider inflation, its effect on credit markets and interest rates, and the impact of monetary and fiscal policy on the individual firm.

THE ROLE OF THE FEDERAL RESERVE SYSTEM

The purpose of the Federal Reserve System is to help achieve stable prices, full employment, and economic growth through the regulation of the supply of credit and money in the economy. Changing the supply of money and credit to achieve these three goals is called **monetary policy.**

MONETARY POLICY
Management of the money supply for the purpose of maintaining stable prices, full employment, and economic growth

The Federal Reserve (the "Fed") has several tools of monetary policy. The primary tool is open market operations, while secondary tools are the discount rate and reserve requirements. The Federal Reserve uses these monetary tools to expand or contract the supply of money to pursue the economic goals of prosperity with full employment and stable prices. When the Federal Reserve seeks to increase the supply of money and credit to help expand the level of income and employment, that is called an "easy" monetary policy. When it seeks to contract the supply of money and credit to help fight inflation, that is referred to as a "tight" monetary policy.

While controlling the supply of money and credit is the primary role of the Federal Reserve, it also serves a variety of other functions. The many roles that the Federal Reserve System plays are mirrored by the assets and liabilities on its balance sheet. A simplified balance sheet for the Federal Reserve is shown in Exhibit 4.1. The majority of the Federal Reserve's assets are gold certificates and the debt of the United States government.

The Federal Reserve's Assets and Liabilities

The **gold certificates** are warehouse receipts for gold held by the Treasury. Until the Gold Reserve Act of 1934, there had to be a dollar's worth of gold for every dollar in Federal Reserve Notes. The gold was held in vaults (Fort Knox, for example) for safekeeping, and paper money, which could be converted into gold, was used as a substitute for gold. In 1934 the nation changed its monetary system so that only a fraction of its paper money was backed by gold. The fraction of gold necessary to cover the money supply was established by the federal government. Eventually this gold requirement was completely eliminated, and today the public's faith in the purchase power of the money supply "backs" the currency. The Treasury, however, still owns the gold and can sell the certificates to the Federal Reserve to raise funds.

GOLD CERTIFICATES
Warehouse receipts issued by the United States Treasury for gold it holds

EXHIBIT 4.1

Simplified Federal Reserve Balance Sheet as of July 31, 1999 (in millions)

Assets		
Gold certificates	$ 11,048	2.0%
U.S. government securities	489,298	88.6
Loans to depository institutions	348	0.1
Cash items in process of collection	5,087	0.9
Other assets	46,597	8.4
Total assets	$552,378	100.0%
Liabilities		
Federal Reserve notes	$506,746	91.7
Deposits:		
Member bank reserves	16,642	3.0
U.S. Treasury	4,984	0.9
Foreign	257	0.0
Other liabilities	9,762	1.7
Capital	13,987	2.7
Total liabilities and capital	$451,890	100.0%

Source: *Federal Reserve Bulletin, December 1999, A10.*

The major asset of the Federal Reserve is the debt of the federal government. As is explained later, this debt is bought and sold by the Federal Reserve through open market operations. These purchases and sales alter the money supply and the ability of banks to create credit and are the most important tool of monetary policy. The Federal Reserve balance sheet mirrors the importance of this element of monetary policy by the large amount of Treasury debt owned by the central bank. The interest paid by this debt is the primary source of revenues to operate the Federal Reserve System. In fact, the Federal Reserve collects sufficient interest to meet its expenses and have a profit. It pays banks a dividend of 6 percent on the amount these banks are required to invest in the Federal Reserve. If there is a residual profit after these dividends, the funds are returned to the Treasury.

CASH ITEMS IN PROCESS
Checks that have not cleared: the float

The remaining assets of the Federal Reserve include **cash items in process** and loans to banks. The term "cash items" is misleading because it does not involve cash but is concerned with the clearing of checks. This clearing of checks is one of the most important services provided to banks by the Federal Reserve. At a given moment there are always checks being cleared, and they appear on the Federal Reserve's balance sheet as cash items in process.

This process of check clearing is illustrated by the flow chart in Exhibit 4.2. When a $100 check is drawn on an account (a deposit in bank A), the funds remain in that bank until the check clears. The bank that receives the check (bank B) credits $100 to the account in which the check was deposited (that is, its

EXHIBIT 4.2

The Process of Clearing Checks

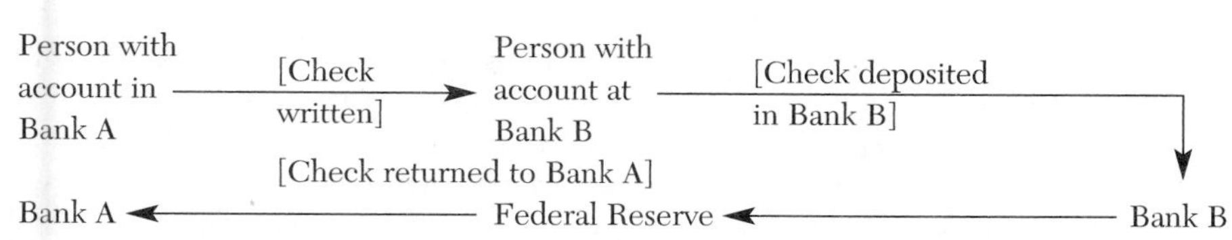

demand deposits increase). The second bank processes the check by sending it to the Federal Reserve for clearing. The Federal Reserve sends the check to bank A, but for a few days that deposit exists in two banks. Both banks may have the reserves because after two days the Federal Reserve credits the second bank with $100 in reserves. In effect the reserves and the deposits are being double-counted.

This double-counting is called the **float.** If checks take longer to clear, the float increases. This is expansionary because the money is in two places at the same time. For example, if checks take four days instead of two days to clear, both banks have the use of the reserves for two additional days. Thus, changes in the float are important because they affect the reserves of commercial banks and alter the ability of these banks to lend and create credit. Of course, once the entire check-clearing process is completed, the float disappears, and the reserves are transferred from one bank to the other (from bank A to bank B).

FLOAT
Checks in the process of clearing that are simultaneously counted as deposits in two banks

The Federal Reserve may lend reserves to depository institutions; thus, the promises of banks to repay these loans constitute additional assets. As is discussed later in this chapter, banks borrow reserves from the Federal Reserve to meet their reserve requirements. Borrowing reserves is not free, and the discount rate, which is the interest rate charged for borrowing from the Federal Reserve, is one of the major tools of monetary policy.

The miscellaneous assets of the Federal Reserve include foreign currencies. Foreign trade involves foreign currencies. American dollars flow abroad when Americans travel in foreign countries, when American firms invest abroad, or when the U.S. government spends money in or gives aid to a foreign country. These dollars must be exchanged for the local currency, and central banks are the mechanisms through which foreign currencies are converted into domestic currencies. Thus, the Federal Reserve has holdings of foreign currencies, just as the banks in other countries have holdings of dollars.

The largest liability of the Federal Reserve is the paper currency held by the general public (that is, **Federal Reserve Notes**). The Federal Reserve also serves as a depository for banks, the Treasury, and foreign financial institutions.[2] Banks deposit their reserves in the Federal Reserve, and the Treasury may deposit its funds, such as tax receipts, in the Federal Reserve banks. The foreign deposits arise as the

FEDERAL RESERVE NOTES
Paper currency of the United States issued by the Federal Reserve

[2] Commercial banks, savings and loan associations, mutual savings banks, and credit unions may deposit reserves with the Federal Reserve.

result of international monetary transactions. Of all the different deposits, the most important are the reserves of depository institutions. By altering these reserves and the amount of Federal Reserve Notes outstanding, the Federal Reserve is able to alter the supply of money and the ability of these institutions to create loans. It is through the power of the Federal Reserve to create and destroy these liabilities that credit is eased or tightened. Presently there are no constraints on the Federal Reserve's power to create or destroy these liabilities. Only the goals of public policy, such as price stability or full employment, constrain the central bank: it is assumed that the Federal Reserve will act to help achieve these economic goals.

Under the Monetary Control Act of 1980, Congress has also given the Federal Reserve vast supervisory power over depository institutions. The purpose of this power is not only to control the supply of money and credit but also to protect the depositors from poor financial management by individual banks. The supervisory power of the Federal Reserve includes the enforcement of bank regulations and periodic examination of banks. Periodic reports to the Federal Reserve concerning an individual bank's loans, expenses, and earnings are also required. If the examinations and reports indicate that a bank is following unsound financial policies, the Federal Reserve can require the bank's management to correct these policies. This ability to force a bank's management to change policy gives the Federal Reserve's supervisory powers real force. The mere existence of this force is sufficient to keep the majority of banks pursuing sound financial policies.

Structure of the Federal Reserve

BOARD OF GOVERNORS
Controlling body of the Federal Reserve whose members are appointed by the president of the United States

The power in the Federal Reserve System is concentrated in a **Board of Governors,** consisting of seven people appointed by the president of the United States with the confirmation of the Senate. The appointments are for 14 years, and the terms are staggered so that one new appointment is made every two years. The long terms and the staggering of these terms reduce political pressures and thus contribute to the federal system of checks and balances. The chairman of the Board of Governors is usually the major spokesperson for monetary policy and may act as an advisor to the president on economic policy. The power of the Board of Governors manifests itself in several ways through its power of appointment and control of open market operations.

DISTRICT BANK
Twelve banks that comprise the Federal Reserve

The country is divided into 12 districts, with a Federal Reserve bank in each district. Each **district bank** is managed by nine directors, three of whom are appointed by the Board of Governors. The remaining six directors are elected by member banks and represent the member banks, industry, commerce, and agriculture. By dividing the nation into districts, it is possible to have an individual reserve bank perform specialized financial services pertaining to its region. For example, the financial problems of rural regions may differ from those of urban areas. Decentralizing the central bank into districts permits a more flexible approach to regional financial problems. Since the city of New York is the financial center of the nation, the district bank in New York is the largest and most important individual reserve bank.

Member banks constitute the next component of the Federal Reserve System. Commercial banks have either state or national charters. All banks with

FIGURE 4.1

Structure of the Federal Reserve

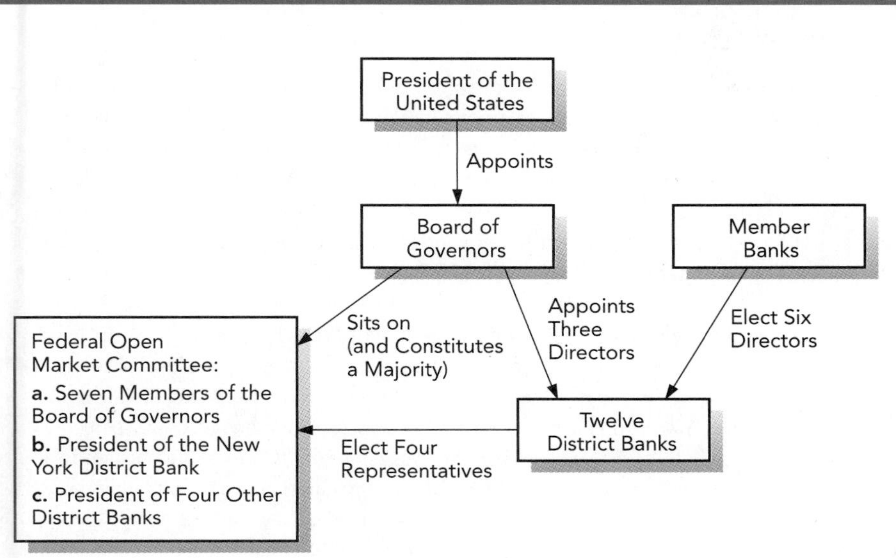

national charters must join the Federal Reserve. State banks have the option to join, but many do not choose to join. Since the Federal Reserve permits non-member banks to use its check-clearing facilities and to borrow reserves, these services are available to all banks without their joining the system.

The member banks are required to invest capital in their district's Federal Reserve bank. The members are the owners of the Federal Reserve banks, and for this investment they receive a modest return on their capital from the earnings of the Federal Reserve. As was explained previously, the source of these earnings is the interest earned on the U.S. government debt owned by the Federal Reserve. If the Federal Reserve earns profits that exceed its required dividends to member banks, the excess profits are returned to the Treasury.

The last component of the Federal Reserve is the **Federal Open Market Committee,** which has control over open market operations. Because open market operations are the most important tool of monetary policy, this committee is a powerful component of the system. The committee consists of the seven members of the Board of Governors and five presidents of the district banks. The president of the New York district bank is a permanent member of the committee, while the four remaining positions rotate among the district bank presidents. By voting as a bloc, the Board of Governors has a majority on the committee, and has control of open market operations.

FEDERAL OPEN MARKET COMMITTEE
Part of the Federal Reserve that establishes and executes monetary policy

In summary, the important components of the Federal Reserve System are (1) the Board of Governors, (2) the district reserve banks, (3) the member banks, and (4) the Federal Open Market Committee. This structure is summarized by Figure 4.1. Although the president of the United States appoints the Board of Governors,

FINANCIAL FACTS

Fed Watching

Because changes in monetary policy rates can have a major impact on interest rates, security prices, and the economy, it is not surprising that investors and financial managers watch the Fed with the hope of determining the next shift in monetary policy. Such monitoring primarily involves the meetings of the Federal Open Market Committee and the Congressional testimony of the chairman of the Board of Governors of the Federal Reserve. A major goal of the Fed is price stability, which suggests that the Fed will raise interest rates at the first whiff of increased prices. These higher prices will tend to depress security prices, increase the cost of credit, and dampen economic activity. ¶ The Federal Open Market Committee is individually the most powerful component of the Fed since it has control over open market operations. The most important individual member of the Fed is the chairman of the Board of Governors. During the 1990s, Alan Greenspan served as chairman. An economist who served as head of the Council of Economic Advisers to President Ford, Chairman Greenspan is an economic conservative who has tended to follow a moderately expansionary monetary policy with a primary emphasis on stabilizing prices. However, the goal of stable prices does not mean that the Fed will not take action to stimulate economic growth. During the 1990 recession, the Federal Reserve put reserves into the banking system and lowered the discount rate to stimulate economic expansion. During the late 1990s, the Fed again lowered interest rates to maintain economic growth as the Asian economies declined and the fear arose that the Asian economic problems would cause the U.S. economy to falter and enter a recession. ¶ As chairman of the Board of Governors, Alan Greenspan is the chief spokesman for the Fed. His frequent testimony to Congress is eagerly watched for clues to future Fed actions. The financial markets do react to his statements. For example, in December 1996, Chairman Greenspan remarked that recent increases in stock prices exhibited "irrational exuberance." The next day, the Dow Jones industrial average declined 145 points. Greenspan's remarks may also cause stock prices to rise. In September 1998, after a one-day drop of more than 500 points, Chairman Greenspan hinted that interest rates may be reduced. The Dow Jones industrial average rose over 380 points the next day. These illustrations indicate that Chairman Greenspan's remarks can have an impact on the market, but the impact may be short lived. The market rose over 1,000 points within six months after the "irrational exuberance" statement and lost more than 380 points within a week after the hint of lower interest rates. ¶

and the member banks own the Federal Reserve, the real power rests with the Board of Governors. It has this power because it (1) appoints three of the nine directors of the district reserve banks, (2) comprises a majority of the Federal Open Market Committee, and (3) has regulatory authority over the commercial banks. Thus, the Board of Governors is individually the most important part of the Federal Reserve System.

THE EXPANSION OF MONEY AND CREDIT

The Federal Reserve affects the supply of money and credit through its impact on the reserves of banks, which alters their lending capacity. A small change in banks' reserves can produce a much larger change in the money supply because of the fractional reserve system. Understanding the potential impact of monetary policy requires understanding how the banking system expands and contracts the supply of money and credit—that is, understanding how a fractional reserve banking system alters the supply of money.

Banks' ability to lend comes from investors: the depositors, general creditors, and owners who invest in various types of instruments (such as certificates of deposit or the bank's stock) issued by each bank. An individual bank can only lend what it obtains from its sources of finance, but, as is subsequently explained, the aggregate banking system can expand the supply of money. As this money flows among banks, the aggregate supply is increased. This increase is the result of the fractional reserve requirements established by the Federal Reserve.

This section is concerned with the banking system's ability to expand and contract the supply of money and credit. The next section will consider how the Federal Reserve affects the capacity of banks to lend and thus affects the supply of money and credit. Although the following discussion could become quite involved as different scenarios are considered, only one simple case is given, since the purpose of the discussion is to illustrate the expansion of money and credit and not to illustrate how differing assumptions may alter the amount of change in the money supply.[3]

The process of loan creation will be illustrated under the following assumptions: (1) Cash is always deposited in a demand deposit, and none is held in the form of cash. (2) Banks hold no excess reserves: all excess reserves are loaned. (3) There are sufficient borrowers to consume the excess reserves of the banks. If these assumptions are violated, there are leakages within the system that decrease the potential expansion. For example, if individuals hold cash, that money is not deposited in a bank and hence cannot be lent by a bank. Such a holding of cash reduces the assets of banks and reduces their capacity to expand the supply of money and credit.

What is the potential effect of cash deposited in a checking account? As was explained in Chapter 2, the money supply (M-1) is the sum of demand deposits plus coins and currency in circulation. Cash deposited into checking accounts does not change the money supply. All that is changed is the form of the money from cash to demand deposits. Such transactions, however, are extremely important, for they increase the banks' ability to lend. When the banks use this ability and make loans, they expand the supply of money.

Consider what happens when $100 is deposited in a checking account. The $100 has been removed from circulation and replaced by the demand deposit.

[3] For a discussion of different scenarios under different assumptions, consult a money and banking text, such as Frederic S. Miskin. *The Economics of Money, Banking, and Financial Markets,* 5th ed. (Reading, Mass.: Addison-Wesley, 1998).

After the bank receives the $100 cash deposit, the $100 becomes part of the reserves of the bank. This $100 reserve is divided into two categories: (1) those reserves that must be held against the demand deposit, the required reserves: and (2) those reserves in excess of the reserve requirement, which are called excess reserves. If the reserve requirement is 10 percent, then $10 of the $100 cash reserve is required and $90 is excess reserves.[4] These excess reserves are very important because commercial banks use their excess reserves to acquire income-earning assets such as loans and securities. Depositing cash in a commercial bank thus gives it the ability to create loans, because the bank obtains a resource that it may lend—excess reserves. Banks do not lend and cannot lend their deposit liabilities.

If the bank grants a borrower a loan of $90, what effect will this transaction have on (1) the depositor, (2) the bank, and (3) the borrower? Since this transaction does not concern the depositor, it has no effect on the depositor. As far as the depositor is concerned, the bank still owes on demand $100. The borrower receives an asset—a demand deposit at the bank—and also incurs a liability, the IOU to the bank. The bank acquires an asset, the $90 loan, and the bank incurs a new liability, the $90 demand deposit. This deposit is the money that the borrower receives for the loan.

Why does the commercial bank create a new demand deposit instead of just lending the person the cash? The answer is that the bank does not want the borrower to remove the cash from the bank. The bank wants to keep that cash as long as possible, for it is part of the bank's reserves. The bank does realize that the borrower will spend the money and the reserves will probably be transferred to another bank, but the bank still wants the use of the reserves as long as possible.

Why does the borrower take out the loan? Obviously, the borrower does not want to leave the money in the bank and pay interest on the loan but intends to spend it. When the borrower does spend the money, the recipient of the check will either cash it or deposit it in a commercial bank. When the check is deposited, the probability of this bank and the borrower's bank being the same is quite small, since there are thousands of commercial banks in the country. When the check is deposited in the second bank, that bank sends the check to the first bank for payment. The first bank transfers $90 worth of reserves (the cash) to the second bank. This flow of deposits and reserves may be summarized by the following figure:

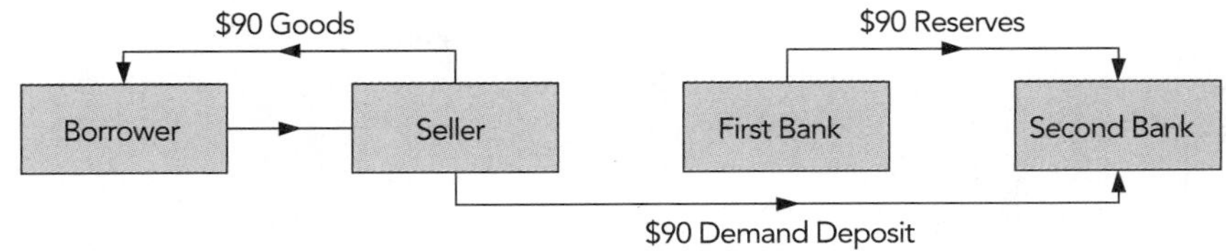

[4] As of January 1, 2000, the reserve requirement was 10 percent.

In summary, the loan made possible a purchase by the borrower, and thus a seller has made a sale that may not have occurred without the creation of the loan. Goods have flowed from the seller to the buyer. When the seller deposited the payment in a commercial bank, this caused reserves to flow between the seller's bank and the borrower's bank.

What is the net effect of this transaction on the money supply and amount of credit? Both have increased. There are $190 in demand deposits—the initial deposit of $100 in the first bank and the new deposit of $90 in the second bank. There has been a net increase in the money supply of $90. This $90 increase came through the process of loan creation, for there is now $90 in new credit. The act of depositing cash in a checking account led to a net increase in the supply of money through the process of loan creation.

The process of loan creation is not limited to the initial expansion of $90, for the second bank now has a new deposit. It must hold reserves against the new checking account. Since the reserve requirement is 10 percent, the bank must hold in reserve $9 ($90 × 0.1). It received $90 in reserves from the first bank when the check cleared. Thus, $81 of these reserves are excess reserves that the second bank may use to purchase an income-earning asset or grant a new loan. If the second bank grants a loan for $81, it creates a new demand deposit of $81. The borrower then purchases goods and services and pays for them with a check drawn on the new demand deposit. The $81 check then is deposited in a third bank and is cleared. This creates for the third bank a new deposit and transfers to it $81 in reserves from the second bank. The third bank divides these reserves into required reserves ($81 × 0.1 = $8.10) and excess reserves of $72.90. The third bank now has the capacity to acquire income-earning assets and create new loans.

This process of lending and passing reserves among commercial banks may continue until there are no more excess reserves. With each new loan there is expansion in the money supply. The net increase in new credit and in demand deposits is many times the initial deposit. This expansion is illustrated in Exhibit 4.3, which continues the multiple expansion for the first eight rounds. As may be seen in the table, each additional loan and new demand deposit (column 1) is smaller, but the sum of the new loans increases (column 2). As the total of demand deposits rises, required reserves also rise (column 3), so excess reserves must decline (column 4). Of course, it is this decline in excess reserves that causes each new loan to be smaller. Eventually, if the expansion continues indefinitely, the excess reserves will become zero and the total $100 in reserves will be required reserves.

If the expansion continues until there are no excess reserves, how much will the money supply increase? What is the increase in new loans? These questions may be answered by the following simple equation:

$$\frac{\text{Change in excess reserves}}{\text{Reserve requirement}} = \text{Change in the money supply.} \qquad \text{4.1}$$

Equation 4.1 gives the increase in *both* new credit and the money supply. In the previous example, the cash deposit of $100 increased excess reserves by $90. Since

EXHIBIT 4.3

Multiple Expansion of the Supply of Money

	Initial Deposit = $100		Reserve Requirement = 10%	
	New Demand Deposits	Cumulative New Credit Created	Cumulative Required Reserves	Excess Reserves
1st bank	$100.00	$ 0.00	$ 10.00	$90.00
2nd bank	90.00	90.00	19.00	81.00
3rd bank	81.00	171.00	27.10	72.90
4th bank	72.90	243.90	34.39	65.61
5th bank	65.61	309.51	40.95	59.05
6th bank	59.05	368.56	46.86	53.14
7th bank	53.14	421.70	52.17	47.83
8th bank	47.83	469.53	56.95	43.05
Final round	0	$900.00	$100.00	0

the reserve requirement was 10 percent, the maximum possible expansion in the money supply and new credit is

$$\$90/0.1 = \$900.$$

Depositing $100 in a demand deposit permits an expansion of $900 of new money. Since the new money came through the creation of new credit, $900 is also the maximum possible increase in new credit. The change in the money supply and the change in credit thus is ten times the initial change in the excess reserves.

Cash Withdrawals and the Reduction in Reserves

In the previous example, cash was deposited in an account, which created new excess reserves and led to the expansion in the supply of money and credit. A cash withdrawal from a bank reverses the process and reduces the bank's reserves. If the bank has excess reserves, the withdrawal creates no problems for the bank, because it takes the funds out of its excess reserves. After the withdrawal, the bank's lending capacity is reduced because the bank has lost excess reserves.

The situation is different if the bank has no excess reserves. While the bank may be able to meet the withdrawal from its existing (and required) reserves, it now has a major problem: Its reserves are insufficient to meet its reserve requirements against its deposit liabilities. Thus, the bank must take some action to restore its reserves.

One possibility is to borrow the reserves from another bank. If bank A borrows reserves from bank B, bank A will now meet its reserve requirement. Will bank B meet its reserve requirement? The answer should be obvious. Bank B can only make this loan if it has excess reserves! The borrowing of reserves transfers reserves from one bank to another; it does not alter the total supply of reserves in the banking system. All that changes is the location of the reserves from bank B to bank A.

The market for these reserves is called the **federal funds market.** Federal funds is one of the most well developed of all short-term credit markets. If a commercial bank lacks sufficient reserves against its deposit liabilities, it can borrow reserves from a commercial bank that has excess reserves. If a bank has excess reserves, it can put these funds to work by lending them in the federal funds market. Thus, the bank converts a sterile asset, the excess reserves, into an income-earning asset, for it charges the borrowing bank interest for the use of the reserves.

FEDERAL FUNDS MARKET
Market in which banks borrow and lend excess reserves

Since the reserves may be needed for only a very short time, the loans made in the federal funds market are usually for extremely short periods (for example, a day). Thus, any commercial bank that has a temporary surplus of loanable funds may briefly lend them in the federal funds market and earn interest on the funds. The rate of interest is referred to as the **federal funds rate.** (This is somewhat of a misnomer because the loans involve neither the federal government nor the Federal Reserve.) Any commercial bank that has a deficit in its reserves is able to borrow them for as short a period as necessary.

FEDERAL FUNDS RATE
Interest rate charged by banks on overnight loans of reserves

The federal funds market illustrates the importance of good management of short-term assets. Because the loans may be for as short a period as *a day,* a bank with excess reserves may put this asset to work for this brief period. Because these loans are of such short duration, the interest rate on federal funds can fluctuate quickly. When excess reserves exist in the banking system, the interest rate may fall to nothing because the quantity of the excess reserves supplied exceeds the quantity demanded. But during periods of excess demand, commercial banks may pay a substantial rate of interest for these loans in order to meet their reserve requirement.

If the banking system lacks excess reserves, the bank that experienced the cash withdrawal could borrow the reserves from the Federal Reserve. Unlike the banking system, the Federal Reserve has the power to create reserves. If bank A is short and all other banks lack excess reserves, then borrowing from the Federal Reserve creates the reserves needed by bank A. Of course, the Federal Reserve charges interest on this loan, just as bank B would charge bank A interest for the use of its reserves. This interest rate, called the **discount rate,** is a major tool of monetary policy and is discussed in detail in the next section on the tools of monetary policy.

DISCOUNT RATE
Interest rate charged banks for borrowing reserves from the Federal Reserve

Suppose, however, that the banking system has no excess reserves and bank A does not want to borrow reserves from the Federal Reserve. What will happen? The bank will have to liquidate some of its assets, and because there are no excess reserves in the banking system, the multiple expansion illustrated previously works in reverse. The reduction in reserves will cause the supply of money and credit to contract. Just as the cash deposit leads to a multiple expansion, the withdrawal of cash when the banking system is fully loaned up will cause a multiple contraction in the money supply and in the supply of credit.

This process of a multiple contraction is illustrated in Exhibit 4.4, which essentially reverses the procedure illustrated in Exhibit 4.3. The initial cash

EXHIBIT 4.4

Multiple Contraction in the Supply of Money

	Initial Withdrawal = $100		Reserve Requirement = 10%	
Final round	**Change in Demand Deposits**	**Cumulative Change in Demand Deposits**	**Reduction in Required Reserves**	**Cumulative Change in Required Reserves**
1st bank	−$100.00	−$100.00	−$10.00	−$10.00
2nd bank	−90.00	−190.00	−9.00	−19.00
3rd bank	−81.00	−271.00	−8.10	−27.10
4th bank	−72.40	−343.90	−7.29	−34.39
.	.	.	.	.
.	.	.	.	.
.	.	.	.	.
Final round	0	−$900.00	0	−$100.00

withdrawal of $100 reduces demand deposits by $100 (column 1). Total reserves also decline by $100, but since required reserves decline by only $10 (column 3), the decline in total reserves of $100 means the bank is now short reserves by $90. The bank liquidates an asset worth $90 to replace its lost reserves and the shortage is transferred to the second bank. The second bank now loses $90 in deposits and reserves and the process is repeated. Unless the cash is returned to the banking system, the system must contract. The cumulative decline in demand deposits is given in the second column, and the fourth column presents the cumulative change in required reserves with each subsequent contraction. As in the case of the expansion in demand deposits, the maximum decrease in the money supply is −$900 (−$90/0.1) and the cumulative change in required reserves is −$100, which is the amount of the initial cash withdrawal.

This contraction is precisely what happened during the Great Depression. (Remember the run on the bank George Bailey experienced in *It's a Wonderful Life*?) Banks had insufficient liquidity to meet withdrawals. Because the Federal Reserve did not put reserves into the system, many commercial banks were unable to meet the withdrawals and had to close their doors. Thus, a major role of the central bank should be to act as a source of reserves and liquidity to commercial banks when all other sources have been drained. The Federal Reserve, by its ability to create bank reserves, is able to create liquidity for banks when such liquidity is needed to meet withdrawals.

The previous discussion suggests that a flow of funds out of a bank can create a significant liquidity problem. An outflow of deposits reduces the individual bank's reserves. (Such cash withdrawals need not affect the reserves of the banking system if the funds are deposited in another bank.) The management of a bank is conscious of the impact of a flow of funds from the bank and takes steps to reduce the impact by seeking to match their loan portfolio and anticipated cash drains. Such matching would be simple if all deposits were 30-day certificates of deposit. The bank could assure having the funds to meet the CDs by only making 30-day loans. The maturing loans would cover the maturing CDs. If the CDs were renewed, then the banks could make new loans for an additional 30 days.

Of course, portfolio management of banks is not that simple because banks issue a variety of instruments to induce deposits. These range from very short-term deposits (such as demand deposits) to instruments that may not mature for many years (for example, a five-year CD). In addition, as is explained in Chapter 21, commercial banks grant lines of credit that permit the creditor to borrow varying amounts over a period of time. (Individuals also have access to lines of credit through credit cards such as VISA that offer cash advances.) Such loans mean that bankers do not know from day to day exactly how much will be loaned, nor do they know exactly when the loans will be repaid.

Management will have had experience with the rate at which deposits flow into and out of the bank, how many loans will be granted, and when they will be repaid. This knowledge permits the bank to construct a portfolio consistent with management's anticipated need for funds to meet withdrawals. However, there have been periods when a bank's managers have found themselves in precarious situations. This is especially true during periods when interest rates rise rapidly. Depositors may withdraw more funds than had been anticipated by the bank's management. Presumably these withdrawals are being made by savers seeking to earn a higher return in an alternative institution that competes with the accounts offered by the bank. Meeting these withdrawals can hurt the individual bank, especially if it must pay higher interest rates to raise the funds to meet the withdrawals. Unless the bank is also able to raise the rates it charges on its loans, the profitability of the bank is hurt, since its cost of funds is increased.

THE TOOLS OF MONETARY POLICY

As the previous discussion indicates, the reserves of commercial banks are an important component of the financial system. Anything that affects these reserves affects the ability of commercial banks to create money and credit. Ultimately, the control of the supply of money rests with the Federal Reserve. It is through the impact on banks' reserves that the Fed is able to alter the supply of money.

The Federal Reserve has three primary tools for affecting the reserves of depository institutions: the reserve requirement, the discount rate, and open market operations. Each is important through its ability to change excess reserves and hence affect banks' lending capacity. In addition to these primary tools of monetary policy, the Federal Reserve has selective credit controls concerning real estate and consumer loans and purchase of securities with borrowed funds (the margin requirement discussed in Chapter 6). However, the primary tools of monetary policy give the Federal Reserve its power to affect the economy. The ensuing discussion explains how each is used to alter the reserves of banks and thus affect the supply of money and credit in the economy.

Reserve Requirement

Changing the reserve requirement against bank deposits is a major tool of monetary policy. Because all depository institutions must maintain reserves against their deposit liabilities, any change in these required reserves alters all banks' ability to lend. For example, if the 12 percent reserve requirement for demand deposits is raised to 15 percent, every depository institution will need to increase its required reserves. While they previously had to hold $12 in reserves against every $100 in demand deposits, these banks will now have to hold $15 in reserves. Therefore, by simply increasing the reserve requirement, the Federal Reserve immediately decreases banks' capacity to grant loans. A decrease in the reserve requirement has the opposite effect, for it immediately increases banks' ability to lend.

Obviously this tool of monetary policy cannot be used to fine-tune the money supply to changing liquidity needs. For example, how could this tool be used to put liquidity into the system for seasonal changes in the demand for money? Changing the reserve requirement is unable to produce subtle changes in the money supply, so it is rarely used as a tool of monetary policy. During the period 1963 to 1999, the reserve requirement against demand deposits was changed on only eight occasions. The major advantage of changing the reserve requirement is to release or absorb a large amount of excess reserves in one act. In addition, a change in the reserve requirement has an "announcement effect" that serves to indicate the seriousness of a particular policy of the Federal Reserve.

Discount Rate

As was previously explained, the discount rate is the interest rate that the Federal Reserve charges banks when they borrow reserves to meet temporary shortages in their required reserves. A change in the cost of borrowing reserves alters banks' willingness to borrow from the Federal Reserve. A decrease in the discount rate may stimulate increased borrowing. An increase in the discount rate should discourage further borrowing and may cause banks to retire debt owed the Federal Reserve.

Although the discount rate may induce banks' behavior, it is a passive tool of monetary policy. The initiative for changes in the level of borrowing rests with the banks. The Federal Reserve may alter the discount rate, but it cannot force banks to borrow or to cease borrowing. An increase in the discount rate does not mean that the banks will cease borrowing and retire existing debt owed the Federal Reserve. If the banks are able to pass on to their customers the higher cost of borrowing, there may be little contraction in the level of credit. Furthermore, not all banks borrow from the Federal Reserve. Some banks prefer to remain free of this obligation. Thus, an increase in the discount rate will not affect the lending behavior of these banks.

During the 1960s, the Federal Reserve changed the discount rate infrequently. From 1960 to 1968 the rate was changed only seven times. In the 1970s the Federal Reserve altered the discount rate more frequently in response to changing economic conditions. These fluctuations in the discount rate are illustrated in Figure 4.2. For example, there was a rapid increase in the rate from 6½ percent in 1978 to a high of 13 percent in 1980. This doubling of the discount rate occurred during a period of inflation and high interest rates, when the Federal

FIGURE 4.2
Discount Rate (1974–2000)

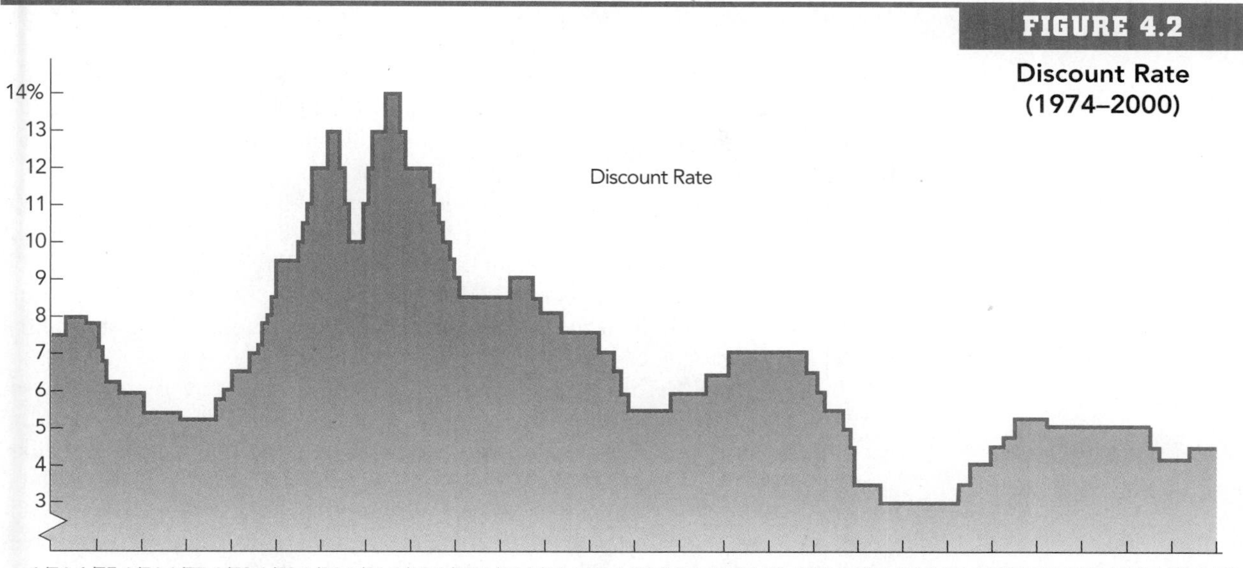

Source: Federal Reserve Bulletin, *various issues.*

Reserve sought to restore more stable prices. As inflation and interest rates subsided, the Federal Reserve lowered the discount rate to encourage economic growth and higher levels of employment.

Although changes in the reserve requirement and the discount rate can affect the supply of money and credit, they are rarely used. This infrequent use of the reserve requirement and the discount rate is the result of more effective (and subtle) means to alter the supply of money and credit.

Instead, the Federal Reserve relies on the federal funds rate and open market operations. The federal funds rate should not be confused with the discount rate. Recall that the federal funds rate is the interest charged by banks when they lend reserves to each other. Banks with excess reserves can put those funds to work by lending them to other banks in the federal funds market.

Unlike the discount rate, the federal funds rate is not set by the Federal Reserve. Instead, it is established by the interaction of the demand and supply of funds available in the federal funds market. The Federal Reserve, however, can affect the supply of funds and thereby affect the federal funds rate. During the 1990s, the Federal Reserve preferred to set a target federal funds rate and changed that target as a tool of monetary policy instead of changing the discount rate.

Open Market Operations

OPEN MARKET OPERATIONS
Buying and selling of U.S. Treasury securities by the Federal Reserve

The target federal funds rate is achieved through the most important tool of monetary policy, **open market operations,** which refer to the purchase and sale of government securities by the Federal Reserve. By buying and selling these securities, the Federal Reserve is able to alter the supply of money in circulation and the reserves of the banking system. The Federal Reserve may buy and sell securities at any time and in any volume. Open market operations, then, are not only a means of changing the money supply and the availability of credit but also of fine-tuning the supply of money on a day-by-day basis.

The Federal Reserve does not directly buy and sell securities to the general public or banks. The transactions are negotiated through private U.S. government security dealers who make markets in these securities. The dealers in turn sell the government securities to the general public and to banks. Since the sales and purchases are in many millions of dollars, the security dealers must have substantial capital and borrowing capacity to make these markets.

If the Federal Reserve seeks to expand the supply of money, it purchases securities. After the transactions are negotiated, payments must be made, and the act of paying for the securities alters the money supply and the reserves of banks. Ownership of the securities is transferred to the Federal Reserve, and the Federal Reserve pays for the securities by writing a check drawn on itself, which the sellers deposit in banks. The banks clear the checks and receive payment in the form of reserves from the Federal Reserve. The total effect of these transactions is (1) to increase the supply of money because demand deposits are increased, and (2) to increase the reserves of the banking system. The required reserves of the banks rise, for the bank's deposit liabilities have risen. However, only a fraction of the increase in reserves will be required reserves. Thus, the excess reserves of the banks also rise.

When the Federal Reserve seeks to contract the money supply, it sells government securities. Once again, it is the payment for the purchased securities that alters the money supply and the capacity of banks to lend. If the public buys the securities, it draws down demand deposits, and the money supply and reserves of banks are decreased. The total effect of these transactions is (1) to decrease the money supply, because demand deposits are decreased, and (2) to decrease the total reserves of the banking system, because banks have fewer reserves on deposit in the Federal Reserve. Since only a percentage of these reserves was required against the deposit liabilities, the excess reserves of the bank were also decreased. Thus, by selling securities, the Federal Reserve decreases the supply of money and decreases the excess reserves of the banks, which reduces their ability to lend and create credit.

FISCAL POLICY

Even though the Federal Reserve can affect the supply of money and credit in the economy, it does not have complete control over them. There are forces beyond its control that can affect the supply of money and credit. One of these forces is the fiscal policy of the federal government.

FISCAL POLICY
Taxation, expenditures, and debt management of the federal government

Fiscal policy is taxation, expenditures, and debt management by the federal government. Like monetary policy, fiscal policy may be used to pursue the economic goals of full employment, price stability, and economic growth. Like monetary policy, fiscal policy can affect the supply of money and the capacity of the banking system to lend.

Taxation or government expenditures by themselves do not alter the money supply. However, when government expenditures exceed revenues, this **deficit** must be financed. When government revenues exceed expenditures, the government must do something with this **surplus.** It is the financing of the deficit or disposing of the surplus that may affect the supply of money and the capacity of banks to lend.

DEFICIT
Disbursements exceeding receipts

SURPLUS
Receipts exceeding disbursements

Prior to the late 1990s, the federal government had not had a budgetary surplus since the Nixon administration. The question was always the deficit's potential impact on the banking system and the supply of credit. Once receipts exceeded disbursements, the question of what to do with the surplus arose. How the surplus is used, however, also has implications for the banking system and supply of credit.

As may be expected, politicians had a variety of ideas for using the surplus. These included reducing taxes and increasing spending on specific programs. The former would decrease government revenues while the latter would increase disbursements, either of which could consume the surplus. Other suggestions included reducing part of the outstanding federal debt and supporting social security. As is discussed in the following section, reducing the debt would, of course, restore the funds to the general public or commercial banks if these investors sell their securities back to the federal government.

Supporting social security could also return the funds to the private sector. Social security payments go into trust funds that hold federal government debt. An influx of funds into these accounts would be invested in government securities. If the federal government is running a surplus, it is reasonable to assume it is not issuing new bonds in excess of what is required to roll over existing debt. Thus, the surplus money contributed to the social security trust funds would not be used to buy new bonds but to purchase existing debt. If this debt is held by the general public and the banking system, money taken out through the taxation that generated the surplus would be returned.

If the federal government runs a deficit, it may obtain funds to finance the deficit by borrowing from (1) the general public, (2) banks, (3) the Federal Reserve, and (4) foreign investors. If the federal government runs a surplus, it may retire debt held by (1) the general public, (2) banks, (3) the Federal Reserve, and (4) foreign investors. Securities issued to finance the deficit compete with other securities. A surplus has the opposite effect. In either case, a deficit or a surplus, the security markets and the banking system are not immune to the fiscal policy of the federal government. Financing a government deficit or investing any government surplus can have an impact on the money supply and commercial banks' reserves and, thus, have an impact on the supply and cost of credit.

Borrowing from the General Public

When the federal government operates at a deficit, it issues securities to finance the deficit. If the general public purchases the securities, funds are transferred from the general public to the Treasury. The Treasury, however, then spends the money to buy goods and services. (If the government did not spend the money, there would be no deficit!) When the Treasury pays for these goods and services, the public's bank deposits are restored as the money is transferred from the Treasury's account to the general public's accounts.

What is the change in the money supply and the reserves of the banks as a result of these transactions? The answer is none. There is no change in the money supply because there is no change in total demand deposits or cash. There is also no change in banks' ability to lend. All that occurs is that the government obtained goods and services from the public by borrowing from the public. In doing so, the Treasury's deficit did not affect the supply of money or the ability of banks to lend.

If the federal government were to run a surplus and use the funds to retire debt held by the general public, the preceding analysis still applies except in reverse. More money is received than spent (the surplus), but when the money is used to retire debt held by the general public, the funds are returned to the private sector. Money that initially flowed out of the private sector is returned. The money supply and the reserves of the banking system are not affected.

Borrowing from Banks

Suppose the federal government's deficit is financed by the banks—that is, the banks buy the government securities. For these purchases to occur, the banks must have excess reserves. From the banks' perspective, lending to the Treasury is essentially no different than lending to businesses or individuals. The money supply is expanded, but the capacity of the banks to lend is decreased because excess reserves are reduced. (The process of lending to the government at the expense of the private sector is sometimes referred to as "crowding out.")

The retiring of debt held by the banks has the opposite effect. The funds are returned to the bank system, which increases the bank's capacity to lend. It makes no difference if General Motors retires a debt owed a commercial bank or if the Treasury pays off a Treasury security owned by the bank. In either case, the excess reserves of the banks are increased, and their capacity to lend is restored.

Borrowing from the Federal Reserve

Borrowing from the Fed to finance a deficit, however, is different from borrowing from the banking system. When the Federal Reserve buys the securities, the Treasury account at the Fed is increased. The Treasury spends these funds to buy goods and services, and the public deposits the payments in commercial banks. The Federal Reserve transfers funds from the Treasury's account to the banks' accounts.

The crucial question then becomes: What is the impact on the money supply and the ability of banks to lend when funds are transferred from the Treasury's account to the banks' account? The answer is twofold: (1) Total demand deposits rise when the public makes the deposits, and (2) total reserves of the banks are increased. (Remember that the banks' accounts at the Federal Reserve are reserves.) While required reserves increase to cover the new demand deposits, excess reserves are also increased. The ability of banks to create additional loans and further expand the money supply is enhanced. Thus, the net effect of the

Federal Reserve's financing a federal government deficit is to increase both the money supply and the ability of banks to lend.[5]

Once again the impact of a surplus is the exact opposite. If the Treasury were to run a surplus and use the funds to retire debt owed the Federal Reserve, both the money supply and the lending capacity of the banks are reduced. The tax collections that generate the surplus reduce the private sector's accounts at the banks. When the funds are transferred to the Treasury account, they reduce the deposit liabilities of the banks. This causes the money supply to decline and reduces the total reserves of the banking system. The reduction in the reserves decreases banks' excess reserves and, hence, decreases their ability to lend.

Borrowing from Foreign Sources

The federal government may also borrow abroad, in which case the securities are sold in foreign countries. When the funds from the sale are deposited in domestic banks, the banks' reserves are increased. From a domestic perspective, borrowing from abroad has the same impact as borrowing from the Federal Reserve. The money supply and the reserves of domestic banks are increased. The money supply and reserves of foreign banks, however, are *decreased*. (This conclusion assumes that the funds borrowed abroad by the Treasury are spent domestically. If the funds are spent abroad, the money flows back out of the country, so there is no net impact on the domestic monetary system.)

Retiring debt owed abroad reverses the flow of deposits. If a surplus is used to retire Treasury securities held by foreigners, the money flows out of the country. The outflow reduces the domestic money supply and the reserves of domestic banks. (If the foreigners were to deposit the proceeds in domestic banks, the net effect would be nil.) Just as selling securities abroad causes a domestic expansion in the money supply and the reserves of banks, retiring debt held abroad contracts the domestic money supply and reserves of banks.

The impact on the money supply and banks' reserves of these cases is summarized in Exhibit 4.5. Of these possibilities to finance a deficit or to replay existing debt, the greatest impact occurs when the transfers involve the Federal Reserve or foreign investors, because both the domestic money supply and the reserves of the banking system are affected. Financing a deficit by selling securities to the Federal Reserve or abroad has expansionary implications. Retiring debt held by the Federal Reserve or foreign investors will have the opposite effect. The domestic money supply and the reserves of domestic banks are decreased.

As this discussion indicates, a federal government deficit or surplus may have an impact on the supply of money and credit. If the Federal Reserve deems this

[5] The process is more subtle than the discussion in the text suggests. Initially the Treasury sells the securities, which are bought by banks and security dealers. These purchases diminish excess reserves, and interest rates tend to rise as the Treasury's sale of securities increases the demand for funds. If the Federal Reserve does not want interest rates to rise, it restores banks' reserves through open market operations. The effect is the same as if the Federal Reserve had directly purchased the debt: The money supply and the reserves of the banks are increased.

EXHIBIT 4.5

Summary of the Impact of Fiscal Policy on the Money Supply and the Reserves of Commercial Banks

	Change in Money Supply	Change in Total Reserves of Banks*	Change in Excess Reserves of Banks
Case 1			
Borrowing from General Public	None	None	None
Retiring Debt Owed General Public	None	None	None
Case II			
Borrowing from Banks	Increase	None	Decrease
Retiring Debt Owed Banks	Decrease	None	Increase
Case III			
Borrowing from the Federal Reserve	Increase	Increase	Increase
Retiring Debt Owned the Federal Reserve	Decrease	Decrease	Decrease
Case IV			
Borrowing from Abroad	Increase	Increase	Increase
Retiring Debt Held Abroad	Decrease	Decrease	Decrease

**Excess reserves plus required reserves.*

impact to be undesirable, it may take actions to offset the impact. For example, if the deficit is financed by banks and this results in fewer loans to businesses and households, the Federal Reserve could create more reserves. The increase in reserves would be accomplished through open market operations. The Federal Reserve would buy securities, which restores reserves to the banking system. Thus, while the Federal Reserve cannot control the federal government's deficit or surplus, it can take action to reduce the impact on the supply of credit and on financial markets.

IMPACT OF AN INFLATIONARY ECONOMIC ENVIRONMENT ON CREDIT MARKETS

INFLATION
General increase in prices with special emphasis on increases in consumer prices

Inflation is a general increase in prices. That is a very simple definition with two crucial words: *prices* and *general*. The first important word is *prices*, indicating what consumers pay to obtain goods and services. (*Prices* could also mean what producers must pay for plant and equipment, but when the word *inflation* is used, the implication is that the prices of consumer goods and services are rising.) The second important word is *general*. Inflation does not mean that all prices are rising but that the prices of most goods and services are increasing. The prices of some specific goods could be falling while most prices were rising.

Inflation is frequently expressed as a rate of increase in an index. The index that is most often used is the Consumer Price Index or CPI. The CPI is compiled monthly by the Bureau of Labor Statistics and is an aggregate of the prices of goods and services paid by consumers. Changes in the CPI are usually expressed in percentages. For example, newspapers may report that the rate of inflation is 3 percent. This usually means that prices as measured by the CPI are rising annually at a rate of 3 percent.

That inflation has occurred is obvious from Figure 4.3, which shows the Consumer Price Index from 1970 to 1999 in the top half of the graph and the annual percentage change in the index in the bottom half. Although the top half of Figure 4.3 shows a steady climb in consumer prices, the bottom half indicates considerable change from year to year in the rate of inflation. While consumer prices rose over 12 percent in 1980, they rose about 3 percent annually for 1992 through 1999.

Although several explanations of inflation have been put forth, the most frequently offered is excessive spending. This spending could come from consumers, firms, or governments, but the effect on prices is the same no matter what the source of the spending. Generally this excess spending is financed by or results from *excessive creation of money* and credit by the Federal Reserve. This cause of inflation is often summarized by the expression "too much money chasing too few goods."

The traditional tools for fighting inflation created by excessive demand are fiscal policy and monetary policy. With fiscal policy, government spending is reduced or taxes are increased. The reduction in government spending should decrease the demand for goods and services and help reduce the inflationary pressure. An increase in corporate income taxes reduces corporate profits, which cuts into the capacity of corporations to pay dividends and reinvest earnings. An increase in personal taxes reduces individuals' disposable income. All these tax increases reduce aggregate demand for goods and services and, therefore, should reduce the tendency for prices to rise.

If monetary policy is used to fight inflation, the Federal Reserve sells securities, raises the reserve requirement, and raises the discount rate. These actions reduce the supply of money, reduce banks' excess reserves, and increase the cost of credit that is, interest rates). The reduction in the supply of money and the higher interest rates should reduce aggregate demand, which is causing prices to rise.

Even if the Federal Reserve does not raise interest rates, inflation will cause interest rates to rise. Inflation can redistribute resources from creditors to debtors (from lenders to borrowers), since the debtors will repay the creditors in the future with funds that purchase less. However, for such a redistribution to occur, the lenders would have to lack an awareness of inflation. If the lenders do anticipate the inflation, they certainly will take steps to protect the purchasing power of their funds. Such protection is achieved by charging more interest so their return equals or exceeds the rate of inflation.

If lenders do not fully anticipate inflation and do not earn a sufficient rate of interest, there will be a transfer of resources to borrowers from the lenders. The

FIGURE 4.3

Consumer Price Index and Annual Percentage Change in the CPI (1970–1998)

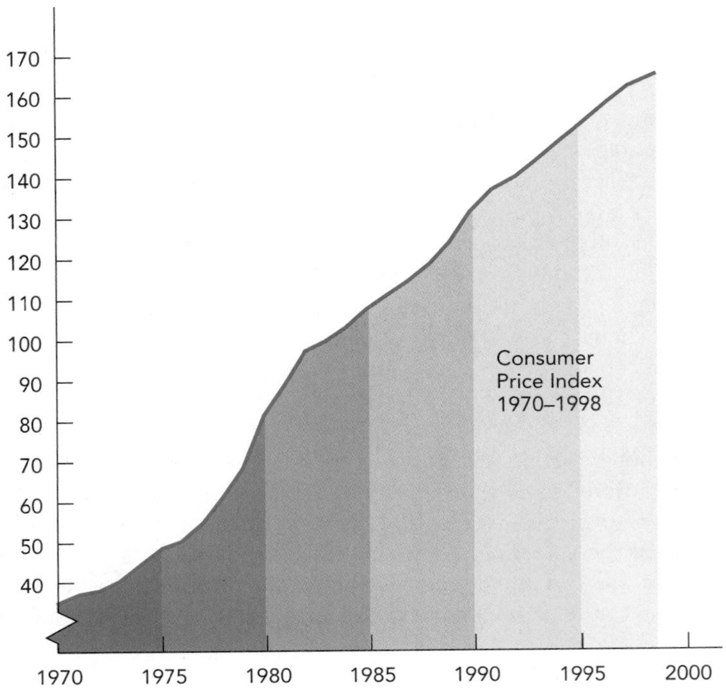

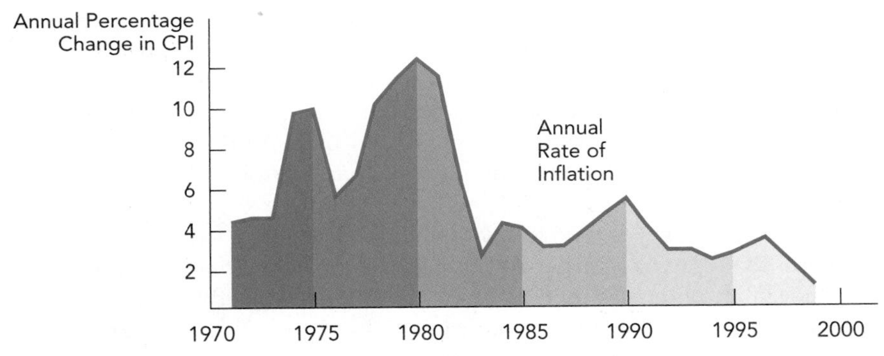

belief that savers will not correctly anticipate the severity of inflation has encouraged some individuals and firms to finance purchases through issuing debt. Thus, inflation (or at least the expectation of it) alters economic decision making and affects credit markets. Inflation encourages the use of debt financing to make current purchases.

Lenders, however, may certainly anticipate inflation just as borrowers may anticipate it. Expectations of inflation, then, should tend to drive up interest rates as

FIGURE 4.4

Rate of Inflation and the Real Rate of Interest (1973–1998)

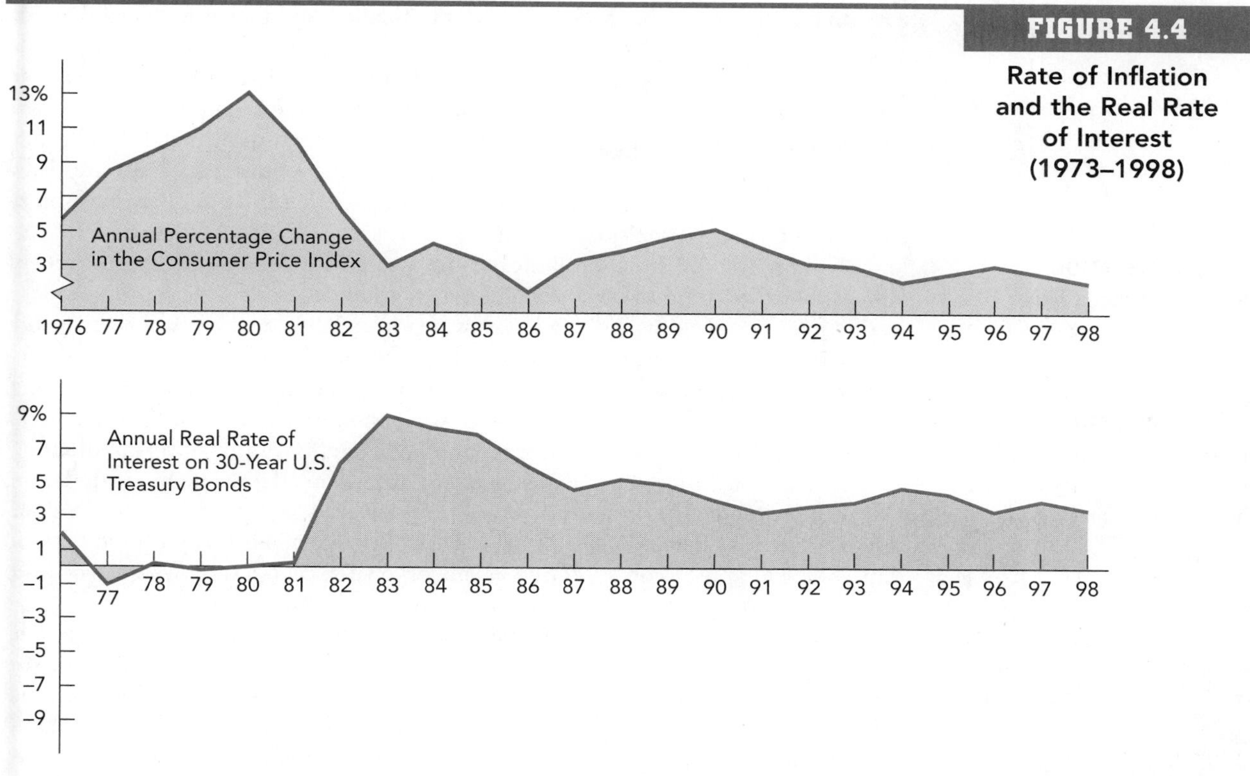

(1) borrowers seek to obtain funds to purchase goods before their prices rise, (2) lenders seek to protect the purchasing power of their funds by requiring higher rates to compensate them for lending, and (3) the Federal Reserve tightens credit in an effort to retard the inflationary pressure.

Certainly the high interest rates of the early 1980s and the lower rates of the early 1990s confirm that inflation is associated with higher rates. The top half of Figure 4.4 presents the annual rate of inflation. The bottom half of the figure shows the difference between the rate of inflation and the nominal interest rate and indicates the purchasing power of the interest. Thus, in 1997 the rate of inflation was about 2 percent but the nominal interest rate was 6.6 percent, so the difference was 4.6 percent. This 4.6 percent is sometimes referred to as the **real rate of interest** that lenders are earning.

REAL RATE OF INTEREST
Purchasing power of the rate of interest: interest rate minus the rate of inflation

The real rate is a measure of the purchasing power that the lenders are receiving on their funds. As may be seen in Figure 4.4, this real rate has fluctuated. Lenders lost purchasing power between 1977 and 1980, but the real rate subsequently rose dramatically from 1982 through 1985 as inflation abated and interest rates declined only moderately.

In addition to raising the cost of credit, inflation also makes financial decision making more difficult. Forecasts of sales and earnings will have to account for the anticipated inflation. Financial analysts who use financial statements will have to be more careful when comparing a firm's performance over a period of years, as the data may not be comparable. As plant and equipment wear out, firms have to raise even larger sums of money just to maintain its operations. These are just a few of many possible examples of the broad impact that inflation may have on financial analysis and decision making.

DEFLATION
General decline in prices

RECESSION
Period (at least six months) of increased unemployment and negative economic growth

The opposite of inflation is **deflation,** which is a general decline in prices.[6] Prices, however, tend to be sticky and may not fall. If prices were more volatile, a reduction in demand would result in lower prices. Since the prices of many goods and services are not responsive to a decline in demand, such reductions result in a decline in the quantity of goods and services produced. Instead of prices declining, workers are laid off. The result is a **recession:** an increase in unemployment and a reduction in the nation's output for a period of time (for example, six months).[7]

During the 1990s, some firms began to experience the problems of deflation. After the extended period of inflation, the prices of some goods, especially commodities such as metals, started to fall. These price declines caused some firms to fail. For example, Global Marine, a major owner of oil rigs, was forced into bankruptcy when lower oil prices resulted in less drilling for oil.

While some firms and individuals may be hurt by falling prices, others may benefit. Lower prices will mean lower cost of goods sold, which should increase profits for some firms. Lower oil prices may have caused the bankruptcy of Global Marine, but lower oil prices benefit any firms or individuals that use oil. Electric utilities that burn oil to generate electricity and individuals who heat their homes with oil furnaces obviously benefit from lower energy costs.

Lower prices also benefit retired individuals and others who live on a fixed income. The real purchasing power of their income is increased by lower prices. Creditors benefit as the purchasing power of the interest they earn is increased. Banks may benefit from lower interest rates that tend to accompany lower prices of goods and services. While banks may pay their depositors a lower rate of interest, they may also charge borrowers a lower rate of interest. Individuals may then be able to purchase homes because the cost of mortgage loans is reduced. Obviously, contractors and those in the building trades benefit from increased demand for housing that is stimulated by the lower cost of credit.

Lower prices, just like higher prices, tend to benefit some individuals and firms but hurt others. Higher prices are not necessarily "good" nor are lower prices necessarily "bad." Just as expected inflation induces certain types of behavior, such as increased borrowing in anticipation of higher interest rates, expectations of lower

[6] Deflation should not be confused with "disinflation," a term that is sometimes used to indicate a decline in the rate of inflation.

[7] Higher unemployment and a stagnating economy can also coexist with continued inflation. Such a scenario has been dubbed "stagflation" and is the result of the inertia associated with the inflationary process. If production costs continue to rise even in the face of increased unemployment, price increases will persist, thus creating higher unemployment and inflation.

prices encourage certain types of behavior. Individuals may postpone purchases in anticipation of lower prices. Investors may seek to lock in yields and thus make long-term investments before interest rates decline. To the extent that individuals or managers correctly anticipate changes in prices in either direction, they may take steps that are beneficial.

IMPACT OF MONETARY AND FISCAL POLICY ON THE FIRM

To financial managers, monetary and fiscal policy are important because of their impact on money and credit and the firm's earnings. As the previous discussion suggests, the actions of the Federal Reserve can affect the supply and, hence, the cost of credit. A tight monetary policy designed to fight inflation will increase interest rates. A monetary policy that is expansionary will initially decrease interest rates. As is explained in Chapter 16, the cost of credit is an important component of the firm's cost of capital. Increases in interest rates, caused by the Federal Reserve's tightening of credit or by increased demand for funds resulting from larger deficit spending by the federal government, will make financing a firm's operations more expensive. Unless this cost can be passed on through price increases, the effect will be to reduce the firm's earnings.

While monetary policy affects the cost of a firm's sources of finance, fiscal policy can affect a firm in other ways. Taxation and spending by the federal government can have a very powerful and direct impact on individual firms. Taxation of earnings affects all profitable firms, since it lowers their net earnings, thus reducing the firms' capacity to pay dividends or to expand through investing retained earnings. Other tax policies, such as the speed with which the firm is permitted to depreciate investments in plant and equipment, also affect the earnings and cash flow of a firm's operations.

In addition, spending by the federal government can affect the well-being of selected firms. A large proportion of the federal government's expenditures is directed to firms (such as defense contractors or road construction companies). Other disbursements (for example, social security payments) are directed to individuals, who in turn buy goods and services from firms. Thus, many firms may experience increased demand and increased earnings as a result of the federal government's spending.

Firms and their financial managers do not live in a vacuum. They cannot be oblivious to the impact of monetary and fiscal policy on the firm's cost of funds or demand for its products. The ability to anticipate changes in monetary and fiscal policy can help the financial manager plan the firm's financial strategy. For example, if higher interest rates are anticipated, long-term funds should be borrowed before the rates increase. If interest rates are expected to decline, the financial manager should postpone long-term borrowing until the rates have fallen. Of course, the expected changes may not occur, and the financial manager may make a costly error (e.g., postpone borrowing in anticipation of lower rates only to have interest rates rise). However, the financial manager cannot ignore the potential impact of monetary and fiscal policy and take no actions based on expected future changes in these policies.

SUMMARY

The Federal Reserve is the nation's central bank. Its purpose is to control the supply of money and credit in the nation. Through this control the Federal Reserve pursues the goals of monetary policy: higher levels of employment, stable prices, and economic growth.

Monetary policy works through its impact on banks' reserves. Since banking is organized under a system of fractional reserves, any transaction that puts reserves into the system will lead to expansion in the supply of money and credit. Transactions that take reserves out of the system will cause the supply of money and credit to contract unless there are excess reserves in the system to meet the reduction in the reserves.

The tools of monetary policy include open market operations, the reserve requirement, and the discount rate. Open market operations—the buying and selling of government securities by the Federal Reserve—are individually the most important tool of monetary policy. When the Federal Reserve seeks to expand the money supply, it buys securities. When it seeks to contract the money supply, it sells securities. Such purchases and sales affect the reserves of banks and thus alter their ability to lend. By altering banks' reserves, the Federal Reserve pursues its economic goals.

The fiscal policy of the federal government, like monetary policy, may have an impact on the money supply and the reserves of banks. When the federal government spends more than it receives in tax revenues, the resulting deficit must be financed. When the Federal Reserve supplies the funds to cover the deficit, the effect is the same as the Federal Reserve's purchasing securities. In both cases the money supply and the reserves of banks are increased.

The reverse occurs when the federal government runs a surplus in which receipts exceed expenses (the federal government's cash inflows exceed cash outflows). Unless the funds are returned to the economy, the money supply and bank reserves are diminished. By increasing expenditures or retiring debt held by the public, the funds are returned, and the impact on the banking system is reduced.

Inflation is a general increase in prices while deflation is a general decrease in prices. Recession is a period of rising unemployment. The anticipation of inflation affects financial decision making as individuals, financial managers, and creditors take actions designed to protect their purchasing power. Inflation encourages spending to acquire goods before prices rise farther and to finance the purchases with borrowed funds. Lenders, however, seek to protect themselves from inflation by charging a higher rate of interest to compensate for the inflation. During a period of inflation, the Federal Reserve will

pursue a tight monetary policy and sell securities to reduce inflationary pressures. During a period of recession, the Federal Reserve does the opposite by purchasing securities and lowering interest rates to stimulate the economy.

Both monetary and fiscal policy may affect the operations and profits of a firm. Monetary policy primarily affects the cost of finance required by the firm's operations. Fiscal policy may directly affect the firm through taxation, which alters the firm's earnings, or through government expenditures, which may alter the demand for the firm's products. Fiscal policy may also indirectly affect the firm's cost of credit because the federal government's securities compete with the securities issued by firms to obtain the funds of savers. Funds that flow to the federal government do not flow to firms, thus increasing the cost of their sources of financing.

Review Questions

1. Why is it correct to suggest that the power within the Federal Reserve rests with the Board of Governors? What happens to the earnings generated by the Federal Reserve?
2. If there are no excess reserves in the banking system and $1 billion in new reserves are created by the Federal Reserve, what should happen to the supply of money? Would your answer be different if the reserve requirement were 10 percent instead of 15 percent?
3. If there were cash withdrawals when the banking system had excess reserves, would the money supply necessarily contract?
4. How does the Federal Reserve use open market operations to contract the supply of money? Will an increase in the discount rate have the same impact?
5. If the federal government runs a surplus during a period of inflation, is it more desirable to retire debt held by commercial banks or by the general public? Why may a U.S. Treasury surplus produce a restraint on the economy?
6. What is recession, and how is it measured? How are monetary and fiscal policy used to combat recession? What impact will inflation or recession have on the level of interest rates?
7. What impact does each of the following have on the capacity of commercial banks to lend?
   a. The Federal Reserve sells bonds that are purchased by the general public.
   b. The Federal Reserve raises the discount rate, and commercial banks decrease their borrowings from the Federal Reserve.
   c. The Federal Reserve raises the reserve requirement on checking accounts.

d. The federal government sells a new issue of bonds that are purchased by the Federal Reserve. The Treasury deposits the proceeds in its accounts at commercial banks.

e. The Treasury borrows from commercial banks and uses the funds to buy defense goods (for example, airplanes).

f. Individuals transfer funds to savings accounts from checking accounts in commercial banks.

g. A corporation issues new stock that is purchased by individual investors.

h. Firms obtain loans from commercial banks.

i. A British citizen deposits pounds in a bank in New York.

8. The Bureau of Labor Statistics, an agency within the U.S. Department of Labor, reports data concerning the aggregate economy. One possible measure of the direction of change is the rate of unemployment, which increases as the economy weakens. Go the bureau's Web page, **stats.bls.gov**, and locate the unemployment rate. (It may be found under a section titled "Economy at a Glance.") Based on recent changes in the unemployment rate, would you expect the Federal Reserve to tighten or ease credit in the immediate future?

9. The Federal Reserve publishes financial data concerning the money supply and interest rates. Go to its Web site address, **www.bog.frb.fed.us** and locate the summary of economic conditions in the *Beige Book.* Does this summary support your answer to the previous question?

10. The Council of Economic Advisors annually issues an *Economic Report to the President* available at **www.access.gpo.gov/eop**. Locate the discussion of the unemployment rate to determine if it confirms your answers to the two previous questions. (The easiest means to obtain the discussion may be to search using the key words, "unemployment rate.")

11. The Council of Economic Advisors *Economic Report to the President* (**www.access.gpo.gov/eop**) is a ready source of information on the federal government's deficit or surplus. From this source, what is the forecasted deficit or surplus for the next two years?

CHAPTER 5
International Finance

Learning Objectives

1. Define foreign exchange and foreign exchange rates.
2. Differentiate devaluations and revaluations, their causes, and their impact on the demand for a nation's exports.
3. Explain how international currency flows may affect a nation's money supply and the reserves of its commercial banks.
4. Describe the components of a nation's balance of payments and the role of the IMF.
5. Define "multinational firm," and explain why such firms developed and how they may be financed.
6. Identify the sources of risk from foreign investments, and explain how these risks may be reduced.

More than 200 years ago, Benjamin Franklin stated, "No nation was ever ruined by trade." Supporters of free, competitive markets believe that maxim today. Even though international markets are not completely competitive and barriers still exist, many goods and services flow across national borders. Nations do not exist in a vacuum. A nation such as the United States exports and imports goods, services, and capital to and from many nations.

Nor do firms operate in a vacuum. Virtually every large American firm has some contact with foreign trade. Many have operations abroad, and others import raw materials or export to foreign markets goods made in the United States. Large American firms may have a substantial part of their operations abroad. Tupperware, for example, reported in its 1998 annual report that the United States accounted for only 15.3 percent of sales while Europe generated 47.9 percent of total sales. Even if a firm has no foreign operations, buys no raw material abroad, or sells no products in foreign countries, it may still face foreign competition for its domestic markets. A textile firm such as Tultex, a manufacturer of fleeced knit apparel and spun yarns, may have no foreign operations but must face stiff foreign competition for its products.

Importing and exporting goods and services and making foreign investments in plant and equipment and financial assets lead to international currency flows. This chapter begins with a discussion of these flows and the rate of exchange. Next follows the impact that currency flows may have on a nation's supply of money and on the capacity of its banks to lend. The third section discusses the balance of payments and how a deficit on a nation's merchandise trade balance must be covered either by foreigners' holding of the country's debt obligations or by the nation's borrowing from the International Monetary Fund. The final sections of the chapter discuss the multinational firm and international financial management along with foreign investments and their sources of risk. The chapter ends with a discussion of risk management and the use of futures contracts to reduce the risk of loss associated with fluctuations in exchange rates.

FOREIGN CURRENCIES AND THE RATE OF EXCHANGE

Demand for foreign goods is also a demand for foreign money. Foreign merchants want payment in their nation's currency, and the buyers must acquire that currency. To acquire this money, the buyers use their nation's currency, which they offer in exchange for the foreign currency. If Americans want British goods, they must convert U.S. dollars into pounds. They offer (that is, supply) American dollars in exchange for British pounds. The opposite is true when British citizens buy American goods. To acquire the goods, they must have American dollars, and to obtain these dollars they supply British pounds in exchange for American dollars. Thus, demand for foreign goods, and demand for foreign currency, implies supplying the domestic currency.

FOREIGN EXCHANGE MARKET
Market for the purchase and sale of currencies

EXCHANGE RATE
Price of a foreign currency; the value of one currency in terms of another

The market for foreign currencies is called the **foreign exchange market.** Billions of dollars' worth of currencies are traded daily in the financial centers: New York, London, Tokyo, and Zurich. The price of one currency in terms of another is referred to as the **exchange rate,** and the prices of major currencies are reported in the financial press. While prices change frequently, a person needing British pounds or any other reported currency has a reasonable idea of their current prices.

Exhibit 5.1, a clipping from *The Wall Street Journal,* gives selected currency prices as of January 4, 2000. At that time the price (called the "spot" price) of a British pound was \$1.6370. The exhibit also expresses the value of each currency in terms of a dollar. Thus, \$1 purchased 0.6109 British pounds. These amounts may be derived by dividing \$1 by the dollar price of the foreign currency. For example, \$1/1.637 = 0.6109 units of the British pound.

As may be seen in Exhibit 5.1, there are many different currencies, because each country has its own currency. However, effective January 4, 1999, eleven European nations joined the Economic Monetary Union (EMU) and adopted a common monetary unit, the euro. The phase in of the new currency will occur over time, but by July 2002, French francs, Italian lira, German marks, and the currencies of the other member nations will cease to exist. (The other countries are Austria, Belgium, Finland, Ireland, Luxembourg, Netherlands, Portugal, and Spain. Denmark, Sweden, Switzerland, and the United Kingdom chose not to join.) In addition to a common monetary unit, the countries that joined the Economic Monetary Union agreed on the creation of a new European Central Bank. Each country had to relinquish control of its domestic supply of money and the level of interest rates. The new central bank will establish monetary policy for the area just as the Federal Reserve sets monetary policy in the United States.

EXHIBIT 5.1

Foreign Exchange Rates

CURRENCY TRADING

Tuesday, January 4, 2000

EXCHANGE RATES

The New York foreign exchange mid-range rates below apply to trading among banks in amounts of $1 million and more, as quoted at 4 p.m. Eastern time by Reuters and other sources. Retail transactions provide fewer units of foreign currency per dollar. Rates for the 11 Euro currency countries are derived from the latest dollar-euro rate using the exchange ratios set 1/1/99.

Country	U.S. $ equiv. Tue	U.S. $ equiv. Mon	Currency per U.S. $ Tue	Currency per U.S. $ Mon
Argentina (Peso)	1.0001	1.0002	.9999	.9998
Australia (Dollar)	.6551	.6582	1.5266	1.5192
Austria (Schilling)	.07491	.07462	13.349	13.402
Bahrain (Dinar)	2.6525	2.6525	.3770	.3770
Belgium (Franc)	.0256	.0255	39.1325	39.2885
Brazil (Real)	.5406	.5495	1.8490	1.8200
Britain (Pound)	1.6370	1.6371	.6109	.6108
1-month forward	1.6372	1.6373	.6108	.6108
3-months forward	1.6371	1.6373	.6108	.6108
6-months forward	1.6365	1.6368	.6111	.6109
Canada (Dollar)	.6887	.6913	1.4521	1.4465
1-month forward	.6892	.6919	1.4510	1.4453
3-months forward	.6902	.6929	1.4489	1.4433
6-months forward	.6915	.6943	1.4462	1.4404
Chile (Peso) (d)	.001890	.001894	529.05	527.85
China (Renminbi)	.1208	.1208	8.2799	8.2798
Colombia (Peso)	.0005238	.0005306	1909.00	1884.50
Czech. Rep. (Koruna)				
Commercial rate	.02839	.02814	35.226	35.541
Denmark (Krone)	.1385	.1379	7.2186	7.2491
Ecuador (Sucre)				
Floating rate	.00004202	.00004598	23800.00	21750.00
Finland (Markka)	.1734	.1727	5.7678	5.7908
France (Franc)	.1572	.1565	6.3633	6.3887
1-month forward	.1575	.1569	6.3488	6.3736
3-months forward	.1582	.1576	6.3205	6.3460
6-months forward	.1592	.1586	6.2800	6.3054
Germany (Mark)	.5273	.5250	1.8966	1.9049
1-month forward	.5285	.5262	1.8922	1.9004
3-months forward	.5308	.5285	1.8838	1.8921
6-months forward	.5343	.5319	1.8717	1.8800
Greece (Drachma)	.003120	.003113	320.52	321.26
Hong Kong (Dollar)	.1286	.1286	7.7773	7.7763
Hungary (Forint)	.004044	.004034	247.30	247.90
India (Rupee)	.02300	.02302	43.480	43.435
Indonesia (Rupiah)	.0001396	.0001417	7165.00	7055.00
3-months forward	.009825	.009989	101.79	100.11
6-months forward	.009974	.010141	100.26	98.61
Jordan (Dinar)	1.4085	1.4085	.7100	.7100
Kuwait (Dinar)	3.2927	3.2895	.3037	.3040
Lebanon (Pound)	.0006634	.0006634	1507.50	1507.50
Malaysia (Ringgit)	.2632	.2632	3.8001	3.8000
Malta (Lira)	2.4691	2.4643	.4050	.4058
Mexico (Peso)				
Floating rate	.1045	.1063	9.5700	9.4050
Netherland (Guilder)	.4678	.4659	2.1378	2.1463
New Zealand (Dollar)	.5209	.5255	1.9198	1.9029
Norway (Krone)	.1260	.1266	[illegible]	7.8969
Pakistan (Rupee)	.01929	.01927	51.850	51.890
Peru (new Sol)	.2841	.2840	3.5200	3.5215
Philippines (Peso)	.02509	.02503	39.850	39.950
Poland (Zloty)	.2427	.2418	4.1195	4.1350
Portugal (Escudo)	.005142	.005121	194.49	195.26
Russia (Ruble) (a)	.03632	.03643	27.530	27.450
Saudi Arabia (Riyal)	.2666	.2666	3.7510	3.7508
Singapore (Dollar)	.6039	.6038	1.6560	1.6562
Slovak Rep. (Koruna)	.02434	.02427	41.077	41.202
South Africa (Rand)	.1643	.1632	6.0875	6.1288
South Korea (Won)	.0008909	.0008869	1122.50	1127.50
Spain (Peseta)	.006196	.006171	161.41	162.05
Sweden (Krona)	.1195	.1195	8.3671	8.3668
Switzerland (Franc)	.6429	.6391	1.5555	1.5647
1-month forward	.6454	.6416	1.5494	1.5585
3-months forward	.6498	.6459	1.5389	1.5483
6-months forward	.6567	.6527	1.5228	1.5321
Taiwan (Dollar)	.03276	.03188	30.525	31.365
Thailand (Baht)	.02683	.02702	37.265	37.015
Turkey (Lira)	.00000186	.00000185	536260.00	539255.00
United Arab (Dirham)	.2722	.2723	3.6731	3.672
Uruguay (New Peso)				
Financial	.08607	.08608	11.619	11.61
Venezuela (Bolivar)	.001538	.001540	650.00	649.2
SDR	1.3820	1.3761	.7236	
Euro	1.0313	1.0268	.9696	

Special Drawing Rights (SDR) are based on exchange for the U.S., German, British, French , and Japanese cu cies. Source: International Monetary Fund.

a-Russian Central Bank rate. Trading band lowe 8/17/98. b-Government rate. d-Floating rate; trading b pended on 9/2/99.

The 3-month and 6-month

Price of the British Pound in Dollars

Price of $1.00 in British Pounds

Source: The Wall Street Journal, January 5, 2000, p. C19.

The demand for foreign money arises in many ways that are not limited to the importing of foreign goods and services. Travel abroad requires foreign currency; its effect is no different from importing goods and services. Investing in foreign securities or in plant and equipment in foreign nations also requires foreign funds, as does federal government foreign aid or military spending in foreign countries. If one thinks about all the transactions that Americans have with foreign firms, individuals, and governments, a substantial demand exists for foreign moneys by Americans. Of course, this large demand may be balanced by foreigners buying American goods and securities and foreign firms investing in plant and equipment in the United States.

The price of a currency depends on the supply of and the demand for that currency. An imbalance in the demand for or the supply of a currency causes its price to change. Excess demand generates a higher price, while excess supply depresses the price. Such price changes are often referred to as devaluations and revaluations. A **devaluation** (or depreciation) implies that one currency's value declines relative to all other currencies. A **revaluation** (or appreciation) implies that one currency's value rises relative to all other currencies.

DEVALUATION
Decrease (depreciation) in the price of one currency relative to other currencies

REVALUATION
Increase (appreciation) in the price of one currency relative to other currencies

How devaluation changes the price of one currency relative to all other currencies may be explained by a simple example. Assume that the British pound costs $1.50 in American dollars. If a good is priced at 2.5 pounds, it costs $3.75 in American money (2.5 times $1.50). If the British pound depreciated, it would take fewer dollars to buy a pound. Thus, if the pound were devalued by 10 percent, it would take 10 percent fewer dollars to buy a pound. The pound's price in terms of dollars would fall from $1.50 to $1.35. The good would now cost $3.375, because Americans could buy pounds at a lower price. The price of the good in terms of pounds would not be reduced. It would still cost 2.5 pounds, and hence its price to anyone holding pounds would be unaltered. However, anyone holding a different currency could purchase pounds at the lower, devalued price. Thus depreciation does not lower prices to the domestic population but lowers the price of domestic goods to foreigners.

Conversely, devaluation also raises all foreign prices to the domestic population. The British now would have to pay more pounds for foreign goods. Previously, a British pound could purchase $1.50 worth of American goods. If a good cost $2.25, it cost 1.5 pounds ($2.25/$1.50). After the devaluation, the number of pounds necessary to purchase the good would increase to 1.67 ($2.25/$1.35) because the value of the pound in terms of dollars has been lowered. Thus, all foreign goods would be more expensive to holders of British pounds because the pound would buy smaller amounts of foreign currencies.

Since prices of goods and services have been altered by the depreciation in the pound, the quantity demanded will also be altered. Holders of British pounds would demand fewer foreign goods because their prices are higher. Simultaneously, since all other currencies can purchase more pounds, the quantity demanded of British goods will increase. British citizens will import fewer foreign goods, and the rest of the world will buy more British goods.

The opposite is true for a revaluation, which increases the value of one currency relative to another and raises the price of domestic goods to foreigners and lowers the price of all foreign goods to the domestic population. For example, if the British pound appreciated by 10 percent, the price of a pound in terms of dollars would rise from $1.50 to $1.65. To foreigners, the prices of all British goods would increase. Simultaneously, the British pound would now buy more foreign money, for a pound would purchase $1.65 worth of American goods. The increased prices of British goods should reduce the quantity demanded, while the reduced price of imports would increase the quantity demanded. Thus, the appreciation reduces the demand for domestically produced goods and increases the demand for imports.

Under the current international monetary system, such price changes occur daily. If the demand for a particular currency rises so that demand exceeds supply,

FIGURE 5.1

Price of the British Pound in Dollars (1980–1999)

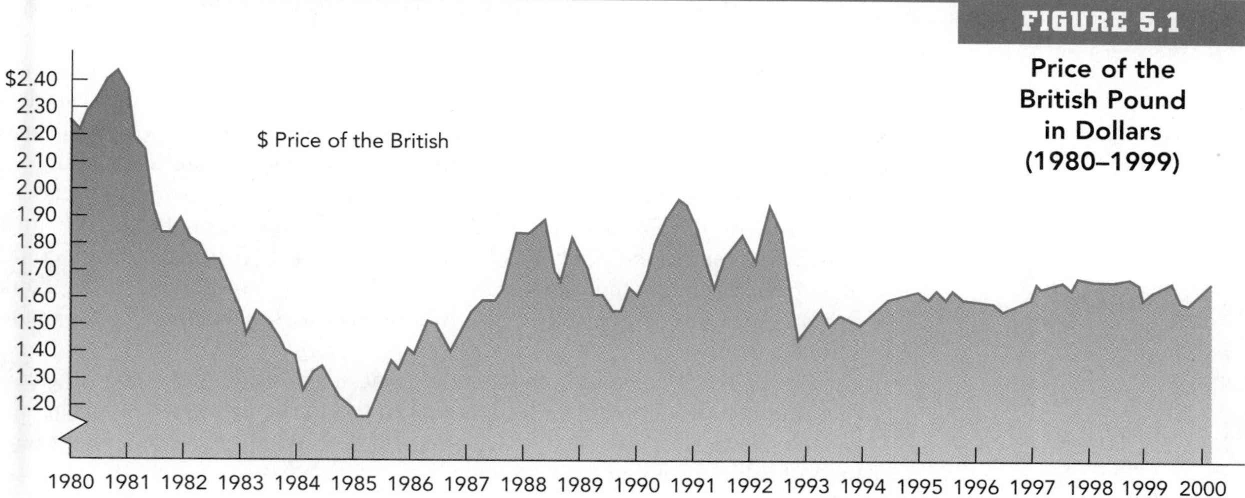

the price of that currency rises relative to other currencies. If the supply of the currency exceeds the demand, the price falls. Because prices fluctuate every day, continual devaluations and revaluations occur as the prices of currencies vary in accordance with supply and demand. These fluctuations are illustrated by Figure 5.1, which plots the price of a pound in dollars from 1980 through 1999. As may be seen in this chart, the pound's price literally varied day by day and experienced a considerable decline in terms of dollars from a high of more than $2.40 in early 1981 to less than $1.20 in 1985. While the pound subsequently rose from its lows of 1985, in 1999 it was worth in dollars about 70 percent of its value in 1980.

EFFECT ON BANKS' RESERVES AND THE DOMESTIC MONEY SUPPLY

As was explained in the first section of this chapter, purchases cause international currency flows. The effect of these flows may be to alter the ability of domestic and foreign banks to create credit. This effect on bank's ability to create credit may be illustrated by the following example in which United States citizens buy goods in England. When the purchases are made, the Americans acquire goods and pay for them with a check drawn on an American bank. The British merchant deposits the check in a bank and obtains a new demand deposit.

The British bank has a new demand deposit and a check drawn on an American bank. The British bank cannot present the check to another British bank for payment, because the check is drawn on an American bank. Thus the check is sent to the British central bank, the Bank of England. The Bank of England sends the check to the Federal Reserve, through which foreign banking transactions are cleared for payment.

Payment from the Federal Reserve can take a variety of forms. For example, the British central bank can request payment in British pounds or American dollars. The Bank of England need not take physical delivery of the dollars but can accept an account at the Federal Reserve. Foreign central banks maintain accounts at the Federal Reserve just as the United States federal government keeps an account with the Federal Reserve. Such accounts can supply funds to British citizens when they make purchases in the United States. The British bank could request payment in another currency, such as European euros. Thus if the Bank of England needs a currency other than American dollars, payment could be made in a third currency.

If the Bank of England accepts an account at the Federal Reserve, the following transactions occur. The check is sent to the Federal Reserve for payment. The Bank of England receives the account, and the Federal Reserve issues a new claim on itself in payment for the check.

This entire transaction may be illustrated by the flowchart presented below. The check goes from the American citizen to the British citizen to pay for goods and services. For the check to clear, it passes through a British bank to the Bank of England to the Federal Reserve to the bank on which it was drawn.

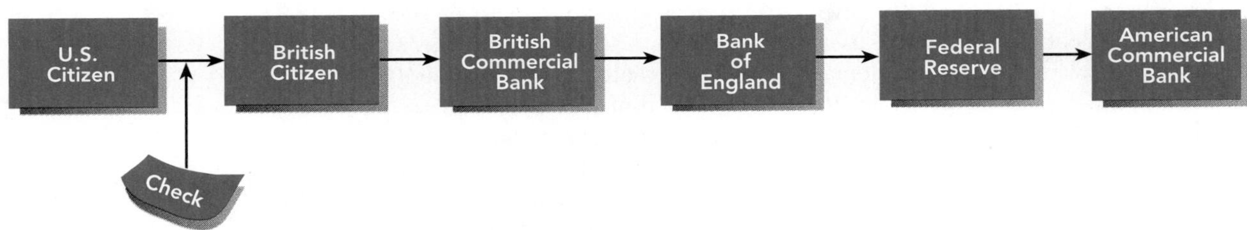

There has been a flow of funds abroad that are lodged in the British banking system and have increased demand deposits and the reserves of the British banks. Since the funds are abroad, they are no longer part of the United States money supply. Demand deposits and reserves of banks in the United States are reduced. In effect, Americans now have British goods and services, and the British have a claim (represented by the account of the Bank of England at the Federal Reserve) on American goods and services.

If the British purchase American goods, they may use the American dollars that were used to purchase British goods. The money that flowed to Great Britain when the Americans purchased British goods is returned to the United States. Hence, if British people are purchasing American goods and services at the same time and at the same value at which Americans are buying British goods and services, the currency flows cancel each other. The dollars that go abroad are returned when the British purchase American goods, and there will be no net effect on the banking system. The same conclusion holds if the British use the American dollars to buy goods in another country, such as Germany, and if the Germans use the dollars to buy American goods. The only difference is that this is a three-way transaction. Americans sell goods to Britain: the British use the dollars to buy German goods; and the Germans use the dollars to buy American goods. The dollars that flowed out to purchase English goods are returned to America. There is a balance in the flow of currencies, and the foreign transactions of all three nations are in balance.

If, however, the British do not exercise the claim on American goods or do not pass the claim to a third party that exercises the claim, the value of purchases of goods and services among nations is not equal, and one nation's currency is lodging itself in another nation. As is explained in the next section, the country doing the purchasing has a deficit in its balance of trade, while the other country has a surplus. The deficit nation is losing currency and receiving goods while the surplus nation is losing goods and receiving money. The importance of these transactions on the banking system in each nation is the effect the currency flows have on reserves of banks and on each nation's money supply. The reserves of banks and the money supply of the deficit nation are reduced, while the reserves of banks and the money supply of the surplus nation are increased. The potential for banks to expand and create credit is reduced in the deficit nation. But the converse is true in the surplus nation, for the ability of its banks to expand the money supply is increased.

BALANCE OF PAYMENTS

The balance of payments is a record of all monetary transactions between a country and the rest of the world during a period of time.[1] While the general time period is a year, many countries compile and report the data quarterly. The balance of payments records transactions by double entry bookkeeping. Each transaction is recorded as both a debit and a credit, so the total of all debits must equal credits. However, individual parts or subsets of the balance of payments statement may have a surplus or deficit.

Although an elaborate discussion of all the parts of the balance of payments is beyond the scope of this text, the essential parts are (1) the current account, (2) the capital account, and (3) the official reserve account. The **current account** enumerates the value of goods and services imported and exported, government spending abroad, and foreign investment income for the time period. It is the broadest measure of a country's international trade in goods and services.

CURRENT ACCOUNT
Part of the balance of payments that enumerates the importing and exporting of goods and services by a national over a period of time

The difference between the value of imports and exports is often referred to as a country's "balance of trade." If a country imports more goods than it exports, it is running a deficit in its "merchandise trade" account. If a country is exporting more goods than it imports, it is running a surplus. A country can run a surplus or

[1] Some transactions do avoid being counted. The value of goods smuggled because they are illegal or because the smugglers wish to avoid tariffs is obviously excluded. In addition, the flight of capital from politically unstable countries may also evade being counted.

a deficit in its balance of trade but not in its balance of payments. For every credit in the balance of payments, there is a corresponding and offsetting debit, so the balance of payments must balance even though the current account may have a surplus or deficit.

CAPITAL ACCOUNT
Part of the balance of payments that enumerates the importing and exporting of investments and long-term securities

The **capital account** consists of investment flows and measures capital investments made between the domestic country and all other countries. Capital investments include direct investments in plant and equipment in a foreign country and the purchases of foreign securities. Security transactions may be long or short term. Long-term transactions are purchases and sales of foreign bonds and stocks. Short-term capital transactions primarily take the form of changes in bank balances held abroad and in foreign money market instruments.

OFFICIAL RESERVE ACCOUNT
Part of the balance of payments that enumerates changes in a country's international reserves

The third account, the **official reserve account,** is a balancing account and reflects the change in a country's international reserves. If a country imports more than it exports or makes more foreign investments, its foreign reserves will decline. If a country exports more than it imports and experiences foreign investments, its holding of foreign reserves will rise. These changes in its reserves may also affect its drawing rights on its account with the International Monetary Fund (IMF).[2]

An illustration of a balance of payments is presented in Exhibit 5.2. The exhibit is divided into the current account, the capital account, and the official reserve account. The vertical columns give the debits (−) and the credits (+). Credits represent currency inflows while debits are currency outflows, and the sum of the debits and credits must be equal.

The current account starts with merchandise exports, a credit of $224.40, and merchandise imports, a debit of $368.70. The difference ($224.40 − $368.70 = −$144.30) is the merchandise balance of trade, and since the amount is a negative number, that indicates a net currency outflow. The next entry is government spending abroad, a debit of $15.30. If a government spends abroad, that has the same impact on currency flows as individuals' spending abroad. It does not matter whether the government buys goods and services abroad or the nation's citizens buy foreign goods and services. Both are currency outflows (that is, both are debits).

Net income from investments abroad, a credit of $20.80, is a currency inflow. This currency inflow is the result of previous currency outflows. Current foreign investments in plant and equipment or in foreign securities require currency outflows that are reported in the capital account. These investments may generate future income that will produce a currency inflow in the current account. Of course, foreign investors will also be earning income on their investments in the domestic country. For the country to experience a net currency inflow, the income received from the foreign investments must exceed the income paid foreign investors. In this illustration, the net investment income is a currency inflow of $20.80, which is reported in the credit column. A currency outflow would have been reported in the debit column.

[2] The rule of the IMF is discussed in the next section.

EXHIBIT 5.2

Simplified Balance of Payments for the Time Period 12/31/X0 through 12/31/X1

	Debit (−)	Credit (+)	Balance
Current Account			
Exports		$224.40	
Imports	$368.70		
Balance of trade			$(144.30)
Government spending abroad	15.30		
Net income from investment abroad		20.80	
Balance on current account			$(138.80)
Capital Account			
Long-term			
Direct investment abroad	130.10		
Foreign investments in the country		117.60	
Purchases of foreign securities	27.40		
Foreign purchase of domestic securities		41.00	
Short-term			
Purchases of short-term foreign investments	9.30		
Foreign purchases of short-term investments		95.70	
Balance on capital account			87.50
Official Reserves			
Statistical adjustment		3.90	
Net change in foreign reserves		47.40	
	$550.80	$550.80	

The sum of all these transactions (−$138.80) is the balance on the current account. In this illustration, the net income from previous investments helped offset some of the currency outflow from the merchandise trade balance, but the total on the current account indicates a currency outflow.

The capital account represents currency flows resulting from investments in physical assets, such as plant and equipment, and financial assets, such as stocks and bonds. It also includes investments in short-term financial assets. If a country has a net currency outflow in the current account, that outflow may be offset by an inflow in the capital account. If foreigners use the currency to make investments in that country, the money is returned. Correspondingly, if a country is running a surplus in its current account, it is receiving money it may use to invest in the foreign country. Such investments, of course, may be in actual physical assets or in financial assets. If the receiving country just holds the other country's cash, it is investing in a financial asset. However, the currency is usually invested in an income-earning asset, since holding the money itself earns nothing.

In this illustration, direct investments generate an outflow (a debit of $130.10), while direct foreign investments in the country generate an inflow (a credit of $117.60). Purchases of long-term foreign securities were $27.40, and foreign purchases were $41.00. Purchases of short-term foreign securities were $9.30, while foreign purchases were $95.70. The total credits on the capital account exceeded the debits by $87.50, indicating a cash inflow. If there had been a currency outflow (in other words, debits exceeded credits), the balance would be negative.

The sum of the currency inflows and outflows on the current and capital accounts still may not balance. The official reserve account is the final balancing item that equates the currency inflows and outflows. If there is a net credit balance on the current and capital accounts, there has to be a debit on the official reserve account. A net credit balance on the official reserve account indicates the opposite, a net debit on the current and capital accounts.

Transactions involving the reserve account can result when the country borrows or repays credit granted by the International Monetary Fund and when it uses or adds to its international reserves created by the IMF. Also, there is a statistical discrepancy account for errors and omissions. These errors can occur when transactions are not recorded (such as illegal transactions). For example, if individuals in a politically unstable country smuggle out money to invest in a safe haven, the transaction may not be recorded on the country's current or capital accounts.

Of all the three accounts in the balance of payments, the merchandise trade balance receives the most publicity. A debit on the merchandise trade account indicates that the country is importing more goods than it is exporting. Money is flowing out of the country into other countries. That money does not disappear, so the question becomes: What happens to this money and what are the implications of the cash outflow? These are not easy questions to answer but are important from the perspective of the country, its commercial banks, and financial managers. The merchandise trade balance for the United States from 1970 through 1997 is presented in Figure 5.2. In recent years the United States has imported more goods than it has exported, so dollars have been flowing out of the country.

Until August 15, 1971, foreigners could demand payment for dollars in gold. When they bought the gold, the currency would be returned to the United States. Today the dollar is not convertible into gold, so foreigners must take another course of action. They may simply hold the dollars. However, since dollars do not earn anything, they will be used to acquire something, such as short-term federal government securities (Treasury bills). Thus, the willingness of foreigners to hold U.S. financial assets absorbs a large amount of the dollars that flow abroad as a result of the merchandise trade deficit. The purchase of these securities, of course, returns the dollars to the United States.

Even if the foreigners do not return the dollars by purchasing financial assets issued in the United States, they do not retain dollars as such. Instead, the holders deposit the dollars in foreign commercial banks. These deposits may be denominated in dollars instead of the local currency (that is, the dollars are not

FIGURE 5.2

U.S. Merchandise Trade Balance, 1970–1997 (in billions)

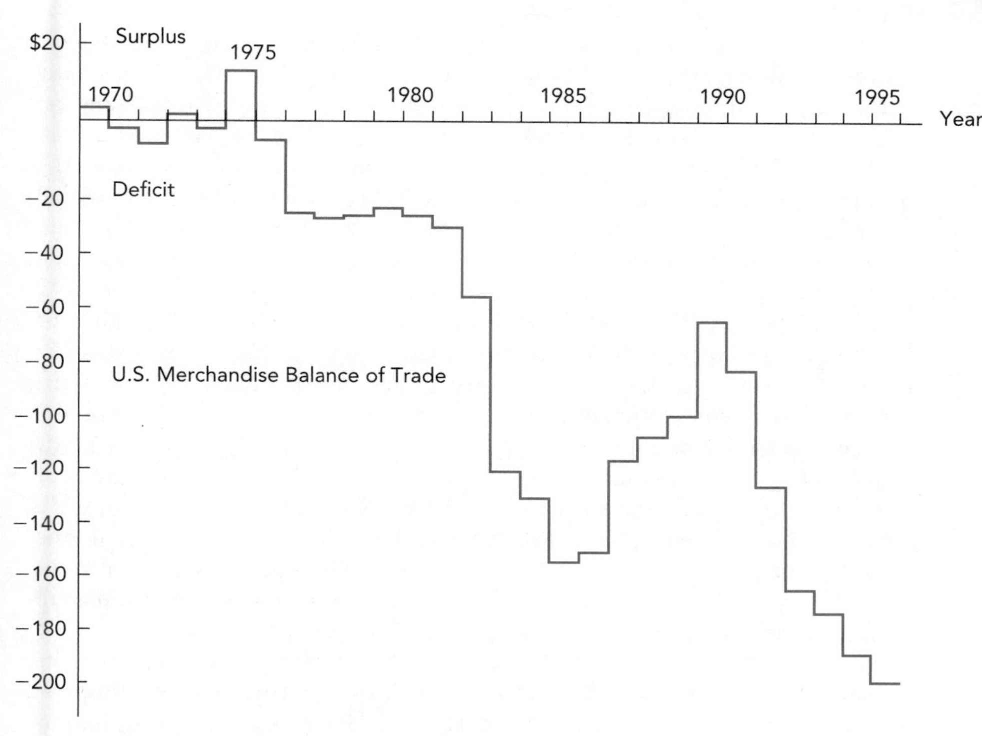

converted into the local currency). Such dollar-denominated deposits placed in banks in Europe are referred to as **Eurodollars.** A Eurodollar, then, is a deposit in any foreign bank that is denominated in dollars. (The bank need not be located in Europe: a dollar-denominated deposit located in a Hong Kong bank is still called a Eurodollar.)

EURODOLLARS
Deposit in a foreign bank denominated in dollars

The creation of Eurodollar deposits led large European banks to accept deposits in other currencies. For example, a bank in London could have deposits denominated in euros, dollars, and yen as well as British pounds. Such deposits, like any deposits, are a source of funds that the bank can lend. Thus, foreign banks may create loans that are denominated in many currencies, as well as loans denominated in their local currency.

The Role of the International Monetary Fund

If a country consistently has a deficit on the current account, the potential for a disequilibrium exists. If foreigners become unwilling to accept the additional currency and to hold additional financial assets, a disequilibrium will occur. Such a situation cannot exist indefinitely. One country cannot continually experience a currency outflow. Eventually the other countries will cease to hold the currency or financial assets denominated in that currency.

One temporary solution to a currency outflow is for a country to draw on its reserves at the International Monetary Fund (IMF). The IMF, which was created by the Bretton Woods agreements of 1944, oversees the international monetary order. It is a sort of central bank for the world's central banks. The initial agreement created the IMF as a pool of currencies contributed by the countries that joined the IMF. These funds are made available to countries with temporary balance of payments difficulties. The primary contributors to this fund are the major economic powers: the United States, the United Kingdom, Germany, France, and Japan.

If a country experiences a currency outflow, it may draw from the pool of currencies. The drawings are, in effect, a purchase of foreign currencies that is paid for by the country's currency. Each drawing increases the amount of the deficit country's currency held by the IMF. The drawings are to be reversed in three to five years by the country's repurchasing of its currency with foreign exchange. Of course, to acquire the foreign exchange, the country must cease experiencing currency outflows and start experiencing currency inflows.

As the country draws currencies from the IMF, it is required to take corrective action to stop the currency outflow. Responsibility for this action generally falls on the country experiencing the currency outflow and not on the countries receiving the currency inflow. Under a system of flexible exchange rates, the adjustment comes through changes in the value of currencies. An excess supply of one currency relative to other currencies causes its price to decline, which increases the quantity demanded of its products and hence of its currency. An excessive currency inflow would have the opposite effect. The increased demand for its currency (the currency inflow) causes the value of the currency to rise, making goods more expensive to foreigners and reducing the quantity demanded.

The importance of the IMF primarily revolves around the less-developed world economies. The more advanced economies (developed countries, or DCs) are often differentiated from the emerging economies (or "less-developed countries," or LDCs) such as Chile, Korea, or Thailand. Freely fluctuating exchange rates act as a constraint on the advanced economies by allocating their currencies. Such countries may not need to borrow funds from the IMF, as changes in exchange rates alter the demand for and supply of their currencies. For less-developed nations, however, the ability to borrow funds may be crucial for continued economic growth. When the IMF grants these countries loans, it also lends credibility to their debt. A country that complies with the IMF's demand for corrective action is able to borrow from other sources.

While the major free-world economic powers operate under a system of fluctuating rates, some countries do not permit the value of their currency to freely fluctuate. Instead they "peg" the value of their currency to a particular currency (for example, the U.S. dollar) or to an index or "basket" of currencies. Since the value of a basket of currencies may be more stable than the value of an individual currency, the value of the currency pegged to the basket may be more stable than if the currency were tied to the U.S. dollar or the euro. If a country that pegs its currency to another currency or basket of currencies experiences a consistent outflow, it has to adjust the value of its currency relative to the pegged currency or basket of currencies. A large devaluation (say, 10 percent) may occur overnight as the deficit nation's government lowers the value of its currency to discourage imports and encourage exports in an effort to stop the currency outflow. For example, Finland devaluated the markka (Fmk) in an effort to encourage exports and tourism. The devaluation made Finland one of the cheapest European countries to visit. If foreign travel in Finland did increase, the influx of tourists would, of course, generate a currency inflow.

FOREIGN TRADE AND MULTINATIONAL FIRMS

The ending of World War II, the rebuilding of Europe and Japan, the reduction in trade barriers, and the development of international trade agreements to facilitate trade led to a large number of American firms expanding their operations by investing abroad. This expansion of firms beyond their home borders has resulted in the development of large multinational firms with operations in many countries. Exxon typifies a multinational corporate giant. Its 1998 annual report discusses operations in many geographical areas, such as the North Sea (with the cooperation of Great Britain and Norway), and in many countries (such as Venezuela, Russia, Malaysia, Kazakhstan, Australia, and Yemen). Exxon's products, which include chemicals, coal, and nuclear fuel, as well as petroleum products, are sold throughout the world, and its fleet of tankers plow the world's major bodies of water.

The initial pattern was for American firms to invest abroad; however, with the increase in foreign income, many foreign firms now invest in the United States. Examples of foreign firms with large investments in the United States are given in Exhibit 5.3.

Growth through international investments has special risks and rewards. Conceptually, the decision to invest in a foreign country is no different from the decision to expand domestic production. In each case management is seeking those investments that maximize the value of the firm. Management identifies and quantifies the factors that affect the cash flow from the foreign investment and then determine which investments are the most profitable. But management also needs to be aware that while foreign investments may offer the firm opportunities for growth, they may also subject the firm to special risks. These risk factors, which are discussed later in this chapter, must be considered when the decision is made to invest abroad.

The potential returns are obvious. Foreign countries offer new markets for existing products (for example, Exxon's petroleum products). The firm already has the technology and usually can transfer that technology from one country to another. Also, operating a plant abroad may be less expensive than expanding a domestic plant, for foreign labor costs may be cheaper. Hence, a new foreign plant that combines a new market with less-expensive labor and the latest in equipment and technology can result in considerable profit. Even if a new plant is not built, exporting domestically produced goods to the new market may increase profits if existing facilities can operate at a higher level of efficiency.

EXHIBIT 5.3

Foreign Firms with Substantial Exports to or Investments in the United States

Firm	Country	Industry
ICI Chemical	Great Britain	Chemicals
Matsushita Electric	Japan	Electronics
Seagrams	Canada	Distillery
SONY	Japan	Electronics
Hoffman-La Roche	Switzerland	Drugs
BASF	Germany	Electronics
Unilever	Netherlands	Consumer products (Lever Brothers, Lipton)
Royal Dutch/Shell	Netherlands/ Great Britain	Petroleum
Alcan	Canada	Aluminum
Saint-Gobain-Pont-a-Mousson	France	Building supplies (Certain-Teed)

Financing Foreign Investments

When an American firm invests abroad, it may use its traditional sources of capital to finance investments. The firm may use internally generated funds, such as retained earnings, or it may borrow from American banks or use other sources, such as commercial paper. The firm then takes the funds abroad and converts them into the foreign currency. It may, however, borrow funds or sell securities abroad. These funds may be denominated in the local currency or, if the firm borrows in the Eurodollar market, be denominated in dollars.

Funds borrowed in the local currency must be retired with the local currency, while funds borrowed in the Eurodollar market must be retired with dollars. Of course, the firm may buy and sell currencies to obtain the funds needed to retire the debt. If a firm has an outstanding loan denominated in British pounds, it could sell dollars to obtain pounds. Of course, if the value of the pound rose, the number of dollars necessary to repay the loan would increase. The converse would be true if the price of the pound fell; then the firm would have to expend fewer dollars to obtain the pounds to retire the debt.

LIBOR
Short-term interest rate for highest quality international loans among international banks

Many large multinational firms with investments in several foreign countries finance their operations by borrowing short- and intermediate-term funds in the Eurodollar market. Such loans are usually unsecured, with maturities from 30 days to several years. The interest rates vary with the creditworthiness of the borrowers and tend to fluctuate with the "London interbank offer rate" (**LIBOR**). The safest (prime) borrowers generally receive a rate that is ¾ to 1 percent above the LIBOR rate.

EUROBONDS
Bonds issued abroad denominated in dollars or a strong currency

Firms may also issue long-term debt called **Eurobonds.** Eurobonds may be denominated in dollars or another strong currency, such as the euro. Part of an issue of Eurobonds may be denominated in one currency while the remainder is denominated in a second currency. Many American firms issue substantial amounts of Eurobonds and other securities outside the United States. For example, Exxon reported in its 1998 annual report that $252 million of its $4.5 billion long-term debt (that is, 5.6 percent of its total long-term debt) was payable in foreign currencies. Public sales of securities by American companies in foreign countries are not subject to the Securities and Exchange Commission's disclosure requirements. Foreign security issues thus avoid the costs associated with the disclosure rules. In addition, the terms of foreign securities may be more advantageous to the issuing firm than if the funds were borrowed in the United States and invested abroad. This is particularly true if the host country promotes economic development by offering generous terms for investments within the country.

The Eurodollar and Eurobond markets have grown rapidly. The large increase in international trade and continued deficits in the U.S. balance of trade have resulted in a substantial increase in Eurodollars. In addition, increased foreign demand for American securities has resulted in a worldwide market for the stocks of large American companies. Firms such as IBM or Ford have their securities listed on foreign exchanges in major foreign financial centers such as London or Paris. The stocks of these companies trade abroad in much the same way that they trade in the United States. The active secondary markets increase foreign interest in the companies, and their investors become potential sources of funds for future sales of securities.

Risk and Foreign Investments

While offering acceptable returns, foreign investments may significantly alter the firm's risk position. The firm may become less risky as the result of foreign investments. If a firm is in a cyclical industry, foreign investments may reduce the variability of its earnings. While economic conditions may be similar in many countries, foreign investments may lessen the effect of a domestic recession. If the domestic market is weak and foreign markets continue to be strong, the impact of the weak domestic market on the firm's earnings is reduced. Besides reducing the impact of the economic cycle, foreign investments may reduce risk by assuring the firm a supply of raw materials. For example, a smelter and fabricator of metal (say, Alcoa) needs a supply of ore and invests in foreign mining operations. By assuring itself of a source of supply, the firm reduces the riskiness of its operations.

International investment, however, may subject the firm to increases in risk. Such risks are the result of local politics, fluctuations in the local economy, and exchange rate fluctuations. The political climate in the United States is stable. Such stability may not exist in foreign countries, or, if it does exist, the political climate can change dramatically. Many American firms with investments abroad have experienced the nationalization and expropriation of their investments. These firms may not receive compensation for the seized assets. For example, Cuba did not offer compensation when Fidel Castro came to power and nationalized the facilities of American firms. Venezuela, however, nationalized Exxon's oil investments in that country and agreed to compensate Exxon by paying $72 million in cash and $435 million in interest-bearing bonds. The amount of compensation and the

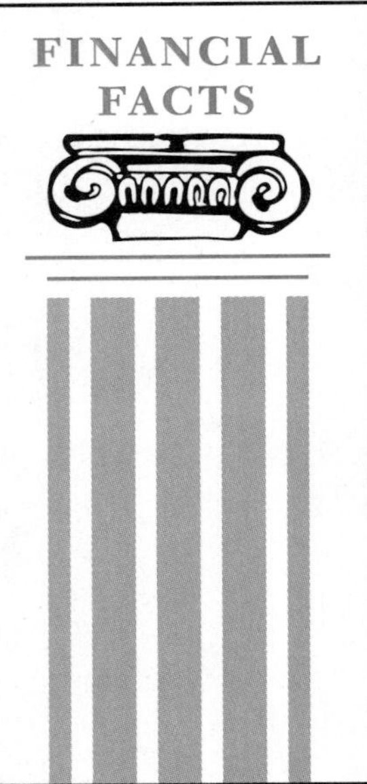

Fluor Corporation's Currency Hedges

Many firms with international operations enter into contracts for the future purchase or sale of currencies. For example, Fluor Corporation is a large engineering, construction, and resource company that builds generation stations, processing plants, and pipelines worldwide. These construction projects take time and require entering into contracts. Some of the contracts are for the future purchase (receipt) of raw materials; other contracts are for the sale (delivery) of finished projects. Because many of Fluor's operations are in foreign countries, the contracts may be denominated in the local currency. ¶ To reduce the risk from fluctuations in exchange rates, Fluor enters into contracts for the future delivery or purchase of foreign currencies. In its 1998 annual report, Fluor had over $100 million in contracts to sell, within 18 months, Australian dollars, Korean won, Dutch guilders, and German marks for U.S. dollars. The firm also had contracts to sell U.S. dollars for British pounds. None of these contracts was premised on profiting from an anticipated change in the value of the currencies. Each contract was a hedge designed to lock in the future price of the currency and, hence, reduce the risk of loss from fluctuations in the exchange rate. ¶

means of payment are political questions that are negotiated between governments as well as between a government and the firm whose facilities are being expropriated. Such power plays and political maneuverings are beyond the discipline of finance, but if a firm makes foreign investments that subject it to these problems, the firm's risk exposure is increased.

One method to reduce political risk is for the firm to join with the foreign government in a joint venture. For example, Exxon and other oil companies have had working relationships with several Arab countries that produce oil. The exact relationship between the firm and the host country varies with each agreement, but the effect is to provide payment to the foreign government. The payment increases cooperation between the firm and the foreign government and may also result in lower taxes and reduced chances of nationalization. Such agreements, however, usually have time limits, after which they must be renegotiated. And if there is a change in the government, the new politicians may repudiate old agreements. Hence, joint ventures may reduce political risks, but they cannot erase them.

Foreign governments can also burden the investing firm with legal constraints. For example, the country can require the firm to hire domestic labor, thus limiting the ability of the firm to import specialized labor to operate foreign plants. The foreign government may also have special laws limiting the ability of the firm to convert currencies. In this case if a firm invests capital in the country, it may be unable to take the funds out of the country. Any profits earned are effectively locked into the country and cannot be returned to the parent company. Certainly one of the most important constraints is the local government's tax laws. Foreign governments may tax income, the property, or the value added by the production process. The latter tax, the so-called value-added tax, is popular in European countries. The foreign government, however, may use tax laws to encourage investment by granting special tax concessions, such as no income or property tax for a specified period. Such concessions are specifically designed to encourage foreign investment and are used by underdeveloped nations to attract capital.

In addition to political and legal problems, local economic conditions may increase the firm's risk exposure. While foreign investments may expand the firm's markets or permit it to produce goods more cheaply, these goals may not be achieved. Anticipated markets may not materialize. Labor unrest or raw material shortages may develop. The foreign country may experience recession or inflation. While the financial manager seeks to anticipate these problems and their solutions before making foreign investments, uncertainties concerning the foreign economy expose the firm to increased risk.

There is also the risk associated with fluctuations in exchange rates.[3] As was explained earlier, the prices of foreign moneys change daily in relation to the demand for and supply of each currency. Such exchange rate fluctuations can have a severe impact on a firm that invests abroad. Some of the largest American firms (Xerox, for example) have lost millions of dollars through exchange rate fluctuations.

How such fluctuations may produce losses can be demonstrated by the following examples. If a firm accepts a bid for plant and equipment in Germany and the euro subsequently rises by 10 percent, the cost of the facility will increase by 10 percent. Such an increase in cost may convert a profitable investment into a losing operation. Another example of a potential loss from an increase in exchange rates occurs when a firm borrows in another country and must repay in the country's own currency. If the value of that currency appreciates, more American dollars are required to retire the loan.

Exchange rate variations may also benefit the firm. For example, if a country's currency rises in price, previous investments are worth more. If the firm in the preceding example already had a plant in Germany, any cash flow generated by the operation would convert into 10 percent more dollars. Such a 10 percent increase in the price of the euro increases the firm's profitability when the euros are converted into dollars. Thus, exchange rate fluctuations may help as well as hurt the firm's financial position.

[3] One of the most important implications of the euro is the elimination of exchange risk for the participating nations. Businesses, investors, and even consumers will no longer have to convert one currency to another. A German company will not have to convert marks to francs when it invests in France and will not have to convert francs back to marks to repatriate its profits. Thus, the uncertainty concerning exchange rates ceases.

The potential economic impact of this change in the financial structure is substantial and should stimulate economic activity in the countries that join the Economic Monetary Union. For example, the existence of a common monetary unit in each of the 11 countries will facilitate the comparison of prices by consumers. Individual firms should achieve operating efficiencies, and increased merger activity may also result as European firms combine to better compete in global markets.

Because exchange rates vary daily, the firm continuously runs the risk of loss through a decline in a country's currency. Management may be able to reduce this risk by trading currencies. The financial manager would sell currencies whose price may decline and purchase currencies appreciating in value. If the financial manager expects the value of the Canadian dollar to decline and the value of the British pound to increase, he or she may sell Canadian dollars for pounds. If the price of the Canadian dollar declines, the pounds will buy more dollars in the future. Of course, if the financial manager is wrong and the price of the Canadian dollar rises while the British pound declines, this transaction produces a loss because the pounds now buy fewer Canadian dollars.

The essential job of the financial manager is not to forecast changes in the value of one currency relative to another, but to ensure there are sufficient funds to pay bills as they come due and to reduce the firm's risk exposure. The preceding sale of one currency and purchase of another may not necessarily reduce risk, because the forecasted direction of change in the value of the currencies may not occur. There has to be a better alternative to reduce the risk associated with fluctuations in exchange rates.

RISK REDUCTION WITH FUTURES CONTRACTS

One means to reduce risk of loss from exchange rate fluctuation is to enter a contract, which establishes the future price of the currency.[4] For example, a firm contracts to buy a plant in Germany for 40,000,000 euros in six months (line 1 in Exhibit 5.4). If the current price of the euro is \$0.80, the cost of the plant is \$32,000,000 (\$0.80 × 40,000,000 in line 2). If the price of the euro were to fall to \$0.75, the cost of the plant would decline to \$30,000,000 and save the firm \$2,000,000 (line 4). However, if the price of the euro were to rise to \$0.85, the cost would increase to \$34,000,000, for a net increase of \$2,000,000 (line 6).

Since the payment will be made in the future, the cost of the euro necessary to make the future payment may rise or fall depending on fluctuations in the demand for and supply of euros. To avoid the possibility of loss through an increase in the price, the financial manager enters into a contract for the purchase of euros (in other words, to sell dollars) after six months for a specified price. If the current six-month price of the euro is \$0.805, the financial manager can enter a contract to purchase euros for delivery in six months for \$0.805. The total cost of the euros necessary to pay for the plant will then be \$32,200,000 (line 7). If the firm does enter the contract, it has a hedged position. In effect, the firm has agreed to purchase 40,000,000 for \$32,200,000; the firm then can use these euros to pay for the plant. The net effect is to increase the cost of the plant by \$200,000 (line 8).

[4] Standardized contracts for future purchase or sale (called "futures") are explained in Chapter 13 on derivatives. Although you may defer this section until after completing that discussion, this presentation does not require understanding the material in Chapter 13.

EXHIBIT 5.4

Gains or Losses from Changes in the Value of the Euro Relative to the U.S. Dollar

Current Cost of the Plant	
1. Cost of the plant in euros	$40,000,000
2. Cost of the plant in dollars (based on an $0.80 price of euros)	$32,000,000
Possible Gain from Decrease in the Cost of the Euro	
3. Cost of the plant in dollars (if the price of the euro declines to $0.75)	$30,000,000
4. Decrease in cost from the depreciation in the euro (line 2 minus line 3)	$2,000,000
Possible Loss from Increase in the Cost of the Euro	
5. Cost of the plant in dollars (if the price of the euro rises to $0.85)	$34,000,000
6. Increase in cost from the appreciation in the euro (line 5 minus line 2)	$2,000,000
Impact of Hedging	
7. Cost of the plant in dollars (based on the future contract price of euros)	$32,200,000
8. Cost of hedging (line 7 minus line 2)	$200,000

By constructing a hedge, the financial manager protects the firm against an increase in the price of the euro, because the firm now has a contract to buy euros for $0.805. If the value of the euro did increase to $0.85, the contract for future delivery at $0.805 would appreciate in value, offsetting the increased cost of the currency. The price of the euro, and thus the price of the plant, cannot exceed $32,200,000. By hedging, the financial manager has locked in the price of the currency. However, while the firm is protected if the price of the euro were to increase, the firm would not gain from a decline in the value of the euro. If the price declined to $0.75, the value of the contract to buy in the future would also decline, thus offsetting the firm's gain from the euro's price decline.

A firm expecting to receive payment in the future would use the opposite procedure. For example, if a firm anticipates a payment in British pounds after three months, it would enter a contract to sell pounds. If the current price of the pound is $1.95 and the future price is $1.94, the firm is assured of receiving $1.94 for a pound. Thus, for the cost of 1 cent per pound, the firm is protected from an exchange rate fluctuation. If the pound were to decline to $1.75, the firm would still receive $1.94. Conversely, the possibility of gain is lost. If the pound were to rise to $2.18, the firm would receive only $1.94. Of course, the purpose of entering into the contract is to reduce the risk of loss from changes in exchange rates. To achieve this reduction in risk, the firm must give up the potential for profit from a price increase.

Entering contracts for the future purchase or sale (i.e., hedging) reduces the risk of loss from unexpected fluctuations in currency values. If a price change in a currency is widely anticipated, the future price will indicate that expectation. In the preceding example, the current price of the British pound was $1.95, and the future price was $1.94. If there were widespread belief that the pound would decline in value, the future price would be lower. No one would want to enter into a contract to buy the pounds for $1.94 if they expected the value of the pounds to be $1.80 after three months. If a substantial price decline were anticipated, there might be no buyers for future delivery of pounds, or the future price might be so low that sellers would prefer to hold the currency and bear the risk.

SUMMARY

This chapter has presented a brief introduction to multinational finance and the international monetary system. The demand for a nation's products is also a demand for its currency. Currencies (foreign exchange) are traded daily in the foreign exchange market. The price of a currency varies daily with the demand for and supply of that currency.

If a country imports more than it exports, it experiences a deficit in its merchandise trade balance, and currency flows out of the country. If a country exports more than it imports, it has a surplus in its merchandise balance of trade, and foreign currencies flow into the country. Imbalances in the demand for and supply of a currency result in changes in its value relative to other currencies. Deficits result in a devaluation or depreciation while a surplus leads to a revaluation or appreciation.

Currency flows arising from foreign trade and foreign investments are recorded on a nation's balance of payments, which is a system of double entry bookkeeping for recording international monetary transactions. While a nation may have a deficit or surplus in its current account or capital accounts, the balance of payments must balance. If a country has a short-term problem, especially a deficit, in its balance of trade, it may purchase foreign exchange from the International Monetary Fund. The nation is then required to take corrective action to stop the outflow of currency and to repurchase its currency with foreign exchange within three to five years.

The reduction in trade barriers, the development of an international monetary system, and expanding economies have led to a large expansion in international trade. Initially, many U.S. corporations expanded their foreign operations to take advantage of potentially profitable investment opportunities, but foreign corporations currently also have substantial investments in the United States. The results of these investments have been the development of large multinational firms that are global in scope.

Foreign investments may be financed by internally generated funds or by borrowing and selling securities abroad. Funds borrowed abroad may be denominated in the local currency or in dollars. Eurobonds and short-term Eurodollar loans are a major source of capital to finance foreign investments.

Foreign investments involve special risks, including political risks, local legal constraints, problems with local economic conditions, and the risk associated with fluctuations in exchange rates. Management may reduce the latter risk by entering contracts to buy or sell currencies in the future. By using these contracts, the financial manager locks in the value of the currency and reduces the risk of loss from changes in the value of one currency relative to the other.

Review Questions

1. If the value of the Canadian dollar rises, what does that imply about demand for its products in the United States? What may have caused the value of the Canadian dollar to rise? Since the Canadian dollar rose, could you conclude that the country was running a deficit on its merchandise trade balance?
2. If a country has a consistent surplus in its balance of trade, what impact may that have on its commercial banks? Why may the surplus in the balance of trade make it easier for this nation to finance long-term investments in other countries?
3. If the IMF is supplying a country with foreign exchange, what does that action imply? What would you expect to happen to the value of that nation's currency?
4. Why may a domestic firm seek to make investments abroad, and why may foreign firms seek to make investments in the United States? If the value of the American dollar rises after the investments are made, what does that imply about their profitability?
5. Why do American firms issue dollar-denominated Eurobonds instead of bonds denominated in the local currency? If the firm borrows the funds in another currency, what risk does it bear?
6. All business ventures involve risk. Foreign investments have additional risks. How do joint ventures and futures contracts reduce risk?
7. If you expect the value of the dollar to rise against the British pound and anticipate receiving a future payment denominated in pounds, do you enter into a contract to sell (that is, deliver) pounds or into a contract to sell dollars?

Problems

1. If the price of a British pound is \$1.50, how many pounds are necessary to purchase \$1.00? If the value of a European euro is \$0.90, how many euros are necessary to purchase \$1.00?
2. Last year, U.S. Leather and Boot had inventory in London valued at 500,000 pounds. At that time, 1£ = \$1.50. Today the pound has strengthened against the dollar; the current exchange rate is 1£ = \$1.65. If the inventory continues to be worth 500,000 pounds, what is the gain or loss in U.S. dollars as a result of the change in the exchange rate?
3. The spot rate for the Japanese yen is 113 yen per dollar. If the forward (or futures) rate is 120 yen per dollar, is the forward rate selling at a premium or a discount to the current (spot) rate?
4. Given the following information, determine the balance on the United States' current account and capital accounts:

imports	$211.5
net income from foreign investments	32.3
foreign investments in U.S.	7.7
government spending abroad	4.6
exports	182.1
U.S. investments abroad	24.7
foreign securities bought by U.S.	4.9
U.S. securities bought by foreigners	2.8
purchase of short-term foreign securities	6.5
foreign purchases of U.S. short-term securities	9.1

Is there a net inflow or outflow of currency into the United States?

5. An American firm expects to pay 20 million Finnish markka in six months. Management fears that the value of the markka will rise. What course of action should it take? The current (that is, spot) price of the markka is $0.50 and the future price is $0.51. What would be the cost to the firm of the course of action you recommend?

6. You expect to receive a payment of 1 million British pounds after six months. The pound is currently worth $1.60 (£1 = $1.60), but the future price is $1.56 (£1 = $1.56). You expect the price of the pound to decline (that is, the value of the dollar to rise). If this expectation is fulfilled, you will suffer a loss when the pounds are converted into dollars when you receive them six months in the future.

a. Given the current exchange rate, what is the expected payment in dollars?
b. Given the future exchange rate, how much would you receive in dollars?
c. If, after six months, the pound is worth $1.40, what is your loss from the decline in the value of the pound?
d. To avoid this potential loss, you enter a contract for the future delivery of pounds at the future price of $1.56. What is the cost to you of this protection from the possible decline in the value of the pound?
e. If, after entering the contract, the price of the pound falls to $1.40, what is the maximum amount that you lose? (Why is your answer different from your answer to part c?)
f. If, after entering the contract, the price of the pound rises to $1.80, how much do you gain from your position?
g. How would your answer to part f be different if you had not made the contract and the price of the pound had risen to $1.80?

CHAPTER 6
The Role of Security Markets

Learning Objectives

1 Differentiate (a) organized exchanges from the over-the-counter markets, (b) brokers from dealers, (c) market orders from limit orders.
2 Trace the mechanics of a security purchase.
3 Explain the advantage and risk associated with buying stock on margin.
4 Contrast a short sale with a purchase of a stock.
5 Distinguish among various aggregate measures of the stock market.
6 Identify the regulatory body that enforces the federal security laws and state its objectives.
7 Determine how American Depository Receipts (ADRs) facilitate purchasing foreign securities.
8 Explain why an investor should not expect to outperform the market consistently.

An anonymous sage once suggested, "A fool and his money are soon parted." The stock market is definitely one place where such separation may occur. On Monday, October 19, 1987, the Dow Jones Industrial Average plummeted 508 points, a 22.6 percent decline in the market in one day. That decline exceeded the decline that occurred October 28, 1929. On that fateful day the value of the market declined only 12.8 percent!

The stock market may also generate large increases in wealth. While excess speculation may lead to financial ruin, prudent investing in stocks and bonds can be a means to store wealth from the present to the future. The individual who purchased 1,000 shares of Maytag in 1981 for $2,800 had stock worth over $40,000 in 1999 (an annualized return of about 16 percent). Certainly such an investment is an important alternative to the savings and time deposits offered by depository institutions.

The stock market is probably the most fascinating and well-known financial institution. The Dow Jones averages and the happenings on Wall Street are newsworthy events that are reported here and abroad. But even with all the publicity, the role of security markets is rarely understood. A security market is *not* a financial intermediary, for it does not transfer funds from lenders to borrowers. Instead, it is a *secondary* market that transfers securities from sellers to buyers. Firms do not receive the proceeds of the sales. The one and only time that a firm receives proceeds from the sale of securities occurs when the securities are issued and sold for the first time in the *primary* market.

Security markets transfer existing securities from owners who no longer desire to maintain their investments to buyers who wish to increase those specific investments. There is no net change in the number of securities in existence, for there is only a transfer of ownership. The role of security markets is to facilitate this transfer of ownership. This transfer of securities is extremely important, for security holders know that a secondary market exists in which they may sell their security holdings. The ease with which securities may be sold and converted into cash increases the willingness of people to hold securities and thus increases the ability of firms to issue securities.

Initially this chapter considers many of the basic elements of investing. The mechanics of investing, measures of stock prices, the regulation of security markets, and the mechanics of buying foreign stock are covered. The chapter ends with a discussion of the efficient market hypothesis, which suggests that over a period of years few investors will outperform the market.

SECURITY TRANSACTIONS

Market Makers

After stocks and bonds are issued, they may subsequently be sold in the secondary markets. Securities are bought and sold every day by investors who never meet each other. The market impersonally transfers the securities from the sellers to the buyers. This transfer may occur on an **organized exchange,** such as the New York Stock Exchange, or an unorganized, informal market, called an **over-the-counter (OTC) market.** In both cases a professional security dealer makes a market in the security. The Securities and Exchange Act of 1934 defines a **dealer** as anyone who engages in the "business of buying and selling for his *own account*." Buying and selling for your own account has the effect of making a market in the security, and dealers in over-the-counter securities are referred to as "market makers." Dealers for securities traded on the New York Stock Exchange and the American Stock Exchange are referred to as **specialists.** These specialists offer to buy securities from any seller and to sell securities to any purchaser. In effect, specialists make a market in the stock.[1] These market makers set a specified price at which they will buy and sell the security. For example, a market maker may be willing to purchase stock at $20 a share and sell at $21. The security is then quoted 20–21, which are the **bid and ask prices.** The market maker is willing to purchase (bid) the stock at $20 and to sell (ask) the stock for $21.

Transactions are either **round lots** or **odd lots.** A round lot is the basic unit for a transaction and for stock is usually 100 shares. Smaller transactions, like 37 shares, are odd lots. For some stocks the round lot is different from 100 shares. For example, for very inexpensive stocks a round lot may be 500 or 1,000 shares.

ORGANIZED EXCHANGE
Organized secondary market for the buying and selling of securities

OVER-THE-COUNTER (OTC) MARKET
Informal, unorganized secondary market for the buying and selling of securities

DEALER
Market maker in unlisted, OTC securities

SPECIALIST
Market maker on an organized exchange

BID AND ASK PRICES
Security prices quoted by market makers at which they are willing to buy and sell securities

ROUND LOT
Normal unit of trading in a security

ODD LOT
Unit of trading that is less than a round lot

[1]As of January 1, 1999, 481 individuals operated as specialists on the New York Stock Exchange. New York Stock Exchange, 1998 *Annual Report*, available at **www.nyse.com**.

For bonds a round lot may be five $1,000 bonds ($5,000), or $10,000, or even $100,000 face value of the bonds.

SPREAD
Difference between the bid and ask prices

The difference between the bid and the ask is the **spread,** and this spread, like brokerage commissions, is part of the cost of investing. When an investor buys a security, the value of the security is the bid price, but the investor pays the ask price. Thus, the difference between the bid and the ask is a cost to the investor. If there are several market makers in a particular security, this spread will be small. If, however, there are only one or two market makers, the spread may be quite large (at least as a percentage of the bid price). The spread is also affected by the volume of transactions in the security and the number of shares the firm has outstanding. If there is a large volume of transactions or the number of outstanding shares is large, then there is usually a larger number of market makers. This increased competition reduces the spread between the bid and the ask. If the number of outstanding shares is small, the spread is usually larger.

The spread is one source of market makers' profits as they turn over the securities in their portfolios. Market makers profit as well when the prices of the securities rise, for the value of their inventory of securities rises. (They also bear the risk if the value of any securities they hold were to fall.) The profits are a necessary facet of security markets, for the profits induce the market makers to serve the crucial function of buying and selling securities. These market makers guarantee to buy and sell at the prices they announce. Thus an investor knows (1) what the securities are worth at a point in time and (2) that there is a place to sell current security holdings or to purchase additional securities. For this service the market makers must be compensated, and this compensation is generated through the spread between the bid and the ask, dividends and interest earned, and profits on the inventory of securities (if their prices rise).

While the bid and ask prices are set by the market makers, the level of these security prices is set by investors. The market maker only guarantees to make a transaction at the bid-ask prices. If the market maker sets too low a price for a stock, a large quantity of shares will be demanded by investors. If the market maker is unable or does not want to satisfy this demand for the stock, this dealer (or specialist) will sell one round lot and increase the bid-ask prices. The increase in the price of the stock will (1) induce some holders of the stock to sell their shares and thereby replenish the market maker's inventory and (2) induce some investors seeking the stock to drop out of the market.

If the market maker sets too high a price for the stock, there will be a large quantity of shares offered for sale. If the market maker is unable or does not want to absorb all these shares, the dealer may purchase a round lot and lower the bid-ask prices. The decline in the price of the stock will (1) induce some potential sellers to hold their stock and (2) induce some investors to enter the market and purchase the shares, thereby reducing any excess buildup of inventory by the market maker. Thus, while market makers may set the bid and ask prices for a security, they cannot set the general level of security prices.

To set the general price level, market makers must be able to absorb excess securities into their inventory when excess supply exists and to sell securities from their inventory when excess demand exists. Buying these excess securities will require that the market makers pay for them, and selling securities will require that the market makers deliver the securities sold. No market maker has an infinite source of money or securities. Although market makers may build up or decrease their inventory, they cannot indefinitely support the price by buying, nor can they stop a price increase by selling. The market maker's function is not to set the level of security prices; all investors do that through buying and selling. The market maker's function is to facilitate the orderly process by which buyers and sellers of securities are brought together.

Security Exchanges

When a company first sells its securities to the public, the securities may be initially traded in the over-the-counter market. However, the firm may subsequently have its securities listed on one of the major organized exchanges: the New York Stock Exchange (NYSE, or "the big board") or the American Stock Exchange (AMEX, or "the curb"). (Although the inclusion of the word *stock* in the names implies a market that deals solely in stock, some bond issues are also traded on these exchanges.) The listing of a firm's securities on a major exchange has an element of prestige, for it indicates that the company has attained a specified size and level of profitability.

The NYSE is the largest exchange and lists the securities of companies of national interest that are expected to maintain their relative positions in their respective industries. The AMEX is smaller than the NYSE. Many of the firms listed on the NYSE were originally listed on the AMEX. After achieving larger earnings and size, these firms transferred their securities from the AMEX to the NYSE.[2]

Once the securities are accepted for trading on an exchange, the firm must continue to conform to certain procedures, including publishing quarterly reports, soliciting proxies, and announcing any development that may affect the value of the securities. The exchange may delist the securities if the firm is unable to meet the listing criteria or is not timely in publishing information that may affect the value of the stock. Such delisting does occur, but over a period of years the number of listed securities has increased. Whereas 1,253 stocks were traded on the NYSE in 1965, the number had grown to 3,114 companies as of 1999.[3]

Reporting of Transactions

Trading in listed and over-the-counter securities is reported in the financial press and other daily newspapers. The amount of information reported depends on the space that the publication chooses to give to the transactions. Exhibit 6.1 reproduces part of the trades in stocks listed on the New York Stock Exchange and OTC transactions. These illustrations are typical of financial reporting of security transactions.

[2] For histories of the New York and American stock exchanges, consult: Robert Sobel, *The Big Board: A History of the New York Stock Market* (New York: The Free Press, 1965; and Robert Sobel, *The Curbstone Brokers: The Origins of the American Stock Exchange* (New York: Macmillan, 1970).

[3] New York Stock Exchange, *1998 Fact Book,* available at **www.nyse.com**.

EXHIBIT 6.1

Reporting of Security Transactions

NEW YORK STOCK EXCHANGE COMPOSITE TRANSACTIONS

Quotations as of 4 p.m. Eastern Time
Tuesday, January 4, 2000

	52 Weeks Hi	Lo	Stock	Sym	Div	Yld %	PE	Vol 100s	Hi	Lo	Close	Net Chg
			-A-A-A-									
	23 3/8	14 5/8	AAR	AIR	.34	1.9	11	517	18	17 1/4	17 5/8	+ 1/16
	33 3/4	20	ABM Indus	ABM	.62f	3.0	12	624	20 3/8	20	20 3/8	+ 1/16
	25 13/16	**19**	**ABN Am ADR**	**ABN**	**.65e**	**2.7**	**...**	**328**	**24 3/16**	**23 3/4**	**23 3/4**	**– 1 5/16**
	26 3/16	19 3/16	ABN Am pfA		1.88	9.1	...	485	20 7/8	20 1/2	20 3/4	– 1/16
n	25 1/2	19 1/8	ABN Am pfB		1.78	9.0	...	1125	19 13/16	19 5/8	19 13/16	+ 1/16
▼	35 1/4	15 1/2	♣ACE Ltd	ACL	.44	2.7	8	12822	16 1/4	15 7/16	16 1/8	– 3/16
	9 1/2	6 5/16	ACM GvtFd	ACG	.90	13.2	...	1678	6 13/16	6 5/8	6 13/16	+ 3/16
	7 15/16	6 1/4	ACM OppFd	AOF	.51a	7.2	...	84	7 1/8	6 15/16	7 1/16	+ 1/16
	8 3/4	6 3/16	ACM SecFd	GSF	.90	13.7	...	1995	6 5/8	6 1/2	6 9/16	+ 1/16
	6 1/4	5 3/8	ACM SpctmFd	SI	.60	10.8	...	794	5 9/16	5 7/16	5 9/16	+ 1/8
	11 1/2	8 1/4	ACM MgdDlr	ADF	1.35a	16.0	...	567	8 1/2	8 3/8	8 7/16	+ 1/16
	9 1/4	5 5/8	ACM MgdInco	AMF	.30	5.2	...	700	5 7/8	5 11/16	5 13/16	...
	14 1/4	10 1/8	ACM MuniSec	AMU	.87	8.2	...	176	10 3/4	10 5/8	10 5/8	– 1/16
s	9 1/4	4 3/16	♣ACX Tch A	ACX		...	5	1212	8 3/4	8	8 7/16	...
	76 3/8	32 13/16	♣AES Cp	AES		...	65	7401	71 15/16	69 1/4	69 5/8	– 2 7/8
n	62	47 1/4	AES Tr			...	...	1066	59 1/2	58	58 1/2	– 2
	56 3/4	39	AFLAC	AFL	.30	.7	21	6789	45 1/8	43 1/4	43 13/16	– 15/16
	14 1/8	6	AGCO Cp	AG	.04	.3	dd	1789	12 9/16	12 1/8	12 9/16	+ 5/16
	23 5/16	15 9/16	AGL Res	ATG	1.08	6.4	13	1173	16 15/16	16 1/2	16 3/4	...
	18 1/16	**13**	**AgSvcAm**	**ASV**		**...**	**11**	**410**	**15 5/8**	**14 11/16**	**15 5/8**	**+ 7/8**

LATE MOST ACTIVE ISSUES

ISSUE	EXCH	VOL (000)	LAST	CH
AriadPharm	(Nq)	4,741.6	5.156	+
DellCptr	(Nq)	792.8	45.875	–
CiscoSys	(Nq)	726.0	100.750	
Microsft	(Nq)	663.1	111.500	
Qualcomm	(Nq)	628.7	158.000	
Amgen	(Nq)	625.5	58.375	
Intel	(Nq)	587.2	82.250	
GlblCross	(Nq)	566.5	46.750	
SunMicrsys	(Nq)	561.9	71.750	
MCI Wrldcm	(Nq)	537.6	49.438	

LATE PRICE PERCENTAGE G

ISSUE	EXCH	VOL (000)	LAST
AriadPharm	(Nq)	4,741.6	5.156
AriadPhrm wt	(Nq)	3.4	1.000
PowerCerv	(Nq)	244.2	9.063
DamarkInt	(Nq)	10.2	18.000
LaJolla wt	(Nq)	5.5	0.21

NASDAQ NATIONAL MARKET ISSUES

Quotations as of 4 p.m. Eastern Time
Tuesday, January 4, 2000

	52 Weeks Hi	Lo	Stock	Sym	Div	Yld %	PE	Vol 100s	Hi	Lo	Close	Net Chg
			-A-A-A-									
	16 3/16	8 1/8	AAON Inc	AAON		...	11	584	15	13 5/8	14 1/16	+ 9/16
s	12 59/64	9 3/8	ABC Bcp	ABCB	.33	3.1	9	59	10 5/8	10 1/2	10 5/8	– 1/8
▼	**21**	**7 7/8**	**ABC NACO**	**ABCR**		**...**	**dd**	**1417**	**7 7/8**	**7 5/16**	**7 7/16**	**– 1/2**
	10 3/8	8 1/8	ABI Cap pf	ABANP	.85	9.7	...	13	8 3/4	8 3/4	8 3/4	+ 1/8
	12	**1 13/16**	**ACE COMM**	**ACEC**		**...**	**72**	**8293**	**9 15/16**	**7**	**8 11/16**	**+ 1 5/16**
	20 7/8	5 7/8	ACLN Ltd	ACLNF		...	6	62	16 1/4	16 1/16	16 1/4	+ 1/16
	6 7/8	4	♣AC MooreArt	ACMR		...	10	60	5 5/8	5 3/8	5 5/8	+ 1/8
	39 1/2	11 7/8	ACT Mfg	ACTM		...	73	1612	35 1/16	33 3/4	34 3/8	– 1
	25 5/8	**4 15/16**	**ACT Netwk**	**ANET**		**...**	**dd**	**1721**	**9 3/4**	**8 3/4**	**9 1/16**	**– 9/16**
	10	3 5/8	♣A CnsltgTm	TACX		...	17	58	4 7/8	4 3/4	4 7/8	– 1/8
	75 3/4	**34 3/8**	**♣ADC Tel**	**ADCT**		**...**	**cc**	**17442**	**71 3/8**	**65 1/16**	**65 1/8**	**– 7 3/8**
	19 1/2	8 1/16	ADE Cp	ADEX		...	dd	167	16 7/8	16 7/16	16 3/4	– 1/4
	55 1/2	15 3/4	ADTRAN Inc	ADTN		...	45	1417	51 5/8	49 1/16	49 9/16	– 1 19/32
	39	17 7/8	AEP Ind	AEPI		...	dd	1	24 3/4	24 3/4	24 3/4	...
	37 5/8	15 3/4	♣AHL Svcs	AHLS		...	17	969	21 11/16	20 7/8	21 1/2	– 1/8
	6 15/16	1 3/4	AHT	AHTC		...	dd	971	4 15/32	4	4 1/16	– 1/8
	3 7/8	**1 1/16**	**♣AMBI Inc**	**AMBI**		**...**	**12**	**1221**	**2 5/8**	**2 11/32**	[illegible]	[illegible]

	52 Weeks Hi	Lo	Stock	Sym	Div	Yld %	PE	Vol 100s	Hi	Lo	Close	Net Chg
	3/4	1/32	AdvAero wtB	AASIZ		...	...	71	11/32	7/32	7/32	– 3/32
	19 1/8	9 13/16	AdvCommSys	ACSC		...	45	703	18 13/16	18 3/8	18 9/16	– 3/16
s	58 9/16	6 19/32	♣AdvDgtlInfo	ADIC		...	70	3056	52	49 3/16	50 7/8	– 1/2
	49 7/8	17 7/8	AdvEngy	AEIS		...	cc	1919	47	44 7/8	45	– 3/8
	47 1/2	**6 3/4**	**AdvFibComm**	**AFCI**		**...**	**cc**	**20681**	**40 7/8**	**36 13/16**	**37 1/4**	**– 4 1/2**
	13 15/16	4 3/4	AdvLightTch	ADLT		...	dd	422	6 1/8	5 9/16	5 29/32	+ 1/32
s	29 1/2	10 3/4	♣AdvMktg	ADMS	.08	.3	18	84	29 1/2	28 7/16	28 1/2	– 3/8
	11 1/2	6 3/16	AdvNeuromod	ANSI		...	14	96	10	9 11/16	9 15/16	– 1/16
	7 1/4	2 3/4	♣AdvPolymer	APOS		...	28	297	3 11/16	3 7/16	3 5/8	...
	25	**6**	**AdvRdioTele**	**ARTT**		**...**	**dd**	**4795**	**22**	**19**	**19 1/2**	**– 1 1/2**
	14 1/4	7 1/2	AdvTechPdts	ATPX		...	11	20	13 15/16	13 15/16	13 15/16	...
	6	1 25/32	AdvTissue	ATIS		...	dd	2837	2 15/16	2 3/4	2 25/32	– 1/32
	23 15/16	9 5/8	Advanta A	ADVNA	.25	1.4	1	738	17 3/4	16 15/16	17 3/8	– 3/8
	19 1/8	**7 19/32**	**Advanta B**	**ADVNB**	**.30**	**2.5**	**1**	**688**	**13 1/8**	**11 15/16**	**12 1/8**	**– 1 1/8**
s	**43**	**10**	**AdvntgLearn**	**ALSI**		**...**	**23**	**6263**	**13 5/16**	**12 1/8**	**13**	**+ 1 5/16**
s	70 1/4	26 21/64	♣AdvntSftwr	ADVS		...	79	515	66 47/64	62 1/8	65 1/8	– 1/8
	7 3/8	3 5/8	AehrTstSys	AEHR		...	dd	194	5 1/8	4 13/16	4 13/16	...
	61 5/8	5	AerialComm	AERL		...	dd	2793	55 1/2	49 7/8	52 3/16	– 2 9/16
	4 3/8	**2 1/16**	**Aerovox**	**ARVX**		**...**	**12**	**88**	[illegible]	**3 1/8**	**3 1/8**	**–**

	52 Weeks Hi	Lo	Stock	Sym	Div	Yld %	PE	Vol 100s	Hi	Lo
s	**112 3/8**	**41**	**Amazon.com**	**AMZN**		**...**	**dd**	**172571**	**91 1/2**	**81 3/4**
	18 3/4	14	AmbancHldg	AHCI	.40f	2.7	...	46	15 1/8	14 5/8
	16 5/8	9 7/8	AmbssdrInt	AMIE		...	12	39	11 1/8	10 1/8
	25 1/4	**19 1/2**	**AmcoreFnl**	**AMFI**	**.56**	**2.8**	**15**	**363**	**21 7/8**	**20 1/8**
	30 1/4	18 5/8	Amerco	UHAL		...	9	137	25	24 1/8
▼	17 5/8	14 3/8	AmerianaBcp	ASBI	.60	4.2	13	29	14 1/2	14 1/8
	9 7/8	**7 3/4**	**AmFstApt**	**APROZ**	**.85**	**10.0**	**...**	**10**	**8 1/2**	**8 1/2**
	6 3/4	4	AmFstTxEx	ATAXZ	.54	10.2	...	433	5 3/8	5
	17 1/2	9 1/2	AmSvcGp	ASGR		...	13	2	14 21/32	[illegible]
	12 1/2	6 5/8	AmAircarriers	AIRS		...	...	66	8 1/8	
	22 3/4	13 1/8	♣AmBcp	AMBC	.60	3.7	10	9	17	
	15	7 7/8	AmBancFL	ABAN		...	28	291	12 1/2	
	18 15/16	**9 3/8**	**♣AmBusFnl**	**ABFI**	**.28**	**2.2**	**3**	**1098**	[illegible]	
	23 1/2	14	♣AmCapStrg	ACAS	1.76a	7.8	...	874	[illegible]	
	36	**15 1/2**	**AmClassic**	**AMCV**		**...**	**cc**	**136**	[illegible]	
	8 1/2	**2**	**♣AmCnMdse**	**AMCN**		**...**	**dd**	**208**	[illegible]	
	13 3/8	6 5/8	AmDntlPtnr	ADPI		...	9	265		
	4 7/8	1 1/32	AmDntlTch	ADLI						

NASDAQ SMALL-CAP ISSUES

	Issue Div	Vol 100s	Last	Chg
	DialCpA	543	5 5/8	– 11/16
	DialCp wt	717	1 13/16	– 7/16
	DiehlG	98	7 1/4	+ 1/4
	DigtlOrgn	1110	11 7/8	+ 1/8
	DigitRec	130	3 19/32	– 19/32
	DigVd wtA	1470	1/8	+ 1/32
	DigtlVid	116	10 1/2	– 1/8
	DiscGph n	59	2 15/16	– 1/8
♣	DiscvLabs	1365	2 7/8	+ 7/16
♣	DscLb wtA	25	5/32	+ 1/32
♣	DscLbs un	6	2 7/8	+ 1 1/16
	Divrsnt g	6447	21 7/8	– 1 1/16
	DblEgl wt	36	1 1/16	+ 1/32
	DblEgl	166	3 11/32	+ 7/32
	DrChina n	57	4 5/16	– 3/16
	Drypers	503	2 7/32	– 1/8
	Dynacq	288	20	+ 1 7/16
	DynHom	2	1 23/64	+ 7/64
♣	DynOil	108	1	...
	Dyntcl	1	1 1/4	+ 7/32
	DyntrCp	256	13/16	[illegible]
	E-Cruitr n	[illegible]		
	e-Net			

	Issue Div	Vol 100s	Last	Chg
♣	GoldRs	628	13/16	...
	GoldStd	116	1 7/16	+ 3/16
	GoldIsl	6	6 3/4	– 1/8
	GoldSt wt	216	5 1/4	– 9/16
	GoldTri	5	2	– 1/4
	GolfEnt	20	15/16	– 1/16
	GoodTm	17	2 1/4	...
	GrndAdv	32	3 5/16	...
	GrandCtrl .24f	5	15 1/4	+ 1 1/4
	GrndToy	544	6 9/32	– 15/32
	GraphOn n	1067	15 3/8	– 1 5/8
	GrOn wtA	79	10 1/4	– 1 3/16
	GrOn wtB	154	8 1/2	– 1 3/4
	GtLkeAv	41	2 1/16	+ 1/16
	GrnDan	75	3 27/32	– 1/8
	GrnCnty n stk	107	8 13/16	+ 1/8
	GuarFin .24	10	8 1/4	– 1/4
	GuardTc	10	2	...
	Gyrody	1	20 3/[illegible]	

	Issue Div	Vol 100s	Last	Chg
	IxysCp	114	6 1/4	– 1/8
	JB Oxfrd	5791	8	+ 1/32
	JLM Ctre	72	1 11/16	+ 1/16
	J2 Com	23	14 3/8	+ 1/8
	JksnvSB .30	82	8 1/8	...
	JadeFncl n	22	8 1/2	– 1/16
	Jffrsnvll .72f	23	20 1/2	– 3/4
	Jenkonl	404	3 7/8	– 1/16
♣	Jmar wt	945	1 1/16	– 3/16
	JunipGrp	658	2	– 1/2
	K2Desgn n	2351	8 21/32	+ 17/32
	K2Dsgn wt	500	1 9/16	+ 1/16
	KMG Ch .04a	56	5 1/8	– 3/8
	KnCtyL s .96	554	33 1/2	– 1/2
	KentFn	1	3 3/4	+ 1/16
	Kyzen n	513	25/32	+ 3/32
	LML Pay	611	[illegible]	[illegible]

	Issue Div	Vol 100s	Last
	NtwkCn	637	5 3/8
	NtwkSix	15	3 3/8
	NetwSys n	248	3 9/16
♣	Network1	1897	9
	NetwNrth	95	[illegible]
	NtrlPst n	99	[illegible]
	NewFrnt	2437	[illegible]
	NHKidQ n	94	[illegible]
	NYHlthC	228	[illegible]
	NewStar	1464	[illegible]
	NexusTl	657	[illegible]
	Nhncmnt	1162	[illegible]
♣	NichFncl	18	[illegible]
	Nitches .25e	20	[illegible]
	NogaElc	194	[illegible]
	NogaEl wt	[illegible]	

The information is fairly obvious. Consider the entries for a company such as AT&T:

52 Weeks High	Low	Stock	Dividend	Yield	P/E	Sales 100s	High	Low	Close	Net Change
64	32	AT&T	0.88	1.9	20	18151	47	46	46.50	−0.50

The high and the low (64 and 32) represent the highest and lowest prices achieved by the security during the past 12 months. After the abbreviated name of the firm comes the annual dividend currently being paid ($0.88) and the current yield on the stock.[4] This is the annual dividend divided by the closing price ($0.88/$46.50 = 1.9%). Next is the ratio of the stock's price to per share earnings (20 for AT&T). This price/earnings (P/E) ratio is a measure of what the market is willing to pay for the firm's earnings. Firms that are expected to grow rapidly tend to have higher P/E ratios. After the P/E ratio comes information concerning the day's trading. First is the volume (18151) expressed in hundreds of shares. Thus, 18151 means 1,815,100 shares were traded. The high, low, and closing prices were 47, 46, and 46.50, respectively. The net change for the day was −0.50.

Securities of companies with shares issued to the general public that are not traded on an exchange are traded over-the-counter through a national market system. The prices of many of these securities are also reported daily in the financial sections of newspapers. In *The Wall Street Journal* these entries are subdivided into the NASDAQ national market and small-cap issues. (Small-cap refers to small firms with modest amounts of equity.) **NASDAQ** is an acronym for National Association of Security Dealers Automated Quotation system, which is the impressive system of communication for over-the-counter price quotations. All major unlisted stocks are included in this system. Investors may readily obtain the bid and ask prices for most stocks by simply entering the firm's ticker symbol into the NASDAQ system.

NASDAQ
National Association of Security Dealers Automated Quotation system; quotation system for over-the-counter securities

As may be seen in Exhibit 6.1, the reporting of the NASDAQ national market issues is the same as the reporting of listed securities. The information given includes the 52-week high and low prices; the firm's dividend; the current dividend yield; the P/E ratio; the volume of transactions; the high, low, and closing prices; and the net change from the previous day.

In addition to the NASDAQ national market issues, *The Wall Street Journal* and other papers that give extensive coverage of security prices report the NASDAQ Small-Cap Issues, which consist of small firms (in other words, small capitalization). This reporting is generally limited to the name, dividend (if any), the volume of transactions, the closing price, and the change from the previous day. For example, Gold Resources pays no dividend, traded 62,800 shares, and closed at 13⁄16, which was unchanged from the previous day.

[4] Dividends and stock valuation are covered in more detail in Chapters 10 and 11.

THE MECHANICS OF INVESTING IN SECURITIES

After deciding to purchase a security, an investor places a purchase order with a broker whose role is to buy and sell securities for customers. The broker and the market maker (the security dealer) should not be confused since they perform different, but crucial, roles in the mechanics of purchasing and selling securities. Brokers are agents who execute orders for customers. Security dealers act as principals who, in the process of making a market, buy and sell securities for their own accounts. Dealers bear the risk associated with their purchases and sales. Because brokers buy and sell for their customers' accounts, they do not bear the risk associated with fluctuations in security prices. These risks are borne by the investors.

MARKET ORDER
Order to buy or sell a security at the best current price

DAY ORDER
Order to buy or sell at a specified price that is canceled at the end of the day if it is not executed

GOOD-TILL-CANCELED ORDER
Order to buy or sell at a specified price that remains in effect until it is executed by the broker or canceled by the investor

COMMISSION
Payment to broker for executing an investor's buy and sell orders

SETTLEMENT DATE
Date by which payment for the purchase of securities must be made; date by which delivery of securities sold must be made

The investor may ask the broker to buy the security at the best price currently available, which is the asking price set by the market maker. Such a request is a **market order.** The investor is not assured of receiving the security at the currently quoted price, since that price may change by the time the order is executed. However, the order is generally executed at or very near the asking price.

The investor may enter a **limit order** and specify a price below the current asking price and wait until the price declines to the specified level. Such an order may be placed for one day (a **day order**), or the order may remain in effect indefinitely (a **good-till-canceled order**). Such an order remains on the books of the broker until it is either executed or canceled. If the price of the security does not decline to the specified level, the purchase is never made.

Once the purchase has been made, the broker sends the investor a confirmation statement (Exhibit 6.2). This confirmation statement gives the number of shares and type of security purchased (100 shares of Clevepak Corporation), the per unit price (12⅛ or $12.125), and the total amount due ($1,264.26). The amount due includes the price of the security and the transaction fees. The major transaction fee is the brokerage firm's **commission,** but there may also be state transfer taxes and other miscellaneous fees. Effective in June 1995, the investor has three business days after the date of purchase (8/16/XX) to pay the amount due and must make payment by the **settlement date** (8/19/XX). (The difference in the two dates is referred to as $t + 3$.)

Brokerage firms establish their own commission schedules, and it may pay the small investor to shop around for the best rates. Large investors are able to negotiate commissions, so that the brokerage costs are less than 1 percent of the value of the securities. Some brokerage firms offer investors discount rates that may reduce brokerage fees. However, these firms generally do not offer other services, such as research and investment advice.

Investors may further reduce commission costs by using online brokerage firms. Firms that offer this service initially charged substantially lower commissions than were assessed by discount brokers. Even discount brokerage firms, such as Charles Schwab, offer customers discounts from regular commissions if investors use their electronic trading systems. Obviously individuals who feel comfortable using online trading and who do not need regular brokerage services may be able to obtain substantial reductions in commission costs by buying and selling securities over the Internet.

EXHIBIT 6.2

Confirmation Statement of a Security Purchase

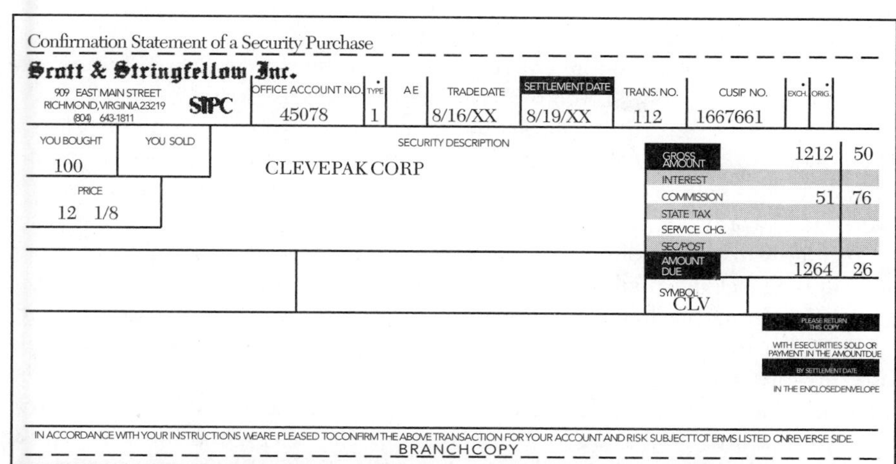

Confirmation Statement of a Security Purchase

Scott & Stringfellow, Inc.
909 EAST MAIN STREET
RICHMOND, VIRGINIA 23219
(804) 643-1811
SIPC

OFFICE ACCOUNT NO.	TYPE	AE	TRADE DATE	SETTLEMENT DATE	TRANS. NO.	CUSIP NO.	EXCH.	ORIG.
45078	1		8/16/XX	8/19/XX	112	1667661		

YOU BOUGHT	YOU SOLD	SECURITY DESCRIPTION
100		CLEVEPAK CORP

PRICE
12 1/8

GROSS AMOUNT	1212 50
INTEREST	
COMMISSION	51 76
STATE TAX	
SERVICE CHG.	
SEC/POST	
AMOUNT DUE	1264 26
SYMBOL	CLV

PLEASE RETURN THIS COPY WITH SECURITIES SOLD OR PAYMENT IN THE AMOUNT DUE BY SETTLEMENT DATE IN THE ENCLOSED ENVELOPE

IN ACCORDANCE WITH YOUR INSTRUCTIONS WE ARE PLEASED TO CONFIRM THE ABOVE TRANSACTION FOR YOUR ACCOUNT AND RISK SUBJECT TO TERMS LISTED ON REVERSE SIDE.

BRANCH COPY

The investor may purchase the security on **margin,** which is buying the stock with a combination of the investor's cash and credit supplied by the broker. The phrase "on margin" can be confusing since it is similar to buying "on credit." Margin is not the amount borrowed but is the investor's equity in the security. This amount is often expressed as a percentage:

MARGIN
Investor's equity in a security position

$$\text{Margin} = \text{Equity/Total value of the portfolio},$$

so if the investor owns stock worth $10,000 but owes $2,000, the individual's margin is 80 percent ($8,000/$10,000).

MARGIN REQUIREMENT
Minimum percentage set by the Federal Reserve of the total price that must be put up to buy securities

The **margin requirement** is the minimum percentage of the total price that the investor must pay and is set by the Federal Reserve Board. Individual brokers, however, may require more margin. The minimum payment required of the investor is the value of the securities times the margin requirement. Thus, if the margin requirement is 60 percent and the price plus the commission on 100 shares of Clevepak Corporation is $1,264.26, the investor must supply $758.56 in cash and borrow $505.70 from the broker, who in turn borrows the funds from a commercial bank. The investor pays interest to the broker on $505.70. The interest rate will depend on the rate that the broker must pay to the lending institution. The investor, of course, may avoid the interest charges by paying the entire $1,264.26 and not using borrowed funds.

Investors use margin to increase the potential return on the investment. Suppose you buy 50 shares at $20 a share for a total cost (excluding commissions) of $1,000. If the margin requirement is 60 percent, you put up $600 in cash and borrow $400 from your broker. If the price of the stock rises to $30, your position in the stock is worth $1,500. Your profit is $500, and you make 83.3 percent

($500/$600) on your funds invested in the stock. If you had not used margin and covered the entire cost ($1,000), your percentage return would have been 50 percent. The use of margin magnified your return.[5]

Using margin works both ways. If the price of the stock fell to $15, the value of the 50 shares is now $750. You have lost $250 on the investment. Your percentage loss is 25 percent if you buy the stock with cash, but your percent loss is 41.7 percent ($250/$600) if you buy the stock on margin. If you borrow money and commit less of your own funds, the percentage loss is magnified. Leverage is a two-edged sword!

An individual's use of margin could increase the broker's risk exposure. If the price of the stock declined sufficiently, it would wipe out the investor's margin, but the investor would still owe the broker the funds borrowed to purchase the securities. If the investor then defaulted (did not pay off the loan), the broker would lose. Obviously brokers do not want to be at risk, so as the security's price and the investor's margin decline, the broker will request additional collateral. This request, referred to as a "margin call," may be met by having the investor deposit cash or additional securities in the account. Once the cash and/or securities are placed in the account, the investor's margin is increased. The restoration of the margin means that the investor, and not the broker, is at risk.

Delivery of Securities

STREET NAME
Registration of securities in a broker's name instead of in the buyer's name

Once the shares have been purchased and paid for, the investor must decide whether to leave the securities with the broker or to take delivery. (In the case of a margin account, the investor *must* leave the securities with the broker.) If the shares are left with the broker, they will be registered in the broker's name (that is, in the **street name**). The broker then becomes custodian of the securities and sends a monthly statement of the securities that are being held in the street name to the investor. The monthly statement also includes any transactions that have taken place during the month and any dividends and interest that have been received. The investor may either leave the dividends and interest payments to accumulate with the broker or receive payment from the broker.

The main advantage of leaving securities with the broker is convenience, and the vast majority of investors (probably more than 95 percent) have their securities registered in the street name. The investor does not have to store the securities and can readily sell them, because they are in the broker's possession. Interest and dividend payments are received by the broker. The investor may have the money transferred to a bank account or held for subsequent investment. (The brokerage firm may also permit checks to be drawn against the account.)

There are disadvantages of leaving the securities in the broker's name. If the brokerage firm fails or becomes insolvent, investors may have difficulty having the

[5] The use of margin is an illustration of financial leverage. (Firms' use of financial leverage is covered in Chapter 16.) The illustrations in the text do not include (1) commissions on the stock purchases and sales and (2) interest on the borrowed funds. Both commissions and interest reduce the return the investor earns. Problems 5 and 6 at the end of this chapter add the interest expense, which reduces the profits on the stocks purchased through the use of margin.

securities transferred into their name and collecting any dividends or interest owed them by the brokerage firm.[6] Second, because the securities are registered in the brokerage firm's name, interim financial statements, annual reports, and other announcements sent by the firm to its security holders are sent to the brokerage firm and not to the investors. The brokerage firm should forward each investor this material but may not. To overcome this, an investor may ask to be placed on the firm's mailing list or may access the information through the Internet.

Whether the investor ultimately decides to leave the securities with the broker or take delivery depends on the individual investor. If the securities are purchased on margin, the investor must leave the securities with the broker. If the investor frequently buys and sells securities (in other words, is a "trader"), then the securities have to be left with the broker in order to facilitate the transactions. If the investor is satisfied with the services of the broker and is convinced that the firm is financially secure, then he or she may also decide to have the securities registered in the street name of the broker for reasons of convenience.

If the investor chooses to take delivery of the securities, the investor receives the **stock certificates,** such as the Clean Harbors, Inc. certificate illustrated in Exhibit 6.3. The front of the stock certificate identifies the name of the owner, the number of shares, and the name of the transfer agent who transferred the certificates from the seller to the buyer. To transfer ownership, the investor must endorse the certificate on the back, just like endorsing a check before depositing or cashing it. Since the certificates may become negotiable if stolen, the investor should take caution to store them in a safe place (for example, a lockbox in a bank). If the certificates are lost or destroyed, they can be replaced, but only at a considerable expense, both money and time.

STOCK CERTIFICATES
Documents evidencing a share of ownership in a corporation

The Short Sale

The previous discussion was limited to what is called a **long position** in which the investor purchases a stock and profits when its price rises. Of course, this individual will sustain a loss if the price of the stock declines. Can the investor earn a profit from a decline in the price of a stock? The answer is yes if the individual establishes a **short-position.** In a short sale, the investor *borrows* stock and sells it. If the price declines, the individual buys back the stock and pays off the loan (that is, returns the borrowed stock). The investor earns a profit because the stock is bought for less than it was sold.

LONG POSITION
Purchase of securities in anticipation of a price increase

SHORT POSITION
Sale of borrowed securities in anticipation of a price decrease

Perhaps this process is best understood through a simple illustration. A stock is selling for $39. The investor believes that the stock is overvalued and that the price will decline. The investor then borrows the stock through a broker and sells it for $39. Several weeks later the stock is selling for $25. The individual buys the stock for $25 and repays the loan (that is, returns the stock to the broker). The investor made $14 a share because he or she purchased the stock for $25 and sold it for $39. Of course, if the price rises to $46, the individual loses because the stock

[6] As is discussed later under the regulation of security markets, most accounts with brokers are insured by the Securities Investor Protection Corporation (SIPC).

EXHIBIT 6.3

Example of Stock Certificate

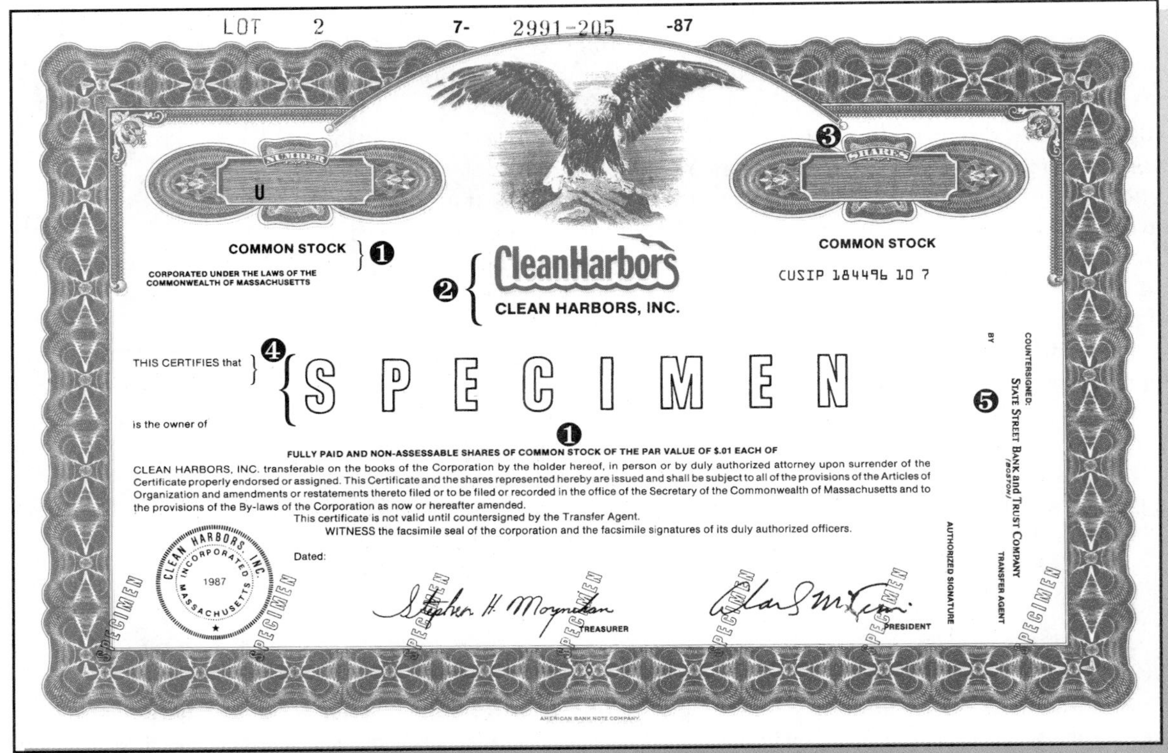

❶ Type of Stock
❷ Issuing Company
❸ Number of Shares
❹ Name of Registered Owner
❺ Transfer Agent

Source: *Reproduced with the permission of Clean Harbors, Inc.*

would have to be bought at the higher price. In that case, the stock would be sold for $39 but would be bought at $46.

Short sales are common in business because a short sale is simply a contract for future delivery. When a school takes a student's tuition money before the semester begins, it enters into a contract for the future delivery of services (courses). This is a short position because if the price of providing the services falls, the school profits. If, however, the price of providing the services rises, the school loses. Entering into contracts for the future delivery of goods and services is common practice in business. In each case, the firm has made a short sale.

MEASURES OF SECURITY PRICES

Security prices fluctuate daily, and several indexes have been developed to measure the price performance of securities. The best known and most widely quoted is the Dow Jones Industrial Average of 30 industrial stocks. Dow Jones and Company also computes averages for 15 utility stocks and 20 transportation stocks as well as a composite index of all 65 stocks. The companies that comprise the Dow Jones averages are among the largest, most well established firms in the nation. Small firms and many firms that have grown into prominence during the last decade are excluded from this average. This has led to criticism of the Dow Jones averages on the basis that they are too narrow and not representative of the stock market.[7] This criticism has led to the development of other indexes, such as the Standard and Poor's 500 Stock Index and the New York Stock Exchange Index.[8] The Standard and Poor's 500 includes 425 industrials, 25 railroads, and 50 utility stocks. The New York Stock Exchange Common Stock Index includes all listed common stocks. The American Stock Exchange also publishes an index that includes all securities traded on that exchange. These three indexes encompass more securities than the Dow Jones Industrials and, therefore, may be better indicators of general price movements in the stock market.

How have stock prices performed? The answer in part depends on the time period selected. Figure 6.1 is based on the high and low values of the Dow Jones Industrial Average from 1970 through 1999. The figure is constructed in two ways. In both cases the horizontal scale is in years, but the vertical scales differ. In part a, the units are expressed in absolute dollars; in part b, the units are in percentage changes. In part a, a price movement from 1,000 to 2,000 is smaller than a movement from 2,000 to 4,000, but in part b they are identical. Because stock returns are often expressed in percentages, stock price movements are frequently presented as in part b. It is immediately apparent when parts a and b are compared that the large absolute price movements experienced during the 1990s are perceptibly less impressive when expressed in percentages instead of absolute dollars.

[7] On November 1, 1999, the composition of the Dow Jones Industrial Average was changed. Four older companies (Chevron, Goodyear, Sears, and Union Carbide) were dropped and replaced with younger companies (Home Depot, Intel, Microsoft, and SBC Communications) that have recently grown into prominence. The rationale for the change was to make the DJIA more representative of the current stock market.

[8] The Dow Jones Industrial Average, the S&P 500, and the NYSE Index differ in two important ways: (1) which securities are included and (2) how the measure is calculated. The Dow Jones Industrials is a simple average of 30 stocks. Although the prices of 30 stocks are summed and divided, the divisor is not 30 because it has been adjusted over time for stock splits and for the substitution of one company for another when a stock is deleted.

The S&P 500 and NYSE indexes use more stocks and are value-weighted rather than simple averages. The price of each stock is multiplied by the number of shares outstanding. Thus, such firms as AT&T and IBM with over 1,350,000,000 and 570,000,000 shares, respectively, have more impact on the S&P 500 and the NYSE indexes than a firm like American Brands, which has 201,000,000 shares.

FIGURE 6.1 High and Low Values (the range) of the Dow Jones Industrial Average, 1970–1999

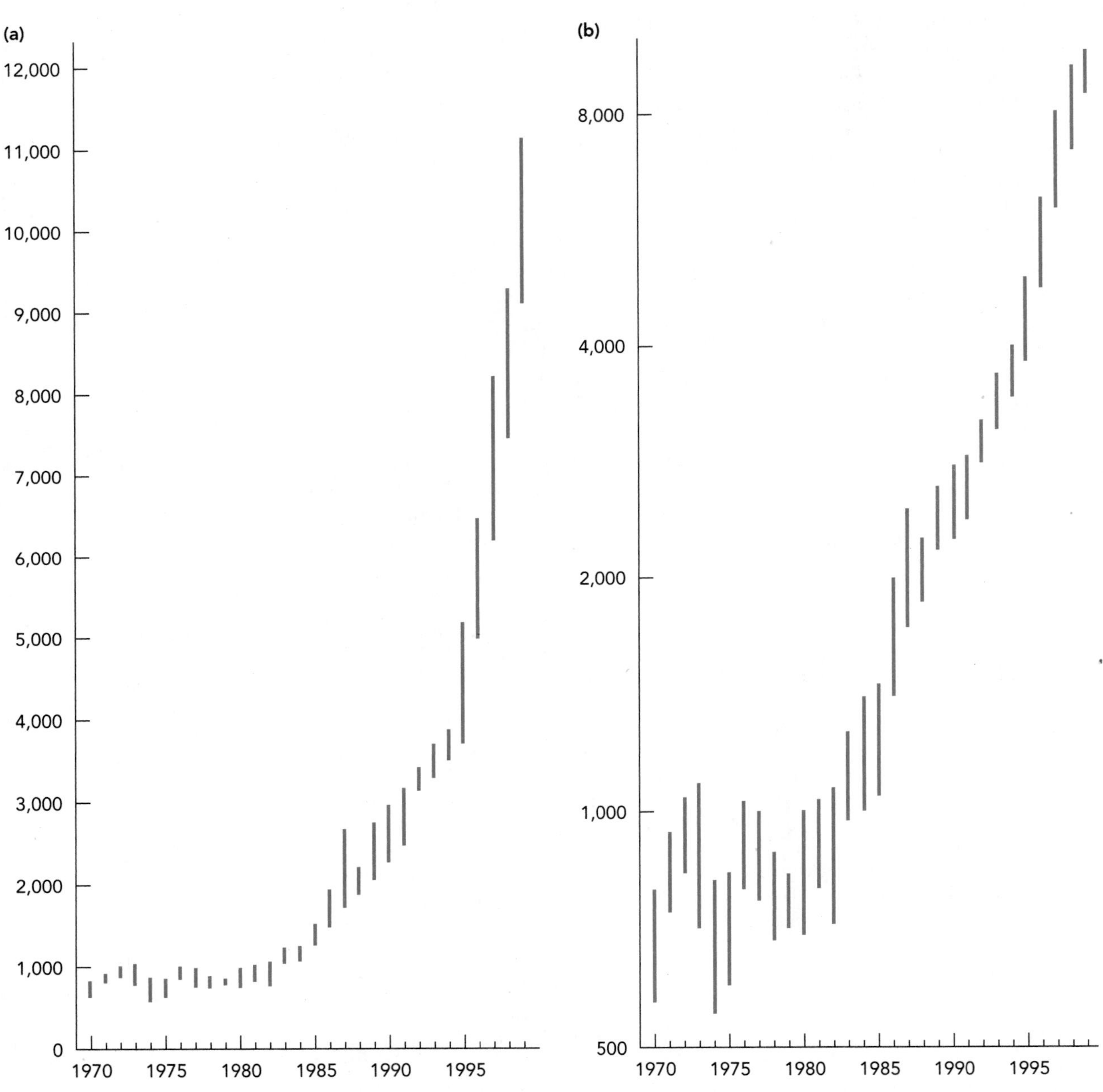

Major Indexes of Stock Prices

Although the Dow Jones Industrial Average, the Standard & Poor's 500 stock index (S&P 500), and the New York Stock Exchange composite are among the most important measures of U.S. stock prices, there are many other indexes of stock prices. Several of these indexes and their composition are as follows:

Russell 1000: The largest 1,000 firms

Russell 2000: The next-largest 2,000 firms

Russell 3000: Combines the firms in the Russell 1000 and Russell 2000

Standard & Poor's 400 MidCap: Index of moderate-sized firms

Standard & Poor's 600 Small Cap: Index of relatively small firms

Standard & Poor's 1500 Index: Combines all the stocks in the S&P 500, S&P 400 MidCap, and the S&P 600 Small Cap

Value Line Stock Index: Index of all stocks covered by the Value Line Investment Survey.

Wilshire 5000: Index of the market value of all NYSE, AMEX, and actively traded NASDAQ stocks. (Although the name implies that the index covers 5,000 stocks, the actual composition exceeds 7,000 issues and covers virtually all publicly traded companies.)

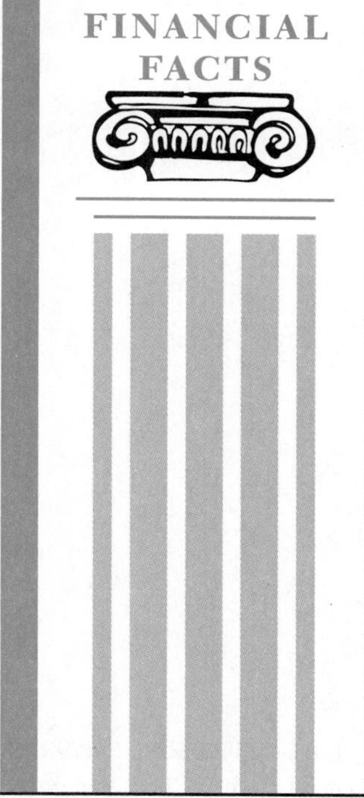

As may be seen in Figure 6.1, stock prices have risen over time; however, periods have occurred when security prices fell. The decline experienced from 1972 to 1974 was particularly severe, for the Dow Jones Industrial Average declined from 1020 at the end of 1972 to 607 in September 1974. That is a 40 percent decline in the average and was the worst setback the market experienced since the great stock market crash in 1929 . (The Dow Jones fell from 2709 to 1738 in 1987, but that is only a 35.8 percent decline.)

Investors who purchased stock and held their positions probably experienced profits on the investments. However, just because security prices rose, it does not follow that an individual investor experienced profits. An individual's securities may decline in price even though the majority of stock prices rise, but in general the price performance of a diversified portfolio should tend to follow the market.

Many security profits are only **paper profits** because the investors do not sell the securities and realize the profits. The tax laws encourage such retention of securities, for the gains are taxed only when realized. Realized profits are taxed as **capital gains.** As of 2000, long-term capital gains (that is, securities held for more than a year) were taxed at a lower rate than ordinary income for the highest income brackets.[9] These tax considerations encourage the retention of securities

PAPER PROFITS
Unrealized profits

CAPITAL GAINS
Increase in the value of a capital asset, such as a stock

[9] As of January 1, 2000, the highest federal tax bracket was 39.6 percent for income and short-term capital gains. The highest tax rate on the sale of securities held for more than a year (that is, long-term capital gains) was 20 percent.

that have risen in price. Unfortunately, security prices that have risen may not continue to rise, and many investors who retained securities have watched their paper profits melt away when security prices subsequently declined.

REGULATION

The securities industry is subject to a large amount of regulation. Since the majority of securities cross state borders, the primary regulation is at the federal level. The purpose of this regulation is to protect the investing public by providing investors with information to help prevent fraud and the manipulation of security prices. The regulation in no way assures investors that they will make profits on their investments. It is not the purpose of the regulation to protect investors from their own mistakes.

Federal regulation developed as a direct result of the debacle in the security markets during the early 1930s. The first major pieces of legislation were the Securities Act of 1933 and the Securities Exchange Act of 1934. These are concerned with issuing and trading securities. The 1933 act is concerned with new issues of securities, and the 1934 act is concerned with the trading of securities. To administer these acts, the Securities and Exchange Commission (commonly called the SEC) was established.

FULL-DISCLOSURE LAWS
Federal security laws requiring the timely disclosure of information that may affect the value of a firm's securities

These acts are also referred to as the **full-disclosure laws,** for their intent is to require companies with publicly held securities to inform the public of facts relating to the companies. As is explained in Chapter 2, a firm can issue new securities only after filing a registration statement with the SEC. The SEC will not clear the securities for sale until it appears that all material facts that may affect the value of the securities have been disclosed. The SEC does not comment on the worthiness of the securities as an investment. It is assumed that the investor who has received the required information can make his or her own determination of the quality of the securities as an investment.

10-K REPORT
Required annual report filed with the SEC by publicly held firms

Once the securities are sold, the companies are required to keep current the information on file with the SEC. This is achieved by having the firm file a report (called the **10-K report**) with the SEC annually. The 10-K report has a substantial amount of factual information concerning the firm, and this information is usually sent in summary form to the stockholders in the company's annual report. (Companies will, on request, also send stockholders a copy of the 10-K report without charge.)

Firms are also required to release during the year any information that may materially affect the value of their securities. Information concerning new discoveries or major lawsuits or strikes is disseminated to the general public. The SEC has the power to suspend trading in a firm's securities if the firm does not release this information. This is a drastic act and is seldom used, for most firms continually have news releases that inform the investing public of significant changes affecting the firm. Sometimes the firm itself will ask to have trading in its securities stopped until a news release can be prepared and disseminated.

The disclosure requirements do not insist that the firm tell everything about its operations. The firm, of course, has trade secrets that it does not want known

Illegal Use of Inside Information

The use of inside (privileged) information for personal gain is illegal. Management cannot buy a stock, make an announcement that causes the values of the stock to rise, and then sell the stock for a profit. If insiders do this, the corporation or its stockholders may sue, and if the defendants are found guilty, any profits must be returned to the corporation. ¶ The law does not forbid insiders from buying and subsequently selling the stock. However, the Securities Exchange Act of 1934 requires that each officer, director, and major stockholder (that is, any individual who owns more than 5 percent of the stock) of a publicly held corporation must file a report with the SEC disclosing the amount of stock held. These individuals must also file a monthly report if there are any changes in the holdings. This information is subsequently published by the SEC. If these insiders make a profit on a transaction that is completed (that is, the stock is bought and sold) within six months, it is assumed the profits is the result of illelgally using confidential corporate information. ¶ Individuals who may be considered insiders are not limited to the corporation's officers and directors. An insider is any individual with "material information" not yet disclosed to the public. Material information implies information that could reasonably be expected to affect the value of the firm's securities. The individual need not necessarily be employed by the firm but could have access to inside information through business relationships, family ties, or being informed (tipped off) by insiders. Use of such privileged information even by nonemployees is also illegal. In one of the most famous cases concerning the illegal use of inside information, several officers and directors of Texas Gulf Sulfur became aware of new mineral discoveries. Not only were their purchases ruled illegal, but purchases made by individuals they had informed were also ruled illegal. Thus, an insider who may not directly profit through the use of inside information cannot pass that information to another party who profits from using that knowledge. ¶

by its competitors. The purpose of full disclosure is not to stifle the corporation but (1) to notify the investors so they can make informed decisions and (2) to prevent the firm's employees from using privileged information for personal gain. It should be obvious that employees may have access to information before it reaches the general public. Such inside information can enhance their ability to profit by buying or selling the company's securities before the announcement is made. Such profiteering from inside information is illegal. Officers and directors of the company must report their holdings and any changes in their holdings of the firm's securities with the SEC. Thus, it is possible for the SEC to determine if transactions are made prior to public announcements.

Inside information, however, is not limited to individuals who work for a firm. The concept applies to people who work for another firm that has access to privileged information. For example, accountants, lawyers, advertising agency employees, and creditors, have access to inside information. Certainly a firm's investment bankers will know if a firm is anticipating a merger, seeking to take over another company, or intending to issue new securities. These investment bankers are, in effect, insiders. Neither they, nor anyone to whom they give this information, may legally use the information for personal gain.

SECURITIES INVESTOR PROTECTION CORPORATION (SIPC)
Federal agency that insures investors against failure by brokerage firms

Another source of regulation of security markets is the **Securities Investor Protection Corporation (SIPC).** This agency is similar in purpose to FDIC, for SIPC is designed to protect investors from failure by brokerage firms. SIPC insurance applies to those investors who leave securities and cash with brokerage firms. If the firm were to fail, these investors might lose part of their funds and investments. SIPC insurance is designed to protect investors from this type of loss. The insurance, however, is limited to $500,000 per customer, of which only $100,000 applies to cash balances. Hence, if an investor leaves a substantial amount of securities and cash with a brokerage firm that fails, the investor is not fully protected by the insurance. To increase coverage, some brokerage firms carry additional insurance with private companies to protect their customers.

FOREIGN SECURITIES

In addition to domestic securities, Americans may purchase foreign stocks and bonds. Foreign companies, like American companies, issue a variety of securities as a means to acquire funds. These securities subsequently trade on foreign exchanges or foreign over-the-counter markets. There are stock exchanges in London, Paris, Tokyo, and other foreign financial centers. Unless Americans and other foreigners are forbidden to acquire these securities, Americans can buy and sell stocks through these exchanges in much the same way that they purchase domestic American stocks and bonds. Thus, foreign securities may be purchased through the use of American brokers who have access to trading on these exchanges. In many cases this access is obtained through a correspondent relationship with foreign security brokers.

By far the easiest way to buy foreign stocks is to purchase the shares of firms that are traded on American exchanges or through American over-the-counter markets (through NASDAQ). To be eligible for such trading, the foreign securities must be registered with the SEC. About 300 foreign stocks are listed on the New York and American stock exchanges and many more are traded through NASDAQ.

Exhibit 6.4 lists several foreign firms whose shares are traded in the United States. The exhibit gives the company, its country of origin, its primary industry, and where the shares are traded. As may be seen in the exhibit, many foreign stocks, such as SONY and KLM Royal Dutch Airlines, are traded on the New York Stock Exchange. Others, such as Dunlop Holdings, trade on the American Stock Exchange, and many others trade through NASDAQ.[10] The majority of the firms whose securities are actively traded in the United States are either Japanese or Canadian.

[10] Foreign stock exchanges also list American securities. For example, Coca-Cola is listed on the Frankfurt and Zurich exchanges.

EXHIBIT 6.4

Selected Foreign Securities Traded on the New York Stock Exchange, on the American Stock Exchange, and through NASDAQ

Firm	Country of Origin	Primary Industry	Where Traded in the United States
Alcan Aluminum	Canada	Aluminum	NYSE
Campbell Red Lakes	Canada	Gold mining	NYSE
Dunlop Holdings	Britain	Tires, sporting goods	AMEX
Hitachi	Japan	Electronics	NYSE
Imperial Group	Britain	Tobacco, food	AMEX
Japan Airlines	Japan	Airline	NASDAQ
KLM Royal Dutch Airlines	Netherlands	Airline	NYSE
Kloof Gold Mines	South Africa	Gold mining	NASDAQ
Plessey	Britain	Electronics equipment	NYSE
SONY	Japan	Electronics	NYSE
TDK	Japan	Electronics	NYSE
Volkswagenwerk	Germany	Automobiles	NASDAQ

These domestic markets do not actually trade the foreign shares but trade receipts for the stock called **American Depository Receipts** or **ADRs.** (ADRs are also referred to as American Depository Shares.) Such receipts are created by large financial institutions, such as commercial banks, and are denominated in dollars. The ADRs are then sold to the American public and continue to trade in the United States.

AMERICAN DEPOSITORY RECEIPTS (ADRs)
Receipts issued for foreign securities held by a trustee

The creation of ADRs greatly facilitates trading in foreign securities. First, ADRs reduce the risk of fraud. If the investor purchased a foreign stock issued by a Japanese firm, the stock certificate would be written in Japanese. It is highly unlikely that the American investor could read the language, and thus he or she could become prey to bogus certificates. ADRs erase that risk, since the certificates are in English and their authenticity is certified by the issuing agent. The investor is assured that the receipt is genuine even though it is an obligation of the issuing agent. The ADR represents only the underlying securities held by the agent and is not an obligation of the firm that issued the stock.

Besides reducing the risk of fraud, ADRs are convenient. Securities do not have to be delivered through international mail, prices are quoted in dollars, and dividend payments are received in dollars. The ADR can represent any number of foreign shares. For example, each share of Telefonos de Mexico traded on the New York Stock Exchange represents 20 ordinary Mexican shares. The regular shares would be considered penny stocks in the United States. To make the prices comparable to U.S. security prices, an ADR may represent 10 or 15 Mexican shares.[11]

[11] Once the number of shares is determined, it remains fixed.

The prices of a number of foreign stocks are given daily in the American financial press. For example, *The Wall Street Journal* gives prices for selected securities traded on several foreign exchanges. The information is limited to prices—there is no reporting of volume of transactions, dividends, or P/E ratios. Because the number of foreign stock prices reported in the American press is small, an investor seeking to track the prices of many foreign stocks will require access to a foreign publication, such as the *Financial Times*, a British newspaper that is comparable to *The Wall Street Journal*.

In addition to stocks, Americans may also acquire bonds sold in foreign countries. There are basically three general types: (1) bonds issued by foreign firms; (2) bonds issued by foreign governments; and (3) bonds issued in foreign countries by American firms.

Bonds issued abroad by American firms are basically of two types, depending on the currency in which they are denominated. The American firms can sell bonds denominated in the local currency (for example, British pounds or French francs), or the firm can sell abroad bonds denominated in American dollars, called Eurobonds. This term applies even though the bonds may be issued in Asia instead of Europe. When a firm issues a Eurobond, the American firm promises to make payments in dollars. In this case the American investor will not have to convert the payments from the local currency (such as British pounds) back into dollars.

COMPETITION IN THE SECURITY MARKETS

Economics teaches that the market will be very competitive if there are many informed participants who may readily enter and exit. Both the stock and bond markets meet these conditions. Individuals may readily buy and sell securities; information is rapidly disseminated, and prices quickly change in reaction to changes in the economic and financial environment. The securities markets are among the most competitive markets in existence.

EFFICIENT MARKET HYPOTHESIS
Theory that securities prices correctly measure the current value of a firm's future earnings and dividends

This competition among investors has led to the **efficient market hypothesis,** which asserts that security markets are so competitive that the current price of a stock properly values the firm's future prospects—that is, the firm's future earnings and its dividends. If a firm's stock were perceived as undervalued, investors (especially professional portfolio managers) would rush to buy it, thus driving up its price. The converse would occur if the stock were perceived as overvalued, and the price would be driven down. Hence the current price is a true measure of the security's worth. For the individual investor, therefore, a security analysis designed to determine if a stock is overpriced or underpriced is futile, because the stock is neither.

An important implication of this theory of efficient markets is that the individual investor cannot consistently beat the market; rather, he or she will earn a return consistent with the market return and the amount of risk borne by the investor. The efficient market hypothesis suggests that the individual investor should realize that the probability of outperforming the market over any extended period is very small. That does not mean an investor cannot outperform (or underperform) the market during a short period of time. During a brief period, such as a

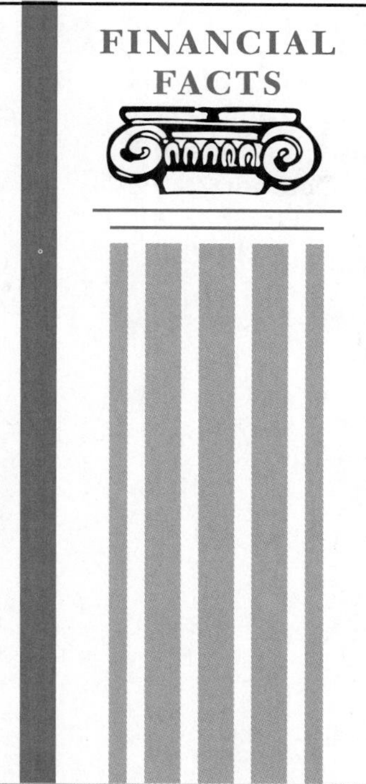

Investing in Third World Countries and the Eastern Bloc

Foreign investments by U.S. investors generally imply the acquisition of assets in advanced economies, but emerging economies, such as Chile, Korea, or Thailand, could offer superior opportunities. Firms in emerging economies may grow more rapidly and be less responsive to global economic changes than firms in advanced economies. More rapid economic growth suggests higher potential returns, and less sensitivity to recession experienced by advanced economies suggests more opportunities for diversification. ¶ In addition to emerging economies, the sudden change in the political environment in eastern Europe and the former Soviet Union may also offer opportunities for the adventurous investor. Although it is premature to determine how security markets will develop in formerly Communist countries, certainly American, Japanese, and western European firms will seek to enter these potential markets. Even if it is not possible for investors to participate directly in these economies through equity investments, individuals may purchase the shares of firms seeking to expand operations into eastern Europe and Russia. Of course, for that strategy to generate a positive return, the firms' earnings must increase as a result of these foreign investments. Because most of the firms capable of making these investments will tend to be large, global firms, it may be impossible to isolate the impact that eastern European investments have on these firms, bottom lines (that is, their earnings). ¶

year, some investors will earn a return that is higher than the return earned by the market. However, there is little chance that those individuals will be able to achieve superior results for an extended period of time (in other words, to outperform the market consistently).

One primary reason for the efficient market hypothesis is the speed with which security prices adjust to new information. The hypothesis requires that prices adjust extremely rapidly as new information is disseminated. In the modern world of advanced communication, information is rapidly dispersed in the investment community. The market then adjusts security prices in accordance with the impact of the news on the firm's future earnings and dividends. By the time that the individual investor has learned the information, security prices probably will have already changed. Thus, the investor will not be able to profit from acting on the information.

This adjustment process is illustrated in Figure 6.2, which plots the daily closing price of AMR (American Airlines) stock during October 1989. In early October, AMR received a buyout offer at \$120, and the stock rose quickly and dramatically. However, the offer was terminated on October 16, and the price of the stock fell 22⅛ points from \$98⅝ to \$76½ in one day. Such price behavior is exactly what the efficient market hypothesis suggests: The market adjusts very rapidly to new information. By the time the announcement was reported in the financial press on October 17, it was too late for the individual investor to react, as the price change had already occurred.

FIGURE 6.2

Price of AMR (American Airlines), October 2, 1989– October 20, 1989

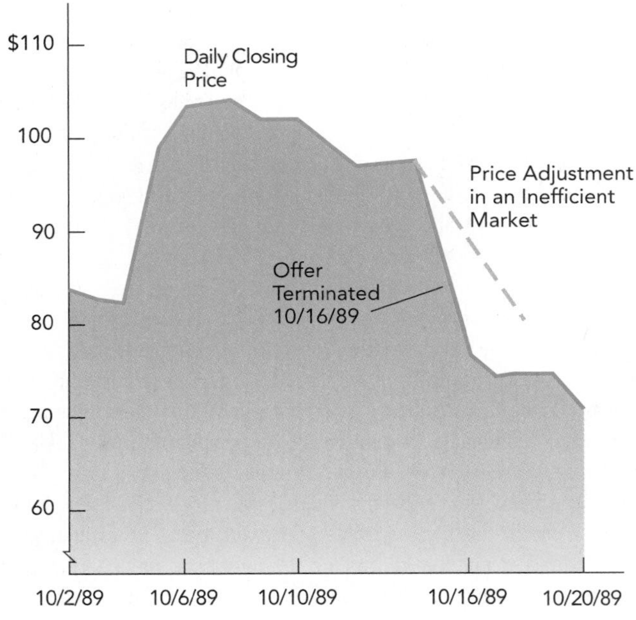

If the market were not so efficient and prices did not adjust rapidly, some investors would be able to adjust their holdings and take advantage of differences in investors' knowledge. Consider the broken line in Figure 6.2. If some investors knew that the agreement had been terminated but others did not, the former could sell their holdings to those who were not informed. The price then may fall over a period of time as the knowledgeable sellers accepted progressively lower prices in order to unload their stock. Of course, if a sufficient number of investors had learned quickly of the termination, the price decline would be rapid as these investors adjusted their valuations of the stock in accordance with the new information. That is exactly what happened, because a sufficient number of investors were rapidly informed and the efficient market quickly adjusted the stock's price.

If an investor were able to anticipate the termination of the merger before it was announced, that individual could avoid the price decline. Obviously some investors did sell their shares just before the announcement, but it is also evident that some individuals bought those shares. Certainly one of the reasons for learning the material and performing the various types of analysis throughout this text is to increase your ability to anticipate events before they occur. However, you should realize that considerable evidence supports the efficient market hypothesis and strongly suggests that few investors will over a period of time outperform the market consistently.

While financial markets appear to be exceedingly efficient, there is some empirical evidence that suggests inefficiencies do exist. These inefficiencies are often referred to as "anomalies." As applied to financial markets, an anomaly is an investment strategy whose return exceeds the return that should be earned if the market were completely efficient.[12] Such inefficiencies tend to revolve around particular investment strategies such as buying stocks in which insiders (e.g., management) are investing or buying stocks after an unusual event occurs since the market may overreact. For example, an unexpected decline in earnings may lead to a large price decline in the price of the stock. After the market has digested the new earnings information, the price of the stock may subsequently rise.

Whether the inefficiencies are sufficiently large that investors can take advantage of the anomaly and generate an excess return is open to debate. Essentially the argument becomes, if an investment strategy increases my return from 12.3 percent to 12.6 percent *but* I have more expenses (such as more commissions or higher taxes from security trading), the increased return may not cover the additional costs. Thus, an anomaly could exist but its magnitude is insufficient to justify using it as an investment strategy. Or the anomaly may apply to large institutional investors but individuals may be unable to take advantage of the inefficiency.

[12] Various anomalies are covered in textbooks on investments. See, for instance, Herbert Mayo. *Investments: An Introduction.* 6th ed., (Fort Worth, Texas: The Dryden Press, 2000) or Zvi Bodie, Alex Kane, and Alan Marcus. *Essentials of Investments,* 3rd ed., (Boston, Mass.: Irwin McGraw-Hill, 1998).

For an excellent lay discussion of efficient markets, possible anomalies, and the implications of efficient markets for investing, see Burton Malkiel. *A Random Walk Down Wall Street.* (New York: W.W. Norton & Company, 1996). One implication of efficient markets is the use of a passive investment strategy. One possible passive strategy is explained in Richard Evans. *The Index Fund Solution,* (New York: Simon & Schuster, 1999).

SUMMARY

This chapter has covered security markets and the mechanics of buying securities. Securities are traded on organized exchanges, such as the NYSE, or in the informal over-the-counter markets (NASDAQ). Securities are primarily bought through brokers, who buy and sell for their customers' accounts. The brokers obtain the securities from dealers, who make markets in them. These dealers offer to buy and sell at specified prices (quotes), which are called the bid and the ask. Brokers and investors obtain these prices through an electronic system that transmits the quotes from the various dealers.

After securities are purchased, the investor must pay for them with either cash or a combination of cash and borrowed funds. When the investor uses borrowed funds, that individual is buying on margin. Buying on margin increases both the potential return and the potential risk of loss for the investor.

Investors may take delivery of their securities or leave them with the broker. Leaving securities registered in the street name offers the advantage of convenience because the broker becomes the custodian of the certificates. Since the advent of the SIPC and its insurance protection, there is little risk of loss to the investor from leaving securities with the broker.

Investors establish long or short positions. With a long position, the investor purchases stock in anticipation of its price rising. If the price of the stock rises, the individual may sell it for a profit. With a short position, the individual sells borrowed stock in anticipation of its price declining. If the price of the stock falls, the individual may repurchase it at the lower price and return it to the lender. The position generates a profit because the selling price exceeds the purchase price.

Both the long and short positions are the logical outcomes of security analysis. If the investor thinks a stock is underpriced, a long position (purchase of the stock) should be established. If the investor believes a stock is overvalued, a short position (the sale of borrowed securities) is established. In either case if the investor is correct, the position will generate a profit. Either position may, however, generate a loss if prices move against the investor's prediction.

The issuing and subsequent trading of securities is regulated by the federal government, and the laws are enforced by the Securities and Exchange Commission. The primary purpose of the security laws is to provide individuals with information so they may make informed investment decisions. The laws prohibit the use of privileged information ("inside information") for personal gain. Federal security legislation also created the SIPC, the Securities Investor Protection Corporation, which insures investors from failure by brokerage firms.

American investors may purchase securities issued by foreign firms. This is usually accomplished through the purchase of American Depository Receipts, or ADRs, which are issued by financial institutions and represent the foreign securities. Americans may also acquire securities such as Eurobonds—debt instruments issued abroad by American firms that are denominated in dollars instead of the foreign currency.

Security markets are very competitive and efficient. New information is disseminated rapidly, and prices adjust quickly in response to the new information. The efficient market hypothesis suggests that few investors will be able to outperform the market. Although an individual may outperform (or underperform) the market for a given period, consistently superior returns may be impossible to achieve.

REVIEW QUESTIONS

1. Why are organized exchanges examples of secondary markets? How do brokers differ from bankers?
2. Securities are purchased through brokers from dealers who "make a market." What does it mean to make a market? How does the market maker earn a profit? What is the essential difference between a broker and a market maker?
3. If a stock is quoted 45–45.50, does that mean the investor can buy the stock for a price between \$45 and \$45.50? If you owned the stock and wanted to sell, how much could you expect to receive before commissions on the sale?
4. What does it mean to buy a stock on margin? If a stock sold for \$36 and the margin requirement was 60 percent, how much would the individual have to commit (excluding commissions) of his or her own funds? If the stock's price subsequently declined to \$27, what is (*a*) the percentage decline in the value of the stock, and (*b*) the percentage loss the investor would realize? Why are these two percentages different?
5. If a stock is selling for \$26 but you anticipate its price declining, what strategy might you follow?
6. How may Americans purchase foreign securities? Are foreign stocks traded on the organized American stock exchanges? How do ADRs facilitate the purchasing of foreign stocks?
7. The security industry, like the banking industry, is regulated. What is the purpose of this regulation? How is this purpose different from the purpose of the regulation of commercial banks?
8. What are the roles of the SEC and SIPC? How is SIPC similar to FDIC?

9. Can an investor expect to outperform the market over an extended period? How rapidly do changes in stock prices occur when a firm makes an announcement, such as a dividend increase?

10. What are the current listing requirements for having a stock listed on the New York Stock Exchange? Find the answer at the NSYE's web site: **www.nyse.com**.

11. Many investors now buy and sell stock online. What is the minimum cost of a purchase of 100 shares of AT&T through Schwab (**www.schwab.com**), Ameritrade (**www.ameritrade.com**) and E*Trade securities (**www.etrade.com**)? What may explain any difference(s) in the commissions?

12. One means to obtain information on foreign companies is to use **www.adr.com**. Do the following foreign firms have stock traded in the United States, and, if so, on which markets are the stocks traded (1) DeBeers Consolidated Mines, (2) Kyocera Corporation, (3) Tele Brasil/Telebras.

13. Information concerning the Dow Jones averages may be obtained from Dow Jones web sites: **averages.dowjones.com** and **indexes.dowjones.com**. What was the percentage change in the Dow Jones Industrial Average from January 1 through December 31 for the following years, (*a*) 1968, (*b*) 1974, (*c*) 1987, and (*d*) 1991? Compare these percentage changes with the percentage changes in 1997 and 1998.

14. From the information obtained through the SEC's website (**www.sec.gov**), what are the SEC's primary objectives and how may the EDGAR database contribute to the efficiency of financial markets?

PROBLEMS

1. You purchase 100 shares for $50 a share ($5,000), and after a year the price rises to $60. What will be the percentage return on your investment if you bought the stock on margin and the margin requirement was (*a*) 25 percent, (*b*) 50 percent, and (*c*) 75 percent? (Ignore commissions, dividends, and interest expense.)
2. Repeat Problem 1 to determine the percentage return on your investment but in this case suppose the price of the stock falls to $40 per share. What generalization can be inferred from your answers to Problems 1 and 2?
3. A stock is currently selling for $45 a share. What is the gain or loss on the following transactions?
   a. You take a long position and the stock's price declines to $41.50.
   b. You sell the stock short and the price declines to $41.50.
   c. You take a long position and the price rises to $54.
   d. You sell the stock short and the price rises to $54.
4. A sophisticated investor, B. Graham, sold 500 shares short of Amwell, Inc. at $42 a share. The price of the stock subsequently fell to $38 before rising to $49 at which time Graham covered the position (that is, closed the short position). What was the percentage gain or loss on this investment?

5. A year ago, Dara Kingston purchased 200 shares of BLK, Inc. for $25.50 on margin. At that time the margin requirement was 40 percent. If the interest rate on borrowed funds were 9 percent and she sold the stock for $34, what is the percentage return on the funds she invested in the stock?

6. Barbara buys 100 shares of DEM at $35 a share and 200 shares of GOP at $40 a share. She buys on margin and the broker charges interest of 10 percent on the loan.
   a. If the margin requirement is 55 percent, what is the maximum amount she can borrow?
   b. If she buys the stocks using the borrowed money and holds the securities for a year, how much interest must she pay?
   c. If after a year she sells DEM for $29 a share and GOP for $32 a share, how much did she lose on her investment?
   d. What is the percentage loss on the funds she invested if the interest payment is included in the calculation?

7. After an analysis of Lion/Bear, Inc., Hamilton H has concluded that the firm will face financial difficulty within a year. The stock is currently selling for $5 and Mr. H wants to sell it short. His broker is willing to execute the transaction but only if Mr. H puts up cash as collateral equal to the amount of the short sale. If Mr. H does sell the stock short, what is the percentage return he loses if the price of the stock rises to $7? What would be the percentage return if the firm went bankrupt and folded?

8. Clare Lasher buys 400 shares of stock on margin at $18 per share. If the margin requirement is 50 percent, how much must the stock rise for her to realize a 25 percent return on her invested funds? (Ignore dividends, commissions, and interest on borrowed funds.)

STOCKS
THE WALL STREET

PART II

INVESTMENTS

Virtually everyone makes investment decisions. My youngest daughter had a savings account before she was a year old. My late father owned stock in Ford at the age of 90. In between these extremes, every member of my family has made an investment in some type of asset.

The same is true for most families. Individuals purchase homes, make contributions to tax-deferred pension plans, acquire shares in mutual funds, and purchase precious metals, such as gold. Some individuals actively manage their portfolios and make their own investment decisions, such as which specific stocks or bonds to buy and sell. Other individuals delegate this decision making. They may purchase the shares in an investment company or participate in a pension plan and let management decide which specific assets to acquire.

Part Two is concerned with the financial assets the individual or portfolio manager may acquire. These assets range from relatively safe debt obligations, such as the bonds issued by the federal government, to extremely risky investments, such as futures contracts. Of course, a person should first decide why he or she is investing (in other words, what are the financial goals of the portfolio?) before making investment decisions. Because not all assets are appropriate to meet every financial goal, portfolio constructing should begin with specifying the investor's objectives. Then the assets considered in the following chapters can be allocated to meet the financial goals.

CHAPTER 7
The Time Value of Money

Learning Objectives

1. Explain why a dollar received tomorrow is not equal in value to a dollar received today.
2. Differentiate between compounding and discounting.
3. Distinguish between the present value of a dollar and the present value of an annuity.
4. Determine the future value of a dollar and the present value of a dollar to be received in the future.
5. Solve problems concerning the time value of money.

As Benjamin Franklin so aptly expressed, "Money makes money. And the money that money makes makes more money." That is the essence of the time value of money: A dollar received in the future is not equivalent in value to a dollar received in the present. The concept of the time value of money answers such questions as: If $100 is deposited in a savings account in a commercial bank today, how much will be in the account ten years from now if the funds earn 4 percent annually? Should a firm whose cost of funds is 9 percent acquire equipment that costs $12 million and offers cash inflows of $1.5 million a year for twelve years? If an investor buys a stock for $50 and sells it after two years for $60, what was the return on the investment?

The time value of money is one of the most crucial concepts in finance. An investment decision is made at a given time, but the return on that investment will be earned in the future. There has to be a means to compare the future results of investments with their present cost. Such comparisons require an understanding of the time value of money.

The chapter considers four concepts: (1) the future value of a dollar, (2) the present value of a dollar, (3) the future value of an annuity, and (4) the present value of an annuity. After each has been explained, several examples will illustrate how the four cases are applied to solve problems concerning the time value of money.

THE FUTURE VALUE OF A DOLLAR

If $100 is deposited in a savings account that pays 5 percent annually, how much money will be in the account at the end of the year? The answer is easy to determine: \$100 plus \$5 interest, for a total of \$105. The answer is derived by multiplying \$100 by 5 percent, which gives the interest earned during the year, and by adding this interest to the initial principal. That is,

$$\text{Initial principal} + (\text{Interest rate} \times \text{Initial principal}) = \text{Principal after one year.}$$

If the initial principal is \$100 and the interest rate is 5 percent, the principal after one year will be

$$\$100 + 0.05(\$100) = \$105.$$

How much will be in the account after two years? This answer is obtained in the same manner by adding the interest earned during the second year to the principal at the beginning of the second year; that is, \$105 plus 0.05 times \$105 equals \$110.25. After two years the initial deposit of \$100 will have grown to \$110.25; the savings account will have earned \$10.25 in interest. This total interest is composed of \$10, representing interest on the initial principal, and \$0.25, representing interest that has accrued during the second year on the \$5 in interest earned during the first year. This earning of interest on interest is called **compounding.** Money that is deposited in savings accounts is frequently referred to as being compounded, for interest is earned on both the principal and the previously earned interest.

COMPOUNDING
Process by which interest is paid on interest that was previously earned

The words *interest* and *compounded* are frequently used together. For example, banks may advertise that interest is compounded daily for savings accounts, or the yield on a bond is 8.0 percent but interest is compounded semiannually. In the previous example, interest was earned only once during the year—that is, compounded annually. In many cases interest is not compounded annually but quarterly, semiannually, or even daily. The more frequently it is compounded (the more frequently the interest is added to the principal), the more rapidly the interest is put to work to earn even more interest.

How much will be in the account at the end of three years? This answer can be determined by the same general formula that was previously used. The amount in the account at the end of the second year (\$110.25) is added to the interest that is earned during the third year (0.05 × \$110.25). That is,

$$\$110.25 + \$5.5125 = \$115.76.$$

By continuing this method, it is possible to determine the amount that will be in the account at the end of 20 or more years, but doing so is obviously a lot of tedious work. Fortunately, there are simpler ways to determine how much will be in the account after any given number of years. This is done by using (1) an interest table, (2) an electronic calculator, or (3) a computer program. This discussion initially employs interest tables and financial calculators. Later in the chapter the use of a computer is illustrated.

Appendix A at the end of the text is an interest table that gives the interest factor for the **future value of a dollar.** The interest rates at which a dollar is compounded are read horizontally at the top of the table. The number of periods (such

FUTURE VALUE OF A DOLLAR
Amount to which a single payment will grow at some rate of interest

as years) is read vertically along the left-hand margin. To determine the amount to which \$100 will grow in three years at 5 percent interest, find the interest factor (1.158) and multiply it by \$100. That calculation yields \$115.80, which is the answer that was derived previously by working out the equations (except for rounding off). To ascertain the amount to which \$100 will grow in 25 years at 5 percent interest compounded annually, multiply \$100 by the interest factor, 3.386, to obtain the answer, \$338.60. Thus, if \$100 were placed in a savings account that paid 5 percent interest annually, \$338.60 would be in the account after 25 years.

The equation for the future value of a dollar is as follows:

$$P_0(1 + i)^n = P_n. \quad \textbf{7.1}$$

P represents the present amount (principal), *i* is the rate of interest, and *n* is the number of time periods. The subscript 0 represents the present and subscripts 1, 2 . . . *n* represent periods 1, 2, and on through the *n*th period. In this form, the equation for the future value of a dollar is a simple equation in the following general form:

$$A \times B = C.$$

A is the present amount, *B* is the interest factor, and *C* is the future amount. Thus, the future value equation states:

$$\text{Present amount} \times \text{Interest factor} = \text{Future amount;}$$

that is,

$$P_0 \times (1 + i)^n = P_n.$$

Notice that the interest factor for the future value of a dollar (*FVIF*) is

$$FVIF = (1 + i)^n. \quad \textbf{7.2}$$

The interest factor for the future value of one dollar (and all subsequent interest factors in this chapter) has two components: a percentage or interest rate (*i*), and the number of time periods (*n*). Throughout this text, these components will be symbolized in the following general form: *IF*(*I,N*). For example, the future value of \$100 at 8 percent at the end of 20 years will be written as

$$P_0 \times FVIF\ (8I,\ 20N) = P_{20}.$$

FVIF indicates the interest factor for the future value of a dollar; 8*I* represents the 8 percent, and 20*N* represents the 20 time periods. This form is used to be consistent with most financial calculators.

Time-value problems may be illustrated with time lines, which place time periods, such as a year, on the horizontal axis and dollars on the vertical axis. The line in the figure represents the value of the money over time. For the previous example in which the value of $100 grew to $466.10 over 20 years at 8 percent, the time line is

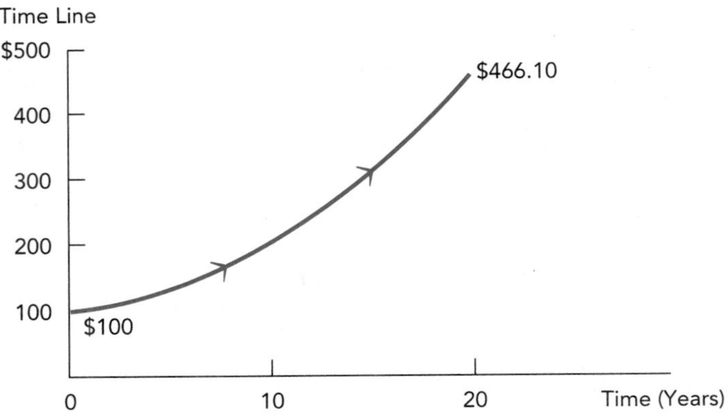

Notice that the arrows indicate the direction of time. In this case the dollar is growing over time from the present to the future, which is indicated by the arrows pointing to the right. When the process is reversed and the future is being brought back to the present, the arrow will point to the left.

The future value of a dollar grows with increases in the length of time and in the rate of interest. These relationships are illustrated in Figure 7.1. If $1 is compounded at 5 percent interest (AB on the graph), it will grow to $1.28 after five years and to $1.63 after ten years. However, if $1 is compounded at 10 percent interest (AC on the graph), it will grow to $2.59 in ten years. These cases illustrate the basic nature of compounding: The longer the funds continue to grow and the higher in the interest rate, the higher will be the final value.

Notice that doubling the interest rate more than doubles the amount of interest. When the interest rate is doubled from 5 percent to 10 percent, interest accumulated in ten years rises from $0.63 at 5 percent to $1.59 at 10 percent. The same conclusion applies to doubling the number of years. When the dollar is compounded annually for five years at 5 percent, the interest earned is $0.28 but rises to $0.63 after ten years. These conclusions are the result of the fact that compounding involves a geometric progression. The $(1 + i)$ is raised to some power (n).

Future-value problems may be easily solved by using a financial calculator designed for business applications. These calculators have been programmed with interest factors and readily solve time-value problems. (Some financial calculators also have other business applications, such as determining depreciation expense and statistical analysis. Many employers expect new employees to be able to use financial calculators, so an inability to use them may put you at a disadvantage.)

Although differences exist among models, financial calculators generally have five special function keys:

N I or % PV PMT FV

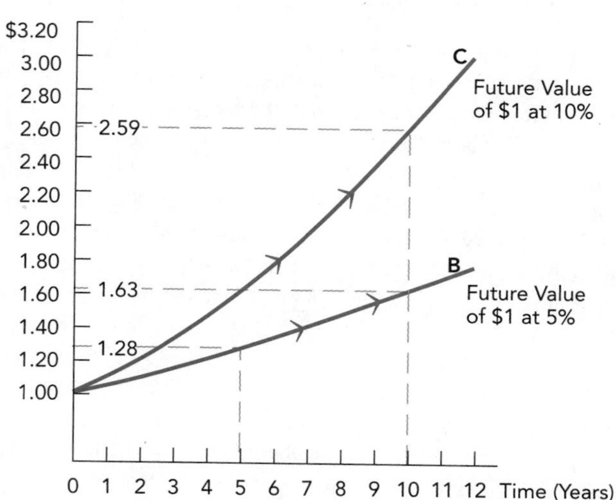

FIGURE 7.1

Future Value of One Dollar

These keys represent the time period (N), the interest rate (I or %), the amount in the present (PV for *present value*), the periodic payment (PMT for *annuity payment,* which will be discussed later in this chapter), and the amount in the future (FV for *future value*).

To illustrate how easy financial calculators are to use, consider the previous example of the future value of a dollar in which $100 grew to $466.10 after 20 years when the annual interest rate was 8 percent. Using a financial calculator, enter the present amount (PV = −100), the interest rate (I = 8), and time (N = 20). Since there are no annual payments, be certain that PMT is set equal to zero (PMT = 0). Then instruct the calculator to determine the future value (FV = ?). The calculator should arrive at a future value of $466.10, which is almost the same amount derived using the interest table for the future value of $1. (Any differences in the answers would be the result of the interest tables being rounded off to three places.)

You may wonder why the present value was entered as a *negative* number. Financial calculators consider payments as either cash inflows or cash outflows. Cash inflows are entered as positive numbers, and cash outflows are entered as negative numbers. One of the cash flows must be an inflow (a positive number), and one must be an outflow (a negative number). In the above example, the initial amount is an outflow because the individual invests the $100. The resulting future amount is a cash inflow because the investor receives the terminal amount. That is, the investor gives up the $100 (the outflow) and after 20 years receives the $466.10 (the inflow). The use of negative numbers should not pose a problem if you understand the reasoning behind their use.

Problems involving time value permeate this text and are illustrated both with the use of interest tables and with financial calculators. Illustrations using interest

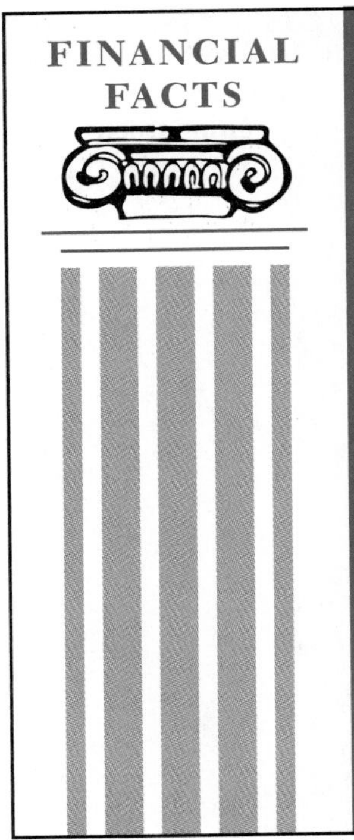

Simple versus Compound Interest

"Simple interest" does not consider the earning of interest on interest; "compound interest" does take into consideration the earning of interest on interest. The calculation of compound interest uses the equations and tables presented in the body of this chapter. To calculate simple interest, multiply the principal by the interest rate by the number of years. For example, the amount of simple interest earned for three years on \$1,000 at 5 percent would be \$1,000 × 0.05 × 3 = \$150. ¶ By the same reasoning, the interest earned over 20 years would be \$1,000 × 0.05 × 20 = \$1,000. ¶ On first impression it might appear that the difference between simple interest and compound interest is so small that the calculation of simple interest is sufficient. (Your banker might agree as far as deposits are concerned but certainly not in regard to borrowings). A compound interest table will show, however, that \$1,000 compounded annually at 5 percent for 20 years will grow to \$2,653 (\$1,000 × 2.653). The amount of interest is \$1,653, and the difference is \$653. ¶ The difference between simple and compound interest is even larger if the number of years or the rate of interest is increased. For example, \$1,000 invested for 25 years at 10 percent yields simple interest of \$1,000 × 0.1 × 25 = \$2,500. Compound interest, however, yields interest of \$9,835 [(\$1,000 × 10.835) − \$1,000]. The difference in the calculations is \$7,335. So borrow from your younger brother using simple interest, but lend to him using compound interest. ¶

tables employ the following general form: *FVIF*(*I,N*) to represent the interest factor, with the *FV* indicating the future value of a dollar and the *i* indicating the interest rate for *n* time periods. Financial calculator illustrations use the following general form:

PV = ?
I = ?
N = ?
PMT = ?
FV = ?

followed by the answer. When applied to the preceding illustration, the form is

PV = \$−100
I = 8
N = 20
PMT = 0
FV = ?
FV = \$466.10

The illustration is placed in the margin, so that it does not break the flow of the written text.

THE PRESENT VALUE OF A DOLLAR

In the preceding section, we examined the way in which a dollar is compounded over time. In this section, we will consider the reverse situation. How much is a dollar that will be received in the future worth today? For example, how much will a payment of $1,000 after 20 years be worth today if the funds earn 5 percent annually? Instead of asking how much a dollar will be worth at some future date, the question asks how much that future dollar is worth today. This is a question of **present value.** The process by which this question is answered is called **discounting.** Discounting determines the worth of funds that are to be received in the future in terms of their present value.

PRESENT VALUE
Current value of a dollar to be received in the future

DISCOUNTING
Process of determining present value

In the earlier section, the future value of a dollar was calculated by Equation 7.1:

$$P_0(1 + i)^n = P_n.$$

Discounting reverses this equation. The present value (P_0) is determined by dividing the future value (P_n) by the interest factor $(1 + i)^n$. This is expressed in Equation 7.3.

$$P_0 = \frac{P_n}{(1 + i)^n}. \qquad (7.3)$$

The future amount is discounted by the appropriate interest factor to determine the present value. For example, if the interest rate is 6 percent, the present value of $100 to be received five years from today is

$$P_0 = \frac{\$100}{(1 + 0.06)^5},$$

$$P_0 = \frac{\$100}{(1.338)},$$

$$P_0 = \$74.73.$$

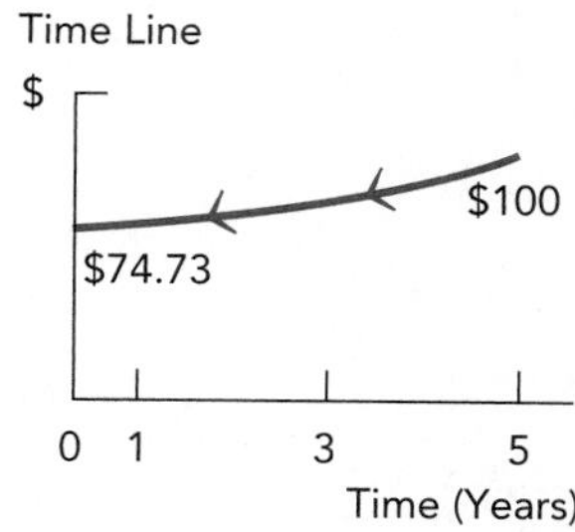

Equation 7.3, like the equation for the future value of $1, breaks down into three simple components: the amount in the future, the amount in the present, and the interest factor that links the present and future values. Thus, the future amount times the interest factor for the present value of $1 is

$$A \times B = C$$

$$P_n \times \text{PVIF(I,N)} = P_0.$$

PVIF(I,N) represents the interest factor for the present value of a dollar:

$$PVIF = \frac{1}{(1 + i)^n}. \quad (7.4)$$

For example, if the interest rate is 6 percent, the present value of \$100 to be received five years from today is

$$P_0 = \$100 \times \text{PVIF(6I,5N)}.$$

CALCULATOR SOLUTION

Function Key		Data Input
FV	=	100
I	=	6
N	=	5
PMT	=	0
PV	=	?
Function Key		Answer
PV	=	−74.73

You may determine the present value by using the interest table for the present value of \$1 (Appendix B). This table presents the interest factors for selected interest rates and periods. The interest rates are read horizontally at the top, and the number of periods is read vertically along the left-hand side. To determine the present value of \$100 that will be received in five years if the current interest rate is 6 percent, multiply \$100 by the interest factor, which is found in the table under the vertical column for 6 percent and in the horizontal column for five years. The present value of \$100 is

$$\$100 \times 0.747 = \$74.70.$$

Thus, \$100 that will be received after five years is currently worth only \$74.70 if the interest rate is 6 percent. This is the same answer that was determined with Equation 7.3 (except for rounding off).[1]

The present value of a dollar depends on the length of time before it will be received and the interest rate. The farther into the future the dollar will be received and the higher the interest rate, the lower is the present value of the dollar. This is illustrated by Figure 7.2, which gives the relationship between the present value of a dollar and the length of time at various interest rates. Lines AB and AC give the present value of a dollar at 4 percent and 7 percent, respectively. As may be seen in this graph, a dollar to be received after 20 years is worth considerably less than a dollar to be received after five years when both are discounted at the same percentage. At 4 percent (line AB) the current value of \$1 to be received after 20 years is only \$0.456, whereas \$1 to be received after five years is worth \$0.822. Also, the higher the interest rate (or discount factor), the lower is the present value of a dollar. For example, the present value of \$1 to be received after five years is \$0.822 at 4 percent, but it is only \$0.713 at 7 percent.

[1]Notice that the table is constructed so you multiply even though according to Equation 7.4 you are dividing. Thus, $\$100/(1 + 0.06)^5$ equals $\$100 \times 0.747$ because $1/(1 + 0.06)^5 = 0.747$.

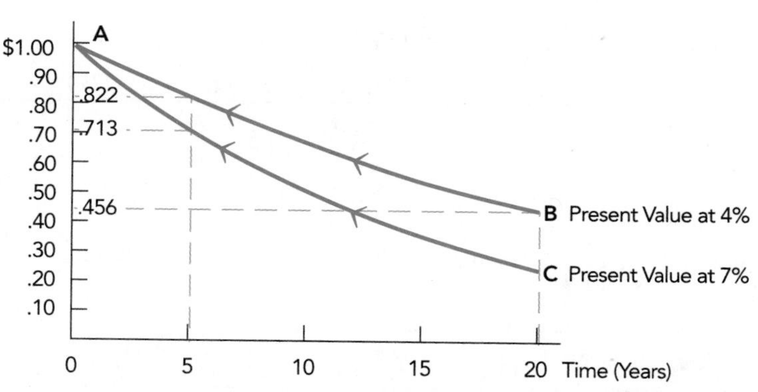

FIGURE 7.2

Present Value of One Dollar to Be Received in the Future

THE FUTURE VALUE OF AN ANNUITY

How much will be in a savings account after three years if $100 is deposited annually and the account pays 5 percent interest? This is similar to the future value of a dollar except that the payment is not a single deposit but a series of annual deposits. If the payments are equal (for example, rent or a loan repayment schedule), the series is called an **annuity.** The above question illustrates the **future value of an annuity.**

ANNUITY
Series of equal, annual payments

FUTURE VALUE OF AN ANNUITY
Amount to which a series of equal payments will grow at some rate of interest

ANNUITY DUE
Annuity in which the payments are made at the beginning of the time period

ORDINARY ANNUITY
Annuity in which the payments are made at the end of the time period

To determine how much will be in the account we must consider not only the interest rate earned but also whether deposits are made at the beginning of the year or the end of the year. If each deposit is made at the beginning of the year, the series is called an **annuity due.** If the deposits are made at the end of the year, the series is an **ordinary annuity.** A car loan with an initial down payment and payments made at the end of each month is an illustration of an ordinary annuity. An apartment lease with payments at the beginning of each month is an illustration of an annuity due.

What is the future value of an annuity due if $100 is deposited in an account for three years starting right now? What is the future value of an ordinary annuity if $100 is placed in an account for three years starting at the end of the year? The flow of deposits is illustrated in Exhibit 7.1. In both cases the $100 is deposited for three years in a savings account that pays 5 percent interest. The top half of the figure shows the annuity due, while the bottom half illustrates the ordinary annuity. In both cases, three years elapse from the present to when the final amount is determined. The difference in the timing of the deposits results in a difference in the interest earned. For example, the initial $100 deposit for the annuity due earns three interest payments ($5.00, $5.25, and $5.51 for a total of $15.76 in interest). The initial $100 deposit for the ordinary annuity earns only two interest payments ($5.00 and $5.25 for a total of $10.25 in interest). Because the deposits are made

EXHIBIT 7.1

Flow of Deposits and Interest for the Future Value of an Annuity Due and an Ordinary Annuity

ANNUITY DUE

	1/1/x0	1/1/x1	1/1/x2	1/1/x3	Sum
Interest earned	—	5.00	5.25	5.51	$115.76
			5.00	5.25	110.25
The deposits	$100.00	100.00	100.00	5.00	105.00
Amount in the account	$100.00	205.00	315.25	331.01	$331.01

ORDINARY ANNUITY

	1/1/x0	1/1/x1	1/1/x2	1/1/x3	Sum
Interest earned	—	—	5.00	5.25	$110.25
				5.00	105.00
The deposits	—	$100.00	100.00	100.00	100.00
Amount in the account	—	100.00	205.00	315.25	$315.25

at the beginning of each year, the annuity due earns more interest ($31.01 versus $15.25) and thus has the higher terminal value ($331.01 versus $315.25). As will be illustrated later in the chapter, the greater the interest rate and the longer the time, the greater will be this difference in terminal values.

The procedures for determining the future value of an annuity due (*FVAD*) and the future value of an ordinary annuity (*FVOA*) are stated formally in Equations 7.5 and 7.6, respectively. In each equation, *PMT* represents the equal, periodic payment, *i* represents the rate of interest, and *n* represents the number of years that elapse from the present until the end of the period. For the annuity due, the equation is

7.5

$$FVAD = PMT(1) + (i)^1 + PMT(1 + i)^2 + \cdots + PMT(1 + i)^n.$$

When this equation is applied to the previous example in which $i = 0.05$, $n = 3$, and the annual payment $PMT = \$100$, the accumulated sum is

$$\begin{aligned} FVAD &= \$100(1 + 0.05)^1 + \$100(1 + 0.05)^2 + \$100(1 + 0.05)^3 \\ &= \$105 + \$110.25 + \$115.76 \\ &= \$331.01. \end{aligned}$$

For the ordinary annuity, the equation is

7.6

$$FVOA = PMT(1 + i)^0 + PMT(1 + i)^1 + \cdots + PMT(1 + i)^{n-1}.$$

When this equation is applied to the above example, the accumulated sum is

$$FVOA = \$100(1 + 0.05)^0 + \$100(1 + 0.05)^1 + \$100(1 + 0.05)^{3-1}$$
$$= \$100 + \$105 + \$110.25$$
$$= \$315.25.$$

(a) Time Line Annuity Due

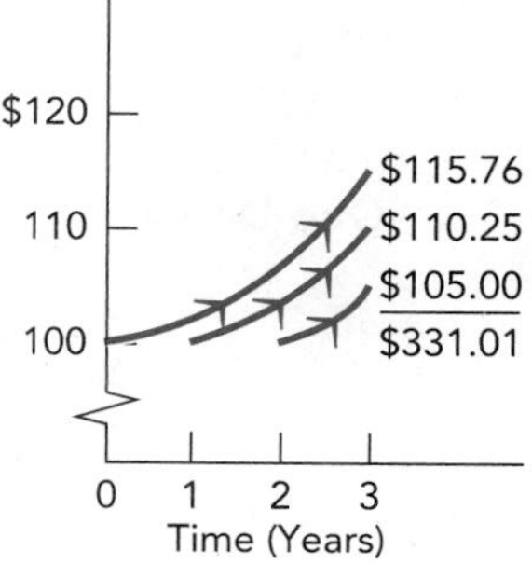

As with the future value of $1 and the present value of $1, the future value of an annuity is determined by the simple equation:

$$A \times B = C.$$

In this case, that is

(b) Time Line Ordinary Annuity

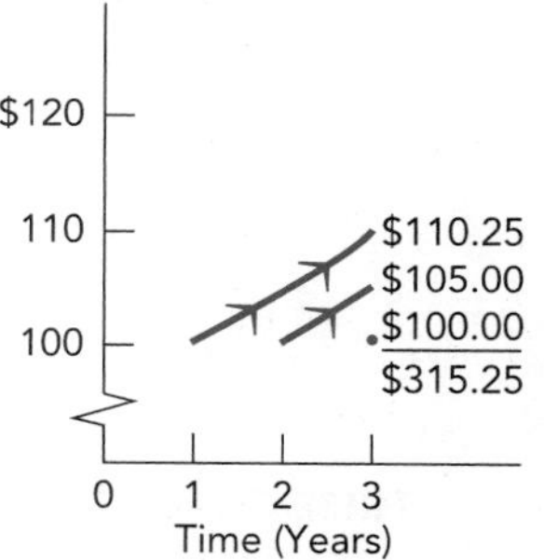

$$PMT \times FVAIF(I,N) = FVA,$$

in which PMT represents the periodic payment, the annuity, and $FVAIF(I,N)$ is the interest factor for the future value of an annuity at I percent and N time periods.

The value of the interest factor for the future value of an annuity may be found in the appropriate interest table. Appendix C presents the interest factors for the future value of an ordinary annuity. (Interest tables are usually given only for ordinary annuities. How these interest factors may be converted into the interest factor for an annuity due is illustrated in the appendix to this chapter.) The number of periods is read vertically at the left, and the interest rates are read horizontally at the top. To ascertain the future value of the ordinary annuity in the previous example, find the interest factor for the future value of an annuity at 5 percent for 3 years (3.152). So the future value of the ordinary annuity is

$$\$100 \times 3.152 = \$315.20.$$

CALCULATOR SOLUTION

Function Key		Data Input
PV	=	0
PMT	=	−100
I	=	5
N	=	3
FV	=	?
Function Key		*Answer*
FV	=	315.25

This is the same answer that was derived by determining the future values of each $100 deposit and totaling them. The slight difference in the two answers is the result of rounding off.

The future value of an annuity of a dollar compounded annually depends on the number of payments (that is, the number of years over which deposits are made) and the interest rate. The longer the time and the higher the interest rate, the greater will be the sum that will have accumulated in the future. This is illustrated by Figure 7.3. Lines AB and AC show the value of the annuity at 4 percent and 8 percent, respectively. After five years the value of the $1 annuity will grow to $5.87 at 8 percent but to only $5.42 at 4 percent. If these annuities are continued for another five years for a total duration of ten years, they will be worth $14.49 and $12.01, respectively. Thus, both the rate at which the annuity compounds and the length of time affect the annuity's value.

FIGURE 7.3

Future Sum (or Value) of an Annuity of One Dollar

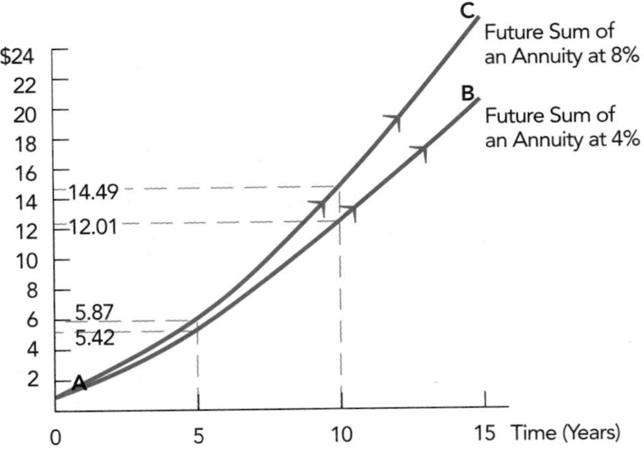

THE PRESENT VALUE OF AN ANNUITY

PRESENT VALUE OF AN ANNUITY
Current value of a series of equal payments to be received in the future

In financial analysis the individual is often concerned not with the future value but with the **present value of an annuity.** The investor or the financial manager who will receive periodic payments often wishes to know the current value of these payments. Of course, the present value of these future payments could be determined by obtaining the present value of each payment and summing these values. This approach is illustrated by the following simple example. The recipient expects to receive $100 at the end of each year for three years and wants to know how much this series of annual payments is currently worth if 6 percent can be earned on invested funds. Notice the payments are made at the end of the year, so this is an illustration of an ordinary annuity. If the payments had been made at the beginning of the year, the series of payments would be an annuity due.

One method for determining the current worth of this ordinary annuity is to calculate the present value of each $100 payment (find the appropriate interest factors in Appendix B and multiple them by $100) and to sum these individual present values, which in this case yields $267.30, as may be seen in Exhibit 7.2.

This process is expressed in more general terms by Equation 7.7. The present value (PV) of the equal, annual payments (PMT) is found by discounting these payments at the appropriate interest rate (i) and summing (Σ) them from the first payment through the last (n) payment.

7.7

$$PV = \frac{PMT}{(1+i)^1} + \cdots + \frac{PMT}{(1+i)^n}$$

$$PV = \sum_{t=1}^{n} \frac{PMT}{(1+i)^t}.$$

EXHIBIT 7.2

Present Value of a $100 Ordinary Annuity at 6 Percent for Three Years

Payment	Year	Interest Factor	Present Value
$100	1	0.943	$ 94.30
100	2	0.890	89.00
100	3	0.840	84.00
			$267.30

When the values from the previous example are inserted into the equation, it reads:

$$PV = \frac{\$100}{(1 + 0.06)} + \frac{\$100}{(1 + 0.06)^2} + \frac{\$100}{(1 + 0.06)^3}$$

$$= \frac{\$100}{1.060} + \frac{\$100}{1.123} + \frac{\$100}{1.191}$$

$$= \$267.30.$$

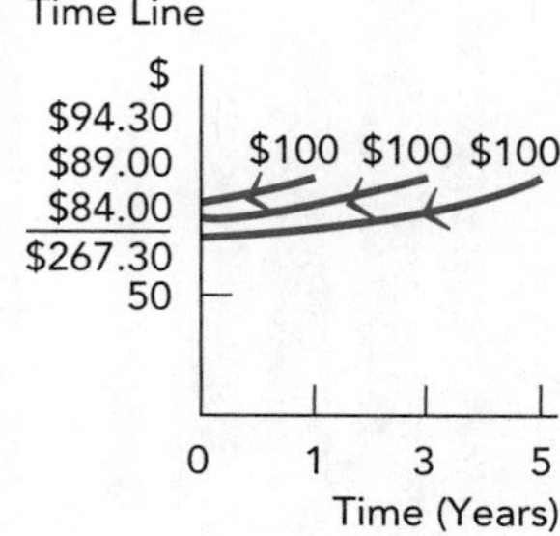

Equation 7.7 may be rewritten as follows:

$$PV = (PMT)\left(\sum_{t=1}^{n} \frac{1}{(1 + i)^t}\right).$$

Once again this is a simple equation in the general form of

$$A \times B = C.$$

The annual annuity payment is multiplied by an interest factor to determine the present value. Thus, the determination of present value of an ordinary annuity is

$$PMT \times PVAIF(I,N) = PV.$$

in which *PMT* is the annuity payment, *PVAIF(I,N)* is the interest factor for the present value of an ordinary annuity at i percent for n time periods, and *PV* is the present value of the annuity. The interest factors for the present value of an ordinary annuity are given in Appendix D. (How these interest factors may be converted into interest factors for an annuity due is explained in the appendix to this chapter.) The selected interest rates are read horizontally along the top, and the number of periods is read vertically at the left. To determine the present value of an annuity of $100 that is to be received for three years when interest rates are 6 percent, find the interest factor for three years at 6 percent (2.673) and then multiply $100 by this interest factor. The present value of this annuity is $267.30, which is the same value (except for rounding off) that was derived by obtaining

CALCULATOR SOLUTION

Function Key		*Data Input*
FV	=	**0**
PMT	=	**100**
I	=	**6**
N	=	**3**
PV	=	**?**
Function Key		*Answer*
PV	=	**−267.30**

The Equations for the Interest Factors

Each of the four cases involving time value has interest factors. Each interest factor has a percentage (interest rate) and time (number of time periods). The equations for the four cases are as follows:

Future value of a dollar *(FVIF)*:

$$(1 + i)^n.$$

Present value of a dollar *(PVIF)*:

$$\frac{1}{(1 + i)^n}.$$

Future value of an ordinary annuity *(FVAIF)*:

$$\frac{(1 + i)^n - 1}{i}.$$

Present value of an ordinary annuity *(PVAIF)*:

$$\frac{1 - \frac{1}{(1 + i)^n}}{i} = \frac{1 - (1 + i)^{-n}}{i}.$$

each of the individual present values and summing them. The price you would be willing to pay at the present time in exchange for three future annual payments of \$100, when the rate of return on alternative investments is 6 percent, is \$267.30.

As with the present value of a dollar, the present value of an annuity is related to the interest rate and the length of time over which the annuity payments are made. The lower the interest rate and the longer the duration of the annuity, the greater is the current value of the annuity. Figure 7.4 illustrates the relationship between the duration of the annuity and the present value of the annuity at various interest rates. As may be seen by comparing lines AB and AC, the lower the interest rate, the higher is the present dollar value. For example, if payments are to be made over five years, the present value of an annuity of \$1 is \$4.45 at 4 percent but only \$3.99 at 8 percent. The longer the duration of the annuity, the higher is the present value; hence, the present value of an annuity of \$1 at 4 percent is \$4.45 for five years, whereas the present value is \$8.11 for ten years.

FIGURE 7.4

Present Value of an Annuity of One Dollar

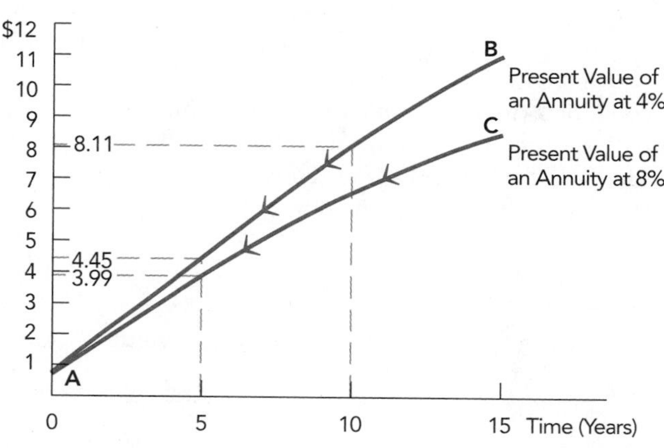

ILLUSTRATIONS OF COMPOUNDING AND DISCOUNTING

The previous sections have explained the various computations involving time value. This section illustrates them in a series of problems that an investor or financial manager may encounter. These illustrations are similar to examples that are used throughout the text. If you understand these examples, comprehending the rest of the text material should be much easier, because the emphasis can then be placed on the analysis instead of on the mechanics of the calculations.

Time-value problems may be solved in several ways. Initially, we will use interest tables in the text with financial calculator solutions in the margin. Later in the chapter, we will use a computer program that was specially written for time-value problems. You may also use computer programs such as Excel, provided, of course, that you are familiar with Excel.

If you use interest tables to solve time-value problems, you must determine which of the four tables to use. The following decision tree may aid in this selection process. First, determine if the problem involves a lump-sum payment or a set of equal payments—that is, an annuity. Then determine if the problem concerns going from the present to the future (future value) or from the future to the present (present value).

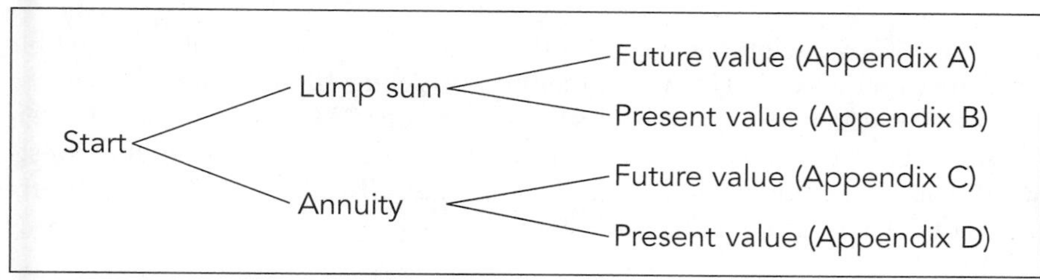

For example, if the total tuition cost of a four-year college education is \$50,000, what will be the cost after ten years if prices rise annually by 6 percent? First, determine if the problem is concerned with an annuity or a lump sum. Since the question asks about total tuition costs, it is an illustration of a lump sum and not an annuity. Second, determine the time dimension. Since the problem is not concerned with the current cost of an education but with future costs, it is an example of future value and not present value. Thus, from the decision tree presented below, the appropriate table is determined to be the future value of a dollar table (Appendix A).

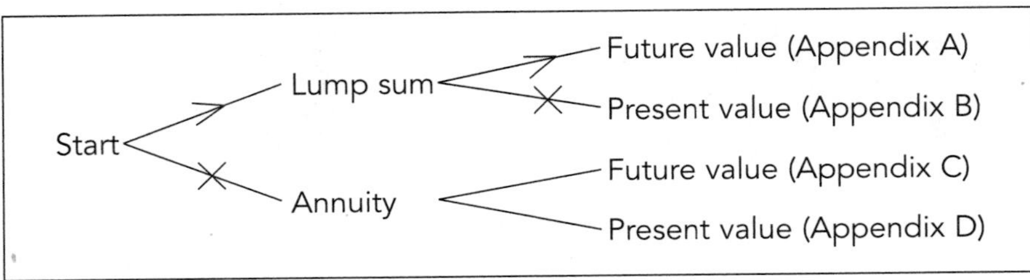

In addition to determining which interest table to use, you need to determine what is known and what is asked for. All time-value problems involve four variables: the present amount, the future amount, the interest rate, and the number of time periods. Since there is only one equation, three of the four variables must be given. That is, three of the variables are independent, and one is dependent.

Consider, for example, an investor who buys a stock for \$10 per share and expects the value of the stock to rise annually at 9 percent. After ten years this investor plans to sell the stock. What is the anticipated sale price? The three known variables (the independent variables) are the present amount (\$10); the rate of growth, which is analogous to the interest rate (9 percent); and the number of years (10). The unknown variable (the dependent variable) is the future sale price. The problem illustrates the future value of a dollar, and that future value is

CALCULATOR SOLUTION

Function Key		Data Input
FV	=	−10
I	=	9
N	=	10
PMT	=	0
FV	=	?
Function Key		*Answer*
FV	=	23.67

$$P_n = P_0(1 + i)^n$$

$$P_{10} = \$10(1 + 0.09)^{10}$$

$$P_{10} = \$10(FVIF\ 9I,\ 10N)$$

$$P_{10} = \$10(2.367) = \$23.67,$$

in which 2.367 is the interest factor for the future value of a dollar at 9 percent for ten years (Appendix A). The investor anticipates selling the stock for \$23.67.

Next, consider that an investor sells a stock for \$23.67 that was held for ten years. A return of 9 percent was earned. What was the original cost of the investment? This is an example of the present value of a dollar discounted back at 9 percent for ten years. The purchase price was

$$P_0 = \frac{P_n}{(1 + i)^n}$$

$$P_0 = \frac{\$23.67}{(1 + 0.09)^{10}}$$

$$P_0 = \$23.67\ (PVIF\ 9I, 10N)$$

$$P_0 = \$23.67(0.422) = \$9.98 \approx \$10,$$

CALCULATOR SOLUTION

Function Key		Data Input
FV	=	23.67
I	=	9
N	=	10
PMT	=	0
PV	=	?
Function Key		*Answer*
PV	=	−10.00

in which 0.422 is the interest factor for the present value of a dollar discounted at 9 percent for ten years (Appendix B). The investment cost \$10 when it was purchased.

These examples are two views of the same investment. In the first example, the \$10 investment grew to \$23.67. In the second example, the value when the stock was sold was brought back to the value of the initial investment. Another variation of this question would be as follows. An investor bought stock for \$10, held it for ten years, and then sold it for \$23.67. What was the return on the investment? In this case, the values of the stock when it was bought and sold are known, but the rate of growth is unknown. The answer can be found by using either the future value of a dollar table or the present value of a dollar table. By solving for either interest factor, the return may be determined.

If the future value table (Appendix A) is used, the question is: At what rate (x) will \$10 grow in ten years to equal \$23.67? The answer is

$$P_0(1 + x)^n = P_n$$

$$\$10(1 + x)^{10} = \$23.67.$$

$$\$10[FVIF(?I, 10N)] = \$23.67$$

$$FVIF(?I, 10N) = 2.367.$$

CALCULATOR SOLUTION

Function Key		Data Input
PV	=	−10
N	=	10
PMT	=	0
FV	=	23.67
I	=	?
Function Key		*Answer*
I	=	9

The interest factor is 2.367, which, according to the future value of a dollar table for ten years, makes the interest rate 9 percent because this interest factor is located under the vertical column for 9 percent and in the horizontal column for ten years.

If the present value table (Appendix B) is used, the question asks what discount rate (x) at ten years will bring \$23.67 back to \$10. The answer is

$$P_0 = \frac{P_n}{(1 + x)^n}$$

$$\$10 = \frac{\$23.67}{(1 + x)^{10}}$$

$$\$10 = \$23.67[(PVIF\ ?I, 10N)]$$

$$PVIF(?I, 10N) = \frac{\$10}{\$23.67} = 0.422.$$

The Annual Increase in the Cost of a College Education

In 1895, annual tuition to attend a major university cost $60. One hundred years later, the tuition was $10,000. In absolute dollars, that is a substantial increase in tuition, but is the increase so astonishing when expressed as an annual rate of growth? ¶ That question may be answered by the use of time value of money. The question is: "In 100 years, $60 grows into $10,000 at what rate?" That is $\$60(1 + g)^{100} = \$10{,}000$, $(1 + g)^{100} = 10{,}000/60 = 166.67$, and $g = {}^{100}\sqrt{1.667} - 1 = 1.0525 - 1 = 5.25\%$. ¶ $60 invested at only 5.25 percent grows into $10,000 after 100 years! From that perspective, the increase in the tuition cost does not seem so astonishing. However, if the 5.25 percent annual rate of growth is maintained, annual tuition in 2095 will be $1,668,055! ¶

The interest factor is 0.422, which may be found in the present value of a dollar table for ten years in the 9 percent column. Thus, this problem may be solved by the proper application of either the compound value or present value tables.

Now consider a third example. An employer offers to start a pension plan for a 45-year-old employee. The plan is to place $1,000 at the end of each year in a savings account that earns 6 percent annually. The employee wants to know how much will have accumulated by retirement at age 65.

This is an example of the future value of an ordinary annuity. The payment is $1,000 annually, and it will grow at 6 percent for 20 years. The fund will thus grow to

CALCULATOR SOLUTION

Function Key		Data Input
PV	=	0
PMT	=	−1,000
I	=	6
N	=	20
FV	=	?
Function Key		*Answer*
FV	=	36,785.59

$$FVA = PMT(1 + i)^0 + \cdots + PMT(1 - i)^{n-1}$$
$$= \$1{,}000(1 + 0.06)^0 + \cdots + \$1{,}000(1 + 0.06)^{19}$$
$$= \$1{,}000[FVAIF(6I, 20N)]$$
$$= \$1{,}000(36.786) = \$36{,}786,$$

in which 36.786 is the interest factor for the future of an annuity of one dollar compounded annually at 6 percent for 20 years (Appendix C).

In a fourth example, the same employer decides to place a lump sum in an account that earns 6 percent and to draw on the account to make the annual payments of $1,000. After 20 years all the funds in the account will be depleted. How much must be deposited initially in the account?

This is an example of the present value of an ordinary annuity. The annuity of $1,000 per year at 6 percent for 20 years is worth how much today? The present value (the amount of the initial deposit necessary to fund the annuity) is

$$PVA = \sum_{1}^{n} \frac{PMT}{(1 + i)} + \cdots + \frac{PMT}{(1 + i)^a}$$

$$= \frac{\$1{,}000}{1 + 0.06} + \cdots + \frac{\$1{,}000}{(1 + 0.06)^{20}}$$

$$= \$1{,}000[PVAIF(6I, 20N)]$$

$$= \$1{,}000(11.470) = \$11{,}470,$$

CALCULATOR SOLUTION

Function Key		Data Input
FV	=	0
PMT	=	1,000
I	=	6
N	=	20
PV	=	?
Function Key		*Answer*
PV	=	−11,469.92

in which 11.470 is the interest factor for the present value of the sum (Σ) of an annuity of a dollar at 6 percent for 20 years (Appendix D). Thus, the employer need deposit only $11,470 in an account that earns 6 percent to meet the $1,000 pension payment for 20 years.

You should notice the difference between the answers in the last two examples. In the first, a set of payments earns interest, and thus the future value is larger than just the sum of the 20 payments of $1,000. In the second, a future set of payments is valued in present terms. Since future payments are worth less today, the current value is less than the sum of the 20 payments of $1,000.

As a final example, consider that an investment pays $50 per year for ten years, after which $1,000 is returned to the investor. If the investor can earn 6 percent, how much is this investment worth? What is its value? This question really contains two questions: What is the present value of the sum (Σ) of an annuity of $50 at 6 percent for ten years, and what is the present value of $1,000 after ten years at 6 percent? The answer is

$$PV = \sum_{1}^{n} \frac{PMT}{(1 + i)^1} + \cdots + \frac{PMT}{(1 + i)^n} + \frac{P_n}{(1 + i)^n}$$

$$= \frac{\$50}{(1 + 0.06)} + \cdots + \frac{\$50}{(1 + 0.06)^{10}} + \frac{\$1{,}000}{(1 + 0.06)^{10}}$$

$$= \$50[PVAIF(6I,10N)] + \cdots + \$1{,}000[PVIF(6I,10N)]$$

$$= \$50(7.360) + \$1{,}000(0.558) = \$926,$$

CALCULATOR SOLUTION

Function Key		Data Input
FV	=	1,000
PMT	=	50
I	=	6
N	=	10
PV	=	?
Function Key		*Answer*
PV	=	−926.40

in which 7.360 and 0.558 are the interest factors for the present value of an annuity of a dollar and the present value of a dollar, respectively, both at 6 percent for ten years (Appendixes D and B, respectively). This example illustrates that many investments may involve both a series of payments (the annuity component) and a lump-sum payment. This particular investment illustrates a bond, the valuation of which is discussed in Chapter 9.

ADDITIONAL APPLICATIONS OF THE TIME VALUE OF MONEY

Throughout the remainder of this text there will be numerous applications of the concept of the time value of money. This concept plays an exceedingly crucial role in finance because decisions must be made today while the returns occur in the future. For example, understanding the time value of money and the processes of

CALCULATOR SOLUTION

Function Key		Data Input
FV	=	0
PMT	=	275
I	=	10
N	=	5
PV	=	?
Function Key		*Answer*
PV	=	−1,042.47

CALCULATOR SOLUTION

Function Key		Data Input
FV	=	1,600
PMT	=	0
I	=	10
N	=	5
PV	=	?
Function Key		*Answer*
PV	=	−993.47

CALCULATOR SOLUTION

C requires a financial calculator that accepts uneven cash inflows. If your calculator accepts uneven cash inflows, enter

Function Key		Data Input
FV	=	0
I	=	10
N	=	5
CF_1	=	300
CF_2	=	300
CF_3	=	250
CF_4	=	250
CF_5	=	250
PV	=	?
Function Key		*Answer*
PV	=	−1,034.25

discounting and compounding are prerequisites to understanding the process of selecting long-term investments (that is, capital budgeting). Suppose the financial manager is faced with the following investments and must choose among them:

A: Generates a cash inflow of $275 a year for five years.

B: Generates $1,600 at the end of the fifth year.

C: Generates $300 a year for two years and $250 for three years.

Although each investment has a life of five years, the timing of the cash inflows generated by each investment differs. How will the financial manager compare the three investments in order to choose among them?

The time value of money facilitates the necessary comparison. If the financial manager computes the present value of each cash inflow, the investments may be compared. If, for example, the cost of funds is 10 percent annually, the present value of each investment is

A: $\$275(3.791) = \$1{,}042.53.$

B: $\$1{,}600(0.621) = \$993.50.$

C: $\$300(0.909) + 300(.826) + 250(0.751) + 250(0.683) + 250(0.621)$
$= \$1{,}034.25$

Having determined the present value of each cash inflow, the financial manager now knows that Investment A has the highest present value and should be preferred.[2]

Time value also has numerous applications for individuals. Suppose you purchase a home for $100,000, making a down payment of 20 percent ($20,000) and borrowing the balance ($80,000). The mortgage loan is for 25 years and the bank charges 8 percent. What is your annual payment required by this loan? (Mortgage payments are usually made monthly, but to keep this illustration simple, assume the payment is made at the end of each year.) This is a common application of the time value of money, and even if the lender makes the calculation, you can perform the following calculation to determine what the mortgage payment will be before asking for the loan.

This problem is harder than those previously used to illustrate the time value of money. In the previous examples used to illustrate the present value of an annuity, annual payment was given, and the example asked for the present value of the annuity. In this case, the present value of the annuity is given and the annual payment is the unknown. As with all time-value problems, identify the known variables. They are the amount borrowed in the present ($80,000), the rate of interest (8 percent), and the term of the loan (25 years). The unknown is the annual payment required to pay the interest and retire the loan. Since the payments will

[2] The same ranking could be made by comparing the future values of the cash flows at the end of the fifth year. Whether the financial manager should acquire any of these investments depends on the present value of the inflows and the current cost (or present outflow) of each investment.

be made at the end of each year, the mortgage is an illustration of an ordinary annuity. Since the loan is being made in the present, the problem requires the use of the present value interest table. That is

$$\$80{,}000 = PMT[PVAIF\ 8I{,}25N)]$$

$$\$80{,}000 = PMT(10.675)$$

$$PMT = \frac{\$80{,}000}{10.675} = \$7{,}494.15$$

CALCULATOR SOLUTION

Function Key		Data Input
PV	=	80,000
I	=	8
N	=	25
FV	=	0
PMT	=	?
Function Key		**Answer**
PMT	=	−7,494.30

(Notice the payments are outflows.)

Thus, the annual mortgage payment is $7,494.15.

Ask yourself, "Does this answer make sense?" If you make 25 payments of $7,494.15, the total amount paid is

$$\$7{,}494.15 \times 25 = \$187{,}353.75$$

That's a lot of money, but remember you are paying interest for 25 years and are retiring a loan of $80,000, so the answer is reasonable. It still may be wrong if you selected the wrong interest factor (for example, the present value of an annuity at 10 percent for 20 years).

If you had set up the problem incorrectly, the answer would make no sense. For example, suppose you thought the problem concerned the future value of an annuity since the payments are made in the future. While that is incorrect, it is easy to fall into that trap. However, when you divide $80,000 by the interest factor for the future value of an annuity (45.762), the answer is $1,748.18. This answer makes no sense, because after making 25 payments of $1,748.18, your total payments would be only $43,704.38, which obviously does not retire the $80,000 loan. You should always ask yourself upon completing the problem. "Does the answer make sense?" If it does, your reasoning should be correct even if your eyes selected the wrong interest factor, you made an arithmetic error, or, if you were using a financial calculator, you entered an incorrect number.

Now that we know your annual payment required to make the loan is $7,494.15, you can split the payment into the interest payment and the principal repayment. (This division may be important, since you may be able to deduct the interest payment on the mortgage for federal income taxation.) Since the interest rate is 8 percent and the initial amount of the loan is $80,000, the interest during the first year is $6,400. The balance of the payment ($1,094.15) reduces the amount owed to $78,905.85.

Since the amount owed is reduced, the interest paid during the second year declines to $6,312.47 (0.08 × $78,905.85). The annual payment remains $7,494.15, so the balance owed is reduced by $1,181.68 ($7,494.15 − 6,312.47). The balance owed after the second year is $77,724.17. This type of calculation is used to generate a repayment schedule, which is referred to as a *loan amortization schedule.*

Such a schedule is illustrated in Exhibit 7.3. The first column gives the number of the payment, and the second and third columns break the payment into the payments for interest and principal repayment. The last column gives the balance

EXHIBIT 7.3

Selections from a Loan Amortization Schedule for an $80,000 Mortgage at 8 Percent for 25 Years (Annual Payment = $7,494.15)

Number of Payment	Interest Payment	Principal Repayment	Balance of Loan
1	$6,400.00	$1,094.15	$78,905.85
2	6,312.47	1,181.68	77,724.17
—			
—			
12	4,942.78	2,551.52	59,233.29
13	4,738.66	2,755.64	56,477.65
—			
—			
24	1,069.15	6,425.16	6,939.17
25	555.13	6,939.17	.00

due on the loan. As may be seen from the table, as payments are made (1) the amount of the outstanding principal declines, (2) the amount of interest paid each month declines, and (3) the rate at which the principal is repaid increases. In the early years of a mortgage, most of the payment covers the interest charges, but during the later life of the mortgage, most of the payment retires the principal.

In the first application illustrated in this section, the financial manager used time value to compare three investments. In the second application, a potential home owner used the concept to determine the repayment of a mortgage loan. Many more applications are given in the problems at the end of this chapter. However, before leaving this section, let's consider two final applications. Suppose your 85-year-old Auntie Bea has to enter a nursing home that charges $2,000 a month ($24,000 a year). You have power of attorney and sell her home for $115,000. Excluding any other sources of income (such as social security payments) and any other expenses (for example, doctors), how long will her money last if you are able to earn 8 percent annually? This may strike you as a morbid situation, but it is a real problem facing many elderly individuals and their families. Actually your Auntie Bea is better off than many elderly. She had a house and was able to live in it until age 85.

Once again this problem is an illustration of an annuity. The known variables are (1) the amount of money Auntie Bea has in the present ($115,000), (2) the rate she will earn on the funds (8 percent), and (3) the amount of the annuity payment ($24,000). The unknown is the number of years that the funds will last. Since she has the money now, this is another illustration of the present value of an annuity. Auntie Bea's problem is set up as follows:

CALCULATOR SOLUTION

Function Key		*Data Input*
PV	=	115,000
I	=	8
FV	=	0
PMT	=	−24,000
N	=	?
Function Key		*Answer*
N	=	6.28

$$\$115{,}000 = \$24{,}000[PVAIF(8I,?N)]$$

$$PVAIF(8I,?N) = \frac{\$115{,}000}{\$24{,}000} = 4.792.$$

Looking up this factor in the table for the present value of an annuity at 8 percent derives an answer of six to seven years. Auntie Bea's assets will cover the nursing home until after she reaches the age of 91. Since life expectancy for a female age 85 is about 6.5 to 7.0 years, Auntie Bea is in relatively good shape financially. Of course, if she lives longer than her life expectancy, there may be a financial problem unless a greater rate of return can be earned on her funds or if she has other sources of income. There may also be a problem if she earns a return of less than 8 percent. For example, at 4 percent, her funds will be exhausted in slightly more than five years, which is less than her life expectancy.

For the last illustration, you have $1,000 to invest. Investment A will pay you $271.37 per year (a total of $1,628.22) for six years, while investment B will pay you $2,195 after six years. Which investment offers you the higher rate of interest (or rate of return)? You know the present amount ($1,000), the time (six years), and the future amount ($271.37 for investment A and $2,195 for investment B). The question is: What rate of interest will equate these future amounts with the present cost of the investment? For investment A, the equation is

$$\$1{,}000 = \$271.37\ [PVAIF(?I,6N)]$$

$$PVAIF = \$1{,}000/\$271.37 = 3.685.$$

CALCULATOR SOLUTION

Function Key		Data Input
PV	=	−1,000
FV	=	0
PMT	=	271.37
N	=	6
I	=	?
Function Key		Answer
I	=	16

Looking up this factor in the table for the present value of an annuity derives an answer of 16 percent. For investment B, the equation is

$$\$1{,}000 = \$2{,}195(PVIF(?I,6N)]$$

$$PVIF = \$1{,}000/\$2{,}195 = 0.456.$$

CALCULATOR SOLUTION

Function Key		Data Input
PV	=	−1,000
FV	=	2,195
PMT	=	0
N	=	6
I	=	?
Function Key		Answer
I	=	14

Looking up this factor in the table for the present value of a dollar derives an answer of 14 percent. Investment A offers the higher rate of return. (However, you cannot conclude that it is to be preferred, because that decision will also depend upon the risk associated with each investment.)

NONANNUAL COMPOUNDING

You should have noticed that in all the previous examples, compounding occurred only once a year. Compounding can and often does occur more frequently, such as twice a year (or semiannually). **Nonannual compounding** requires that the equations presented earlier be adjusted. This section extends the discussion of the compound value of a dollar to include compounding for periods other than a year.

NONANNUAL COMPOUNDING
Payment of interest more frequently than once a year

This explanation, however, is limited to the future value of a dollar. Similar adjustments must be made in the future value of an annuity, the present value of a dollar, or the present value of an annuity when the funds are compounded more frequently than annually.

Converting annual compounding to other time periods necessitates two adjustments in Equation 7.1. First, a year is divided into the same number of time periods as the funds that are being compounded. For semiannual compounding, a year consists of two time periods, whereas for quarterly compounding the year comprises four time periods.

After adjusting for the number of time periods, the individual adjusts the interest rate to find the rate per time period. This is done by dividing the stated interest rate by the number of time periods per year. If the interest rate is 8 percent compounded semiannually, 8 percent is divided by 2, giving an interest rate of 4 percent earned in *each* time period. If the annual rate of interest is 8 percent compounded quarterly, the interest rate is 2 percent (0.08 ÷ 4) in each of the four time periods.

These adjustments may be expressed in more formal terms by modifying Equation 7.1 as follows:

7.8
$$P_0\left(1 + \frac{i}{c}\right)^{n \times c} = P_n.$$

The only new symbol is c, which represents the frequency of compounding. The interest rate (i) is divided by the frequency of compounding (c) to determine the interest rate in each period. The number of years (n) is multiplied by the frequency of compounding to determine the number of time periods.

The application of this equation may be illustrated by a simple example. An individual invests \$100 in an asset that pays 8 percent compounded quarterly. What will the future value of this asset be after five years? In other words, \$100 will grow to what amount after five years if it is compounded quarterly at 8 percent? Algebraically, that is

CALCULATOR SOLUTION

Function Key		Data Input
PV	=	−100
I	=	8/4 = 2
N	=	5 × 4 = 20
PMT	=	0
FV	=	?
Function Key		*Answer*
N	=	148.59

$$P_5 = P_0\left(1 + \frac{i}{c}\right)^{n \times c}$$

$$= \$100\left(1 + \frac{0.08}{4}\right)^{5 \times 4}$$

$$= \$100(1 + 0.02)^{20}.$$

In this formulation the investor is earning 2 percent for 20 time periods. To solve this equation, the interest factor for the compound value of a dollar at 2 percent for 20 periods (1.486) is multiplied by \$100. Thus, the future value is

$$P_5 = \$100(1.486) = \$148.60.$$

The difference between compounding annually and compounding more frequently can be seen by comparing this problem with a problem in which the values are identical except that the interest is compounded annually. The question then is: \$100 will grow to what amount after five years at 8 percent compounded annually? The answer is

$$P_5 = \$100(1 + 0.08)^5$$

$$= \$100(1.469)$$

$$= \$146.90.$$

This sum, $146.90, is less than the amount that was earned when the funds were compounded quarterly. We may conclude that the more frequently interest is compounded, the greater will be the future amount.

PERIODS OF LESS THAN ONE YEAR

All the previous illustrations and problems had time periods of a year or more. There are, however, many situations in finance that occur in time periods of less than a year. For example, a wholesaler may lend to a retailer for a period of 30 days, or a cash manager may acquire a three-month short-term security. The retailer may need to know the annual cost of the credit and the cash manager may want to determine the annual rate of return being earned on the security. These are but two illustrations that involve the time value of money for less than a year.

As with nonannual compounding, the basic time value of money equations may be applied to solve these problems. Suppose the cash manager invests $98,543 that will return $100,000 at the end of 45 days. What is the annual rate of return? The future value of a dollar Equation 7.1 may be used to solve the problem as follows:

$$P_0(1 + i)^n = P_n.$$

P_0 is the initial amount ($98,543) and P_n is the terminal amount ($100,000) received after the 45-day time period (n = 45 days or 45/365 = 0.1233 of a year). Thus the equation is

$$\$98{,}543(1 + i)^{0.1233} = \$100{,}000.$$

To isolate the unknown, divide $100,000 by $98,543 and raise both sides of the equation by reciprocal of 0.1233 (1/0.1233 = 8.1103):

$$[(1 + i)^{0.1233}]^{8.1103} = [\$100{,}000/\$98.543]^{8.1103}$$

$$(1 + i) = 1.014785^{8.1103} = 1.12641,$$

and subtract 1:

$$i = 1.12641 - 1 = 12.641\%.$$

CALCULATOR SOLUTION

Function Key		Data Input
PV	=	−98,543
N	=	0.1233
PMT	=	0
FV	=	100,000
I	=	?
Function Key		*Answer*
I	=	12.64

The annualized rate of interest to the borrower (the rate of return to the lender) is 12.641 percent.[3]

Many situations in short-term financial decision making involve this type of calculation. A financial manager or corporate treasurer may borrow short-term funds, receiving an amount such as $98,543 and agreeing to repay $100,000 after

[3] This is a compound rate of interest that assumes that the cash manager is able to invest $98,543 and have it grow to $100,000 every 45 days.

a specified period of time. Such discounted loans are common, especially for short periods of time less than a year). The determination of the annualized percentage cost of the loans to the borrowers (or the yields to the lenders) is essentially the same as any time-value problem, only the period is less than a year instead of greater than a year.

COMPUTER SOLUTIONS: THE *INVESTMENT ANALYSIS CALCULATOR*

Previously, time value of money problems were solved in the body of the text using interest tables and in the margin using a financial calculator. These problems may also be solved using computer programs. (For example, performing time value calculations is part of Microsoft's Excel® package.) In this section, the use of the *Investment Analysis Calculator* to solve time value problems is illustrated. *Investment Analysis Calculator* is a set of programs designed for Herbert B. Mayo, *Investments: An Introduction*, sixth edition, (The Dryden Press, 2000). The software may also be used to solve many of the problems in this introductory text. The software may be accessed through the Web page for this text: **www.harcourtcollege.com/finance/mayo**.

To run the software, go to "starthere," which takes you to the title screen: Investment Analysis Calculator. Clicking on this screen brings up the main menu, which gives the following table of contents:

Financial Calculator
Statistical Calculator
Portfolio Standard Deviation
Common Stock Valuation
Capital Asset Pricing Model
Rate of Return (Dollar-Weighted)
Rate of Return (Time-Weighted)
Financial Statement Analysis
Bond Valuation and Duration
Yields
Convertible Bond Calculations
Option Valuation
Portfolio Evaluation

The section titled "Financial Calculator" can be used to solve the time value problems illustrated in this chapter.

Several of the sections of the software have subsections (or submenus). A listing of the table of contents and the submenus is provided in Exhibit 7.4. Many of the topics in this software can be used to solve financial problems that are illustrated in the remainder of this text. Where appropriate, the text refers you to the

Contents and Submenus of the Investment Analysis Calculator

EXHIBIT 7.4

Contents

- Financial Calculator
  - Basic Future Value
  - Basic Present Value
  - Future Value of an Ordinary Annuity
  - Future Value of an Annuity Due
  - Future Value of a Lump Sum and an Ordinary Annuity
  - Present Value of an Ordinary Annuity
  - Present Value of an Annuity Due
  - Ordinary Annuity Payment to Accumulate a Future Value
  - Annuity Due Payment to Accumulate a Future Value
  - Payments from a Present Value
  - Growth Rate
  - Number of Periods
    - Number of Periods, Given PV, FV, and an Interest Rate
    - Number of Periods, Given PV, Ordinary Annuity PMT, and an Interest Rate
    - Number of Periods, Given FV, Ordinary Annuity PMT, and an Interest Rate
  - Future Value—Unequal Payments
  - Present Value—Unequal Payments
  - Mortgage Balance
  - Present and Future Value Graphs
    - Basic Present Value Graph
    - Basic Future Value Graph
    - Present Value of Ordinary Annuity Graph
    - Future Value of Ordinary Annuity Graph
- Statistical Calculator
  - Expected Value and Descriptive Statistics for a Probability Distribution
  - Arithmetic Mean, Geometric Mean, and Descriptive Statistics for a Historic Series
  - Simple Linear Regression
- Portfolio Standard Deviation
- Common Stock Valuation
  - Valuation of a Zero or Constant Growth Stock
  - Valuation of a Supernormal Growth Stock
- Capital Asset Pricing Model
  - Beta Calculation
  - Required Rate of Return Calculation (Security Market Line)
  - Common Stock Valuation
    - Valuation of a Zero or Constant Growth Stock
    - Valuation of a Supernormal Growth Stock
  - Required Rate of Return Calculation and Common Stock Valuation in Sequence
- Rate of Return (Dollar-Weighted)
  - Holding Period Return
  - Rate of Return, Given a PV and a FV
  - Rate of Return, Given PV and a Series of Ordinary Annuity Payments
  - Rate of Return, Given PV and a Series of Unequal Payments at End of Equal Time Periods
  - Portfolio Weighted Average Return and Average Beta
- Rate of Return (Time-Weighted)
- Financial Statement Analysis
- Bond Valuation and Duration
- Yields
  - Current Yield and Yield to Maturity
  - Taxable Equivalent Yield
- Convertible Bond Calculations
  - Given Conversion Price
  - Given Conversion Ratio
- Option Valuation
  - Calculate Option Value
  - Implied Variability of Underlying Stock
- Portfolio Evaluation

specific section in the *Investment Analysis Calculator*, so it may be beneficial to spend time now to become comfortable using the software. The software also permits you to print answers and to export the results to another document. To print, use the print command. To export, highlight what you wish to copy as you would in a Word® document and paste it into your Excel® or Word® document.

Let's demonstrate how you can use the *Investment Analysis Calculator* to solve time value problems illustrated in this chapter. In the chapter's first section (the future value of a dollar), interest tables and a financial calculator are used to illustrate how $100 grows into $466.10 after 20 years at 8 percent. How much $100 will grow to after 20 years at 8 percent may also be determined by using the *Investment Analysis Calculator.* Since this is a future value problem, click on Financial Calculator to obtain the submenus. Now click on Basic Future Value. You will be asked for the nominal rate, periods per year, number of years, and the present value. Enter the nominal rate (8 percent), periods per year (1), number of years (20), and the present value ($100). (You may use your mouse or the tab key to move from space to space.) Once you have entered the data, press enter and the answer ($466.10) appears. You can readily determine the impact of a change in the interest rate from 8 percent to 10 percent by substituting 10 for 8 percent and clicking on enter. The new future value ($672.75) appears.

For a second illustration, consider the third problem in the section entitled "Illustrations of Compounding and Discounting." In that problem you bought a stock for $10, sold it after 10 years for $23.67 and are asked to determine the annual return on the investment. To solve this problem using the *Investment Analysis Calculator,* you could go either to the submenu on computing a "Growth Rate" under Financial Calculator or to the submenu for on computing "Rate of Return, Given a *PV* and a *FV*" under the section of Rates of Return (Dollar-Weighted). If you use the Growth Rate program, you are asked to enter present value, periods per year, number of years, and future value. Enter the cost of the investment as the present value ($10), the number of periods in a year (1), the sale price as a future value ($23.67), and the number of years (10). The answer (10.0 percent) appears in the answer space. If you had sold the stock for $32 and entered that number in the appropriate space, the answer is immediately recalculated (12.33 percent).

Let's do two more problems, which illustrate the versatility of the *Investment Analysis Calculator.* Consider the loan amortization schedule in Exhibit 7.3 for a $80,000 loan at 8 percent for 25 years. To get the annual payment, go to the submenu "Mortgage Balance." Enter the interest rate (8 percent), the number of periods per year (1), the number of years (25), the amount of the loan ($80,000), and the pay period for which you want to determine the balance owed (e.g., the amount owed at the end of year 1). The software provides the answers to the amount of each payment ($7,494.30) and the balanced owed at the end of the period ($78,905.70).

You may quickly determine the impact of accepting a shorter mortgage (e.g., 20 years instead of 25 years) or having to pay a higher rate of interest (10 percent instead of 8 percent.) You may also determine the required *monthly* payments for an 8-percent, 25-year mortgage. Enter 12 periods per year instead of 1, and the monthly payment for a $80,000 mortgage at 8 percent for 25 years is $617.45. (Determining monthly payments is virtually impossible using interest tables since they are constructed with numbers such as 8, 9 or 10 percent per period and not 0.75 or 1.2 percent, which would be necessary to determine monthly payments.)

Let's consider one final problem, Investment C in the section on Applications of the Time Value of Money. In this problem, the investment generates cash flow of $300 a year for two years and $250 for the next three years. Since the annual cash flows differ, you cannot use the interest factor for the present value of an annuity to determine the present value. Each individual cash flow must be discounted at 10 percent, a tedious process. If a financial calculator is used, the process is easier but requires the calculator to accept uneven cash inflows.

The calculation of the present value for an investment with uneven cash inflows is easily performed with the *Investment Analysis Calculator.* Go to the submenu "Present Value – Unequal Payments." Enter the number of periods per years (1), the number of years (5), and then enter each of the individual cash flows ($300 for the years 1 and 2 and $250 for years 3, 4, and 5) and the nominal rate (10 percent). This cost of funds will be referred to as the firm's cost of capital in Chapter 16. Almost instantaneously, the present value of the cash flows is determined to be $1,034.47 if the payments are received at the end of each pay period and $1,137.92 if the payments are received at the beginning of each period.

SUMMARY

Money has time value. A dollar to be received in the future is worth less than a dollar received today. People will forgo current consumption only if future growth in their funds is possible. Such appreciation is called compounding. The longer the funds compound and the higher the rate at which they compound, the greater will be the amount of funds in the future.

The opposite of compounding is discounting, which determines the present value of funds that are to be received in the future. The present value of a future sum depends both on how far in the future the funds are to be received and on the discount rate.

Compounding and discounting are applied both to single payments and to series of payments. If the payments in a series are equal and made annually, the series is called an annuity.

The ability to compare future dollars with present dollars is crucial to financial decision making. Many financial decisions involve the current outlay of funds, for investments are made in the present. The returns on these investments occur in the future. The concepts presented in this chapter are basic to an understanding of the valuation of securities, the cost of a loan, and capital budgeting.

REVIEW QUESTIONS

1. What is the difference between a lump-sum payment and an annuity? Are all series of payments annuities?

2. What is the difference between compounding (the determination of future value) and discounting (the determination of present value)?

3. For a given interest rate, what happens to the numerical value of the interest factor as time increases for the
a. future value of a dollar;
b. future value of an annuity;
c. present value of a dollar;
d. present value of an annuity?

4. For a given time period, what happens to the numerical value of the interest factor as the interest rate increases for the
a. future value of a dollar;
b. future value of an annuity;
c. present value of a dollar;
d. present value of an annuity?

5. What does the phrase "discounting the future at a high rate" imply?

6. As is explained in subsequent chapters, increases in interest rates cause the value of assets to decline. Why would you expect this relationship?

PROBLEMS

1. A saver places $1,000 in a certificate of deposit that matures after ten years and pays 5 percent interest, which is compounded annually until the certificate matures.
   a. How much interest will the saver earn if the interest is left to accumulate?
   b. How much interest will the saver earn if the interest is withdrawn each year?
   c. Why are the answers to *a* and *b* different?
2. At 7 percent compounded annually, how many years are necessary for
   a. $200 to grow to $245?
   b. $2,500 to grow to $4,295?
   c. $10,000 to grow to $19,670?
3. A self-employed person deposits $3,000 annually in a retirement account that earns 8 percent.
   a. How much will be in the account when the individual retires at the age of 65 if the savings program starts when the person is age 40?
   b. How much additional money will be in the account if the saver defers retirement until age 70?
   c. How much additional money will be in the account if the saver discontinues the contributions but does not retire until age 70?
4. A 45-year-old woman decides to put funds into a retirement plan. She can save $2,000 a year and earn 9 percent on this savings. How much will she have accumulated if she retires at age 65? At retirement how much can she withdraw each year for 20 years from the accumulated savings if the savings continue to earn 9 percent?

   (Problems 3 and 4 illustrate the basic elements of pension plans. A sum of money is systematically set aside. It earns interest so that by retirement a considerable amount has been accumulated. Then the retired person draws on the fund until it is exhausted, or until death occurs, in which case the remainder of the fund becomes part of the estate. Of course, while the retired person draws on the fund, the remaining principal continues to earn interest.)
5. You annually invest $1,500 in an individual retirement account (IRA) starting at the age of 20 and make the contributions for 10 years. Your twin sister does the same starting at age 30 and makes the contributions for 30 years. Both of you earn 7 percent annually on your investment. Who has the larger amount at age 60?
6. If a father wants to have $100,000 to send a newborn child to college, how much must he invest annually for 18 years if he earns 9 percent on his funds? (Any current student who subsequently becomes a parent and wants to send a child to college should make this calculation early in the child's life.)

7. A widow currently has a $93,000 investment yielding 9 percent annually. Can she withdraw $16,000 a year for the next 10 years?

8. An investment generates $10,000 per year for 25 years. If an investor can earn 10 percent on other investments, what is the current value of this investment? If its current price is $120,000, should the investor buy it?

9. A company has two investment possibilities, with the following inflows of cash:

	Year 1	Year 2	Year 3
A	$1,400	$1,700	$1,800
B	1,500	1,500	1,500

If the firm can earn 7 percent in other investments, what is the present value of investments A and B? If each investment costs $4,000, is the present value of each investment greater than the cost of the investment? (This question is a very simple example of one method of capital budgeting [Chapter 17]. This technique permits the firm to rank alternative investments and help select the potentially most profitable investment.)

10. *a.* If a person currently earns $10,000 and inflation continues at 4 percent for ten years, how much must the person make to maintain purchasing power?
b. If a person bought a $50,000 home in 1970 and sold it in 2000, what would be the value of the house if the annual rate of price appreciation were 5 percent during the 30 years?

11. You purchase a stock for $20 and expect its price to grow annually at a rate of 8 percent.
a. What price are you expecting after five years?
b. If the rate of increase in the price doubled from 8 percent to 16 percent, would that double the *increase* in the price? Why?

12. You are 25 years old and inherit $65,000 from your grandmother. If you wish to purchase a $100,000 yacht to celebrate your 30th birthday, what compound annual rate of return must you earn?

13. An investment offers to pay you $10,000 a year for five years. If it costs $33,520, what will be your rate of return on the investment?

14. An investment costs $61,446 and offers a return of 10 percent annually for ten years. What are the annual cash inflows anticipated from this investment?

15. You are offered $900 after five years or $150 a year for five years. If you can earn 6 percent on your funds, which offer will you accept? If you can earn 14 percent on your funds, which offer will you accept? Why are your answers different?

16. You purchase a townhouse for $85,000. After a down payment of $18,000, you obtain a mortgage loan at 9 percent that requires annual payments for 15 years.
a. What are the annual payments?
b. How much of the first payment goes to pay the interest?
c. What is the remaining mortgage balance after the first payment is made?

17. You are offered an annuity that will pay $10,000 a year for ten years (that is, ten payments) starting after five years have elapsed. If you seek an annual return of 8 percent, what is the maximum amount you should pay for this annuity?

18. You want your salary to double in six years. At what annual rate of growth must your salary increase to achieve your goal?

19. Each year you invest $2,000 in an account that earns 10 percent annually. How long will it take for you to accumulate $50,000?

20. Auntie Bea sells her house for $100,000, which is then invested to earn 7 percent annually. If her life expectancy is ten years, what is the maximum amount she can annually spend on a nursing home, doctors, and taxes?

21. You win a judgment in an auto accident for $100,000. You immediately receive $25,000 but must pay your lawyer's fee of $15,000. In addition, you will receive $2,500 a year for 20 years for a total of $50,000, after which the balance owed ($25,000) will be paid. If the interest rate is 7 percent, what is the current value of your settlement?

22. A firm must choose between two investment alternatives each costing $100,000. The first alternative generates $35,000 a year for four years. The second pays one large lump sum of $157,400 at the end of the fourth year. If the firm can raise the required funds to make the investment at an annual cost of 10 percent, which alternative should be preferred?

23. You wish to retire in 12 years and currently have $50,000 in a savings account yielding 5 percent annually and $100,000 in quality "blue chip" stocks yielding 10 percent. If you expect to add $10,000 at the end of each year and $20,000 to your stock portfolios, how much will you have in your retirement fund when you retire? What rate of return must you earn on your retirement funds if you want to withdraw $102,000 per year for the next 15 years?

24. Uncle Fred recently died and left $325,000 to his 50-year-old favorite niece. She immediately spent $100,000 on a town home but decided to invest the balance for her retirement at age 65. What rate of return must she earn on her investment over the next 15 years to permit her to withdraw $75,000 at the end of each year through age 80 if her funds earn 10 percent annually during retirement?

25. A savings and loan association finances your 25-year, $100,000, 9-percent mortgage. How much interest does the S&L collect on the loan in the second year?

26. You purchase a stock for $10,000 and collect $400 at the end of each year in dividends. You sell the stock for $11,300 after four years. What was the annual return on your $10,000 investment?

27. A $1,000,000 state lottery prize is spread evenly over 10 years ($100,000 a year), or you may take a lump distribution of $654,000. If you can earn 7 percent, which alternative is better?

28. You purchase a building for $900,000, collect annual rent (after expenses) of $120,000 and sell the building for $1,000,000 after three years. What is the annual return on this investment?

29. You buy a stock for $1000 and expect to sell it for $900 after four years but also expect to collect dividends of $120 a year. Prove that the return on this investment is less than 10 percent.

30. You contribute $1,000 annually to a retirement account and stop making payments after 8 years at the age of 25. Your twin brother (or sister . . . which ever applies) also opens an account and contributes $1,000 a year until retirement at age 65 (40 years). You both earn 10 percent on your investments. How much can each of you withdraw for 20 years (that is, ages 66 through 85) from the retirement accounts?

CASE

Funding a Pension Plan

Erin MacDowell was recently employed in the benefits division of a moderate size engineering firm. The firm has adopted a pension plan in which it promises to pay a maximum of 75 percent of an individual's last year salary if the employee has worked for the firm for 25 years. The amount of the pension is to be reduced by 3 percent for every year less than 25, so that an individual who has been employed for 15 years will receive a pension of 45 percent of the last year's salary [75 percent − 10(3 percent)]. Pension payments will start at age 65, provided the individual retired. There is no provision for early retirement. Continuing to work after age 65 may increase the individual's pension if he or she has worked for less than 25 years or if his or her salary were to increase.

One of the first tasks given Ms. MacDowell is to estimate the amount that the firm must set aside today to fund pensions. Although management plans to hire actuaries to make the final determination, the managers believe the exercise may highlight some problems that they will want to be able to discuss with the actuaries. Ms. MacDowell was instructed to select two representative employees and estimate their annual pensions as well as the annual contributions necessary to fund the pensions.

Ms. MacDowell decided to select Arnold Berg and Vanessa Barber. Berg is 58 years old, has been with the firm for 27 years, and is earning $34,000. Ms. Barber is 47, has been with the firm for three years, and earns $42,000 annually. Ms. MacDowell believes that Berg will be with the firm until he retires: he is a competent worker whose salary will not increase by more than 4 percent annually, and it is anticipated he will retire at age 65. Ms. Barber is considerably different. She is considered a rising star, and Ms. MacDowell expects her salary to rise at least 7 percent annually in order to retain her until retirement at age 65.

To determine the amount that must be invested annually to fund the pension, Ms. MacDowell needs (in addition to an estimate of the amount of the pension) an estimate of how long the pension will be distributed (that is, life expectancy) and how much the invested funds will earn. Since the firm must pay an interest rate of 8 percent to borrow money, she decides that the invested funds should be able to earn at least that amount.

Case Problems

1. If each individual retires at age 65, how much will be their estimated pensions if life expectancy is 15 years?
2. If the firm buys an annuity from an insurance company to fund each pension and the insurance company is able to earn 9 percent on the funds invested in the annuity, what is the amount required to purchase the annuity contracts?
3. If the firm can earn 8 percent on the money it must set aside each year to fund the pension, how much will the firm have to invest annually to have the money necessary to purchase the annuities?
4. What would be the impact of each of the following on the amount that the firm must invest annually to fund the pension?
   a. Life expectancy is increased to 20 years.
   b. The rate of interest on the annuity contract with the insurance company is reduced to 7 percent.
   c. Ms. Barber retires at age 62 instead of 65.

APPENDIX to Chapter 7

ORDINARY ANNUITIES AND ANNUITIES DUE

Annuity payments may be made at the beginning or at the end of the year. If the payments are made at the end of the year, such annuities are called ordinary annuities. These annuities should be differentiated from annuities due, in which the payments are made at the beginning of the year. This difference in the timing of payments may be seen in the following time lines for an annuity of $100 for three years.

Time Payments:	1/1/x1	12/31/x1	1/1/x2	12/31/x2	1/1/x3	12/31/x3
Ordinary Annuity	—	$100	—	$100	—	$100
Annuity Due	$100	—	$100	—	$100	—

In each annuity, three $100 payments are made; however, in the ordinary annuity, the payments occur at the end of the year while the annuity due payments occur at the beginning of the year.

The Future Value of an Annuity Due

The impact of the difference in the timing of payments (deposits) was illustrated in Exhibit 7.1. In both cases $100 is deposited for three years in a savings account that pays 5 percent annually. The top half of the exhibit illustrated the annuity due, while the bottom half illustrated the ordinary annuity. In both cases, three years elapse from the present to the time when the final amount is determined, and in each case three payments are made. The difference in the timing of the payments results in a difference in the interest earned. Since payments for an annuity due are made at the beginning of each year, the annuity earns more interest ($31.01 versus $15.25) and thus has the higher terminal value ($331.01 versus $315.25).

The equations for the determination of the future values of an ordinary annuity and an annuity due were given in the body of the chapter. When applied to the previous example in which i = 5 percent = 0.05, n = 3 years, and PMT = $100, the accumulated sum for the future value of the ordinary annuity was

$$\$100(1 + 0.05)^0 + \$100(1 + 0.05)^1 + \$100(1 + 0.05)^2 =$$

$$\$100 + \$105 + \$110.25 = \$315.25.$$

The accumulated sum for the future value of the annuity due was

$$\$100(1 + 0.05)^1 + \$100(1 + 0.05)^2 + \$100(1 + 0.05)^3 =$$

$$\$105 + \$110.25 + \$115.76 = \$331.01.$$

Although it is possible to calculate the future sum of an ordinary annuity or an annuity due by performing each calculation and summing them, that technique is obviously tedious. This chapter used an interest table presented in Appendix C to calculate the future sum for an ordinary annuity. The interest factors may be converted into the interest factors for an annuity due. When the $100 was deposited annually in the savings account for three years at 5 percent, the interest factor for the ordinary annuity was 3.152. This interest factor may be converted for an annuity due at 5 percent for three years by multiplying 3.152 by 1 + 0.05. That is,

$$3.152(1 + 0.05) = 3.3096.$$

When this interest factor is applied to the example of $100 deposited in the bank at 5 percent for three years with the deposits starting immediately, the resulting terminal value is

$$\$100(3.3096) = \$330.96.$$

This is the same answer as derived by making each calculation individually and summing them. (Once again the small difference in the two answers is the result of rounding off.)

The difference between the terminal value of the two kinds of annuity payments can be substantial as the number of years increases or the interest rate rises. Consider an individual retirement account (IRA) in which the saver places $2,000 annually for 20 years. If the deposits are made at the end of the year (an ordinary annuity) and the rate of interest is 7 percent, the terminal amount will be

$$\$2{,}000(40.995) = \$81{,}990.$$

However, if the deposits had been made at the beginning of each year (an annuity due), the terminal amount would be

$$\$2{,}000(40.995)(1 + 0.07) = \$87{,}729.30.$$

The difference is $5,739.30! Almost $6,000 in additional interest is earned if the deposits are made at the beginning, not at the end, of each year.

The difference between the ordinary annuity and the annuity due becomes even more dramatic if the interest rate rises. Suppose the above IRA offered 12 percent instead of 7 percent. If the deposits are made at the end of each year, the terminal value is

$$\$2{,}000(72.052) = \$144{,}104.$$

If the deposits are made at the beginning of the year, the terminal value will be

$$\$2{,}000(72.052)(1 + 0.12) = \$161{,}396.48.$$

The difference is now $17,292.48.

The Present Value of an Annuity Due

The present value of an annuity, like the future value of an annuity, is affected by the timing of the payments. Many payments in finance are received at the end of the time period and are ordinary annuities. There are, however, payments that may occur at the beginning of the time period, such as the distributions from a pension plan: these would be examples of annuities due.

The difference in the flow of payments and the determination of the present values of an ordinary annuity and an annuity due are illustrated in Exhibit 7A.1. In each case the annuity is for $2,000 a year for three years and the interest rate is 10 percent. In the top half of the exhibit, the payments are made at the end of the year (an ordinary annuity). In the bottom half of the exhibit, the payments are

EXHIBIT 7.A.1

Flow of Payments and Determination of the Present Value of an Ordinary Annuity and an Annuity Due at 10 Percent for Three Years

Ordinary Annuity

1/1/x0	1/1/x1	1/1/x2	1/1/x3
$1.818 ←	(0.909) 2.000		
1.652 ←		(0.826) 2.000	
1.502 ←			(0.751) 2.000
$4.972			

Annuity Due

1/1/x0	1/1/x1	1/1/x2	1/1/x3
$2.000			
1.818 ←	(0.909) 2.000		
1.652 ←		(0.826) 2.000	
$5.470			

made at the beginning of the year (an annuity due). As may be seen by the totals, the present value of the annuity due is higher (\$5,470 versus \$4,972). This is because the payments are received sooner and, hence, are more valuable. As may also be seen in the illustration, since the first payment of the annuity due is made immediately, its present value is the actual amount received. Because the first payment of the ordinary annuity is made at the end of the first year, that amount is discounted, and, hence, its present value is less than the actual amount received.

The interest tables for the present value of an annuity presented in this text (and in other finance and investment texts) apply to ordinary annuities. These interest factors may be converted into annuity due factors by multiplying them by $(1 + i)$. Thus the interest factor for the present value of an ordinary annuity for \$1 at 10 percent for three years (2.487) may be converted into the interest factor for an annuity due of \$1 at 10 percent for three years as follows:

$$2.487(1 + i) = 2.487(1 + 0.1) = 2.736.$$

When this interest factor is used to determine the present value of an annuity due of \$2,000 for three years at 10 percent, the present value is

$$\$2{,}000(2.736) = \$5.472.$$

The present value of an ordinary annuity of \$2,000 at 10 percent for three years is

$$\$2{,}000(2.487) = \$4{,}974.$$

These are essentially the same answers given in Exhibit 7A.1 with the small differences being the result of rounding.

PROBLEMS

1. Bob places \$2,000 in his retirement account at the end of each year, while Betty places \$2,000 in her account at the beginning of each year. If they both earn 8 percent annually on their funds and make contributions for 20 years, how much will each have in his or her account?
2. Investment A offers to pay you \$1,000 a year for ten years with the payments occurring at the end of each year. Investment B pays \$925 a year for ten years, but the payments commence at the beginning of each year. If you can earn 10 percent on your funds, which investment should be preferred?
3. A parent decides to put aside \$1,000 annually toward a child's education. If the investment is made for ten years and earns 9 percent annually, what is the difference in the final amount if the contribution is made at the beginning of the year instead of at the end of the year?
4. A firm is facing two possible financing alternatives. The first requires the payment of \$1,000 a year at the end of the year for ten years. The second requires an annual payment of \$940 for ten years, but the payments must be made at the beginning of each year. Which alternative is preferred if the firm earns 5 percent on its funds? Would your answer be different if the firm could earn 10 percent? Explain.

CHAPTER 8
Risk and Its Measurement

Learning Objectives

1. Be able to compute the expected return and the required return on an investment.
2. Contrast the sources of risk.
3. Explain the impact that diversification has on the different sources of risk.
4. Explain what condition must be met for diversification to occur.
5. Differentiate the standard deviation and the beta coefficient as measures of risk.
6. Illustrate how beta coefficients affect the required return on an investment

In *War As I Knew It,* George Patton wrote, "Take calculated risks; that is quite different from being rash." Investors and financial managers should realize that because the future is uncertain, they too must take calculated risks. Purchasing the bonds of Trump Taj Mahal when the potential return exceeded 25 percent annually may have been rash because the firm subsequently declared bankruptcy. Purchasing the bonds of AT&T, however, which offered less than 8 percent annually—a yield almost double what was available in a savings account—may have been a calculated but prudent risk.

The reward for bearing risk is the anticipated return. Until the 1950s, investors and financial analysts dealt with risk and return on an intuitive basis; there were no theoretical models to indicate the interrelationships between risk and return. However, a theory of portfolio behavior and measures of risk and return developed because of the work of several financial analysts and economists.

This chapter gives a brief introduction to the sources and analysis of risk and its use in modern portfolio construction. Risk may be measured by a standard deviation, which measures the dispersion around a central tendency, such as an average return. Risk may also be measured by a beta coefficient, which is an index of the volatility of a security's return relative to the return on the market. Much of this chapter is devoted to these measures of risk and the reduction of risk through diversification. The chapter ends with a discussion of the use of beta coefficients in the capital asset pricing model to help determine the required return that is necessary to justify the purchase of a common stock.

THE RETURN ON AN INVESTMENT

RETURN
What is earned on an investment: the sum of income and capital gains generated by an investment

All investments are made in anticipation of a **return.** This applies not only to individuals but also to the financial managers of firms. An investment may offer a return from either of two sources. The first is the flow of income. A savings account yields the holder a flow of interest income. The second source of return is capital appreciation. If an investor buys stock and its price increases, the investor earns a capital gain. All investments offer the investor either potential income and/or capital appreciation. Some investments, like the savings account, offer only income. Other investments, such as an investment in land, may offer only capital appreciation. In fact, some investments may require expenditures (for example, property tax) on the part of the investor.

REQUIRED RETURN
Return necessary to induce an individual to make an investment

Investors and financial managers make investments because they anticipate a return. They will not know the actual return until the investment is sold and converted to cash. It is important to differentiate between *the expected return* and *the realized return*. The expected return is the incentive for accepting risk, and it must be compared with the **required return,** which is the return necessary to induce the investor to bear the risk. The required return includes (1) what the investor may earn on alternative investments, such as the risk-free return available on Treasury bills,[1] and (2) a premium for bearing risk that includes compensation for the expected inflation rate and for fluctuations in security prices. Specification of this required return, however, requires a measurement of risk. Thus, discussion of the required return will be deferred until after the discussion of the measures of risk.

Expected return depends on individual expected outcomes and the probability of their occurrence. For example, an investor may say, "Under normal economic conditions, which occur 60 percent of the time, I expect to earn a return of 10 percent on an investment in this stock. However, there is a 20 percent chance the economy will grow more rapidly and the company will do well, in which case I will earn 15 percent. Conversely, there is a 20 percent chance the economy will enter a recession and the company will do poorly, in which case I will earn only 5 percent." Given the possible outcomes and their probabilities, what is the return this investor can anticipate?

The answer to this question depends on the outcomes and the probability of their occurring (in other words, the probability of the economy growing more rapidly, growing at a normal rate, or entering into a recession). Since the investor believes these probabilities are 20 percent, 60 percent, and 20 percent, respectively, the expected return on the investment is

$$0.2 \times 15\% + 0.6 \times 10\% + 0.2 \times 5\% = 10\%.$$

Notice that the expected return is a weighted average of the individual expected outcomes and the probability of occurrence. If the individual expected outcomes had been different, the expected return would differ. For example, if the investor

[1] Treasury bills are discussed in Chapter 3 in the section on money market instruments.

had expected the returns to be 19 percent, 9 percent, and 2 percent, the expected return on the investment would be

$$0.2 \times 19\% + 0.6 \times 9\% + 0.2 \times 2\% = 9.6\%.$$

If the probabilities had been different, the expected return would also differ. If, in the first illustration, the probabilities had been 15 percent, 50 percent, and 35 percent, the expected return would be

$$0.15 \times 15\% + 0.5 \times 10\% + 0.35 \times 5\% = 9\%.$$

Thus, a change in either the expected returns of the individual outcomes or their probability of occurrence causes the expected return on the investment to change.

THE SOURCES OF RISK

Risk is the uncertainty that the realized return will not equal the expected return (that is, the expected return may not be achieved). If there were no uncertainty, there would be no risk. In the real world, there is uncertainty, which requires the financial manager or investor to analyze possible outcomes and assess the investment's risk. Of course, the realized outcome may be better than expected, but the emphasis in the analysis of risk is on the negative: the outcome will be worse than expected.

RISK
Possibility of loss; the uncertainty that the anticipated return will not be achieved

Since financial decisions are made in the present but the results occur in the future, risk permeates all financial decision making. The future is not certain; it is only expected. However, sources of risk can be identified. These are frequently classified into "diversifiable" risk and "nondiversifiable" risk or "unsystematic risk" and "systematic risk." (Both sets of terms are used to differentiate the sources of risk.) A **diversifiable risk** (or **unsystematic risk**) refers to the risk associated with the individual asset. Since the investor buys specific assets, such as the stock of IBM or the bonds of AT&T, that individual must bear the risk associated with each specific investment.

DIVERSIFIABLE RISK (UNSYSTEMATIC RISK)
Risk associated with individual events that affect a particular asset; firm-specific risk that is reduced through the construction of diversified portfolios

The sources of diversifiable risk are the business and financial risks associated with the individual firm. **Business risk** refers to the nature of the firm's operations, and **financial risk** refers to how the firm finances its assets (that is, whether the firm uses a substantial or modest amount of debt financing). For example, the business risk of US Air depends on such factors as the cost of fuel, the capacity of planes, and changes in demand. The financial risk associated with US Air depends on how it finances its planes. Were the assets acquired by leasing, by retaining earnings, or by issuing bonds, preferred stock, or common stock? The use of debt obligations and lease obligations increases financial risk while the use of equity financing reduces financial risk.

BUSINESS RISK
Risk associated with the nature of a business

FINANCIAL RISK
Risk associated with the types of financing used to acquired assets

Although business and financial risk differ (one is concerned with the nature of the firm's operations and the other with how management chooses to finance its operations), management uses financial leverage to affect the firm's total risk exposure. As is explained in Chapter 16 on the cost of capital, management may reduce the firm's cost of funds by using financial leverage. However, increased use of financial leverage increases risk and raises the cost of funds. The problem facing management is to determine what combination of debt and equity financing minimizes the cost of funds. That combination is the firm's optimal capital structure and uses debt financing without excessively increasing the firm's financial risk.

Business and financial risk are firm specific and are the source of unsystematic, diversifiable risk. As is illustrated later in this chapter, the construction of a diversified portfolio reduces diversifiable risk. This reduction occurs because the events that decrease the return on one asset may increase the return on another. Notice there is little relationship between the returns on the individual assets; hence the name "unsystematic risk."

The possible beneficial effect of combining different assets in a portfolio may be intuitively grasped by considering the purchase of the stocks of an airline and an oil driller (for example, US Air and Schlumberger). Higher oil prices may reduce the earnings of the airline but increase the profits of the drilling operation. Lower oil prices may have the opposite impact; thus, combining the stocks of these two firms will reduce the risk associated with the portfolio. Of course, the risk associated with each individual asset remains the same, but from the investor's perspective, the risk associated with the portfolio is what matters and not the risk associated with the individual asset.

Although the previous illustration applies to an individual's portfolio, the same concept applies to a firm. The financial managers of firms also bear the risk associated with specific assets. A firm invests in particular pieces of inventory, acquires specialized plant and equipment, and extends credit to specific buyers (that is, accounts receivable). Inventory may not sell, equipment may become obsolete, and debtors may default. The financial manager thus bears the unsystematic risk associated with each individual asset acquired by the firm in much the same way that the individual bears the unsystematic risk associated with individual stocks and bonds.

Because firms face unsystematic risk, the advantages associated with diversification may also apply. For example, Chesapeake Corporation stated in a quarterly report to stockholders that "our corporate strategy to move the company into more profitable and less volatile niche markets will be beneficial." Such a strategy reduces the unsystematic risk associated with the individual "niche" markets. Many mergers have been justified (perhaps rationalized) on the grounds that combining two firms with similar, but different, product lines will create a stronger firm with a better and more diversified assortment of goods and services for sale.

Even though a firm may seek a broader mix of products, diversification primarily remains the responsibility of investors. Firms cannot achieve as diversified a mix of assets that is possible in an individual's portfolio, which can include real estate, savings accounts, collectibles, and shares in mutual funds as well as the stocks and bonds issued by a variety of firms and governments.

NONDIVERSIFIABLE RISK (SYSTEMATIC RISK)
Risk associated with fluctuations in security prices and other non-firm-specific factors: market risk that is not reduced through the construction of diversified portfolios

Nondiversifiable (or **systematic risk**) refers to those sources that are not reduced through the construction of a diversified portfolio. These include fluctuations in security prices, changes in interest rates, reinvestment rates, inflation, and fluctuations in exchange rates.

Market risk is the risk associated with movements in security prices, especially stock prices. If an individual buys a stock and the market as a whole declines, the price of the specific stock will probably fall. Conversely, if the market increases, the price of the stock will probably also tend to increase.

MARKET RISK
Risk associated with fluctuations in security prices

Interest rate risk is the risk associated with fluctuations in interest rates. Suppose that a financial manager borrows funds under one set of terms only to have interest rates subsequently fall. If the financial manager had waited, the cost of these borrowed funds would have been lower. Movements in interest rates also affect security prices, especially the prices of fixed income securities, such as bonds and preferred stock. As explained in Chapter 9, there is an inverse relationship between changes in interest rates and security prices. Thus, a rise in interest rates will drive down security prices and inflict a loss on investors.

INTEREST RATE RISK
Risk associated with changes in interest rates

Reinvestment rate risk refers to the risk associated with reinvesting funds generated by an investment. If an individual receives interest or dividends, these funds could be spent on goods and services. For example, individuals who live on a pension consume a substantial portion, and perhaps all, of the income generated by their assets. Other investors, however, will reinvest their investment earnings in order to accumulate wealth.

REINVESTMENT RATE RISK
The risk associated with reinvesting earnings on principal at a lower rate than was initially earned

Consider an individual who wants to accumulate a sum of money and purchases a $1,000 bond that pays $100 a year and matures after ten years. The anticipated annual return based on the annual interest and the amount invested is 10 percent ($100/$1,000). The investor wants to reinvest the annual interest, and the question then becomes what rate will be earned on these reinvested funds: Will the return be more or less than the 10 percent initially earned? The essence of reinvestment rate risk is this: Will the investor earn more or less than the return anticipated when the investment was initially made?

Purchasing power risk is the risk associated with inflation. A conservative investor may deposit funds in a savings account that pays a modest rate of interest. If the rate of inflation exceeds the rate of interest, the investor sustains a loss.

PURCHASING POWER RISK
Uncertainty that future inflation will erode the purchasing power of assets and income

The rate of inflation has varied perceptibly. During the early 1980s, the annual rate of inflation rose to over 10 percent, and purchasing power risk became a major concern of financial managers and investors. These individuals were forced to take actions designed to reduce the impact of inflation. Variable interest rate bonds and variable rate mortgages are examples of two debt instruments that were developed in response to the risk associated with the loss of purchasing power. Subsequently, the rate of inflation declined and the impact of purchasing power risk diminished. However, inflation has not disappeared. The risk still exists and must be considered when making financial decisions.

Although the rate of inflation has declined, another source of risk has become more prominent: fluctuations in the value of the dollar relative to other currencies. This **exchange rate risk** is the risk associated with fluctuations in the prices of foreign moneys. Many firms make and receive payments in foreign countries, and Americans travel abroad, making payments in foreign currencies. In addition, many individuals and financial managers make foreign investments. Any foreign investment subjects the investor to risk from changes in the value of the foreign currency. The dollar value of a foreign currency can rise, thus increasing the

EXCHANGE RATE RISK
Risk of loss from changes in the value of foreign currencies

return when the funds are converted back to dollars. The value of the foreign currency can also fall, however, reducing the return on the investment when converted back to dollars.

These various sources of risk appear repeatedly throughout this text, since risk is an integral part of financial decision making. Neither the financial manager nor the investor can stop fluctuations in stock prices or interest rates. Nor can they stop inflation or fluctuations in exchange rates. They will, however, seek to earn a return that compensates them for bearing nondiversifiable risk.

The Standard Deviation as a Measure of Risk

STANDARD DEVIATION
Measure of dispersion around an average value; a measure of risk

BETA COEFFICIENT
Index of systematic risk; measure of the volatility of a stock's return relative to the market return

As was stated earlier, risk is concerned with the uncertainty that the realized return will not equal the expected return. One measure of risk, the **standard deviation,** emphasizes the extent to which the return differs from the average or expected return. An alternative measure of risk, a **beta coefficient,** is an index of the return on an asset relative to the return on a portfolio of assets (for example, the return on a stock relative to the return on the Standard and Poor's 500 stock index). This section considers the standard deviation as it is used to measure risk, while beta coefficients are explained later in the chapter.

The standard deviation measures the dispersion around an average value. As applied to investments, it considers an average return and the extent to which individual returns deviate from the average. If there is very little difference between the average return and the individual returns, the dispersion will be small. If there is a large difference between the average return and the individual returns, the dispersion will be large. The larger this dispersion, the greater the risk associated with the investment.

This measurement is perhaps best illustrated by a simple example. Consider the returns on two mutual funds over a period of nine years:

Return Year	Return Fund A	Return Fund B
1	13.5%	11%
2	14	11.5
3	14.25	12
4	14.5	12.5
5	15	15
6	15.5	17.5
7	15.75	18
8	16	18.5
9	16.5	19
average return	15.0%	15.0%

The average return over the nine years is the same for both mutual funds, 15 percent, but annual returns differ. Mutual fund A's individual returns were close to the average return. The worst year generated a 13.5 percent return while the best year generated a 16.5 percent return. None of the individual returns deviated from the average by more than 1.5 percent. Mutual fund B's individual returns differ from the average return, ranging from a low of 11 percent to a high of 19 percent. With the exception of year 5, all the returns deviate from the average by more than 1.5 percent.

Even though both mutual funds achieved the same average return, common sense suggests that B was riskier than A. The individual returns are more dispersed around the average return and this implies greater risk. The larger dispersion means there were periods with smaller returns (or larger losses, if applicable) from the investment. Of course, there were periods when the returns were greater, which would be expected if the risk were greater, but even so, the average return from B only matched the average return from A.

How may this dispersion be measured? One possible answer is the standard deviation. Since the standard deviation measures the tendency of the individual returns to cluster around the average return, it may be used as a measure of risk. The larger the dispersion, the greater the standard deviation and the larger the risk associated with the particular investment.

The standard deviation is calculated as follows:

1. Subtract the individual observations from the average return.
2. Square this difference.
3. Add these squared differences.
4. Divide this sum by the number of observations less 1.
5. Take the square root.

For stock A the standard deviation is determined as follows:

Average Return	Individual Return	Difference	Difference Squared
15	13.50	1.5	2.2500
15	14	1	1.0000
15	14.25	0.75	0.5625
15	14.50	0.5	0.25
15	15	0	0
15	15.50	−0.5	0.25
15	15.75	−0.75	0.5625
15	16	−1	1.000
15	16.50	−1.5	2.2500
		The sum of the squared differences:	8.1250

The sum of the squared differences divided by the number of observations less 1:

$$\frac{8.1250}{9-1} = 1.0156.$$

The square root: $\sqrt{1.0156} = 1.01.$

Thus, the standard deviation is 1.01.

The investor must then interpret this result. Plus and minus one standard deviation has been shown for normal distributions to encompass approximately 68 percent of all observations (in this case, that is 68 percent of the returns). The standard deviation for stock A is 1.01, which means that approximately two-thirds of the returns fall between 13.99 percent and 16.01 percent.[2] These returns are simply the average return (15 percent) plus 1.01 and minus 1.01 percent (that is, plus and minus the standard deviation).

For stock B the standard deviation is 3.30, which means that approximately 68 percent of the returns fall between 11.7 percent and 18.3 percent. Fund B's returns have a wider dispersion from the average return, and this fact is indicated by a greater standard deviation.

These differences in the standard deviations are illustrated in Figure 8.1, which plots the various returns on the horizontal axis and the frequency of their occurrence on the vertical axis. While the example used only nine years, Figure 8.1 is drawn as if there were a large number of observations. Most of fund A's returns are close to the average return, so the frequency distribution is narrower and taller. The frequency distribution for B's returns is lower and wider, which indicates the greater dispersion in that fund's returns (that is, the standard deviation for fund B is 3.30 versus 1.01 for A).

In the previous example, historical returns were used to illustrate the standard deviation as a measure of risk. The same concept may be used to measure the risk associated with expected returns. Consider stock A: An investor believes there is a 20 percent chance of a 15 percent return, a 60 percent chance of a 10 percent return, and a 20 percent chance of a 5 percent return. The expected average return is 10 percent. However, there is dispersion around that expected return, and once again this dispersion may be measured by the standard deviation. In this case, the standard deviation is 3.162, which is calculated as follows:

(1) Expected Average Return	(2) Expected Individual Return	(3) Difference (1) − (2)	(4) Difference Squared	(5) Probability of Occurrence	(6) Difference Squared Times the Probability (4) × (5)
10	15	−5	25	0.2	5.0
10	10	0	0	0.6	0.0
10	5	5	25	0.2	5.0
Sum of the weighted squared differences:					10.0
Square root of 10 (the standard deviation):			3.162		

[2] A square root is a positive (+) or negative (−) number. The square root of 9 is +3 and −3 because (3) (3) = 9 and (−3) (−3) = 9. However, in the calculation of the standard deviation, only positive numbers are used (that is, the sum of the squared differences), so the square root must be a positive number.

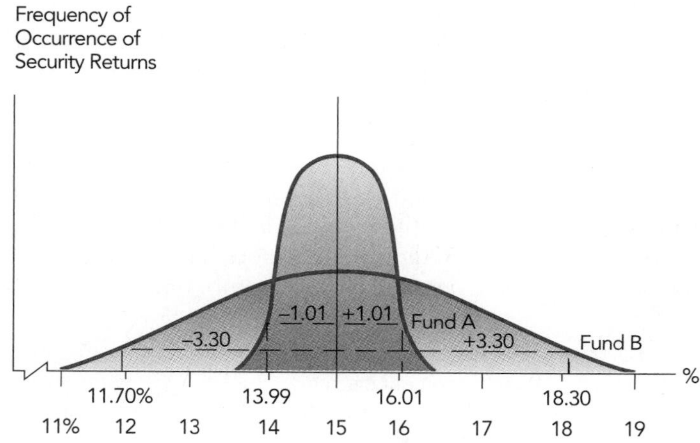

FIGURE 8.1

Distribution of the Returns of Two Mutual Funds

If the individual expected returns or the probabilities of occurrence were different, the standard deviation would be different. For example, if the individual expected returns for stock B were 20 percent, 10 percent, and 0 percent and the probabilities were the same, the expected return would be 10 percent (0.2(20%) + 0.1(60%) + 0.0(20%) = 10%). The standard deviation around stock B's expected return is 6.325. Since 6.325 is larger than 3.162, this indicates a larger dispersion in the expected return for stock B.

The larger dispersion around the expected return implies that the investment is riskier, because the investor is less certain of the return. The larger the dispersion, the greater is the chance of a smaller gain (or larger loss). Correspondingly, there is a greater chance of a larger return. However, this potential for increased gain is concomitant with bearing additional risk. Stock A involves less risk; it has the smaller dispersion. Because the expected returns on both investments are the same, obviously stock A is to be preferred since it has less risk.

Although the preceding discussion was limited to the return on an individual security and the dispersion around that return, the concepts can be applied to an entire portfolio, such as a mutual fund's portfolio.[3] A portfolio also has an average return and dispersion around that return. The investor is concerned not only with the return and the risk associated with each investment, but also with the return and risk associated with the portfolio as a whole. This aggregate is, of course, the result of the individual investments and of each one's weight in the portfolio (that is, the value of each asset, expressed in percentages, in proportion to the total value of the portfolio).

[3] For instance, Morningstar provides the standard deviation of mutual fund returns in its database.

Consider a portfolio consisting of the following three stocks:

Stock	Return
1	8.3%
2	10.6
3	12.3

If 25 percent of the total value of the portfolio is invested in stocks 1 and 2 and 50 percent is invested in stock 3, the return is more heavily weighted in favor of stock 3. The return is a weighted average of each return times its proportion in the portfolio.

Return	×	Weight (percentage value of stock in proportion to total value of portfolio)	=	Weighted average
8.3%	×	0.25	=	2.075%.
10.6	×	0.25	=	2.650.
12.3	×	0.50	=	6.150.

The return is the sum of these weighted averages.

$$\begin{array}{r} 2.075\% \\ 2.650 \\ \underline{6.150} \\ 10.875\% \end{array}$$

The previous example is generalized in Equation 8.1, which states that the return on a portfolio r_p is a weighted average of the returns of the individual assets $[(r_1) \ldots (r_n)]$, each weighted by its proportion in the portfolio $(w_1 \ldots w_n)$:

8.1 $$r_p = w_1(r_1) + w_2(r_2) + \ldots w_n(r_n).$$

Thus, if a portfolio has 20 securities, each plays a role in the determination of the portfolio's return. The extent of that role depends on the weight that each asset has in the portfolio. Obviously those securities that compose the largest part of the individual's portfolio have the largest impact on the portfolio's return.[4]

Unfortunately, an aggregate measure of the portfolio's risk (or the portfolio's standard deviation) is more difficult to construct than the weighted average of the returns. This happens because security prices are not independent of each other.

[4] The same general equation may be applied to expected returns, in which case the expected return on a portfolio, $E(r_p)$, is a weighted average of the expected returns of the individual assets $[E(r_1) \ldots E(r_n)]$ each weighted by its proportion in the portfolio $(w_1 \ldots w_n)$:

$$E(r_p) = w_1E(r_1) + w_2E(r_2) + \ldots + w_nE(r_n).$$

However, although security prices do move together, there can be a difference in these price movements. For example, prices of stocks of firms in homebuilding may be more sensitive to recession than stock prices of utilities, whose prices may decline only moderately. These relationships among the assets in the portfolio must be considered in the construction of a measure of risk associated with the entire portfolio. In more advanced texts, these inner relationships among stocks are called *covariation*.

Risk Reduction through Diversification— An Illustration

The development of a measure of covariation and the calculation of a portfolio's standard deviation go beyond the scope of this text. The concept, however, may be illustrated by considering the returns earned on two specific stocks, Public Service Enterprise Group and Mobil Corporation, for 1971–1990. Public Service Enterprise Group is an electric and gas utility whose stock price fell with higher interest rates and inflation. Mobil is a resource company whose stock price rose during inflation in response to higher oil prices but fell during the 1980s as oil prices weakened and inflation receded. Thus, what was positive for one company was negative for the other.

The annual returns (dividends plus price change) on investments in these two stocks are given in Figure 8.2. As may be seen in the graph, there were periods when the returns on the two stocks moved in opposite directions. For example, during 1978, an investment in Public Service Enterprise Group generated a loss while an investment in Mobil produced profits. The converse occurred during 1981 as Public Service Enterprise Group's stock price rose. From 1980 to 1985, the stock price of Public Service Enterprise Group doubled, but the price of Mobil's stock declined.

Figure 8.3 presents a scatter diagram of the returns on these two stocks. The horizontal axis presents the annual return on Public Service Enterprise Group, while the vertical axis presents the annual return on Mobil Corporation. As may be seen in the graph, the individual points lie throughout the plane representing the returns. For example, point A represents a positive return on Mobil but a negative return on Public Service Enterprise Group, and point B represents a positive return on Public Service Enterprise Group but a negative return on Mobil.

Combining these securities in a portfolio reduced the individual's risk exposure. For the years 1971 through 1985, the line representing the composite return runs between the lines representing the returns on the individual securities. Over the entire period, the average annual returns on Mobil and Public Service Enterprise Group were 15.7 percent and 14.7 percent, respectively. The average annual return on the composite was 15.2 percent. The risk reduction (the reduction in the dispersion of the returns) can be seen by comparing the standard deviations of the returns. For the individual stocks, the standard deviations were 27.8 percent and 21.5 percent, respectively, for Mobil and Public Service Enterprise Group. However, the standard deviation for the composite return was 19.4 percent, so the dispersion of the returns associated with the portfolio is less than the dispersion of the returns on either stock by itself.

FIGURE 8.2

Annual Returns

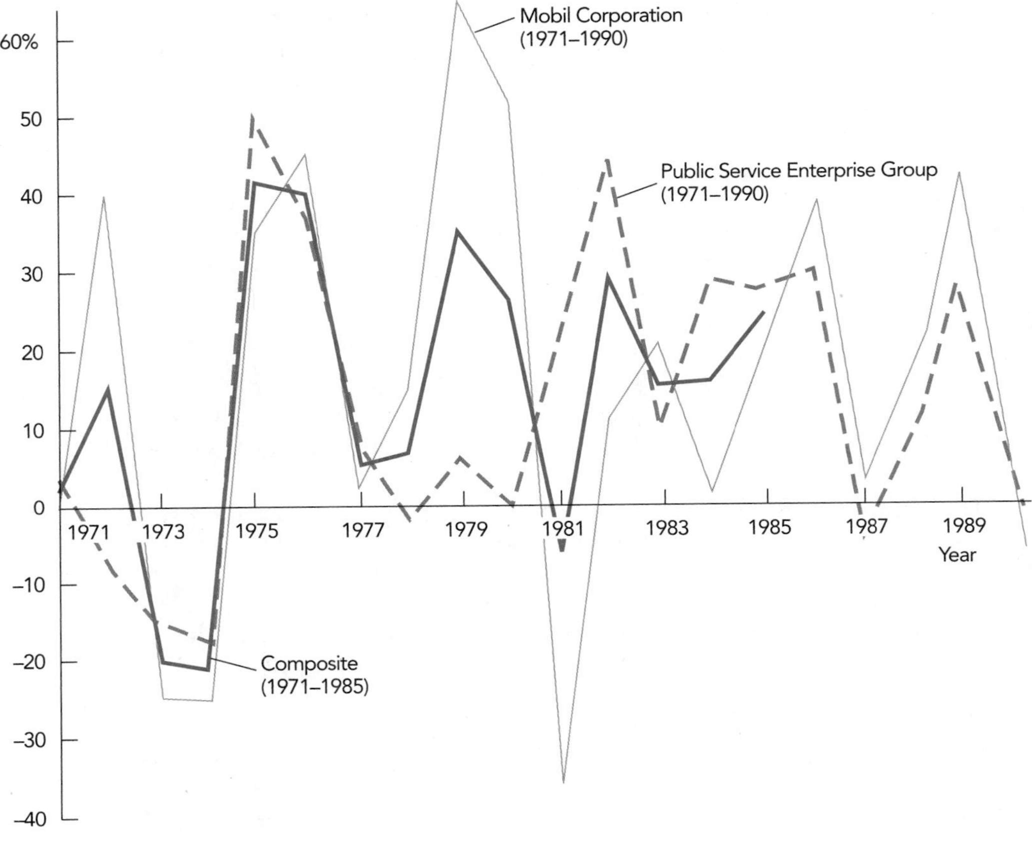

Why is there less dispersion for the portfolio than for the individual stocks? The answer is that the returns are not highly correlated. Correlation may be measured by a statistical concept: the "correlation coefficient." The numerical value of the correlation coefficient ranges from +1.0 to −1.0.[5] If the two variables move exactly together (that is, if there is a perfect positive correlation between the two variables), the numerical value of the correlation coefficient is 1.0. If the two

[5] The computation of the correlation coefficient is explained in statistics textbooks. See, for instance, Morris Hamburg and Peg Young, *Statistical Analysis for Decision Making,* 6th ed. (Fort Worth, Texas: The Dryden Press, 1994). For the purpose of this discussion, all that is necessary is that low values (i.e., 0.2 to −0.2) indicate, at best, a weak relationship between the two variables.

FIGURE 8.3

Scatter Diagram of Returns

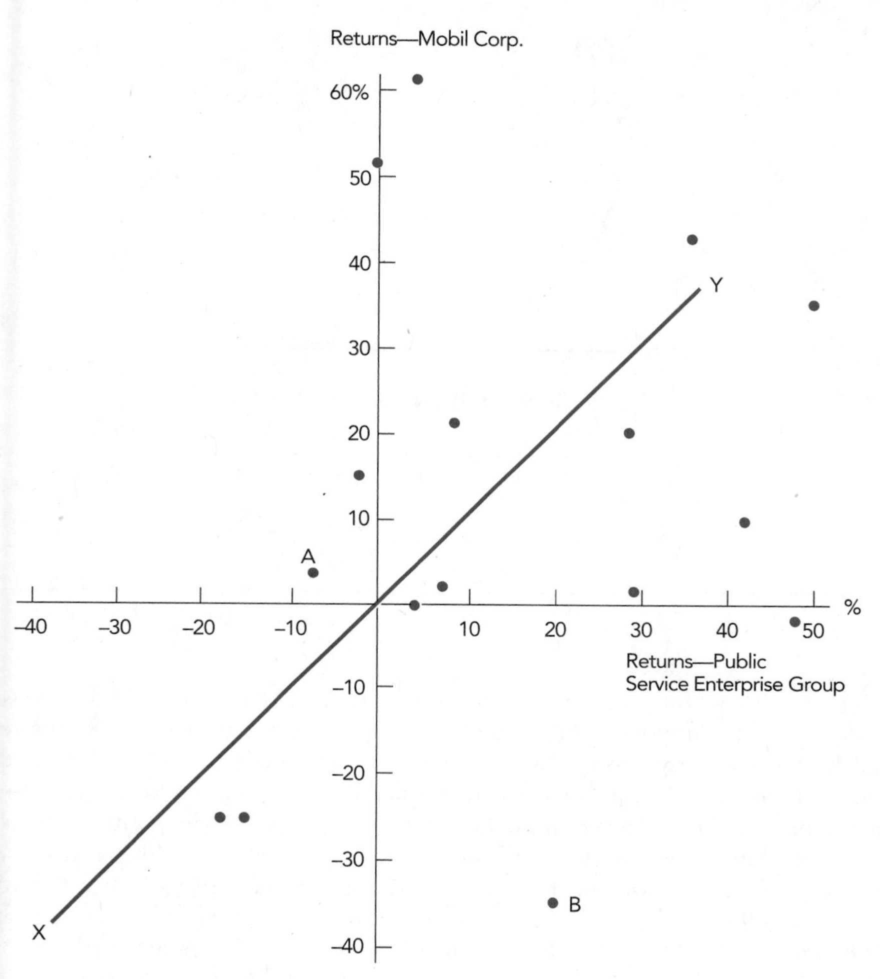

variables move exactly opposite of each other, the correlation coefficient equals −1.0. All other possible values lie between these two extremes. Low numerical values, such as −0.12 or +0.19, indicate little relationship between the two variables.

The correlation coefficient relating the returns on Mobil and Public Service Enterprise Group stocks is 0.148, so there was little relationship between the returns on the two stocks. This lack of correlation is visible in Figure 8.3. If there were a high positive correlation between the two returns, the points would lie close to the line XY. Instead, the points are scattered throughout the figure. Thus, there is little correlation between the two returns, which is why combining the two securities reduces the individual's risk exposure.

FIGURE 8.4

Portfolio Risk Consisting of Systematic and Unsystematic Risk

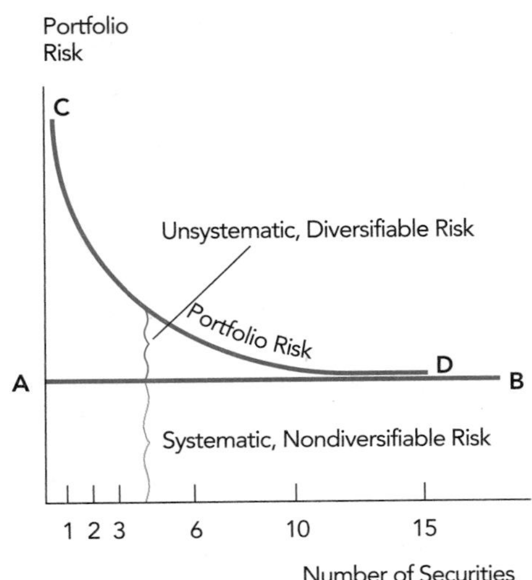

Combining Mobil and Public Service Enterprise Group reduced risk because it decreased the dispersion of the portfolio, and this lower dispersion was the result of the low correlation between the returns. However, two additional points should be made. First, just because diversification was achieved in the past does not imply it will be achieved in the future. If the returns become positively correlated, combining the two stocks will not achieve diversification. This positive correlation appears to have occurred since 1985 because the returns appear to have moved together during that period. (The composite return has been omitted from 1985 through 1990 to better illustrate the close movement between the returns on the two stocks.) This suggests that investing in Mobil and Public Service Enterprise Group during 1985 to 1990 had little impact on diversification. Second, to the extent that diversification reduces risk, it only affects the risk associated with specific assets. Other sources of risk remain. Diversification does not reduce the risk associated with fluctuations in security prices, inflation, changes in interest rates, the reinvestment rate, or fluctuations in exchange rates.

In effect, a diversified portfolio reduces the element of unsystematic risk. The risk associated with each individual investment is reduced by accumulating a diversified portfolio of assets. Even if one company fails (or does extremely well), the impact on the portfolio as a whole is reduced through diversification. Distributing investments among different industries, however, does not eliminate the other sources of risk. For example, the value of a group of securities will tend to follow the market values in general. The price movements of securities will be mirrored by the diversified portfolio; hence the investor cannot eliminate this source of systematic risk.

This reduction in unsystematic risk is illustrated in Figure 8.4. The vertical axis measures units of risk, and the horizontal axis gives the number of securities. Since market risk is independent of the number of securities in the portfolio, this element of risk is illustrated by a line, AB, that runs parallel to the horizontal axis. Regardless of the number of securities that an individual owns, the amount of market risk remains the same.

PORTFOLIO RISK
Total risk associated with owning a portfolio; sum of systematic and unsystematic risk

Portfolio risk (or the sum of systematic and unsystematic risk) is indicated by line CD. The difference between line AB and line CD is the unsystematic risk associated with the specific securities in the portfolio. The amount of unsystematic risk depends on the number of securities held. As this number increases, unsystematic risk diminishes; this reduction in risk is illustrated in Figure 8.4, in which line CD approaches line AB. For portfolios consisting of ten or more securities, the risk involved is primarily systematic.

Such diversified portfolios, of course, do not consist of ten public utilities but of a cross section of American businesses. Investing $20,000 in ten stocks ($2,000 for each) may achieve a reasonably well diversified portfolio. Although such a portfolio may cost somewhat more in commissions than two $10,000 purchases, the small investor achieves a diversified mixture of securities, which should reduce the risk of loss associated with investment in a specific security. Unfortunately, the investor must still bear the systematic risk associated with investing.[6]

BETA COEFFICIENTS

The computation of a standard deviation for a portfolio of any size is impractical for the individual investor, because it requires the correlation among the individual stock returns. For a portfolio of three stocks (A, B, and C), the investor needs to know the correlation among stocks A and B, A and C, and B and C. If the portfolio has four stocks (A, B, C, and D), then you need the correlation between A and B, A and C, A and D, B and C, B and D, and C and D. Consider the number of correlations that would be necessary for a portfolio of 20 stocks! To make matters worse, data relating returns between stocks are not generally available. The investor would have to compute the individual correlation coefficients before computing the portfolio's standard deviation.

Fortunately there is an alternative. The previous discussion of diversification suggested that if a portfolio is sufficiently diversified, unsystematic risk is virtually erased. The remaining risk is the result of nondiversifiable, systematic risk. Is there a measure of systematic risk and may it be used instead of a standard deviation to indicate the risk associated with an asset or with a well-diversified portfolio?

The answer is yes. This measure of the systematic risk associated with an asset is called a *beta coefficient.* While the concept may be applied to any asset, the usual explanation employs common stock. A beta coefficient is an index of risk that quantifies the responsiveness of a stock's return to changes in the return on the

[6] Instant diversification is a prime advantage offered by an investment in a stock mutual fund.

market. Since a beta coefficient measures a stock's return relative to the return on the market, it measures the systematic risk associated with the stock.

Beta coefficients have become widely used by financial analysts to measure the risk associated with individual stocks. The concept is also applied to portfolios, as betas are computed for mutual funds, in which case they compare the return on the fund with the return on the market. Portfolio betas are simply weighted averages of the individual betas in the portfolio. While the use of betas permeates finance, it is important to realize that these coefficients are only a *relative measure of risk*. They tell you nothing about how the market itself will fluctuate!

A beta coefficient of 1 means that the stock's return moves exactly with an index of the market as a whole. A 10 percent increase in the market produces a 10 percent increase in the return on the specific stock. Correspondingly, a 10 percent decline in the market results in a 10 percent decline in the return on the stock. A beta coefficient of less than 1 implies that the return on the stock tends to fluctuate less than the market as a whole. A coefficient of 0.7 indicates that the stock's return will rise only 7 percent as a result of a 10 percent increase in the market but will fall by only 7 percent when the market declines by 10 percent. A coefficient of 1.2 means that the return on the stock will rise by 12 percent if the market increases by 10 percent, but the return on the stock will decline by 12 percent when the market declines by 10 percent.

The greater the beta coefficient, the more market (systematic) risk is associated with the individual stock. High beta coefficients may indicate higher profits during rising markets, but they also indicate greater losses during declining markets. Stocks with high beta coefficients are referred to as "aggressive." The converse is true for stocks with low beta coefficients, which should underperform the market during periods of rising stock prices but outperform the market as a whole during periods of declining prices. Such stocks are referred to as "defensive."

This relationship between the return on a specific security and the market index as a whole is illustrated in parts a and b of Figure 8.5. In each graph, the horizontal axis represents the percentage return on the market index, and the vertical axis represents the percentage return on the individual stock. The line AB, which represents the market, is the same in both graphs. It is a positively sloped line that runs through the point of origin and is equidistant from both axes (it makes a 45-degree angle with each axis).

The left side of Figure 8.5 illustrates a stock with a beta coefficient greater than 1. Line CD represents a stock whose return rises and declines more than the market's return. In this case, the beta coefficient is 1.2, so when the market index is 10 percent, this stock's return is 12 percent.

The right side of Figure 8.5 illustrates a stock with a beta coefficient of less than 1. Line EF represents a stock whose return rises (and declines) more slowly than that of the market. In this case, the beta coefficient is 0.8, so when the market's return is 10 percent, this stock's return is 8 percent.

Because a beta coefficient indicates the systematic risk associated with a particular stock, it can be used in security selection and portfolio construction. Some assets offer the investor modest returns for taking very little risk. Insured savings accounts and short-term obligations of the federal government are virtually

FIGURE 8.5

Differences in Beta Coefficients (a) Stock with a Beta Coefficient Greater Than 1.0 (b) Stock with a Beta Coefficient Less Than 1.0

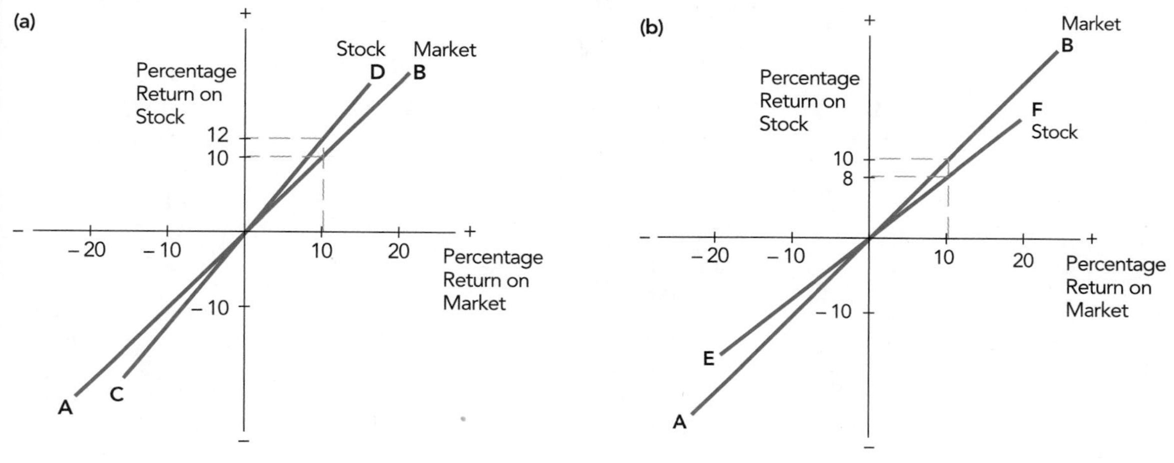

risk-free. To induce investors to purchase risky securities, such as common stock, the anticipated return must be sufficient to compensate the investor for the additional risk. Since unsystematic risk is reduced by diversification, systematic risk becomes very important in the selection of an asset. The investor must anticipate a sufficient return for bearing systematic risk, and increases in systematic risk will require larger expected returns. (How beta coefficients may be used in the valuation of a stock is explained in Chapter 11.)

Beta coefficients do vary among firms. This is illustrated in Exhibit 8.1, which presents the beta coefficients for selected firms as computed by *Value Line.* As may be seen in the table, some firms (such as Alcoa) have relatively low beta coefficients, while the coefficients for other firms (such as LSI Logic) are much higher. Investors who are willing to bear more risk may be attracted to those stocks with the higher beta coefficients, because when stock market prices rise, these stocks tend to outperform the market. Investors who are less inclined to bear risk may prefer the stocks with low beta coefficients. Although these investors may forgo some potential return during rising market prices, they should suffer milder losses during periods of declining stock prices.

To be useful, beta coefficients must be reliable predictors of future stock price behavior. For example, an investor who desires stocks that will be stable will probably purchase stocks with low beta coefficients. An investor selecting a stock with a beta coefficient of 0.6 will certainly be upset if the market prices decline by 10 percent and this stock's price falls by 15 percent, since a beta coefficient of 0.6 indicates that the stock price should decline by only 6 percent when market prices decline by 10 percent.

EXHIBIT 8.1

Selected Beta Coefficients

Company	*Value Line* Beta Coefficient
Piedmont Natural Gas	0.55
Hershey Foods	0.70
Aluminum Company of America (ALCOA)	0.80
ExxonMobil	0.80
E.I. duPont de Nemours Co.	1.05
Boeing	1.05
IBM Corp.	1.05
Boston Scientific	1.25
General Electric Co.	1.25
Compaq Computer	1.35
LSI Logic	1.45

Source: Value Line *Publishing, Inc.*

Unfortunately, beta coefficients can and do change over time. Therefore, the investor should not rely solely on these coefficients in selecting a particular security. However, beta coefficients do give the investor some indication of the systematic risk associated with specific stocks and thus can play an important role in the selection of a security.

Unlike the beta coefficients for individual securities, the beta coefficient for a portfolio composed of several securities is fairly stable over time. Changes in the different beta coefficients tend to average out; while one stock's beta coefficient is increasing, the beta coefficient of another stock is declining. A portfolio's historical beta coefficients, then, can be used as a tool to forecast its future beta coefficient, and this projection should be more accurate than forecasts of an individual security's beta coefficient.

Since a portfolio's beta coefficient is stable, the investor can construct a portfolio that responds in a desired way to market changes. For example, the average beta coefficient of the portfolio illustrated in Exhibit 8.1 is approximately 1.00. If an equal dollar amount were invested in each security, the value of the portfolio should follow the market values closely, even though individual beta coefficients are greater or less than 1. This tendency of the portfolio to mirror the performance of the market should hold true, even though selected securities may achieve a return that is greater (or less) than that of the market as a whole. Hence, the beta coefficient for the portfolio may be a more useful tool than the beta coefficients for individual securities.

Regression Analysis and the Estimation of Beta Coefficients[7]

A statistical technique, regression analysis, is used to estimate a stock's beta coefficient. As was previously explained, a beta coefficient is a measure of the responsiveness of a stock's return to movements in security prices in general. While it is not known exactly how a stock's return will react to changes in the market in the future, it is possible to measure historical responsiveness. For example, observations of the past relationship between the return on the market (r_m) and the return on stock A (r_s) are as follows:

Return on the Market (r_m)	Return on Stock A (r_s)
14%	13%
12	13
10	12
10	9
5	4
2	−1
−1	−2
−5	−7
−7	−8
−12	−10

Each observation represents the return on the stock and the return on the market for a period of time (for instance, a week). These data are plotted in Figure 8.6 with each point representing one set of observations. For example, point A represents a 4 percent increase in the return on the stock in response to a 5 percent increase in the market. Point B represents a 7 percent decrease in the return on the stock in response to a 5 percent decline in the return on the market.

Individual observations, like points A and B, tell very little about the systematic risk of the stock, but all the observations, taken as a whole, may. The individual observations are summarized by linear regression analysis, which is used to compute an equation relating the return on the stock (r_s, the dependent variable) to the return on the market (r_m, the independent variable). The regression analysis computes the y-intercept (a) and the slope (b) for the following equation:

$$r_s = a + br_m.$$

This slope is the beta coefficient.

[7] This section may be omitted without loss of continuity. For an extensive bibliography on the determination of beta and its estimation, see: Carolyn M. Callahan and Rosanne M. Mohr, "The Determinants of Systematic Risk: A Synthesis," *Financial Review* (May 1989): 157–181.

FIGURE 8.6

Observations Relating the Return on a Stock to the Return on the Market

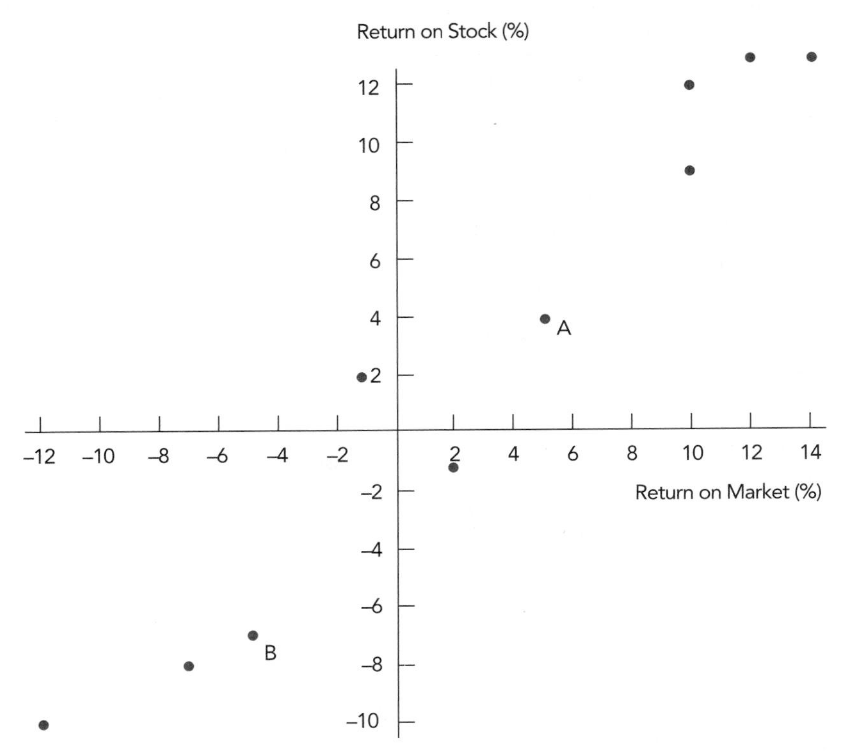

Like the correlation coefficient presented earlier in this chapter, regression analysis is a statistical concept. The actual computations of the intercept and the slope are generally performed by a computer program. A manual demonstration of the process is presented in Exhibit 8.2, in which the following equation is derived:

$$r_s = -0.000597 + 0.9856r_m.$$

This equation is given as line XY in Figure 8.7, which reproduces Figure 8.6 and adds the regression line. As may be seen from the graph, line XY runs through the individual points. Some of the observations are above the line while others are below it. However, all the points are close to the line.

This regression equation can be used to forecast the expected return on the stock. If the individual anticipates that the market return will be 20 percent, the stock should yield a return of

$$r_s = -0.000597 + 0.9856(20\%) = 19.7\%.$$

EXHIBIT 8.2

The Computation of a Beta Coefficient

X (r_m)	Y (r_s)	X^2	Y^2	XY
0.14	0.13	0.0196	0.0169	0.0182
0.12	0.13	0.0144	0.0169	0.0156
0.10	0.12	0.0100	0.0144	0.0120
0.10	0.09	0.0100	0.0081	0.0090
0.05	0.04	0.0025	0.0016	0.0020
0.02	−0.01	0.0004	0.0001	−0.0002
−0.01	0.02	0.0001	0.0004	−0.0002
−0.05	−0.07	0.0025	0.0049	0.0035
−0.07	−0.08	0.0049	0.0064	0.0056
−0.12	−0.10	0.0144	0.0100	0.0120
$\Sigma X = 0.28$	$\Sigma Y = 0.27$	$\Sigma X^2 = 0.0788$	$\Sigma Y^2 = 0.0797$	$\Sigma XY = 0.0775$

n = the number of observations (10).

$$b = \frac{n\Sigma XY - (\Sigma X)(\Sigma Y)}{n\Sigma X^2 - (\Sigma X)^2}$$

$$= \frac{(10)(0.0775) - (0.28)(0.27)}{(10)(0.0788) - (0.28)(0.28)}$$

$$= \frac{0.7750 - 0.0756}{0.7880 - 0.0784} = 0.9856.$$

The a is computed as follows:

$$a = \frac{\Sigma Y}{n} - b\frac{\Sigma X}{n}$$

$$= \frac{0.27}{10} - (0.9856)\frac{0.28}{10} = -0.000597.$$

The estimated equation is $r_s = -0.000597 + 0.9856\ r_m$.

As with any forecast, this result may not be realized, because factors other than the increase in the market may affect the stock's return. (These factors are the unsystematic risk associated with the stock.) The predictive power of this particular beta may be excellent, because the individual observations lie close to the estimated regression line. That indicates a high correlation between the two variables. The actual correlation coefficient is 0.976, which indicates a strong, positive relationship between the return on the stock and the return on the market. A correlation coefficient of 1.0 indicates a perfect, positive relationship. Most of the fluctuations

FIGURE 8.7

Regression Equation Relating the Return on a Stock to the Return on the Market

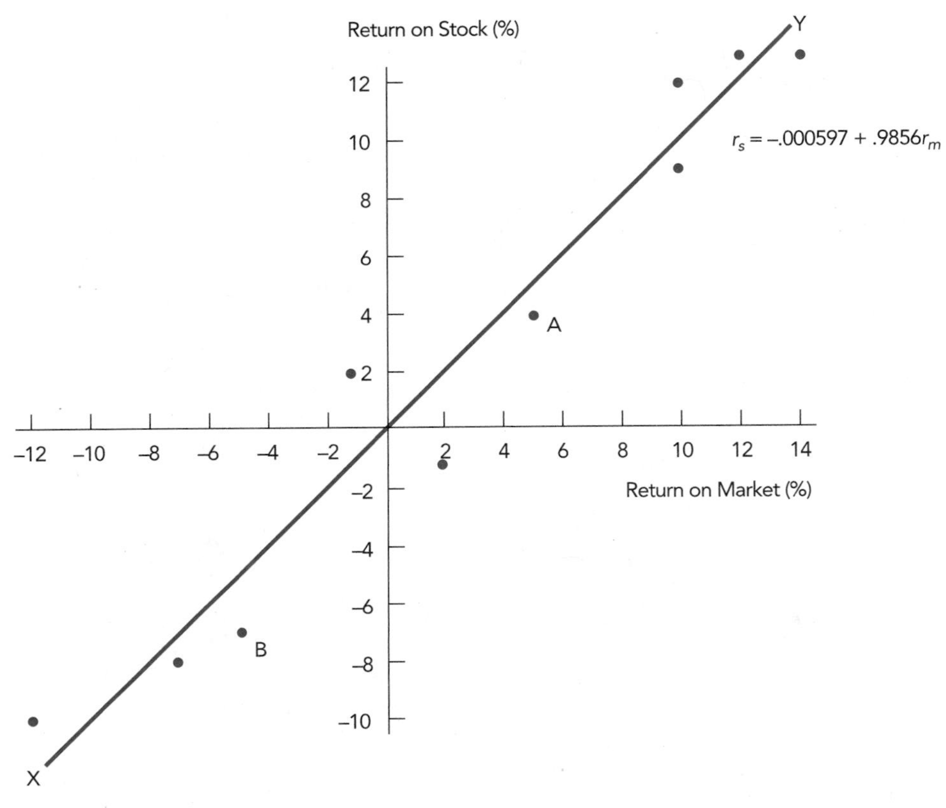

in the individual returns on the stock were caused by fluctuations in the return on the market. Of course, this high correlation may not continue in the future, but unless some fundamental change in the firm were to occur, the beta coefficient may be an excellent forecaster of the future responsiveness of the stock to changes in the market.

The development of beta coefficients and a theory of the reduction of risk through diversification was exceedingly important to the formation of a theory of asset valuation. This theory led to the development of the capital asset pricing model, which specifies the relationship between risk and return and determines the required return for an asset. This required return is discussed in the next section and will be used subsequently to value investments, such as the purchase of common stock by individuals or plant and equipment by a firm's management.

THE CAPITAL ASSET PRICING MODEL AND AN INVESTMENT'S REQUIRED RETURN[8]

One important decision facing a financial manager or an investor is whether to acquire an asset. This decision requires a determination of either (1) an asset's value, which is compared to its cost, or (2) an asset's expected return, which is compared to the required return. It is not necessary to do both, because either technique uses the same information.

When valuation is employed, the analyst uses the required return to discount future cash flows to determine what the asset is worth. This valuation is compared to the asset's current price. If the value exceeds the cost, the asset should be acquired. This technique will subsequently be used in the dividend-growth model for selecting stocks in Chapter 11 and in the net present value technique for selecting investments in plant and equipment in Chapter 17.

While valuation expresses an asset in monetary units (that is, dollars), the required return and the expected return use percentages. The asset's cash flows are compared to its cost to determine an expected return, which is compared to the investor's required rate of return. If the anticipated return exceeds the required return, the asset is acquired. The primary use for this technique is the computation of an investment's internal rate of return (Chapter 17), but it may also be used for the selection of stock (Chapter 11).

Both techniques need a required return, which has led to a general framework for analyzing risk and return called the **capital asset pricing model** or **CAPM.** The CAPM specifies the relationship between risk and return that is used either to value an asset or to judge an asset's expected return. While the model may be applied to any type of investment, it is generally explained in terms of acquiring common stock, so the following explanation is presented from the perspective of the individual investor.

CAPITAL ASSET PRICING MODEL (CAPM)
Model used in the valuation of an asset that specifies the required return for different levels of risk

The CAPM builds on the proposition that additional risk requires a higher return. This return has two components: (1) what may be earned on a risk-free asset, such as a federally insured savings account or a U.S. Treasury bill, plus (2) a premium for bearing risk. Since unsystematic risk is reduced through diversification, a stock's risk premium is the additional return required to bear the nondiversifiable, systematic risk associated with the stock.

This risk-adjusted required return (k) is expressed in Equation 8.2:

$$k = \text{risk-free rate} + \text{risk premium}. \quad (8.2)$$

The risk premium is composed of two components: (1) the additional return that investing in securities in general offers above the risk-free rate and (2) the volatility of the particular security relative to the market as a whole. The volatility of the

[8] A more advanced discussion of portfolio theory and security valuation may be found in specialized textbooks on investments, such as William F. Sharpe, Gordon J. Alexander, and Jeffrey V. Bailey, *Investments*, 5th ed. (Upper Saddle River, N.J.: Prentice Hall, 1999).

FIGURE 8.8

Relationship between Risk and the Required Return

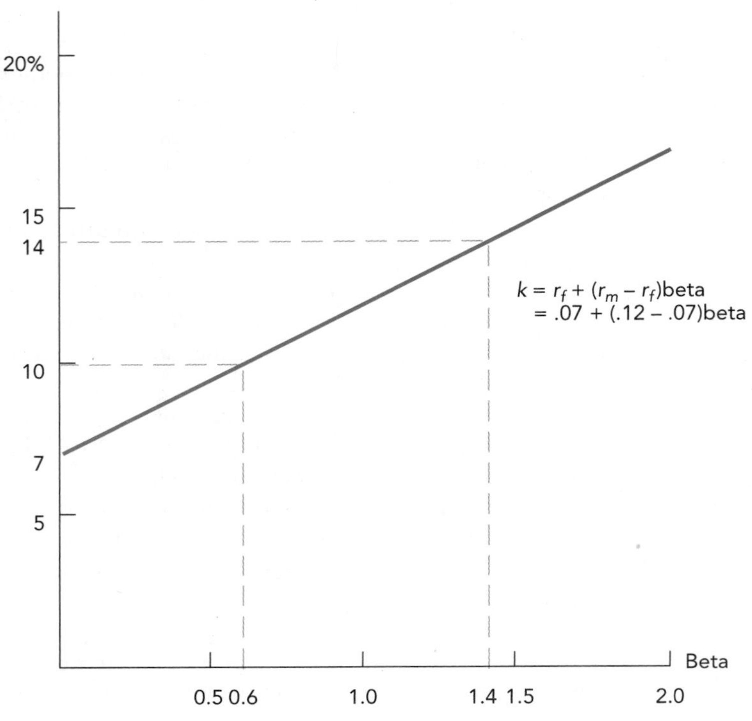

individual stock is measured by the beta coefficient (β), and the additional return is measured by the difference between the expected return on the market (r_m) and the risk-free rate (r_f). This differential ($r_m - r_f$) is the risk premium that is required to induce the individual to purchase risky assets.

To induce the investor to purchase a particular stock, the risk premium associated with the market must be adjusted by the market risk associated with the individual security. This risk adjustment uses the stock's beta coefficient, which indicates the stock's volatility relative to the market. The risk adjustment is achieved by multiplying the security's beta coefficient by the difference between the expected return on the market and the risk-free rate. Thus the risk premium for the individual stock is

$$\text{risk premium} = (r_m - r_f) \text{ beta coefficient.}$$

The return required for investing in a particular stock is found by substituting this risk premium into Equation 8.2. Thus the required return is

8.3 $$\text{required return} = r_f + (r_m - r_f) \text{ beta coefficient}$$

The relationship between various levels of risk and the required return indicated by Equation 8.3 is illustrated in Figure 8.8. Risk, as measured by the beta coefficient, is given on the horizontal axis while the required return, measured as a percentage, is on the vertical axis. If the risk-free rate is 7 percent and the expected return on the market is 12 percent, then the required rate of return on a stock with a beta coefficient of 0.6 is

$$k_A = 0.07 + (0.12 - 0.07)0.6 = 0.10 = 10\%.$$

If a stock has a beta coefficient equal to 1.4, the required return is

$$k_B = 0.07 + (0.12 - 0.07)1.4 = 0.14 = 14\%.$$

The stock with the higher beta coefficient has the higher required return because it is riskier.

The preceding specification of the required rate of return reappears several times in this text. It is used to value common stock in Chapter 11 and is part of the firm's cost of capital in Chapter 16. Since the cost of capital is part of the capital budgeting models covered in Chapter 17, the required return has an impact on the financial manager's decision to invest in plant and equipment.

INVESTMENT ANALYSIS CALCULATOR APPLICATIONS

This chapter considers the sources of risk and return and suggests means for measuring both risk and return. The *Investment Analysis Calculator* may be used to facilitate the calculations of returns, both expected and historical, and the calculations of an investment's standard deviation and the calculation of a stock's beta. The beta then is used as part of the calculation of an investor's required return.

To calculate the expected and historical returns and their standard deviations, use the section entitled Statistical Calculator. (Remember that you may access the software at **www.harcourtcollege.com/finance/mayo**.) The estimation of beta and the required return are found in the section devoted to the Capital Asset Pricing Model. (Since a beta coefficient is an example of regression analysis, it may also be calculated in the submenu "Simple Linear Regression" in the section Statistical Calculator.)

Suppose you want to compare the expected returns and risk (as measured by the standard deviation) of the following two investments:

Investment A	Return	Probability of Occurrence
	7%	10%
	10	40
	12	30
	20	20

Investment B	Return	Probability of Occurrence
	4%	40%
	7	30
	8	20
	10	10

Go to the section "Expected Value and Descriptive Statistics for a Probability Distribution" in the Statistical Calculator section. Enter the number of occurrences in the distribution (4), the returns and the probabilities. The software then calculates the average expected return and various descriptive statistics, which include the standard deviation of the returns. The software indicates that the expected average returns for A and B are 12.3 percent and 6.3 percent with standard deviations of 4.1 and 2.05.

Suppose you had two investments and you wanted to compare the following historical returns and risk (as measured by the standard deviation) for each investment.

Investment A	Year	Return
	1	−6
	2	10
	3	24
	4	4
Investment B	**Year**	**Return**
	1	12
	2	14
	3	5
	4	8

Go to the section "Arithmetic Mean, Geometric Mean, and Descriptive Statistics for a Historic Series" in the Statistical Calculator section. Enter the number of data points (4) and the returns. The software calculates the average return (both the arithmetic and geometric averages) and various descriptive statistics. In this example the arithmetic average historical returns are 8.0 percent for investment A and 9.75 percent for investment B. (You may, however, prefer the geometric averages since the geometric averages gives the compound return. If you prefer the geometric averages, they are 7.5 and 9.7 percent, respectively.) The standard deviations are 12.5 for investment A and 4.0 for investment B.

The Investment Analysis Calculator also computes the coefficient of variation, which is the standard deviation divided by the average. The coefficient of variation is used to adjust for differences in scale. While a large standard deviation suggests greater variability (and hence more risk), it is difficult to compare investments when the scales differ. If two investments have the same return and hence have the same scale, then the investment with the higher standard deviation is riskier and inferior.

If two investments have different returns but the investment with a higher return also has a higher standard deviation, then the investor is earning more for bearing more risk. The standard deviation is not sufficient evidence to rank the two investments. The coefficient of variation, however, facilities a comparison since it views risk relative to the return. (The use of the coefficient of variation discussed in more depth in Chapter 18 on the adjustment of returns for risk used in capital budgeting.)

Beta coefficients are available from a variety of sources. (See Question 8 for possible sources.) To see how a beta may be estimated by using the Investment Analysis Calculator, enter the data from Exhibit 8.2 into the section "Beta Calculation" under Capital Asset Pricing Model. The number of observations is 10, the return on the market (X) is given in the first column of the exhibit, and the return on the stock (Y) is given in the second column. After entering the data, click on enter, and the beta coefficient (0.986) is estimated.

Notice that the software provides not only the beta but also the Y intercept (-0.001) and the correlation coefficient ($R = 0.976$) and the coefficient of determination (R^2), which gives the proportion of the variability in the beta that is explained by the variability in the market. In this illustration, the $R^2 = 0.952$, so that less than 5 percent of the variability in the stock's return is explained by something other than the movement in the market.

Beta coefficients are a crucial ingredient in the capital asset model and the determination of the required rate of return. Once you have the beta, the risk-free rate, and the return on the market, you can determine the required return on a stock. This return relates (1) the market risk associated with the stock and (2) the return necessary to purchase the stock. Equation 8.3 summarizes the required return for various betas and is illustrated in Figure 8.8. The line generated by the equation is generally referred to as the "Security Market Line."

The program for the calculation of the required return is found under the submenu "Required Rate of Return Calculation" in the section for the Capital Asset Pricing Model. To determine the required rate of return, enter the beta coefficient, the risk-free rate, and the return on the market. To use the illustrations in the text, enter the beta (0.6), the risk-free rate (7 percent) and the return on the market (12 percent). The software determines the required return to be 10 percent. If the beta had been 1.4, the required return is 14 percent.

SUMMARY

Investments are made in anticipation of a return, which is a flow of income and/or price appreciation. Individuals and financial managers make investments in anticipation of a return, but the realized return may differ from the expected return. That is the element of risk. The future is uncertain.

There are several sources of risk. These include the risk associated with the specific asset (diversifiable, unsystematic risk) and the non-diversifiable, systematic risk from fluctuations in security prices, changes in interest rates, reinvestment rates, inflation, and fluctuations in exchange rates.

The construction of a diversified portfolio reduces the risk associated with the particular asset. By owning a variety of assets whose returns are not highly positively correlated, the investor reduces unsystematic risk without necessarily reducing the potential return on the portfolio as a whole. Unfortunately, the construction of a diversified portfolio does not reduce the other sources of risk.

Risk may be measured by an asset's (or portfolio's) standard deviation, which measures the dispersion around the realized return (in the case of historical returns) or the expected return (in the case of anticipated returns). The larger the dispersion of the returns, the greater the risk.

An alternative measure of risk determines the responsiveness of an asset's return relative to the market as a whole. This measure, called a beta coefficient, is an index of the systematic risk associated with the asset. The larger the beta coefficient, the greater the systematic risk associated with the security since its return has risen or fallen more rapidly than the return on the market as a whole.

Beta coefficients are used to determine an investor's required rate of return. This capital asset pricing model specifies the required return and includes (1) the risk-free rate that may be earned on very safe investments plus (2) a risk premium. The risk premium includes a premium for purchasing risky assets instead of the risk-free asset, plus an adjustment for the systematic risk associated with the particular investment.

REVIEW QUESTIONS

1. What are the sources of return on an investment? What are the differences among the expected return, the required return, and the realized return?

2. Why does a diversified portfolio reduce unsystematic risk but have no impact on systematic risk? What condition must be met for a portfolio to be diversified? How many securities are necessary to achieve diversification?

3. What is a beta coefficient? What do beta coefficients of 0.5, 1.0, and 1.5 imply? How may beta coefficients be used in the capital asset pricing model to help determine the required return on an investment?

4. What is the difference between beta coefficients and standard deviations as measures of risk?

5. What impact would each of the following have on a well-diversified portfolio?
   a. The stock market declines by 10 percent.
   b. One of the stocks in the portfolio suspends its dividend.
   c. The rate of inflation decreases.

6. You compute the following expected returns and standard deviations of three portfolios.

Portfolio	Expected Return	Standard Deviation
1	18%	5%
2	9	2
3	12	6

   Would you prefer portfolio 1 to 2? Would you prefer portfolio 1 to 3?

7. If stock A's beta coefficient is 1.5 while stock B's beta coefficient is 1.2, what does that suggest about their relative risks? Is this information sufficient to prefer either stock A or B?

8. Beta coefficients may change over time. Betas also may differ if you obtain them from different sources. These discrepancies occur because various sources use different time periods or a different measure of the market when calculating beta coefficients. Exhibit 4.1 illustrates beta coefficients obtained from the Value Line Investment Survey. Obtain beta coefficients for the same companies from another source and compare with the betas in Exhibit 4.1. Are the numerical values of the betas different? (Possible sources for obtaining betas include Yahoo! (**biz.yahoo.com**), Wall Street Research Network (**www.wsrn.com**), moneynet (**www.moneynet.com**), and Market Guide (**www.marketguide.com**). Since the location of the beta coefficients varies in each web site, you will have to search to find the beta. A good starting point may be the sections called "company profile", "company snapshot", or "company statistics".)

Problems

1. You are considering buying stock A. If the economy grows rapidly, you may earn 30 percent on the investment while a declining economy could result in a 20 percent loss. Slow economic growth may generate a return of 6 percent. If the

probability of rapid growth is 15 percent, 20 percent for a declining economy, and 65 percent for slow growth, what is the expected return on this investment?

2. You are considering investing in three stocks with the following expected returns:

Stock A	7%
Stock B	12
Stock C	20

What is the expected return on the portfolio if an equal amount is invested in each stock? What would be the expected return if 50 percent of your funds is invested in stock A and the remaining funds are split evenly between stocks B and C?

3. A portfolio consists of assets with the following expected returns:

Technology stocks	20%
Pharmaceutical stocks	15
Utility stocks	10
Savings account	5

a. What is the expected return on the portfolio if the investor spends an equal amount on each asset?
b. What is the expected return on the portfolio if the investor puts 50 percent of available funds in technology stocks, 10 percent in pharmaceutical stocks, 24 percent in utility stocks, and 16 percent in the savings account?

4. Consider a $30,000 portfolio consisting of three stocks. Their values and expected returns are as follows:

Stock	Investment	Expected Return
A	$ 5,000	12%
B	10,000	10
C	15,000	14

What is the weighted-average expected return on the portfolio?

5. Two investments generated the following annual returns:

	Investment X	Investment Y
19X0	10%	16%
19X1	20	18
19X2	30	15
19X3	20	20
19X4	10	21

a. What is the average annual return on each investment?
b. What is the standard deviation of the return on investments X and Y?
c. Based on the standard deviation, which investment was riskier?

6. You expect to invest your funds equally in four stocks with the following expected returns:

Stock	Expected Return
A	16%
B	14
C	10
D	8

At the end of the year, each stock had the following realized returns:

Stock	Realized Return
A	−6%
B	18
C	3
D	−2

Compare the portfolio's expected and realized returns.

7. You are considering two stocks and have determined the following information:

Stock A	Return	Probability of the Return
	18%	25%
	14	50
	10	25
Stock B	**Return**	**Probability of the Return**
	22%	10%
	12	60
	11	30

a. Which of the two stocks has the higher expected return?
b. Which stock is riskier?
c. Given your answers to the two previous questions, what stock is preferred?

8. Two stocks, A and B, have beta coefficients of 0.8 and 1.4, respectively. If the expected return on the market is 10 percent and the risk-free rate is 5 percent, what is the risk premium associated with each stock?

9. Stock A has a risk premium of 6.5 percent. If Treasury bills yield 6.2 percent and the expected return on the market is 10.5 percent, what is the stock's beta coefficient?

10. What is the required return on an investment with a beta of 1.3 if the risk-free rate is 4 percent and the return on the market is 11 percent? If the expected return on the investment is 14 percent, what should you do?

CHAPTER 9
Investing in Long-Term Debt (Bonds)

Learning Objectives

1. Identify the general characteristics of all long-term debt instruments.
2. Isolate the feature(s) that distinguish each type of corporate bond.
3. State the role of bond ratings.
4. Calculate the price of a bond, the current yield and the yield to maturity.
5. Explain the inverse relationship between interest rates and the price of a bond.
6. Explain the difference between sinking funds and call features.
7. Recognize the advantage offered by municipal bonds.

In *The Merchant of Venice,* Antonio sealed his debt to Shylock with a "pound of flesh." Today the terms of a bond are not so severe—creditors cannot require borrowers to offer their flesh as collateral. However, the terms of a debt can still kill a firm. When Eastern Airlines filed for bankruptcy, the secured creditors with liens on the airline's planes had the right to take possession of the aircraft. Without its planes, Eastern was dead; it would never fly again.

Many corporations issue long-term debt (bonds) to finance expansion of plant and equipment when the firm's internally generated funds are insufficient to finance the expansion. For example, as of 1999, AT&T had over $6.6 billion in bonds outstanding. Financing fixed assets with long-term debt offers the firm the advantage of financial leverage, and the debt may be retired by the cash flow generated by the plant and equipment.

This chapter is concerned with the long-term debt, especially bonds issued by corporations. It covers the characteristics common to all long-term debt and the different types of corporate debt. Bonds may be purchased by institutions in a private placement or by individuals through a public offering. Once the bonds have been issued, they may be bought and sold on organized security exchanges or in the over-the-counter market. Thus, bonds must have a market price, and this chapter considers how that price is determined.

A bond's price may exceed the principal amount of the debt, in which case the bond sells for a premium. A bond's price may also be less than the face amount, in which case the bond sells for a discount. The chapter explains how the premium or discount affects a bond's current yield and its yield to maturity and illustrates how these yields are calculated.

All debt must be retired. The last section on corporate debt considers the retirement of bonds. The chapter closes with a brief discussion of the bonds issued by various levels of government and how government debt differs from corporate debt.

CHARACTERISTICS OF ALL DEBT INSTRUMENTS

All **bonds** (that is, long-term debt instruments) share a number of characteristics. They are liabilities of their issuers for a specified amount, called the **principal.** Virtually all debt has a **maturity date;** it must be paid off by a specified date. If maturity occurs after a year, it is long-term debt. When this debt is issued, the length of time to maturity can range from a few years to 20 or 30 years. (Coca-Cola has a bond outstanding that matures in 2093!) The owners of debt instruments receive payments **(interest).** Interest should not be confused with other forms of income, such as cash dividends paid by common and preferred stock. Dividends come from the firm's earnings, while interest is an expense. Sometimes interest is called **yield** and may be expressed in two ways: **current yield** and **yield to maturity.** The difference between the two is discussed subsequently in the section on yields.

BOND
Long-term debt instrument which specifies (1) the *principal* (amount owed), (2) the *interest* (payment for the use of the principal), and (3) the *maturity date* (the day on which the debt must be repaid)

YIELD
Return on a bond expressed as (1) a *current yield* (interest divided by the current price of the bond) or (2) the *yield to maturity* (return earned from holding the bond until it matures)

Each debt agreement has terms that the debtor must meet, and these are stated in a legal document called the **indenture.** One of the most frequent requirements is the pledging of collateral that the borrower must put up to secure the loan. For example, the collateral for a mortgage loan is the building and land. Other assets, such as securities or inventory owned by the borrower, may also be pledged to secure the loan. If the borrower **defaults** on the loan (in other words, if the borrower fails to pay the interest or fails to meet other terms of the indenture), the creditor may seize the collateral and sell it to recoup the principal.

INDENTURE
Document specifying the terms of a debt issue

DEFAULT
Failure to meet the terms specified in the indenture of a debt issue

Other examples of common loan restrictions are (1) limits on dividend payments, (2) limits on the issue of additional debt, and (3) the requirement to periodically retire a proportion of the debt. These examples do not exhaust all the possible conditions of a given loan. Since each loan is separately negotiated, there is ample opportunity for subtle differences among loan agreements. The important point, however, is that if any part of the loan agreement is violated, the creditor may declare that the debt is in default and the entire loan is due. Default is not just the failure to pay the interest. Failure to meet any of the indenture provisions places the loan in default, even though the interest is still being paid.

Many debt instruments are purchased by investors who may be unaware of the terms of the indenture. Even if they are aware of the terms, the investors may be too geographically dispersed to take concerted action in case of default. To protect their interests, a **trustee** is appointed for each publicly held bond issue. It is the trustee's job to see that the terms of the indenture are upheld and to take remedial action if the company should default on the terms of the indenture. If the firm should default on the interest payments or other terms of the indenture, the trustee may take the firm to court on behalf of all the bondholders in order to protect their principal.

TRUSTEE
Representative of the rights of bondholders who enforces the terms of the indenture

Another characteristic of all debt is risk—risk that the interest will not be paid, risk that the principal will not be repaid, risk that the price of the debt instrument may decline, and risk that inflation will continue.[1] Risk of default on interest and principal payments varies with different types of debt. The debt of the federal government has no risk of default on its interest payments and principal repayments. The reason for this absolute safety is that the government has the power to print money. The government can always issue the money necessary to pay the interest and repay the principal.

CREDIT RATINGS
Classification schemes designed to indicate the risks associated with a particular debt instrument

The debt of firms and individuals is not so riskless, for both may default on their obligations. To aid potential buyers of debt instruments, **credit rating** services have developed (Moody's, Dun & Bradstreet, and Standard & Poor's). These services rate the degree of risk of a debt instrument. Exhibit 9.1 illustrates the risk classifications offered by Moody's and Standard & Poor's. High-quality debt receives a rating of triple A, while poorer-quality debt receives progressively lower ratings. Although not all debt instruments are rated, the services do cover a significant number of debt obligations.

Ratings play an important role in the marketing of debt obligations. Since the risk of default may be substantial for poor-quality debt, some financial institutions and investors will not purchase debt with a low credit rating. If a firm's or municipality's debt rating falls, the entity may have difficulty selling its debt. Corporations and municipal governments thus seek to maintain good credit, for good credit ratings reduce the cost of borrowing and increase the marketability of the debt.

Debt is also subject to the risk of price fluctuations. Once it has been issued, the market price of the debt will rise or fall depending on market conditions. If interest rates rise, the price of debt must fall so that its fixed interest payment is competitive. The opposite is true if interest rates decline. The price of debt will rise, for the fixed interest payment makes it more attractive, and buyers bid up the debt's price. Why these fluctuations in the price of debt instruments occur is explained in more detail in the subsequent section on the pricing of debt instruments.

There is, however, one feature of debt that partially compensates for the risk of price fluctuations. The holder knows that the debt ultimately matures; the principal must be repaid. Thus, if the price falls and the debt instrument sells for a discount (less than the face value), the value of the debt must appreciate as it approaches maturity. For on the day it matures, the full amount of the principal must be repaid.

The final risk that all creditors must endure is inflation, which reduces the value of money. During inflation the debtor repays the loan in money that purchases less. If the lenders anticipate inflation, they will demand a higher rate of interest to help protect their purchasing power. For example, if the rate of inflation is 4 percent, the creditors may demand 6 percent, which nets them 2 percent in real terms. While the inflation causes the real value of the capital to deteriorate, the interest rate partially offsets the effects of inflation. Thus creditors must

[1] The risk of default is firm specific, so the impact of a bond's failure to pay interest or be retired is reduced through the construction of a diversified bond portfolio. The other sources of risk, however, apply to all bonds and cannot be reduced through the construction of a diversified portfolio.

EXHIBIT 9.1

Bond Ratings

Moody's Bond Ratings

Rating	Description	Rating	Description
Aaa	Bonds of highest quality	Ba	Bonds of speculative quality whose features cannot be considered well assured
Aa	Bonds of high quality	B	Bonds that lack characteristics of a desirable investment
A	Bonds whose security of principal and interest is considered adequate but may be impaired in the future	Caa	Bonds in poor standing that may be defaulted
Baa	Bonds of medium grade that are neither highly protected nor poorly secured	Ca	Speculative bonds that are often in default
		C	Bonds with little probability of any investment value (lowest rating)

For ratings Aa through B, 1, 2, and 3 represent the high, middle, and low ratings within the class.

Standard & Poor's Ratings

Rating	Description	Rating	Description
AAA	Bonds of highest quality	BB	Bonds of lower medium grade with few desirable investment characteristics
AA	High-quality debt obligations	B and CCC	Primarily speculative bonds with great uncertainties and major risk if exposed to adverse conditions.
A	Bonds that have a strong capacity to pay interest and principal but may be susceptible to adverse effects	C	Income bonds on which no interest is being paid
BBB	Bonds that have an adequate capacity to pay interest and principal but are more vulnerable to adverse economic conditions or changing circumstances	D	Bonds in default

Plus (+) and minus (−) are used to show relative strength within a rating category.

Source: *Adapted from Moody's Bond Record and Standard and Poor's Bond Guide.*

demand a rate of interest at least equal to the rate of inflation to maintain purchasing power.

TYPES OF CORPORATE BONDS

Many types of bonds are issued by corporations. These bonds may be issued in this country or abroad, in which case they are called Eurobonds. The following list indicates the categories of corporate bonds:

- mortgage bonds
- equipment trust certificates
- debentures
- subordinated debentures
- income bonds
- convertible bonds
- variable interest rate bonds
- zero coupon bonds

Each type of bond has characteristics that differentiate it from the others. Purchasers should be aware of the differences, for some types of bonds are decidedly more risky.

Mortgage Bonds

MORTGAGE BONDS
Bonds secured by a claim on real estate

COLLATERAL
Assets used to secure a loan or debt instrument

Mortgage bonds are issued to purchase specified real estate assets, and the acquired assets serve as **collateral.** That means the assets are pledged to secure the debt. If the firm should default on the interest or principal repayment, the creditors may take title to the pledged property. They may then choose to operate the fixed asset or to sell it. While the pledging of property may decrease the lender's risk of loss, the lender is not interested in taking possession and operating the property. Lenders earn their income through interest payments, not by the operation of the fixed assets. Creditors are rarely qualified to operate the assets if they were to take possession of them. If they were forced to sell the assets, they might find few buyers and have to sell at distress prices. For example, if a school defaults on interest on the mortgage payments for its dormitories, what can the creditors do with the buildings if they take possession of them? While the pledging of the assets increases the safety of the principal, the lenders prefer the prompt payment of interest and principal.

Equipment Trust Certificates

EQUIPMENT TRUST CERTIFICATES
Serial bonds issued by transportation companies that are secured by the equipment purchased with the proceeds of the loan

Equipment trust certificates are issued to finance specified equipment, and the assets are pledged as collateral. These certificates are primarily issued by railroads (for example, Southern Pacific) and airlines (for example, Delta Airlines) to finance rolling stock and airplanes, and this equipment is the collateral. This collateral is considered to be of excellent quality, for unlike fixed assets, this equipment can be readily *moved* and sold to other railroads and airlines should the firm default on the certificates.

A typical illustration of this type of bond is the 8.41 percent equipment trust certificates issued by CSX. The $93,568,000 raised by selling the certificates was used to acquire railroad gondola cars. CSX is required to retire annually a specified amount of the certificates, starting with $3,289,427 in 1993 and rising to $10,647,655 in 2006. The revenues generated by the railroad cars secure the interest and principal repayment. In case of default, the trustee may sell the equipment to recoup funds due owed the owners of the certificates.

Debentures

Debentures are unsecured bonds supported by the general credit of the firm. This type of debt is more risky, for in case of default or bankruptcy, the secured debt is redeemed before the debentures. Some debentures are **subordinated debentures,** and these are even riskier because they are subordinate to other debts of the firm. Even unsecured debt has a superior position to the subordinated debenture. These bonds are among the riskiest types of debt issued and usually have higher interest rates or other features, such as convertibility into the stock of the company, to compensate the lenders for the increased risk.

DEBENTURES
Unsecured bonds

SUBORDINATED DEBENTURES
Bonds with a lower (subordinate) claim on the firm's assets than the claims of other debt instruments

Financial institutions often prefer a firm to sell debentures to the general public. Since the debentures are general obligations of the company, they do not tie up its assets. If the firm needs additional money, it can use these assets as collateral. The financial institutions will be more willing to lend the firm the additional funds because of the collateral. If the assets had been previously pledged, the firm would lack this flexibility in its financing.

While the use of debentures may not decrease the ability of the firm to issue additional debt, default on the debentures usually means that all superior debt is in default. A frequent indenture clause stipulates that if any of the firm's debt is in default, all debt issues are in default, in which case the creditor may declare the entire debt to be due. Thus, a firm should not overextend itself through excessive use of unsecured debt any more than it should use excessive amounts of secured debt.

Income Bonds

Income Bonds require that the interest be paid only if the firm earns it. If the firm is unable to cover its other expenses, it is not legally obligated to pay the interest on these bonds. These are among the riskiest of all types of bonds and are rarely issued today by corporations. There is, however, a type of bond frequently issued by state and local governments that is similar to income bonds. These are **revenue bonds,** which pay the interest only if the revenue is earned. Examples of this type are the bonds issued to finance toll roads (for example, the New Jersey Turnpike). The interest on the debt is paid if the tolls generate sufficient revenue (after operating expenses) to cover the interest payments.

INCOME BONDS
Bonds whose interest is paid only if it is earned by the firm

REVENUE BONDS
Bonds supported by the assets the bonds financed; income bonds issued by state and local governments

Convertible Bonds

Convertible bonds are a hybrid type of security. Technically they are debt: The bonds pay interest that is a fixed obligation of the firm, and the bonds have a maturity date. But these bonds have a special feature—they may be converted into a specified number of shares of common stock. For example, the Hilton Hotel convertible bonds may be exchanged for 30.98 shares of Hilton Hotel's common stock. The value or market price of these bonds depends on both the value of the stock and the interest that the bonds pay.

CONVERTIBLE BONDS
Bonds that may be converted into (exchanged for) stock at the option of the bondholder

This type of bond offers the investor the advantages of both debt and equity. If the price of the common stock rises, the value of the bond must rise. The investor has the opportunity for capital gain should the price of the common stock rise. If, however, the price of the common stock does not appreciate, the investor still owns a debt obligation of the company. The company must pay interest on this debt and must retire it at maturity. Thus, the investor has the safety of an investment in a debt instrument.

The convertible bond also offers the firm several advantages. First, if the firm gives investors the conversion feature, it is able to issue the bond with a lower rate of interest. Second, the conversion price is set above the market price of the stock when the bond is issued. If the bond is converted, the firm issues fewer shares than would have been issued if the firm had sold common stock. Therefore, the current stockholders' position is diluted less by the issuing of convertible bonds. Third, when the convertible bond is issued, the management of the firm does not anticipate having to retire the bond. Instead, management anticipates that the bond will be converted into stock, and this conversion ends the necessity to retire the debt. Fourth, when the bond is converted, the transfer of debt to common stock increases the equity base of the firm. Since the firm will then be less financially leveraged, it may be able to issue additional debt.

Convertible bonds appear to offer advantages to both investors and firms. They have been a popular financing vehicle for firms ranging from large established firms like IBM to small firms. However, since convertible bonds are a hybrid security that mixes elements of debts and equity, they are difficult to analyze. For this reason, a detailed discussion is deferred to Chapter 13, which follows the material on common stock.

Variable Interest Rate Bonds

Prior to the mid-1970s, once bonds were issued the amount of interest was fixed. With the advent of increased inflation in the 1970s, corporations started issuing bonds with variable interest rates. Citicorp was the first major American firm to offer **variable interest rate bonds** to the general public. These bonds were not the first examples of variable interest rate bonds, however, for there had been prior issues in the United States, and variable interest rate mortgages have existed in other countries for years.

VARIABLE INTEREST RATE BONDS
Long-term debt instruments whose interest payments vary with changes in short-term interest rates

Two features of the Citicorp bond were unique: (1) a variable interest rate tied to the interest rate on Treasury bills, and (2) the right of the holder of the bond to redeem it at its face value. The interest rate of the Citicorp bond was 1 percent above the average Treasury bill rate during a specified time period. This variability of the interest rate meant that if short-term interest rates rose, the interest rate paid by this bond would increase. The bond's owner would participate in any increase in short-term interest rates. Of course, if the short-term interest rates declined, the holder of the bond would earn a lower rate of interest.

The second unique feature of the Citicorp bond was that the holder of the bond had the option to redeem the bond for its face value two years after it was issued. This option would subsequently recur every six months. The holder knew that the principal could be obtained twice a year. If the holder needed the money quicker, the bond could be sold, for there existed an active secondary market in these debt instruments.

After these variable interest rate bonds were issued, short-term interest rates did, in fact, decline. The Citicorp bond paid 9.7 percent in the first year but only 6.6 percent during the second year. The decline in short-term interest rates resulted in a decline in investor fascination with variable interest rate bonds.

Zero Coupon Bonds

In 1981 a new type of bond was sold to the general public. These bonds pay no interest and are sold at large discounts. The path-breaking issue was the JC Penney **zero coupon bond.** This bond was initially sold in 1981 for a discount ($330) but paid $1,000 at maturity in 1989. The investor's funds grew from $330 to $1,000 after eight years. The rate of growth (the yield on the bond) was 14.86 percent.[2]

ZERO COUPON BONDS
Bonds that are initially sold at a discount and on which interest accrues and is paid at maturity

After the initial success of this issue, several other firms, including IBM Credit Corporation (the financing arm of IBM), issued similar bonds. In each case the firm makes no cash interest payments. The bond sells for a discount, and the investor's return accrues from the appreciation of the bond's value as it approaches maturity.

One tax feature, however, reduces the attractiveness of zero coupon bonds. The IRS taxes the accrued interest as if it were received. The investor must pay federal income tax on the earned interest even though the investor receives the funds only when the bond matures. Thus, zero coupon bonds are of little interest to investors except as part of tax-deferred pension plans, because the tax on the accrued interest in the account is deferred until the funds are withdrawn. Therefore, the primary reason for acquiring a zero coupon bond is to use it in conjunction with a tax-deferred pension plan.

High-Yield Securities—Junk Bonds

High-yield securities **(junk bonds)** are not a particular type of bond but a name given to debt of low quality (that is, bonds rated below triple B). Junk bonds are usually debentures and may be subordinated to the firm's other debt obligations. The poor quality of this debt requires that junk bonds offer high yields, which may be three to four percentage points greater than the yield available on high-quality bonds. Junk bonds are bought by financial institutions and individuals who are accustomed to investing in poor-quality bonds and who are willing to accept the larger risk in order to earn the higher yields.

JUNK BONDS
Poor-quality debt with high yields and high probability of default

[2] This yield is calculated as follows:

$$\$330(1 + i)^8 = \$1{,}000$$
$$(1 + i)^8 = \$1{,}000/\$330 = 3.0303$$
$$i = (3.0303)^{.125} - 1 = 14.86$$

If a financial calculator is used, the yield is determined as follows: PV = −330; N = 8; PMT = 0; FV = 1,000, and I = ? When these data are entered into the calculator, I = 14.86 percent.

FOREIGN BONDS

U.S. firms may also issue bonds in foreign countries to raise funds for foreign investments, such as plant and equipment. For example, Mobil reported in its 1998 annual report that it had long-term debt of $3,670 billion, of which $1,739 billion (47 percent) was payable in foreign countries. These bonds fall into two basic types, depending on the currency in which they are denominated. U.S. companies can sell bonds denominated in the local currency (for example, British pounds, or the firm can sell abroad bonds denominated in U.S. dollars. Correspondingly, non–U.S. firms can sell bonds denominated in their local currency or a foreign currency. If these bonds are issued in the United States by a foreign company and denominated in U.S. dollars, they are referred to as "Yankee bonds."

Firms that sell bonds denominated in another currency have the risk associated with changes in exchange rates. Thus, issuers of Yankee bonds bear the risk associated with fluctuations in the value of the dollar. If the value of the dollar were to rise, more domestic currency would be required to retire the debt. Of course, the converse also applies. If the value of the dollar were to fall, the firm profits because less domestic currency would be needed to pay off the bonds.

EUROBOND
Bond sold in a foreign country but denominated in the currency of the issuing firm

Eurobonds are sold outside of the country of issue but denominated in the currency of the issuing company. Such bonds can be denominated in pounds or yen, so the term is not limited to European currencies. If IBM sells Eurobonds in Europe, it promises to make payments in dollars and avoids the risk associated with changes in exchange rates. U.S. investors who purchase these bonds also do not have to convert the payments from the local currency into dollars and thereby also avoid currency risk. Foreign investors, however, do have to convert the dollar payments into their currency, and do not avoid exchange rate risk. This brings up an essential point: When investments and currencies cross international borders, someone must bear the risk associated with fluctuations in exchange rates.

Although Eurobonds are debt instruments, they are different from bonds issued in the United States. First, they pay interest annually instead of semiannually so their yields are not comparable to yields on U.S. bonds unless adjusted for the differences in compounding. Second, Eurobonds are not registered with the SEC for sale in the United States, so American investors must purchase them in another country. Third, although the interest is subject to federal income tax, no taxes are withheld, so these bonds may be acquired by individuals (both American and non-American) for the purpose of illegally evading taxes. To the extent that the latter is true, the prices of Eurobonds may be artificially bid up, so their yields are less than those on comparable bonds subject to the withholding of taxes.

REGISTERED AND BOOK ENTRY BONDS

In the past, bonds were issued in bearer form with physical coupons attached. Possession of the bond was evidence of ownership, and the owner would detach the interest coupons and send them to the paying agent for collection. Individuals who owned these bonds and lived on the fixed interest payments were referred to as "coupon clippers." Under current law, new issues of coupon bonds are no longer

EXHIBIT 9.2

Example of a Registered Bond

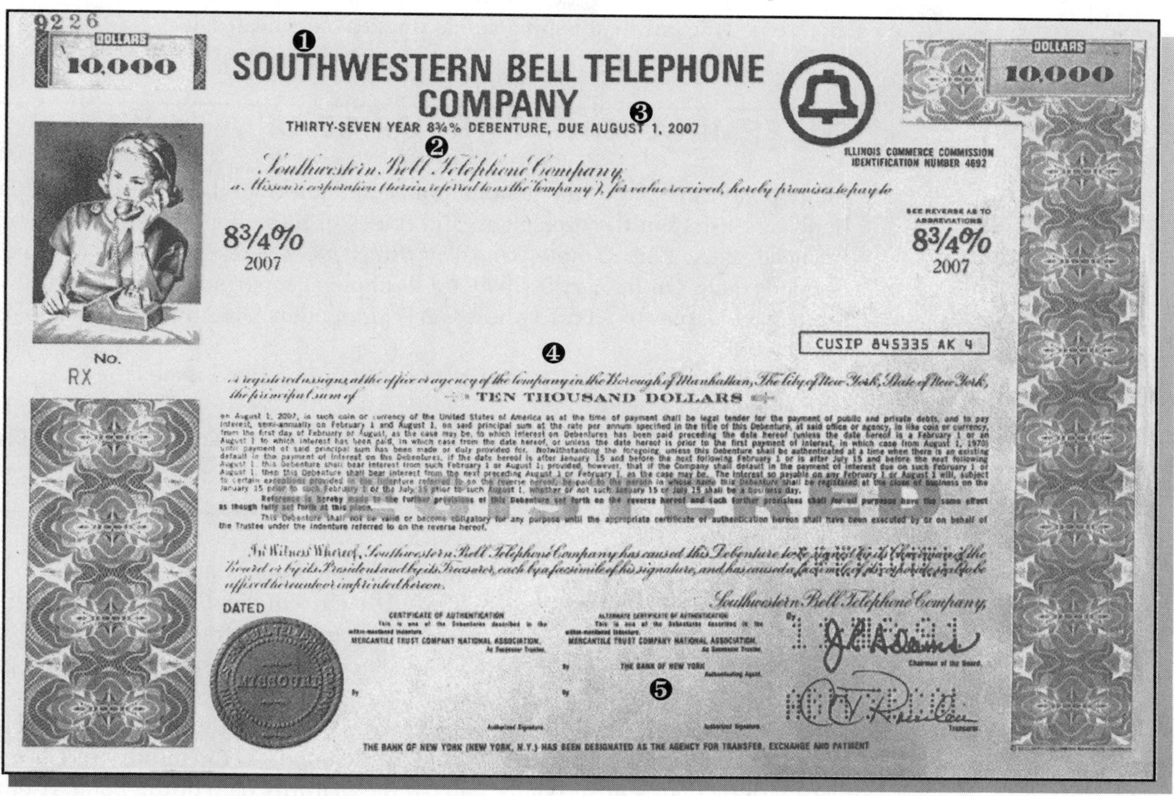

9226

DOLLARS 10,000

SOUTHWESTERN BELL TELEPHONE COMPANY

THIRTY-SEVEN YEAR 8¾% DEBENTURE, DUE AUGUST 1, 2007

ILLINOIS COMMERCE COMMISSION IDENTIFICATION NUMBER 4692

Southwestern Bell Telephone Company, a Missouri corporation (herein referred to as the "Company"), for value received, hereby promises to pay to

SEE REVERSE AS TO ABBREVIATIONS

8¾% 2007

CUSIP 845335 AK 4

No. RX

or registered assigns, at the office or agency of the Company in the Borough of Manhattan, The City of New York, State of New York, the principal sum of TEN THOUSAND DOLLARS

on August 1, 2007, in such coin or currency of the United States of America as at the time of payment shall be legal tender for the payment of public and private debts, and to pay interest, semi-annually on February 1 and August 1, on said principal sum at the rate per annum specified in the title of this Debenture, at said office or agency, in like coin or currency, from the first day of February or August, as the case may be, to which interest on Debentures has been paid preceding the date hereof (unless the date hereof is a February 1 or an August 1 to which interest has been paid, in which case from the date hereof, or unless the date hereof is prior to the first payment of interest, in which case from August 1, 1970) until payment of said principal sum has been made or duly provided for. Notwithstanding the foregoing, unless this Debenture shall be authenticated at a time when there is an existing default in the payment of interest on the Debentures, if the date hereof is after January 15 and before the next following February 1 or is after July 15 and before the next following August 1, this Debenture shall bear interest from such February 1 or August 1; provided, however, that if the Company shall default in the payment of interest due on such February 1 or August 1, then this Debenture shall bear interest from the next preceding August 1 or February 1, as the case may be. The interest so payable on any February 1 or August 1 will, subject to certain exceptions provided in the Indenture referred to on the reverse hereof, be paid to the person in whose name this Debenture shall be registered at the close of business on the January 15 prior to such February 1 or the July 15 prior to such August 1, whether or not such January 15 or July 15 shall be a business day.

Reference is hereby made to the further provisions of this Debenture set forth on the reverse hereof and such further provisions shall for all purposes have the same effect as though fully set forth at this place.

This Debenture shall not be valid or become obligatory for any purpose until the appropriate certificate of authentication hereon shall have been executed by or on behalf of the Trustee under the Indenture referred to on the reverse hereof.

In Witness Whereof, Southwestern Bell Telephone Company has caused this Debenture to be signed by its Chairman of the Board or by its President and by its Treasurer, each by a facsimile of his signature, and has caused a facsimile of its corporate seal to be affixed hereunto or imprinted hereon.

DATED

CERTIFICATE OF AUTHENTICATION

MERCANTILE TRUST COMPANY NATIONAL ASSOCIATION

ALTERNATE CERTIFICATE OF AUTHENTICATION

MERCANTILE TRUST COMPANY NATIONAL ASSOCIATION

THE BANK OF NEW YORK

Southwestern Bell Telephone Company

Chairman of the Board

Treasurer

THE BANK OF NEW YORK (NEW YORK, N.Y.) HAS BEEN DESIGNATED AS THE AGENCY FOR TRANSFER, EXCHANGE AND PAYMENT

❶ Company
❷ Coupon
❸ Maturity Date
❹ Name of Registered Owner
❺ Trustee

permitted. (They are too easy to use as a means to evade income and estate taxes.) Some coupon bonds, however, still exist, but these will disappear as they mature and are retired.

Even though coupon bonds will cease to exist, the word *coupon* continues to be used to mean the periodic interest payment made by a bond. Today bonds are issued either in registered or book entry form. Registered bonds are registered as to principal and interest and are similar in appearance to stock certificates, as is illustrated by the 8¾ percent Southwestern Bell bond in Exhibit 9.2. In this illustration, the interest payment or "coupon" is $43.75 semiannually per $1,000 and is sent to the registered owner.

Even registered bonds are ceasing to exist because the current trend is to issue bonds as book entries. All U.S. Treasury bonds are now issued in book entry form, and the same applies to many corporate and municipal bonds. No actual physical bonds are issued; instead a record of owners is maintained by the issuer (or the bank that acts as the transfer and paying agent). Such a system is obviously more cost efficient than issuing actual physical certificates.

DETERMINATION OF THE PRICE OF A BOND

Many bonds are sold to the general public and are traded daily like stocks. Some bonds are listed on the exchanges, and trades in these bonds are reported by the financial press. For example, *The Wall Street Journal* reports trades in hundreds of bonds daily. On January 5, 2000, for example, it reported transactions in 13 different bond issues of AT&T (whereas AT&T, of course, has only one issue of common stock).

The general form for reporting transactions in a bond issue is

Bonds	Current Yield	Volume	Close	Net Change
ATT 5⅜ 22	5.2	20	103	+½

The first entries describe the bond, which in this example is an AT&T bond with a 5⅜ coupon that matures in 2022. The current yield (discussed later in this chapter) is 5.2 percent; 20 of these $1,000 bonds were traded. The closing price was 103 ($1,030), which was ½ ($50) greater than the closing price on the previous day.

While bond prices fluctuate daily, the price of a bond (in a given risk class) is primarily related to (1) the interest paid by the bond, (2) the interest rate investors may earn on competitive bonds, and (3) the maturity date of the bond. A bond is a debt instrument that makes periodic interest payments (usually semiannually) that are similar to annuity payments. Part of the bond's value is in the present value of these interest payments. At maturity the principal is repaid. The rest of the bond's value is in the present value of this principal repayment. Thus, the price of a bond today is determined by the present value of the interest payments and the present value of the principal repayment.

The value of a bond is expressed algebraically in Equation 9.1 and subsequently in terms of the present value formulas discussed in Chapter 7. A bond's value is

9.1

$$P_B = \frac{PMT}{(1+i)^1} + \frac{PMT}{(1+i)^2} + \cdots + \frac{PMT}{(1+i)^n} + \frac{FV}{(1+i)^n},$$

in which P_B indicates the current price of the bond; *PMT,* the periodic interest payment; *n,* the number of years (payments) to maturity; *FV,* the principal amount to be received in the future; and *i,* the current interest rate.

The calculation of a bond's price using Equation 9.1 may be illustrated by a simple example. A firm has a $1,000 bond outstanding that matures in three years with a 6 percent coupon rate ($60 annually). All that is needed to determine the price of the bond is the current interest rate, which is the interest rate that is being paid by newly issued, competitive bonds with the same length of time to maturity and the same degree of risk. If the competitive bonds yield 6 percent, then the price of this bond will be par ($1,000), for:

$$
\begin{aligned}
P_B &= \frac{\$60}{(1+0.06)^1} + \frac{\$60}{(1+0.06)^2} + \frac{\$60}{(1+0.06)^3} + \frac{\$1{,}000}{(1+0.06)^3} \\
&= \$56.60 + \$53.40 + \$50.38 + \$839.62 \\
&= \$1{,}000.00.
\end{aligned}
$$

If competitive bonds are selling to yield 8 percent, this bond will be unattractive to investors. They will not be willing to pay $1,000 for a bond yielding 6 percent when they could buy competing bonds at the same price that yield 8 percent. In order for this bond to compete with the others, its price must decline sufficiently to yield 8 percent. In terms of Equation 9.1, the price must be

$$
\begin{aligned}
P_B &= \frac{\$60}{(1+0.08)^1} + \frac{\$60}{(1+0.08)^2} + \frac{\$60}{(1+0.08)^3} + \frac{\$1{,}000}{(1+0.08)^3} \\
&= \$60(0.926) + \$60(0.857) + \$60(0.794) + \$1{,}000(0.794) \\
&= \$55.56 + \$51.42 + \$47.64 + \$794 \\
&= \$948.62.
\end{aligned}
$$

The price of the bond must decline to approximately $950, which means it must sell for a *discount* (a price less than the stated principal) to be competitive with comparable bonds. At that price, investors will earn $60 per year in interest and approximately $50 in capital gains over the three years, for a total annual return of 8 percent on their investment. The capital gain occurs because the bond is purchased for $948.62, but when it matures, the holder will receive $1,000.

If comparable debt were to yield 4 percent, the price of the bond in the previous example would rise. In this case the price of the bond would be

$$
\begin{aligned}
P_B &= \frac{\$60}{(1+0.04)^1} + \frac{\$60}{(1+0.04)^2} + \frac{\$60}{(1+0.04)^3} + \frac{\$1{,}000}{(1+0.04)^3} \\
&= \$60(0.962) + \$60(0.925) + \$60(0.889) + \$1{,}000(0.889) \\
&= \$1{,}055.56.
\end{aligned}
$$

The bond, therefore, would sell at a *premium* (in other words, a price greater than the stated principal). Although it may seem implausible for the bond to sell at a premium, this would occur if the market interest rate were to fall below the coupon rate of interest stated on the bond.

These price calculations are lengthy, but the number of computations can be reduced when you realize that the valuation of a bond has two components: a flow of interest payments and a final repayment of principal. Since interest payments are fixed and are paid every year, they may be treated as an annuity. The principal repayment may be treated as a simple lump-sum payment. Thus the price of a bond is

$$\text{Price of bond} = \text{coupon} \times \text{interest factor for the present value of an annuity} + \text{principal} \times \text{interest factor for the present value of \$1.00}$$

$$= \text{coupon} \times PVAIF + \text{principal} \times PVIF.$$

If a $1,000 bond pays $60 per year in interest and matures after three years, its current value is the present value of the $60 annuity for three years and the present value of the $1,000 that will be received after three years. If the interest rate is 8 percent, the current value of the bond is

$$P_B = \$60(PVAIF\ 8I,\ 3N) + \$1{,}000(\text{PVIF}\ 8I,\ 3N)$$

$$P_B = \$60(2.577) + \$1{,}000(0.794) = \$948.62,$$

in which 2.577 is the interest factor for the present value of a $1 annuity at 8 percent for three years and 0.794 is the interest factor for the present value of $1 at 8 percent after three years. This is the same answer that was derived earlier, but the amount of arithmetic has been reduced.

Since most bonds pay interest semiannually, the above illustration should be adjusted for semiannual interest payments. First, divide the coupon by 2 to determine the six-month payment ($60/2 = $30); second, divide the rate of interest by 2 to determine the semiannual interest rate (8%/2 = 4%); and third, multiply the number of years by 2 to determine the number of time periods, denoted by the letter n when other than one year (3 × 2 = 6). After these adjustments, the value of the bond is

$$P_B = \$30(PVAIF\ 4I,\ 6N) + \$1{,}000(PVIF\ 4I,\ 6N)$$

$$= \$30(5.242) + \$1{,}000(0.790) = \$947.26.$$

This valuation is marginally smaller than when annual compounding was used since the bond's price must decline slightly more to compensate for the more frequent compounding. If interest rates rise and bond prices fall, the decline will be greater when the price is calculated using semiannual payments, because the investor forgos more lost interest from the higher rates when interest is paid semiannually. The lower price compensates the buyer for the lost interest.

A bond's price is easy to compute when you use a financial calculator. In the previous example, a 6 percent coupon bond that matures in three years sold for $947.26 when the comparable interest rate was 8 percent. To use a financial calculator to determine the price of the bond (*PV*), enter the principal repayment as the future value (*FV* = 1,000), the annual interest payments (*PMT* = 30), the time

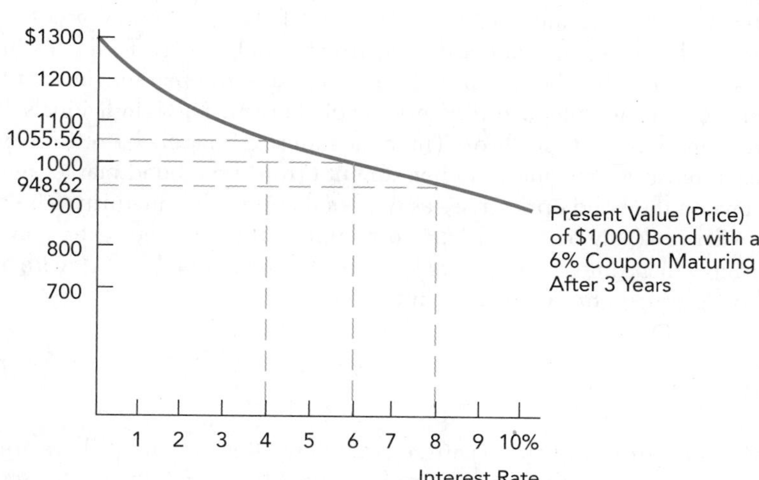

FIGURE 9.1

Relationship between a Bond's Price and Interest Rates

to maturity ($N = 6$), and the yield on comparable debt ($I = 4$). The calculator determines the present value to be $947.58, which, except for rounding off, is the same price derived using the interest tables.

The preceding examples illustrate an important general conclusion: Bond prices and changes in market interest are inversely related. *When market interest rates rise, bond prices decline. When market interest rates fall, bond prices rise.* Higher interest rates depressed the bond's current value. This general conclusion is illustrated in Figure 9.1. The bond's price declined from $1,000 to $948.62 when interest rates rose from 6 percent to 8 percent, but the price rose to $1,055.56 when interest rates declined to 4 percent (assuming annual interest payments).

This negative relationship between the price of a bond and changes in current interest rates is, of course, the interest rate risk discussed in Chapter 8. Although all bonds exhibit this price volatility, the price fluctuations of bonds with longer terms to maturity tend to be greater than the price fluctuations of bonds with shorter terms to maturity. In the previous example, the price of the three-year bond declined from $1,000 to $948.62 when interest rates rose from 6 percent to 8 percent. If the bond had had a 20-year term to maturity, its price would have fallen to $803.59. The increased price volatility also applies if interest rates fall. Thus the price of a 20-year bond that pays $60 annually would rise to $1,271.82 if interest rates were to fall from 6 percent to 4 percent.

If investors anticipate that interest rates will decline, they are expecting the price of previously issued bonds to rise. This price increase must occur for previously issued bonds to have the same yield as bonds being currently issued. The converse is also true, for if investors anticipate that interest rates will rise, they are also anticipating that the price of currently available bonds will decline. This decline must occur for previously issued bonds to offer the same yield as currently issued bonds. Therefore, if investors can anticipate the direction of change in interest rates, they can also anticipate the direction of change in bond prices.

Investors, however, may anticipate incorrectly and thus suffer losses in the bond market. If they buy bonds and interest rates rise, the market value of their bonds must decline and the investors suffer capital losses. These individuals, however, have something in their favor: The bonds must ultimately be retired. Since the principal must be redeemed, an investment error in the bond market may be corrected when the bond's price rises as the bond approaches maturity. The capital losses will eventually be erased. The correction of the error, however, may take years, during which time the investors have lost the higher yields that were available on bonds issued after their initial investments.

YIELDS

The word *yield* is frequently used with regard to investing in bonds. There are two important types of yield: the current yield and the yield to maturity. This section will differentiate between these two yields.

The Current Yield

The current yield (CY) is the percentage that the investor earns annually. It is simply

9.2

$$CY = \frac{\text{Annual interest payment}}{\text{Price of the bond}}.$$

The bond used in the previous example has a coupon rate of 6 percent. Thus, when the price of the bond is $948.62, the current yield is

$$\frac{\$60}{\$948.62} = 6.3\%.$$

The current yield is important because it gives the investor an indication of the current return that will be earned on the investment. Investors who seek high current income prefer bonds that offer a high current yield.

The current yield, however, can be very misleading, for it fails to consider any change in the price of the bond that may occur if the bond is held to maturity. Obviously, if a bond is bought at a discount, its value must rise as it approaches maturity. The opposite occurs if the bond is purchased for a premium, for its price will decline as maturity approaches. For this reason it is desirable to know the bond's yield to maturity.

The Yield to Maturity

The yield to maturity considers not only the current income that is generated by the bond but also any change in its value when it is held to maturity. If the bond referred to earlier is purchased for \$948.62 and is held to maturity, after three years the investor will receive a return of 8 percent. This is the yield to maturity, because this return considers not only the current interest return of 6.3 percent but also the price appreciation of the bond from \$948.62 at the time of purchase to \$1,000 at maturity. Since the yield to maturity considers both the flow of interest income and the price change, it is a more accurate measure of the return offered to investors by a particular bond issue than the current yield.

The yield to maturity may be determined by using Equation 9.1. That equation reads:

$$P_B = \frac{PMT}{(1+i)^1} + \frac{PMT}{(1+i)^2} + \cdots + \frac{PMT}{(1+i)^n} + \frac{FV}{(1+i)^n}.$$

The i, which was defined as the rate of interest paid by newly issued bonds, is also the yield to maturity. It is that rate which equates the present value of the interest payments plus the present value of the principal repayment with the cost of the bond when the bond is held to maturity. If the investor buys a bond and holds it until maturity, the return is the yield to maturity, and that rate has to be the current rate of interest being paid by comparable bonds with the same term and credit ratings.

Determining the yield to maturity when the coupon rate of interest, the bond's price, and the maturity date are known is not easy. For example, if a \$1,000 bond that matures in three years and pays \$100 annually were selling for \$952 and the investor wanted to know the yield to maturity, the calculation would be

$$\$952 = \frac{\$100}{(1+i)^1} + \frac{\$100}{(1+i)^2} + \frac{\$100}{(1+i)^3} + \frac{\$1{,}000}{(1+i)^3}.$$

Solving this equation can be a formidable task because there is no simple arithmetical computation to determine the value of i. Instead, the investor selects a value for i and plugs it into the equation. If this value equates the left-hand and right-hand sides of the equation, then that value of i is the yield to maturity.

If the value does not equate the two sides of the equation, another value must be selected. This process is repeated until a value for i is found that equates both sides of the equation. Obviously, that can be a long process. For example, suppose the investor selects 14 percent and substitutes it into the right-hand side of the equation:

$$P_B = \frac{\$100}{(1+0.14)^1} + \frac{\$100}{(1+0.14)^2} + \frac{\$100}{(1+0.14)^3} + \frac{\$1{,}000}{(1+0.14)^3}.$$

Since the individual has both an interest rate (0.14 percent) and the number of years (3 years), the interest factors for the present value of an annuity and of a dollar may be obtained from the appropriate interest tables and used to determine the value of the bond at that rate for that term to maturity. That is,

$$P_B = \$100(\text{PVAIF 14I, 3N}) + \$1{,}000(\text{PVIF 14I, 3N})$$
$$= \$100(2.322) + \$1{,}000(0.675)$$
$$= \$907.20.$$

If the yield to maturity were 14 percent, the bond would sell for $907.20; however, the bond is selling for $952, so 14 percent cannot be its yield to maturity. The selected yield was too high, which caused the present value (the price of the bond) to be too low. The investor must select another, lower rate and repeat the process. (If the investor had obtained a value greater than the current price, the selected rate was too low, and the investor should select a higher rate.) If the investor had selected 12 percent, then

$$P_B = \$100(\text{PVAIF 12I, 3N}) + \$1{,}000(\mathit{PVIF}\ \text{12I, 3N})$$
$$= \$100(2.402) + \$1{,}000(0.712)$$
$$= \$952.20.$$

Thus, the yield to maturity, compounded annually, is 12 percent.

The above process to determine the yield to maturity is tedious, and since interest tables have only discrete rates and numbers of years, the resulting yield is often only approximate. The yield to maturity is readily determined by the use of a financial calculator. Enter the price of the bond ($PV = -952.20$, the maturity value ($FV = 1{,}000$), the interest payment ($PMT = 100$), and the number of payments to maturity ($N = 3$), and instruct the calculator to determine the rate (I = 11.99). The 11.99 percent interest rate is essentially equal to 12 percent and is the bond's yield to maturity.

A Comparison of the Current Yield and the Yield to Maturity

The current yield and the yield to maturity are equal only if the bond sells for its principal amount or par. If the bond sells at a discount, the yield to maturity exceeds the current yield. This may be illustrated by the bond in the previous example. When it sells at a discount (such as $952), the current yield is only 10.5 percent. However, the yield to maturity is 12 percent. The appreciation on the value of the bond increases the return, so the yield to maturity exceeds the current yield.

If the bond sells at a premium, the current yield exceeds the yield to maturity. For example, if the bond sells for $1,052, the current yield is 9.5 percent ($100 ÷ $1,052) and the yield to maturity is 8 percent. The yield to maturity is less because the loss that occurs when the price of the bond declines from $1,052 to $1,000 at maturity has been incorporated into the calculation of the yield.

Exhibit 9.3 presents the current yield and the yield to maturity at different prices for a bond with an 8 percent coupon that matures in ten years. As may be seen in the table, the larger the discount (or the smaller the premium), the greater are both the current yield and the yield to maturity. For example, when the bond

EXHIBIT 9.3

Current Yields and Yields to Maturity for a Ten-Year Bond with an 8 Percent Annual Coupon

Price of Bond	Coupon	Current Yield	Yield to Maturity
$1,107	8.0%	7.2%	6.5%
1,048	8.0	7.6	7.3
1,000	8.0	8.0	8.0
967	8.0	8.3	8.5
911	8.0	8.8	9.4
882	8.0	9.1	9.9
883	8.0	9.6	10.8
798	8.0	10.0	11.5

sells for $882, the yield to maturity is 9.9 percent, but it rises to 11.5 percent when the price declines to $798.

RETIRING DEBT

Debt must ultimately be retired. This retirement may occur on or before the maturity date of the debt. When the bond is issued, a method for periodic retirement is usually specified, for very few debt issues are retired in one lump payment at the final maturity date. Instead, part of the issue is systematically retired each year. This systematic retirement may be achieved by issuing the bond in series or by having a sinking fund. In addition, dramatic changes in interest rates may cause a corporation to retire bonds before maturity by repurchasing or by calling the debt.

Serial Bonds

In an issue of **serial bonds,** some bonds mature each year. This type of bond is usually issued by a corporation to finance specific equipment (for example, railroad cars), and the equipment is pledged as collateral. As the equipment is depreciated, the cash flow generated by the profits and depreciation expense is used to retire the bonds in series as they mature.

SERIAL BONDS
Debt issued in a series so that some of the bonds periodically mature

Exhibit 9.4 presents the repayment schedule for a typical issue to serial bonds. The entire issue of Norfolk Redevelopment and Housing Authority Educational Facility Revenue Bonds is for $9,115,000. Most the bonds are retired in a series over a period of 14 years. The amount of debt redeemed each year starts at $280,000 in the year 2000 and rises to $515,000 in 2013. (Notice that the interest rate paid by each bond in the series rises as the time to maturity increases. This positive relationship between time and the interest rate was initially illustrated in Figure 2.1, which depicted a positive yield curve.) This particular issue also includes $3,775,000 of term bonds, which mature in 2019.

While a few corporate bonds are issued in series such as the CSX equipment trust certificates referred to earlier in this chapter, most serial bonds are issued by state and local governments. The funds raised by issuing the bonds are used for

EXHIBIT 9.4

Example of a Serial Bond

$9,115,000
Norfolk Redevelopment and Housing Authority
Educational Facility Revenue Bonds
Tidewater Community College
Series of 1999

Maturity Date	Amounts	Interest Rates
2000	$280,000	3.65%
2001	290,000	4.15
2002	305,000	4.30
2003	315,000	4.40
2004	330,000	4.50
2005	345,000	4.65
2006	365,000	4.75
2007	380,000	4.85
2008	400,000	4.95
2009	420,000	5.05
2010	440,000	5.15
2011	465,000	5.25
2012	490,000	5.35
2013	515,000	5.40
2019	3,775,000	5.65

capital improvements such as new school buildings. The serial bonds are then retired over a number of years by the tax revenues or fees changed by the governmental unit. (Municipal bonds are covered later in the section on government securities.)

Sinking Funds

SINKING FUND
Series of periodic payments to retire a bond issue

Sinking funds are generally employed to ease the retirement of bonds. A **sinking fund** is a periodic payment for the purpose of retiring the debt issue. The payment may be made to a trustee, who invests the money to earn interest. The periodic payments plus the accumulated interest retire the debt when it matures.

In another type of sinking fund, the firm is required to retire a specified amount of the principal each year. The firm may randomly identify the bonds to be retired. Once the sinking fund has selected the individual bonds, the holders must surrender the bonds to receive the principal. There is no reason for the bondholders to continue to hold the bonds, for interest payments cease.

A variation on this type of sinking fund permits the firm to buy back the bonds on the open market instead of randomly selecting and retiring them at par. If the bonds are currently selling at a discount, the firm does not have to expend $1,000 to retire the bonds. For example, if the current price of a bond is $800, the firm can retire a $1,000 bond with an outlay of only $800. Such a repurchase meets the sinking fund requirement and obviously is advantageous for the firm.

Repurchasing Debt

If interest rates have risen and bond prices have declined, a firm may retire debt by purchasing it. The purchases may be made from time to time, and sellers of the bonds need not know that the company is purchasing and retiring the bonds. The company may also announce the intention to purchase and retire the bonds at a specified price. The bondholders then may sell their bonds at the specified price.

The advantage to the firm of retiring debt that is selling at a discount is the immediate savings. If $1,000 bonds are currently selling for $600, the firm reduces its debt by $1,000 with only a $600 outlay in cash. There is a $400 saving (in other words, extraordinary gain) from purchasing and retiring the debt at a discount. This gain generates income for the firm's stockholders. For example, General Cinema earned over $419.6 million from repurchasing $1.8 billion of its long-term debt at a discount.

On the surface, this method may appear to be a desirable means to retire debt, but such appearances may be deceiving. Using money to repurchase debt is an investment decision just like buying plant and equipment. If the firm repurchases the debt, it cannot use the money for other purposes. The question is, which is the better use of the money: purchasing other income-earning assets, or retiring the debt? Unlike a sinking fund requirement (which management must meet), repurchasing the debt is a voluntary act. The lower the price of the debt, the greater the potential benefit from the purchase, but the firm's management must determine if it is the best use of the firm's scarce resource—cash.

Calling the Debt

Some bonds have a **call feature,** which permits the issuer to redeem the bond prior to maturity. If interest rates fall after a bond has been issued, it may be advantageous for the company to issue a new bond at the lower interest rates. The proceeds then can be used to retire the older bond with the higher interest rates. The company "calls" the older bond and retires it.

CALL FEATURE
Right of a debtor to retire (call) a bond prior to maturity

Of course, such a refunding hurts the bondholders, who lose the higher yielding instruments. To protect these creditors, a call feature usually has a call penalty, such as a year's interest. If the initial issue had a 9 percent interest rate, the company would have to pay $1,090 to retire $1,000 worth of debt. While such a call penalty does protect bondholders, a company can still refinance if interest rates decline enough to justify paying the call penalty.

Such refinancing frequently occurred during the early 1990s, when interest rates fell significantly below the levels of the 1980s. Firms that had previously issued debt with high interest rates issued new bonds with lower interest coupons, called the old debt, and paid any applicable penalties. For example, Textron redeemed all of its 9½ percent bonds due in 2016. The firm paid $1,056.10 per $1,000 bond to retire the debt prior to maturity. The lower cost of new debt sufficiently reduced interest expense to justify paying the $56.10 call penalty.

GOVERNMENT SECURITIES

The federal, state, and local governments issue a variety of debt instruments to tap the funds of individuals, firms, and other governments with funds to invest. The general features of these securities are essentially the same as corporate debt; they pay interest and must be retired at some specified time in the future. The bonds may be callable, and while many do not have sinking funds, the debt is often issued in series, so that a specified series periodically matures.

Federal Government Debt

The federal government issues securities that range from short-term Treasury bills to long-term Treasury bonds with denominations ranging from $50 to $1,000,000. The variety of this debt is illustrated in Exhibit 9.5, which gives the type of debt, the term, the amount outstanding, and the percentage of the total debt comprised by each issue. The emphasis is on short- to intermediate-term financing, primarily because, as was illustrated in Figure 2.1, interest rates on short-term debt are usually less than on long-term debt. Thus, the use of short-term debt reduces the Treasury's interest expense.

Perhaps the most widely held federal government debt is the Series EE savings bond, which is issued in denominations as small as $50 and sold at a discount, so the earned interest accrues but is not paid until the bond is redeemed or matures.[3] EE bonds are designed to attract the funds of modest investors and compete directly with other savings vehicles, such as savings accounts or certificates of deposit issued by banks. EE bonds have one significant feature that differentiates them from traditional savings vehicles: The earned interest may be tax deferred until the individual redeems the bond or it matures (whichever comes first). While the investor can choose to pay the tax as the interest accrues, most individuals take advantage of the tax deferral.

Series EE bonds are an illustration of a bond with no secondary market. The majority of federal government Treasury bills and bonds may be bought and sold in the secondary markets. Treasury bills are short-term securities issued by the federal government that compete against other money market instruments. (See the discussion of money market instruments in Chapter 3.)

Intermediate-term federal government debt consists of Treasury notes, which are issued in denominations of $1,000 to more than $100,000 and mature in one

[3] Effective May 1, 1995, the term of the new EE bond was set at 17 years. If the bonds are not redeemed at maturity, they will continue to earn interest for an additional 13 years, for a total of 30 years. The rate of interest was divided into a short-term rate that applies for the first 5 years and a long-term rate that applies to the last 12 years. The interest rates are announced every May 1 and November 1 and apply for the following six months. For years 1 through 5, the rate will be 85 percent of an average of the rate paid by six-month Treasury securities for the preceding three months. For years 6 through 17, the rate will be 85 percent of an average of the rate paid by five-year Treasury securities for the preceding three months. Interest is added to the value of the bonds every six months after they are purchased.

EXHIBIT 9.5

The Variety of Federal Government Debt as of June 30, 1999

	Length of Time to Maturity	Value (in Billions of dollars)	Percentage of Total Debt
Treasury bills	Up to 1 year	$ 647.8	11.5%
Intermediate-term notes	1 to 10 years	1,868.5	33.1
Long-term bonds	10 or more years	692.4	12.3
Savings bonds	Various maturities	180.0	3.2
Other debt*	Various maturities	2,250.1	39.9
		$5,638.8	100.0

Source: Federal Reserve Bulletin, December 1999, A27.

*Primarily debt held by U.S. government agencies, trust funds, and state and local governments

to ten years. Treasury bonds are issued in denominations of $1,000 to $1,000,000 and mature in more than ten years from date of issue. New issues of Treasury bonds may be purchased through banks and brokerage firms. These firms charge commissions, but the investor may avoid such fees by purchasing the bonds directly through any of the Federal Reserve banks.

Once purchased, the bonds may be readily resold in the active secondary markets. Like corporate stocks and bonds, Treasury bonds are quoted in the financial press under the general heading "Treasury Bonds, Notes & Bills." Such quotes are illustrated in Exhibit 9.6, which presents the quotes for selected bonds, notes, and bills. These quotes, however, do differ from the reporting of corporate bonds, which gives only a bond's closing price and the current yield. Treasury bonds are quoted in 32nds, so a price such as 90.26 means $90 26/32 per $100 face amount of debt. Thus, the 6 of August 2009, which was quoted 96:16–96:17, had a bid price of $96 16/32 and an asking price of $96 17/32 (that is, $965.00 and $965.13, respectively, per $1,000 bond).

Treasuring securities are among the safest investments available to investors because there is no question that the federal government can pay interest and refund its debt. There are, however, ways in which the holder of Treasury notes and bonds can sustain losses. Acquiring Treasury notes and bonds requires the investor to bear purchasing power risk, interest rate risk, and reinvestment rate risk. Treasury notes and bonds pay a fixed amount of interest that is determined when they are issued. If the rate of inflation increases, the investor sustains a loss of purchasing power. If interest rates rise, the market prices of the bonds fall, and the investor sustains a capital loss if the bonds are sold. If interest rates fall, the investor will be unable to reinvest interest payments at the previous, higher interest rate. Thus, while federal government securities are among the safest of all investments with regard to the certainty of the payment of interest and principal, some elements of risk still exist.

EXHIBIT 9.6 Price Quotes and Yields on Federal Government Securities as of January 4, 2000

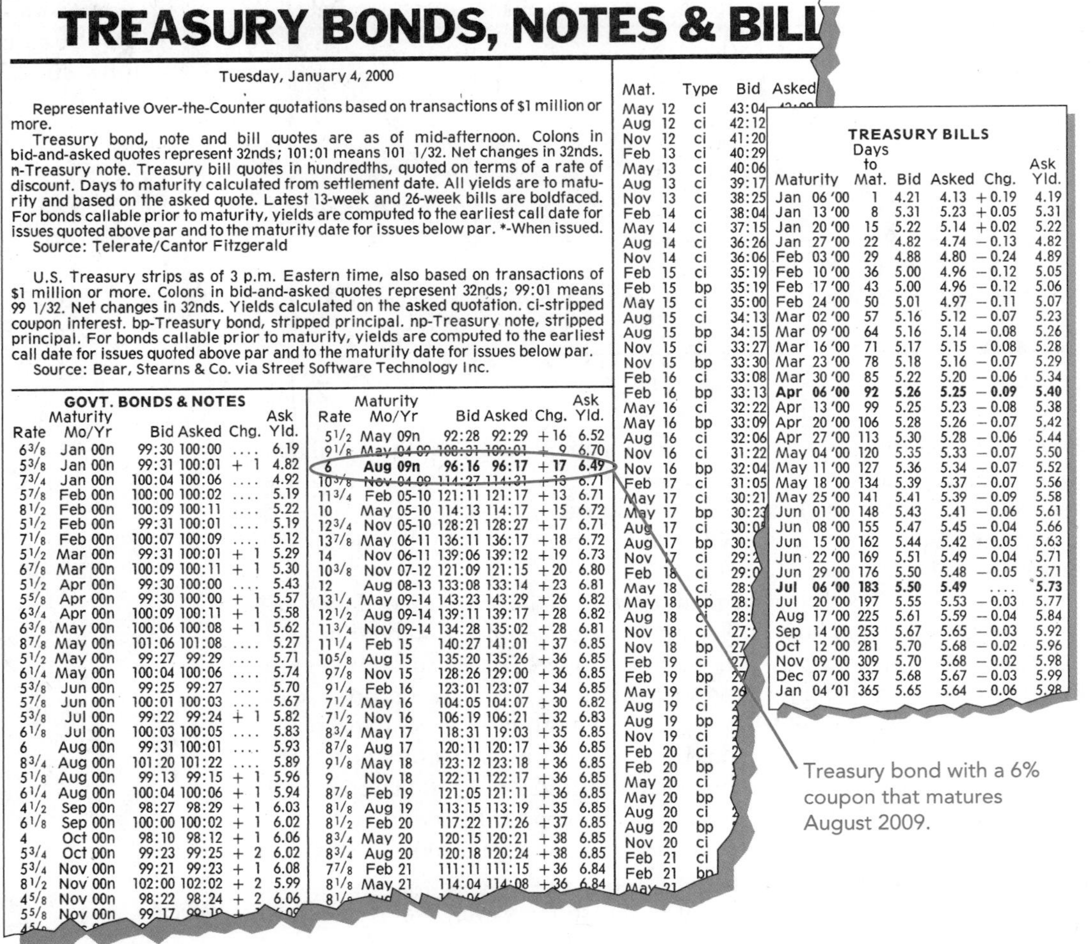

TREASURY BONDS, NOTES & BILLS

Tuesday, January 4, 2000

Representative Over-the-Counter quotations based on transactions of $1 million or more.

Treasury bond, note and bill quotes are as of mid-afternoon. Colons in bid-and-asked quotes represent 32nds; 101:01 means 101 1/32. Net changes in 32nds. n-Treasury note. Treasury bill quotes in hundredths, quoted on terms of a rate of discount. Days to maturity calculated from settlement date. All yields are to maturity and based on the asked quote. Latest 13-week and 26-week bills are boldfaced. For bonds callable prior to maturity, yields are computed to the earliest call date for issues quoted above par and to the maturity date for issues below par. *-When issued.

Source: Telerate/Cantor Fitzgerald

U.S. Treasury strips as of 3 p.m. Eastern time, also based on transactions of $1 million or more. Colons in bid-and-asked quotes represent 32nds; 99:01 means 99 1/32. Net changes in 32nds. Yields calculated on the asked quotation. ci-stripped coupon interest. bp-Treasury bond, stripped principal. np-Treasury note, stripped principal. For bonds callable prior to maturity, yields are computed to the earliest call date for issues quoted above par and to the maturity date for issues below par.

Source: Bear, Stearns & Co. via Street Software Technology Inc.

GOVT. BONDS & NOTES

Rate	Maturity Mo/Yr	Bid	Asked	Chg.	Ask Yld.
6 3/8	Jan 00n	99:30	100:00	....	6.19
5 3/8	Jan 00n	99:31	100:01	+ 1	4.82
7 3/4	Jan 00n	100:04	100:06	....	4.92
5 7/8	Feb 00n	100:00	100:02	....	5.19
8 1/2	Feb 00n	100:09	100:11	....	5.22
5 1/2	Feb 00n	99:31	100:01	....	5.19
7 1/8	Feb 00n	100:07	100:09	....	5.12
5 1/2	Mar 00n	99:31	100:01	+ 1	5.29
6 7/8	Mar 00n	100:09	100:11	+ 1	5.30
5 1/2	Apr 00n	99:30	100:00	....	5.43
5 5/8	Apr 00n	99:30	100:00	+ 1	5.57
6 3/4	Apr 00n	100:09	100:11	+ 1	5.58
6 3/8	May 00n	100:06	100:08	+ 1	5.62
8 7/8	May 00n	101:06	101:08	....	5.27
5 1/2	May 00n	99:27	99:29	....	5.71
6 1/4	May 00n	100:04	100:06	....	5.74
5 3/8	Jun 00n	99:25	99:27	....	5.70
5 7/8	Jun 00n	100:01	100:03	....	5.67
5 3/8	Jul 00n	99:22	99:24	+ 1	5.82
6 1/8	Jul 00n	100:03	100:05	....	5.83
6	Aug 00n	99:31	100:01	....	5.93
8 3/4	Aug 00n	101:20	101:22	....	5.89
5 1/8	Aug 00n	99:13	99:15	+ 1	5.96
6 1/4	Aug 00n	100:04	100:06	+ 1	5.94
4 1/2	Sep 00n	98:27	98:29	+ 1	6.03
6 1/8	Sep 00n	100:00	100:02	+ 1	6.02
4	Oct 00n	98:10	98:12	+ 1	6.06
5 3/4	Oct 00n	99:23	99:25	+ 2	6.02
5 3/4	Nov 00n	99:21	99:23	+ 1	6.08
8 1/2	Nov 00n	102:00	102:02	+ 2	5.99
4 5/8	Nov 00n	98:22	98:24	+ 2	6.06
5 5/8	Nov 00n	99:17	[illegible]	[illegible]	6.09
5 1/2	May 09n	92:28	92:29	+16	6.52
9 1/8	May 04-09	108:31	109:01	+ 9	6.70
6	**Aug 09n**	**96:16**	**96:17**	**+17**	**6.49**
10 3/8	Nov 04-09	114:27	114:31	+13	6.71
11 3/4	Feb 05-10	121:11	121:17	+13	6.71
10	May 05-10	114:13	114:17	+15	6.72
12 3/4	Nov 05-10	128:21	128:27	+17	6.71
13 7/8	May 06-11	136:11	136:17	+18	6.72
14	Nov 06-11	139:06	139:12	+19	6.73
10 3/8	Nov 07-12	121:09	121:15	+20	6.80
12	Aug 08-13	133:08	133:14	+23	6.81
13 1/4	May 09-14	143:23	143:29	+26	6.82
12 1/2	Aug 09-14	139:11	139:17	+28	6.82
11 3/4	Nov 09-14	134:28	135:02	+28	6.81
11 1/4	Feb 15	140:27	141:01	+37	6.85
10 5/8	Aug 15	135:20	135:26	+36	6.85
9 7/8	Nov 15	128:26	129:00	+36	6.85
9 1/4	Feb 16	123:01	123:07	+34	6.85
7 1/4	May 16	104:05	104:07	+30	6.82
7 1/2	Nov 16	106:19	106:21	+32	6.83
8 3/4	May 17	118:31	119:03	+35	6.85
8 7/8	Aug 17	120:11	120:17	+36	6.85
9 1/8	May 18	123:12	123:18	+36	6.85
9	Nov 18	122:11	122:17	+36	6.85
8 7/8	Feb 19	121:05	121:11	+36	6.85
8 1/8	Aug 19	113:15	113:19	+35	6.85
8 1/2	Feb 20	117:22	117:26	+37	6.85
8 3/4	May 20	120:15	120:21	+38	6.85
8 3/4	Aug 20	120:18	120:24	+38	6.85
7 7/8	Feb 21	111:11	111:15	+36	6.84
8 1/8	May 21	114:04	114:08	+36	6.84

Mat.	Type	Bid	Asked
May 12	ci	43:04	[illegible]
Aug 12	ci	42:12	
Nov 12	ci	41:20	
Feb 13	ci	40:29	
May 13	ci	40:06	
Aug 13	ci	39:17	
Nov 13	ci	38:25	
Feb 14	ci	38:04	
May 14	ci	37:15	
Aug 14	ci	36:26	
Nov 14	ci	36:06	
Feb 15	ci	35:19	
Feb 15	bp	35:19	
May 15	ci	35:00	
Aug 15	ci	34:13	
Aug 15	bp	34:15	
Nov 15	ci	33:27	
Nov 15	bp	33:30	
Feb 16	ci	33:08	
Feb 16	bp	33:13	
May 16	ci	32:22	
May 16	bp	33:09	
Aug 16	ci	32:06	
Nov 16	ci	31:22	
Nov 16	bp	32:04	
Feb 17	ci	31:05	
May 17	ci	30:21	
May 17	bp	30:23	
Aug 17	ci	[illegible]	
Aug 17	bp	[illegible]	
Nov 17	ci	[illegible]	
Feb 18	ci	[illegible]	
May 18	ci	[illegible]	
May 18	bp	[illegible]	
Aug 18	ci	[illegible]	
Nov 18	ci	[illegible]	
Nov 18	bp	[illegible]	
Feb 19	ci	[illegible]	
Feb 19	bp	[illegible]	
May 19	ci	[illegible]	
Aug 19	ci	[illegible]	
Aug 19	bp	[illegible]	
Nov 19	ci	[illegible]	
Feb 20	ci	[illegible]	
Feb 20	bp	[illegible]	
May 20	ci	[illegible]	
May 20	bp	[illegible]	
Aug 20	ci	[illegible]	
Aug 20	bp	[illegible]	
Nov 20	ci	[illegible]	
Feb 21	ci	[illegible]	
Feb 21	bp	[illegible]	

TREASURY BILLS

Maturity	Days to Mat.	Bid	Asked	Chg.	Ask Yld.
Jan 06 '00	1	4.21	4.13	+0.19	4.19
Jan 13 '00	8	5.31	5.23	+0.05	5.31
Jan 20 '00	15	5.22	5.14	+0.02	5.22
Jan 27 '00	22	4.82	4.74	−0.13	4.82
Feb 03 '00	29	4.88	4.80	−0.24	4.89
Feb 10 '00	36	5.00	4.96	−0.12	5.05
Feb 17 '00	43	5.00	4.96	−0.12	5.06
Feb 24 '00	50	5.01	4.97	−0.11	5.07
Mar 02 '00	57	5.16	5.12	−0.07	5.23
Mar 09 '00	64	5.16	5.14	−0.08	5.26
Mar 16 '00	71	5.17	5.15	−0.08	5.28
Mar 23 '00	78	5.18	5.16	−0.07	5.29
Mar 30 '00	85	5.22	5.20	−0.06	5.34
Apr 06 '00	**92**	**5.26**	**5.25**	**−0.09**	**5.40**
Apr 13 '00	99	5.25	5.23	−0.08	5.38
Apr 20 '00	106	5.28	5.26	−0.07	5.42
Apr 27 '00	113	5.30	5.28	−0.06	5.44
May 04 '00	120	5.35	5.33	−0.07	5.50
May 11 '00	127	5.36	5.34	−0.07	5.52
May 18 '00	134	5.39	5.37	−0.07	5.56
May 25 '00	141	5.41	5.39	−0.09	5.58
Jun 01 '00	148	5.43	5.41	−0.06	5.61
Jun 08 '00	155	5.47	5.45	−0.04	5.66
Jun 15 '00	162	5.44	5.42	−0.05	5.63
Jun 22 '00	169	5.51	5.49	−0.04	5.71
Jun 29 '00	176	5.50	5.48	−0.05	5.71
Jul 06 '00	**183**	**5.50**	**5.49**	....	**5.73**
Jul 20 '00	197	5.55	5.53	−0.03	5.77
Aug 17 '00	225	5.61	5.59	−0.04	5.84
Sep 14 '00	253	5.67	5.65	−0.03	5.92
Oct 12 '00	281	5.70	5.68	−0.02	5.96
Nov 09 '00	309	5.70	5.68	−0.02	5.98
Dec 07 '00	337	5.68	5.67	−0.03	5.99
Jan 04 '01	365	5.65	5.64	−0.06	5.98

Treasury bond with a 6% coupon that matures August 2009.

Source: The Wall Street Journal, *January 5, 2000, C19. Reprinted by permission of The Wall Street Journal © 2000 Dow Jones & Company, Inc. All rights reserved worldwide.*

Municipal Bonds

State and local governments also issue a variety of debt instruments to finance capital expenditures, such as schools or roads. The government then retires the debt as the facilities are utilized. The funds used to retire the debt may be raised through taxes, such as property taxes, or through revenues generated by the facilities, such as the tolls collected by the New Jersey Turnpike.

The primary factor that differentiates state and local government securities from other forms of debt is the tax advantage they offer investors. The interest earned on state and municipal debt is exempt from federal income taxation. Although state and local governments may tax the interest, the federal government may not. Hence, these bonds are frequently referred to as **tax-exempt bonds.** (Conversely, the interest earned on federal government debt is exempt from state and local government income taxation.) Since the interest paid by all other debt, including federal government and corporate bonds, is subject to federal income taxation, this exemption is advantageous to state and local governments. They are able to issue debt with substantially lower interest costs.

TAX-EXEMPT BONDS
Bonds issued by a state or municipal government whose interest is exempt from federal income taxation

Investors are willing to accept a lower interest rate on state and local government debt because the after-tax return is equivalent to higher yields on other debt. For example, if the individual is in the 36 percent federal income tax bracket, the return after taxes is the same for a corporate bond paying 7.5 percent as a municipal bond that pays 4.8 percent. The after-tax return is 4.8 percent in either case.

The individual investor may determine the equivalent yields on tax-exempt bonds and nonexempt bonds by using the following equation:

$$i_c(1 - t) = i_m, \quad \text{9.3}$$

in which i_c is the interest rate paid on the corporate debt, i_m is the interest rate paid by the municipal bond, and t is the individual's tax bracket. Thus, if the corporate bond pays 7.5 and the individual's tax bracket is 36 percent, the equivalent yield on a municipal bond is $0.075\ (1 - 0.36) = 0.048 = 4.8\%$.

Although state and municipal bonds offer an important tax advantage, they do subject the investor to risk. Inflation erodes the purchasing power of the interest and the principal, and fluctuations in interest rates cause the prices of municipal bonds to fluctuate. Lower interest rates reduce the investor's ability to reinvest at the previous, higher rates, and there is the possibility of default.

While investors can do little to reduce the risks associated with inflation and fluctuations in interest rates, they may reduce the impact of the risk of default. First, they should acquire a well-diversified portfolio of tax-exempt bonds that spreads the risk over many state and local governments. Second, they may limit purchases to bonds with high credit ratings, such as triple or double A. Third, they may acquire bonds that are insured. Several insurance companies guarantee municipal bonds with regard to the payment of interest and repayment of principal. By purchasing insured bonds, the investor has a claim on both the government that issued the bonds and the insurance company that guaranteed them.

INVESTMENT ANALYSIS CALCULATOR APPLICATIONS

This chapter covers the features of bonds and how these securities are valued. The chapter also illustrates the determination of the yield to maturity when the price of a bond is known. The text illustrates the calculations using interest tables and financial calculators. The price of a bond and the yield to maturity may also be

calculated using the *Investment Analysis Calculator.* (Remember you may reach this software at **www.harcourtcollege.com/finance/mayo**.)

To calculate the value of a bond, go to the menu Bond Valuation and Duration.[4] Suppose you want to determine the current price of a 6 percent bond (interest paid semiannually) that matures after three years assuming that the current rate of interest is 8 percent. Enter the current or market rate of interest (8 percent), the coupon rate of interest (6 percent), the number of years to maturity (3), and the face value of the bond ($1,000). Next, answer the question as to whether the bond pays interest annually or semi-annually. The market value (price) of the bond is then determined to be $947.58, which is the same answer derived using a financial calculator.

To calculate a bond's yield to maturity, go to the submenu "Current Yield and Yield to Maturity" under Yields. Suppose you need to determine the current yield and the yield to maturity of a three year, 10 percent bond ($100 interest paid annually) that is currently selling for $952. Enter the price of the bond ($952), the coupon rate of interest (10 percent), the number of years to maturity (3), and the face value of the bond ($1,000). Next, answer the question as to whether the bond pays interest annually or semi-annually. The software determines the current yield (10.5 percent) and the yield to maturity (11.99 percent). A yield of 11.99 percent is the same answer derived using a financial calculator.

[4] Duration is a measure of the average life of a bond's expected cash inflows. For an explanation of duration, see Herbert B. Mayo, *Investments: An Introduction,* 6th ed. (Fort Worth, Texas: The Dryden Press, 2000), pp. 555–560.

SUMMARY

This chapter has discussed the general features of long-term debt (bonds). While a corporation may issue a variety of bonds, ranging from secured mortgage bonds to unsecured subordinated debentures and income bonds, the general terms of each issue include the coupon rate of interest and the maturity date. A trustee is appointed for each bond issue to protect the rights of the individual investors. The risks associated with investing in bonds include default on interest and principal repayment, increased interest rates that decrease the current market value of the bond, and loss of purchasing power through inflation.

The current price of a bond depends on the bond's coupon, its term to maturity, and the current interest rates being paid on comparable debt. When interest rates rise, the market price of previously issued bonds declines, but the price of a bond rises when interest rates fall. These price fluctuations are the result of bonds paying a fixed amount of interest each year.

Since a bond's price fluctuates, it may sell for a discount below the face value or for a premium over its face value. The current yield expresses the bond's interest relative to its price. The yield to maturity equates the bond's price with the present value of the interest payments and the principal repayment. If a bond sells for a discount, its yield to maturity exceeds the coupon yield. If a bond sells for a premium, the yield to maturity is less than the coupon yield. Since the yield to maturity factors in any premium or discount in the calculation of the yield, it is a better indicator of the return an investor actually earns from date of purchase to the bond's maturity.

Bonds may be retired through the use of a sinking fund, which requires the issuer to retire a specified amount of the bonds each year or make a periodic payment to retire the debt issue. Some bonds are issued in series; each year one of the series within the issue is retired. Bonds may also be callable, which permits the issuer to pay off the entire issue prior to maturity. A bond will be called only if interest rates have fallen. If interest rates rise and cause a bond's price to fall, it would be more advantageous for the issuer to repurchase the bonds than to call and retire them at par.

Governments as well as corporations issue bonds. The general features and risks associated with investing in government bonds are the same as with corporate bonds. The big difference between government bonds and corporate bonds is the taxation of the interest income. The interest on state and local government bonds is exempt from federal income taxation, while the interest on federal government debt is exempt from state taxation. The interest earned on an investment in

corporate debt may be taxed by the federal, state, or local government. The tax exemption of interest earned on state and local government debt increases the appeal of municipal bonds, as investors seek to reduce their tax obligations.

REVIEW QUESTIONS

1. Given:

Issuer of Bond	Maturity Date	Credit Rating	Yield to Maturity
ABC, Inc.	10 years	AAA	6.2%
DEF, Inc.	20 years	A	8.0
GHI, Inc.	20 years	B	9.5
JKL, Inc.	10 years	B	8.8

   How would you explain the differences in the rates of interest? What do these yields imply about (a) the effect of time and (b) the effect of risk?

2. What is the difference between the current yield and the yield to maturity? When would these two yields be equal? When would the yield to maturity exceed the current yield? If you thought that interest rates were going to decline, should you buy or sell bonds?
3. Debt must eventually be repaid. What is the difference between a serial bond issue and a bond issue with a sinking fund?
4. Why may equipment trust certificates be safer than debentures? Why may debentures be safer from the investor's perspective than income bonds?
5. If you expected interest rates to rise, should you buy bonds or sell those you already own?
6. If interest rates fall after a bond is issued, why might you expect the firm to call the bond?
7. How is a call feature different from a sinking fund? From the firm's perspective, which is preferable? If a bond issue lacks a call feature, how may a company retire the bonds prior to maturity?
8. Which is more important to the determination of the price of a 20-year bond: the interest payments or the principal repayment? Would your answer be different if the bond matured in five years?
9. If municipal bonds were not tax-exempt, what would happen to the cost of borrowing for state and local governments?

10. The federal government's public debt web site (**www.publicdebt.tres.gov**) provides yields on Treasury securities and interest rates on savings bonds. What is the current interest rate being paid by EE bonds?

11. The Securities and Exchange Commission's EDGAR database (**www.sec.gov**) is a major source of data on firms, since it includes the information that publicly held companies must file with the SEC. As of January 1999, AT&T's long-term debt exceeded $6.6 billion. Based on information found in EDGAR, has AT&T's long-term debt increased?

12. Material on bonds may be found at Equity Analytics, Ltd's bond page (**www.e-analytics.com/bonds**) or at Bondsonline (**www.bonds-online.com**). From these sources determine, what are the current prices and yields on Treasury bonds that mature after 5, 10, and 20 years?

13. Go to Moody's Investors Services (**www.moodys.com**). Has this credit rating agency recently lowered the ratings of any bonds from investment grade (triple B or better) to high-yield (junk) status?

PROBLEMS*

1. Blackstone, Inc. has a five-year bond outstanding that pays $60 annually. The face value of each bond is $1,000, and the bond sells for $890.
   a. What is the bond's coupon rate?
   b. What is the current yield?
   c. What is the yield to maturity?

2. A bond with 15 years to maturity has a semiannual interest payment of $40. If the bond sells for its par value, what are the bond's current yield and yield to maturity?

3. A $1,000 bond has the following terms:
   - Coupon rate of interest: 6%
   - Interest paid semiannually: $30
   - Maturity: 10 years

   a. What would be the bond's price if comparable debt yields 8 percent?
   b. What would be the price if comparable debt yields 8 percent and the bond matures after five years?
   c. Why are the prices different in a and b?
   d. What proportion of the bond's prices in a and b is attributable to the interest payments and to the principal repayment?
   e. What are the current yields and the yields to maturity in a and b?

4. A $1,000 bond that matures in ten years and has a coupon of 5 percent ($50 a year) is selling for $690.
   a. What is the current yield?
   b. What is the yield to maturity?
   c. If five years later the yield to maturity is 10 percent, what will be the price of the bond?

*The first problem assumes annual interest payments to facilitate practice. All remaining problems assume semiannual interest payments.

5. *a.* A $1,000 bond pays $75 a year (that is, 7½ percent coupon) and matures after 10 years. If current interest rates are 10 percent, what should be the price of the bond?
   b. If after six years interest rates are still 10 percent, what should be the price of the bond?
   c. Even though interest rates did not change in a and b, why did the price of the bond change?
   d. Change the interest rate in a and b to 6 percent and rework your answers. Even though the interest rate is 6 percent in both calculations, why are the bond prices different?

6. Your broker offers to sell for $1,200 a AAA-rated bond with a coupon rate of 10 percent and a maturity of 8 years. Given that the interest rate on comparable debt is 8 percent, is your broker fairly pricing the bond?

7. Ten years ago your grandfather purchased for you a 25-year $1,000 bond with a coupon rate of 10 percent. You now wish to sell the bond and read that yields are 8 percent. What price should you receive for the bond?

8. Bond A has the following terms:
   - Coupon rate of interest: 10%
   - Principal: $1,000
   - Term to maturity: 8 years

   Bond B has the following terms:
   - Coupon rate of interest: 5%
   - Principal: $1,000
   - Term to maturity: 8 years

   a. What should be the price of each bond if interest rates are 10 percent?
   b. What will be the price of each bond if, after five years have elapsed, interest rates are 10 percent?
   c. What will be the price of each bond if, after eight years have elapsed, interest rates are 8 percent?

9. A bond has the following features:
   - Coupon rate of interest: 8% (4%, semiannual)
   - Principal: $1,000
   - Term to maturity: 10 years

   a. What will the holder receive when the bond matures?
   b. If the current rate of interest on comparable debt is 12 percent, what should be the price of this bond? Would you expect the firm to call this bond? Why?
   c. If the bond has a sinking fund that requires the firm to set aside annually with a trustee sufficient funds to retire the entire issue at maturity, how much must the firm remit each year for ten years if the funds earn 9 percent annually and there is $10 million outstanding?

10. You are given the following information concerning a noncallable, sinking fund debenture:
    - Principal: $1,000
    - Coupon rate of interest: 7% paid semiannually
    - Term to maturity: 15 years
    - Sinking fund: 5 percent of outstanding bonds retired annually; the balance at maturity

    a. If you buy the bond today at its face amount and interest rates rise to 12 percent after three years have passed, what is your capital gain (loss)?
    b. If you hold the bond 15 years, what do you receive at maturity?
    c. What is the bond's current yield as of right now?
    d. Given your price in a, what is the yield of maturity?
    e. Is there any reason to believe that the bond will be called after three years have elapsed if interest rates decline?
    f. What proportion of the total debt issue is retired by the sinking fund?
    g. What assets secure this bond?
    h. If the final payment to retire this bond is $1,000,000, how much must the firm invest annually to accumulate this sum if the firm is able to earn 7 percent on the invested funds?
11. Your federal income tax bracket is 36 percent. Corporate debt currently yields 7.3 percent. What is the comparable yield on municipal debt?
12. Your broker offers you a municipal bond with a yield of 5.1 percent. Corporate debt with the same credit rating and term to maturity has a yield of 6.9 percent. Based solely on after-tax returns, which security is to be preferred if you are in the 25 percent federal income tax bracket? Would your answer be different if your bracket were 39.6 percent?

BUILDING A BOND PORTFOLIO

CASE

Nancy Pallette, a very conservative individual seeking financial advice, recently had an initial consultation with Robert Frederick Strauss (old "RF"), a personable financial planner. Ms. Pallette has $500,000 invested in certificates of deposit with maturities of one to three years and interest rates of 2.75 percent to 3.50 percent. Old RF thought this amount tied up in one type of asset is a decidedly inferior investment strategy, but he immediately realized that Ms. Pallette would not be willing to alter the portfolio if the change would have a large impact on risk.

Since Ms. Pallette is primarily concerned with income and safety of principal, RF decided that initially the best strategy would be to alter the portfolio by substituting quality bonds for a substantial proportion of the certificates of deposit. He suggested that $400,000 be invested in bonds and the remaining $100,000 be held in CDs. Fifty thousand dollars would be invested in triple A or double A rated bonds with one year to maturity; $50,000 with two years to maturity, and so on until the last $50,000 would be invested in bonds with eight years to maturity.

Thus, none of the bonds would have a maturity exceeding eight years, none of the bonds would have a rating of less than double A, and $50,000 face amount of the bonds would mature each year.

Ms. Pallette agreed to the basic strategy but required that all the bonds be federal government obligations. Currently the structure of interest rates is as follows:

Term to Maturity	Coupon Rate of Interest
1	4.0%
2	4.0
3	5.0
4	5.0
5	6.0
6	6.0
7	7.0
8	7.0

All bonds are currently selling at par (that is, $1,000 per $1,000 face amount). Ms. Pallette still had doubts concerning risk of loss of principal, but she liked the additional income that would be generated by the bonds with the higher coupons. She asked RF what the advantage was of placing $50,000 in bonds maturing each year versus investing the entire $400,000 in eight-year federal government bonds.

Case Problems

1. How should RF respond to this question?
2. How much could Ms. Pallette lose of the $400,000 if she follows the recommended strategy and, after one year, interest rates rise one percentage point? (To ease the calculations, assume annual payments.)
3. Would the interest earned offset the loss?
4. How much additional loss would be incurred compared to the loss in Question 2 if Ms. Pallette invests the $400,000 in eight-year bonds and one year later the rate rises to 10 percent?

CHAPTER 10
Equity: Preferred and Common Stock

Learning Objectives

1 Differentiate preferred stock from bonds.
2 Analyze the firm's capacity to pay preferred stock dividends.
3 Enumerate cash dividend policies.
4 Illustrate the effect that income taxes have on cash dividends and the retention of earnings.
5 Explain the time line of a dividend payment.
6 Determine the impact of cash dividends, stock dividends, and stock splits on the firm's earnings, assets, equity, and stock price.
7 Describe dividend reinvestment plans and their advantages.

The seventeenth-century English poet George Herbert wrote, "By no means run in debt: take thine own measure." While a few firms are able to operate without some debt financing, equity is a necessary source of funds for every business. The single proprietor invests money and other assets in the business and thus has equity in the firm. Partners invest funds into the partnership and have an equity claim on the firm.

Corporations raise funds by selling preferred and common stock to individuals and other investors who become the owners (shareholders) of the firm. While preferred stock is similar to debt, it is still a form of equity. Many corporations do not issue preferred stock, but all issue common stock. These stockholders are the ultimate owners of the firm and bear the risk associated with that ownership. For bearing that risk, these investors anticipate a return on their funds, either through dividends or through price appreciation.

Companies that experience consistent growth in earnings tend to increase their dividends periodically. As of 1999, GT&E had annually increased its dividend in 43 of the last 45 years. Many firms have paid dividends for over a century. The Bank of Boston and the Bank of New York started paying dividends in 1784 and 1785, respectively. Of course, some firms reduce or suspend dividends (for example, Freeport McMoRan Copper and Gold) when their financial condition deteriorates sufficiently so that continuing the dividend may threaten the firm's continued existence.

Chapters 10 and 11 are devoted to stock. Chapter 10 is descriptive and covers the features of preferred and common stock, the voting right of stockholders, dividend payments, stock splits, divided reinvestment plans, and corporate repurchases of stock. Chapter 11 is more theoretical and is devoted to the valuation of stock. It covers models that are used to determine if a particular stock is undervalued and should be purchased or if it is overvalued and should be avoided.

EQUITY

A firm's capital (that is, its sources of finance) is either debt or equity. As was discussed in the previous chapter, a variety of debt instruments are issued to tap the funds of savers who invest in fixed income securities. Each debt instrument is differentiated by its terms; a debenture differs from a mortgage, for example, because the former is unsecured while the latter is secured by property. However, in both cases, the issuing firm must meet the terms of the bond's indenture. Both are legal obligations of the firm.

Equity represents ownership in a firm. Like creditors, the holders of equity instruments such as common stock have a claim on the firm. Since the firm's debt obligations have a prior claim, equity represents a residual claim. Interest on debt must be paid before there are any earnings available to the owners. If the firm is dissolved, debts must be paid, and any remaining assets are distributed to the owners.

Being the residual claim is one of the reasons why equity is riskier than debt. If the firm performs poorly, there may be little or nothing available to the owners. However, a profitable firm can generate a large return for its owners, since after the debt obligations are met, the residual accrues solely to the equity. Higher earnings, thus, accrue solely to the owners.

Stock represents equity in a corporation. While there may be many different types of debt instruments, there are only two types of stock: preferred stock and common stock.[1] As the name implies, preferred stock has a preferred or superior position. Common stock thus represents the final claim on a corporation's earnings and assets. While equity (ownership) represents the residual claim on a firm's earnings and assets, it still is a claim. The managers and employees of the firm work for and are responsible to the owners.

For the vast majority of firms, the owners, managers, and employees are one and the same. The owner of a small store must perform all the roles required to operate and manage the business. While the owner may employ individuals with special skills (for example, an accountant or a lawyer) to perform specific tasks, management, marketing, and financing decisions all fall on the owner/manager. Since the owner and manager are one and the same, it seems reasonable to assume that management decisions are made with the welfare of the owner as a primary consideration.

[1] Some corporations have also issued a "preference" stock. This stock is subordinated to preferred stock but has preference over common stock with regard to the payment of dividends. Such stock is another level of preferred stock, and this text makes no distinction between the two.

In large corporations, the owners, managers, and employees differ. As is explained later in this chapter, the owners are represented by an elected board of directors. The board employs management who, in turn, hires the various individuals that staff the operation. It could be assumed that the goals of management are consistent with the owners' goals, since the managers have a fiduciary responsibility to the corporate owners (that is, they are the "agents" of the owners). However, such an assumption may be at odds with reality.[2] For example, higher salaries may be a goal of individual managers, but higher salaries will reduce earnings and come at the expense of the owners.

Owners, therefore, must monitor managerial decisions and take steps to reduce the potential conflict between managers and owners. These actions may include (1) developing a structure in which the chain of command and responsibility starts with the owners and flows to the employees, (2) forming a system for the removal of employees who act in a way that is harmful to owners, or (3) instituting a system of rewards that is tied to performance so that the welfare of the owners, managers, and employees is interrelated. For example, Lucent Technologies has an employee stock option award that grants most of its employees the right to purchase stock at a set price. If the firm prospers, the value of the stock and the rights will increase and reward employees as well as stockholders.

Linking the welfare of owners, managers, and employees will involve expenses. These expenditures are sometimes referred to as the "agency costs" that owners must bear to insure that management acts in the best interests of the owners and not solely on its own behalf. Creditors also have similar costs since owners and managers can take actions that reduce the safety of debt instruments. For example, the paying of bonuses and stock options may reward management, but such payments reduce the money available to pay interest and repay principal.

THE FEATURES OF PREFERRED STOCK

Preferred stock is an equity instrument that usually pays a fixed dividend. While most firms have only one issue of common stock, they may have several issues of preferred stock. Virginia Electric and Power (a subsidiary of Dominion Resources) has 15 issues of preferred stock. In nine cases the dividend rate is fixed. Thus for the series $5.58 preferred, the annual dividend is $5.58, which is distributed at the rate of $1.395 per share quarterly. For the remaining six issues, the dividend is tied to the yields on short-term money market securities and changes quarterly.

PREFERRED STOCK
Class of stock (equity) that has a claim prior to common stock on the firm's earnings and assets

The dividend is paid from the firm's earnings. If the firm does not have the earnings, it may not declare and pay the preferred stock dividends. If the firm

[2] This "agency" issue exists throughout organizations. In business the assumption is that the top managers of publicly held corporations will act responsibly on behalf of stockholders and not for the benefit of themselves. A similar situation exists in colleges, since your professor is an agent of the school. It is his or her responsibility to explain finance clearly to you. (I'd like to thank Alan Severn for this insightful observation.)

ARREARS
Dividends on a cumulative preferred stock that have not been paid and have accumulated

CUMULATIVE PREFERRED STOCK
Preferred stock whose dividends accumulate (accrue) if not paid

NONCUMULATIVE PREFERRED STOCK
Preferred stock whose dividends do not accumulate if the firm misses a dividend payment

should omit the preferred stock's dividend, the dividend is said to be in **arrears.** The firm does not have to remove this arrearage. In most cases, however, any omitted dividends have to be paid in the future before any dividends may be paid to the holders of the common stock. Such cases, in which the preferred stock's dividends accumulate, are called **cumulative preferred stocks.** Most preferred stock is cumulative, but there are examples of **noncumulative preferred stocks** whose dividends do not have to be made up if missed. For investors holding preferred stock in firms having financial difficulty, the difference between cumulative and noncumulative may be immaterial. Forcing the firm to pay dividends to erase the arrearage may further weaken the firm and hurt the owner of the preferred stock more than would forgoing the dividends. Once the firm has regained its profitability, erasing the arrearage may become important not only to holders of the stock but also to the company as a demonstration of its improved financial condition.

An example of a firm clearing the arrearage on its preferred stock is Unisys, which suspended preferred stock dividends in 1991 and resumed in 1993. The 1993 payments totaled $5.625 a share, which consisted of $3.75 for the current year and $1.875 toward the arrearage.

Once the preferred stock is issued, the firm may never retire it. The security is perpetual. This may be both an advantage and a disadvantage. Since the firm may never have to retire the preferred stock, it does not have to generate the money to retire it. The firm may instead use its funds elsewhere (for example, to purchase equipment). However, should the firm ever want to change its capital structure and substitute debt financing for the preferred stock, the firm may have difficulty in retiring the preferred stock. The firm may have to purchase the preferred stock on the open market, and, in order to induce the holders to sell the preferred shares, the firm will probably have to bid up the price of the preferred stock.

To maintain some control over the preferred stock, the firm may seek to add to the preferred issue a call feature. This gives the firm the option to call and redeem the issue. (For example, the Unisys convertible preferred referred to above is callable.) Although the actual terms of a call feature will vary with each preferred stock issue, the general features are similar. First, the call is at the option of the firm. Second, the call price is specified. Third, the firm may pay a call penalty (for example, a year's dividends). Fourth, after the issue is called, future dividend payments will cease; this, of course, forces any recalcitrant holders to surrender their certificates.

In addition to a call feature, some preferred stocks have mandatory sinking fund requirements. These sinking funds require that the firm periodically retire some of the issue. For example, the Virginia Electric and Power $7.30 preferred stock has a mandatory sinking fund that requires the firm to redeem annually 15,000 shares at $100 per share. Such issues of preferred stock with mandatory sinking funds are very similar to bonds, which also are not perpetual and must be retired.

PREFERRED STOCK AND BONDS CONTRASTED

Because preferred stock pays a fixed dividend, it is purchased primarily by investors seeking a fixed flow of income. Since preferred stock pays a fixed dividend, it is analyzed and valued like a bond. But preferred stock differs from long-term debt, as the subsequent discussion will demonstrate, and these differences are significant.

First, for investors, preferred stock is riskier than debt. The terms of a bond are legal obligations of the firm. If the corporation fails to pay the interest or meet any of the terms of the indenture, the bondholders may take the firm to court to force payment of the interest or to seek liquidation of the firm in order to protect the bondholders' principal. Preferred stockholders do not have that power, for the firm is not legally obligated to pay the preferred stock dividends.

In addition, debt must be retired, while preferred stock is often perpetual. If the security is perpetual, the only means to recoup the amount invested is to sell the preferred stock in the secondary market. The investor cannot expect the firm to redeem the security. Market price fluctuations tend to be greater for preferred stock than for long-term bonds. Price fluctuations for long-term bonds are greater than price fluctuations experienced by short-term debt. This principle holds when comparing long-term bonds and preferred stock. The price of a perpetual preferred stock will fluctuate more than the price of a long-term bond with a finite life.

Second, the yield differential between preferred stock and bonds is smaller than would be expected on the basis of risk differentials. This small differential between the yields on bonds and preferred stock may be explained by the corporate income tax laws. Dividends paid by one corporation to another receive favorable tax treatment. Only 30 percent of the dividends are taxed as income of the corporation receiving the dividends. Thus for a firm such as an insurance company in the 34 percent corporate income tax bracket, this shelter is very important. If the company receives $100 in interest, it nets only $66 as $34 is taxed away. However, if this company were to receive $100 in preferred stock dividends, only $30 would be subject to federal income tax. Thus the firm pays only $10.20 ($30 × 0.34) in taxes and gets to keep the remaining $89.80 of the dividends.

For this reason, a corporate investor may choose to purchase preferred stocks instead of long-term bonds. The impact of this preference is to drive up the price of preferred stocks, which reduces their yields. Since individual investors do not enjoy this tax break, they may prefer bonds that offer comparable yields to preferred stock but are less risky. To induce these investors to purchase preferred stock, the firm often offers other features, such as the convertibility of the preferred stock into the firm's common stock.

A third important difference (from the viewpoint of the issuing corporation) between debt and preferred stock is that the interest on debt is a tax-deductible expense while the dividend on preferred stock is not. Preferred dividends are paid out of earnings. This difference in the tax treatment of interest expense and preferred stock dividends affects the firm's earnings available to its common stockholders. The use of debt instead of preferred stock as a source of funds will result in higher earnings per common share.

Consider a firm with operating income of $1,000,000 (that is, earnings before interest and taxes). The firm has 100,000 common shares outstanding and is in the 40 percent corporate income tax bracket. If the firm issues $2,000,000 of *debt* with a 10 percent rate of interest, is earnings per common share are

Earnings before interest and taxes	$1,000,000
Interest	200,000
Earnings before taxes	800,000
Taxes	320,000
Net income	$ 480,000

Earnings per common share: $480,000/100,000 = $4.80

If the firm had issued $2,000,000 in *preferred stock* that also paid 10 percent, the earnings per common share would be

Earnings before interest and taxes	$1,000,000
Interest	00
Earnings before taxes	1,000,000
Taxes	400,000
Earnings before preferred stock dividends	600,000
Preferred stock dividends	200,000
Earnings available to common stock	$ 400,000

Earnings per common share: $400,000/100,000 = $4.00

The use of preferred stock has resulted in lower earnings per common share. This reduction in earnings is the result of the different tax treatment of interest, which is a tax-deductible expense, and the preferred stock dividends, which are not deductible.

ANALYSIS OF PREFERRED STOCK

Because preferred stock is an income-producing investment, the analysis is primarily concerned with the capacity of the firm to meet the dividend payments. Although dividends must ultimately be related to current earnings and the firm's future earning capacity, preferred dividends are paid from cash. Even if the firm is operating at a loss, it may still be able to pay dividends to the preferred stockholders if it has sufficient cash. In fact, cash dividends might be paid despite the earnings deficit to indicate that the losses are expected to be temporary and that the firm is financially strong.

An analysis of the firm's financial statements (such as the ratios used to analyze a firm's financial condition in Chapter 12) may reveal the liquidity position and profitability of the firm. The more liquid and profitable the firm, the safer should be the dividend payment. The investor may also analyze how well the firm covers its preferred dividend by computing the **times-dividend-earned** ratio:

TIMES-DIVIDEND-EARNED
Ratio of earnings divided by preferred dividend requirements

$$\frac{\text{Earnings after taxes}}{\text{Dividends on preferred stock}}.$$

The larger this ratio, the safer should be the preferred stock's dividend. Notice that the numerator consists of *total* earnings. Although the preferred stock dividends are subtracted from the total earnings to derive the earnings that are available to the common stockholders, all of the firm's earnings are available to pay the preferred stock dividend.

A variation on this ratio is **earnings per preferred share.** This ratio is

EARNINGS PER PREFERRED SHARE
Total earnings dividend by the number of preferred shares outstanding

$$\frac{\text{Earnings after taxes}}{\text{Number of preferred shares outstanding}}.$$

The larger the earnings per preferred share, the safer is the dividend payment. However, neither of these ratios indicates whether the firm has sufficient cash to pay the dividends. They can only indicate the extent to which earnings cover the dividend requirements of the preferred stock.

How each ratio is computed can be illustrated by the following simple example. A firm has earnings of $6 million and is in the 40 percent tax bracket. It has 100,000 shares of preferred stock outstanding, and each share pays a dividend of $5. The times-dividend-earned ratio is

$$\frac{\$6{,}000{,}000 - \$2{,}400{,}000}{\$500{,}000} = 7.2,$$

and the earnings per preferred share are

$$\frac{\$6{,}000{,}000 - \$2{,}400{,}000}{100{,}000} = \$36.$$

Both ratios, in effect, show the same thing. In the first, the preferred dividend is covered by a multiple of 7.2:1. The second ratio shows an earnings per preferred share of $36, which is 7.2 times the $5 dividend paid for each share.

DISADVANTAGES OF PREFERRED STOCK

Although most preferred stock does offer the investor the advantage of a fixed flow of income, this advantage may be more than offset by several disadvantages. Like any fixed income security, preferred stock offers no protection from inflation. If the rate of inflation increases, the real purchasing power of the dividend is diminished. In addition, increased inflation will probably lead to higher interest rates, which will drive down the market value of all fixed income securities, including preferred stock. Thus, higher rates of inflation doubly curse preferred stock as the purchasing power of the dividend and the market value of the stock will both be diminished. (This disadvantage, of course, applies to all fixed income, long-term securities.)

Preferred stock also tends to be less marketable than other securities. Marketability of a particular preferred stock depends on the size of the issue. However, most preferred stock is bought by insurance companies and pension plans. The market for the remaining shares may be quite small, so the spread between the bid and ask prices can be substantial. While this may not be a disadvantage if the investor intends to hold the security indefinitely, it will reduce the attractiveness of the preferred stock in cases in which investors desire marketability.

The impact of inflation and reduced marketability are not the only disadvantages associated with preferred stock. Other disadvantages were alluded to earlier in the chapter but were not explicitly stated as disadvantages. The first of these is the inferior position of preferred stock to debt obligations. The investor must realize that preferred stock is perceptibly riskier than bonds. For example, Zapata Corporation omitted dividends on its two issues of preferred stock but continued to make the interest payments on its debentures. One of these preferred stocks is noncumulative, so those dividend payments are lost forever.

The second disadvantage that was previously alluded to is that the yields offered by preferred stock are probably insufficient to justify the additional risk. The yields on preferred stock are not necessarily higher than those available on bonds because of the tax advantages that preferred stock offers corporate investors. Only 30 percent of the dividends paid by one corporation and received by a second corporation are subject to corporate income tax. This tax advantage artificially drives up the price of preferred stock and drives down the yield. Since individual investors cannot take advantage of the tax break, they may earn an inferior yield after adjusting for the additional risk associated with investing in a security that is subordinated to the firm's bonds.

COMMON STOCK

COMMON STOCK
Security representing ownership in a corporation; common stock owners have a final claim on the firm's assets and earnings after the firm has met its obligations to creditors and preferred stockholders

BOARD OF DIRECTORS
Body elected by and responsible to stockholders to set policy and hire management to run a corporation

Although preferred stock legally is equity and hence represents ownership, in financial reality it is similar to debt, while common stock represents the bottom line. **Common stock** represents the residual claim on the assets and earnings of a corporation. In case of liquidation, the holder of common stock receives whatever is left after all other claims have been satisfied; he or she receives earnings that have accrued after expenses, interest, and preferred stock dividends are paid. In effect, these investors bear the risk and reap the rewards associated with the ownership of a corporation.

The investors who purchase common stock receive all the rights of ownership. These rights include the option to vote the shares.[3] The stockholders elect a **board of directors** that selects the firm's management. Management is then responsible to the board of directors, which, in turn, is responsible to the firm's stockholders. If the stockholders do not think that the board is doing a competent job, they may elect another board to represent them.

Previously for publicly held corporations, stockholder democracy may not have worked. Stockholders were usually widely dispersed, while the firm's

[3] Stockholders may vote their shares over the Internet. Go to **www.proxyvote.com** and follow the instructions. Companies are also beginning to permit (and even encourage) voting via the Internet, since there is an obvious cost advantage.

management and board of directors generally formed a cohesive unit in which the board supported management. However, the recent explosive growth in institutional investors (that is, mutual funds and pension plans with common stock investments) has changed the relationship between stockholders and management. Professional money managers often press corporate executives to achieve higher earnings and returns for stockholders. If management is unable to achieve these goals, the money managers may seek the replacement of management or the acquisition of the corporation by another firm whose goal is higher stock returns. The threat of a change in management or a takeover often encourages a corporation's board of directors and current executives to pursue strategies that increase the value of the firm's stock.[4]

A stockholder generally has one vote for each share owned, but there are two ways to distribute this vote. The difference between these two methods is best explained by an example. Suppose a firm has 1,000 shares outstanding and a board of directors composed of five members. With the traditional method of voting, each share gives the stockholder the right to vote for one individual for each seat on the board. Under this system, if a majority group voted as a block, a minority group could not select a representative. For example, a majority group of 70 percent of the stockholders could give each of its candidates 70 percent of the vote, thus denying representation to a minority group of 30 percent of the stockholders.

Another system, called **cumulative voting,** gives minority stockholders a means to obtain representation, but not a majority, on the firm's board of directors. Under cumulative voting, the stockholder in the previous example who owns one share has a total of five votes (one vote for each seat on the board of directors). That stockholder may cast up to five votes for one candidate. (Of course, then the stockholder could not vote for anyone else running for the remaining seats.) The 70 percent majority would have a total of 3,500 votes (700 shares × 5). The 30 percent minority would have 1,500 votes (300 shares × 5), and by voting as a block for specific candidates could assure itself of representation on the board of directors.

CUMULATIVE VOTING
Voting system that encourages minority representation by permitting stockholders to cast all their shares (votes) for one candidate for the firm's board of directors

For example, if the 30 percent minority ran two candidates against the five candidates of the majority, the following voting could occur:

Majority Candidates	Votes
A	700
B	700
C	700
D	700
E	700
Minority Candidates	**Votes**
F	750
G	750

[4] This development of "investor capitalism" is discussed by Michael Useem in *Investor Capitalism* (New York: Basic Books, 1996). Similar material is covered in Robert Monks and Nell Minow, *Watching the Watchers* (Cambridge, Mass.: Blackwell Business, 1996).

The majority has cast its 3,500 votes evenly among its candidates, and the minority has also cast its 1,500 votes evenly between its two candidates. In this election the minority wins two seats. Even if the majority were to cast more votes for candidates A through D, these votes would be at the expense of candidate E. For example, if the majority cast 800 votes for each of candidates A through D, it would have only 300 votes available for candidate E. These 300 votes are not enough to gain election, and the minority would still win one seat on the board of directors.[5]

Although cumulative voting can help a minority group obtain representation, it cannot assure representation if the minority is too small. If the minority in this example had been 15 percent, it would have had 750 votes and the 85 percent majority would have had 4,250 votes. Each of the five majority candidates would have received 850 votes (4,250/5) and would have beaten any single minority candidate with 750 votes. For the minority to win representation, the total of its combined votes must be large enough to exceed the majority's per-seat voting capacity.

Preemptive Rights

PREEMPTIVE RIGHTS
Right of current stockholders to maintain their proportionate ownership in the firm

RIGHTS OFFERING
Sale of new securities to stockholders by offering them the option (right) to purchase new shares.

Some stockholders have **preemptive rights,** which is their prerogative to maintain their proportionate ownership in the firm. If the firm wants to sell additional shares to the general public, these new shares must be offered initially to the existing stockholders in a sale called a **rights offering.** If the stockholders wish to maintain their proportionate ownership in the firm, they can exercise their rights by purchasing the new shares. However, if they do not want to take advantage of this offering, they may sell their privilege to whomever wants to purchase the new shares.

Preemptive rights may be illustrated by a simple example. If a firm has 1,000 shares outstanding and an individual has 100 shares, that individual owns 10 percent of the firm's stock. If the firm wants to sell 400 new shares and the stockholders have preemptive rights, these new shares must be offered to the existing stockholders

[5] The number of shares (S) required to elect a specific number of seats can be determined by the following equation:

$$S = \frac{V \times P}{D + 1} + 1$$

The definition of each symbol is

V: number of voting shares,
P: number of positions desired on the board of directors,
D: total number of directors to be elected.

Thus, in the above example, if the minority wanted to elect two seats, it would have to control 334 shares. That is,

$$S = \frac{1{,}000 \times 2}{5 + 1} + 1 = 334.33$$

Since it controls only 300 shares, the minority can be assured of electing only one director.

Voting by Proxy

A corporation's board of directors holds at least one stockholders meeting a year. At the meeting stockholders vote on a variety of issues, including the election of the members of the board, the approval of the firm's auditors, the authority to issue additional shares, and any other matters that may arise. The board may also call a special meeting to vote upon a specific topic, such as the approval of a merger. ¶ Stockholders of a publicly held corporation are dispersed throughout the country and, in the case of large firms like AT&T, throughout the world. Obviously, most stockholders are not going to make the trip to the meeting to vote their shares. Instead they vote by proxy, which is a document giving the power to vote the shares to the holder of the proxy. Management solicits proxies to vote on stockholders' behalf. Even if the investor signs and submits the proxy, he or she can later rescind the authorization to vote the shares. If a dissident group wants to gain control of the company, it also may solicit proxies in which case a "proxy fight" could erupt. One such proxy fight occurred in 1999 when ASARCO and Cyprus Minerals agreed to merge. After the announcement, Phelps Dodge offered to buy ASARCO and Cyprus Minerals. What followed was a proxy fight in which the managements of ASARCO and Cyprus Minerals sought stockholders votes to thwart the takeover while the management of Phelps Dodge sought votes in support of the takeover. Ultimately, Phelps Dodge won by raising its offer price. ¶ Even if the individual signs the proxy, he or she may attend the stockholders meeting. Besides conducting the formal voting, management often reviews the firm's accomplishments and future goals. Good news such as a dividend increase may be announced at the meeting and samples of the firm's products, especially if the corporation makes consumer products, may be distributed to stockholders. ¶

before they are sold to the general public. The individual who owns 100 shares would have the right to purchase 40, or 10 percent, of the new shares. If the purchase is made, then the stockholder's relative position is maintained, for the stockholder owns 10 percent of the firm both before and after the sale of the new stock.

Although preemptive rights are required in some states for incorporation, their importance has diminished. (Rights offerings are more common in foreign countries, such as the United Kingdom.) Some firms have changed their bylaws to eliminate preemptive rights. For example, AT&T asked its stockholders to relinquish these rights. The rationale was that issuing new shares through rights offerings was more expensive than selling the shares to the general public through an underwriting. Investors who desired to maintain their relative position could still purchase the new shares, and all stockholders would benefit through the cost savings and the flexibility given to the firm's management. Most stockholders accepted the management's request and voted to relinquish their preemptive rights. Now AT&T does not have to offer any new shares to its current stockholders before it offers them publicly.

DIVIDEND POLICY

CASH DIVIDENDS
Distribution from earnings paid in the form of cash

After a corporation has earned profits, management must decide what to do with these earnings: return them and increase each stockholder's investment in the firm, or distribute them in **cash dividends.** If the earnings are distributed, the cash flows out of the firm. If the earnings are retained, management will put the funds to work by purchasing income-earning assets or retiring outstanding debt. The retained earnings will *not be held in cash.*

Suppose a firm begins the year with the following balance sheet:

ASSETS		LIABILITIES AND EQUITY	
Assets	$10,000	Debt	$3,000
		Equity	7,000
	$10,000		$10,000

During the year the firm earns $1,000. The impact of the dividend policy on the firm's balance sheet depends on whether it (1) distributes the earnings, (2) retains the earnings and acquires more assets, or (3) retains the earnings and retires debt. The impact on the balance sheet of these alternatives is as follows:

The firm's balance sheet after earning $1,000 and

1. distributing the earnings:

ASSETS		LIABILITIES AND EQUITY	
Assets	$10,000	Debt	$3,000
		Equity	7,000
	$10,000		$10,000

2. retaining the earnings and investing the funds in income-earning assets:

ASSETS		LIABILITIES AND EQUITY	
Assets	$11,000	Debt	$3,000
		Equity	8,000
	$11,000		$11,000

3. retaining the earnings and using the funds to retire outstanding debt:

ASSETS		LIABILITIES AND EQUITY	
Assets	$10,000	Debt	$2,000
		Equity	8,000
	$10,000		$10,000

As the first case illustrates, if earnings are distributed as cash dividends, the firm's equity is not increased. If management wants to invest in additional assets, it will have to use an alternative source of funds. This money may be borrowed, which may increase the financial risk of the firm. Or the funds may be obtained by issuing additional stock, but it may not make sense to distribute earnings and then issue new shares to raise equity. The retention of the earnings would achieve the same effect and not involve the costs associated with selling new stock.

Since the stockholders are the owners of the firm and are entitled to the earnings, the question becomes: What do the stockholders want? What is best for them, additional investment in the firm or cash dividends? This would seem to be an easy question to answer but, in reality, is not. Usually, many different stockholders own shares, and some may seek income through dividends while others may seek capital gains.

The decision concerning the distribution of earnings is sometimes viewed as that of management serving various clients. The intent is to identify what the clients (the stockholders) want and to satisfy that want. Retirees, individuals seeking supplementary income, managers of pension plans and trust funds, and corporate stockholders may prefer dividends to capital gains. Other investors with current income may prefer capital gains that may be realized in the future when the funds are needed. If management can identify which of these groups are the primary stockholders, then dividend policy may be designed to meet the needs of those stockholders.

Actually, the decision to retain versus distribute may be irrelevant. Suppose that at the beginning of the year a stock is selling for $100 and an individual buys 100 shares ($10,000). During the year, the firm earns $10 per share. As a result of the earnings growth, the value of a share rises to $110, and the stockholder's shares are now worth $11,000.

If the firm distributes the earnings, the stockholder receives $1,000 ($10 × 100 shares). However, the value of the share will fall by the amount of the dividend, so the price returns to the original $100.[6] The investor experiences neither a capital gain nor a loss and will have earned 10 percent on the investment (the $1,000 in dividends divided by the $10,000 cost of the investment).

Suppose the firm does not distribute the earnings, and the investor needs the cash. The individual could sell 9 shares to obtain $990 (9 shares × $110 a share). Of course, the investor still has 91 shares worth $10,010. Except for the $10 difference resulting from the inability to sell fractional shares, the investor's position is the same as before when earnings were distributed. In either case, the investor has $1,000 in cash and $10,000 worth of stock.

This discussion suggests that the stockholder's position is unaffected by the dividend policy of the firm; thus, dividend policy is irrelevant.[7] There are,

[6] That the price of a stock declines by the amount of the dividend is explained in the next section on cash dividends.

[7] For a discussion of the irrelevancy of dividends, see an advanced test on financial management, such as Eugene F. Brigham, Louis S. Gapenski, and Michael C. Ehrhardt, *Financial Management,* 9th ed. (Fort Worth, Texas: The Dryden Press, 1999), Chapter 17.

however, considerations that may affect dividend policy and hence suggest that in the real world in which management and investors make decisions, dividend policy is not relevant. Transaction costs, such as commissions on the purchase and sale of securities or investment banking fees from the sale of new securities, taxation, and the firm's cash needs affect the dividend policy of the individual firm.

Impact of Transaction Costs

A situation in which an investor must sell part of his or her holdings in order to generate cash argues for a cash dividend policy. In the previous illustration, it would not be cost-effective to sell 9 shares of stock. Commissions would consume a large proportion of the proceeds of the sale, and this expense is avoided by the receipt of dividends. However, if management paid dividends and then had to sell additional shares to raise funds, the firm would incur investment banking fees that would have been avoided if earnings had been retained.

These transaction costs do not conclusively argue for or against the distribution of dividends. If the corporation's primary stockholders desire dividends, then there may be a net cost saving from the distribution of earnings and flotation of new shares. Those stockholders who want the additional shares could purchase them, in which case they bear the expense. If the corporation's primary stockholders seek capital gains, then there may be a net cost saving from retaining the earnings. Those stockholders who want cash could sell part of their holdings, in which case they bear the expense.

Impact of Taxation

Taxes have a major impact on financial decisions and dividend policy is no exception. Consider the earlier example in which the stockholder received either a cash dividend or sold some of the stock. Dividends are subject to federal income taxes, while profits from security sales are subject to federal capital gains taxes. If these taxes are the same, then taxation does not matter. As of 2000, the federal income tax rates on dividend income could be as high as 39.6 percent while the maximum rate on long-term capital gains (gains held for more than a year) was 20 percent. Such taxation argues in favor of capital gains over dividend income.

Even if dividends and capital gains were taxed at the same rate, there is still an argument in favor of capital gains. Dividends are taxed when they are received; the tax on capital gains is deferred until the gains are realized (in other words, when the shares are sold). If the corporation retains earnings and grows, and the value of the shares rises in response to the growth, stockholders will not pay any tax as long as they hold their shares and do not realize the gains.

Even if the gains are realized after a number of years and taxed at the same rate as dividends, the ability to defer the tax permits the investor to take advantage of compounding. The following example illustrates how federal income taxes favor the retention of earnings through compounding. The example assumes that the stockholder is in the 28 percent income tax bracket and invests $1,000 in a firm. The firm earns 10 percent on the individual's equity in the firm. Case A illustrates the retention of earnings and the growth in the individual's investment in the firm.

CASE A INITIAL FUNDS $1,000

	Earnings	Earnings Retained	Stockholder's Investment
Year 1	$100.00	$100.00	$1,100.00
Year 2	110.00	110.00	1,210.00
Year 3	121.00	121.00	1,331.00
Year 4	133.10	133.10	1,464.10

During the first year, the firm earns $100 for the investor (0.1 × $1,000) and retains the earnings so the investor's equity rises to $1,100 ($1,000 + $100). After four years, the investor's equity in the firm grows to $1,464. If the shares are sold for $1,464, the investor has a capital gain of $464 ($1,464 − $1,000), which is taxed at 20 percent. The investor thus pays $92.80 (0.20 × $464) in taxes and nets $371.20 after taxes.

In Case B, the firm distributes the annual earnings in cash dividends. Since there is no retention of earnings, the firm earns and distributes $100 each year. The investor then pays personal income tax of $28 and nets $72 after tax.

CASE B INITIAL FUNDS $1,000

	Earnings	Earnings Distributed	Income Tax	After-Tax Income	Stockholder's Investment
Year 1	$100	$100	$28	$72	$1,000
Year 2	100	100	28	72	1,000
Year 3	100	100	28	72	1,000
Year 4	100	100	28	72	1,000

After four years, the stockholder will have received $400 in cash dividends, paid $112 in taxes, and netted $288. The $288 is less than the $371.20 netted in the first case, in which the earnings were allowed to grow (and compound) and the tax was deferred.

As may be seen from cases A and B, compounding and differences in tax rates on dividends and long-term capital gains favor the retention of earnings rather than cash dividends. The difference in the after-tax return, however, would be smaller if the investor had invested the dividends elsewhere and earned more than the firm earned on the retained earnings. Thus, an investor would be better off receiving the earnings if there were a use for the money that overcame the deferral of the tax and the lower long-term capital gains tax rate. Many investors, however, may not have such investment opportunities, so the retention of earnings is often viewed as being in the best interests of the firm and its stockholders who are seeking growth in capital.

Impact on the Firm's Need for Cash

The previous discussion suggested that transaction costs and taxation may affect a firm's dividend policy. The firm's need for cash may also have an impact. For

FINANCIAL FACTS

Classes of Common Stock

Suppose some stockholders want management to distribute cash dividends while others want management to retain earnings to finance future growth. Can management distribute earnings to one group and retain earnings for the other stockholders? Essentially, the answer is no; some owners of a class of stock cannot receive cash dividends while others have their earnings reinvested. What applies to one applies to all. Of course, some stockholders may opt to have their cash dividends reinvested in additional shares through dividend reinvestment plans. This choice to have cash dividends reinvested is made by the individual and not by management. ¶ Although the preceding paragraph states that all stockholders in a class are treated the same, there is a very important qualifying phrase: "in a class." Some companies have more than one class of common stock. For example, Oshkosh B'Gosh has two classes of common stock. Class A shares have limited voting rights and receive 15 percent higher dividends than the Class B shares. Other publicly held corporations with two classes of common stock include Food Lion and Media General. ¶ While the stockholders of the different classes of common stock may receive different cash dividends, the purpose of two classes is not the distribution of dividends but the distribution of voting power. Often one of the classes has no or only limited voting rights. Thus, voting power can be concentrated in the hands of a few stockholders who own the class of stock with voting power, which virtually assures them control over the firm. ¶

example, in Chapter 19, a cash budget will illustrate a case in which the firm's needs for cash fluctuate during the year. Such variations in cash requirements affect the firm's capacity to pay dividends. If management must pay dividends during a period when the firm has insufficient cash, such payments will require the firm to borrow money. Management may be reluctant to borrow funds just to pay the dividend, since such borrowings will require interest payments and principal repayment. Thus, the fluctuation in the firm's cash needs can have an impact on the desirability of distributing cash dividends as well as the firm's capacity to pay the dividend.

Firms in cyclical industries have a similar problem except that it is spread over a longer period. These firms are primarily in industries that produce capital goods (manufacturers of machinery and machine tools) or durable goods (automobiles and housing). Firms in cyclical industries experience fluctuations in earnings that affect both their capacity to pay dividends and their need to retain earnings. During periods of economic prosperity their earnings tend to expand, which would permit higher dividends. However, management may prefer to retain the earnings to help finance the firm's operations during periods of economic slowdown and stagnation. During recessions the firm's earnings may decline severely, or the firm may even operate at a loss. If the firm had previously retained earnings, its capacity to endure economic stagnation would be increased.

Inflation also has an impact on dividends. Since the cost of plant and equipment rises during a period of inflation, the firm will need more sources of funds to finance the replacement of worn-out assets. Notice that this replacement of plant and equipment is not the same as expansion of the firm's operations; inflation means that the firm will have to spend more just to maintain its current operations. Such expenditures require financing, and the retention of earnings is a source of those funds. Of course, if the firm distributes its earnings, it will have to find other sources of funds to replace the obsolete plant and equipment.

The preceding discussion has indicated that there is no unique dividend policy that all firms follow. Such reasons as saving brokerage commission explain why the individual investor may prefer cash to capital gains. Any reasons, such as deferring capital gains taxes, explains why the individual investor may prefer the retention of earnings. There are also reasons, such as the availability of investment opportunities or the need for cash, that explain why management may prefer to retain earnings.

If management seeks to maximize the wealth of the stockholders, the dividend decision basically depends on who has the better use for the money—the stockholders or the firm. Management, however, may not know the stockholders' alternative uses for the money, or may choose to ignore the stockholders' alleged uses, and decide to retain the earnings. Stockholders who do not like the firm's dividend policy may then sell their shares. If stockholders like the dividend policy, they may purchase more shares. If the sellers exceed the buyers, the value of the shares will fall, and management will become aware of the stockholders' preference for the cash dividends instead of the retention of earnings.

CASH DIVIDENDS

Dividend policy is a question of how much of a firm's earnings should be distributed. Companies that do pay cash dividends usually have a policy that is either stated or implicitly known by the investment community. If an American company pays a cash dividend, the dollar amount is often stable and well known. The proportion of the earnings distributed is measured by the **payout ratio,** which is the cash dividend divided by earnings per share. If the dollar amount of the dividend is stable, the payout ratio will fluctuate with fluctuations in earnings. The stability of dividends coupled with fluctuations in earnings means that the amount of earnings retained varies each year and that management has decided to maintain a stable dividend at the expense of stable increases in retained earnings.

PAYOUT RATIO
Ratio of cash dividends to earnings

American companies that pay cash dividends distribute a regular cash dividend on a quarterly basis. A few companies make monthly distributions (for example, Winn-Dixie), and some pay semiannually or annually.[8] In the case of semiannual and annual payments, the dollar amount is small. Instead of paying 2½ cents a share quarterly, the company pays 10 cents annually, which reduces the expense of distributing the dividend.

[8]Foreign firms typically pay cash dividends semiannually. For example, British Airways paid $0.84 in November 1998, and $2.26 in June 1999. Even if the amount of the dividend is stable, fluctuations in exchange rates imply that the amount of the dividend received varies with each payment.

While most companies with cash dividend policies pay regular quarterly dividends, there are other types of dividend policies. Some companies pay quarterly dividends plus extras. Chicago Rivet and Machine pays a quarterly dividend ($0.18) but may distribute an extra dividend at year end if the company has a good year. In 1998, the firm paid an additional $0.40 extra dividend. Such a policy is appropriate for a firm in a cyclical industry because earnings fluctuate, and the firm may be hard pressed to maintain a higher level of regular quarterly dividends. By having a set cash payment supplemented with extras in good years, the firm maintains a fixed payment and supplements the dividend when appropriate.

Some firms pay cash dividends that are irregular; there is no set dividend payment. For example, to maintain favorable tax treatment, real estate investment trusts are required by law to distribute their earnings. These earnings fluctuate, causing the cash dividends to fluctuate. For example, BRT Realty Trust paid $2.43 in 1988, $1.46 in 1990, and $0 in 1995 when it sustained a loss.

As earnings grow, the firm can increase its cash dividends. There is, however, a reluctance to increase the cash dividend immediately with an increase in earnings. This lag occurs because of management's reluctance to reduce cash dividends if earnings decline. Management apparently fears that the reduction will be interpreted as a sign of financial weakness. The unwillingness to cut dividends has resulted in a tendency for management to raise dividends only when it is certain that the higher level of earnings can be maintained.

Distributing dividends takes time. The first step is the dividend meeting of the firm's directors. If they decide to distribute a cash dividend, two important dates are established. The first date determines who is to receive the dividend. On a particular day the ownership books of the corporation are closed, and everyone owning stock in the company at the end of that day receives the dividend. This is called the **date of record.** If investors buy the stock after the date of record, they do not receive the dividend. The stock is purchased excluding the dividend; this is referred to as **ex dividend,** for the price of the stock does not include the dividend payment. The ex dividend day is two working days before the date of record, because the settlement date is three working days after the transaction.

DATE OF RECORD
Day on which an investor must own stock in order to receive the dividend payment

EX DIVIDEND
Stock purchases exclusive of any dividend payment

The second important date is the day that the dividend is distributed, or the **pay date** or **distribution date.** The distribution date may be several weeks after the record date, as the company must determine the owners on the record date and process the checks. The company may not perform this task itself; instead it uses its commercial bank, for which service the bank charges a fee. The day that the dividend is received by the stockholder is thus likely to be many weeks after the board of directors announced the dividend payment.

PAY DATE OR DISTRIBUTION DATE
Day on which a dividend is paid to stockholders

The time frame for the declaration and payment of a dividend is illustrated by the following time line:

Declaration Date (July 1)	Ex Div Date (July 29)	Date of Record (August 1)	Distribution Date (September 1)

On July 1, the board of directors declares a dividend to be paid September 1 to all stockholders of record August 1. To receive the dividend, the individual must own the stock at the close of trading on August 1. To own the stock August 1, the stock must have been purchased on or before July 28. If the stock is bought July 28, settlement will occur after three days on July 31 (assuming three workdays), so the investor owns the stock on August 1. If the investor buys the stock on July 29, that individual does not own the stock on August 1 (the seller owns the stock) and cannot be the owner of record on August 1. On July 29, the stock trades ex dividend, or "ex div," and the buyer does not receive the dividend.

In the financial papers, purchases of the stock on the ex dividend day are indicated by an X next to sales volume. The following entry indicates that the stock of Sun Company traded on that day was purchased exclusive of the dividend.

Stock	Dividend	Sales	High	Low	Close	Net Change
Sun Co.	2	X 135	48	47	47.25	+0.25

The $0.50 ($2.00/4) quarterly dividend will be paid to the owners of record of the previous day and not to the investors who purchased the stock on the ex dividend day. In this example there was a net change of 0.25 in the price of the stock for the ex dividend day. This indicates that the closing price on the previous day was $47.50 and not $47 as might be expected from the increase of .25 for the day. Since the current buyers will not receive the $0.50 dividend, the price of the stock is reduced for the dividend. The net change in the stock's price from the previous day's trading is figured from the adjusted price ($47.50 minus the $0.50 dividend).

STOCK DIVIDENDS

STOCK DIVIDENDS
Distribution from earnings paid in additional shares of stock

Some firms pay **stock dividends** in addition to or instead of cash dividends. For example, Bear Sterns periodically distributes a 5 percent dividend in addition to its cash dividends. Unfortunately, the recipients may misunderstand what they are receiving. Although stock dividends alter the entries in the firm's equity section of its balance sheet, they do *not* increase the firm's assets.[9] Because the assets and their management produce the firm's income, a stock dividend does not by itself increase the potential earning power of the company.

The following equity section (on page 260) of a balance sheet is used to illustrate a stock dividend:

[9]For an explanation of the components of the balance sheet, including the equity section, see Chapter 12 on the analysis of a firm's financial statements.

Equity: \$1 par common stock (2,000,000 shares authorized; 1,000,000 outstanding)	\$1,000,000
Additional paid-in capital	500,000
Retained earnings	5,000,000
	\$6,500,000

A stock dividend does not affect a firm's assets and liabilities. Only the entries in the equity section of the balance sheet are affected by a stock dividend. The stock dividend transfers amounts from retained earnings to common stock and additional paid-in capital. The amount transferred depends on (1) the number of new shares issued through the stock dividend and (2) the market price of the stock. If the above company issued a 10 percent stock dividend when the market price of the common stock was \$20 a share, this would cause the issuing of 100,000 shares with a value of \$2,000,000. This amount is subtracted from the retained earnings and transferred to the common stock and additional paid-in capital. The amount transferred to common stock will be 100,000 times the par value of the stock (\$1 × 100,000 = \$100,000). The remaining amount (\$1,900,000) is transferred to additional paid-in capital. The equity section then becomes:

Equity: \$1 par common stock (2,000,000 shares authorized; 1,100,000 outstanding)	\$1,100,000
Additional paid-in capital	2,400,000
Retained earnings	3,000,000
	\$6,500,000

Although there has been an increase in the number of shares outstanding, there has been no increase in cash and no increase in assets that may be used to earn profits. All that has happened is a recapitalization: The equity entries have been altered.[10]

The stock dividend does not increase the wealth of the stockholder but does increase the number of shares owned. In the above example, a stockholder who owned 100 shares before the stock dividend had stock worth \$2,000. After the stock dividend, this stockholder owns 110 shares, and the 110 shares are also worth \$2,000, for the price per share falls from \$20 to \$18.18 (\$2,000/110 = \$18.18). Why does the price of the stock fall? The answer is that there are 10 percent more shares outstanding, but there has been no increase in the firm's assets and earning power. The old shares have been *diluted* and hence the price of the stock must decline to indicate this **dilution.** If the price of the stock did not fall, all companies could make their stockholders wealthier by declaring stock dividends. But

DILUTION
Reduction in earnings per share as the result of issuing additional shares

[10] Since cash dividends are paid from earnings, this transfer of capital from retained earnings to common stock and paid-in capital reduces the firm's ability to pay cash dividends, because retained earnings are decreased.

investors would soon realize that the stock dividend does not increase the assets and earning power of the firm, and they would not be willing to pay the old price for a larger number of shares. The market price would fall to adjust for the dilution of the old shares, and that is what happens.

The major misconception concerning the stock dividend is that it increases the ability of the firm to grow. If the stock dividend were a substitute for a cash dividend, the statement would be partially true, because the firm still has the asset cash that would have been paid to stockholders if a cash dividend had been declared. The firm, however, would still have the cash if it did not pay the stock dividend, for a firm may retain its cash and not pay a stock dividend. Hence, the decision to pay the stock dividend does not increase the firm's cash; it is the decision *not to pay the cash dividend* that conserves the cash.

STOCK SPLITS

After the price of a stock has risen substantially, management may choose to split the stock. This **stock split** lowers the price of the stock and makes it more accessible to investors. Implicit in this statement is the belief that investors prefer lower-priced shares and that reducing the price of the stock benefits the current stockholders by widening the market for their stock.

STOCK SPLIT
Recapitalization achieved by changing the number of shares outstanding

Like the stock dividend, the stock split is a recapitalization that alters the equity section on the balance sheet.[11] It does not affect the assets or liabilities of the firm. It does not increase the earning power of the firm, and the wealth of the stockholder is not increased unless other investors prefer lower-priced stocks and increase the demand for this stock.

The equity section of a balance sheet used previously for illustrating the stock dividend will now be employed to demonstrate a two-for-one stock split. In a two-for-one stock split, one old share becomes two new shares, and the par value of the stock is halved from $1.00 to $0.50. There are no changes in the additional paid-in capital, retained earnings, or total equity. All that has happened is that there are now twice as many shares outstanding, and each share is worth half as much as an old share.

Equity: $0.50 par common stock (2,000,000 shares authorized: 2,000,000 outstanding)	$1,000,000
Additional paid-in capital	500,000
Retained earnings	5,000,000
	$6,500,000

[11]A stock split may be differentiated from a stock dividend by the number of shares issued. If the number of shares is increased by 25 percent or more, the recapitalization is considered a stock split. If the number of shares increases by less than 25 percent, the recapitalization is a stock dividend. An eleven for ten stock split would, in effect, be a 10 percent stock dividend.

EXHIBIT 10.1

Selected Stock Splits Distributed in 2000

Firm	Terms of Split
General Electric	3 for 1
Novellus	3 for 1
CMGI, Inc.	2 for 1
Hormel Foods	2 for 1
KLA-Tencor	2 for 1
MGM Grand	2 for 1
Oracle	2 for 1
Sprint PCS Group	2 for 1
Home Depot	3 for 2

Stock splits may be in any combination of terms, as can be seen in Exhibit 10.1, which gives the terms of several stock splits. The most common splits are two for one or three for two. There are also reverse splits, which reduce the number of shares and raise the price of the stock. For example, Transcend Services split its stock one for five in 1999. Thus, 100 shares became 20 shares after the split.

All stock splits affect the price of the stock. With a two-for-one split, the stock's price is cut in half. A one-for-ten split raises the price by a factor of ten. An easy method for finding the price of the stock after the split is to multiply the stock's price before the split by the reciprocal of the terms of the split. For example, if a stock is selling for $54 a share and is split 3 for 2, then the price of the stock after the split will be $\$54 \times 2/3 = \$36$.

Stock splits, like stock dividends, do not by themselves increase the wealth of the stockholder, for the stock split does not increase the assets and earning power of the firm. All that changes is the number of shares and their price. A stock split is like a pie that is cut into eight instead of four pieces. The size of the pie remains the same, but each piece is smaller.[12]

The usual rationale given by management for splitting a stock is that a lower selling price increases the marketability of the shares. That is, the split produces a wider distribution of ownership and increases investor interest in the company. This increased interest and marketability may ultimately cause the value of the stock to appreciate. For example, if Ford splits its stock (as it did in 1988), the wider distribution may lead to an increase in sales. Larger sales then produce higher earnings and an increase in the price of the shares. If such a scenario were to occur (and there is no evidence that it will), the current stockholders would

[12] In a scene in that wonderful movie *Rainman,* Raymond (the Rainman, played by Dustin Hoffman) receives four fish sticks. Raymond says that he always gets eight fish sticks, so his brother (played by Tom Cruise) cuts them in half and says "You now have eight."

That's a two-for-one stock split. Four fish sticks become eight fish sticks. It's like cutting a pizza into eight slices instead of four. The size of the pizza remains the same; you just get more slices.

Stock Splits and Investing

When a stock is split, its price is adjusted for the split. If the price were $50 and the stock is split two for one, your 100 shares become 200 shares and the price becomes $25. You have $5,000 worth of stock in either case. After receiving the additional shares, it is easy to say, "If the stock rises $5, I will now make $1,000 instead of $500." This line of reasoning assumes that a $25 stock will rise by 20 percent while the $50 stock will rise by only 10 percent. If they both rise by 10 percent (or 20 percent), it does not matter if you have 100 shares at $50 or 200 shares at $25. Ten percent is 10 percent in either case. ¶ There is another reason not to buy stocks after they split. Full-service brokerage firms tend to base commissions on the number of shares sold as well as the price. The commission on 200 shares at $25 is greater than the commission on 100 shares at $50. (Discount brokers tend to base commissions on the dollar value of the purchase or sale and not on the number of shares. Online brokers may charge a flat fee that is independent of the number of shares.) I once heard two brokers discussing the commission on Disney after it split four for one. The difference in commissions before and after the split exceeded $100. That will pay a couple of days' admissions to Disneyland. ¶ The above suggests that buying split stocks is not a superior investment decision. Empirical results also support the conclusion that splits do not increase stockholders' wealth. But, as is often the case, there is some evidence that stock splits may increase investors' wealth. For a balanced view of stock splits, you should also consult David L. Ikenberry, Graeme Rankine, and Earl K. Stice, "What Do Stock Splits Really Signal," *Journal of Financial and Quantitative Analysis* (September 1996): 357–375. ¶

benefit; however, the source of a subsequent price increase in the stock's value would still be the increase in earnings and not the stock split.

DIVIDEND REINVESTMENT PLANS

Many corporations that pay cash dividends also have **dividend reinvestment plans** (sometimes referred to as DRIPs). These permit stockholders to have cash dividends used to purchase additional shares of stock. The potential returns to stockholders are substantial. Washington Real Estate Investment Trust reported that if an investor had purchased 100 shares in 1973 for $1,387 and had all dividends reinvested, that individual would have accumulated 3,986 shares (adjusted for stock splits) worth $80,216 in 20 years.

DIVIDEND REINVESTMENT PLANS (DRIPs)
Plans that permit stockholders to have cash dividends reinvested in additional shares instead of receiving the cash

There are two types of dividend reinvestment plans. In most plans a bank acts on behalf of the corporation and its stockholders. The bank collects the cash dividends for the stockholders and, in some plans, offers the stockholders the option of making additional cash contributions. The bank pools all the funds and purchases the stock in the secondary market. Since the bank purchases a large block of shares, it receives a substantial reduction in the per-share commission cost of the purchase. This reduced brokerage fee is spread over all the shares, so even the smallest investor receives the advantage of the reduced brokerage fees. The bank does charge a fee for its service, but this fee is usually modest and does not offset the potential savings in brokerage fees.

In the second type of reinvestment plan, the company issues new shares of stock, and the money goes directly to the company. The investor may also have the option of making additional cash contributions. This type of plan offers the investor a further advantage in that the brokerage fees are entirely circumvented. The entire amount of the cash dividend is used to purchase shares, with the issuing cost paid by the company.

Besides the potential lost savings, the major advantage to investors of dividend reinvestment plans is the "forced savings." Such forced saving may be desirable for investors who wish to save but have a tendency to spend money once it is received. The plans also offer advantages to the firm. They create goodwill and may result in some cost savings (for instance, lower costs of preparing and mailing dividend checks). The reinvestment plans that result in the new issue of stock also increase the company's equity base.

REPURCHASE OF STOCK

A firm with cash may choose to repurchase some of its stock. Stock repurchases decrease the number of shares outstanding. Since the earnings will be spread over fewer shares, the earnings per share should increase. The higher per share earnings then may lead to a higher stock price in the future.

The repurchasing of shares is another example of the question of selecting among alternatives. The company repurchases shares because management believes that it is the best use of the money. The shares may then be used in the future in merger agreements or for exercising stock options. Repurchases also occur because management believes that the price of the stock is too low and the shares are undervalued. Repurchasing the shares, then, is viewed as the best investment currently available to the firm.

Repurchasing shares may be viewed as an alternative to paying cash dividends. Instead of distributing the money as cash dividends, the firm offers to purchase the shares from the stockholders. This offers the stockholders a major advantage. They have the option to sell or retain their shares. If the stockholders believe that the firm's potential is sufficient to warrant retention of the shares, they do not have to sell them. The decision to sell the shares rests with the stockholder.

Perhaps the most spectacular repurchase occurred when Teledyne bought 8.7 million of its shares at $200 each for a total outlay of $1.74 billion. Teledyne initially offered to repurchase 5 million shares at $200. At that time the stock was selling for $156, so the offer represented a 28 percent premium over the current price. The large premium probably caused more shares to be tendered than 5 million. While Teledyne could have prorated its purchases, it instead chose to accept all the shares. The result was to reduce the amount of outstanding stock from

20.4 million to 11.7 million shares—a reduction of 40 percent. The reduction in the number of shares outstanding increased Teledyne's earnings per share by more than $7. After the repurchase had been completed, the stock's price continued to increase and sold for more than $240 a share within a few weeks. Obviously the security market believed that the repurchase was in the best interests of the remaining stockholders.

SUMMARY

Corporations issue and sell stock to individuals as a means to raise equity funds. The stockholders are the owners of the corporation. Although preferred stock is legally considered to be equity, its features make it similar to debt. Preferred stock pays a fixed dividend. If the firm misses a payment, the amount of the dividend usually accumulates and must be paid before dividends can be paid to the common stockholders. While some preferred stock is perpetual, other preferred issues have a sinking fund or call feature. The investor can expect these issues of preferred stock to have a finite life.

Although preferred stock is similar to debt, in some ways it is different. From the investor's perspective, it is riskier than bonds because the terms of preferred stock are not legal obligations of the firm. From the firm's viewpoint, preferred stock is less attractive than debt because the dividends are paid from earnings and are not tax deductible. Interest on bonds is a tax-deductible expense.

Common stock represents the residual claim on the corporation's earnings and assets. The owners of common stock have the right to vote their shares. Once a corporation has achieved earnings, the earnings are either distributed or retained. Retained earnings, which are an important source of funds for corporations, increase the stockholders' investment in the firm and permit the firm to retire debt or increase its assets. Thus, retained earnings finance further growth, which, if achieved, should tend to increase the value of the shares.

Some corporations pay stock dividends, which increase the number of shares outstanding. Stock dividends are perceptibly different from cash dividends, which require the firm to distribute funds. Stock dividends (and stock splits) do not change the firm's assets, liabilities, or total equity and do not affect the firm's earning capacity. They do, however, lower the stock's price in proportion to the number of new shares issued.

Many firms offer dividend reinvestment plans that permit stockholders to accumulate additional shares at little or no brokerage cost. Occasionally, a firm will elect to repurchase shares instead of making a cash distribution. Such repurchases generally occur if management believes that the shares are undervalued.

REVIEW QUESTIONS

1. What are the features common to most preferred stock?
2. Must a firm pay preferred stock dividends? What does being in arrears mean? What is the advantage offered to investors by having a cumulative preferred stock?

3. From the viewpoint of the corporation, preferred stock is less risky than bonds. From the viewpoint of the investor, preferred stock is riskier. Why are these statements concerning risk true?
4. Why is earnings per preferred share a measure of the safety of preferred stock?
5. If you were a minority stockholder, why might you support cumulative voting?
6. What impact may federal personal income taxes have on the decision to retain earnings?
7. Which dividend policy, a constant payout or a stable dollar, would a retired individual prefer?
8. Why does the price of a stock decline after a 10 percent stock dividend?
9. If you purchase a stock on the ex dividend day, do you receive the dividend?
10. What is a dividend reinvestment plan, and what advantages does it offer investors?
11. Information on dividend reinvestment plans is available through the DRIP Investor (**www.dripinvestor.com**), DRIP Central (**www.dripcentral.com**) and Netstock Direct (**www.netstockdirect.com**). What are the features of the Exxon and IBM dividend reinvestment plans? Do the plans permit investors to purchase additional shares? Do any dividend reinvestment plans permits investors to purchase additional shares at a discount?

12. While stock splits may not increase the wealth of stockholders, many companies do split their stock. A calendar of stock splits is available at several Internet sites such as Yahoo! (**www.biz.yahoo.com/s/s.html**) and Money Central (**www.moneycentral.msn.com/investor/calendar/splits/current.asp**). How many stocks will split during the next month, and what proportion of the splits are 2 for 1?

PROBLEMS

1. West Wind, Inc. has 5,000,000 shares of common stock outstanding with a market value of $60 per share. Net income for the coming year is expected to be $6,900,000. What impact will a three-for-one stock split have on the earnings per share and on the price of the stock?
2. Sharon Bohnette owns 1,000 shares of Northern Chime Company. There are four seats on the board of directors up for election and Ms. Bohnette is one of the nominees. Under the traditional method of voting, how many votes may she cast for herself? How many votes may she cast for herself under the cumulative method of voting?
3. Jersey Mining earns $9.50 a share, sells for $90, and pays a $5 per share dividend. The stock is split two for one and a $3 per share cash dividend is declared.
   a. What will be the new price of the stock?
   b. If the firm's total earnings do not change, what is the payout ratio before and after the stock split?

4. Firm A had the following selected items on its balance sheet:

Cash	$28,000,000
Common stock (2,000,000 shares; $50 par)	100,000,000
Paid-in capital	10,000,000
Retained earnings	62,000,000

How would each of these accounts appear after:
a. a cash dividend of $1 per share?
b. a 5 percent stock dividend (fair market value is $100 per share)?
c. a one-for-two reverse split?

5. Jackson Enterprises has the following capital (equity) accounts:

Common stock (100,000 shares at $1 par)	$100,000
Paid-in capital	200,000
Retained earnings	225,000

The board of directors has declared a 20 percent stock dividend on January 1 and a $0.25 cash dividend on March 1. What changes occur in the capital accounts after each transaction if the price of the stock is $4?

6. A firm's balance sheet has the following entries:

Cash	$10,000,000
Total liabilities	30,000,000
Common stock (2,000,000 shares outstanding; $5 par)	10,000,000
Paid-in capital	3,000,000
Retained earnings	42,000,000

What will be each of these balance sheet entries after:
a. a three-for-one stock split?
b. a $1.25 per share cash dividend?
c. a 10 percent stock dividend (current price of the stock is $15 per share)?

7. What effect will a two-for-one stock split have on the following items found on a firm's financial statements?
a. Earnings per share $4.20
b. Total equity $10,000,000
c. Long-term debt $4,300,000
d. Paid-in capital $1,534,000
e. Number of shares outstanding 1,000,000
f. Earnings $4,200,000

8. You are considering purchasing the preferred stock of a firm but are concerned with its capacity to pay the dividend. To help allay that fear, you compute the times-dividend-earned ratio for the past three years from the following data taken from the firm's financial statements:

Year	X1	X2	X3
Operating income	$12,000,000	$15,000,000	$17,000,000
Interest	3,000,000	5,900,000	11,000,000
Taxes	4,000,000	5,400,000	4,000,000
Preferred dividends	1,000,000	1,000,000	1,500,000
Common dividends	3,000,000	2,000,000	—

What does your analysis indicate concerning the firm's capacity to pay the preferred stock dividends?

9. A firm has the following balance sheet:

ASSETS		LIABILITIES AND EQUITY	
Cash	$ 20,000	Accounts payable	$ 20,000
Accounts receivable	110,000	Long-term debt	100,000
Inventory	120,000	Common stock ($8 par; 4,000 shares outstanding)	32,000
Plant and equipment	250,000	Paid-in capital	148,000
		Retained earnings	200,000
	$500,000		$500,000

a. Construct a new balance sheet showing the impact of a three-for-one split. If the current market price of the stock is $54, what is the price after the split?

ASSETS		LIABILITIES AND EQUITY	
Cash	$____	Accounts payable	$____
Accounts receivable	____	Long-term debt	____
Inventory	____	Common stock ($___ par; ____ shares outstanding)	____
Plant and equipment	____	Paid in capital	____
	____	Retained earnings	____
	$____		$____

b. Construct a new balance sheet showing the impact of a 10 percent stock dividend. After the stock dividend, what is the new price of the common stock?

ASSETS		LIABILITIES AND EQUITY	
Cash	$____	Accounts payable	$____
Accounts receivable	____	Long-term debt	____
Inventory	____	Common stock ($___ par; ____ shares outstanding)	____
Plant and equipment	____	Paid in capital	____
	____	Retained earnings	____
	$____		$____

CASE

STRATEGIES TO INCREASE EQUITY

Kathy Tiller is preparing for a meeting of the board of directors of the Delaware Bay Corporation, a developer of moderately priced homes and vacation homes in the Delaware Bay area. The combination of the location near major metropolitan areas with the recreational facilities associated with the Delaware Bay has made the firm one of the most successful homebuilders in the nation. During the last five years, the firm's cash dividend has risen from $2.10 to $3.74, and the price of its stock has risen from $36 to $75. Since the firm has 1,200,000 shares outstanding, the market value of the stock is $90,000,000. Given the volatile nature of the building industry, the increases in the price of the stock and in the dividend were substantial achievements.

Management, however, is considering entering into nonbuilding areas in an effort to diversify the firm. These new investments will require more financing. Although additional debt financing is a possibility, management believes that it is unwise to issue only new debt and not increase the firm's equity base. New equity could be obtained by issuing additional stock or reducing the dividend, and thus retaining a larger proportion of the firm's earnings. Two major points had previously been raised against these strategies: Issuing additional shares may dilute the existing stockholders' position, and reducing the dividend could cause the value of the stock to decline.

Even though it is possible that no change will be made and that the firm will continue its present course, the board believes that a thorough discussion of all possibilities is desirable. Ms. Tiller has been instructed to develop alternatives to the two strategies for the next meeting of the board in two weeks.

The short period for preparation means that a thorough analysis may be impossible, especially of the possible impact of a dividend cut on the value of the stock, but Ms. Tiller presumes that some additional alternatives do exist. One of her assistants suggested that the firm institute a dividend reinvestment plan, in which additional shares would be sold to stockholders to raise additional equity capital. Her other assistant suggested that the company substitute a 5 percent stock dividend for the cash dividend. Before making either (or both) suggestions to the board, Ms. Tiller decided to answer several questions:

CASE PROBLEMS

1. Would implementing the suggestions dilute the existing stockholders' position?
2. How much new equity would be raised by each action?
3. What may happen to the price of the stock?
4. What are the costs associated with each strategy?
5. Would a stock split combined with either strategy help raise additional equity financing?

6. Would an increase in the cash dividend coupled with the divided reinvestment plan help raise additional equity financing?
7. Is there any reason to prefer or exclude any one of the four strategies (that is, issuing new shares, reducing the dividend, instituting a dividend reinvestment plan, or substituting a stock dividend for the cash dividend)?

CHAPTER 11
Valuation of Stock

Learning Objectives

1. Illustrate the pricing of preferred stock.
2. Show the relationship between changes in interest rates and the value of preferred stock.
3. Calculate the value of a common stock using the dividend-growth model to determine if stock is undervalued or overvalued.
4. Adjust the dividend-growth model for differences in risk.
5. Illustrate the impact of changes in the expected return on the market or in the risk-free rate on the value of a common stock.
6. Use price/earnings (P/E) ratios as a means to value common stock.

In *Lady Windermere's Fan,* Oscar Wilde defines a cynic as "a man who knows the price of everything, and the value of nothing." This quote could be paraphrased as "an uninformed investor is a person who knows the price of every stock, and the value of none." Anybody can find the price of a stock. Yesterday's prices are reported in newspapers, and current quotes may be obtained from brokers or services like America Online. But the current price does not tell an investor if the stock is a good purchase. To answer that question, the investor needs to know what the stock is worth: its value.

One individual who learned how to determine the value of a stock was Warren Buffett. A $10,000 investment in a partnership he started in 1956 grew into $1,500,000 worth of Berkshire Hathaway stock in 1990. Buffett's success resulted from his capacity to identify excellent management and to find undervalued stocks by using security analysis and valuation techniques.[1]

This chapter is devoted to the valuation of stock. The first section describes the valuation of preferred stock. Since preferred stock is similar to bonds (that is, they both are fixed income securities), the valuation of preferred stock is essentially the same as the valuation of bonds.

[1]Warren Buffett's success is chronicled in John Train, *The Midas Touch* (New York: Harper and Row, 1987). For a biography of Warren Buffett, obtain Roger Lowenstein, *Buffett: The Making of an American Capitalist* (New York: Random House, 1995). Techniques used by Buffett are discussed in Robert G. Hagstrom, *The Warren Buffett Way* (New York: John Wiley & Sons, 1994), and Robert G. Hagstrom, *The Warren Buffett Portfolio* (New York: John Wiley & Sons, 1999).

The next section, which forms the bulk of the chapter, centers around the valuation of common stock. Although this can be an elusive topic, the individual needs to know what a stock is worth in order to determine if it should be purchased. If a stock is selling for $15 and the individual determines it is only worth $13, the stock is not a good investment.

The valuation of common stock revolves around the firm's earnings, its dividend, the future growth in dividends, and the amount that the investor can earn on alternative investments. The standard dividend-growth model used in finance is explained and illustrated, and an adjustment for risk is introduced into the dividend-growth model. The chapter ends with a description of the use of price-to-earnings and other ratios to select stocks.

VALUATION OF PREFERRED STOCK

The process of valuing (pricing) preferred stock is essentially the same as that used to price debt. The future dividend payments are brought back to the present at the appropriate discount rate. If the preferred stock does not have a required sinking fund or call feature, it may be viewed as a perpetual debt instrument. The fixed dividend (D_p) will continue indefinitely. These dividends must be discounted by the yield being earned on newly issued preferred stock (k_p). The process for determining the present value of a preferred stock (P_p) is given in Equation 11.1:

$$P_p = \frac{D_p}{(1+k_p)^1} + \frac{D_p}{(1+k_p)^2} + \frac{D_p}{(1+k_p)^3} + \ldots \tag{11.1}$$

This equation reduces to

$$P_p = \frac{D_p}{k_p}. \tag{11.2}$$

Thus, if a preferred stock pays an annual dividend of $4 and the appropriate discount rate is 8 percent, the present value of the stock is

$$P_p = \frac{\$4}{(1+0.08)^1} + \frac{\$4}{(1+0.08)^2} + \frac{\$4}{(1+0.08)^3} + \ldots$$

$$P_p = \frac{\$4}{0.08} = \$50.$$

If an investor buys this preferred stock for $50, he or she can expect to earn 8 percent ($50 × 0.08 = $4) on the investment. Of course, the realized rate of return on the investment will not be known until the investor sells the stock and adjusts this 8 percent return for any capital gain or loss. However, at the current price, the preferred stock is selling for an 8 percent dividend yield.

If the preferred stock has a finite life, this fact must be considered in determining its value. As with the valuation of long-term debt, the amount is repaid when the preferred stock is retired must be discounted back to the present value. Thus, when preferred stock has a finite life, the valuation equation becomes

11.3

$$P_p = \frac{D_p}{(1+k_p)^1} + \frac{D_p}{(1+k_p)^2} + \cdots + \frac{D_p}{(1+k_p)^n} + \frac{S}{(1+k_p)^n}.$$

CALCULATOR SOLUTION

Function Key	Data Input
PMT =	4
FV =	100
I =	8
N =	30
PV =	?
Function Key	Answer
PV =	−54.97

in which S represents the amount that is returned to the stockholder when the preferred stock is retired after n number of years. If the preferred stock in the previous example is retired after 30 years for \$100 per share, its current value would be

$$\begin{aligned} P_p &= \frac{\$4}{(1+0.08)^1} + \cdots + \frac{\$4}{(1+0.08)^{30}} + \frac{\$100}{(1+0.08)^{30}} \\ &= \$4(PVAIF\ 8I,\ 30N) + \$100(PVIF\ 8I,\ 30N) \\ &= \$4(11.258) + \$100(0.099) \\ &= \$54.93. \end{aligned}$$

in which 11.258 is the interest factor for the present value of an annuity of \$1 for 30 years at 8 percent (Appendix D), and 0.099 is the interest factor for the present value of \$1 to be received after 30 years when yields are 8 percent (Appendix B). Instead of being valued at \$50, the preferred stock would be valued at \$54.93. This yield is still 8 percent, but the return in this case consists of a current dividend yield of 7.28 percent (\$4 ÷ \$54.93) and a capital gain as the price of the stock rises from \$54.93 to \$100 when it is retired after 30 years.

Since preferred stock pays a fixed dividend and is priced like a debt instrument, its price rises and declines with changes in interest rates. If interest rates rise, the rate at which preferred stock is discounted also rises, causing the price of preferred stock to decline. Conversely, when interest rates fall, the rate at which preferred stock is discounted falls, causing its price to rise. Like bond prices, the price of preferred stock moves inversely with changes in interest rates.

Individuals who desire income from their investments may find preferred stock attractive. However, these investors should realize that the firm is not bound to pay dividends on preferred stock. Unlike debt, which imposes legal obligations on the firm, preferred stock imposes only moral obligations. Therefore, from the investor's point of view, preferred stock is riskier than debt. Income-seeking investors would probably do better buying long-term debt than owning preferred stock, unless the stock has certain features that make it more attractive. For this reason, some preferred stock that is issued by industrial firms is convertible into the firm's common stock. As is explained in Chapter 13, convertible preferred stock is perceptibly different from nonconvertible preferred stock because its price rises and declines with the price of the stock into which it may be converted. Whereas nonconvertible stock is analyzed as if it were debt, convertible preferred stock is analyzed as both debt and equity.

VALUATION OF COMMON STOCK: THE PRESENT VALUE AND THE GROWTH OF DIVIDENDS

As with the valuation of debt and preferred stock, the valuation of common stock involves bringing future payments back to the present at the appropriate discount factor. The discount factor is the required rate of return for an investment in common stock. Thus, the valuation involves discounting future cash flows (dividends) back to the present at the investor's required rate of return. The present value is then compared with the current price to determine if the stock is a good purchase.

Constant Dividends

The process of valuation and security selection is readily illustrated by the simple case in which the stock pays a fixed dividend of $1 that is not expected to change. That is, anticipated flow of dividend payments is

Year	1	2	3	4	. . .
	$1	$1	$1	$1	. . .

The current value of this indefinite flow of payments (the dividend) depends on the discount rate (the investor's required rate of return). If this rate is 10 percent, the stock's value (V) is

$$V = \frac{\$1}{(1+0.1)^1} + \frac{\$1}{(1+0.1)^2} + \frac{\$1}{(1+0.1)^3} + \frac{\$1}{(1+0.1)^4} + \cdots$$

$$V = \$10.00.$$

This process is expressed in the following equation in which the new variables are the dividend (D) and the required rate of return (k):

$$V = \frac{D}{(1+k)^1} + \frac{D}{(1+k)^2} + \cdots + \frac{D}{(1+k)^n},$$

which simplifies to

$$V = \frac{D}{k}. \qquad (11.4)$$

If a stock pays a dividend of $1 and the investor's required rate of return is 10 percent, the valuation is

$$V = \frac{D}{k} = \frac{\$1}{0.1} = \$10.00.$$

If the stock pays a fixed annual dividend of $1 and the required return is 10 percent, the stock is worth $10.00. Conversely, if the investor buys this stock for $10.00, the return is 10 percent ($1/$10.00). Any price greater than $10.00 will result in a return that is less than 10 percent. Therefore, for this investor to achieve the required rate of return of 10 percent, the price of the stock must not exceed $10.00.

Growth in the Dividend

There is, however, no reason to anticipate that common stock dividends will be fixed indefinitely into the future. Common stocks offer the potential for growth, both in value and in dividends. For example, if the investor expects the $1 dividend to grow annually at 6 percent, the anticipated dividend payments are

Year	1	2	3	4	. . .
	$1	$1.06	$1.124	$1.191	. . .

The current value of this flow of growing dividend payments also depends on the discount rate (the investor's required rate of return). If this rate is 10 percent, the stock's value is

$$V = \frac{\$1}{(1 + 0.1)^1} + \frac{\$1.06}{(1 + 0.1)^2} + \frac{\$1.124}{(1 + 0.1)^3} + \frac{\$1.191}{(1 + 0.1)^4} + \cdots$$

DIVIDEND-GROWTH MODEL
Valuation model for common stock that discounts future dividends

In this form, the value cannot be determined. If, however, it is assumed that the dividend will grow (g) indefinitely at the same rate, the **dividend-growth model** is

$$V = \frac{D(1 + g)^1}{(1 + k)^1} + \frac{D(1 + g)^2}{(1 + k)^2} + \frac{D(1 + g)^3}{(1 + k)^3} + \cdots + \frac{D(1 + g)^n}{(1 + k)^n},$$

which simplifies to

11.5

$$V = \frac{D_0(1 + g)}{k - g}.$$

The stock's intrinsic value depends on (1) the current dividend, (2) the growth in dividends, and (3) the required rate of return. The application of this model may be illustrated by a simple example. If the investor's required return is 10 percent and the stock is currently paying a $1 per share dividend and is growing indefinitely into the future at 6 percent annually, its value is

$$V = \frac{\$1(1 + 0.06)}{0.10 - 0.06} = \$26.50.$$

Any price greater than \$26.50 will result in a total yield of less than 10 percent. Conversely, a price less than \$26.50 will produce a return in excess of 10 percent. This return can be determined by rearranging the equation and substituting the current price for the value of the stock. Thus the return (r) on an investment in stock is

$$r = \frac{D_0(1 + g)}{P} + g. \tag{11.6}$$

The $D_0(1 + g)/P$ is the dividend yield, and g is the expected rate of growth in the dividend. If the price were \$30, the return would be

$$\begin{aligned} r &= \frac{\$1(1 + 0.06)}{\$30} + 0.06 \\ &= 9.5\%. \end{aligned}$$

Since 9.5 percent is less than the required 10 percent, investors will not purchase the stock. If the price is \$15, the return is

$$\begin{aligned} r &= \frac{\$1(1 + 0.06)}{\$15} + 0.06 \\ &= 13.1\% \end{aligned}$$

This return is greater than the 10 percent required by the investor. Since the stock offers a superior return, it is undervalued, and the investor would buy it.[2]

Only at a price of \$26.50 does the stock offer a return of 10 percent. At that price the stock's anticipated return equals the required return, which is the return available on alternative investments of the same risk (that is, $r = k$). The investment will yield 10 percent because the dividend yield during the year is 4 percent and dividends are growing annually at the rate of 6 percent (that is, the anticipated capital gain is 6 percent). These relationships are illustrated in Figure 11.1, which shows the growth in dividends and the price of the stock that will produce a constant return of 10 percent. After 12 years the dividend will have grown to \$2.01, and the price of the stock will be \$53.32. The total return on this investment will still be 10 percent. During the year the dividend grows to \$2.13, giving a 4 percent dividend yield, and the price appreciates annually at the 6 percent growth rate in dividends.

You should notice that the lines in Figure 11.1 representing the dividend and the price of the stock are curved. The dividends and the price of the stock are growing at the same rate, but they are not growing by the same amount each year.

[2]Valuation compares dollar amounts. That is, the dollar value of the stock is compared with its price. Returns compare percentages. That is, the expected percentage return is compared with the required return. In either case, the decision will be the same. If the valuation exceeds the price, the expected return exceeds the required return.

FIGURE 11.1

Dividends and Price of Stock over Time Yielding 10 Percent Annually

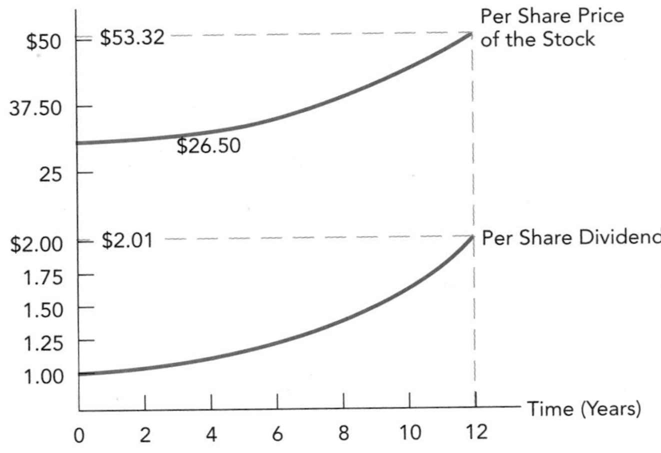

This is another illustration of the time value of money, as the dividends (and presumably earnings) and the price of the stock are compounded annually at 6 percent.

A firm's earnings need not grow steadily at this rate. Figure 11.2 illustrates a case in which the firm's earnings grow annually at an average of 6 percent, but the year-to-year changes stray considerably from 6 percent. These fluctuations are not in themselves necessarily reason for concern. The firm exists within the economic environment, which fluctuates over time. Exogenous factors, such as a strike or an energy curtailment, may affect earnings during a particular year. If these factors continue to plague the firm, they will obviously play an important role in the valuation of the shares. However, the emphasis in valuation is on the growth of dividends and the growth in earnings to pay the dividend over a period of years. This longer time dimension smooths out temporary fluctuations in earnings and dividends.

The common stock valuation model presented thus far assumes that (1) the firm's dividends will grow indefinitely at a certain rate and (2) the firm's earnings increase so the dividend may also grow. These assumptions, however, need not apply; the model may be modified so that different growth patterns can be built into the valuation.

Uneven Dividend Growth

Dividends can increase (or decrease), and these increments need not be at a constant rate. For example, an emerging firm may not pay any dividends initially but retain all earnings to finance expansion. After achieving a certain level of growth, management may start to pay cash dividends. The initial rate of growth in the dividend may be very large, if for no other reason than that an increment from $0.02

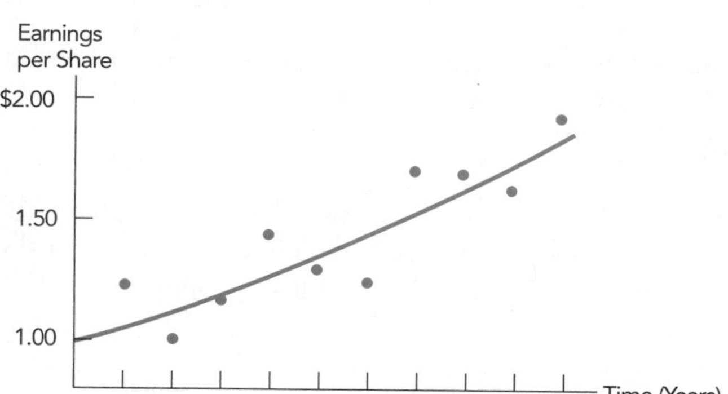

FIGURE 11.2

Earnings Growth Averaging 6 Percent Annually

to $0.04 is a 100 percent increase. As the firm matures and the rate of growth in earnings declines, the rate of growth in the dividend will also decline. The firm's dividend may then increase at a stable rate. This pattern of dividends is illustrated in the following table, which represents the cash dividend and the percentage change from the preceding year:

Year	Cash Dividend	Percentage Change in the Dividend
1	—	—
2	—	—
3	$0.10	—
4	0.20	100.0%
5	0.35	75.0
6	0.50	42.9
7	0.60	20.0
8	0.66	10.0
9	0.726	10.0
10	0.799	10.0
.	.	.
.	.	.

Initially (years 1 and 2), the firm did not distribute a cash dividend. Years 3 through 7 represent a period during which the dividend rose rapidly. From year 8 into the indefinite future, the dividend grows at a constant rate of 10 percent.

The dividend-growth model may still be used to value this stock. Each of the individual dividend payments for years 1 through 7 are discounted back to the present at the required rate (for example, 12 percent) and are summed:

$$V = \frac{\$0.00}{(1.12)^1} + \frac{0.00}{(1.12)^2} + \frac{0.10}{(1.12)^3} + \frac{0.20}{(1.12)^4} + \frac{0.35}{(1.12)^5} + \frac{0.50}{(1.12)^6} + \frac{0.60}{(1.12)^7}$$

$$= \$0.00 + 0.00 + 0.10(0.712) + 0.20(0.636) + 0.35(0.567) + 0.50(0.507) + 0.60(0.452)$$

$$= \$0.92.$$

Thus the flow of dividends during years 1 through 7 is currently worth $0.92.

For year 8 and all subsequent years, the dividend grows annually at 10 percent, so the constant dividend-growth model may be applied. The value of future dividends is

$$V = \frac{\$0.60(1 + 0.1)}{0.12 - 0.10} = \$33.$$

This value, however, is as of the end of year 7, so the $33 must be discounted back to the present at 12 percent to determine its current value:

$$\frac{\$33}{(1.12)^7} = \$33(0.452) = \$14.92.$$

(The 0.452 is the interest factor for the present value of $1 at 12 percent for seven years.)

The value of the stock is the sum of the two pieces: the present value of the dividends during the period of variable growth ($0.92) plus the present value of the dividends during the period of stable growth ($14.92). Thus the value of the stock is

$$V = \$0.92 + \$14.92 = \$15.84.$$

Although the preceding illustration appears complicated, the valuation process is not. Valuation remains the present value of future cash flows (that is, the dividend payments). Each anticipated future payment is discounted back to the present at the required rate of return, and the present value of each payment is summed to determine the current value of the stock. Thus, the valuation of a common stock and the valuations of preferred stocks and bonds all involve the same basic process. Each asset is worth the present value of the expected cash payments that the asset will generate.

RISK AND STOCK VALUATION

The previous discussion presented models for the valuation of stock. However, no statement was made concerning the risk associated with an individual stock. Not all firms are equally risky, and the investor would require a higher return for riskier stocks.

FIGURE 11.3

Relation between Beta and Required Return

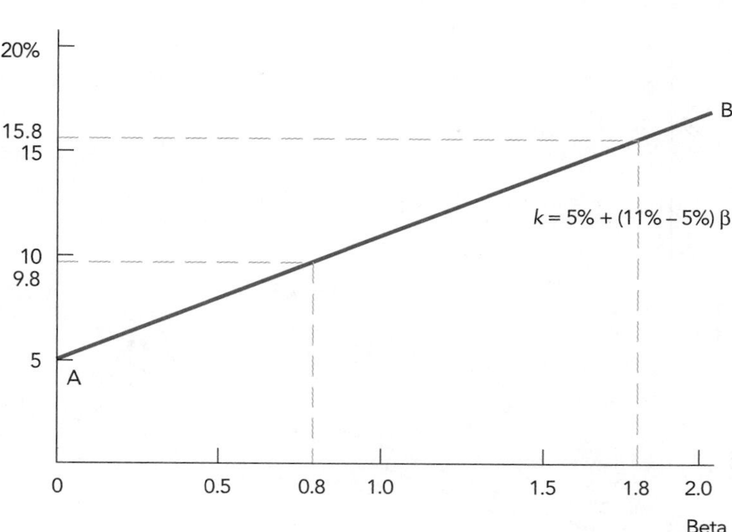

Such a risk adjustment is part of the valuation process, for the investor's required return (k) adjusts for risk. In Chapter 8, the required return was divided into two components: (1) the risk-free return that an investor can earn on a risk-free security such as a Treasury bill and (2) a risk premium. The risk premium is also composed of two components: (1) the additional return that investing in securities offers above the risk-free rate and (2) the volatility of the particular stock relative to the market as a whole. The volatility of the individual stock is measured by beta (β), and the additional return is measured by the difference between the expected return on the market (r_m) and the risk-free rate (r_f). This differential ($r_m - r_f$) is the risk premium that is required to induce individuals to purchase stocks.

To induce the investor to purchase a particular security, the risk premium associated with the market must be adjusted by the risk associated with the individual security. This adjustment is achieved by using the stock's beta, so the required return for investing in a particular stock, as specified in Equation 8.3, is

$$k = r_f + (r_m - r_f)\beta.$$

The relationship between the required return and beta is illustrated in Figure 11.3. The **security market line** (AB) represents all the required returns associated with each level of risk. In this figure, the risk-free rate is 5 percent and the expected return on the market is 11 percent. Thus for a beta of 0.8, the required return is 9.8 percent [0.05 + (0.11 − 0.05)0.8 = 9.8 percent], and for a beta of 1.8, the required return is 15.8 percent [0.05 + (0.11 − 0.05)1.8 = 15.8 percent].

SECURITY MARKET LINE
Line specifying the required return for different levels of risk

FIGURE 11.4

Relation between Beta and Required Return After a Change in Interest Rates

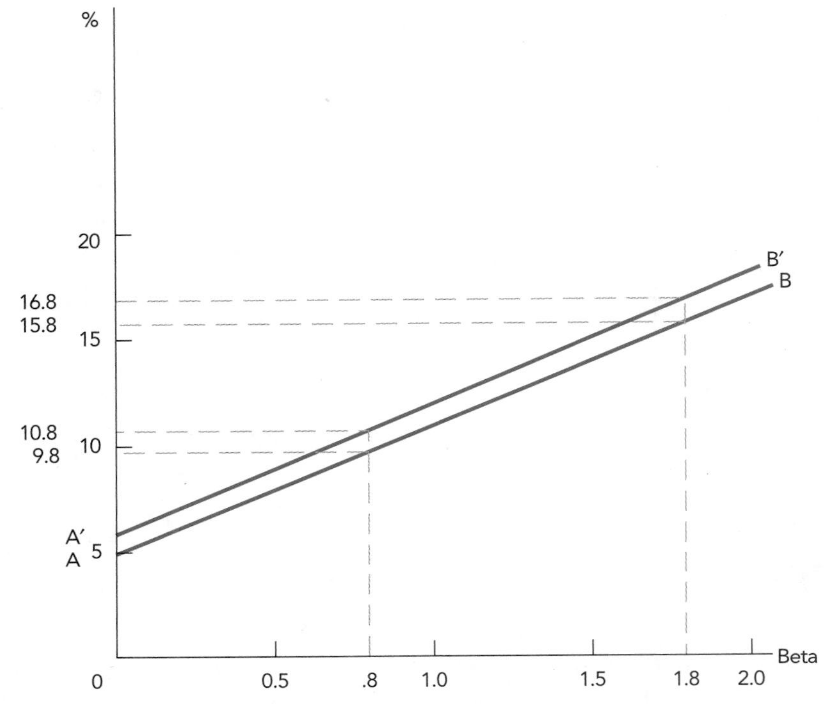

Line AB crosses the vertical axis at the current risk-free rate (5 percent). The slope of the line is the difference between the market return and the risk-free rate (0.11 − 0.05). Movements along the line represent changes in risk as measured by beta (that is, the increase in beta from 0.8 to 1.8 and the corresponding increase in the required return from 9.8 percent to 15.8 percent). The line shifts if either the risk-free rate or the expected return on the market changes. Such a shift is illustrated in Figure 11.4, in which the risk-free rate rises from 5 percent to 6 percent and the expected return on the market rises from 11 percent to 12 percent. The security market line shifts from AB to A′B′. Thus, the required return at each level of risk (at each beta) correspondingly increases. The required return for a stock with a beta of 0.8 now becomes 10.8 percent, while the required return for a stock with a beta of 1.8 rises to 16.8 percent.

How this risk-adjusted discount may be applied to the valuation of a specific stock is illustrated by the following example. From 1991 through 1996, ExxonMobil's dividend rose from $1.34 to $1.64 for an annual compound growth rate of approximately 2.6 percent. According to the *Value Line Investment Survey,* the stock has a beta of 0.8. If (1) U.S. Treasury bills of 6-month duration offered a

Historical Returns

There have been several studies of security returns, but the returns updated and published annually by Ibbotson Associates in the *Stocks, Bonds, Bills, and Inflation* (*SBBI*) *Yearbook* are generally considered to be the definitive studies of stock returns. These returns cover the period from 1926 to the present and provide annual returns and annualized returns for longer periods, such as five years and ten years. ¶ The annual returns for 1926–1997 are as follows:

	Annual Return	**Standard Deviation of Return**
Large company stocks	11.0%	20.3
Small company stocks	12.7	33.9
Long-term corporate bonds	5.7	8.7
Long-term government bonds	5.2	9.2
Rate of inflation	3.1	4.5

Source: Stocks, Bonds, Bills, and Inflation, 1998 Yearbook *(Chicago: Ibbotson Associates, 1998).*

Large companies are those that comprise the Standard & Poor's 500 Index. Small companies are the smallest one-fifth of NYSE listed stocks. They are not just small companies in general and are, in reality, large firms compared to the many corporations whose shares trade through NASDAQ. ¶ Notice that the Ibbotson data include both annual returns and their standard deviations. This inclusion of the standard deviation gives investors a measure of the risk associated with each type of investment. The above returns and their standard deviations may be interpreted as follows: For the entire time period, small company stocks earned 12.7 percent annually but for approximately 67 percent of the 71-year period, the returns ranged between 46.6 and −21.2 percent. Obviously, there were some years when investors in small company stocks sustained substantial losses. For example, during 1990, small company stocks declined 21.6 percent. ¶ The data also indicate the relatively small rate of inflation over the entire period (3.1 percent). However, the rate of inflation exceeded 18 percent in 1945. Although the 1990s were a period of relative price stability, the rate of inflation exceeded 6 percent as recently as 1990. ¶

risk-free return of 3.5 percent, (2) an investor anticipated that the market would rise annually at a compound rate of 9.5 percent (about 6 percentage points more than the risk-free rate), and (3) the dividend growth would continue indefinitely at 2.6 percent, what would be the maximum price this investor should pay for the stock?

The first step in answering the question is to determine the risk-adjusted required return:

$$k = r_f + (r_m - r_f)\beta$$
$$= 0.035 + (0.095 - 0.035)0.8$$
$$= 0.083 = 8.3\%.$$

Next, this risk-adjusted required return is used in the dividend-growth model presented earlier:

$$V = \frac{D_0(1 + g)}{k - g}$$
$$= \frac{1.64(1 + 0.026)}{0.083 - 0.026}$$
$$= \$29.52.$$

If the price of the stock is less than \$29.52, the stock is underpriced and should be bought. Conversely, if the price exceeds \$29.52, the stock is overpriced and should be sold.

Although this procedure does bring a risk adjustment into the valuation model, remember that the results or conclusions can only be as good as the data employed. While this model and others presented in this text (for example, the net present value of an investment presented in Chapter 17) are theoretically sound, their accuracy depends on the data used. The possibility of inaccurate data should be obvious in the above valuation model. Any of the estimates—the growth rate, the expected return on the market, the beta coefficient—may be incorrect, in which case the resulting valuation is incorrect. For example, if the expected growth rate were increased from 2.6 percent to 4.6 percent, the effect would be to increase the valuation from \$29.52 to \$46.36. As may be seen in this illustration, the modest change in the growth rate produces a large change in the stock valuation.

The problem of inaccurate data does not mean that the use of models in financial decision making is undesirable. Without such models there would be no means to value an asset. Hunches, intuition, or just plain guessing would then be used to value and select assets. Theoretical models force investors and financial managers to identify real economic forces (such as earnings and growth rates) and alternatives (for example, the risk-free rate and the return earned by the market as a whole). Even if the analysis may sometimes be inaccurate, it is still fundamentally sound and should prove better than random guessing or intuitive feelings.

ALTERNATIVE VALUATION TECHNIQUES

Although the dividend-growth model may be theoretically sound, it is difficult to make operational. There are, for instance, problems associated with estimating future growth rates and determining the appropriate required return. In addition, not all common stocks currently pay a cash dividend. In fact, the vast majority of stocks traded through NASDAQ do not pay dividends and cannot be expected to distribute dividends for the foreseeable future. Without a dividend payment, the numerator in the dividend-growth model is \$0.00, which makes the value equal to \$0.00.

Price-to-Earnings (P/E) Ratio

An alternative to the dividend-growth model is to use a type of ratio analysis. The most often used ratio is price to earnings, the **P/E ratio,** but such ratios as price to sales or price to book value are also used. (All of these ratios are expressed in per share terms: price to earnings per share, price to sales per share, and price to per share book value.)

P/E RATIO
The ratio of a stock's price to earnings per share

The P/E technique is essentially very easy. The value of the stock is a specified multiple of earnings (or sales or book value). That is,

$$\text{Value of the stock} = \text{Earnings} \times \text{Earnings multiple}. \qquad 11.7$$

To use this technique, the investor only needs earnings and the appropriate earnings multiple. For example, if the earnings are \$2.45 and the appropriate multiple is 13 (that is, the appropriate P/E ratio is 13), then the value of the stock is

$$\$2.45 \times 13 = \$31.45.$$

This value is then compared to the current price of the stock. If the price is less than \$31.45, the stock is undervalued and should be purchased. If the price of the stock is greater than \$31.45, the stock is overvalued and should not be purchased.

The use of P/E ratios, however, is not without problems. First, what earnings should be used in the calculation? You could select either historical earnings or forecasted earnings. If historical earnings, do you use earnings before extraordinary, nonrecurring earnings or net earnings? If forecasted earnings, which forecast? Forecasted earnings may be available from investment advisory services, such the *Value Line Investment Survey,* or through the Internet. Estimates, however, will differ, so the question remains which estimate to use.

The next problem is to determine the appropriate multiple. One possible solution is to use the historic P/E ratios. Most firms tend to trade within a range of P/E values. For example, the historic low P/E ratio for Bristol-Myers Squibb has averaged 11.8 while the historic high P/E ratio has averaged 16.7. Thus, if the estimated earnings are \$3.50, the price of the stock should tend to trade between \$41.30 (\$3.50 × 11.8) and \$58.45 (\$3.50 × 16.7). If the stock is trading outside this range, that would suggest it may be currently undervalued or overvalued.

This use of P/E ratios provides a range of values but not a unique value. To obtain a unique value, the individual would have to determine a unique earnings multiple. If the average P/E ratio of all firms in an industry is 13.2, then that earnings multiple may be applied to a specific firm within the industry. For example, if the average P/E ratio for household products, toiletries, and drugs is 13.2 and

Bristol-Myers Squibb is expected to earn \$3.50, then the value of the stock is \$46.20 (13.2 × \$3.50).

Such application of P/E ratios for valuation suggests that there is a unique P/E ratio for all firms within an industry. This is, of course, an oversimplification since there are differences among firms within an industry, such as size, product lines, sources of finance, and domestic versus foreign operations. These factors can affect the risk associated with a particular firm, so using a unique average P/E ratio to value all firms may be inappropriate.

Price-to-Sales (P/S) Ratio

An alternative valuation ratio that has achieved some prominence is the ratio of the stock price to per share sales (P/S). This ratio offers one particular advantage over the P/E ratio. If a firm has no earnings (and many firms, especially small firms that are just beginning, operate at a loss), the P/E ratio has no meaning. The P/S ratio, however, can be computed even if the firm is operating at a loss, thus permitting comparisons of all firms, including those that are not profitable.

Even if the firm has earnings and thus has a positive P/E ratio, the price-to-sales ratio remains a useful analytical tool. Earnings are ultimately related to sales. A low P/S ratio indicates a low valuation; the stock market is not placing a large value on the firm's sales. Even if the firm is operating at a loss, a low P/S ratio may indicate an undervalued investment. A small increase in profitability may translate these sales into a large increase in the stock's price. When the firm returns to profitability, the market may respond to the earnings, and both the P/E and P/S ratios increase. Thus, a current low price-to-sales ratio may suggest that there is considerable potential for the stock's price to increase. Such potential would not exist if the stock were selling for a high price-to-sales ratio.

The essential weakness that applies to P/E ratios also applies to price-to-sales ratios. Essentially there is no appropriate or correct ratio to use for the valuation of a stock. While one investor may believe that a low P/E ratio is indicative of financial weakness, another investor may draw the opposite conclusion. The same applies to price-to-sales ratios. While some investors and financial analysts isolate firms with low ratios, other analysts would argue the opposite. Low price-to-sales ratios are characteristic of firms that are performing poorly and not worth a higher price. The low ratio then does not indicate undervaluation but is a mirror of financial weakness.

Price to Book (P/B) Value

An alternative to P/E and P/S ratios for the selection of stocks is the ratio of the price of the stock to the per share book value. (*Book value* is another term for the firm's equity found on a firm's balance sheet.) Essentially, the application is the same as with the other two ratios. The investor or security analyst compares the price of the stock with its per share book value. A low ratio suggests that the stock is undervalued while a high ratio suggests the opposite. Once again, determining what constitutes a low or a high value is left to the discretion of the analyst, but the ratio (like all ratios) does facilitate comparisons of firms.

INVESTMENT ANALYSIS CALCULATOR APPLICATIONS

This chapter considers the valuation of preferred and common stock. The *Investment Analysis Calculator* may be used to facilitate these calculations. (This software is available at www.harcourtcollege.com/finance/mayo.) For the valuation of preferred stock, go to the main menu and use the section on Bond Valuation and Duration. The application of the software for preferred stock valuation is essentially the same as the application for a bond except you use the dividend payment instead of the interest payment.

To apply the software, consider a $100 par preferred stock pays a $6 dividend and the stock is to be retired after 20 years at par. What is the value of this stock if the return on comparable preferred stock is 8.6 percent? Enter the yield on comparable preferred stock (8.6 percent), the dividend as a percent of the par value (6 percent), the number of years to maturity or redemption (20), and the face value or par value of the stock ($100). The software determines that the value is $75.57.

To value a stock using the dividend-growth model, go the Common Stock Valuation menu. The submenus apply the model assuming either constant growth or periods of variable growth. Consider the first application of the dividend-growth model presented earlier in the text. The stock pays a $1.00 dividend, which is increasing annually at 6 percent, and the required return is 10 percent. Go to the appropriate submenu, Valuation of a Zero or Constant Growth Stock. Enter the dividend ($1.00), the required return (10), and the expected rate of growth. (If you need to calculate the required return prior to applying the valuation model, use the section on the Capital Asset Pricing Model. This section computes the beta coefficient and the required return and then goes to the dividend-growth valuation model.) Once the data are entered, the value of the stock ($26.50) is determined, which is the same value derived in the illustration presented earlier in this chapter.

SUMMARY

Although preferred stock is legally equity, its valuation is identical to that of a long-term bond. Both bonds and preferred stock are fixed income securities whose value is the present value of their future payments (interest or dividends and the repayment of the principal). The value of all fixed income securities moves inversely with changes in interest rates. Thus, if interest rates rise, the price of preferred stock falls; if interest rates fall, the price of preferred stock rises.

Common stock is more difficult to value than preferred stock because it is not a fixed income security. The dividend-growth model may be used to value common stock. In its simplest form, the model assumes that the current dividend will grow indefinitely into the future at a constant rate. This growing dividend is discounted back to the present using the investor's required rate of return. The required rate of return is specified by the capital asset pricing model in which the return depends on the risk-free rate plus a risk premium. The risk premium depends on the return on the market and the systematic risk associated with the stock as measured by its beta coefficient.

Once the value of the stock has been determined, this value is compared to the current market price of the stock. If the current price exceeds the valuation, the stock is overpriced and should not be purchased. If the current price is less than the valuation, the stock is undervalued and should be purchased.

Alternatives to the dividend-growth model use ratios to determine the value of a stock. These methods include the price-to-earnings (P/E) ratio, the price-to-sales (P/S) ratio, and the price-to-book-value (P/B) ratio. In each case, the firm's earnings, sales, or book value are multiplied by an appropriate factor to value the stock. This value is then compared to the price of the stock to determine if the stock should be bought or sold.

Review Questions

1. Why is the valuation of preferred stock more similar to the valuation of bonds than to the valuation of common stock?
2. According to the dividend-growth model, what variables affect the value of common stock? If the required return increases, what should happen to the value of the stock?
3. Is it necessary to assume that the rate of growth in a firm's cash dividend is constant in order to value the firm's common stock?
4. How can the analysis of risk be integrated into the valuation of common stock? What should happen to the value of a common stock if its beta increases?

5. Why should the value of both preferred stock and common stock fall when interest rates rise?
6. What impact does each of the following (taken by itself) have on the value of a common stock:
   a. an increase in earnings and dividends
   b. an increase in the appropriate P/E ratio
   c. an increase in the expected return on the market
   d. a decrease in the risk-free rate and the return on the market
7. The use of P/E ratios to value securities requires earnings, which may be historical or estimated. Several Internet sources provide security analysts' estimates to per share earnings.
   a. What were Bristol-Myers Squibb's earnings for the last fiscal year?
   b. Obtain earnings estimates for Bristol-Myers Squibb from at least three sources. Possible sources include Quicken: **www.quicken.com/**, INVESTools: **www.investools.com/**, Motley Fool: **www.fool.com/**, Quote.Com: **www.quote.com/**, SmartMoney.com: **www.smartmoney.com/**, Wall Street City: **www.wallstreetcity.com/** and Yahoo! Finance: **quote.yahoo.com/**. (You should be warned that not all of these sources may provide earnings estimates as part of their complementary services.) Do the estimates vary, and, if so, what accounts for the differences?
   c. If the appropriate P/E for a pharmaceutical firm is 13.2, what is the value of the stock based on the estimates? Given the current price of the stock, is it undervalued?
   d. If the appropriate P/E ratio is 25, is the stock undervalued?

PROBLEMS

1. Big Oil Inc. has a preferred stock outstanding that pays a $9 annual dividend. If investors' required rate of return is 13 percent, what is the market value of the shares? If the required return declines to 11 percent, what is the change in the price of the stock?
2. What should be the prices of the following preferred stocks if comparable securities yield 7 percent? Why are the valuations different?
   a. MN Inc., $8 preferred ($100 par)
   b. CH Inc., $8 preferred ($100 par) with mandatory retirement after 20 years
3. Repeat the previous problem but assume that comparable yields are 10 percent.
4. What will be the capital losses if an investor purchases the following securities when yields on comparable securities are 6 percent but subsequently rise to 9 percent?
   a. 100 shares of $10 par, preferred stock with a $0.60 per share dividend (an investment of $1,000)
   b. $1,000 face amount, 6 percent debenture that matures after ten years

   Why are the losses different?

5. The dividend-growth model may be used to value a stock:

$$V = \frac{D_0(1 + g)}{k - g}.$$

a. What is the value of a stock if:

$$D_0 = \$2$$
$$k = 10\%$$
$$g = 6\%$$

b. What is the value of this stock if the dividend is increased to $3 and the other variables remain constant?

c. What is the value of this stock if the required return declines to 7.5 percent and the other variables remain constant?

d. What is the value of this stock if the growth rate declines to 4 percent and the other variables remain constant?

e. What is the value of this stock if the dividend is increased to $2.30, the growth rate declines to 4 percent, and the required return remains 10 percent?

6. Last year Artworks, Inc. paid a dividend of $3.50. You anticipate that the company's growth rate is 10 percent and have a required rate of return of 15 percent for this type of equity investment. What is the maximum price you would be willing to pay for the stock?

7. An investor with a required return of 14 percent for very risky investments in common stock has analyzed three firms and must decide which, if any, to purchase. The information is as follows:

Firm	A	B	C
Current earnings	$2.00	$3.20	$7.00
Current dividend	$1.00	$3.00	$7.50
Expected annual growth rate in dividends and earnings	7%	2%	−1%
Current market price	$23	$47	$60

a. What is the maximum price that the investor should pay for each stock based on the dividend-growth model?

b. If the investor does buy stock A, what is the implied percentage return?

c. If the appropriate P/E ratio is 12, what is the maximum price the investor should pay for each stock? Would your answers be different if the appropriate P/E were 7?

d. What does stock C's negative growth rate imply?

8. TSC, Inc. sells for $26 and pays an annual per share dividend of $1.30, which you expect to grow at 12 percent. What is your expected return on this stock? What would be the expected return if the price were $40 a share?

9. Jersey Jewel Mining has a beta coefficient of 1.2. Currently the risk-free rate is 5 percent and the anticipated return on the market is 11 percent. JJM pays a $4.50 dividend that is growing at 6 percent annually.

a. What is the required return for JJM?

b. Given the required return, what is the value of the stock?

c. If the stock is selling for $80, what should you do?

d. If the beta coefficient declines to 1.0, what is the new value of the stock? If the price remains $80, what course of action should you take?

10. The risk-free rate of return is 3 percent, and the expected return on the market is 8.7 percent. Stock A has a beta coefficient of 1.4, an earnings and dividend growth rate of 5 percent, and a current dividend of $2.60 a share.

a. What should be the market price of the stock?

b. If the current market price of the stock is $27, what should you do?

c. If the expected return on the market rises to 10 percent and the other variables remain constant, what will be the value of the stock?

d. If the risk-free return rises to 4.5 percent and the return on the market rises to 10.2 percent, what will be the value of the stock?

e. If the beta coefficient falls to 1.1 and the other variables remain constant, what will be the value of the stock?

f. Explain why the stock's value changes in c through e.

11. The security market line is estimated to be

$$k = 5\% + (10.4\% - 5\%)\beta.$$

You are considering two stocks. The beta of A is 1.4. The firm offers a dividend yield during the year of 4 percent and a growth rate of 7 percent. The beta of B is 0.8. The firm offers a dividend yield during the year of 5 percent and a growth rate of 3.8 percent.

a. What is the required return for each security?

b. Why are the required rates of return different?

c. Since A offers higher potential growth, should it be purchased?

d. Since B offers higher dividend yield, should it be purchased?

e. Which stock(s) should be purchased?

12. Two stocks each currently pay a dividend of $1.75 per share. It is anticipated that both firms' dividends will grow annually at the rate of 8 percent. Firm A has a beta coefficient of 0.88 while the beta coefficient of firm B is 1.35.

a. If U.S. Treasury bills currently yield 6.4 percent and you expect the market to increase at an annual rate of 12.1 percent, what are the valuations of these two stocks using the dividend-growth model?

b. Why are your valuations different?

c. If stock A's price were $51 and stock B's price were $42, what would you do?

13. The dividend-growth model,

$$V = \frac{D_0(1 + g)}{k - g},$$

suggests that an increase in the dividend growth rate will increase the value of a stock. However, an increase in the growth may require an increase in retained earnings and a reduction in the current dividend. Thus, management may be faced with a dilemma: current dividends versus future growth. As of now, investors' required return is 13 percent. The current dividend is $1 a share and is expected to grow annually by 7 percent, so the current market price of the stock is $17.80. Management may make an investment that will increase the firm's growth rate to 10 percent, but the investment will require an increase in retained earnings, so the firm's dividend must be cut to $0.60 a share. Should management make the investment and reduce the dividend?

CASE

DETERMINING THE VALUE OF A BUSINESS

Erik Satie has just inherited his father's company. Prior to his death, Mr. Satie was the sole stockholder, and he left the entire company to his only son. Although Erik has worked for the firm for many years as a commercial artist, he does not feel qualified to manage the operation. He has considered selling the firm while it is still a viable operation and before his father's absence causes the value of the firm to deteriorate. Erik realizes that selling the firm will result in his losing control, but his father granted him a long-term contract that guarantees employment or a generous severance package. Furthermore, if Erik were to sell for cash, he should receive a substantial amount of money, so his financial position would be secure.

Even though Erik would like to sell out, he has enough business sense to realize that he does not know how to place an asking price (a value) on the firm. The IRS had established a value on his father's stock of $100 a share, and since he owned 100,000 shares, the value of the company for estate tax purposes was $10,000,000. Erik thought that was a reasonable amount but decided to consult with Sophie Wagner, a CPA who completed the estate tax return.

Ms. Wagner suggested that the firm could be valuated using a discounted cash flow method in which the current and future dividends are discounted back to the present to determine the value of the firm. She explained to Erik that this technique, the dividend-growth model, is an important theoretical model used for the valuation of companies. In addition, she suggested that the price/earnings ratio of similar firms may be used as a guide to the value of the firm. Erik asked Ms. Wagner to prepare a valuation of the stock based on P/E ratios and the dividend-growth model. While Erik realized that he could get only one price, he requested a range of values from an optimistic price to a minimum, rock-bottom value below which he should not accept.

To aid in the valuation process, Ms. Wagner assembled the following information. The firm earned $8.50 a share and distributed 60 percent in cash dividends during its last fiscal year. This payout ratio had been maintained for several years, with 40 percent of the earnings being retained to finance future growth. The per share earnings for the past five years were

Year	Per Share Earnings
X1	$6.70
X2	7.40
X3	7.85
X4	8.20
X5	8.50

Publicly held firms in the industry have an average P/E ratio of 12 with the highest being 17 and the lowest, 9. The betas of these firms tend to be less than 1.0 with 0.85 being typical. While the firm is not publicly held, it is similar in structure to other firms in the industry. It is, however, perceptibly smaller than the publicly held firms. The Treasury bill rate is currently 5.2 percent, and most financial analysts anticipate that the market as a whole will average a return of 6 percent to 6.5 percent greater than the Treasury bill rate.

Case Problems

1. What are the lowest and highest values based on P/E ratios and the dividend-growth model?
2. What assumptions must be made to determine these values?

CHAPTER 12
Analysis of Financial Statements

Learning Objectives

1. Define assets, liabilities, equity, book value, and net worth.
2. Differentiate among revenues, income, cash, and retained earnings.
3. Differentiate the accounting statements covered in the text.
4. Illustrate the difference between cross-sectional analysis and time series analysis.
5. Be able to compute and interpret the ratios covered in the text.
6. Understand the limitations of accounting data and of the analysis that employs this data.

"Annual income twenty pounds, annual expenditure nineteen nineteen six, result happiness. Annual income twenty pounds, annual expenditure twenty pounds ought and six, result misery." As Charles Dickens so aptly expressed it in *David Copperfield,* the difference between operating at a profit or at a loss may be just a few pennies. This bottom line, however, plays an important role both in the financial decisions made by management and in how management's performance is perceived by the public. Management wants to make those decisions that increase the value of the firm, which include decisions affecting the firm's profitability.

By enumerating revenues and expenses in a firm's income statement (or statement of profit or loss, as it is sometimes called), accountants determine if a firm's operations are profitable. Profits are not, however, synonymous with cash. Revenues and expenses are not the same as receipts and disbursements. Not all sales are for cash; some are for credit. Not all expenses require the disbursement of cash; depreciation is a noncash expense.

This chapter is initially concerned with a firm's financial statements, such as the balance sheet or the income statement. If you are already familiar with the basic content of financial statements, the first half of the chapter may be omitted, and you can progress to the second half: the study of a firm's financial statements through ratio analysis. Ratio analysis is a popular tool with creditors, investors, and management because the ratios may be easily computed and readily interpreted. Creditors and investors employ ratio analysis to establish the ability of the firm to service its debt and earn profits for the owners. Management may use the analysis as (1) a planning device, (2) a tool for control, or (3) a means to identify weaknesses in the firm.

The many ratios that the financial manager may use can be classified into five groups. Liquidity ratios seek to determine if a firm can meet its current obligations as they come due. Activity ratios tell how rapidly assets flow through the firm. Profitability ratios measure performance, while leverage ratios measure the extent to which the firm uses debt financing. Coverage ratios measure the ability to make (or cover) specific payments.

GENERAL ACCOUNTING PRINCIPLES

Accounting statements provide financial information concerning an enterprise. Although the emphasis in this text is the statements' applications to firms, financial statements may be constructed for governments (for example, the local municipality), nonprofit organizations (such as the Metropolitan Opera), or individuals. In all cases these statements show the financial condition of the entity and its assets and how they were financed. This information can then be used to aid financial decision making.

To be useful in decision making, financial statements must be reliable, understandable, and comparable. Reliability requires the statements to be objective and unbiased. The data included on the statements should be verifiable by independent experts. This does not mean that two accountants working with the same information will construct identical financial statements. Individual opinions and judgments may lead to different financial statements. For example, as is illustrated in Chapter 20, the decision to use last-in-first-out (LIFO) instead of first-in-first-out (FIFO) inventory valuation may affect the cost of goods sold and thus affect earnings. Another example that involves the accountant's judgment is the allowance for doubtful accounts receivable. Two accountants may establish differing amounts that will affect the firm's financial statements. However, it should not be concluded that two accountants will construct widely different statements. While the financial statements may differ, the amount of differentiation should be modest.

Accountants' second goal is that financial statements be understandable. The statement should be presented in an orderly manner and be readable by informed laypersons as well as professionals. Investors and other individuals who use financial statements need not know all the principles used to construct a financial statement. However, an intelligent individual should be able to read a firm's financial statements and have some idea of the firm's profitability, its assets and liabilities, and its cash flow.

Comparability requires that one set of financial statements can be compared to the same financial statements constructed over different accounting periods. The principles used to construct one year's statements should be used for subsequent years. If the principles being applied are changed, the previous years' statements should be restated. If the firm's operations change, the financial statements should also reflect these changes. If, for example, the firm discontinues part of its operations, its sales, expenses, and profits for previous years should be restated. If this adjustment is not made, the users of the financial statements will be unable to compare the firm's financial condition and performance over a period of time for its continuing operations.

To increase the objectivity of financial statements, a general framework for accounting and financial reports has been established by the Financial Accounting Standards Board (FASB). Accounting principles that are "generally accepted" also receive the support of the American Institute of Certified Public Accountants and the Securities and Exchange Commission (SEC). Although these bodies establish the principles under which financial statements are constructed, it should not be concluded that the principles are static. Their conceptual framework changes over time with changes in the business environment and the needs of the statements' users. For example, increases in foreign investments and fluctuations in the value of foreign currencies have generated a need for better methods of accounting for these foreign investments. This problem, plus others such as inflation, pension liabilities, and stock options, have resulted in changes in accounting principles as the profession seeks to improve the informational content of financial statements.

BALANCE SHEET
Financial statement that enumerates (as of a point in time) what an economic unit owns and owes and its net worth

ASSETS
Items or property owned by a firm, household, or government and valued in monetary terms

LIABILITIES
What an economic unit owes

STOCKHOLDERS' EQUITY
Firm's net worth; stockholders' investment in the firm; the sum of stock, paid-in capital, and retained earnings

CONSOLIDATED BALANCE SHEET
Parent company's balance sheet, which summarizes and combines the balance sheets of the firm's various subsidiaries

CURRENT ASSETS
Short-term assets that are expected to be converted into cash during the fiscal year

LONG-TERM ASSETS
Assets that are expected to be held for more than a year, such as plant and equipment

INVENTORY
Raw materials, work-in-process, and finished goods; what a firm has available to sell

THE BALANCE SHEET

What have the owners invested in a firm? One method of answering this question is to construct a **balance sheet** that enumerates what a business owns (that is, its **assets**) and what it owes (that is, its **liabilities**) and to calculate the difference. This difference is called the net worth or the **stockholders' equity** in the firm.

Exhibit 12.1 presents simplified balance sheets for Pier 1 Imports. These balance sheets (and the other financial statements presented later in this chapter) are published in the firm's annual report. These balance sheets combine the financial information for all the firm's subsidiaries and hence is called a **consolidated balance sheet.** The assets are divided into three groups: (1) **current assets,** which are expected to be used and converted into cash within a relatively short period of time; (2) **long-term assets,** which are those assets with a life span exceeding a year; and (3) other assets, such as investments in other firms' stocks. The liabilities and stockholders' equity are presented next, frequently on the right-hand side of the balance sheet across from the assets. Although it is not necessary for a balance sheet to be arranged in this manner, many firms use this general form because it clearly enumerates the assets, liabilities, and equity of the firm.

While current assets are listed in order of liquidity (cash, accounts receivable, and inventory), the following discussion considers each asset in reverse order. Raw materials are first acquired and converted into finished goods. This inventory is then sold, at which time the firm receives either an account receivable or cash.

Firms must have goods or services (or both) to sell. These goods are the firm's **inventory.** Not all inventory is ready for sale. Some of the goods may be unfinished ("work-in-process"), and there also may be inventories of raw materials. According to the Pier 1 balance sheet, total inventory amounted to $258,773 in 1999. The balance sheet does not subdivide the inventory into finished goods, work-in-process, and raw materials. The financial analyst should remember that only finished items are available for sale. Considerable time and cost may be involved in

EXHIBIT 12.1

Pier I Imports Consolidated Balance Sheet (in Thousands except Per Share Data)

	As of End of Fiscal Year	
	1999	1998
Assets		
Current assets		
Cash and cash equivalents	$ 41,945	$ 80,729
Accounts receivable, less allowance for doubtful accounts	9,060	12,638
Inventory	258,773	234,180
Other current assets	72,165	74,834
Total current assets	381,943	402,381
Property, plant, and equipment		
Land	31,620	42,445
Buildings	67,253	76,586
Machinery and equipment	310,613	253,347
Less accumulated depreciation	(183,224)	(156,048)
Net property, plant and equipment	226,262	216,330
Other assets	45,786	34,699
Total assets	$653,991	$653,410
Liabilities		
Current liabilities		
Current maturities of long-term debt	$ 350	$ 1,994
Accounts payable and accrued liabilities	119,215	110,116
Notes payable to banks	—	—
Taxes due	10,267	9,430
Total current liabilities	129,832	121,590
Long-term debt	96,008	114,881
Other non-current liabilities	24,257	24,208
Total liabilities	$250,097	$260,679
Shareholders' equity		
Common stock ($1.00 par, 500,000,000 shares authorized, 100,799,000 and 67,903,000 issued, respectively)	$100,779	$ 67,903
Paid-in capital	159,631	166,824
Retained earnings	201,457	165,345
Adjustments	(3,319)	(4,192)
Shares repurchased and held in treasury, at cost, respectively	(54,654)	(3,149)
Total equity	$403,894	392,731
Liabilities and shareholders' equity	$653,991	$653,410

Adapted from Pier 1 Imports, Annual Report 1999.

ACCOUNT RECEIVABLE
Account rising from a credit sale that has not been collected.

processing raw materials into finished goods. Therefore, much of a firm's inventory may not be salable and cannot readily be converted into cash.[1]

When goods or services are sold, the firm receives either cash or a promise of payment in the future. A credit sale generates an **account receivable,** which represents money that is due to the firm. Pier 1 has $9,060 in receivables; this is a net figure obtained by subtracting the doubtful accounts from the total amount of receivables. Since a firm does not always obtain payment from all its accounts receivable, it is necessary to make an allowance for these "doubtful accounts." Thus, only the net realizable figure is included in the tabulation of the firm's assets.

A cash sale generates the asset "cash" for the firm. Since holding cash will earn nothing, some of it may be invested in short-term money instruments (often referred to as "cash equivalents"). Cash and short-term money instruments may be combined under a classification called cash and cash equivalents. For Pier 1, cash and short-term marketable securities total $41,945. This money is available to meet the firm's immediate financial obligations.

Cash and cash equivalents, accounts receivable, and inventory are the major short-term assets.[2] In 1999, total current assets amounted to $381,943. These short-term assets will flow through the firm during its fiscal year and will be used to meet its financial obligations that must be paid during the year. The total value and the nature of these assets are important in determining the firm's ability to meet its current obligations.

Long-term assets include the firm's property, plant, and equipment, which are used for many years. The firm's employees utilize these long-term assets in conjunction with the current assets to create the products or services that the company offers for sale. The type and quantity of long-term assets that a company uses vary with the industry. Some industries, such as utilities and transportation, require numerous plants and extensive equipment. Firms in these industries must have substantial investments in long-term assets in order to operate. Not all companies choose to own these assets; instead, they may rent them, which is called *leasing.* Regardless of whether the firm leases or owns these assets, it must have the use of the long-term assets to produce the company's output.

At the end of fiscal 1999, Pier 1 Imports had $226,262 invested in long-term assets. The balance sheet indicates that the firm initially invested 67,253 in buildings and $310,613 in equipment. These assets have depreciated by $183,224 and are currently being carried on the books at $194,642 ($226,262 minus the value of the land). As is explained in Chapter 15, depreciation is important because it is the process of allocating the cost of the plant and equipment over a period of time.

[1] Balance sheets sent to stockholders present only aggregate numbers. Presumably management would have access to disaggregated figures and thus would know the amount of inventory that is finished goods and the amount that is raw materials.

[2] Other current assets include the "prepaid expense," which arises when an expense is paid before it occurs. For example, an insurance premium is paid at the beginning of the policy. The premium payment generates the asset, prepaid expenses. This asset is consumed (reduced) while the policy is in force, so at the end of the term of the policy, the prepaid expense account is reduced to zero.

Thus, the value of long-term assets on the balance sheet is reduced over time as the assets are used by the firm.

Pier 1 owns land that is worth $31,620. Land does not depreciate with use, and hence the book value of the land is usually the purchase price. However, the value of the land may rise, in which case the accountants could increase the land's value on the books. Such revaluations rarely occur, so many firms have **hidden assets,** such as land whose market value is understated.[3]

HIDDEN ASSETS
Assets that have appreciated in value but are carried on the balance sheet at a lower value, such as their original cost

The remaining entry on the asset side of the balance sheet is "other" ($45,786), which may include securities, such as stock in other companies. Even though such stock can be sold and converted into cash, it may be considered separately from the firm's current assets. For example, if the securities were purchased with the intention of holding them for several years as an investment, they would be placed in a separate category on the balance sheet.

The total assets owned are the sum of the short-term assets ($381,943), the long-term assets ($226,262), and the other ($45,786). These assets are financed by the claims of creditors and stockholders—the firm's liabilities and equity—which are presented on the other half of the balance sheet.

The firm's liabilities are divided into two groups: **current liabilities,** which must be paid during the fiscal year, and **long-term liabilities,** which are due after the fiscal year. Current liabilities are primarily accounts payable and short-term loans. Just as the firm may sell goods on credit, it may also purchase goods and raw materials on credit. This trade credit is short-term and is retired as goods are produced and sold. In the balance sheet for Pier 1, accounts payable ($119,215 in 1999) also includes wages and salaries that have been earned but not paid out. (Many balance sheets have a separate entry called *accrued liabilities* to cover these current liabilities.) In addition to accounts payable, the firm has other short-term debt that must be paid during the fiscal year. This includes short-term notes for funds that the company has borrowed from commercial banks or other lending institutions ($0 in 1999) and that portion of its long-term debt that must be retired this year ($350). The taxes that must be paid during the year ($10,267) constitute the remaining current obligation.

CURRENT LIABILITY
Debt that must be paid during the fiscal year

LONG-TERM LIABILITY
Debt that becomes due after one year

Long-term debt obligations must be retired at some time after the current fiscal year. Such obligations may include bonds that are outstanding and mortgages on real estate. These long-term debts represent part of the permanent financing of the firm because these funds are committed to financing the business for a long time. Short-term liabilities are usually not considered part of the firm's permanent financing because these liabilities must be paid within a relatively short period.[4] For Pier 1, the long-term liabilities consist primarily of long-term debt ($96,008 in 1999). On other financial statements, a breakdown of the various debt issues (if the debt consists of more than one issue) may be given in a footnote that appears after the body of the financial statement.

[3] The revaluation of an asset would create taxable income, so there is little reason to appreciate the value of the asset on the firm's balance sheet.

[4] Since some short-term liabilities (for example, accrued wages) are always carried by the firm, these may be treated as part of the firm's permanent financing.

Other noncurrent liabilities may include deferred taxes, which arise from the differences in the timing of when the taxes are incurred and when they are paid. For example, a firm may make a profitable installment sale and report the earnings in its current fiscal year. Even though the tax liability is incurred during the present year, the firm does not make the tax payment until it receives the installments. Thus, the tax payments are deferred. These deferred taxes appear on the balance sheet in a separate account from the current taxes due, which must be paid within the fiscal year and hence are a current liability.

On most balance sheets, the stockholders' equity is listed after the liabilities and deferred taxes. There are three essential entries: the stock outstanding, additional paid-in capital, and the earnings that have been retained. A fourth entry, treasury stock, may appear if the firm has repurchased some of its common stock. The stock outstanding shows the various types of stock that have been issued and their quantities. Pier 1 Imports has only one issue—common stock. Many firms, however, have not only common stock but also preferred stock.

Additional paid-in capital represents the funds paid for the common stock in excess of the stock's par value. For example, if a stock's par value is $0.25 and the shares are sold for $1.00, then $0.25 is credited to common stock and the balance ($0.75) is considered additional paid-in capital. In 1999, Pier 1 had 100,799 shares of $1.00 par-value common stock outstanding. Thus, the common stock entry would be $100,799 ($1.00 × 100,799). Additional paid-in capital was $159,631.

RETAINED EARNINGS
The sum of a firm's income earned over a period of time that has not been distributed

The third entry under common stock is **retained earnings,** which represent the accumulated earnings of the firm that have not been distributed. (This entry could be negative if the firm has operated at a loss.) In 1999, retained earnings were $201,457. This represents the firm's undistributed earnings since its inception. Retained earnings, like the common stock and paid-in capital, represent an investment in the firm by common stockholders. Because these stockholders would receive the earnings if they were distributed, retained earnings are part of the stockholders' contribution to the financing of the firm.

Some firms repurchase their stock and hold these shares "in their treasury." These shares could be retired, but if the firm desired to resell them to the general public, the shares would have to be reregistered with the SEC. Because treasury stock is held for future purposes, it is not retired, which avoids the cost associated with registering the shares. Over time, Pier 1 has repurchased stock for which it paid $54,654. This reduces the total equity of the firm from $458,548 to $403,894. Notice that the reduction in equity is the cost to repurchase the shares (and not what the shares initially sold for).

Such repurchases have been common after periods of falling stock prices, such as occurred during October 1987 and after the invasion of Kuwait in 1990. Repurchases also occur when management believes the shares to be undervalued and uses the firm's cash to reduce the number of shares outstanding instead of using the cash for other purposes. The purchases may be made on the open market or through privately negotiated sales. The latter may occur when one stockholder seeks to sell a large block, in which case the seller may approach management concerning the possible sale of the shares back to the firm.

Firms may also repurchase their stock as a defense tactic against an attempted takeover. The repurchase of shares owned by public stockholders increases management's proportionate ownership in the firm. The repurchased shares may be resold to "friendly hands," an investor who will support current management. For example, the shares may be repurchased by the employee pension plan. If the trustees of the pension plan support current management, the sale strengthens management's position against a hostile takeover.

The **book value** of a firm is the equity that the investors have in the firm—the sum of common stock, additional paid-in capital, and retained earnings ($403,894). This sum represents the common stockholders' investment in the firm. Individual investors are primarily concerned with the value of a share of stock and not with the value of all the shares. To obtain the **book value per share,** the total equity available to common stock is divided by the number of shares outstanding.[5] For Pier 1, the per share book value in 1999 was $4.01 ($403,894/100,799). This amount is the accounting value of each of the shares held by the firm's stockholders.

BOOK VALUE
Firm's total assets minus total liabilities; equity; net worth

BOOK VALUE PER SHARE
Book value divided by number of shares outstanding

If Pier 1 were to cease operations, sell its assets, and pay off its liabilities, the owners would receive the remainder. If the assets and liabilities are accurately measured by their dollar values on the balance sheet, the book value equals the amount that stockholders would receive in the liquidation. However, as we will discuss later, the book value may not be an accurate measure of the market value of the firm or its assets.

Since a balance sheet presents a firm's assets, liabilities, and equity, it is a summary of the firm's financial condition at a particular point in time. It shows how funds were raised and how they were allocated. The balance sheet for Pier 1 indicates that in 1999, Pier 1 owned total assets valued at $653,991. These are the resources that the firm has to use, and (excluding the investment in the common stock of other firms) these resources are almost evenly allocated between short-term and long-term assets.

Pier 1 had liabilities of $250,097 and equity of $403,894 in 1999. The sum of the liabilities and equity must equal the sum of the assets, for it is the liabilities and equity that finance the acquisition of the assets. The assets could not have been acquired if creditors and owners had not provided the funds. For Pier 1, the balance sheet indicates that liabilities finance 38.2 percent ($250,097/$653,991) and that equity finances 61.8 percent ($403,894/$653,991) of the total assets. Thus, the balance sheet indicates the proportion of the assets financed with debt and the proportion financed with equity.

Two additional points need to be made about balance sheets. First, a balance sheet is constructed at the end of a fiscal period (for example, a year). It indicates the value of the assets and liabilities and the net worth at that particular time. Since financial transactions occur continuously, the information contained in a balance sheet may become outdated rapidly. Second, the values assigned to the assets need not mirror their market value. Instead, the values of the assets may be overstated or understated. For example, the firm owns accounts receivable, not all of

[5] An alternative definition of per share book value is equity divided by the number of shares outstanding minus repurchased shares. Since 3,107 shares have been repurchased, per share book value would be $4.13 ($403,894/97,692).

Capitalization

The sources of a firm's finance are also referred to as its capitalization. Capitalization, however, generally does not refer to the firm's book value of its equity. Instead, capitalization refers to the market value of its securities. As of August 1, 1999, the market value of Pier 1 Imports stock was approximately $9, so the total value of the firm's stock was $907,191,000 ($9 × 100,799,000). During the preceding 12 months, the stock's price ranged from about $6 to $20, so the capitalization ranged from $604,794,000 to $2,015,980,000. During the same period, the book value remained essentially unchanged at approximately $4 a share. ¶ As is discussed in Chapter 14 on mutual funds, capitalization is important because some mutual funds specialize in portfolios of large-capitalization ("large-cap") stocks while other mutual funds invest only in medium-sized or small-cap stocks. For these funds, consideration of which firms to purchase depends on the total market value of the shares and not on the book values. Book value may be an important consideration for selecting stocks based on the price of the stock relative to the book value. But that book value is different from the stock's capitalization. ¶

which will be paid. Although the firm does allow for these potential losses in an effort to make the balance sheet entries more accurate, the allowances may be insufficient, and the value of the assets may be overstated. Conversely, the value of other assets may be understated. The land on which the plant is built may have increased in value but may continue to be carried on the company's books at its cost.

For the book value of the firm to be a true indication of its worth, all the assets on the balance sheet should be valued at their market prices; however, this practice is not necessarily followed. Accountants suggest that assets be valued conservatively: (1) at the cost of the asset, or (2) at its market value, depending on which is less. Such conservatism is prudent but may result in assets having hidden or understated value if their appreciation is not recognized. Because of these accounting methods, the book value of the equity or net worth of a firm may not be a good measure of its liquidation or market value.

THE INCOME STATEMENT

INCOME STATEMENT
Financial statement that summarizes revenues and expenses for a period of time to determine profit or loss

The **income statement** tells investors how much accounting income or profits the company has earned during a period of time (for example, its fiscal year). It is a summary of revenues and expenses and indicates the firm's accounting profits or losses. It is not, however, a summary of cash receipts and disbursements.[6]

Exhibit 12.2 provides the 1998 and 1999 income statements for Pier 1 Imports. The statements start with a summary of the firm's sources of revenues: net

[6] Receipts and disbursements are considered in the cash budget, which is discussed in Chapter 19.

EXHIBIT 12.2

Pier I Imports Consolidated Statement of Operations (in Thousands except Per Share Amounts)

	For the Fiscal Year Ended	
	1999	**1998**
Net Sales	$1,138,590	$1,075,405
Cost of goods sold	638,173	613,937
Gross profit	500,417	461,468
Operating expenses	334,629	315,788
Depreciation	31,130	23,946
Income before interest and taxes	134,658	121,734
Net interest expense	5,048	6,824
Income taxes	49,253	45,964
Net earnings	$ 80,357	$ 78,047
Earnings per share	$0.82	$0.77
Fully diluted earnings per share	$0.77	$0.72

Adapted from Pier 1 Imports, Annual Report 1999.

sales (total sales minus returns) of $1,138,590 in 1999. Next follows a summary of the cost of goods sold ($638,173). The difference between the net sales and the cost of goods sold is the gross profit ($500,417). Then the selling, administrative expenses, and depreciation are subtracted to determine the operating earnings ($134,658). (If the firm has other sources of income—for instance, dividends received—they are added to the operating earnings to determine the company's total earnings before interest and taxes.) To determine net earnings, interest expense ($5,048) and taxes ($49,253) must be subtracted from the $134,658, which yields net earnings of $80,357.

EARNINGS PER SHARE
Earnings divided by number of outstanding common shares

Stockholders are generally not concerned with total earnings but with **earnings per share.** The bottom line of the income statement shows the earnings per share (EPS = $0.82), which is net earnings divided by the number of shares outstanding. This $0.82 is the amount of earnings available to each share of common stock.

Notice that earnings per share ($0.82) may not be simply the earnings divided by the number of shares outstanding at the end of the year ($80,357/100,799 = $0.7972). Since the firm may issue stock throughout the year, it does not have the use of the funds for the entire year. The funds raised by issuing these shares could not generate current income. Thus, shares outstanding are averaged over the year, and this average is used to determine earnings per share.

Also notice that two earnings per share figures are provided. Earnings per share uses outstanding shares (or an average of outstanding shares). Fully diluted earnings per share includes shares that will be issued when stock options are exercised. Although these shares are not currently outstanding, it is reasonable to assume they will become outstanding as employees exercise their options to buy the stock. Providing fully diluted earnings per share acknowledges that the earnings will be spread over more shares when (and if) the options are exercised and more shares become outstanding.

When the firm earns profits, management must decide what to do with these earnings. There are two choices: (1) to pay out the earnings to stockholders in the form of cash dividends, or (2) to retain the earnings. The retained earnings on the balance sheet are the sum of all the firm's undistributed earnings that have accumulated but that have not been paid out in dividends during the company's life. These retained earnings are used to finance the purchase of assets or to retire debt. How this year's earnings were used does not appear on the income statement. The income statement merely summarizes revenues and expenses during the fiscal year and indicates whether the firm produced a net profit or loss.

STATEMENT OF CASH FLOWS

Accountants, financial managers, and investors have increased their emphasis on analyzing a firm's ability to generate cash. This emphasis has led to the creation of the "statement of cash flows," which determines the changes in the firm's holdings of cash and cash equivalents and serves as a linkage between the income statement (which determines if the firm operated at a loss or at a profit) and the balance sheet (which enumerates the firm's assets, liabilities, and equity).

STATEMENT OF CASH FLOWS
Financial statement summarizing cash inflows and cash outflows

The **statement of cash flows** is divided into three sections: (1) operating activities, (2) investment activities, and (3) financing activities. In each section it enumerates the inflow and outflow of cash. The cash inflows are

1. a decrease in an asset.
2. an increase in a liability, and
3. an increase in equity.

The cash outflows are

1. an increase in an asset.
2. a decrease in a liability, and
3. a decrease in equity.

The statement of cash flows starts with a firm's earnings and works through various entries to determine the change in the firm's cash and cash equivalents. This process is illustrated in Exhibit 12.3. The firm starts with earnings of $80,357. Since earnings are not synonymous with cash, adjustments must be made to put earnings on a cash basis. The first adjustment is to add back all noncash expenses and deduct noncash revenues.[7] The most important of these adjustments is usually

[7]A firm's income may include earnings from an affiliate even though it receives no cash. These earnings must be subtracted to express the income on a cash basis.

EXHIBIT 12.3

Pier I Imports Consolidated Statement of Cash Flows (in Thousands)

	For the Fiscal Year Ended	
	1999	**1998**
Cash flow from operating activities		
Net income	$ 80,357	$ 78,047
Depreciation	31,130	23,946
Amortization	—	—
Deferred taxes	(2,575)	1,281
Changes in operating assets and liabilities		
Accounts receivable	2,500	(10,302)
Inventory	(24,103)	(13,617)
Accounts payable and accrued expenses	12,826	25,031
Other current liabilities	(4,409)	2,468
Net cash provided by operating activities	$ 95,726	$106,854
Cash flow from investing activities		
Purchases of plant	(78,055)	(49,854)
Proceeds from sale of plant	36,408	8,856
Acquisitions	(4,235)	(1,003)
Other	2,548	(2,201)
Net cash use in investment activities	$(43,334)	$ (44,202)
Cash flow from financing activities		
Cash dividends	(11,522)	(8,934)
Purchases of treasury stock	(65,777)	(10,228)
Proceeds from issuance of long-term debt	—	—
Repayments of long-term debt	(20,325)	—
Net borrowings of short-term bank debt	—	—
Proceeds from sale of stock	6,448	4,959
Net cash used in financing activities	$(91,176)	$ (14,203)
Change in cash and cash equivalents	(38,784)	48,449
Cash and cash equivalents at beginning of the year	80,729	32,280
Cash and cash equivalents at the end of the year	$ 41,945	$ 80,729

Adapted from Pier 1 Imports, Annual Report 1999.

depreciation, the noncash expense that allocates the cost of plant and equipment over a period of time. Other noncash expenses may include depletion of raw materials and amortization of intangible assets, such as goodwill. In this illustration, the firm has depreciation expense of $31,130 but no amortization and no noncash revenues, so only the $31,130 is added to the firm's earnings.

An increase in deferred taxes is added to earnings plus noncash expenses. Earnings are determined after subtracting taxes owed for the time period but not necessarily paid. The firm may be able to defer paying some taxes until the future, so these deferred taxes do not result in an outflow of cash during the current accounting period. Although taxes actually paid are a cash outflow, deferred taxes recognized during the time period are not a cash outflow and are added back to earnings to determine the cash generated by operations.

Although an increase in deferred taxes is added back, a decrease in deferred taxes indicates that taxes previously deferred were paid. This payment is a cash outflow and must be subtracted. In 1998, Pier 1 experienced an increase in deferred taxes, so $1,281 is added back to determine cash. In 1999, however, deferred taxes are negative ($2,575), indicating that the account was reduced. Previously deferred taxes were paid; cash was consumed (that is, there was a cash outflow), and that amount is subtracted to determine cash generated by operations.

The next set of entries refers to changes in the firm's current assets and liabilities resulting from operations. Some of these changes will generate cash while others will consume it. If accounts receivable increase, that means during the accounting period the firm has experienced a net increase in credit sales. These credit sales do not generate cash until the receivables are collected, so an increase in accounts receivable is a cash outflow. In 1998, Pier 1's receivables increased by $10,302, so there was a cash outflow of $10,302. The outflow is represented by the parentheses around the amount. Conversely, if accounts receivable had declined, it would mean the firm collected more receivables than it granted. Such a positive collection would result in a cash inflow. Since a decline in accounts receivable produces a positive inflow, the dollar amount of the decline would not be presented in parentheses on the statement. This occurred in 1999 when the $2,500 decrease in accounts receivable increased cash.

An increase in inventory, like an increase in accounts receivable, is an outflow of cash. If the firm ends the time period with more inventory than when it began the period, it has experienced a cash outflow. In Exhibit 12.3, inventory rose by $24,103 during 1999, so this amount is subtracted to determine cash generated by operations. Once again, the cash outflow is indicated by the dollar amount being in parentheses. If inventory had declined, that would indicate the firm sold more inventory than it acquired. This change would be an inflow of cash, and the amount would not be in parentheses.

These effects on cash by changes in accounts receivable and inventory also apply to other current assets. An increase in any current asset, other than cash or cash equivalents, is a cash outflow, while a decrease is a cash inflow. For example, if the firm prepays an insurance policy or makes a lease or rent payment at the beginning of the month, these payments are cash outflows. However, they are also increases in the asset prepaid expense; thus, the increase in the asset represents a cash outflow.

In addition to changes in current assets, normal day-to-day operations will alter the firm's current liabilities. Wages will accrue and other trade accounts may rise. An increase in the firm's payables is a cash inflow because the cash has not been paid out. During 1999, Pier 1 Imports' creditors lent the firm an additional $12,826 as part of the normal operations of both supplier (the creditor) and user (the borrower or debtor). This $12,826 is an inflow, so the amount is not presented in parentheses. If payables decline, that means the firm experiences a cash outflow as the payables are retired. Such a reduction in a current liability is an outflow, as occurred with the other liabilities, which decreased by $4,409.

The sum of the adjustments and changes in current assets and liabilities gives the net cash generated (or consumed) by operations. In 1999, Pier 1 Imports' operations generated cash of $95,726, slightly less than the $106,854 generated in 1998.

The next part of the statement of cash flows analyzes the firm's investments in long-term assets. The acquisition of plant and equipment requires a cash outflow while the sale of plant and equipment generates cash (an inflow). Expanding firms will need additional investment in plant and equipment, which consumes cash. A firm with excess capacity may sell plant and equipment, which generates cash. During 1999, Pier 1 acquired $78,055 in new plant. This acquisition is a cash outflow, so the amount is in parentheses. The firm also sold plant for $36,408, which is an inflow. After two small additional entries, the net amount of these investment activities is a negative $43,334. The negative number indicates net investments in plant and equipment required a cash outlay.

The third part of the statement of changes in cash flows covers the financing decisions of the firm. Issuing new debt or new stock produces a cash inflow. Retiring debt, redeeming stock, or paying cash dividends are cash outflows. Financing decisions can be either long- or short-term. An increase in a short-term liability, such as a bank loan, or a long-term liability, such as a bond outstanding, is a source of cash. A reduction in these accounts, however, requires a cash outflow. An increase in equity is also an inflow of cash while a reduction in equity is a cash outflow.

Besides paying cash dividends ($11,522), Pier 1's financing decisions are primarily concerned with the repurchase of stock ($65,777) and the retirement of long-term debt ($20,325), both of which are cash outflows. The company did not increase borrowings from commercial banks or issue long-term debt. Although a small amount of cash was generated through the sale of stock, the primary result of the financing activities was a cash outflow of $91,176.

The final part of the statement presents the firm's cash position at the end of the time period. Cash at the end of the accounting period is determined by the amount of initial cash and by the change in cash. Pier 1's cash inflow from operations was $95,726 but its investment activities resulted in a cash outflow of $43,334. Financing activities resulted in a cash outflow of $91,176, so after combining the cash flows from operations, investments, and financing, cash outflows exceeded inflows by $38,784. Since the firm began the year with $80,729, it ends the year with $41,945.

The bottom line of the statement of cash flows is the firm's cash position at the end of the accounting period. If the firm uses more cash than it generated, its cash

EXHIBIT 12.4

Georgia-Pacific Statement of Cash Flows (in Millions)

	Operating Activities	
	Net income	$ 101
	Adjustments	
	Depreciation	131
	Depletion	15
	Deferred taxes	25
	Cash sources from operations	$ 272
	Changes in operating assets and liabilities	
	Accounts receivable	($ 35)
	Inventory	(27)
	Other assets	3
	Trade accounts payable and accruals	1
	Net cash provided by operating activities	$ 214
	Investment Activities	
	Purchases of plant	($ 118)
	Timberlands purchased	(31)
	Proceeds from sale of assets	30
The Purchase	Other	15
(Cash Outflow) ⟶	Acquisition	(3,456)
	Net cash used in investment activities	($3,560)
	Financing Activities	
	Net increase in short-term notes	$ 7
The Financing	Payments of long-term debt	(226)
(Cash Inflow) ⟶	Proceeds from sale of long-term debt (after fees)	3,640
	Proceeds from sale of common stock	—
	Stock repurchases	—
	Dividends paid	(35)
	Net cash provided by financing activities	$3,386
	Increase in cash	$ 40
	Cash at beginning of year	23
	Cash at end of year	$ 63

holdings (or cash equivalents) will decline. Conversely, if the firm's cash inflows exceed the outflows, its cash and cash equivalents will rise.

What does the statement add to the financial analyst's knowledge? By placing the emphasis on cash, the statement permits the analyst to see where the firm generated cash and how this money was used. In the example in Exhibit 12.3, Pier 1 generated cash from earnings and the non-cash depreciation expense. Since these are part of operating activities, they are "internally" generated funds. How was this cash used? The answer is primarily to purchase plant. Since the internally generated cash was sufficient to cover the acquisition of plant, Pier 1 did not need "external" sources to cover operations and its investments in plant and equipment. Some financing decisions were made (for instance, the payment of dividends). These decisions were not forced upon the firm by its operating with a cash drain. Instead, operations generated sufficient cash to cover the expansion in inventory and plant without necessitating an influx of cash from an outside source.

The statement also indicates that cash declined by $38,784 partly as a result of a large repurchase of stock ($65,777) and a reduction in long-term debt of $20,325. While the statement of cash flows cannot explain why management made these decisions, the decisions' impact (the decline in the firm's cash position) is immediately apparent from studying the statement.

Differences between statements of cash flows can be seen by comparing Exhibit 12.3 with Exhibit 12.4. The latter presents the statement of cash flows provided to stockholders by Georgia-Pacific after its acquisition of Great Northern Nekoosa. As may be readily seen from the statement, the acquisition was a large investment that required a substantial outflow of cash ($3,456 million). Where did the cash come from? Was it internally generated by operations? Were the funds borrowed, or did the firm issue new stock to raise the cash to pay for the acquisition?

Studying the statement of cash flows answers these questions. Cash generated by operations, $214 million, was sufficient to cover the increases in inventory and receivables (that is, cash provided by operations was positive) but was certainly insufficient to pay for the acquisition. Instead, Georgia-Pacific issued a substantial amount of long-term debt, $3,640 million, to pay for the investment. The large amount of cash used by investment activities was covered by external financing activities. Whether such actions have a positive or negative impact on the firm is, of course, for the financial analyst or investor to determine.

LIMITATIONS OF ACCOUNTING DATA

There are several weaknesses inherent in accounting statements, but this does not mean that financial analysis employing accounting data should be discounted. The financial analyst, however, needs to be aware of the limitations so that accounting statements may be interpreted in light of these weaknesses.

First, accounting data do not take into account nonmeasurable items, such as the quality of the research department or the marketing performance of the firm. Performance is measured solely in terms of money, and the implication of accounting data is that if the firm consistently leads its industry (or is at least above average), its management and divisions are qualitatively superior to its competitors. A relationship probably does exist between performance and superior financial statements. The strong financial statements of Coca-Cola or Johnson & Johnson mirror the quality of their management and of their research and marketing staffs. However, many firms may be able to improve their financial position temporarily and achieve short-term superior performance that cannot be maintained.

Second, accounting data may not be sufficiently challenged by auditors. Although accounting records are examined for reasonableness and conformity with

The Role of the Auditor

The accounting statements of publicly held firms must be audited by an independent certified public accountant (CPA). These audits, which are an official examination of accounts, must be held annually. After conducting an audit, the CPA issues an auditor's opinion that attests to the "fairness" of the financial statements and their conformity with generally accepted accounting principles. By *fairness,* accountants mean that the statements are not misleading. ¶ The auditor's opinion must be included in the firm's annual report for publicly held firms. It is a brief document that usually consists of a few paragraphs that cover the scope of the examination and give the auditor's opinion. On occasion, the opinion may include a discussion of specific factors that affect specific details in the financial statements. In this case the opinion is said to be "qualified." ¶ Since audits are held by independent accountants, investors can have confidence in the financial statements. Accountants' objectivity enhances the statements' credibility. However, an auditor's opinion does not guarantee the accuracy of the statements. Responsibility for accuracy rests with management. ¶

accounting principles, the auditors may lack knowledge in specific areas pertinent to the firm's accounting statements. For example, the auditors may accept the estimates of the firm's engineers because the auditors lack the specialized knowledge necessary to challenge the estimates. This is not meant to suggest that the auditors are incompetent; they may, however, lack specific knowledge that is necessary to verify the authenticity of some of the data used by the corporation's accountants.

Third, accounting statements that are available to the public give aggregate data. Although the company's management has access to itemized data, individual investors or security analysts may not receive sufficiently detailed information to guide investment decisions. For example, a company may not give its sales figures according to product lines. Aggregate sales data do not inform the public as to which of the company's products are its primary sources of revenue. The use of aggregate numbers in the firm's income statements and balance sheets may hide important information that the investor or security analyst could use in studying the company.

Fourth, accounting data may be biased. For example, the valuation of assets by the lower of either cost or market value may result in biased information if the dollar value of the assets has significantly risen (as may occur during periods of inflation). Such increases in value are hidden by the use of the historical cost, and thus the accounting statements do not give a true indication of the current value of the firm's assets. If the value of the assets has risen and this is not recognized by the accounting data, the return earned by the company on its assets is overstated. If the true value of the assets were used to determine the return that the firm earns on its assets, the rate would be lower. In this case the use of historical cost instead of market value results in inaccurate measures of the company's performance.

Fifth, inflation causes a problem in interpreting accounting data. Items that were purchased a number of years before cannot be replaced at the same prices.

As the firm's plant and equipment wear out, these assets have to be replaced at a higher cost. For the firm to maintain its current capacity, additional financing is required to cover the higher costs. This decline in the purchasing power of money is not indicated by accounting data.

RATIO ANALYSIS

Accounting data are often used to analyze a firm's financial position. Such analysis may be conducted by creditors seeking to measure the safety of their loans. Investors also analyze financial statements to learn how well management is performing. The profitability of the firm and hence the return the firm's owners are achieving may be perceived in the financial statements. In addition, management analyzes the data in financial statements. Such analysis may indicate weaknesses in the firm, which, if corrected, may increase the firm's profitability and value.

The ratios used in financial analysis can be classified into the following groups: (1) liquidity, (2) activity, (3) profitability, (4) leverage, and (5) coverage. Liquidity ratios indicate the ability of the firm to meet its short-term obligations as they come due. Activity ratios are concerned with the amount of assets a firm needs to support its sales. The more rapidly assets turn over, the fewer assets the firm needs to generate sales. High turnover of inventory and accounts receivable also indicates how quickly the firm is able to convert these current assets into cash. Profitability ratios are a measure of performance; they indicate what the firm earns on its sales, assets, and equity. Leverage ratios are concerned with the firm's capital structure, or the extent to which debt is used to finance the firm's assets. Coverage ratios indicate the extent to which the firm generates operating income to cover an expense.

These ratios may be computed and interpreted from two viewpoints. They may be compiled for a period of years to perceive trends; this is **time series** or **trend analysis.** The ratios may be computed at the same time for several firms within an industry; this is **cross-sectional analysis.** Time series and cross-sectional analysis may be used together. Rarely will all the ratios indicate the same general tendency. When they are taken as a group, the ratios should give the investigator an indication of the direction in which the firm is moving and how it compares with other firms in its industry.

TIME SERIES ANALYSIS
Analysis of a firm over a period of time

CROSS-SECTIONAL ANALYSIS
Analysis of several firms in the same industry at a point in time

The analysis of financial statements through ratios can be a very useful tool for financial managers, investors, and creditors, who may use this type of analysis to ascertain how the firm is performing over time and relative to its competition. The ratios will tend to indicate trends, such as a deterioration in the firm's profitability. Such time series analyses of financial statements may indicate future difficulties while there is still time to take remedial action.

Even if the firm is not experiencing a deteriorating financial position, its performance may be inferior to other firms within its industry. A cross-sectional analysis of firms will indicate if the particular firm is performing up to the norms of the industry. To make such comparisons, the financial analysts must have access to industry averages. The most widely known industry averages are the ratios compiled by Dun and Bradstreet and published annually in *Dun's Review.* Firms are classified by their SIC (Standard Industrial Classification) numbers, and the ratios are subdivided by the size of the firm.

Robert Morris Associates, a national association of bank loan officers, also publishes industry averages in its annual publication *Statement Studies*. The sources of its data are financial statements acquired by commercial banks from firms receiving loans. Sixteen ratios are given, and firms are classified by their SIC numbers.

Individual investors and creditors may find calculating their own ratios to be useful, since they may stress the ratios most applicable to the intended use of the analysis. For example, commercial banks and other lending institutions are concerned with the capacity of the borrower to service the loan (to pay the interest and repay the principal). Thus, ratios concerning the borrower's use of debt or the coverage of interest payments are important. Loan officers will use such ratios in credit reviews and in decisions to grant new loans.

Even if the financial analyst uses public sources of industry averages, there may be problems with the data. Published industry averages are based on last year's financial statements, reducing the comparability of the data with current-year financial ratios. Second, the individual firm may not fit neatly into one of the industry categories. Large firms, such as Pepsi, have operations in a variety of related fields (for example, soft drinks *and* snack foods), which reduces the comparability of ratios computed for similar, but not identical, firms (for example, Coca-Cola). Third, even if industry averages are presented for firms in comparable industries, the problem of comparing firms of different sizes remains. This problem is obvious for large size differentials (such as the local "ma and pa" grocery store compared with a large supermarket chain). But the problem may also apply when comparing larger firms in an industry. For example, are the ratios for a small grocery store comparable to the ratios for a large operation, such as Safeway, ACME, or Food Lion?

Although there are problems with the application of ratio analysis, it remains a convenient means to analyze a firm's financial condition. The financial manager (or other analyst) certainly should not discard the analysis because there may be difficulties with its application or interpretation. Used with other tools of financial analysis, ratio analysis of financial statements can give a clear indication of the firm's performance and its direction. The analysis can be a harbinger of things to come and as such may indicate that action should be taken now to correct a small problem before it grows into a major source of financial embarrassment.

In the sections that follow, several ratios are discussed and illustrated. These ratios do not exhaust all the possible ratios, and certainly you may find that in a specific occupation additional ratios or more sophisticated versions of some of the ratios presented here are needed. The purpose of this chapter is only to illustrate how ratios are compiled, interpreted, and used, employing the balance sheet as of the end of the 1999 fiscal year (Exhibit 12.1), and income statement for the 1999 fiscal year (Exhibit 12.2), of Pier 1 Imports.

Before proceeding, you also need to be forewarned that several ratios have more than one definition. The definition used by one analyst may differ from that used by another. These differences can arise from averaging the data in two financial statements. (See, for instance, the two approaches to inventory turnover discussed below.) Another source of differences can be what is included or excluded.

(See, for instance, the various definitions of the debt ratios.) You cannot assume that the analysis obtained from one source is comparable to that provided by an alternative source. This problem may be particularly acute now that analyses of financial statements can be found on the Internet. Of course, you can avoid this problem by performing the analysis yourself!

LIQUIDITY RATIOS

Liquidity is the ease with which assets may be converted into cash without loss. If a firm is liquid, it will be able to meet its bills as they come due. Thus, liquidity ratios are useful not only to short-term creditors of the firm, who are concerned with being paid, but also to the firm's management, who must make the payments.

The Current Ratio

The **current ratio** is the ratio of current assets to current liabilities.

CURRENT RATIO
Ratio of current assets to current liabilities: measure of liquidity

$$\text{Current ratio} = \text{Current assets/Current liabilities.}$$

It indicates how well the current liabilities, which must be paid within a year, are "covered." For Pier 1, the current assets are $381,943 and the current liabilities are $129,832; thus, the current ratio is

$$\frac{\$381{,}943}{\$129{,}832} = 2.94,$$

which indicates that for every dollar that the firm must pay within the year, there is $2.94 in an asset that is either cash or should become cash during the year.[8]

For most industries it is desirable to have more current assets than current liabilities. It is sometimes asserted that it is desirable to have at least $2 in current assets for every dollar in current liabilities (a current ratio of at least 2:1). If the current ratio is 2:1, then the firm's current assets could deteriorate in value by 50 percent and the firm still would be able to meet its short-term liabilities. While such rules of thumb are convenient, they need not apply to all industries. For example, electric utilities usually have current liabilities that exceed their current assets. Does this worry short-term creditors? No, because the short-term assets are of high quality (accounts receivable from electricity users). Should a person fail to pay an electric bill, the company will cut off service, and this threat is usually sufficient to induce payment. The higher the quality of the current assets (in other words, the higher the probability that these assets can be converted to cash at their stated value), the smaller the need for the current ratio to exceed 1:1. The reason for selecting a current ratio such as 2:1 as a rule of thumb is that creditors frequently believe that not all current assets will be converted into cash, and to protect themselves the creditors want a current ratio of at least 2:1.

[8]The use of a year is arbitrary, as the life of current assets and current liabilities varies among industries.

Although management also wants to know if the firm has sufficient liquid assets to meet its bills, the current ratio may have an additional use to management. A low current ratio is undesirable because it indicates financial weakness. A high current ratio may also be undesirable, for it may imply that the firm is not using funds economically. For example, the firm may have issued long-term debt and used it to finance too much inventory or accounts receivable. The high current ratio may also indicate that the firm is not taking advantage of available short-term financing. As was illustrated in Figure 2.1, short-term debt tends to be cheaper than long-term debt; failure to use short-term debt may reduce profitability. Thus, a high or low numerical value for the current ratio could signal that the management of short-term assets and liabilities needs changing.

Although the current ratio gives an indication of the ability of the firm to meet its current liabilities as they come due, the ratio does have limitations. The current ratio may be readily changed, and it is an aggregate measure of liquidity that does not differentiate the degree of liquidity of the different current assets. That the current ratio may be affected with ease is shown by the following examples. Management may sell plant and equipment for cash, which will increase the current assets while holding constant the current liabilities, and thus the current ratio rises. While this does increase the degree of liquidity, it may be detrimental to the firm, for the firm may need plant and equipment in order to produce. Thus, liquidity has been bought at the expense of productive capacity.

Management may retire current liabilities by paying them off with cash. This also will increase the current ratio (as long as the ratio exceeds 1.0), but a firm needs cash to work with. Paying off short-term liabilities solely to improve the current ratio may be detrimental, for the firm has less cash, even though by the current ratio the firm appears to be more liquid.

The second problem with the current ratio is that it is an aggregation of all current assets and does not differentiate among current assets with regard to their degrees of liquidity. The ratio considers inventory that may be sold after three months on credit (payment for which in turn may not be collected for several additional months) as no different from cash or a short-term government security.

The Quick Ratio (Acid Test)

QUICK RATIO (ACID TEST)
Current assets excluding inventory divided by current liabilities; measure of liquidity

Since it may take months before inventory is sold and turned into cash, a variation on the current ratio is the ratio of all current assets except inventory divided by current liabilities. This ratio is called the **quick ratio** or *acid test* (both terms are used for this ratio) and is expressed as follows:[9]

[9]The quick ratio is sometimes defined as

$$\text{Quick ratio} = \frac{\text{Cash} + \text{Marketable securities} + \text{Accounts receivable}}{\text{Current liabilities}}.$$

The two definitions will give the same answer if the firm's current assets are limited to cash, marketable securities, accounts receivable, and inventory. Some firms, however, do have other current assets, such as prepaid expenses, in which case the choice of definition will affect the numerical value of the quick ratio.

$$\text{Quick ratio} = \frac{\text{Current assets} - \text{Inventory}}{\text{Current liabilities}}.$$

For Pier 1 the quick ratio is

$$\frac{\$381{,}943 - \$258{,}773}{\$129{,}832} = 0.95,$$

which is lower than the current ratio of 2.94 determined previously. The difference is, of course, the result of inventory that the company is carrying. A low quick ratio indicates that the firm may have difficulty meeting its obligations as they come due if it must rely on converting its inventory into cash to meet these current liabilities. The quick ratio, however, does not indicate that the firm will fail to pay. The ability to meet the obligations will be influenced by such factors as (1) how quickly cash flows into the firm, (2) the firm's ability to raise additional capital, (3) how rapidly obligations come due, and (4) the relationship the company has with its suppliers and their willingness to extend credit. The quick ratio simply indicates how well the current liabilities are covered by cash and assets that may be converted into cash relatively quickly. In effect, the quick ratio considers that not all current assets are equally liquid and is a more stringent measure of liquidity.

The Components of the Current Assets

Another approach to liquidity is to rank the current assets with regard to their degree of liquidity and determine each one's proportion of total current assets. The most liquid current asset is cash. Next are cash equivalents, such as Treasury bills or negotiable certificates of deposit. Then comes accounts receivable, and, finally, inventory. For Pier 1 the proportion of each asset to total current assets is as follows:

Current Asset	Proportion of Total Current Assets
Cash and cash equivalents	11.0%
Accounts receivable	2.3
Inventory	67.8

The table indicates that 11.0 percent of the firm's assets are cash and short-term securities but inventory accounts for over 67 percent of current assets.

Since this technique determines each asset's proportion of current assets, it gives an indication of the degree of liquidity of the firm's current assets. If a large proportion of the current assets is inventory, the firm is not very liquid. The decomposition of the current assets according to their degree of liquidity, along with the quick ratio, gives management, creditors, and investors a better measure of the ability of the firm to meet its current liabilities as they come due than the current ratio provides. These ratios, then, are a basic supplement to the current ratio and should be used to analyze the liquidity of any firm, such as Pier 1, that carries a significant amount of inventory in its operations.

ACTIVITY RATIOS

Activity ratios indicate how rapidly the firm is turning its assets (for example, inventory and accounts receivable) into cash. Two activity ratios that are frequently encountered are inventory turnover and receivables turnover (the average collection period or days sales outstanding). The more rapidly the firm turns over its inventory and receivables, the more rapidly it acquires cash. Hence, high turnover indicates that the firm is rapidly receiving cash and is more able to pay its liabilities as they come due. High turnover, however, need not imply that the firm is maximizing profits. For example, high inventory turnover may indicate that the firm is selling items for a lower price in order to induce quicker sales. The rapid collection of accounts receivable may indicate that the firm is offering too large a cash discount to buyers to increase collections of receivables. High turnover of inventory or receivables is not desirable by itself and may be indicative of management decisions that reduce earnings. Comparison must be made with industry averages in order to have some basis for making assertions that the turnover is too slow or too rapid.

Inventory Turnover

INVENTORY TURNOVER
Speed with which inventory is sold

Inventory turnover may be defined as annual sales divided by average inventory. That is,

$$\text{Inventory turnover} = \frac{\text{Sales}}{\text{Average inventory}}.$$

Since all assets must be financed the more rapidly the inventory turns over, the less are the financing needs of the firm. Since Pier 1's 1998 year-end inventory was \$234,180, the inventory turnover for 1999 is

$$\frac{\text{Sales}}{\text{Average inventory}} = \frac{\$1{,}138{,}590}{(258{,}773 + \$234{,}180)/2} = 4.6.$$

This indicates that annual sales are 4.6 times the level of inventory. Inventory turns over 4.6 times a year or about every 2.6 months (12/4.6 = 2.6). The turnover may be expressed in days by dividing the number of days in a year by the inventory turnover. Thus, in this illustration the firm holds an average item of inventory for 79 days (365/4.6 = 79). Since management can anticipate that on the average, inventory will be held for 79 days, management will need to find financing for that period of time to carry the inventory.

Inventory turnover may also be defined as cost of goods sold divided by average inventory. Accountants in particular may prefer to use cost of goods sold, because accounting places much emphasis on the determination of cost. Financial analysts and creditors may prefer to use sales in order to stress how rapidly the inventory flows into sales. In addition, Dun and Bradstreet uses sales instead of costs in its "Key Business Ratios." Hence, analysts must use sales to inventory if they are comparing a specific firm with the Dun and Bradstreet industry averages.

Either definition, however, is acceptable provided that the user is consistent. If the cost of goods sold is used instead of annual sales, all inventory turnover ratios used as a basis of comparison must also use cost of goods sold instead of annual sales. This points out the need for the person using ratio analysis to be aware of the definitions and to apply the definitions consistently. Otherwise, the analysis may be biased.

Receivables Turnover

RECEIVABLES TURNOVER
Speed with which accounts receivable are collected

Receivables turnover is defined as annual credit sales divided by receivables. Thus, the receivables turnover ratio is expressed as follows:

$$\text{Receivables turnover} = \frac{\text{Annual credit sales}}{\text{Accounts receivable}}.$$

An alternative definition substitutes annual sales for annual credit sales. That is,

$$\text{Receivables turnover} = \frac{\text{Annual sales}}{\text{Accounts receivable}}$$

Either definition is acceptable as long as it is applied consistently. (The analyst may also use average accounts receivable instead of year-end accounts receivable.) While management can use either definition, investors may be limited to the data provided by the firm. If annual credit sales are not reported by the firm, the investor will have no choice but to use annual sales instead of annual credit sales.

Pier 1's income statement does not give annual credit sales, so the first definition cannot be used. When the second definition is used, receivables turnover is

$$\text{Receivables turnover} = \frac{\$1{,}138{,}590}{\$9{,}060} = 125{,}672.$$

This is a meaningless number; 125,672 times a year makes no sense! This large turnover is simply the result of the fact that Pier 1 Imports has virtually no receivables. Pier 1, of course, does extend credit to its customers but offers credit services, such as VISA or American Express. The credit is extended by the credit card companies, and these companies have to collect the accounts receivable. Pier 1 pays for the service. The credit card company will credit Pier 1 only \$0.98 (or perhaps \$0.985) for every \$1 in credit sales.[10]

[10]A major reason for using the credit companies is that Pier 1 avoids the costs of establishing a credit policy. See the discussion of management of accounts receivable in Chapter 20.

While most retail operations offer credit cards as a means to generate credit sales, other firms directly offer credit. For example, utilities, such as Southern Company, extend service on credit and have accounts receivable. At the end of 1998, Southern had revenues of $11,403 billion and accounts receivables of $1,797 billion. Thus, Southern's receivables turnover was

$$\text{Receivables turnover} = \frac{\$11{,}403}{\$1{,}797} = 6.35.$$

This indicates that annual sales were 6.35 times receivables, which means the receivables are paid off about every two months.

AVERAGE COLLECTION PERIOD (DAYS SALES OUTSTANDING)
Number of days required on the average to collect an account receivable

An alternative means to measure receivables is the **average collection period** or "days sales outstanding." The average collection period is

$$\text{Average collection period} = \frac{\text{Receivables}}{\text{Sales per day}}.$$

For Southern Company, sales per day are $31.675 ($11,403/360). (A 360-day year is often used as a convenience. As stated previously, any definition may be acceptable, as long as it is applied consistently. Sales per day are $31.24 if a 365-day year is used.) The average collection period is

$$\$1{,}797/\$31.675 = 57 \text{ days}$$

This implies that when the firm makes a credit sale instead of a cash sale, it can expect payment in 57 days. This is essentially the same information derived by the receivables turnover rate. If it takes the firm 57 days to collect its receivables, they are turning over about 5½ times a year.[11] This is the same answer given by the ratio of annual sales to accounts receivable. However, by stressing the number of days necessary to collect the receivables, the average collection period may be easier to interpret.

Turnover ratios employing current assets need to be interpreted cautiously. These ratios are dealing with dynamic measurements, since they are concerned with how long it takes for an event to occur. Turnover ratios may be biased if the firm has (1) seasonal sales; (2) sales that do not occur evenly during the fiscal year; or (3) growth in inventory, accounts receivable, or sales during the fiscal year. Under these circumstances, the use of year-end figures may produce ratios that are biased.

The potential bias may be seen in the following example, which presents the monthly inventory of a firm that has a seasonal type of business. During the year, inventory is accumulated in anticipation of large sales during the Christmas season.

[11] The average collection period may also be calculated by dividing 360 by the receivables turnover. For Southern Company, that is 360/6.35 = 57, which is the same average collection period derived in the body of the text.

Month	Inventory at End of Month	Sales during the Month
January	$ 100	$ 50
February	100	50
March	200	50
April	200	50
May	300	50
June	400	50
July	500	50
August	700	50
September	1,000	400
October	1,000	1,300
November	1,200	2,000
December	300	1,200
Total sales		$5,300

If year-end inventory and yearly sales figures are employed, the inventory turnover is 26.5 ($5,300/$200),[12] which indicates that inventory is turning over almost every 14 days (360/26.5). This, however, is misleading because it fails to consider the large buildup of inventory that occurred during the middle of the year. In this case the use of year-end inventory figures increases the inventory turnover. The inventory turnover appears to be more rapid than it actually was.

Several means exist to help alleviate this problem. For example, the average of the monthly inventories may be used instead of the year-end inventory. The monthly average inventory is $500 (total inventory acquired during the year divided by 12). When this figure is used with the annual sales, the turnover is 10.6, or about 34 days. This is much slower than the turnover indicated when the year-end inventory figures were used. Other methods for removing the potential bias may be to construct monthly turnover ages or moving averages. The point is that turnover ratios may be subject to bias and, hence, may be misleading. In order for ratios to be helpful, users need to recognize the potential bias and take steps to remove it.

Fixed Asset and Total Asset Turnover

In addition to the turnover ratios that analyze the speed with which the firm turns over its current assets, there are also turnover ratios that employ the firm's long-term (fixed) assets and total assets. The **fixed asset turnover** ratio is defined as:

FIXED ASSET TURNOVER
Ratio of sales to fixed assets; measure of fixed assets necessary to generate sales

$$\text{Fixed asset turnover} = \frac{\text{Sales}}{\text{Fixed assets}}.$$

[12] Average inventory is ($300 + $100)/2 = $200.

For Pier 1, the fixed asset turnover is

$$\frac{\$1{,}138{,}590}{\$226{,}262} = 5.03.$$

This indicates that sales are 5 times fixed assets (land, plant, and equipment). The more rapidly fixed assets turn over (the higher the ratio), the smaller the amount of plant and equipment the firm is employing. Many firms, such as utilities, must have substantial investment in plant and equipment to produce the output they sell. (Southern Company's fixed asset turnover is 0.47, which indicates the company has over $2 invested in plant and equipment for every $1 of revenues.) Other firms, especially those providing services or retailers, may need only modest amounts of fixed assets.

TOTAL ASSET TURNOVER
Ratio of sales to total assets: measure of total assets required to generate sales

Total asset turnover measures how many assets are used to generate sales. The definition of total asset turnover is

$$\text{Total asset turnover} = \frac{\text{Sales}}{\text{Total assets}}.$$

For Pier 1 the total asset turnover is

$$\frac{\$1{,}138{,}590}{\$653{,}991} = 1.74.$$

This indicates the firm needs $1.00 in assets for every $1.74 generated in revenues.

By computing all the turnover ratios (in other words, the average collection period, inventory turnover, fixed asset turnover, and total asset turnover), the financial manager may be able to identify weak areas. For example, if the firm's accounts receivable and inventory turnover ratios are comparable to those for the industry but its total asset or fixed asset turnover is low, then the problem has to be the management of the firm's fixed assets. Once problems are identified, further analysis and remedial action can be directed toward the source of the problem.

OPERATING PROFIT MARGIN
Ratio of operating income to sales; percentage earned on sales before deducting interest expense and taxes

NET PROFIT MARGIN
Ratio of earnings after interest and taxes to sales; percentage earned on sales

PROFITABILITY RATIOS

Profitability ratios are measures of performance that indicate what the firm is earning on its sales or assets or equity. The **operating profit margin** is earnings before interest and taxes (EBIT) divided by sales, and the **net profit margin** is the ratio of earnings after interest and taxes to sales.[13]

[13]The words *profit, income,* and *earnings* are often synonymous. Operating income is defined as earnings before interest and taxes, and, in most cases, that is sufficient unless the firm has extraordinary or nonrecurring items included in earnings before interest and taxes. Although management will report these items as a separate entry, they may be reported as part of income before interest and taxes, in which case the earnings are not indicative of operating income.

$$\text{Operating profit margin} = \frac{\text{Earnings before interest and taxes}}{\text{Sales}}.$$

$$\text{Net profit margin} = \frac{\text{Earnings after interest and taxes}}{\text{Sales}}.$$

Computing both of these ratios may appear unnecessary, but it is best to compute both. Management then can see the effect of changes in interest expense and taxes on profitability. If management computed only the net profit margin, an increase in tax rates or interest rates would decrease the profit margin even though there had been no internal deterioration in the profitability of the firm's operations.

For Pier 1, the operating profit margin is

$$\text{Operating profit margin} = \frac{\$134{,}658}{\$1{,}138{,}590} = 11.8\%,$$

and the net profit margin is

$$\text{Net profit margin} = \frac{\$80{,}357}{\$1{,}138{,}590} = 7.1\%.$$

These indicate that the company earns $0.118 before interest and taxes for every dollar of sales and $0.071 after interest and taxes for every dollar of sales.

In addition to the operating profit margin and the net profit margin, some financial analysts compute the **gross profit margin,** which is

GROSS PROFIT MARGIN
Ratio of revenues minus cost of goods sold to sales; percentage earnings on sales before considering operating expenses, interest, and taxes

$$\text{Gross profit margin} = \frac{\text{Revenues} - \text{Cost of goods sold}}{\text{Sales}}.$$

For Pier 1, the gross profit margin is

$$\text{Gross profit margin} = \frac{\$500{,}417}{\$1{,}138{,}590} = 44.0\%.$$

This ratio indicates that the firm earns $0.44 on every dollar of sales before considering administrative, advertising, depreciation, and financing expenses. The gross profit margin is sensitive only to changes in the cost of goods sold but is not affected by other operating expenses. The operating profit margin, however, is affected by all operating expenses. By analyzing both the gross profit margin and the operating profit margin, the analyst can determine whether changes in the cost of goods sold or changes in other operating expenses are affecting the firm's earnings before interest and taxes (that is, its operating income).

RETURN ON TOTAL ASSETS
Ratio of earnings to total assets; percentage earned on assets

RETURN ON EQUITY
Ratio of earnings to owners' equity; percentage earned on equity

Other profitability ratios measure the **return on total assets** and the **return on equity.** The return on total assets is earnings divided by assets and measures what a firm earns on its resources.

$$\text{Return on total assets} = \frac{\text{Earnings after interest and taxes}}{\text{Total assets}}.$$

The return on equity is earnings divided by the equity or the net worth of the firm.

$$\text{Return on equity} = \frac{\text{Earnings after interest and taxes}}{\text{Equity}}.$$

Equity is defined as the sum of the common stock, the additional paid-in capital, and the retained earnings. Return on equity measures the return the firm is earning on its stockholders' investment. (If the company has any preferred stock, the ratio must be adjusted by subtracting the dividends paid the preferred stockholders from the earnings and subtracting the par value of the preferred stock from the equity. Since the common stockholders are interested in the return on their investment, the preferred stock should not be included in determining the return on the common stock equity.) For Pier 1, the return on total assets is

$$\text{Return on total assets} = \frac{\$80,357}{\$653,991} = 12.3\%.$$

The return on the equity is

$$\text{Return on equity} = \frac{\$80,357}{\$403,894} = 19.9\%.$$

This indicates that the firm returns \$0.123 for every dollar invested in assets and \$0.199 for every dollar invested by the common stockholders.

In addition to the return on total assets and return on equity, some financial analysts compute the return generated by operating income (earnings before interest and taxes, or EBIT). This ratio, which may be referred to as the **basic earning power,** is

BASIC EARNING POWER
Ratio of operating income to total assets; measure of the firm's ability to generate income before considering interest and taxes

$$\text{Basic earning power} = \frac{\text{EBIT}}{\text{Total assets}},$$

and it measures what the firm earns on its assets independently of (1) how the assets were financed and (2) the taxes the firm has to pay. For Pier 1, its basic earning power is

$$\text{Basic earning power} = \frac{\$134,658}{\$653,991} = 20.6\%,$$

which indicates that \$1 of the firm's assets generates \$0.206 in operating income (that is, income before paying interest and taxes).

This ratio may be particularly important to long-term creditors who are concerned with the capacity of management to generate earnings after meeting operating expenses. Since operating expenses are paid prior to debt service, the greater the basic earning power, the safer should be the creditors' interest payments.

LEVERAGE RATIOS

Among the more frequently computed ratios are leverage ratios, which measure the firm's use of debt financing. The two most commonly used ratios to measure financial leverage are (1) debt to equity, which is often referred to as the **debt/net worth ratio,** and (2) debt to total assets, which is commonly referred to as the **debt ratio.** These ratios are as follows:

DEBT/NET WORTH RATIO
Ratio of debt to equity; debt divided by equity

DEBT RATIO
Total debt divided by total assets; proportion of assets financed by debt; a measure of financial leverage

$$\text{Debt/net worth ratio} = \frac{\text{Debt}}{\text{Equity}}.$$

$$\text{Debt ratio} = \frac{\text{Debt}}{\text{Total assets}}.$$

Because Pier 1 Imports' total debt is $250,097 (that is, the sum of current liabilities and long-term debt), the values of these ratios are

$$\frac{\text{Debt}}{\text{Equity}} = \frac{\$250{,}097}{\$403{,}894} = 61.9\%.$$

$$\frac{\text{Debt}}{\text{Total Assets}} = \frac{\$250{,}097}{\$653{,}991} = 38.2\%.$$

The debt-to-equity ratio indicates that there is $0.619 debt for every dollar of equity. The debt-to-assets ratio indicates that debt is financing 38.2 percent of the firm's assets.

Leverage ratios are aggregate ratios. They use total debt and do not differentiate between short-term and long-term debt. The debt-to-equity ratio uses total equity and does not differentiate between preferred and common stock financing.[14] The debt-to-total-assets ratio uses total assets and does not differentiate between current and long-term assets.

The financial manager may disaggregate the data. For example, if the emphasis is on long-term debt financing, current liabilities may be removed so that the debt ratio becomes

$$\frac{\text{Long-term debt}}{\text{Total assets}}.$$

This ratio indicates the extent to which long-term debt is financing the firm's assets. If the financial manager is primarily concerned with senior or subordinated

[14]If the firm has both preferred and common stock outstanding, the analyst may define the debt-to-net-worth ratio as debt/common equity.

long-term debt, similar adjustments can be made in the ratio (that is, senior debt/total assets or subordinated debt/total assets).[15]

For most purposes the use of aggregate numbers does not pose a problem, for the debt ratio is measuring the proportion of the total assets that creditors (both short- and long-term) are financing. The smaller the proportion of total assets that creditors are financing, the larger the decline in value of the assets that may occur without threatening the creditors' position. Leverage ratios thus give an indication of financial risk. Firms that have high leverage ratios are considered riskier, because there is less cushion to protect creditors if the value of the assets deteriorates. For example, the debt ratio for Pier 1 is 38.2 percent. This indicates that the value of the assets may decline by 61.8 percent (100% − 38.2%) before the equity is destroyed, leaving only enough assets to pay off the debt. If the debt ratio had been 70 percent, then only a 30 percent decline in the value of the assets would endanger the creditors' position.

Leverage ratios are not only an indication of risk to creditors but also of risk to stockholders, for firms that are highly financially leveraged are riskier equity investments. If the value of the assets declines or if the firm should experience declining sales and losses, the equity is wiped out more quickly for financially leveraged firms than for unleveraged firms. Hence, leverage ratios are important indicators of risk for stockholders as well as for creditors.

Leverage ratios differ significantly among firms. The debt ratios (debt to total assets) for several large industrial and telephone companies are presented in Exhibit 12.5.[16] The table has been arranged in descending order from the highest debt ratio to the lowest. The proportion of a firm's total assets financed by debt varies not only across industries but also within an industry. The telephone companies' debt ratios do have less variation than the debt ratios of the industrial firms. While the range for the industrial firms is from 80.4 to 45.3 percent, the range for the phone companies is 69.9 to 47.3 percent.

For the individual firm, there may exist an optimal proportion of debt to total assets. Finding this optimal capital structure of debt and equity financing is important to maximizing the value of a firm, and Chapter 16 discusses the optimal capital structure of a firm. It is sufficient for now to suggest that finding the optimal use of financial leverage may benefit the common stockholder by increasing the per share earnings of the company and permitting faster growth and larger dividends. If, however, the firm is too financially leveraged or *undercapitalized,*

[15] Some analysts add the deferred taxes to debt. Others define the debt ratio as permanent current liabilities plus long-term debt divided by total assets. Since there is no absolute, correct definition, any is acceptable provided the definition is applied consistently.

[16] The debt ratios calculated for Exhibit 12.5 use total debt. The ranking of the ratios may differ if only noncurrent debt is used. For example, the Coca-Cola Company debt ratio declines from 53.9 percent to only 8.8 percent if current liabilities are excluded from the calculation.

The ratios may also differ from debt ratios reported by the firms in their annual reports. For example, the management of the Coca-Cola Company uses a different definition of the leverage ratios: total debt to total capital. Total capital is defined as equity *plus* interest-bearing debt. Since interest-bearing debt excludes accruals and payables, that definition differs from either total assets used in the debt ratio or total equity used in the debt-to-equity ratio.

EXHIBIT 12.5

Ratio of Total Debt to Total Assets

Industrial Firms

Firm	Debt Ratio
GenCorp	80.4%
Heinz	77.6
Atlantic Richfield	69.9
Hershey Foods	69.3
Georgia-Pacific	65.7
Reynolds Metals	60.8
Coca-Cola Company	53.9
VF Corp. (Vanity Fair)	45.3

Telephone/Communications Firms

Firm	Debt Ratio
Bell Atlantic	69.9%
Bell South	59.1
Sprint	53.2
SBC Communications	47.3

Source: *1998 annual reports.*

potential investors may be less willing to invest, and creditors will require a higher interest rate to compensate them for the increased risk. Thus, leverage ratios, which measure the use of financial leverage by the firm, are among the most important ratios that managers, creditors, and investors may calculate.

Several ratios may be combined to analyze a firm. One such technique is the **DuPont system,** which was designed by that firm's management to measure a firm's earning power. The system combines net profit margin, total asset turnover, and leverage to determine the return on the firm's equity. Essentially, the DuPont system determines the return on equity by multiplying three things: (1) the net profit margin, (2) total asset turnover, and (3) an equity multiplier (used to indicate the amount of leverage).

DUPONT SYSTEM
Measure of earning capacity that combines asset turnover, profitability, and financial leverage

The product of the net profit margin and total asset turnover determines the return on assets. That is,

$$\text{Return on assets} = \frac{\text{Net profits}}{\text{Sales}} \times \frac{\text{Sales}}{\text{Assets}} = \frac{\text{Net profit}}{\text{Assets}}.$$

The product of the return on assets and the ratio of assets to equity (the equity multiplier) determines the return on equity. That is,

$$\text{Return on equity} = \frac{\text{Net profits}}{\text{Assets}} \times \frac{\text{Assets}}{\text{Equity}}.$$

EXHIBIT 12.6

The DuPont System of Financial Analysis

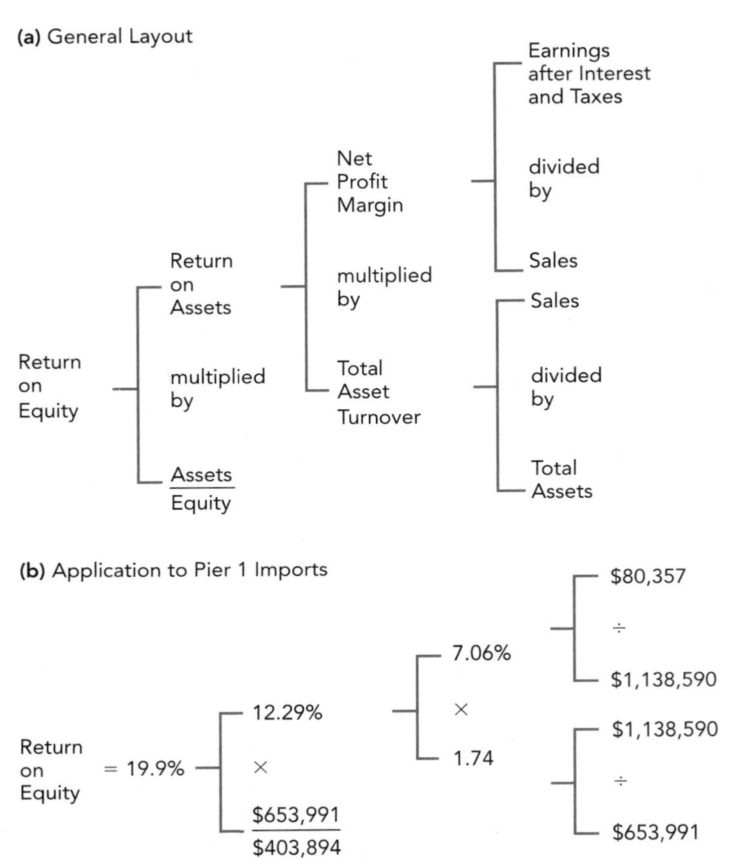

Thus, the DuPont system is

$$\text{Return on equity} = \frac{\text{Net profits}}{\text{Sales}} \times \frac{\text{Sales}}{\text{Assets}} \times \frac{\text{Assets}}{\text{Equity}} = \frac{\text{Net profits}}{\text{Equity}}.$$

In the DuPont system, financial leverage is measured by the ratio of assets to equity (the equity multiplier mentioned earlier). This ratio is the reciprocal of the ratio of equity to total assets. Since the ratio of equity to total assets indicates the proportion of assets financed by equity, it is a measure of financial leverage. The smaller the proportion of assets financed by equity (or the larger the proportion of the assets financed by debt), the larger will be the ratio of assets to equity, and, for a given return on assets, the greater will be the return on equity.

The DuPont system is illustrated in Exhibit 12.6, which presents the general layout of the system and applies it to the financial statements of Pier 1. While the end product of the system (the return on equity) is no different than the simple ratio of earnings to equity, the layout of the analysis facilitates locating internal sources of a firm's problems.

In addition to combining profitability, turnover, and leverage in one analysis, the system facilitates comparisons of firms in one industry with firms in different industries. Some firms, such as grocery stores, have rapid turnover but small profit margins. These low profit margins may appear to indicate that the firms are not very profitable. Other firms, such as furniture stores, may have large profit margins but slow turnover. If profit margins are considered in a vacuum, such firms appear to be very profitable. If these conclusions were true, owners of grocery stores would convert them to furniture stores. This does not occur, however, because the return on equity may be similar for both firms when profitability, turnover, and leverage are considered together. A furniture store may turn over its inventory only twice a year; thus, it has to have large profit margins to compensate for its low turnover. Both firms may earn the same return for their stockholders when profitability, turnover, and leverage are taken together, and the DuPont system does just that by integrating them in one analysis.

COVERAGE RATIOS

In addition to the ratios previously covered in this chapter, the financial analyst may compute coverage ratios, which indicate the ability of the firm to service (to "cover") some payment, such as interest. All coverage ratios consider the funds available to meet a particular expense relative to that expense. The most common coverage ratio is **times-interest-earned,** which measures the ability of the firm to meet its interest obligations.[17] That ratio is

TIMES-INTEREST-EARNED
Ratio of operating income (EBIT) to interest expense; measure of the safety of a debt instrument

$$\text{Times-interest-earned} = \frac{\text{Earnings before interest and taxes}}{\text{Annual interest charges}}.$$

A ratio of 2 indicates that the firm has $2 in operating income for every $1 in interest expense. The numerator uses operating income (EBIT), since interest is paid after other expenses but before taxes. The higher the numerical value of the ratio, the safer should be the interest payment. For Pier 1, the times-interest-earned ratio is

$$\text{Times-interest-earned} = \frac{\$134{,}658}{\$5{,}048} = 26{,}676.$$

[17]Coverage ratios may also be used to analyze the safety of lease payments. See Chapter 21.

This indicates that for every dollar of interest expense, the firm has operating income in excess of $26,675!

Ability to cover interest expense is important, for failure to meet interest payments as they come due may throw the firm into bankruptcy. Deterioration in the times-interest-earned ratio gives an early warning to creditors and investors, as well as to management, of a deteriorating financial position and an increased probability of default on interest payments.

In the above form, the times-interest-earned ratio is an aggregate ratio that lumps together all interest payments. Some debt issues may be subordinated to the other debt issues and are paid only after the senior debt is paid. Thus, it is possible that the senior debt will be paid in full but that nothing remains to pay the interest on the subordinated debt. When this subordination exists, the times-interest-earned ratio may be altered to acknowledge it. For example, consider a firm with $1,000 in earnings before interest and taxes and with $10,000 in debt consisting of two issues. Issue A is $8,000 and carries an interest rate of 5 percent. Issue B is $2,000, carries an interest rate of 7 percent, and is subordinated to issue A. The subordination may explain why the second issue has the higher interest rate, for the creditor demands the higher rate in return for accepting the riskier debt issue.

The times-interest-earned ratio for each debt issue is computed as follows. The interest on issue A is $400 and on issue B is $140. For issue A there is $1,000 available to pay the $400 interest, and thus the coverage ratio is

$$\frac{\$1,000}{\$400} = 2.50.$$

For issue B there is $1,000 to cover the interest on A and B. Thus, for issue B the coverage ratio is

$$\frac{\$1,000}{\$400 + \$140} = 1.85$$

It would be misleading to suggest that the coverage for issue B is the amount available *after* issue A was paid. In such a case, that would indicate coverage of

$$\frac{\$600}{\$140} = 4.29.$$

This is clearly misleading. Issue B has the higher coverage ratio and appears to be safer than the senior debt. The proper way to adjust for subordination is to add the interest charges to the denominator and not subtract the interest paid the senior issue from the numerator. Interest payments for successive issues of subordinated debt are added to the denominator. Since the total amount of earnings available before taxes to pay the interest is spread over ever-increasing interest payments, the coverage ratio declines and hence gives a truer indication of the actual coverage of the subordinated debt.

AN APPLICATION OF RATIO ANALYSIS

The various ratios have been defined and illustrated using Pier 1 Imports' financial statement. The definitions and illustrations are summarized in Exhibit 12.7. The order of presentation is the same as in the body of the chapter.

An obvious question arises: What is the value of this information? A set of ratios by themselves has little meaning; there has to be some comparison. As was mentioned earlier in this chapter, one possible comparison is to compute the ratios over time to determine changes in the firm's financial position (that is, to use time-series analysis). Thus, the analyst would compute the ratios given in Exhibit 12.7 over a period such as five years to determine if the firm's performance or financial condition have changed.

An alternative approach employs competing or comparable firms (a cross-sectional analysis), but an immediate problem arises. Pier 1 Imports is North America's largest specialty retailer of decorative home furnishings. Over 50 percent of sales come from furniture and decorative accessories. Should the firm be compared with other specialty retailers, such as The Gap or dELiA's? Should Pier 1 Imports be compared to firms that sell housewares and textile products (for example, Bed, Bath and Beyond or Linens-n-Things), or should it be compared to furniture retailers, such as Heilig-Myers? There is no obvious or correct answer. Each analyst must come to a personal solution.

ANALYSIS OF FINANCIAL STATEMENTS AND THE INTERNET

If you do not want to calculate the ratios used in an analysis of a firm's financial statements, you can use the Internet.[18] Many of the basic ratios covered in this chapter are readily found on the Internet at no cost. Two possible complimentary sources are Yahoo! (**www.biz.yahoo.com**), which provides ratios calculated by Market Guide and Wall Street Research Net (**www.wsrn.com**), which gives ratios taken from Media General Financial Services. These sources do not necessarily give the same ratios, and the results may differ. These two points are illustrated in Exhibit 12.8, which provides selected financial ratios for Pier 1 Imports from each source.

Immediately it becomes apparent that the ratios available from the two sources differ. Also the values for the ratios may differ among the sources and with the values calculated in this chapter. Such differences could be the result of time periods used. For example, one source may use the firm's last fiscal year (or latest quarter) while an alternative source computes the ratios using the last 12 months.

[18]You may also compute ratios using the *Investment Analysis Calculator*. Go to the menu "Financial Statement Analysis," and follow the instructions.

EXHIBIT 12.7

Summary of Ratios and Their Application to Pier 1 Imports

Ratio			Calculation for Pier 1
I. Liquidity Ratios			
a. Current Ratio			
	(1)	$\frac{\text{Current assets}}{\text{Current liabilities}}$	$\frac{\$381{,}943}{\$129{,}832} = 2.94$
b. Quick Ratio	(2)	$\frac{\text{Current assets} - \text{Inventory}}{\text{Current liabilities}}$	$\frac{\$381{,}943 - 258{,}773}{\$129{,}832} = 0.95$
II. Activity Ratios			
a. Inventory Turnover			
	(3)	$\frac{\text{Sales}}{\text{Average inventory}}$	$\frac{\$1{,}138{,}590}{(\$258{,}773 + \$234{,}180)/2} = 4.6$
	or		
	(4)	$\frac{\text{Cost of goods sold}}{\text{Average inventory}}$	$\frac{\$638{,}173}{(258{,}773 + \$234{,}180)/2} = 2.6$
b. Receivables Turnover			
	(5)	$\frac{\text{Annual credit sales}}{\text{Accounts receivable}}$	$\frac{\text{Not given}}{\$9{,}060} = \text{N.A.}$
	or		
	(6)	$\frac{\text{Annual sales}}{\text{Accounts receivable}}$	$\frac{\$1{,}138{,}590}{\$9{,}060} = \text{N.M.F.}$
c. Average Collection Period (Days Sales Outstanding)			
	(7)	$\frac{\text{Receivables}}{\text{Sales per day}}$	N.M.F.
d. Fixed Asset Turnover			
	(8)	$\frac{\text{Sales}}{\text{Fixed assets}}$	$\frac{\$1{,}138{,}590}{\$226{,}262} = 5.03$
e. Total Asset Turnover			
	(9)	$\frac{\text{Sales}}{\text{Total assets}}$	$\frac{\$1{,}138{,}590}{\$653{,}991} = 1.74$
III. Profitability Ratios			
a. Gross Profit Margin			
	(10)	$\frac{\text{Revenues} - \text{Cost of goods sold}}{\text{Sales}}$	$\frac{\$500{,}417}{\$1{,}138{,}590} = 44.0\%$

Ratio		Calculation for Pier 1
b. Operating Profit Margin (11)	$\frac{\text{Earnings before interest and taxes}}{\text{Sales}}$	$\frac{\$134{,}658}{\$1{,}138{,}590} = 11.8\%$
c. Net Profit Margin (12)	$\frac{\text{Earnings after interest and taxes}}{\text{Sales}}$	$\frac{\$80{,}357}{\$1{,}138{,}590} = 7.1\%$
d. Return on Total Assets (13)	$\frac{\text{Earnings after interest and taxes}}{\text{Total assets}}$	$\frac{\$80{,}357}{\$653{,}991} = 12.3\%$
e. Return on Equity (14)	$\frac{\text{Earnings after interest and taxes}}{\text{Equity}}$	$\frac{\$80{,}357}{\$403{,}894} = 19.9\%$
f. Basic Earning Power (15)	$\frac{\text{Earnings before interest and taxes}}{\text{Total assets}}$	$\frac{\$134{,}658}{\$653{,}991} = 20.6\%$
IV. Leverage Ratios		
a. Debt/Net Worth Ratio (16)	$\frac{\text{Debt}}{\text{Equity}}$	$\frac{\$250{,}097}{\$403{,}894} = 61.9\%$
b. Debt Ratio (17)	$\frac{\text{Debt}}{\text{Total assets}}$	$\frac{\$250{,}097}{\$653{,}991} = 38.2\%$
V. Coverage Ratio		
Times-Interest-Earned (18)	$\frac{\text{Earnings before interest and taxes}}{\text{Annual interest expense}}$	$\frac{\$134{,}658}{\$5{,}048} = \text{N.M.F.}$

N.A. = Not Available

N.M.F. = No Meaningful Figure

EXHIBIT 12.8

Selected Ratios for Pier 1 Imports Using Internet Sources

	Yahoo!	Wall Street Research Net
Ratios		
Current ratio	3.0	—
Profit margin	6.2	6.2
Return on assets	11.1	11.1
Return on equity	18.3	17.3
Debt/equity ratios		
Debt/equity	—	0.21
Long-term debt/equity	0.2	—
Stock selection data		
Beta	0.81	—
Market capitalization	$688.9 million	—
Market/book value ratio	1.66	1.66
Price/earnings ratio	10.08	10.0
Price/sales ratio	0.65	0.59

Different definitions of a particular ratio could also explain the numerical differences (e.g., the return on equity could be earnings divided by total equity or earnings divided by common equity). Even if the definitions are the same, different data may be used in the calculation. For example, the net profit margin is earnings divided by sales. One source may use earnings that have not been adjusted for extraordinary items while another source may use adjusted earnings.

These differences pose a problem for anyone using ratio analysis to make comparisons. One obvious solution is for the individual to compute the ratios, in which case the definitions and time periods can be applied consistently. A more pragmatic solution may be to select one source and use it exclusively. The choice could depend on which source gives the desired ratios. For example, the Yahoo! source provided the current ratio and the beta, but Wall Street Research Net source provided neither. (The beta coefficient is discussed in Chapter 8.) The Wall Street Research Net source, however, included a comparison of the firm to its industry. In addition, information may appear in different files. For example, Yahoo! provides the stock's beta coefficient along with the ratios. Wall Street Research Net does provide a beta coefficient but in a different location, so the investor would have to know to search in a different file to locate the firm's beta coefficient.[19]

[19]To further confuse the issue, Wall Street Research Net also provides a link to Market Guide. If the beta is found through this link, Media General Financial Services did not compute the beta coefficient. Quicken (**www.quicken.com**) is an alternative to Yahoo! as a means to obtain ratios computed by Media General Financial Services. Some of the ratios reported by Quicken, however, are different than the ratios than found through Wall Street Research Net. These problems may be avoided by subscribing to a one source, which provides more information than is available through complimentary sources. Two possible subscription services are Thomson Investors Network (**www.thomsoninvest.net**) and Media General Financial Services (**www.mgfs.com**).

Netscape and Locating Information on Pier 1 Imports

Netscape has a relatively easy process for obtaining general information concerning investing or on a particular company, such as Pier 1 Imports. Start at the Netscape Netcenter (www.netscape.com) and click on "Personal Finance." The section on Personal Finance has links to many investing and financial topics, such as mortgage loans and insurance, as well as links to a specific firm. It is a useful means to obtain general financial information. ¶ If you are on the Personal Finance page and want information on a specific firm, enter the ticker symbol, such as PIR for Pier 1 Imports. This takes you to the "Quote" page for current price information on the stock. (You can avoid going through the Personal Finance section by entering the ticker symbol on the home page.) From the Quote page, you have several choices for additional information concerning PIR. "News" provides current headlines, if any are available. "Charts" shows price movements in the stock for the prior 12 months. "Profile" gives basic financial information, such as earnings, market capitalization, the existence of a dividend reinvestment plan, and ratios, such as price/earnings, price/sales, and price/book. "Financials" gives PIR's income statement and balance sheet and some additional ratios, such as debt/equity and return on equity. "Analysis" and "Insiders" provide earnings estimates and insider transactions and purchases and sales by mutual funds. "SEC Filings" gives a chronological listing on the firm's filings (for example, 10K forms) with the SEC. ¶ Although the preceding process is a means to obtain information and data concerning a company, you will have to process what you find into a useful form. This process provides information on only one firm, and you will have to repeat the process if you wish to compare firms. If you have access to a database, you should be able to compare firms more readily, but databases are generally available only through subscription. The process described here is a means to obtain a considerable amount of complimentary information and data on specific stocks. ¶

SUMMARY

This chapter covered three essential financial statements. A balance sheet enumerates at a point in time what a firm owns (its assets), what it owes (its liabilities), and what owners have invested in a firm (its equity). An income statement enumerates a firm's revenues and expenses over a period of time and determines if a firm operated at a profit or for a loss. The statement of cash flows enumerates the flow of cash into and out of a firm over a period of time.

Ratio analysis provides a convenient method to analyze a firm's financial statements, for the ratios are easily computed and readily permit comparisons. Since publicly held corporations must give financial information to stockholders, ratio analysis may be employed not only by management and creditors but also by stockholders.

Liquidity ratios measure the capacity of the firm to meet its current obligations as they come due. Activity ratios indicate how rapidly assets flow through the firm and how many assets are used to generate sales. Profitability ratios measure performance; leverage ratios indicate the use of debt financing; coverage ratios measure the capacity of the firm to make certain payments, such as interest. Once the ratios have been computed, the results may be compared over a series of years or compared with other firms within the industry. Such comparisons should help the analyst perceive the firm's position within the industry, as well as trends that are developing.

Review Questions

1. Specify which of the following are assets and which are liabilities:
   a. cash
   b. retained earnings
   c. equipment
   d. accounts payable
   e. accrued taxes owed
   f. additional paid-in capital

2. Specify the time period covered by a balance sheet, by an income statement, and by a statement of cash flows.

3. Why may the market value of an asset be different from its book value?

4. Are a firm's profits equal to its cash? What may a corporation do with its earnings? Can retained earnings be negative?

5. Which of the following generate a cash inflow and which a cash outflow?
a. an increase in inventory
b. an increase in accounts payable
c. a decrease in accounts receivable
d. a reduction in long-term debt
e. an increase in equipment
f. an increase in stock

6. Company A sells appliances, and its current ratio recently rose. Can you conclude that the firm's liquidity also rose? Why other test of liquidity would you suggest? If this firm increased its inventory near the end of its fiscal year, why may the inventory turnover be a poor measure of activity?

7. If a firm's current ratio exceeds 1:1, what is the impact on the current ratio and quick ratio if:
a. it buys inventory for cash?
b. it buys inventory on credit?

In which case does the firm appear to be more liquid? What is the source of funds used in a and b to finance the acquisition of the inventory?

8. Why is the times-interest-earned ratio important for an investor in debt but not equity?

9. What are the differences among the gross profit margin, the operating profit margin, and the net profit margin? Why may it be desirable to compute all three ratios?

10. If a firm's profitability improves, does that imply that its liquidity also improved?

11. Obtain Pier 1 Imports' (**www.Pier1.com**) most recent financial statements and update Exhibit 12.7. Have there been any changes in the firm's financial position as indicated by the ratios?

12. Use an Internet source such as Market Guide Inc (**www.marketguide.com**) and compare the profitability and leverage ratios for the following retail firms:

dELiA's

Gap, Inc.

Lands' End

The Limited, Inc.

Rank the firms on the basis of (a) use of debt financing, (b) profitability, and (c) valuation based on P/E and price/sales ratios.

PROBLEMS

1. Find the following information, construct a simple income statement and a balance sheet:

Sales	$1,000,000
Finished goods	200,000
Long-term debt	300,000
Raw materials	100,000
Cash	50,000
Cost of goods sold	600,000
Accounts receivable	250,000
Plant and equipment	400,000
Interest expense	80,000
Number of shares outstanding	100,000
Earnings before taxes	220,000
Taxes	100,000
Accounts payable	200,000
Other current liabilities	50,000
Other expenses	100,000
Equity	450,000

2. Given the following information, determine the per share earnings of the common stock:

Earnings before interest and taxes	$100,000
Debt outstanding	$300,000
Income tax rate	30%
Interest rate on debt	12%
Preferred stock dividends	$20,000
Number of common shares outstanding	10,000

3. Given the following information, construct the firm's balance sheet:

Cash and cash equivalents	$ 300,000
Accumulated depreciation on plant and equipment	800,000
Plant and equipment	5,800,000
Accrued wages	400,000
Long-term debt	4,200,000
Inventory	6,400,000
Accounts receivable	4,100,000
Preferred stock	500,000
Retained earnings	7,700,000
Land	1,000,000

Accounts payable	2,100,000
Taxes due	100,000
Common stock	$ 10 par
Common shares outstanding	150,000
Current portion of long-term debt	$ 300,000

4. Fill in the blanks (______) with the correct entries.

ASSETS		LIABILITIES AND STOCKHOLDERS' EQUITY	
Current assets		Current liabilities	
Cash	$ 250,000	Accounts payable	$ 620,000
Accounts receivable (______ less) allowance for doubtful accounts of $20,000)	1,320,000	Notes payable to banks	130,000
Inventory	1,410,000	Accrued wages	______
Total current assets	______	Taxes owed	100,000
Land	______	Total current liabilities	$1,250,000
Plant and equipment ($2,800,000 less accumulated depreciation ______)	2,110,000	Long-term debt	______
Total assets	$5,390,000	Stockholders' equity	
		Preferred stock	1,000,000
		Common stock ($1 par, 750,000 shares authorized, 700,000 outstanding)	______
		Retained earnings	______
		Total common stockholders' equity	$3,140,000
		Total liabilities and equity	______

5. Given the following information, compute the current and quick ratios:

Cash	$100,000
Accounts receivable	357,000
Inventory	458,000
Current liabilities	498,000
Long-term debt	610,000
Equity	598,000

6. Sean's Boats has a net profit margin of 13 percent and a total asset turnover of 2.0.

a. What is the return on assets?

b. If the company has no debt, what is the return on equity?

7. Specific information concerning a profitable company follows:

Net income	$250,000
Debt ratio (debt/total assets)	45%
Return on assets	23%
Net profit margin	15%

With this information, find the following:
a. sales
b. total assets
c. total asset turnover
d. total debt
e. return on equity

8. If a firm has sales of $25,689,000 a year, and the average collection period for the industry is 45 days, what should this firm's accounts receivable be if the firm is comparable to the industry?
9. ABCD Corp. has credit sales of $10,640,000 and receivables of $1,520,000.
a. What is the receivables turnover?
b. What is the average collection period (days sales outstanding)?
c. If the company offers credit terms of 30 days, are its receivables past due?
10. A firm with sales of $500,000 has average inventory of $200,000. The industry average for inventory turnover is four times a year. What would be the reduction in inventory if this firm were to achieve a turnover comparable to the industry average?
11. A firm with annual sales of $8,700,000 increases its inventory turnover from 4.5 to 6.0. How much would the company save annually in interest expense if the cost of carrying the inventory is 10 percent?
12. Wendy's Wings has a debt ratio of 0.6 and total debt of $175,000. If the company has net income of $45,000, what is the return on assets and the return on equity?
13. Two firms have sales of $1 million each. Other financial information is as follows:

FIRM	A	B
EBIT	$150,000	$150,000
Interest expense	20,000	75,000
Income tax	50,000	30,000
Debt	400,000	700,000
Equity	600,000	300,000

What are the operating profit margins and the net profit margins for these two firms? What are their returns on assets and on equity? Why are they different?

14. If a firm has the following sources of finance,

Current liabilities	$100,000
Long-term debt	350,000
Preferred stock	75,000
Common stock	225,000

earns a profit of $35,000 after taxes, and pays $7,500 in preferred stock dividends, what is the return on assets, the return on total equity, and the return on common equity?

15. Company A has three debt issues of $3,000 each. The interest rate of issue A is 4 percent, on B the rate is 6 percent, and on C the rate is 8 percent. Issue B is subordinate to A, and issue C is subordinate to both A and B. The firm's operating income is $400. Compute the times-interest-earned for issue C. Does the answer mean that the interest will not be paid?

16. If a firm has revenues of $1,220,000 in 20X1, what is the difference in its inventory turnover ratio if the financial analyst uses 20X1 year-end data instead of using average inventory? The firm's inventory was $300,000 in 20X0 and $450,000 in 20X1.

17. You prefer to extend credit on the assumption that you will be paid in full within 30 days of the sales. Firm X has average inventory of $600,000 with all cash sales (no credit sales) of $6,000,000. If you extend credit to this firm, can you expect to be paid on time?

18. Perform a ratio analysis for the years 20X1 and 20X0 using the following financial statements, and answer the subsequent questions.

Firm X Balance Sheet as of 12/31/XX

	20X1	20X0
Assets		
Current Assets		
Cash and cash equivalents	$ 953	$ 631
Accounts receivable	201	59
Inventory	5,824	4,655
Total current assets	$ 6,978	$5,345
Property and equipment	4,635	1,114
Total Assets	$11,613	$6,459
Liabilities		
Current Liabilities		
Accounts payable	$783	$ 685
Accrued expenses	490	496
Rentals owed	241	97
Taxes due	86	84
Total current liabilities	$ 1,600	$1,362
Long-term debt	3,054	564
Total Liabilities	$ 4,654	$1,926
Equity	6,959	4,533
Total Liabilities and Equity	$11,613	$6,459

Income Statement for the Fiscal Year Ended:	12/31/X1	12/31/X0
Sales	$23,117	$18,428
Cost of goods sold	13,174	10,630
Gross profit	9,943	7,798
Selling and administrative expenses	7,460	5,976
Earnings before interest and taxes	2,483	1,822
Interest	317	177
Taxes	1,029	698
Net income	$ 1,137	$ 947

a. Given the following industry averages, are any weaknesses revealed in the ratio analysis?

Current ratio	4:1
Quick ratio	0.4:1
Average collection period	3 days
Inventory turnover	5×
Operating profit margin	11%
Net profit margin	3.5%
Return on assets	10%
Return on equity	22%
Debt ratio	50%
Times-interest-earned	5×

b. What kind of operation would have this firm's average collection period?
c. Why might the firm's operating profit margin be comparable to the industry but the net profit margin exceed the industry average?
d. What is the amount of annual change in the firm's equity from 20X0 to 20X1? Do the firm's earnings account for this change? What must have occurred during the fiscal year?
e. What general operating and financial decisions does management appear to have made and executed during the fiscal year?

CASE

USING RATIO ANALYSIS TO DETERMINE THE SAFETY OF A LOAN

Joseph Berio is a loan officer with the First Bank of Tennessee. Red Brick, Incorporated, a major producer of masonry products, has applied for a short-term loan. Red Brick supplies building material throughout the southern states, with brick plants located in Tennessee, Alabama, Georgia, and Indiana.

Mr. Berio knows that brick production is affected by two factors: the cost of energy and the state of the building industry. First, manufacturing bricks uses a significant amount of energy. Red Brick, Inc. has recently converted many

EXHIBIT 1

Income Statement and Balance Sheet for Red Brick

RED BRICK INCOME STATEMENT (for the period ending December 31, 2000)	
Sales	$210,000,000
Cost of goods sold	170,000,000
Administrative expenses	26,000,000
Operating income	$ 14,000,000
Interest expense	13,000,000
Taxes	400,000
Net income	$ 600,000

RED BRICK BALANCE SHEET AS OF 12/31/2000			
ASSETS		**LIABILITIES AND STOCKHOLDERS' EQUITY**	
Cash	$ 600,000	Accounts payable	$ 39,000,000
Accounts receivable	33,000,000*	Notes payable	11,000,000
Inventory	75,400,000†	Long-term debt	45,000,000
Plant and equipment	132,000,000	Stockholders' equity	146,000,000
	$241,000,000		$241,000,000

**90% of sales are on credit.*

†Previous year's inventory was $52,000,000.

oil-fired kilns to coal kilns, which are cheaper to operate. To finance these conversions, the company has recently issued a substantial amount of long-term debt that must be retired over the next 25 years.

Second, brick sales are very sensitive to activity in the building industry, especially new housing starts. The industry frequently follows a pattern of boom and bust, with sales and earnings responding to changes in the demand for building products.

Currently the economy is experiencing a severe recession, and housing starts have fallen more than 40 percent from the previous year. While the south and southwest have not experienced such a severe decline, housing starts there have declined 25 percent.

Red Brick, Inc. has not been immune to the economic environment. Sales have declined, and although the firm has reduced production, inventory has increased. The firm needs the short-term loan to finance its inventory. Mr. Berio must decide whether to grant or deny the loan. Such loans have been made to Red Brick in the past and have always been repaid when the economic picture improved.

EXHIBIT 2

Selected Ratios for Red Brick and Industry Averages

	Company's Ratios (Previous Year)	Industry Average
Current ratio	4:1	2.2:1
Quick ratio	2:1	0.8:1
Inventory turnover	4.7×	4.6×
Average collection period	39 days	49 days
Debt ratio (debt/total assets)	39%	30%
Times-interest-earned	4.1	3.7
Return on equity	13.8%	14.1%
Return on assets	8.2%	10.2%
Operating profit margin	14.1%	15.2%
Net profit margin	8.8%	8.8%

The firm's income statement and balance sheet are given in Exhibit 1. Exhibit 2 presents both a ratio analysis of Red Brick's previous year's financial statements and the industry averages of the ratios.

To help decide whether to grant the loan, Mr. Berio computes several ratios and compares the results with the ratios given in Exhibit 2.

CASE PROBLEMS

1. What strengths and weaknesses are indicated by this analysis?
2. What may explain why the debt ratio exceeds the industry average? Is that necessarily a weakness in this case?
3. As a banker, is Mr. Berio more concerned with the firm's liquidity or its return on equity?
4. Based on the above analysis, should Mr. Berio grant the loan? Justify your position.

CHAPTER 13

Derivatives

Learning Objectives

1. Describe the features of a call option, a put option, a futures, a contract, a convertible bond, and a convertible preferred stock.
2. Contrast the use of margin in the futures market with its use in the stock market, and explain how options are an alternative to buying stock on margin.
3. Contrast long and short positions in futures with buying and writing options.
4. Explain how individuals earn profits and sustain losses in the markets for futures, options, and convertible securities.
5. Explain how investors and financial managers use options and futures to reduce the risk of loss from fluctuations in prices.
6. Determine the value of a convertible bond in terms of stock and in terms of debt and how these values affect the price of the bond.
7. List the factors that affect the price of a call and a convertible bond, and differentiate the premiums paid for a convertible bond from the time premium paid for an option.
8. Contrast and compare the advantages and risks associated with the securities covered in this chapter.

Bernard Baruch pointed out a fundamental fact concerning free markets: "Markets will fluctuate." That certainly applies to derivatives. The price of an option to buy the stock of NCR traded for $375 on Friday and $2,687.50 the following Monday after it was announced that the company would be sold to AT&T. That's an increase of 500 percent over the weekend!

Investing in derivatives can also generate large losses, and such financial disasters are reported in the financial and popular press. Although such publicity may reduce public confidence in securities in general and derivatives in particular, the importance of these financial assets is not reduced. A basic knowledge of derivatives can only help you better understand investment strategies and risk management.

As the name implies, a derivative is an asset whose value or price depends upon (is derived from) another asset. This chapter considers several derivatives: options to buy or sell stock, future contracts (commonly called "futures") for the purchase or sale of an asset, and convertible bonds and convertible preferred stock.

In each case the value of the financial asset is tied to the value of the underlying asset and, hence, is an illustration of a derivative.

Derivatives can be extremely sophisticated investments, and only the barest of fundamentals can be covered here. The chapter describes these securities, the mechanics of establishing positions, the role of margin, long and short positions, the relationship between the prices of the derivative and its underlying asset, and how these securities may be used to reduce risk. This is a long chapter, but each section is self-contained. Thus, you may cover the material on options without having to read the material on convertible bonds. And the converse is also true: You may cover convertible bonds without reading the material on options.

WARRANT
Option (issued by a corporation) to buy stock at a specified price within the specified time period

CALL
Option (issued by an individual) to buy stock at a specified price within a specified time period

PUT
Option to sell stock at a specified price within a specified time period

PREMIUM
Market price of an option

STRIKE PRICE/ EXERCISE PRICE
Price at which the option holder may buy the underlying stock

EXPIRATION DATE
Date by which an option must be exercised

INTRINSIC VALUE
Value of an option as stock

OPTIONS

An option is the right to do something. When the term *option* is used with regard to securities, it means the right to buy or sell stock. The word *right* is extremely important: the owner of an option is *not obligated* to do anything. The holder of an option to buy stock does not have to buy the stock, nor does the holder of a right to sell stock have to sell the stock. This makes options different from futures contracts, discussed later in this chapter. The individual who acquires a futures contract to buy must either close the position or meet the obligation.

The rights to buy and sell stock are not the only options in finance. For example, many bonds are callable. Such a call feature is an example of an option because the firm has the right to call the bonds and retire them prior to maturity. Many business transactions involve options. For example, a landowner may sell to a developer an option to buy the land. The developer does not have to buy the land but has the right to purchase it.

Options to buy stock are called **warrants** if they are issued by firms and **calls** if they are issued by individuals.[1] A warrant or a call is the right to buy stock at a specified price within a specified time period. Options to sell stock are called **puts.** A put is the right to sell stock at a specified price within a specified time period. In the jargon of option trading, the market price of the option is often referred to as the **premium.** The price at which the holder may buy or sell the shares is called the **strike price** or **exercise price,** and the day on which the option expires is called the **expiration date.**

THE INTRINSIC VALUE OF AN OPTION TO BUY STOCK

What a warrant or call is worth in terms of the underlying stock is the **intrinsic value** of the option. For an option to buy stock, this intrinsic value is the difference

[1]A firm may also issue an option called a "right." Rights are issued to current stockholders when the firm is offering them the privilege of subscribing to a new issue of stock. By exercising the right and buying the new shares, current stockholders maintain their proportionate ownership in the corporation. Rights have a very short duration, such as four weeks, while a warrant may exist for many years.

EXHIBIT 13.1

The Price of a Stock and the Intrinsic Value of an Option to Buy the Stock at $50 per Share

Price of the Stock	Per Share Strike Price of the Option	Intrinsic Value of the Option
$ 0	$50	$ 0
10	50	0
20	50	0
30	50	0
40	50	0
50	50	0
60	50	10
70	50	20
80	50	30
90	50	40

between the price of the stock and the per share exercise price (strike price) of the option. If an option is the right to buy stock at $30 a share and the stock is selling for $40, then the intrinsic value is $10 ($40 − $30 = $10).

If the stock is selling for a price greater than the strike price, the option to buy has positive intrinsic value. This may be referred to as the option's being "in the money." If the common stock is selling for a price that equals the strike price, the option is "at the money." And if the price of the stock is less than the strike price, the option to buy the stock has no intrinsic value. The option is "out of the money." No one would purchase and exercise an option to buy stock for $50 when the stock could be purchased for a price that is less than the strike price of the option (for example, $40).

The relationships among the price of a stock, the strike price (the exercise price of an option), and the option's intrinsic value are illustrated in Exhibit 13.1 and Figure 13.1. In these examples, the option is the right to buy the stock at $50 per share. The first column of the exhibit (the horizontal axis on the graph) gives various prices of the stock. The second column presents the strike price of the option ($50), and the last column gives the intrinsic value of the option (the difference between the values in the first and second columns). The values in this third column are illustrated in the figure by line ABC, which shows the relationship between the price of the stock and the option's intrinsic value. It is evident from both the exhibit and the figure that as the price of the stock rises, the intrinsic value of the option also rises. However, for all stock prices below $50, the intrinsic value is zero, since security prices are never negative. Only after the stock's price has risen above $50 does the option's intrinsic value become positive.

The intrinsic value is important because the market price of an option must approach its intrinsic value as the option approaches its expiration date. On the day that the option is to expire, the market price can be only what the option is worth as stock. It can be worth only the difference between the market price of the stock and the exercise price of the option. This fact means that the investor

FIGURE 13.1

Relationship between the Price of a Stock and the Intrinsic Value of an Option to Buy the Stock at $50 per Share

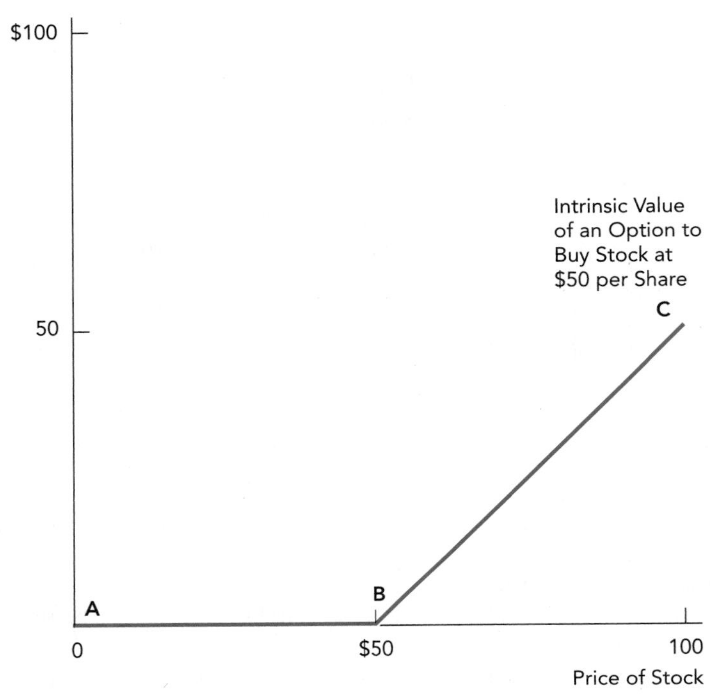

may use the intrinsic value of an option as an indication of the option's future price, for the investor knows that the market price of the option must approach its intrinsic value as the option approaches expiration.

The intrinsic value also sets the minimum price that the option will command.[2] Suppose the price of a stock is $60 and the strike price of the option is $50. The option's intrinsic value is $10 ($60 − $50). If the current market price of the option were $6, an investor could buy the option and exercise it to acquire stock worth $60. The investor could then sell the stock and make a $4 profit.

The act of buying the option and selling the stock will tend to increase the price of the option and decrease the price of the stock. However, as long as the option sells for less than its intrinsic value, investors will buy the option and sell the stock; thus the price of the option rises while the price of the stock declines. Such price changes continue until the option sells for at least its intrinsic value. The intrinsic value thus sets the minimum price that an option will command, for as soon

[2]To be more precise, the minimum value of the option cannot be less than the difference between the price of the stock and the *present value* of the strike price. Unless the interest rate is zero or the option is at expiration, this difference must exceed the option's intrinsic value.

as an option sells for less than its intrinsic value, forces will be set in motion to assure that the option's market price returns to the option's intrinsic value.

LEVERAGE

Although an option is a "right," it represents none of the legal rights of ownership. An option does, however, offer investors one important advantage: leverage. The potential return on an investment in an option may exceed the potential return on an investment in the underlying stock. Like the use of margin, this magnification of the potential return is an example of financial leverage.

Exhibit 13.1, which illustrates the relationship between the price of a stock and an option's intrinsic value, also demonstrates the potential leverage that options offer. For example, if the price of the stock rose from \$60 to \$70, the intrinsic value of the option would rise from \$10 to \$20. The percentage increase in the price of the stock is 16.67 percent ([\$70 − \$60] ÷ \$60), whereas the percentage increase in the intrinsic value of the option is 100 percent ([\$20 − \$10] ÷ \$10). The percentage increase in the intrinsic value of the option exceeds the percentage increase in the price of the stock. If the investor purchased the option for its intrinsic value and the price of the stock then rose, the return on the investment in the option would exceed the return on the investment in the stock.

Leverage, however, works in both directions. Although it may increase the investor's potential return, it may also increase the potential loss if the price of the stock declines. For example, if the price of the stock in Exhibit 13.1 fell from \$70 to \$60 for a 14.3 percent decline, the intrinsic value of the option would fall from \$20 to \$10 for a 50 percent decline. As with any investment, the investor must decide if the increase in the potential return offered by leverage is worth the increased risk.

If an option offers a greater potential return than does the stock, investors may prefer to buy the option. In an effort to purchase the option, investors bid up its price, so the market price exceeds the option's intrinsic value. Since the market price of an option is referred to as the premium, the extent to which this price exceeds the option's intrinsic value is referred to as the **time premium** or time value. Investors are willing to pay this time premium for the potential leverage the option offers. This time premium, however, reduces the potential return and increases the potential loss.

TIME PREMIUM
Amount by which an option's price exceeds its intrinsic value

The time premium is illustrated in Exhibit 13.2, which adds to Exhibit 13.1 a hypothetical set of option prices in column 4. The hypothetical market prices are greater than the intrinsic values of the option because investors have bid up the prices. To purchase the option, an investor must pay the market price and not the intrinsic value. Thus, in this example when the market price of the stock is \$60 and the intrinsic value of the option is \$10, the market price of the option is \$15. The investor must pay \$15 to purchase the option, which is \$5 more than the option's intrinsic value.

The relationships in Exhibit 13.2 among the price of the stock, the intrinsic value of the option, and the hypothetical price of the option are illustrated in Figure 13.2. The time premium paid for the option is easily seen in the graph, for it

EXHIBIT 13.2

Relationships among the Price of Stock, the Intrinsic Value of the Option, and the Hypothetical Market Price of the Option

	OPTION		
Price of the Common Stock	Per Share Strike Price	Intrinsic Value	Hypothetical Market Price
$ 10	$50	$ 0	$ 0
20	50	0	¼
30	50	0	½
40	50	0	1¼
50	50	0	6¾
60	50	10	15
70	50	20	23
80	50	30	32⅝
90	50	40	41¼
100	50	50	50

is the shaded area that is the difference between the line representing the market price of the option (line DE) and the line representing its intrinsic value (line ABC). Thus, when the prices of the stock and option are $60 and $15, respectively, the time premium is $5 [the price of the option ($15) minus its intrinsic value ($10)].

As may be seen in the figure, the amount of the time value varies at the different price levels of the stock. The time premium declines as the price of the stock rises above the option's strike price. Once the price of the stock has risen, the option may command virtually no time premium. At $100 per share, the option is selling at approximately its intrinsic value of $50. The primary reason for this decline in the time premium is that as the price of the stock and the intrinsic value of the option rise, the potential leverage is reduced. In addition, at higher prices the potential price decline in the option is greater if the price of the stock falls. For these reasons investors are less willing to bid up the price of the option as the price of the stock rises, and, hence, the amount of the time premium diminishes.

The time premium decreases the potential leverage and return from investing in options. If, for example, this stock's price rose from $60 to $70 for a 16.7 percent gain, the option's price would rise from $15 to $23 for a 53.3 percent gain. The percentage increase in the price of the option still exceeds the percentage increase in the price of the stock; however, the difference between the two percentage increases is smaller. The time premium has reduced the potential leverage that the option offers investors.

Several factors affect an option's time premium. As an option approaches expiration, its market price must approach the option's intrinsic value. On the expiration date, the option cannot command a price greater than its intrinsic value based on the underlying stock. Thus, as an option nears expiration, it will sell for a lower time premium, and that premium disappears at the option's expiration.

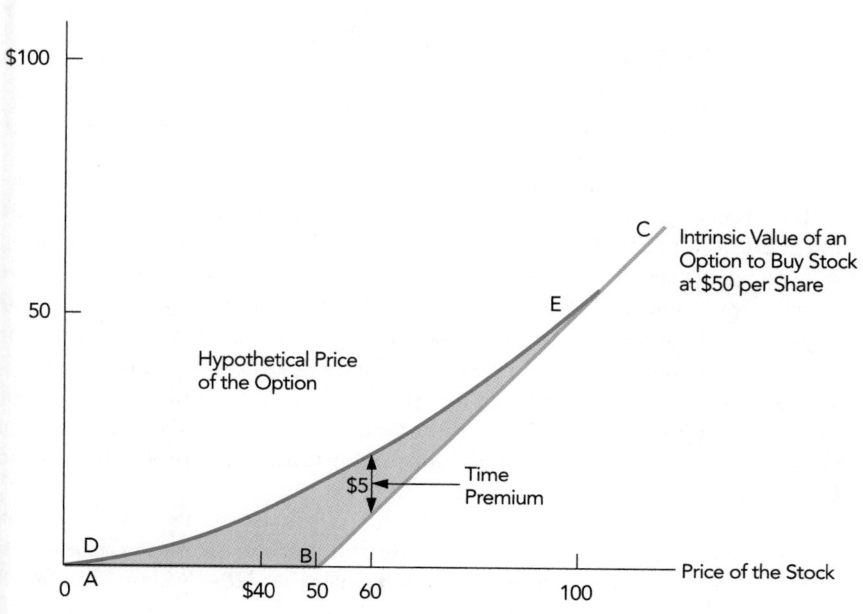

FIGURE 13.2

Relationships among the Price of the Stock, the Intrinsic Value of the Option, and the Hypothetical Price of the Option

Other determinants of an option's time premium include the payment of cash dividends, the volatility of the underlying stock, and interest rates. Options of companies that pay cash dividends tend to sell for lower time premiums. There may be two possible explanations for this relationship. First, companies that retain (do not distribute) earnings have more funds available for investments. By retaining and reinvesting earnings, a company may grow more rapidly, and the potential gain in the price of the option may be greater if the firm retains its earnings and does not pay a cash dividend. Second, if a company pays a dividend, the owner of the option does not receive the cash payment. Since the owner of the option must forgo the dividend, investors will not be willing to pay as much for the option, and it will sell for a lower time premium.

Another factor that affects the time premium paid for an option is the price volatility of the common stock. Since the price of the option follows the price of the underlying stock, fluctuations in the price of the stock will be reflected in the option's price. The more volatile the price of the stock, the more opportunity the option offers for a price increase. Thus, options on volatile stocks tend to be more attractive and command a higher time premium than options on stocks whose prices are more stable and less volatile.

Interest rates affect options by their impact on the present value of the funds necessary to exercise the option. Since options are exercised in the future, higher interest rates imply that the investor must set aside a smaller amount of money to exercise the option. Since an option's intrinsic value is the price of the stock minus the strike price, a lower strike must increase the value of the option. In effect, higher interest rates reduce the present value of the strike price, which makes the option more valuable and increases the time premium.[3]

CALL OPTIONS

While the preceding discussion covered options to buy stock in general, the next section is devoted to specific options known as calls and warrants. A call option is the right to buy a specified number of shares (usually 100) at a specified price (the strike price) within a specified time period. Calls are similar to warrants, but they have several distinguishing features. Warrants are issued by firms, but investors issue call options. The process of creating and issuing a call is often referred to as *writing*. The ability of the individual investor to write call options is very important, for it means the investor can be either a buyer *or* a seller. Because calls enable individuals to write options, they offer opportunities for profit that are not available with warrants.

A second distinction between warrants and calls is the duration of the option. When warrants are issued, their expiration is fixed, but the expiration date is generally several years into the future. Call options have a relatively short duration—three, six, or nine months. (A limited number of call options with lives up to two years, called LEAPS for Long-term Equity Anticipation Securities, are also traded.)

CHICAGO BOARD OPTIONS EXCHANGE (CBOE)
First secondary market in put and call options

The third distinguishing feature of calls occurs when they are exercised. When a warrant is exercised, the firm issues new stock. The writer of a call, however, cannot create the stock but must either purchase it on the open market or surrender the stock from personal holdings. When the stock is supplied to the investor who is exercising the call, the option writer, and not the firm, receives the proceeds. The development of the **Chicago Board Options Exchange (CBOE)** has been the primary reason why calls have replaced warrants in popularity. The CBOE is an organized secondary market in put and call options. An investor who purchases a call through the CBOE knows that a ready market exists in which the option may be sold.

There are several features of the CBOE that are conducive to the development of secondary markets for the calls. First, transactions are continuously reported, and summaries of transactions appear in daily newspapers. Exhibit 13.3 presents a clipping of selected calls and puts traded on various exchanges as reported in *The Wall Street Journal*. As may be seen in the exhibit, several options are traded on each stock. The company, such as Amazon.com, is listed first,

[3]The process of option valuation, such as the Black-Scholes option pricing model, and the use of options in various portfolio strategies are complex topics that are discussed in texts devoted exclusively to derivative securities. See, for example, Don Chance, *An Introduction to Derivatives* 4th ed. (Fort Worth, TX: The Dryden Press, 1998.) For a more pragmatic approach to options, consult Lawrence G. McMillan. *Options as a Strategic Investment* 3rd ed. (New York: New York Institute of Finance, 1993.)

Listing of Selected Options Traded on the CBOE

EXHIBIT 13.3

LISTED OPTIONS QUOTATIONS

Tuesday, January 4, 2000

Composite volume and close for actively traded equity and LEAPS, or long-term options, with results for the corresponding put or call contract. Volume figures are unofficial. Open interest is total outstanding for all exchanges and reflects previous trading day. Close when possible is shown for the underlying stock on primary market. **CB**-Chicago Board Options Exchange. **AM**-American Stock Exchange. **PB**-Philadelphia Stock Exchange. **PC**-Pacific Stock Exchange. **NY**-New York Stock Exchange. **XC**-Composite. **p**-Put.

MOST ACTIVE CONTRACTS

Option/Strike	Vol	Exch	Last	Net Chg	a-Close	Open Int
Micsft Jan 100	p 14,001	XC	3/4	+ 1/4	112 5/8	109,572
AmOnline Jan 80	13,524	XC	4 1/2	− 2 7/8	77 1/4	211,536
Disney Jan 27 1/2	13,413	XC	4 1/8	+ 1 9/16	31 3/4	95,848
Micsft Jan 90	p 10,498	XC	1/4	+ 1/16	112 5/8	140,712
Intel Jan 70	p 9,829	XC	11/16	+ 5/16	82 15/16	158,564
DellCptr Jan 45	p 9,223	XC	1 1/2	+ 7/8	46 5/8	81,720
Compaq Jan 30	8,727	XC	1 1/8	− 15/16	28 5/8	256,144
Intel Jan 90	7,726	XC	1 5/8	− 1	82 15/16	148,840
Disney Feb 30	7,047	XC	2 7/8	+ 1 1/8	31 3/4	4,152
Intel Jan 80	6,763	XC	5 5/8	− 3	82 15/16	169,968
AmOnline Jan 90	6,697	XC	1 15/16	− 1 7/16	77 1/4	211,516
Cisco Jan 90	p 6,595	XC	1	+ 1/2	102	53,396
Yahoo Jan 450	6,564	XC	49	− 14 7/8	443	27,424
Intel Jan 85	6,376	XC	3 1/4	− 1 7/8	82 15/16	148,724
Bk of Am Jan 47 1/2	6,230	XC	1 7/16	− 1 1/4	45 9/16	16,968
Qualcom Jan 77 1/2	p 6,049	XC	1/16	...	162 1/16	31,856
AmOnline Jan 100	6,028	XC	1	− 1/2	77 1/4	261,988
Yahoo Jan 02 135	p 6,002	XC	6 1/8	− 1	443	160
Disney Jan 30	p 5,789	XC	1/2	− 5/8	31 3/4	32,984
DellCptr Jan 50	5,475	XC	1	− 1 7/8	46 5/8	187,664

Option/Strike	Vol	Exch	Last	Net Chg	a-Close	Open Int
CMGI Inc Jan 320	5,244	XC	22	− 17	293 3/4	16,305
Micsft Jan 125	5,205	XC	3/4	− 1/2	112 5/8	65,676
CBS Cp Feb 60	5,020	XC	2 1/16	− 2 1/16	56 5/8	2,211
DellCptr Feb 45	p 4,926	XC	2 13/16	+ 1 1/16	46 5/8	46,540
AmOnline Jan 85	4,624	XC	2 7/8	− 2 1/8	77 1/4	187,732
Disney Jan 30	4,559	XC	2	+ 1	31 3/4	100,672
Atl R Feb 85	4,500	XC	4 3/4	− 2 1/4	80 7/8	740
Cmpuwr Jan 30	4,386	XC	6 1/4	− 3/4	35	15,858
MCI Wrld Jan 46 5/8	p 4,358	XC	1 3/8	+ 5/8	80	49,432
GMagic Feb 5	4,258	XC	1 15/16	+ 1 5/16	5 3/4	156,147
Compaq Apr 20	4,230	XC	9 3/4	− 1	28 5/8	52,660
Caterp Aug 50	4,154	XC	6	+ 1	48	240
Compaq Feb 30	4,121	XC	2 1/8	− 7/8	28 5/8	34,532
Compaq Feb 35	4,115	XC	7/8	− 7/16	28 5/8	11,312
Intel Jan 95	4,108	XC	5/8	− 9/16	82 15/16	70,272
Citigrp Jan 55	4,071	XC	9/16	− 1/2	50 5/8	87,340
Micsft Jan 120	4,037	XC	1 5/8	− 1 3/8	112 5/8	143,600
Intel Jan 85	p 4,026	XC	5	+ 2	82 15/16	53,596
DellCptr Jan 55	3,994	XC	5/16	− 3/4	46 5/8	133,160
Micsft Jan 110	3,917	XC	5 5/8	− 2 3/8	112 5/8	157,088

Complete equity option listings and data are available in The Wall Street Journal Interactive Edition at **http://wsj.com** on the Internet's World Wide Web.

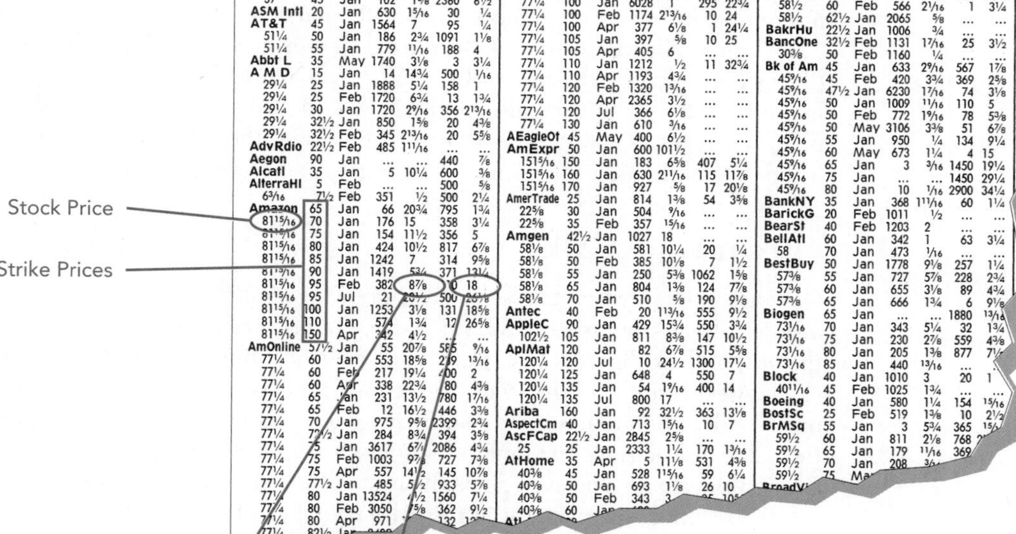

Option/Strike		Exp.	Call Vol.	Call Last	Put Vol.	Put Last
ACTV	35	Jan	186	5 3/8	2503	2 3/16
37	45	Jan	102	1 3/8	2380	8 1/2
ASM Intl	20	Jan	630	1 5/16	30	1/4
AT&T	45	Jan	1564	7	95	1/4
51 1/4	50	Jan	186	2 3/4	1091	1 1/8
51 1/4	55	Jan	779	11/16	188	4
Abbt L	35	May	1740	3 1/8	3	3 1/4
A M D	15	Jan	14	14 3/4	500	1/16
29 1/4	25	Jan	1888	5 1/4	158	1
29 1/4	25	Feb	1720	6 3/4	13	1 3/4
29 1/4	30	Jan	1720	2 9/16	356	2 13/16
29 1/4	32 1/2	Jan	850	1 5/8	20	4 3/8
29 1/4	32 1/2	Feb	345	2 13/16	20	5 5/8
AdvRdio	22 1/2	Feb	485	1 11/16	...	...
Aegon	90	Jan	...	...	440	7/8
Alcatl	35	Jan	5	10 1/4	600	3/8
AlterraHl	5	Feb	...	...	500	5/8
6 3/16	7 1/2	Feb	351	1/2	500	2 1/4
Amazon	65	Jan	66	20 3/4	795	1 3/4
81 15/16	70	Jan	176	15	358	3 1/4
81 15/16	75	Jan	154	11 1/2	356	5
81 15/16	80	Jan	424	10 1/2	817	6 7/8
81 15/16	85	Jan	1242	7	314	9 5/8
81 15/16	90	Jan	1419	[illegible]	371	[illegible]
81 15/16	95	Feb	382	8 7/8	[illegible]	18
81 15/16	95	Jul	21	[illegible]	500	[illegible]
81 15/16	100	Jan	1253	3 1/8	131	18 5/8
81 15/16	110	Jan	574	1 3/4	12	26 5/8
81 15/16	150	Apr	342	4 1/2	...	...
AmOnline	57 1/2	Jan	55	20 7/8	585	9/16
77 1/4	60	Jan	553	18 5/8	239	13/16
77 1/4	60	Feb	217	19 1/4	400	2
77 1/4	60	Apr	338	22 3/4	80	4 3/8
77 1/4	65	Jan	231	13 1/2	780	1 7/16
77 1/4	65	Feb	12	16 1/2	446	3 3/8
77 1/4	70	Jan	975	9 5/8	2399	2 3/4
77 1/4	72 1/2	Jan	284	8 3/4	394	3 5/8
77 1/4	75	Jan	3617	6 7/8	2086	4 3/4
77 1/4	75	Feb	1003	9 7/8	727	7 3/8
77 1/4	75	Apr	557	14 1/2	145	10 7/8
77 1/4	77 1/2	Jan	485	5 1/2	933	5 7/8
77 1/4	80	Jan	13524	4 1/2	1560	7 1/4
77 1/4	80	Feb	3050	7 5/8	362	9 1/2
77 1/4	80	Apr	971	[illegible]	132	[illegible]
77 1/4	82 1/2	Jan	[illegible]	[illegible]	[illegible]	[illegible]

Option/Strike		Exp.	Call Vol.	Call Last	Put Vol.	Put Last
77 1/4	97 1/2	Jan	565	1 1/16	10	20 1/2
77 1/4	100	Jan	6028	1	295	22 3/4
77 1/4	100	Feb	1174	2 13/16	10	24
77 1/4	100	Apr	377	6 1/8	1	24 1/4
77 1/4	105	Jan	397	5/8	10	25
77 1/4	105	Apr	405	6	...	...
77 1/4	110	Jan	1212	1/2	11	32 3/4
77 1/4	110	Apr	1193	4 3/4	...	...
77 1/4	120	Feb	1320	1 3/16	...	...
77 1/4	120	Apr	2365	3 1/2	...	...
77 1/4	120	Jul	366	6 1/8	...	...
77 1/4	130	Jan	610	3/16	...	...
AEagleOt	45	May	400	6 1/2	...	...
AmExpr	50	Jan	600	101 1/2	...	...
151 5/16	150	Jan	183	6 5/8	407	5 1/4
151 5/16	160	Jan	630	2 11/16	115	11 7/8
151 5/16	170	Jan	927	5/8	17	20 1/8
AmerTrade	25	Jan	814	1 3/8	54	3 5/8
22 5/8	30	Jan	504	9/16	...	...
22 5/8	35	Feb	357	15/16	...	...
Amgen	42 1/2	Jan	1027	18	...	...
58 1/8	50	Jan	581	10 1/4	20	1/4
58 1/8	50	Feb	385	10 1/8	7	1 1/2
58 1/8	55	Jan	250	5 3/8	1062	1 5/8
58 1/8	65	Jan	804	1 3/8	124	7 7/8
58 1/8	70	Jan	510	5/8	190	9 1/8
Antec	40	Feb	20	1 13/16	555	9 1/2
AppleC	90	Jan	429	15 3/4	550	3 3/4
102 1/2	105	Jan	811	8 3/8	147	10 1/2
AplMat	120	Jan	82	6 7/8	515	5 5/8
120 1/4	120	Jul	10	24 1/2	1300	17 1/4
120 1/4	125	Jan	648	4	550	7
120 1/4	135	Jan	54	1 9/16	400	14
120 1/4	135	Jul	800	17	...	...
Ariba	160	Jan	92	32 1/2	363	13 1/8
AspectCm	40	Jan	713	1 5/16	10	7
AscFCap	22 1/2	Jan	2845	2 5/8	...	...
25	25	Jan	2333	1 1/4	170	1 3/16
AtHome	35	Apr	5	11 1/8	531	4 3/8
40 3/8	45	Jan	528	1 15/16	59	6 1/4
40 3/8	50	Jan	693	1 1/8	26	10
40 3/8	50	Feb	343	3	[illegible]	[illegible]
40 3/8	60	Jan	[illegible]	[illegible]	[illegible]	[illegible]

Option/Strike		Exp.	Call Vol.	Call Last	Put Vol.	Put Last
BP Amoco	60	Jan	575	1 1/8	515	2 5/16
58 1/2	60	Feb	566	2 1/16	1	3 1/4
58 1/2	62 1/2	Jan	2065	5/8	...	...
BakrHu	22 1/2	Jan	1006	3/4	...	...
BancOne	32 1/2	Feb	1131	1 7/16	25	3 1/2
30 3/8	50	Feb	1160	1/4	...	...
Bk of Am	45	Jan	633	2 9/16	567	1 7/8
45 9/16	45	Feb	420	3 3/4	369	2 5/8
45 9/16	47 1/2	Jan	6230	1 7/16	74	3 1/8
45 9/16	50	Jan	1009	11/16	110	5
45 9/16	50	Feb	772	1 9/16	78	5 3/8
45 9/16	50	May	3106	3 3/8	51	6 7/8
45 9/16	55	Jan	950	1/4	134	9 1/4
45 9/16	60	May	673	1 1/4	4	15
45 9/16	65	Jan	3	3/16	1450	19 1/4
45 9/16	75	Jan	...	...	1450	29 1/4
45 9/16	80	Jan	10	1/16	2900	34 1/4
BankNY	35	Jan	368	1 11/16	60	1 1/4
BarickG	20	Feb	1011	1/2	...	...
BearSt	40	Feb	1203	2	...	...
BellAtl	60	Jan	342	1	63	3 1/4
58	70	Jan	473	1/16	...	...
BestBuy	50	Jan	1778	9 1/8	257	1 1/4
57 3/8	55	Jan	727	5 7/8	228	2 3/4
57 3/8	60	Jan	655	3 1/8	89	4 3/4
57 3/8	65	Jan	666	1 3/4	6	9 1/8
Biogen	65	Jan	...	...	1880	13/16
73 1/16	70	Jan	343	5 1/4	32	1 3/4
73 1/16	75	Jan	230	2 7/8	559	4 3/8
73 1/16	80	Jan	205	1 3/8	877	[illegible]
73 1/16	85	Jan	440	13/16	...	[illegible]
Block	40	Jan	1010	3	20	1
40 11/16	45	Feb	1025	1 3/4	...	...
Boeing	40	Jan	580	1 1/4	154	15/16
BostSc	25	Feb	519	1 3/8	10	2 1/2
BrMSq	55	Jan	3	5 3/4	365	[illegible]
59 1/2	60	Jan	811	2 1/8	768	[illegible]
59 1/2	65	Jan	179	11/16	369	[illegible]
59 1/2	70	Jan	208	[illegible]	[illegible]	[illegible]
59 1/2	75	[illegible]	[illegible]	[illegible]	[illegible]	[illegible]

Option/Str
60 13/16
60 13/16
Cabltrn
CalAmp
Caterp
48
Cellstar
9 1/32
Cendant
23 1/4
23 1/4
23 1/4
Chase n
70 7/8
70 7/8
70 7/8
70 7/8
70 7/8
Cisco
102
102
102
102
102

Source: The Wall Street Journal, *January 5, 2000, p. C16. Reprinted by permission of The Wall Street Journal.*

followed by the strike price and the expiration month. The last four entries are the volume (number of contracts traded) and the closing price for call options at that strike price, followed by the volume and closing price for put options. If there are no entries, the option did not trade or does not exist. The number of existing options, which is referred to as the **open interest,** is also reported for the day's most actively traded options.

OPEN INTEREST
Number of contracts in existence with specified strike price and expiration date on a particular stock

Second, a clearinghouse was established for the CBOE that maintains a daily record of options issued in the accounts of its members. The members are required to keep a continuous record of their customers' positions in options. No actual options certificates are issued; only the bookkeeping is maintained by the clearinghouse. A centralized clearinghouse greatly facilitates trading in the options, for it serves as the intermediary through which purchases and sales of the calls are recorded.

Third, the CBOE is self-regulated. It imposes requirements that must be met before calls may be traded on the exchange, and options on only a selected number of stocks have been accepted for trading on the exchange. Investors must be approved before they can purchase and sell through the CBOE, and there is a limit to the number of options on a single stock that an investor may own. Brokers on the floor of the exchange must have a minimum amount of capital. Although such self-regulation does not guarantee the absence of illegal transactions, it helps to increase investors' confidence in security markets.

The initial success of the CBOE exceeded expectations. Soon after its formation, other exchanges started to list call options. Currently, call options are traded not only on the CBOE but also on the New York, American, Pacific, and Philadelphia exchanges. Although not all companies meet the criteria for having options listed, over a thousand firms now have options on their stock listed and traded.

Purchasing Calls

Calls are primarily purchased by investors who want to leverage their position in a stock. Should the price of the stock rise, the price of the call will also rise. Since the cost of the call is less than the cost of the stock, the percentage increase in the call may exceed that of the stock, so the investor earns a greater percentage return on the call option than on the underlying stock. If the price of the stock declines, the value also falls, so the investor sustains a larger percentage loss on the option than on the stock. However, since the cost of the call is less than the stock, the absolute loss on the investment in the call may be less than the absolute loss on the stock.

The potential profits and losses at expiration on the purchase of the call for $15 when the stock sells for $60 is illustrated in Figure 13.3. As long as the price of the stock is $50 or less, the entire investment in the call ($15) is lost. As the price of the stock rises above $50, the loss is reduced. The investor breaks even at $65, because the intrinsic value of the call is $15—the cost of the option. The investor earns a profit as the price of the stock continues to rise above $65. (Remember that in this illustration the starting price of the stock was $60. The price has to rise only by more than $5 to assure the investor of a profit on the position in the call.)

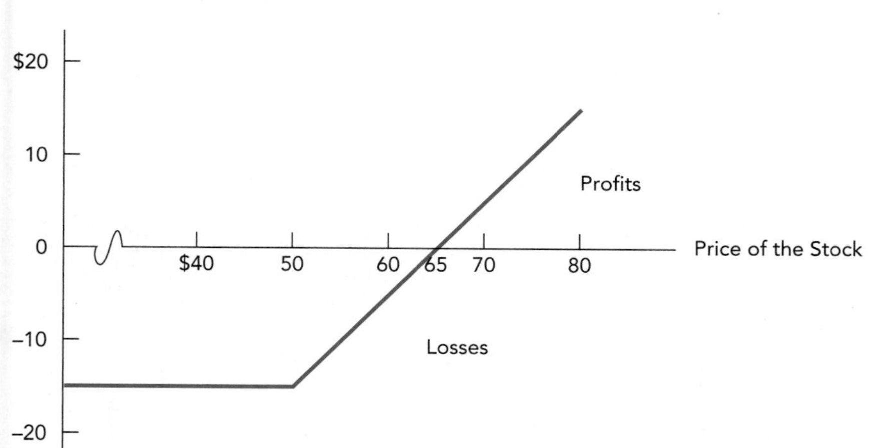

FIGURE 13.3

Profits and Losses at Expiration for the Buyer of a Call

Figure 13.4 adds the profits and losses from buying the stock at $60. Both involve purchases and therefore are *long positions* in the securities. If the price of the stock rises above or declines below $60, the investor earns a profit or sustains a loss. The important difference between the lines indicating the profit and losses on the long positions in the two securities is the possible large dollar loss from buying the stock compared to the limited dollar loss on the call. In the worst case scenario, the investor could lose $60 on the stock but only $15 on the call.

Writing Calls

The preceding section considered the reason for purchasing calls; this section considers the advantages of writing them. (The process of issuing and selling an option is referred to as writing.) While buying calls gives the investor an opportunity to profit from the leverage that call options offer, issuing calls produces revenue from their sale. The investor earns a return from the proceeds of the sale.

There are two ways to write options. The first is the less risky strategy, which is called **covered option writing.** The investor buys the stock and then sells the call. If the option is exercised, the investor supplies the stock that was previously purchased (in other words, "covers" the option with the stock). The second method entails selling the call without owning the stock. This is referred to as **naked option writing,** for the investor is exposed to considerable risk. If the price of the stock rises and the call is exercised, the option writer must buy the stock at the higher market price in order to supply it to the buyer. With naked option writing, the potential for loss is greater than with covered option writing.

COVERED OPTION WRITING
Selling an option when an individual has a position in the underlying stock

NAKED OPTION WRITING
Selling an option when an individual does not have a position in the underlying stock

WRITING THE COVERED CALL The reason for writing options is the income generated by the sale. The potential profit from writing a *covered call*

FIGURE 13.4

Profits and Losses from Purchasing the Stock Compared to Purchasing the Call Option

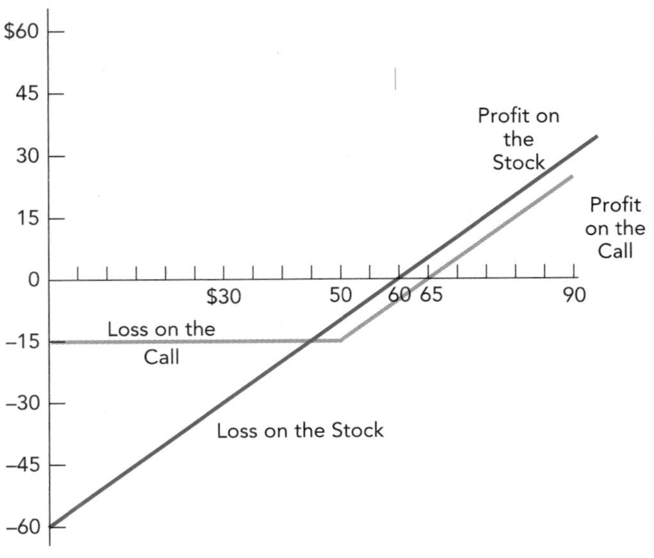

option is shown in Exhibit 13.4. In this example the investor purchases 100 shares of stock at the current market price of $50 per share and simultaneously sells for $5 a call to buy the shares at the strike price of $50. Thus, the investor sells the call for $500 ($5 × 100 shares). Possible future prices for the stock at the expiration of the call are given in column 1. Column 2 presents the net profit to the investor from the purchase of the stock. Column 3 gives the value of the call at expiration, and column 4 presents the profit to the investor from the sale of the call. As may be seen in column 4, the sale of the call is profitable to the investor as long as the price of the common stock remains below $55 per share. The last column gives the net profit on the entire position. As long as the price of the common stock stays *above $45 per share*, the entire position will yield a profit before commissions. The maximum amount of this profit, however, is limited to $500. Thus, by selling the covered call, the investor *forgoes* the possibility of large gains but keeps the premium. For example, if the price of the stock were to rise to $70 per share, the holder of the call would exercise it and purchase the 100 shares from the seller at $50 per share. The seller would then make only the $500 that was received from the sale of the call.

If the price of the stock were to fall below $45, the entire position would result in a loss to the seller. For example, if the price of the common stock fell to $40, the investor would lose $1,000 on the purchase of the stock. However, $500 has been received from the sale of the call. Thus, the net loss is only $500. The investor still owns the stock and may now write another call on that stock. As long as the investor owns the stock, the same 100 shares may be used over and over to

EXHIBIT 13.4

Profits and Losses on a Covered Call Consisting of the Purchase of 100 Shares and the Sale of One Call to Buy 100 Shares at $50 a Share

Price of Stock at Expiration of the Call	New Profit on the Stock	Value of the Call at Expiration	Net Profit on the Sale of the Call	Net Profit on the Position
$40	−$1,000	$ 0	$500	−$500
42	−800	0	500	−300
44	−600	0	500	−100
46	−400	0	500	100
48	−200	0	500	300
50	0	0	500	500
52	200	200	300	500
54	400	400	100	500
56	600	600	−100	500
58	800	800	−300	500
60	1,000	1,000	−500	500

cover the writing of options. Thus, even if the price of the stock does fall, the investor may continue to use it to write more options. The more options that can be written, the more profitable the strategy becomes. For individuals who write covered options, the best possible situation would be for the stock's price to remain stable. In that case the investors would receive the income from writing the options and never suffer a capital loss from a decline in the price of the stock on which the option is being written.

The relationship between the price of the stock and the profit or loss on writing a covered call is illustrated in Figure 13.5, which plots the first and fifth columns of Exhibit 13.4. As may be seen from the figure, the sale of the covered option produces a profit (before commissions) for all prices of the stock above $45. However, the maximum profit (before commissions) is only $500.

WRITING THE NAKED CALL Option writers do not have to own the common stock on which they write calls. Although such naked or uncovered option writing exposes the investor to a large amount of risk, the returns may be considerable. If the writer of the call option given in Exhibit 13.4 had not owned the stock and had sold the option for $500, the position would have been profitable as long as the price of the common stock remained below $55 per share at the expiration of the call. The potential loss, however, is theoretically infinite, for the naked option loses $100 for every $1 increase in the price of the stock above the call's exercise price. For example, if the price of the stock were to rise to $70 per share, the call would be worth $2,000. The owner of the call would exercise it and purchase the 100 shares for $5,000. The writer of the call would then have to purchase the shares in the secondary market for $7,000. Since the writer received only $500 when the call was sold and $5,000 when the call was exercised, the loss is

FIGURE 13.5

Profit or Loss on Selling a Covered Call

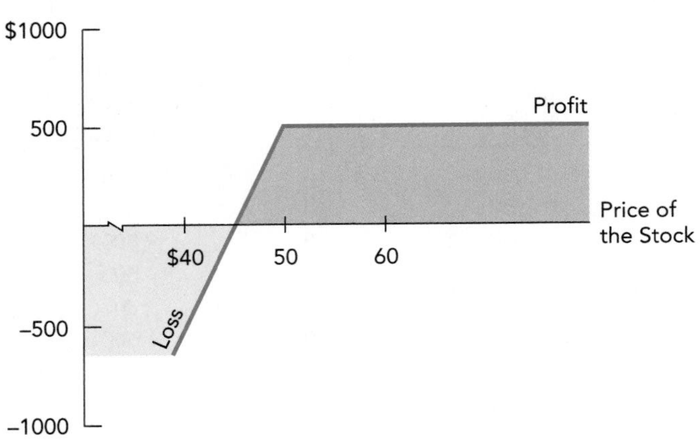

FIGURE 13.6

Profit or Loss on Selling a Naked Call

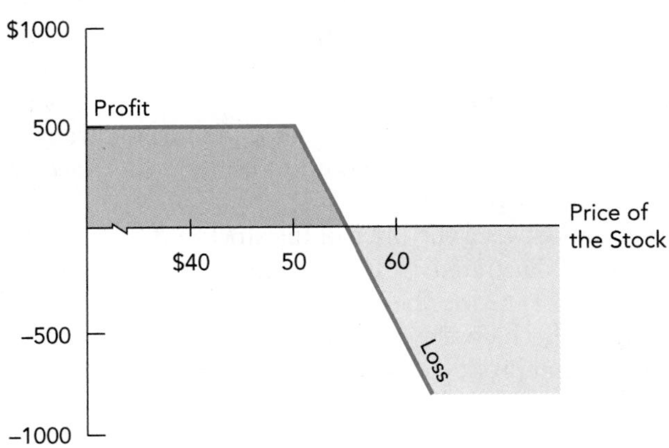

$1,500. Therefore, uncovered option writing exposes the writer to considerable risk if the price of the stock rises.

The relationship between the price of the stock and the profit or loss on writing a naked call option is illustrated in Figure 13.6. In this case the option writer earns a profit (before commissions) as long as the price of the stock does not exceed $55 at the expiration of the call. Notice that the investor earns the entire $500 if the stock's price falls below $50. However, the potential for loss is large if the price of the stock increases.

Investors should write naked call options only if they anticipate a decline (or at least no increase) in the price of the stock. These investors may write covered call options if they believe the price of the stock may rise but are not certain of the price increase. And they may purchase the stock (or the option) and not write calls if they believe there is substantial potential for a price increase.

PUTS

A put option is an option to *sell* stock (usually 100 shares) at a specified price within a specified time period. As with calls, the time period is short—three, six, or nine months. Like all options, a put has an intrinsic value, which is the difference between the strike price of the put and the price of the stock.[4] The relationship between the price of a stock and the intrinsic value of a put is illustrated in Exhibit 13.5. This put is an option to sell 100 shares at $30 per share. The first column gives the strike price of the put, the second column presents the price of the stock, and the third column gives the intrinsic value of the put (the strike price minus the price of the stock).

If the price of the stock is less than the strike price, the put has a positive intrinsic value and is said to be "in the money." If the price of the stock is greater than the strike price, the put has no intrinsic value and is said to be "out of the money." If the price of the stock equals the strike price, the put is "at the money." As with call options, the market price of a put is called "the premium."

As may be seen in the exhibit, when the price of the stock declines, the intrinsic value of the put rises. Since the owner of the put may sell the stock at the price specified in the option agreement, the value of the option rises as the price of the stock falls. Thus, if the price of the stock is $15 and the exercise price of the put is $30, the put's intrinsic value as an option must be $1,500 (for 100 shares). The investor can purchase the 100 shares of stock for $1,500 on the stock market and sell them for $3,000 to the person who issued the put. The put, then, must be worth the $1,500 difference between the purchase and sale prices.

Why should an investor purchase a put? One reason is the same for puts as it is for other options: The put offers potential leverage to the investor. Such leverage may be seen in the example presented in Exhibit 13.5. When the price of the stock declines from $25 to $20 (a 20 percent decrease), the intrinsic value of the put rises from $5 to $10 (a 100 percent increase). In this example, a 20 percent decline in the price of the stock produces a larger percentage increase in the intrinsic value of the put. It is the potential leverage that makes put options attractive to investors.

As with other options, investors pay a price that exceeds the put's intrinsic value: The put commands a time premium above its intrinsic value as an option.

[4]Note that the intrinsic value of a put is the reverse of the intrinsic value of an option to buy. Compare Exhibits 13.1 and 13.5.

EXHIBIT 13.5

Relationships among the Strike Price of the Put, the Price of the Stock, and the Hypothetical Market Price of the Put

Strike Price of the Put	Price of the Stock	Intrinsic Value of the Put	Hypothetical Price of the Put
$30	$15	$15	$15
30	20	10	12
30	25	5	8
30	30	0	6
30	35	0	3
30	40	0	1
30	50	0	—

As with calls, the amount of this time premium depends on such factors as the volatility of the stock's price, the duration of the put, and the potential for decline in the price of the stock.

The relationship between the price of the stock and hypothetical prices of the put are also illustrated in Exhibit 13.5, in which the fourth column presents prices of the put. As may be seen, the price of the put exceeds the intrinsic value, for the put commands a time premium over its intrinsic value as an option.

Figure 13.7 illustrates the relationships among the price of the common stock, the intrinsic value of the put, and the hypothetical market value of the put that were presented in Exhibit 13.5. This figure shows the inverse relationship between the price of the stock and the put's intrinsic value. As the price of the stock declines, the intrinsic value of the put increases (for example, from $5 to $10 when the stock's price declines from $25 to $20). The figure also shows the time premium paid for the option, which is the difference between the price of the put and the option's intrinsic value. If the price of the put is $8 and the intrinsic value is $5, the time premium is $3.

As may be seen in both Exhibit 13.5 and Figure 13.7, the market price of the put converges with the put's intrinsic value as the price of the stock declines. If the price of the stock is sufficiently high (for example, $50), the put will not have any market value because the price of the stock must decline substantially for the put to have any intrinsic value. At the other extreme, when the price of the stock is low (for example, $10), the price of the put is equal to the put's intrinsic value as an option. Once again, there are two reasons for this convergence. First, as the price of the stock declines below the strike price of the put, the potential risk to the investor if the price of the stock should start to rise becomes greater. Thus, put buyers are less willing to pay a time premium above the put's intrinsic value. Second, as the intrinsic value of a put rises when the price of the stock declines, the investor must spend more to buy the put; therefore, the potential return on the investment is less. As the potential return declines, the willingness to pay a time premium diminishes.

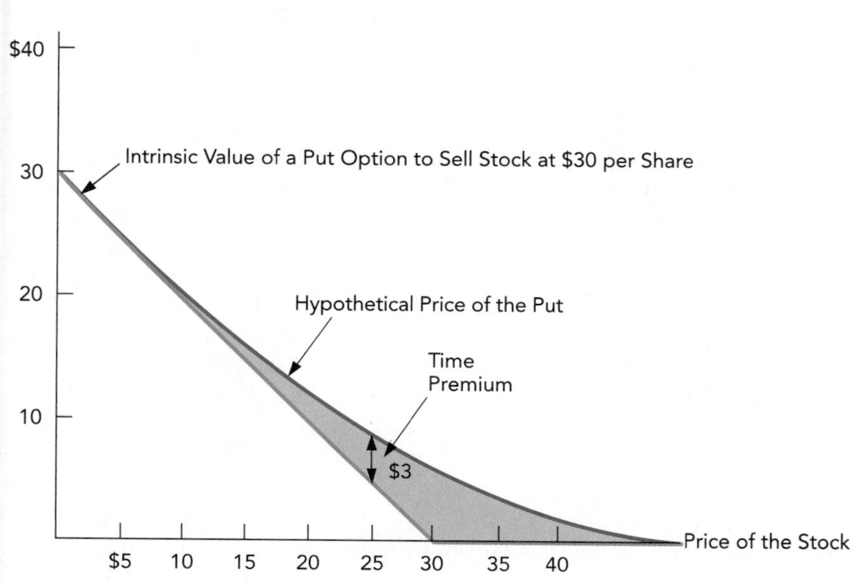

FIGURE 13.7

Relationships among the Price of the Stock, the Intrinsic Value of a Put Option, and the Hypothetical Price of the Option

STOCK INDEX OPTIONS

STOCK INDEX OPTION
Right to buy or sell stock based on an index of stock prices

Although put and call options were initially created for individual stocks, **stock index options** also have developed. These stock index options are similar to options based on individual stocks, but the index option is based on an aggregate measure of the market, such as the Standard & Poor's 500 Index. In addition, there are also options based on subsets of the market, such as computer technology stocks or oil stocks. A listing of selected index options and where they are traded is given in Exhibit 13.6. Stock index options have proved to be particularly popular and account for a substantial proportion of the daily transactions in options.

These options are popular because they permit the investor to take a position in the market or in a group of companies without having to select specific securities. For example, suppose an investor anticipates that the stock market will rise. What does this individual do? He or she cannot buy every stock but must select individual stocks.[5] Remember from the discussion of risk in Chapter 8 that two sources of risk are associated with the individual stock: nondiversifiable, or systematic, risk, and diversifiable, or unsystematic, risk. Systematic risk refers to the tendency of a stock's price to move with the market. Unsystematic risk refers to price movements generated by the security that are independent of the market (for example, a takeover announcement, dividend cut, or large increase in earnings).

[5]As is explained in Chapter 14, the investor could buy an index mutual fund. Such funds construct portfolios that mirror aggregate measures of the stock market.

EXHIBIT 13.6

Selected Index Options and Where They Are Traded

The Option	Where Traded
S&P 100 Index	Chicago Board Options Exchange
S&P 500 Index	Chicago Board Options Exchange
Major Market Index	American Stock Exchange
AMEX Market Value Index	American Stock Exchange
Computer Technology Index	American Stock Exchange
Oil Index	American Stock Exchange
Airline Index	American Stock Exchange
Value Line Index	Philadelphia Exchange
National O-T-C Index	Philadelphia Exchange
Technology Index	Pacific Exchange
NYSE Options Index	New York Stock Exchange

If the investor buys a particular stock on the expectation of a rising market, it does not necessarily follow that the individual stock's price will increase when the market rises. Investors construct diversified portfolios to reduce the unsystematic risk associated with the individual asset. As the portfolio becomes more diversified, unsystematic risk is reduced further and the return on the portfolio mirrors the return on the market.

Index options offer the investor an alternative to creating diversified portfolios as a means to earn the return associated with movements in the market. For example, if the investor anticipates that the market will rise in the near future, he or she may purchase a call option based on an index of the market as a whole. If the market does rise, the value of the call option also increases. The investor has avoided the unsystematic risk associated with the individual stock.

Stock index options also give investors a means to reduce risk (to hedge their existing portfolios). Consider a substantial stock portfolio that has appreciated in value. If the investor anticipates declining stock prices and sells the shares, this transaction is taxable. Instead of selling the stocks, the investor may purchase stock index puts. Then if the market declines, the value of the puts increases, so the profits in the position in the puts will help offset the losses on the individual stocks.

There is one major difference between stock index options and call options on specific stocks. With a call option to buy shares of IBM, the owner may exercise the option and buy the stock. Such purchases are not possible with a stock index option. The owner of the call cannot exercise it and receive the index. Instead stock index options are settled in cash. For example, suppose an investor owns a call based on the Standard & Poor's 500 Index. At expiration the intrinsic value of the option is determined and that amount is paid by the seller of the option to the owner. Of course, if the option has no intrinsic value at expiration, it is worthless and expires. The seller of the option then has no further obligation to the option's owner. In that case the premium paid for the option (that is, its price) becomes profit for the seller.

In addition to stock index options, there are options on debt instruments (such as Treasury bonds) and foreign currencies. Each of these options permits the investor (1) to take positions on the underlying assets without actually acquiring them or (2) to reduce the risk of loss from price fluctuations. For example, if an investor anticipates declining interest rates, he or she will buy a call option to purchase bonds. If interest rates do fall, the value of bonds will rise, increasing the value of the call option. However, if the investor were to purchase the call option and interest rates rose, the investor's maximum possible loss would be limited to the cost of the option.

The same concepts apply to options on foreign currencies. If the investor expects the value of the British pound to rise, that individual buys a call option on the pound. Of course, if the investor anticipates a price decline in the pound, he or she would acquire a put option on the pound. If the anticipated price change were to occur, then the investor would earn a profit. However, if the price were to move in the opposite direction (rise after the purchase of the put), the maximum the investor would lose is the cost of the option.

FUTURES

The preceding discussion considered options to buy and sell stock. Such options are used to magnify the investor's return or, in combination with other securities, to reduce the investor's risk exposure. A futures contract performs the same functions. Futures are used by speculators to increase the potential return or by hedgers to reduce the risk of loss.

A commodity such as wheat or a financial asset such as a Treasury bond may be purchased for current delivery or for future delivery. A **futures contract** is a formal agreement executed through a commodity exchange for the delivery of goods or securities in the future. One party agrees to accept a specific commodity that meets a specified quality in a specified month. The other party agrees to deliver the specified commodity during the designated month.

FUTURES CONTRACT
Agreement for the future delivery or receipt of a commodity or security at a specified price and time

Individuals who enter futures contracts but do not deal in the actual commodities are called **speculators.** This distinguishes them from the growers, processors, warehousers, and other participants who also enter contracts but who deal in the actual commodity. Such participants are the **hedgers,** who use the contracts to reduce the risk of loss from fluctuating prices. (Hedging is explained later in the chapter.)

SPECULATORS
Individuals who are willing to accept substantial risk for the possibility of a large return

HEDGERS
Individuals or firms that enter into offsetting contracts

The appeal of futures contracts to speculators is the potential for a large return on the investment. The large return is the result of the leverage that exists because (1) a futures contract controls a substantial amount of the commodity and (2) the investor must make only a small payment to enter into a contract to buy or sell a commodity (that is, there is a small margin requirement). These two points are discussed in detail later in this chapter.

The Mechanics of Purchasing Futures

Like stocks and bonds, futures contracts are traded in several markets, such as the Chicago Board of Trade, which executes contracts in agricultural commodities,

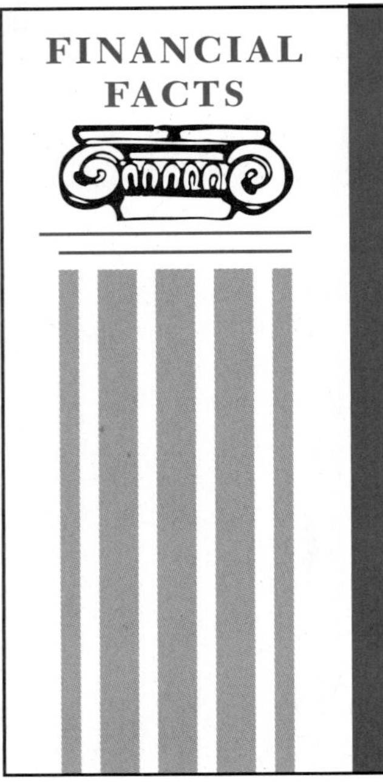

The Price Volatility of Options

The prices of options can be extremely volatile, especially as they approach expiration. In the second week of December 1996, the price of Iomega's stock declined from $23\frac{1}{2}$ to $18\frac{3}{4}$ (a 15.8 percent decline). The December call to buy the stock at 20 fell from $3\frac{3}{4}$ to $\frac{9}{16}$, an 85 percent decline. Simultaneously, the price of a December put to sell the stock at 20 rose from 1 to $3\frac{1}{8}$, a 213 percent increase. ¶ Why did the prices of the options move so dramatically in response to the change in the price of the underlying stock? One reason is the short time to expiration. Both options were due to expire on December 20, only seven days after the large movement in the price of Iomega's stock. The price decline wiped out the call's intrinsic value and simultaneously converted an *out of the money* put into a put with positive intrinsic value. ¶ Such large price changes do not occur every day, but they do occur frequently enough to attract individuals who like to speculate on large and rapid price changes. Of course, you would have to be on the correct side to profit from the price movement. If you had purchased the put or sold the call naked, you would have made large profits, but if you had purchased the call or sold the put, you would have sustained large losses. Price volatility may create an opportunity for gains, but it also can be the source of large losses. ¶

such as wheat, soybeans, and livestock. More than 50 commodities are traded on ten exchanges in the United States and Canada. These markets developed close to the regions in which each commodity is produced. Thus, the markets for wheat are located not only in Chicago but also in Kansas City and Minneapolis.

Futures contracts are entered into through brokers, just as stocks and bonds are bought and sold. Brokerage firms own seats on the commodity exchange. Membership on each exchange is limited, and only members are allowed to execute contracts. If the investor's brokerage firm lacks a seat, that broker must have a correspondent relationship with another firm that does own a seat. Brokers charge a commission fee for executing orders. This fee usually covers both the purchase and subsequent sale of the contract.

The Units of Commodity Contracts

To facilitate trading, contracts must be uniform. For a particular commodity the contracts must be identical. Besides identifying the delivery month, the contract must specify the grade and type of the commodity (for example, a particular type of wheat) and the units of the commodity (such as 5,000 bushels). Thus, when an individual enters a contract, there can be no doubt as to the nature of the obligation. For example, if the investor enters into a contract to buy wheat for January delivery, there can be no confusion with a contract for the purchase of wheat for February delivery. These are two different commodities in the same way that AT&T common stock, AT&T preferred stock, and AT&T bonds are all different securities. Without such standardization of contracts, there would be chaos in the futures (or any) markets.

Commodity Positions

An individual may acquire a contract to accept future delivery (to buy). This is the **long position,** in which the buyer profits if the price of the commodity, and hence the value of the contract, rises. The individual may also enter into a contract to make future delivery (to sell). This is the **short position,** in which the seller agrees to make good the contract (that is, to deliver the goods) sometime in the future. This investor profits if the price of the commodity, and hence the value of the contract, declines.

LONG POSITION
Contract to accept delivery, to buy

SHORT POSITION
Contract to make delivery, to sell

FUTURES PRICE
Price for the future delivery of a commodity or financial asset

How each position generates a profit can be seen in a simple example. Assume that the **futures price** of wheat is $3.50 per bushel. If a contract is made to accept delivery in six months at $3.50 per bushel, the buyer will profit from this long position if the price of wheat *rises.* If the price increases to $4.00 per bushel, the buyer can exercise the contract by taking delivery and paying $3.50 per bushel. The speculator then sells the wheat for $4 per bushel, which produces a profit of $0.50 per bushel.

The opposite occurs when the price of wheat declines. If the price of wheat falls to $3.00 per bushel, the individual who made the contract to accept delivery at $3.50 suffers a loss. But the speculator who made the contract to deliver wheat (the short position) earns a profit from the price decline. The speculator can then buy wheat at the market price of $3.00, deliver it for the contract price of $3.50, and earn a $0.50 profit per bushel.

If the price rises, the short position produces a loss. If the price increases from $3.50 to $4.00 per bushel, the speculator who made the contract to deliver suffers a loss of $0.50 per bushel, because he or she must pay $4.00 to obtain the wheat that will be delivered for $3.50 per bushel.

Actually, these losses and profits are generated without the goods being delivered. Of course, when a speculator makes a contract to accept future delivery, the possibility always exists that this individual will receive the goods and have to buy them. Conversely, if the speculator enters into a contract to make future delivery, the possibility exists that the goods will have to be supplied. Such deliveries occur infrequently, however, because the speculator can offset the contract before the delivery date.

This process of offsetting existing contracts is illustrated as follows. Suppose a speculator has a contract to buy wheat in January. If the individual wants to close the position, he or she can enter a contract to sell wheat in January. The two contracts cancel each other, as one is a purchase and the other is a sale. If the speculator actually received the wheat by executing the purchase agreement, he or she could pass on the wheat by executing the sell agreement. However, since the two contracts offset each other, the actual delivery and subsequent sale are not necessary. Instead, the speculator's position in wheat is closed, and the actual physical transfers do not occur.

Correspondingly, if the speculator has a contract for the sale of wheat in January, he or she can cancel it by entering a contract for the purchase of wheat in January. If the speculator were called upon to deliver wheat as the result of the contract to sell, the individual would exercise the contract to purchase wheat. The buy and sell contracts cancel each other, and no physical transfers of wheat occur.

Once again the speculator has closed the initial position by taking the opposite position (that is, the sales contract is canceled by a purchase contract).

Because these contracts are canceled and actual deliveries do not take place, it should not be assumed that profits or losses do not occur. The two contracts need not be executed at the same price. For example, the speculator may have entered into a contract for the future sale of wheat at \$3.50 per bushel. Any contract for the future purchase of comparable wheat can cancel the contract for the sale. But the cost of the wheat for future delivery could be \$3.60 or \$3.40 (or any conceivable price). If the price of wheat rises (for example, from \$3.50 to \$3.60 per bushel), the speculator with a long position earns a profit, but the short position suffers a loss. If the price declines (for example, from \$3.50 to \$3.40 per bushel), the short seller earns a profit, but the long position sustains a loss.

Reporting on Futures Trading

Futures prices and the number of contracts are reported in the financial press in much the same way as stock and bond transactions. This is illustrated in Exhibit 13.7, which was taken from *The Wall Street Journal*. As may be seen in the exhibit, wheat is traded on the Chicago Board of Trade (CBT) and on the Kansas City Board of Trade (KC). The unit for trading is 5,000 bushels, and prices are quoted in cents per bushel. The opening price for Chicago wheat for September delivery was 276 (\$2.76) per bushel, while the high, low, and closing (the "settle") prices were 277½, 274, and 277½, respectively. This closing price was unchanged from the closing price on the previous day. The high and low prices (prior to the previous day of trading) for the lifetime of the contract were 325 and 266½, respectively. The open interest, which is the number of contracts in existence, was 1,406.

This open interest varies over the life of the contract. Initially, the open interest rises as buyers and sellers establish positions. Then it declines as the delivery date approaches and the positions are closed. This changing number of contracts is illustrated in Figure 13.8, which plots the spot and futures prices and the open interest for a September contract to buy Kansas City wheat. When the contracts were initially traded in November X1, there were only a few contracts in existence. By June X2 the open interest had risen to more than 10,000 contracts. As the remaining life of the contracts declined, the number of contracts fell as the various participants closed their positions. By late September only a few contracts were still outstanding.

SPOT PRICE
Current price of a commodity

Figure 13.8 also shows the **spot price** (the current price) and the futures price for Kansas City wheat. In this case the futures price was generally less than the spot price. This relationship between the two prices occurs when speculators believe that the price of the commodity will decline. These speculators sell contracts now to lock in the higher prices so they may buy back the contracts at a lower price in the future. This selling of the futures drives the futures price down below the spot price.

If speculators had anticipated higher prices for wheat, they would enter contracts to buy (that is, to accept the future delivery of wheat). This would drive up the futures price relative to the spot price. The value of the futures would then exceed the current price of the commodity.

EXHIBIT 13.7

Selected Futures Prices

FUTURES PRICES

Tuesday, January 4, 2000

Open Interest Reflects Previous Trading Day.

GRAINS AND OILSEEDS

CORN (CBT) 5,000 bu.; cents per bu.

	Open	High	Low	Settle	Change	Lifetime High	Lifetime Low	Open Interest
Mar	200¾	203½	200¾	203	+ 2¼	270	195¼	213,948
May	207¾	210¼	207¾	209¾	+ 1¾	261	202½	62,419
July	214½	217	214½	216½	+ 1¾	278½	209	59,436
Sept	222½	223¾	222	223¼	+ 1¼	257	215¾	17,403
Nov	....	....	....	229¾	+ 1	245	222½	561
Dec	232	233	231	232½	+ 1	279½	225¼	35,915
Mr01	240½	241¼	240	241	+ 1¼	246½	233¾	878
Dec	251½	254	251½	253¾	+ 1¾	263	246½	1,132

Est vol 45,000; vol Mon 64,373; open int 391,990, +7,538.

OATS (CBT) 5,000 bu.; cents per bu.

	Open	High	Low	Settle	Change	Lifetime High	Lifetime Low	Open Interest
Mar	108½	109	108	109	+ ¾	135	107	7,329
May	113¾	114¼	113½	114¼	+ ½	133	112¾	2,796
July	111¾	112½	111¾	112½	+ ¾	124¼	110½	1,543
Sept	117	117	117	117	+ ¼	130	115¾	649
Dec	124	124	123½	123¾	+ ½	135	123	821

Est vol 600; vol Mon 1,074; open int 13,138, +456.

SOYBEANS (CBT) 5,000 bu.; cents per bu.

	Open	High	Low	Settle	Change	Lifetime High	Lifetime Low	Open Interest
Jan	456½	466	456½	464¼	+ 7¾	632	415	11,516
Mar	465	474	465	471½	+ 7	598	423½	61,985
May	474	481½	473	479	+ 7¼	554	432	25,181
July	478½	487	478½	485½	+ 7	647	440	23,339
Aug	482	486	482	485	+ 6½	541½	441	2,407
Sept	483½	486	482	486	+ 5½	541	450	678
Nov	487½	495½	487	492½	+ 6	631	453	10,278

Est vol 48,000; vol Mon 41,090; open int 135,418, +993.

SOYBEAN MEAL (CBT) 100 tons; $ per ton.

	Open	High	Low	Settle	Change	Lifetime High	Lifetime Low	Open Interest
Jan	146.90	148.70	146.90	147.90	+ 1.50	164.00	123.30	9,841
Mar	146.70	149.10	146.50	148.60	+ 1.90	162.00	126.30	32,086
May	147.50	149.20	147.20	148.50	+ 2.20	162.60	127.30	20,861
July	148.20	150.20	148.20	149.50	+ 2.00	164.20	130.00	16,684
Aug	149.00	150.30	148.30	149.50	+ 2.30	164.00	131.00	5,449
Sept	149.00	150.30	148.50	149.50	+ 2.30	164.00	132.00	3,123
Dec	151.80	153.40	151.50	153.20	+ 2.40	169.00	135.50	6,832

Est vol 20,000; vol Mon 11,890; open int 97,013, +381.

SOYBEAN OIL (CBT) 60,000 lbs.; cents per lb.

	Open	High	Low	Settle	Change	Lifetime High	Lifetime Low	Open Interest
Jan	15.47	15.65	15.32	15.57	+ .13	24.90	15.32	8,597
Mar	15.70	15.94	15.58	15.82	+ .12	23.95	15.58	53,625
May	16.01	16.20	15.91	16.15	+ .13	23.50	15.91	23,273
July	16.34	16.55	16.21	16.45	+ .13	22.30	16.21	19,790
Aug	16.52	16.60	16.37	16.57	+ .12	21.00	16.37	4,584
Sept	16.68	16.75	16.52	16.73	+ .13	21.70	16.52	2,852
Oct	16.75	16.85	16.65	16.85	+ .10	22.25	16.65	3,244
Dec	17.08	17.30	16.97	17.16	+ .12	20.62	16.97	13,536

Est vol 27,000; vol Mon 17,989; open int 130,411, −1,649.

WHEAT (CBT) 5,000 bu.; cents per bu.

	Open	High	Low	Settle	Change	Lifetime High	Lifetime Low	Open Interest
Mar	247½	248	241	247¼	− ¼	340	236½	85,433
May	258	258½	253	258	....	322	246¾	10,042
July	268	269½	263	268	+ ¼	347	256¾	22,134
Sept	276	277½	274	277½	....	335	266½	1,406
Dec	288	291	287¾	291	− 1¼	345	280½	2,978

Est vol 25,000; vol Mon 16,705; open int 122,038, +1,126.

WHEAT (KC) 5,000 bu.; cents per bu.

	Open	High	Low	Settle	Change	Lifetime High	Lifetime Low	Open Interest
Mar	273¼	274¼	270¼	274	− ¼	361½	262½	41,508
May	283½	285	280¾	284¾	+ ¼	340½	272¾	7,950
July	293¾	295	290¾	295	+ ¼	366	282	11,938
Sept	304	304½	300	304½	+ ½	346	291	690
Dec	315½	316½	312	316½	+ 1	354	302	671

Est vol 5,530; vol Mon 4,972; open int 62,757, +559.

WHEAT (MPLS) 5,000 bu.; cents per bu.

	Open	High	Low	Settle	Change	Lifetime High	Lifetime Low	Open Interest
Mar	316	317½	313	316¼	− ¼	386	312½	11,938
May	325	326¼	321¾	325	[illegible]	380	[illegible]	[illegible]

	Open	High	Low	Settle	Change	Lifetime High	Lifetime Low	Open Interest
Mr01	....	....	....	541.6	− 7.7	520.0	511.0	201
May	....	....	....	541.9	− 7.7	....	....	80
July	....	....	....	542.6	− 7.7	574.0	510.0	1,350
Dec	....	....	....	543.4	− 7.7	680.0	498.0	978
Dc02	....	....	....	537.9	− 7.7	613.0	495.0	492
Dc03	....	....	....	537.9	− 7.7	560.0	510.0	377

Est vol 14,000; vol Thur 16,087; open int 76,387, −2,003.

CRUDE OIL, Light Sweet (NYM) 1,000 bbls.; $ per bbl.

	Open	High	Low	Settle	Change	Lifetime High	Lifetime Low	Open Interest
Feb	25.20	25.69	24.71	25.55	− 0.05	27.02	12.90	122,90
Mar	24.29	25.00	24.11	24.84	+ 0.05	25.99	12.97	66,52
Apr	23.87	24.25	23.45	24.13	+ 0.14	25.01	13.03	40,4
May	22.95	23.60	22.80	23.43	+ 0.20	24.25	13.65	24,4
June	22.45	22.70	22.20	22.79	+ 0.22	23.52	13.26	53,
July	21.70	22.20	21.60	22.23	+ 0.23	22.90	13.70	31,6
Aug	21.30	21.90	21.25	21.79	+ 0.23	22.40	13.78	15,9
Sept	20.80	21.45	20.80	21.42	+ 0.24	22.00	14.40	13,1
Oct	21.00	21.00	21.00	21.09	+ 0.26	21.58	14.22	12,8
Nov	20.66	20.66	20.66	20.77	+ 0.28	21.15	15.60	9,5
Dec	20.30	20.45	20.00	20.50	+ 0.29	21.00	13.85	37,
Ja01	19.87	19.95	19.85	20.24	+ 0.29	20.73	14.25	13
Feb	19.95	19.95	19.95	20.00	+ 0.29	20.44	14.30	3,
Mar	....	....	....	19.79	+ 0.29	20.11	14.44	3,4
Apr	....	....	....	19.59	+ 0.29	19.80	15.80	1,2
May	....	....	....	19.40	+ 0.29	19.27	15.80	1,2
June	....	....	....	19.25	+ 0.29	19.62	14.56	8,6
July	....	....	....	19.13	+ 0.29	19.05	19.05	3
Aug	....	....	....	19.04	+ 0.29	18.40	18.40	[illegible]
Sept	....	....	....	18.96	+ 0.29	18.98	17.96	2,3
Oct	....	....	....	18.89	+ 0.29	....	....	5
Nov	....	....	....	18.82	+ 0.29	19.05	18.20	3
Dec	18.52	18.60	18.52	18.75	+ 0.29	19.10	14.90	17,9
Ja02	....	....	....	18.69	+ 0.29	....	....	3
Feb	....	....	....	18.63	+ 0.29	....	....	1
Mar	....	....	....	18.57	+ 0.29	18.65	18.45	2,2
June	18.00	18.00	18.00	18.42	+ 0.32	18.98	17.35	1,
Dec	17.70	17.70	17.70	18.16	+ 0.32	21.38	15.50	4,
Dc03	....	....	....	17.79	+ 0.32	22.00	15.92	5,
Dc04	....	....	....	17.67	+ 0.32	19.27	16.35	4
Dc05	....	....	....	17.63	+ 0.32	18.40	17.00	

Est vol 122,839; vol Thur 86,498; open int 501,819, +4,331

HEATING OIL NO. 2 (NYM) 42,000 gal; $ per gal.

	Open	High	Low	Settle	Change	Lifetime High	Lifetime Low	Open Interest
Feb	.6720	.6830	.6540	.6778	− .0009	.7070	.3750	
Mar	.6425	.6615	.6380	.6583	+ .0036	.6820	.3760	
Apr	.6115	.6370	.6115	.6318	+ .0041	.6500	.3760	
May	.5830	.6040	.5810	.6043	+ .0056	.6205	.3800	
June	.5610	.5800	.5610	.5833	+ .0066	.6000	.3790	
July	.5620	.5650	.5615	.5728	+ .0081	.5860	.3890	
Aug	.5580	.5580	.5460	.5693	+ .0086	.5860	.3970	
Sept	.5620	.5620	.5620	.5728	+ .0091	.5775	.42	
Oct	....	....	....	.5758	+ .0091	.5755	.4	
Nov	....	....	....	.5788	+ .0091	.5925	.4	
Dec	.5725	.5725	.5725	.5818	+ .0091	.5950		
Ja01	.5650	.5650	.5650	.5823	+ .0091	.5965		
Feb	....	....	....	.5753	+ .0096	.5920		
Mar	....	....	....	.5578	+ .0101	[illegible]		
Apr	....	....	....	.5413	+ .0106			
May	....	....	....	.5248	+ .0111			
June	....	....	....	.5123	+ .0116			

Est vol 37,143; vol Thur 40,373; open int 13

GASOLINE-NY Unleaded (NYM) 42,000

	Open	High	Low	Settle	Change
Feb	.6685	.6890	.6570	.6850	+ .0088
Mar	.6625	.6890	.6590	.6850	+ .0100
Apr	.6950	.7140	.6930	.7140	+ .0100
May	.6875	.6945	.6850	.7058	+ .0093
June	.6775	.6810	.6740	.6930	+ .0095
July	....	....	....	.6750	+ .0075
Sept	....	[illegible]	[illegible]	[illegible]	[illegible]

Est vol 34,2

September Wheat Traded in Chicago

September Wheat Traded in Kansas City

Source: The Wall Street Journal, *January 5, 2000, p. C20. Reprinted by permission of The Wall Street Journal.*

FIGURE 13.8

Spot and Futures Prices and Open Interest for a September Contract for Kansas City Wheat

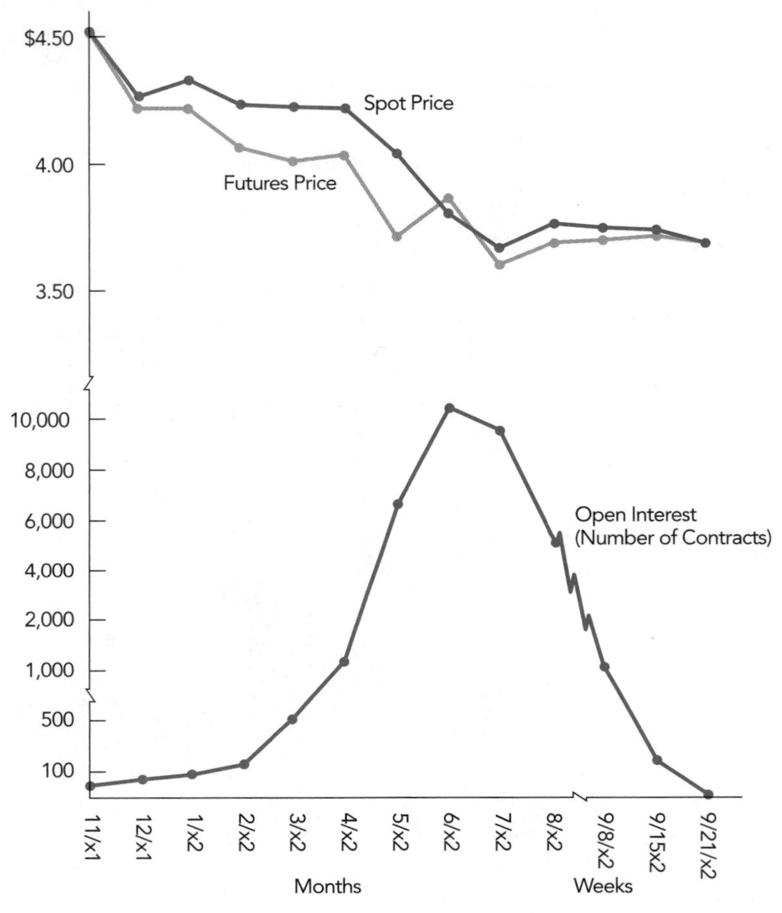

The value of the futures contract can be worth only the value of the underlying commodity at the expiration date. Hence the spot and futures prices must converge with the approach of the expiration date. This pattern of price behavior is also illustrated in Figure 13.8. In March, April, and May, there was a differential between the two prices. However, in late September the futures and spot prices converged and erased the differential.

Leverage

Commodities are paid for on delivery. Thus, when an individual enters into a contract for future delivery, he or she does not pay for the commodity unless actual delivery is made. When the contract is made, the investor provides an amount of money, called **margin,** to guarantee the contract. This margin is not to be confused with the margin that is used in the purchase of stocks and bonds. In the trading of stocks and bonds, margin represents the investor's equity in the position, whereas margin for a commodity contract is a deposit to show the investor's good faith and to protect the broker and the exchange against an adverse change in the price of the commodity.

MARGIN
Good faith deposit used to secure a futures contract

In the stock market, the amount of margin that is required varies with the price of the security, but in the commodity markets the amount of margin does not vary with the dollar value of the transaction. Instead, each contract has a fixed minimum margin requirement. For example, the investor who makes a contract to buy cocoa must put up $1,000. These margin requirements are established by the commodity exchanges, but individual brokers may require more.

The margin requirements are only a small percentage of the value of the contract. For example, the $1,000 margin requirement for cocoa gives the owner of the contract to buy a claim on 10 metric tons of cocoa. If cocoa is selling for $1,400 a metric ton, the total value of the contract is $14,000. The margin requirement as a percentage of the value of the contract is only 7.14 percent ($1,000/$14,000). This small amount of margin is one reason why a commodity contract offers so much potential leverage.

The potential leverage from speculating in commodity futures may be illustrated in a simple example. Consider a contract to buy wheat at $3.50 per bushel. Such a contract controls 5,000 bushels of wheat worth a total of $17,500 (5,000 × $3.50). If the investor owns this contract to buy and the margin requirement is $1,000, the investor must remit $1,000. An increase of only $0.20 per bushel in the price of the commodity produces an increase of $1,000 in the value of the contract. This $1,000 is simply the product of the price change ($0.20) and the number of units in the contract (5,000). The profit on the contract is $1,000.

What is the percentage return on the investment? With a margin of $1,000 the return is 100 percent, because the investor put up $1,000 and then earned an additional $1,000. An increase of less than 6 percent in the price of wheat produced a return on the speculator's money of 100 percent. Such a return is the result of leverage that comes from the small margin requirement and the large amount of the commodity controlled by the contract.

Leverage, of course, works both ways. In the previous example, if the price of the commodity declines by $0.10, the contract will be worth $17,000. A decline of only 2.9 percent in the price reduces the investor's margin from $1,000 to $500. To maintain the position, the investor must deposit additional margin with the broker. The broker's request for additional funds is referred to as a **margin call.** Failure to meet the margin call will result in the broker's closing the position. Should the investor default on the contract, the broker becomes responsible for the execution of the contract. The margin call thus protects the broker.

MARGIN CALL
Request by the broker for an investor to place additional funds to restore the good faith deposit

Actually, there are two margin requirements. The first is the minimum initial deposit, and the second is the maintenance margin. The **maintenance margin** specifies when the investor must deposit additional funds with the broker to cover a decline in the value of a commodity contract. For example, the margin requirement for wheat is $1,000 and the maintenance margin is $750. If the investor owns a contract for the purchase of wheat and the value of the contract declines by $250

MAINTENANCE MARGIN
Minimum level of funds in a margin account that triggers a margin call

to the level of the maintenance margin ($750), the broker makes a margin call. This requires the investor to deposit an additional $250 into the account, which restores the initial $1,000 margin. This additional deposit protects the broker, since the value of the contract has declined and the investor has sustained a loss.

Maintenance margin applies to *both buyers and sellers.* If, in the previous example, the price of wheat were to rise by $250, the speculators who had entered the contract to deliver wheat would see their margin decline from the initial deposit of $1,000 to $750. The broker would then make a margin call, which would require the short sellers to restore the $1,000 margin. Once again this protects the broker, since the value of the contract has risen and the short seller has sustained the loss.

These margin adjustments occur *daily.* After the market closes, the value of each account is totaled. In the jargon of futures trading, each account is *marked to the market.* If the account does not meet the margin requirement, the broker issues a margin call that the individual must meet or the broker will close the position.

HEDGING

HEDGING
Simultaneous purchase and sale designed to reduce risk of loss from price fluctuations

One of the prime reasons for the development of futures markets was the desire of producers to reduce the risk of loss from price fluctuations. The procedure for this reduction in risk is called **hedging,** which consists of taking opposite positions at the same time. In effect, a hedger simultaneously takes the long and the short positions in a particular commodity.

Hedging is best explained by illustrations. In the first example, a wheat farmer expects to harvest a crop at a specified time. Since the costs of production are determined, the farmer knows the price that is necessary to earn a profit. Although the price that will be paid for wheat at harvest time is unknown, the current price of a contract for the future delivery of wheat is known. The farmer can then enter a contract to sell (to make future delivery). Such a contract is a hedged position, because the farmer takes a long position (the wheat in the ground) and a short position (the sale of the contract for future delivery).

Such a position reduces the farmer's risk of loss from a price decline. Suppose the cost to produce the wheat is $3.50 per bushel and September wheat is selling in June for $3.75. If the farmer sells wheat for September delivery, a $0.25 per bushel profit is assured, because the buyer of the contract agrees to pay $3.75 per bushel upon delivery in September. If the price of wheat declines to $3.50, the farmer is still assured $3.75. However, if the price of wheat rises to $4.10 in September, the farmer still gets only $3.75. The additional $0.35 gain goes to the owner of the contract for delivery who buys the wheat for $3.75 but can now sell it for $4.10.

Is this transaction unfair? Remember that the farmer wanted protection against a decline in the price of wheat. If the price had declined to $3.40 and the farmer had not hedged, the farmer would have suffered a loss of $0.10 (the $3.40 price minus the $3.50 cost) per bushel. To obtain protection from this risk of loss, the farmer accepted the profit of $0.25 per bushel and relinquished the possibility of a larger profit. The speculator who entered the contract to buy the wheat bore the risk of loss from a price decline and received the reward from a price increase.

Users of wheat hedge in the opposite direction. A user of wheat (Kellogg) desires to know the future cost of wheat in order to plan production levels and the prices that will be charged to distributors. However, the spot price of wheat need not hold into the future. This company then enters a contract to accept future delivery and thereby hedges the position. This is hedging because Kellogg has a long position (the contract to accept the future delivery of wheat) and a short position (the future production of cereal, which requires the future delivery of wheat).

If Kellogg enters a contract in June for the delivery of wheat in September at \$3.75 per bushel, the future cost of the grain becomes known. The company cannot be hurt by a price increase in wheat from \$3.75 to \$4.10, because the contract is for delivery at \$3.75. However, the company has forgone the chance of profit from a decline in the price of wheat from \$3.75 to \$3.40 per bushel.

Instead, the possibility of profit from a decline in the price of wheat rests with the speculator who entered the contract to deliver wheat. If the price of wheat were to decline, the speculator could buy the wheat in September at the lower price, deliver it, and collect the \$3.75 that is specified in the contract. However, this speculator would suffer a loss if the price of September wheat rose over \$3.75. Then the cost would exceed the delivery price specified in the contract.

These two examples illustrate why growers and users of a commodity hedge. They often take the opposite side of hedge positions. If all growers and users were to agree on prices for future delivery, there would be no need for speculators: but this is not the case. Speculators enter contracts when there is an excess or an insufficient supply. If the farmer in the preceding example could not find a user to enter into the contract to accept the future delivery of wheat, a speculator would make the contract and accept the risk of a price decline. If the user could not find a farmer to supply a contract for the future delivery of wheat, the speculator would make the contract to sell (to deliver) and accept the risk of a price increase.

Of course, farmers, users, and speculators are simultaneously entering contracts. No one knows who buys and who sells at a specific moment. However, if there is an excess or a shortage of one type of contract, the futures price of the commodity changes, which induces a certain behavior. For example, if September wheat is quoted at \$3.75 per bushel, but no one is willing to buy at that price, the price declines. This induces some potential sellers to withdraw from the market and some potential buyers to enter the market. By this process, an imbalance of supply and demand for contracts for a particular delivery date is erased. It is the interaction of the hedgers and the speculators that establishes the futures price of each contract.

FINANCIAL AND CURRENCY FUTURES

FINANCIAL FUTURES
Contract for the future delivery of a financial asset

CURRENCY FUTURES
Contract for the future delivery of a currency

In the previous discussion, futures contracts meant commodity contracts for the delivery of physical goods. However, there are also **financial futures,** which are contracts for the future delivery of a security, such as a Treasury bill, and **currency futures,** which are contracts for the future delivery of currencies (for example, the

British pound or the European euro). The market for financial futures, like the market for commodity futures, has two participants: the speculators and the hedgers. It is the interaction of their demands for and supplies of these contracts that determines the price of a given financial futures contract.

While any speculator may participate in any of the financial or currency futures markets, the hedgers differ from the speculators because they also deal in the security or the currency itself. The hedgers in currency futures are primarily multinational firms that make and receive payments in foreign moneys. Since the value of these currencies can change, the value of payments that the firms must make or receive can change. Firms thus establish hedge positions in order to lock in the price of the currency and thereby avoid the risk associated with fluctuations in the value of one currency relative to another.

Financial futures are used in hedge positions by financial institutions and borrowers to lock in yields. As interest rates and bond prices change, the yields from lending and the cost of borrowing are altered. To reduce the risk of loss from fluctuations in interest rates, borrowers and lenders may establish hedge positions to lock in a particular interest rate.

Speculators, of course, are not seeking to reduce risk but to reap large returns for taking risks. The speculators bear the risk that the hedgers want to avoid. The speculators anticipate changes in the value of currencies and the direction of changes in interest rates and security prices and take positions that will yield profits. The return the speculators earn (if successful) is magnified because of the leverage offered by the small margin requirements necessary to establish the positions.

How financial futures may produce profits for speculators may be illustrated with an example that employs the futures contract for the delivery of U.S. Treasury bonds. Suppose a speculator expects interest rates to fall and bond prices to rise. This individual enters into a contract to accept (to buy) and take delivery of Treasury bonds in the future (the *long* position). If interest rates do fall and bond prices rise, the value of this contract increases, because the speculator has the contract to buy bonds at a lower price (in other words, higher yield). If, however, interest rates rise, bond prices fall, and the value of this contract declines. The decline in the value of the contract inflicts a loss on the speculator who bought the contract when yields were lower.

If speculators expect interest rates to rise, they enter into a contract to sell and to make future delivery of Treasury bonds, thus establishing a *short* position. If interest rates do rise and the value of the bond declines, the value of this contract must decline. The speculators earn a profit because the short sellers can buy the bonds at a lower price and deliver them at the price specified in the contract. Of course, if the speculators are wrong and interest rates fall, the value of the bonds increases, which inflicts a loss on the speculators who must now pay more to buy the bonds to cover the contract.

While speculators use financial futures as a means to take advantage of fluctuations in interest rates and security prices, financial managers or investors may use futures to reduce the risk of loss from the same price fluctuations. For example, suppose a firm has decided to invest in plant and equipment. Building a new plant and installing new equipment takes time, during which the cost of capital may change as interest rates and security prices fluctuate. If the cost of capital falls, the investment may become even more profitable. However, if interest rates rise and security prices fall (that is, the cost of capital rises), an investment that was previously judged to be profitable may now be unprofitable.

It is the risk associated with fluctuations in interest rates and security prices that the financial manager seeks to reduce. One means to avoid this risk is to acquire the funds to finance the investment when the investment decision is made. But this may not be possible, since raising funds may require time. The financial manager then may use financial futures as a means to reduce the risk of loss from an increase in the cost of capital. Of course, hedging reduces the possibility of gain should the cost of capital fall. However, the emphasis is on risk reduction and not on increased profitability through speculating on changes in the cost of funds.

The reduction in risk is achieved by the financial manager entering a contract to make future delivery (taking a short position). The impact of this hedge may be seen in the following illustration. In six months a firm plans to issue $1 million of 20-year bonds. If interest rates increase, the firm will have to pay an additional $10,000 annually for every 1 percent increase in the rate of interest. To hedge against the potential loss if interest rates rise, the financial manager takes a short position in a contract to deliver Treasury bonds. If interest rates do rise, the value of these contracts declines. The financial manager may then close out the position in these contracts at a profit, which will help offset the loss resulting from the increased cost of funds.

The previous illustration considered the borrower's reduction of loss through hedging. Lenders also bear risk associated with fluctuations in interest rates, but the risk is from lower, not higher, interest rates. For example, suppose a financial institution agrees to make a loan in six months at the then current rate of interest. That rate could be higher or lower than the current rate. If interest rates rise, the lender will earn a higher return on the loan; if interest rates fall, the yield will be lower. Lenders can protect themselves from a decline in interest rates by hedging through the use of financial futures.

Unlike borrowers, who enter futures contracts to sell (or deliver) to hedge their positions, lenders enter futures contracts to buy (or accept delivery). If interest rates do fall, the value of the contracts will increase. This increase in the value of the contract will partially offset the interest lost as a result of lower rates. Of course, the lender will have forgone the possibility of earning a higher yield if interest rates were to increase. Higher interest rates would reduce the value of the contract and thus offset the higher rate earned on the loan.

STOCK INDEX FUTURES

The previous section covered financial futures whose value fluctuates with changes in interest rates. This section considers stock index futures whose value is derived from and fluctuates with changes in the stock market. **Stock index futures** are contracts based on an aggregate measure of the stock market, such as the S&P 500, the New York Stock Exchange stock index, or the Value Line stock index. These stock index futures contracts offer speculators and hedgers opportunities for profit or risk reduction that are not possible through the purchase of

STOCK INDEX FUTURES
Contracts based on an index of security prices

individual securities. For example, the NYSE Composite Index futures contracts have a value that is 500 times the value of the NYSE Index. Thus, if the NYSE Index is 100, the contract is worth $50,000. By entering a contract to buy (establishing a long position), the holder profits if the market rises. If the NYSE Index rose to 105, the value of the contract would increase to $52,500. The investor would then earn a profit of $2,500. Of course, if the NYSE Index declined, the buyer would experience a loss.

The sellers of those contracts also participate in the fluctuations of the market, but their positions are the opposite of the buyers (that is, they have established a short position). If the value of the NYSE Index fell from 100 to 95, the value of the contract would decline from $50,000 to $47,500, and the short seller would earn a $2,500 profit. Of course, if the market rose, the short seller would suffer a loss. Obviously, if the individual anticipates a rising market, that investor should take a long position in a stock index futures contract. Conversely, if the investor expects the market to fall, he or she should take a short position.

These contracts may also be used by professional money managers who are not speculating on price movements but who seek to hedge against adverse price movements. For example, suppose a portfolio manager has a well-diversified portfolio of stocks as part of a firm's pension plan. If the market rises, the value of this portfolio appreciates. However, there would be the risk of loss if the market were to decline. The portfolio manager can reduce this risk by entering an NYSE Index futures contract to sell at the specified price (a short position). If the market declines, the losses experienced by the portfolio will at least be partially offset by the appreciation in the value of the short position in the futures contract.

NYSE Index futures contracts are similar to other future contracts. The buyers and sellers must make good faith deposits (margin payments). Since the amount of this margin is modest (only $3,500 per contract), these contracts offer considerable leverage. If stock prices move against the investor and the investor's equity in the position declines, the individual will have to place additional funds in the account to support the contract. Since there is an active market in the contracts, the investor may close a position at any time by taking the opposite position. Thus if the investor has a contract to buy, that long position is closed by a contract to sell. If the investor has a contract to sell (to deliver), that short position is closed by a contract to buy (to accept delivery).

There is one important difference between stock market futures and other futures contracts. Settlement at the expiration or maturity of the contract occurs in cash. There is no physical delivery of securities as could occur with a commodity futures contract to buy or sell wheat or corn. Instead, gains and losses are totaled and are added to or subtracted from the participants' accounts. The long and the short positions are then closed.

CONVERTIBLE BONDS AND CONVERTIBLE PREFERRED STOCK

This chapter has covered options to buy and sell securities, and futures contracts to buy and sell commodities. In each case, the value of the option or the contract was derived from the value of the underlying security or commodity. This section considers convertible bonds and convertible preferred stock whose value is also derived from another asset. As will be explained in the next two sections, the value of a convertible security is partially derived from the price of the stock into which the bond (or preferred stock) may be converted and partially from its value as a nonconvertible bond.

Features of Convertible Bonds

CONVERTIBLE BOND
Bond that may be converted into (exchanged for) stock at the option of the holder

Convertible bonds are debentures (that is, unsecured debt instruments) that may be converted at the holder's option into the stock of the issuing company. As was seen in Chapter 9, firms issue a variety of debt instruments to tap funds in the capital markets. The conversion feature is an option firms grant bondholders to induce them to buy the debt. Since the firm has granted the holder the right to convert the bonds, these bonds are usually subordinated to the firm's other debt. They also tend to offer a lower rate of interest (coupon rate) than is available on nonconvertible debt. Thus, the conversion feature means that the firm can issue lower-quality debt at a lower interest cost. Investors are willing to accept this reduced quality and interest income because the market value of the bond will appreciate *if* the price of the stock rises. These investors are thus trading quality and interest for possible capital gains.

Since convertible bonds are long-term debt instruments, they have features that are common to all bonds. They are usually issued in $1,000 denominations, pay interest semiannually, and have a fixed maturity date. However, if the bonds are converted into stock, the maturity date is irrelevant because the bonds are retired when they are converted. Convertible bonds frequently have a sinking fund requirement, which, like the maturity date, is meaningless once the bonds are converted.

Convertible bonds are always callable. The firm uses the call to force the holders to convert the bonds. Once the bond is called, the owner must convert, or any appreciation in price that has resulted from an increase in the stock's value will be lost. Such forced conversion is extremely important to the issuing firm, because it no longer has to repay the debt.

Convertible bonds are attractive to some investors because they offer the safety features of debt. The firm must meet the terms of the indenture, and the bonds must be retired if they are not converted. The flow of interest income usually exceeds the dividend yield that may be earned on the firm's stock. In addition, since the bonds may be converted into stock, the holder will share in the growth of the company. If the price of the stock rises in response to the firm's growth, the value of the convertible bond must also rise. It is this combination of the safety of debt and the potential for capital gain that makes convertible bonds an attractive investment, particularly to investors who desire income and some capital appreciation.

Like all investments, convertible bonds subject the holder to risk. If the company fails, the holder of a bond stands to lose the funds invested in the debt. This is particularly true with regard to convertible bonds, because they are usually subordinated to the firm's other debt. Thus, convertible bonds are less safe than senior debt or debt that is secured by specific collateral. In case of a default or bankruptcy, holders of convertible bonds may at best realize only a fraction of the principal amount invested. However, their position is still superior to that of the stockholders.

Default is not the only potential source of risk to investors. Convertible bonds are actively traded, and their prices can and do fluctuate. As is explained in the next section, their price is partially derived from the value of the stock into which they may be converted. Fluctuations in the value of the stock produce fluctuations in the price of the bond. These price changes are *in addition* to price movements caused by changes in interest rates. Thus, during periods of higher interest rates and lower stock prices, convertible bonds are doubly cursed. Their lower coupon rates of interest cause their prices to decline more than those of nonconvertible debt. This, in addition to the decline in the value of the stock into which they may be converted, results in considerable price declines for convertible bonds.

The Valuation of Convertible Bonds

The value of a convertible bond is derived from (1) the value of the stock into which it may be converted and (2) the value of the bond as a debt instrument. Although each of these factors affects the market price of the bond, the importance of each element varies with changing conditions in the security markets. In the final analysis, the valuation of a convertible bond is difficult, because it is a hybrid security that combines debt and equity.

This section has three subdivisions. The first considers the value of the bond solely as stock. The second covers the bond's value only as a debt instrument, and the last section combines these values to show the hybrid nature of convertible bonds. In order to differentiate the value of the bond as stock from its value as debt, subscripts are added to the symbols used. *S* will represent stock, and *D* will represent debt.

THE CONVERTIBLE BOND AS STOCK The value of a convertible bond in terms of the stock into which it may be converted (C_S) depends upon (1) the principal amount of the bond or face amount received in the future (FV), (2) the conversion (or exercise) price per share of the bond (P_e), and (3) the market price of the common stock (P_S). The principal divided by the conversion price of the bond gives the number of shares into which the bond may be converted. For example, if a $1,000 bond may be converted at $20 per share, the bond may be converted into 50 shares ($1,000 ÷ $20). The number of shares times the market price of a share gives the value of the bond in terms of stock. If the bond is convertible into 50 shares and the stock sells for $15 per share, the bond is worth $750 in terms of stock.

This conversion value of the bond as stock is expressed in Equation 13.1:

13.1 $$C_S = \frac{FV}{P_e} \times P_S$$

and is illustrated in Exhibit 13.8. In this example a $1,000 bond is convertible into 50 shares (a conversion price of $20 per share). The first column gives various

EXHIBIT 13.8

Relationship between the Price of a Stock and the Value of a Convertible Bond

Price of the Stock	Shares into Which the Bond Is Convertible	Value of the Bond in Terms of Stock
$ 0	50	$ 0
5	50	250
10	50	500
15	50	750
20	50	1,000
25	50	1,250
30	50	1,500

prices of the stock. The second column presents the number of shares into which the bond is convertible (in this case, 50 shares). The third column gives the value of the bond in terms of stock (the product of the values in the first two columns). Thus, if the price of the stock is $15, the conversion value of the bond is $1,000/$20 × $15 = $750. As may be seen in the exhibit, the value of the bond in terms of stock rises as the price of the stock increases.

This relationship between the price of the stock and the conversion value of the bond is illustrated in Figure 13.9. The price of the stock (P_S) is given on the horizontal axis, and the conversion value of the bond (C_S) is shown on the vertical axis. As the price of the stock rises, the conversion value of the bond increases. This is shown in the graph by line C_S, which represents the value of the bond in terms of stock. Line C_S is a straight line running through the origin. If the stock has no value, the value of the bond in terms of stock is also worthless. If the exercise price of the bond and the market price of the stock are equal (that is, $P_S = P_e$, which in this case is $20), the bond's value as stock is equal to the principal amount. As the price of the stock rises above the exercise price of the bond, the value of the bond in terms of stock increases to more than the principal amount of the debt.

The market price of a convertible bond cannot be less than the bond's conversion value as stock. If the price of the bond were less than its value as stock, an opportunity for profit would exist. Investors would purchase the convertible bond, exercise the conversion feature, and sell the shares acquired through the conversion. The investors would then make a profit equal to the difference between the price of the convertible bond and the conversion value of the bond. For example, if in the preceding example the bond were selling for $800 when the stock sold for $20, the bond would be worth $1,000 in terms of the stock ($20 × 50). Investors would buy the bond for $800 and convert it. Then they would sell the 20 shares for $1,000 and earn $200 profit (before commissions).

As investors sought to purchase the bonds, they would drive up the price of the bonds. The price increase would continue until there was no opportunity for profit, which would occur when the price of the bond was equal to or greater than the bond's value as stock. Thus the value of the bond in terms of stock sets the

FIGURE 13.9

Relationship between the Price of a Stock and the Conversion Value of the Bond

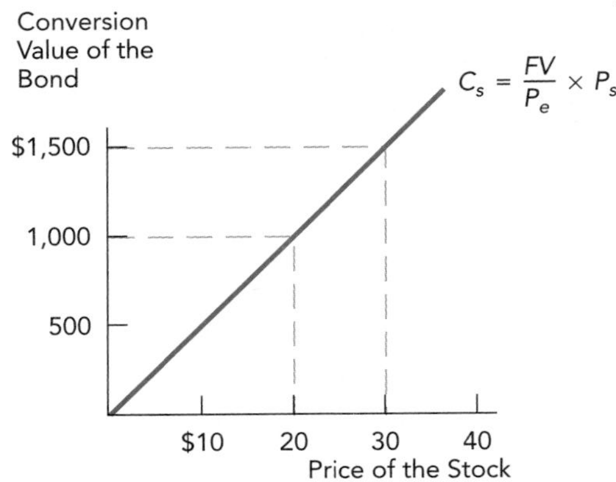

minimum price of the bond. The market price of a convertible bond will be at least equal to its conversion value.

However, the market price of the convertible bond is rarely equal to the conversion value of the bond. The bond frequently sells for a premium over its conversion value, because the convertible bond may also have value as a debt instrument. As a pure (nonconvertible) bond, it competes with other nonconvertible debt. Like the conversion feature, this element of debt may affect the bond's price. Its impact is important, for it has the effect of putting a minimum price on the convertible bond, giving investors in convertible bonds an element of safety that stock lacks.

THE CONVERTIBLE BOND AS DEBT The value of a convertible bond as debt (C_D) is related to (1) the annual interest or coupon rate that the bond pays (PMT), (2) the current interest rate being paid on comparable nonconvertible debt (i), and (3) the requirement that the principal or face value (FV) be retired at maturity (after n years) if the bond is not converted. In terms of present value calculations, the value of a convertible bond as nonconvertible debt is given in Equation 13.2:

13.2

$$C_D = \frac{PMT}{(1+i)^1} + \frac{PMT}{(1+i)^2} + \cdots + \frac{PMT}{(1+i)^n} + \frac{FV}{(1+i)^n}.$$

Equation 13.2 is the value of any bond (Equation 9.1 given in Chapter 9). Thus, the equation used to determine the value of a nonconvertible bond is used to determine the convertible bond's value as debt.

Equation 13.2 may be illustrated by the following example. Assume that the convertible bond in Exhibit 13.8 matures in ten years and pays 5 percent annually.

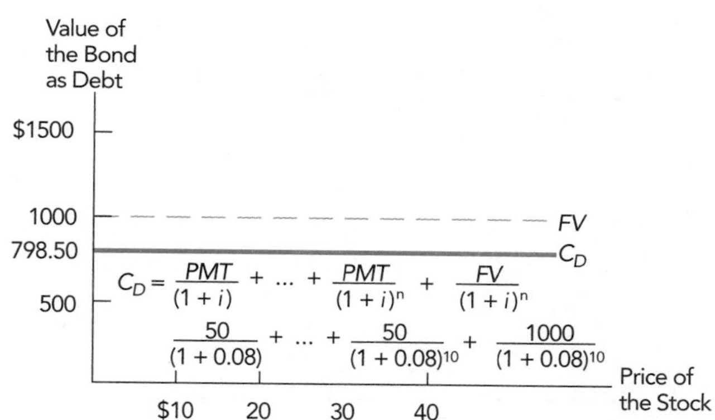

FIGURE 13.10

Relationship between the Price of a Stock and the Value of the Bond as Nonconvertible Debt

Nonconvertible debt of the same risk class currently yields 8 percent. When these values are inserted into Equation 13.2, the value of the bond as nonconvertible debt is $798.50.

$$C_D = \frac{\$50}{(1+0.08)^1} + \frac{\$50}{(1+0.08)^2} + \cdots + \frac{\$50}{(1+0.08)^9}$$

$$+ \frac{\$50}{(1+0.08)^{10}} + \frac{\$1{,}000}{(1+0.08)^{10}}$$

$$= \$50(PVAIF\ 8I,\ 10N) + \$1{,}000(PVIF\ 8I,\ 10N)$$

$$= \$50(6.710) + \$1{,}000(0.463) = \$798.50.$$

CALCULATOR SOLUTION

Function Key		Data Input
FV	=	1,000
PMT	=	50
I	=	8
N	=	10
PV	=	?
Function Key		*Answer*
PV	=	−798.70

The relationship between the price of the common stock and the value of this bond as nonconvertible debt is illustrated in Figure 13.10. This figure consists of a horizontal line (C_D) that shows what the price ($798.50) of the bond would be if it were not convertible into stock, in which case the price is independent of the value of the stock. The principal amount of the bond is also shown in Figure 13.10 by the broken line *FV*, which is above the line C_D. The principal amount exceeds the value of the bond as pure debt because this bond must sell at a discount to be competitive with nonconvertible debt.

The value of the convertible bond as debt varies with market interest rates. Since the interest paid by the bond is fixed, the value of the bond as debt varies inversely with interest rates. An increase in interest rates causes this value to fall; a decline in interest rates causes the value to rise.

The relationship between the value of the preceding convertible bond as debt and various interest rates is presented in Exhibit 13.9. The first column gives various interest rates; the second column gives the nominal (coupon) rate of interest; and the last column gives the value of the bond as nonconvertible debt (as

EXHIBIT 13.9

Relationship between Interest Rates and the Value of a Bond

Interest Rate	Coupon Rate	Value of a Ten-Year Bond
3%	5%	$1,170.60
4	5	1,081.11
5	5	1,000.00
6	5	926.40
7	5	859.53
8	5	798.70
10	5	692.77
12	5	604.48

determined using a financial calculator). The inverse relationship is readily apparent, for as the interest rate rises from 3 percent to 12 percent, the value of the bond declines from $1,170.60 to $604.48.

The value of the bond as nonconvertible debt is important because it sets another minimum value that the bond will command in the market. At that price the convertible bond is competitive with nonconvertible debt of the same maturity and degree of risk. If the bond were to sell below this price, it would offer a yield that is higher than that of nonconvertible debt. Investors would buy the convertible bond to attain this higher yield and bid up the bond's price until its yield was comparable to that of nonconvertible debt. Thus, the bond's value as nonconvertible debt becomes a floor on the price of the convertible bond. Even if the value of the stock into which the bond may be converted were to fall, this floor would halt the decline in the price of the convertible bond.

The actual minimum price of a convertible bond combines its value as stock and its value as debt. This is illustrated in Figure 13.11, which combines the preceding figures for the value of the bond in terms of stock and the value of the bond as nonconvertible debt. The bond's price is always equal to or greater than the higher of the two valuations. If the price of the convertible bond were below its value as common stock, investors would bid up its price. If the bond sold for a price below its value as debt, investors in debt instruments would bid up the price.

While the minimum price of the convertible bond is either its value in terms of stock or its value as nonconvertible debt, the importance of these determinants varies. For low stock prices (stock prices less than P_{s1} in Figure 13.11), the minimum price is set by the bond's value as debt. However, for stock prices greater than P_{s1}, it is the bond's value as stock that determines the minimum price.

THE BOND'S VALUE AS A HYBRID SECURITY The market price (P_m) of the convertible bond combines both the conversion value of the bond and its value as nonconvertible debt. If the price of the stock were to decline below the exercise price of the bond, the market price of the convertible bond would be influenced primarily by the bond's value as nonconvertible debt. In effect, the bond would be priced as if it were a pure debt instrument. As the price of the stock rises,

FIGURE 13.11

Minimum Price of a Convertible Bond

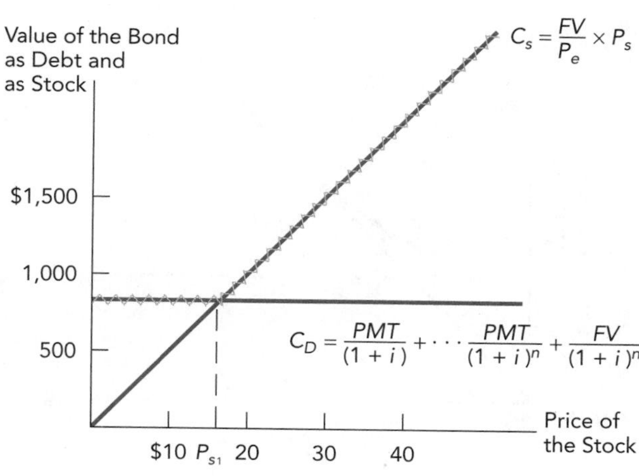

the conversion value of the bond rises and plays an increasingly important role in the determination of the market price of the convertible bond. At sufficiently high stock prices, the market price of the bond is identical with its conversion value.

These relationships are illustrated in Figure 13.12, which reproduces Figure 13.11 and adds to it the market price of the convertible bond (P_m). For prices of the common stock below P_{s1}, the market price is identical to the bond's value as nonconvertible debt. For prices of the common stock above P_{s2}, the price of the bond is identical to its value as common stock. At these extreme stock prices, the bond may be analyzed as if it were either pure debt or stock. For all prices between these two extremes, the market price of the convertible bond is influenced by the bond's value both as nonconvertible debt and as stock.

Premiums Paid for Convertible Debt

One way to analyze a convertible bond is to measure the premium over the bond's value as debt or as stock. For example, if a particular convertible bond is commanding a higher premium than is paid for similar convertible securities, perhaps this bond should be sold. Conversely, if the premium is low, the bond may be a good investment. Of course, the lower premium may indicate financial weakness, in which case the bond would not be a good investment. Thus, a lower premium is not a sufficient reason to acquire a convertible bond, but it may suggest that the bond be considered for purchase after further analysis.

The premiums paid for a convertible bond are illustrated in Exhibit 13.10, which reproduces Exhibit 13.8 and adds the value of the bond as nonconvertible debt (column 4) along with hypothetical market prices for the bond (column 5). The premium that an investor pays for a convertible bond may be viewed in either of two ways: the premium over the bond's value as stock or the premium over the

FIGURE 13.12

Determining the Market Price of a Convertible Bond

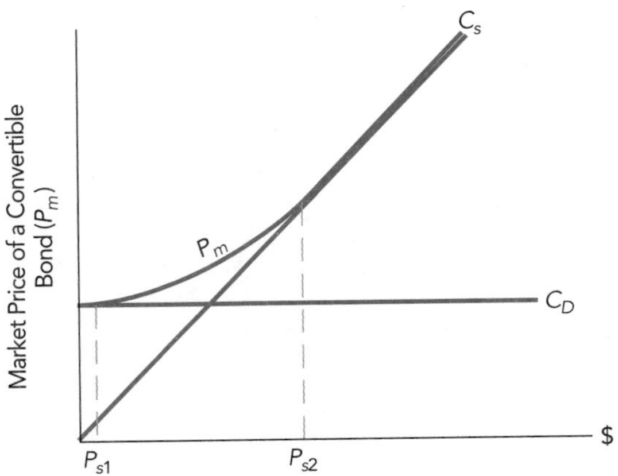

bond's value as debt.[6] Column 6 gives the premium in terms of stock. This is the difference between the bond's market price and its value as stock (the value in column 5 minus the value in column 3). This premium declines as the price of the stock rises and plays a more important role in the determination of the bond's price. Column 7 gives the premium in terms of nonconvertible debt. This is the difference between the bond's market price and its value as debt (the value in column 5 minus the value in column 4). This premium rises as the price of the stock rises, because the debt element of the bond is less important.

The inverse relationship between the two premiums is also illustrated in Figure 13.13. The premiums are shown by the differences between the line representing the market price (P_m) and the lines representing the value of the bond in terms of stock (C_S) and the value of the bond as nonconvertible debt (C_D).

[6] The Investment Analysis Calculator (**www.harcourtcollege/finance/mayo**) may be used to determine convertible bond values and premiums. Go to the submenu "Given Conversion Ratio" under Convertible Bond Calculations. Enter (1) the price of the bond, (2) the coupon rate of interest, (3) the term on the bond, (4) the face value of the bond, (5) the interest rate on comparable non-convertible debt, (6) the conversion ratio, which is the number of shares into which the bond may be converted, (7) the price of the stock, and (8) the stock's dividend. The software then calculates

1. the value of the bond in terms of stock
2. the premium over the bond's value as stock
3. the value of the bond as debt
4. the premium over the bond's value as debt
5. the price of the stock based on the price of the bond
6. the number of years necessary for the bond's interest to cover the bond's premium over its value as stock
7. The bond's yield to maturity.

EXHIBIT 13.10

Premiums Paid for Convertible Debt

Price of the Stock	Shares into Which the Bond May Be Converted	Value of the Bond in Terms of Stock	Value of the Bond as Nonconvertible Debt	Hypothetical Price of the Convertible Bond	Premium in Terms of Stock*	Premium in Terms of Nonconvertible Debt†
$ 0	50	$ 0	$798.50	$ 798.50	$798.50	$ 0.00
5	50	250	798.50	798.50	548.50	0.00
10	50	500	798.50	798.50	298.50	0.00
15	50	750	798.50	900.00	150.00	101.50
20	50	1,000	798.50	1,100.00	100.00	301.50
25	50	1,250	798.50	1,300.00	50.00	501.50
30	50	1,500	798.50	1,500.00	0.00	701.50

**The premium in terms of stock is equal to the hypothetical price of the convertible bond minus the value of the bond in terms of stock.*

†The premium in terms of nonconvertible debt is equal to the hypothetical price of the convertible bond minus the value of the bond as nonconvertible debt.

FIGURE 13.13

Premiums Paid for a Convertible Bond

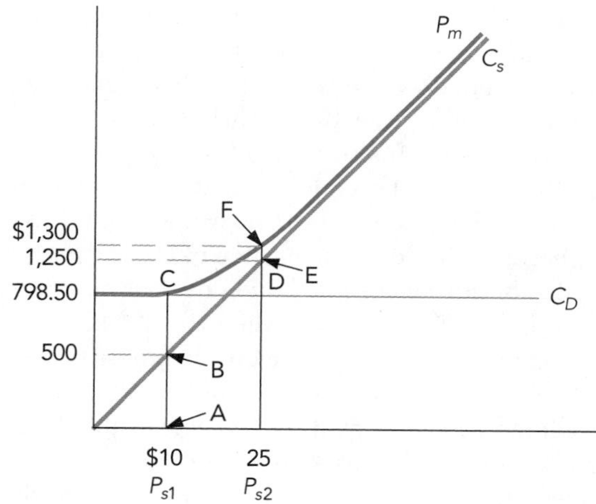

When the price of the stock is low and the bond is selling close to its value as debt, the premium above the bond's value as stock is substantial, but the premium above the bond's value as debt is small. For example, at P_{s1} the price of the stock is $10, the bond's value in terms of stock is $500 (line AB in Figure 13.13), and the premium is $298.50 (line BC). However, the bond is selling for its value as nonconvertible debt ($798.50), and there is no premium over its value as debt. When the price of the stock is $25 and the bond is selling for $1,300, the premium in terms of stock is only $50 (line EF). However, the bond's premium over its value as nonconvertible debt is $501.50 (line DF).

As these examples illustrate, the premium paid for the bond over its value as stock declines as the price of the stock rises. This decline in the premium is the result of the increasing importance of the conversion value on the bond's market price and the decreasing importance of the debt element on the bond's price.

As the price of the stock rises, the safety feature of the debt diminishes. If the price of the common stock ceased to rise and started to fall, then the price of the convertible bond could decline considerably before it reached the floor price set by the nonconvertible debt. For example, if the price of the stock declined from $30 to $15 (a 50 percent decline), the price of the convertible bond could fall from $1,500 to $798.50 (a 46.8 percent decline). Such a price decline would indicate that the floor value of $798.50 had little impact on the decline in the price of the bond.

In addition, as the price of the stock (and hence the price of the convertible bond) rises, the probability that the bond will be called rises. When the bond is called, it can be worth only its value as stock. The call forces the holder to convert the bond into stock. For example, when the price of the stock is $30, the bond is worth $1,500 in terms of stock. Should the company call the bond and offer to retire it for its face value ($1,000), no one would accept the offer. Instead they would convert the bond into $1,500 worth of stock. If the investor paid a premium over this conversion value (such as $1,600) and the bond were called, the investor would suffer a loss. Thus, as the probability of a call increases, the willingness to pay a premium over the bond's value as stock declines, and the price of the convertible bond ultimately converges with its value as stock.

This decline in the premium also means that the price of the stock will rise more rapidly than the price of the bond. As may be seen in both Exhibit 13.10 and Figure 13.13, the market price of the convertible bond rises and falls with the price of the stock, because the conversion value of the bond rises and falls. However, the market price of the convertible bond does not rise as rapidly as the conversion value of the bond. For example, when the stock's price increased from $20 to $25 (a 25 percent increase), the convertible bond's price rose from $1,100 to $1,300 (an 18.2 percent increase). The reason for this difference in the rate of increase is the declining premium paid for the convertible bond. Since the premium declines as the price of the stock rises, the rate of increase in the price of the stock must exceed the rate of increase in the price of the bond. In summary, convertible bonds offer investors the opportunity for some capital growth with less risk.

CONVERTIBLE PREFERRED STOCK

CONVERTIBLE PREFERRED STOCK
Preferred stock that may be converted into common stock at the option of the holder

In addition to convertible bonds, firms may issue **convertible preferred stock.** As its name implies, this stock is convertible into the common stock of the issuing corporation. Although convertible preferred stock is similar to convertible debt,

Swaps

In addition to options and futures, another derivative is the swap. A swap is an agreement between two parties who contract to exchange (that is, swap) payments. A swap is as if I agree to pay your electric bill if you will agree to pay my phone bill. We agree to trade payments. Individuals rarely, if ever, swap payments, but firms and financial institutions often participate in the swap market. Firms make their profits through operations and not from speculating on anticipated price changes. To reduce the risk of loss from price changes, management may enter into a swap agreement. ¶ Swaps occur primarily in one of two cases. One firm swaps a series of fixed payments for a series of variable payments. In the second case, a firm swaps payments in one currency for payments in a different currency. Consider an American firm with operations in the United Kingdom. If the American firm must make payments in British pounds, the dollar cost of the payments rises if the pound increases (the dollar declines). (Correspondingly, the dollar cost declines if the pound decreases and the dollar increases.) The converse is true for a British firm with American operations that must make payments in dollars. The fluctuation in the exchange rate can increase or decrease the firm's earnings. ¶ One means to reduce the risk of loss is to hedge using currency futures. Swapping payments is another means to reduce the foreign exchange risk. The British firm agrees to make the American firm's required payments in pounds, and the American firm agrees to make the British firm's dollar payments. Since both firms are now making the payments in their native currency, neither has the risk associated with changes in the exchange rate. If the dollar rises (pound falls), the effect on both firms is immaterial. ¶ Since firms are generally in business to generate profits from operations and not from exchange rate fluctuations, many firms with international operations participate in swap agreements. For example, in its *1998 Annual Report*, Coca-Cola stated that it had currency swap agreements at the end of 1998 totaling over $1 billion. Coke's total derivative activities using interest rate swaps, currency swaps, and commodity futures exceeded $4 billion. None of these derivatives transactions, however, was to speculate on price changes; all were entered to manage risk. ¶

there are important differences. The differences are primarily the same as those between nonconvertible preferred stock and nonconvertible debt. Preferred stock is an equity instrument. Thus, the firm may not pay the dividend. In addition, the preferred stock may be a perpetual security and may not have to be retired. However, convertible preferred stocks are always callable, so the firm can force investors to convert the preferred stock into common stock.

The value of convertible preferred stock (like convertible bonds) is derived from the price of the stock into which it may be converted and the value of comparable nonconvertible preferred stock. As with convertible bonds, these values set floors on the price of the convertible preferred stock. It cannot sell for any length of time below its value as stock. If it did, investors would buy the preferred stock, which would increase its price. Thus, the minimum value of the convertible preferred stock (like the minimum value of the convertible bond) must be equal to the conversion value of the stock (P_e). In equation form that is

13.3 $$P_e = P_S \times N,$$

in which P_S is the market price of the stock into which the convertible preferred stock may be converted, and N is the number of shares an investor obtains through conversion. Equation 13.3 is similar to Equation 13.1, which gave the value of the convertible bond as stock.

The convertible preferred stock's value as nonconvertible preferred stock (P) is related to the dividend it pays (D) and to the appropriate discount factor (k), which is the yield earned on competitive nonconvertible preferred stock. In equation form that is

13.4 $$P = \frac{D}{k},$$

which is the same as the convertible bond's value as debt, except that the preferred stock has no definite maturity date. However, this value does set a floor on the price of a convertible preferred stock because at that price it is competitive with nonconvertible preferred stock.

As with convertible bonds, the convertible preferred stock is a hybrid security whose value combines its worth both as stock and as nonconvertible preferred stock. Convertible preferred stock tends to sell for a premium over both its value as stock and its value as straight preferred stock. Figures 13.12 and 13.13, which illustrated the value of the convertible bond at various prices of the stock into which it may be converted, also apply to convertible preferred stock. The primary difference is the premium that the preferred stock commands over the value as common stock. This premium tends to be smaller. This reduced premium occurs because the preferred stock does not have the safety associated with debt. Thus, its price usually commands less of a premium over its value as stock.

SUMMARY

A derivative is a financial asset whose value depends upon (is derived from) another asset. This chapter has covered options to buy and sell stock, futures, and convertible bonds and convertible preferred stock. In each case, the value of the financial asset depends upon the underlying asset's value.

Options are the right to buy or sell stock at specified prices within specified time periods. A warrant is an option to buy stock issued by a corporation. When the option is exercised, the firm issues the new stock and receives the proceeds. A call is an option to buy stock issued by an individual. When the option is exercised, the seller (called the "writer") of the option must supply the stock, and he or she receives the proceeds of the sale. A put is an option to sell stock.

Options may have an intrinsic value, which for an option to buy stock is the difference between the market price of the stock and the option's exercise price (called the "strike price"). For a put option, the intrinsic value is the strike price minus the market price of the stock. While an option tends to sell for a time premium over its intrinsic value, the option's price (called the "premium") must equal the option's intrinsic value at the option's expiration.

Individuals buy options as a way to lever their positions. In general, the price of an option experiences larger percentage changes than does the price of the underlying stock. Individuals sell options to hedge their positions or to speculate on an anticipated price change. The existence of stock index options permits individuals to take a position without having to select individual securities; these individuals thus avoid the risk associated with the specific securities.

Futures are contracts for future delivery of a commodity such as wheat or corn. An individual ("speculator") takes a long position by entering into a contract to buy and accept delivery. The opposite, or short, position occurs when the individual enters into a contract to sell and make future delivery. The long position profits if the price of the commodity rises, since the speculator has a contract to buy at a lower price. The short position profits if the price of the commodity falls, since the speculator has a contract to sell at a higher price.

While speculators seek to profit from changes in prices, growers, miners, and other users of commodities want to reduce the risk of loss from price fluctuations. They "hedge" their positions. Growers or miners with long positions in crops and metals sell futures contracts. The sales are short positions that lock in futures prices and reduce the risk of loss from a price decline. Producers who use the crops and the metals do the opposite. They buy futures contracts to lock in prices and reduce the risk of loss from a price increase. It is frequently the speculators who are offering the contracts sought by the hedgers. This process of buying and selling futures contracts passes the risk associated with price fluctuations from the hedges to the speculators.

Besides commodity futures there are also financial futures, currency futures, and stock market futures. Financial futures are contracts for the delivery of financial assets such as U.S. Treasury bills and bonds. Currency futures are contracts for the future delivery of foreign moneys such as European euros or British pounds. Stock market futures are based on a broad measure of the market (for example, the New York Stock Exchange Composite Index). Speculators who anticipate movements in interest rates, foreign currencies, or the stock market can speculate on these anticipated price changes by taking appropriate positions in futures contracts. Financial managers may use these contracts as a means to reduce the risk associated with fluctuations in interest rates, security prices, or currency values.

A convertible bond is a debt instrument that may be converted into stock. The value of this bond depends on the value of the stock into which the bond may be converted and on the value of the bond as a debt instrument. As the value of the stock rises, so does the value of the convertible bond. If the price of the stock declines, the value of the bond will also fall. However, the stock's price will decline faster, because the convertible bond's value as debt will halt the fall in the bond's price.

Since a convertible bond's price rises with the price of the stock, the bond offers the investor an opportunity for appreciation as the value of the firm increases. In addition, the bond's value as a debt sets a floor on the bond's price, which reduces the risk of loss to the investor. Should the stock decline in value, the debt element reduces the risk of loss to the bondholder.

Convertible preferred stock is similar to convertible debt, except that it lacks the safety implied by a debt instrument. Its price is related to its conversion value, the flow of dividend income, and the rate that investors may earn on nonconvertible preferred stock.

Review Questions

1. What differentiates a warrant from a call and what differentiates both a warrant and a call from a put? Why would an investor buy any of these options?
2. What are an option's intrinsic value, its time premium, and its value at expiration? What impact does the time premium have on the option's potential leverage?

3. What is the difference between naked call writing and covered call writing? If an investor writes an option, how is the position closed?
4. If an investor anticipates that stock prices will rise, why may that individual buy a stock index option instead of buying the stock of AT&T?
5. If an investor anticipates that the price of AT&T stock will decline, that individual may buy a put or sell a call. What are the differences in the risk and the potential profits or losses from the two positions?
6. What is the difference between a long and a short position in a futures contract? Who profits if the commodity's price declines? What is the difference between the spot and the futures prices?
7. What is the difference between the margin used to acquire stock and the margin in the futures market? Why is the margin a source of financial leverage? How does a speculator close a position in a futures contract?
8. How does the financial manager of a firm that uses copper hedge against an increase in the price of copper?
9. The loan officer of a commercial bank has made a commitment to grant a loan in three months at the current rate of interest. How can that individual hedge against an increase in interest rates?
10. How is the value of a convertible bond in terms of stock determined? How is its value in terms of debt determined? What impact do these values have on the price of the bond?
11. Why, from the investor's perspective, are convertible bonds less risky than stock but more risky than nonconvertible debt?
12. Why would a company call a convertible bond? What condition must be met for the call to occur?
13. How are convertible preferred stocks different from convertible bonds? If interest rates increase, would you expect the prices of these securities to rise or fall?

PROBLEMS

1. A six-month call is the right to buy stock at $20. Currently, the stock is selling for $22, and the call is selling for $5. You buy 100 shares ($2,200) and sell one call (in other words, you receive $500).
   a. Does this position illustrate covered or naked call writing?
   b. If, at the expiration date of the call, the price of the stock is $29, what is your profit on the combined position?
   c. If, at the expiration date of the call, the price of the stock is $19, what is your profit on the combined position?
2. A put is the option to sell stock at $40. It expires after three months and currently sells for $3 when the price of the stock is $42.
   a. If an investor buys this put, what will the profit be after three months if the price of the stock is $45? $40? $35?
   b. What will be the profit from selling this put after three months if the price of the stock is $45? $40? $35?

3. The price of a stock is $39, and a six-month call with a strike price of $35 sells for $8.
   a. What is the option's intrinsic value?
   b. What is the option's time premium?
   c. If the price of the stock rises, what happens to the price of the call?
   d. If the price of the stock falls to $36, what is the maximum you could lose from buying the call?
   e. What is the maximum profit you could earn by selling the call uncovered (naked)?
   f. If, at the expiration of the call, the price of the stock is $35, what is the profit (or loss) from buying the call?
   g. If, at the expiration of the call, the price of the stock is $35, what is the profit (or loss) from selling the call naked?
   h. If, at the expiration of the call, the price of the stock is $46, what is the profit (or loss) from buying the call?
   i. If, at the expiration of the call, the price of the stock is $46, what is the profit (or loss) from selling the call naked?
4. The price of a stock is $61, and a six-month call with a strike price of $60 sells for $5.
   a. What is the option's intrinsic value?
   b. What is the option's time premium?
   c. If the price of the stock falls, what happens to the price of the call?
   d. If the price of the stock falls to $45, what is the maximum you could lose from buying the call?
   e. What is the maximum profit you could earn by selling the call uncovered (that is, naked)?
   f. If, at the expiration of the call, the price of the stock is $66, what is the profit (or loss) from buying the call?
   g. If, at the expiration of the call, the price of the stock is $66, what is the profit (or loss) from selling the call naked?
   h. If, at the expiration of the call, the price of the stock is $46, what is the profit (or loss) from buying the call?
   i. If, at the expiration of the call, the price of the stock is $46, what is the profit (or loss) from selling the call naked?
5. A warrant is the option to buy stock at $25. It expires after one year and currently sells for $4. The underlying stock is selling for $26.
   a. What is the intrinsic value and the time premium paid for the warrant?
   b. What will be the value of this warrant if the price of the stock at the warrant's expiration is $20? $25? $30? $40?
   c. If the price of the stock is $45 at the expiration of the warrant, what is the percentage return that is earned by an investor in the stock and an investor in the warrant? Why does the warrant in this problem illustrate the successful use of financial leverage?
6. You expect the stock market to increase, but instead of acquiring stock, you decide to acquire a stock index futures contract based on the New York Stock Exchange Composite Index. That index is currently 58.8, and the contract has a

value that is $500 times the amount of the index. The margin requirement is $2,500.

a. When you make the contract, how much must you put up?
b. What is the value of the contract based on the index?
c. If the value of the index rises 1 percent to 59.39, what is the profit on the investment? What is the percentage earned on the funds you put up?
d. If the value of the index declines 1 percent to 58.2, what percentage of your funds will you lose?
e. What is the percentage you earn (or lose) if the index falls to 53.8?

7. Given the following information concerning a convertible bond, answer the following questions:

Principal	$1,000
Coupon	5%
Maturity	15 years
Call price	$1,050
Conversion price	$37 (i.e., 27 shares)
Market price of the common stock	$32
Market price of the bond	$1,040

a. What is the current yield of this bond?
b. What is the value of the bond based on the market price of the common stock?
c. What is the value of the common stock based on the market price of the bond?
d. What is the premium in terms of stock that the investor pays when he or she purchases the convertible bond instead of the stock?
e. Nonconvertible bonds are selling with a yield to maturity of 7 percent. If this bond lacked the conversion feature, what would the approximate price of the bond be?
f. What is the premium in terms of debt that the investor pays when he or she purchases the convertible bond instead of a nonconvertible bond?
g. What is the probability that the corporation will call this bond?
h. Why are investors willing to pay the premiums mentioned in questions d and f?

8. Given the following information concerning a convertible bond:

- Coupon 6% ($50 per $1,000 bond)
- Exercise price: $25
- Maturity date: 20 years
- Call price: $1,040
- Price of the common stock: $30

a. If this bond were nonconvertible, what would be its approximate value if comparable interest rates were 9 percent?
b. How many shares can the bond be converted into?
c. What is the value of the bond in terms of stock?
d. What is the current minimum price that the bond will command?

e. Is there any reason to anticipate that the firm will call the bond?
f. What do investors receive if they do not convert the bond when it is called?
g. If the bond were called, would it be advantageous to convert?

CASE

A Speculator's Choices

Rachel Fried is an optimist who likes to speculate. She enjoys watching prices change rapidly and believes that she could make large profits by judiciously taking advantage of price swings. Thus it is easy to see why she is attracted to options whose prices may change rapidly from day to day. She especially likes the securities associated with Fasolt Construction Corporation, a large building and engineering firm that also has considerable holdings of coal and oil reserves.

Currently the economy is in a recession. Fasolt is doubly cursed: The recession has resulted in a significant decline in construction, and commodity prices, including oil and gas, are declining. These two factors have reduced Fasolt's profit margins so that per share earnings have plummeted from $5.50 to $1.00 during the latest fiscal year. The stock, which at one time had been an outstanding performer, has declined from a high of more than $80 to its current price of $15.

Ms. Fried believes that the stock market has overreacted to the decline in earnings. Furthermore, there are signs that the recession is ending. Retail sales have risen and interest rates are falling. A more robust economy should certainly help Fasolt's sales and earnings, which Ms. Fried believes would result in a higher stock price. Fasolt's fundamentals are sound, as its profit margins have historically been among the highest in the industry. However, the firm has a considerable amount of long-term debt outstanding. Even though the company pays no cash dividends, it has had to issue long-term bonds because retained earnings were insufficient to finance expansion and acquisitions.

Ms. Fried firmly believes that Fasolt Construction offers an excellent opportunity for profit, but she is very uncertain as to the correct strategy to follow. In addition to the stock, the firm has outstanding a convertible debenture with a 7 percent coupon and an exercise price of $30 (33.33 shares per $1,000 bond). The bond is currently selling for $780 per $1,000 face amount and, like the stock, is actively traded. It is rated double B by one rating service but only single B by another service

Options on Fasolt stock are also actively traded. Currently the following options and their prices are available:

	Three-Month		Six-Month		Nine-Month	
Exercise Price	**Call**	**Put**	**Call**	**Put**	**Call**	**Put**
$15	$2	$1.50	$3.50	$2.25	$5	$3
20	0.75	5.50	1.50	6	2	6.25

To help determine the potential returns from the various alternatives, Ms. Fried decided that answers to the following questions may be useful.

1. What is the current yield offered by the stock, the convertible bond, and the calls and puts?
2. What is the conversion value of the bond in terms of the stock?
3. What is the intrinsic value of each option?
4. What are the premiums paid for the bond and the time premiums paid for each option?
5. What will be the price of each security if after six months the fundamental economic picture is not changed and the price of the stock remains $15?
6. While Ms. Fried considered a further decline in Fasolt's situation to be unlikely, the possibility does exist that after six months the stock would fall to $10. What impact would that have on the prices of the various securities?
7. Ms. Fried believes that the price of the stock will rise to $25 a share within six months. What impact would such a price increase have on the prices of the various securities?

Case Problem

As an outside financial advisor to Rachel Fried, what course of action would you suggest with regard to Fasolt's securities? In formulating your answer, consider the pros and cons of each of the alternatives and which conditions favor each security. There is, of course, no one correct strategy.

CHAPTER 14
Investment Companies

Learning Objectives

1. Differentiate between closed-end and open-end investment companies.
2. Identify the costs of investing in mutual funds and in closed-end investment companies.
3. List the advantages offered by investment companies.
4. Distinguish among the types of investment companies.
5. Explain the tax implications of purchasing shares in investment companies.
6. Determine if investment companies consistently outperform the market.

Herodotus suggested in the fifth century B.C. that "great deeds are usually wrought at great risks." Large investment returns usually require great risks, but most investors do not want to bear these risks. They acquire diversified portfolios that reduce the risk of loss but also reduce the chance of a large return. Building and managing a diversified portfolio can be difficult and time-consuming, so many investors purchase shares in investment companies. The managements of these companies construct diversified portfolios and manage them for the benefit of the investment companies' shareholders.

This chapter is concerned with investment companies, especially mutual funds. It covers the mechanics of buying and selling the shares, the taxation of investment companies, the costs associated with these investments, and the potential sources of profit. Also included in the chapter are the specialized investment companies, such as stock index funds and global funds, which offer investors a broad spectrum of investment alternatives to purchasing individual stocks and bonds.

The chapter ends with a discussion of factors to consider when selecting among the thousands of mutual funds and closed-end investment companies. The investor's allocation of funds among various investment alternatives, the fees associated with investing in mutual funds, and mutual funds' performance relative to the market as a whole (especially in an efficient market) are important considerations when choosing mutual funds. These factors are covered after the factual material concerning investment companies.

INVESTMENT COMPANIES: ORIGINS AND TERMINOLOGY

Investment companies are not a recent development but were established in Britain during the 1860s. Initially, these investment companies were referred to as *trusts* because the securities were held in trust for the firm's stockholders. These firms sold a specified number of shares and used the proceeds to acquire shares of other firms. Today the descendants of these companies are referred to as **closed-end investment companies** because the number of shares is fixed (that is, closed).

CLOSED-END INVESTMENT COMPANY
Investment company with a fixed number of outstanding shares that are bought and sold through secondary markets

The first trusts offered a specified number of shares. Today, however, the most common type of investment company does not. Instead, the number of shares varies as investors purchase more shares or sell them back. This **open-end investment company** is commonly called a **mutual fund.** Such funds started in 1924 when Massachusetts Investor Trust offered new shares and redeemed (bought) existing shares on demand by stockholders.

OPEN-END INVESTMENT COMPANY
Mutual fund that issues new shares and agrees to redeem the shares on the demand of the shareholder

MUTUAL FUND
Open-end investment company that stands to issue and redeem its shares on demand

The rationale for investment companies is both simple and appealing. The firms receive the funds from many investors, pool them, and purchase securities. The individual investors receive (1) the advantage of professional management of their money, (2) the benefit of ownership in a diversified portfolio, (3) the potential savings in commissions, as the investment company buys and sells in large blocks, and (4) custodial services, such as the storing of certificates and the collecting and disbursing of funds.

The advantages and services help to explain why both the number of mutual funds and the dollar value of their shares have grown since the 1940s. This growth is illustrated in Figure 14.1, which presents mutual funds' net assets from 1965 through 1998.[1] Net sales are gross sales minus redemptions, which are shares sold back to the mutual fund. Thus, net sales indicate the flow of money into mutual funds. During the 1990s sales of shares plus the general increase in security prices dramatically increased mutual funds' net assets from \$472.3 billion in 1989 to over \$4,173.5 billion in 1998, a growth of over 780 percent in ten years.[2]

Investment companies receive special tax treatment. Their dividend and interest income and realized capital gains are exempt from taxation at the corporate level. Instead, these profits are taxed through their stockholders' income tax returns.

For this reason, income that is received by investment companies and realized capital gains are distributed. The companies, however, offer their stockholders the option of having the fund reinvest these distributions. While such reinvestments do not erase the stockholders' tax liabilities, they are a convenient means to accumulate shares. The advantages offered by the dividend reinvestment plans of

[1] The annual, compound growth rate exceeded 24 percent. The assets of money market mutual funds are excluded.

[2] The value of closed-end investment companies has also grown, but the total value of their assets is less than one-tenth the value of mutual funds' assets.

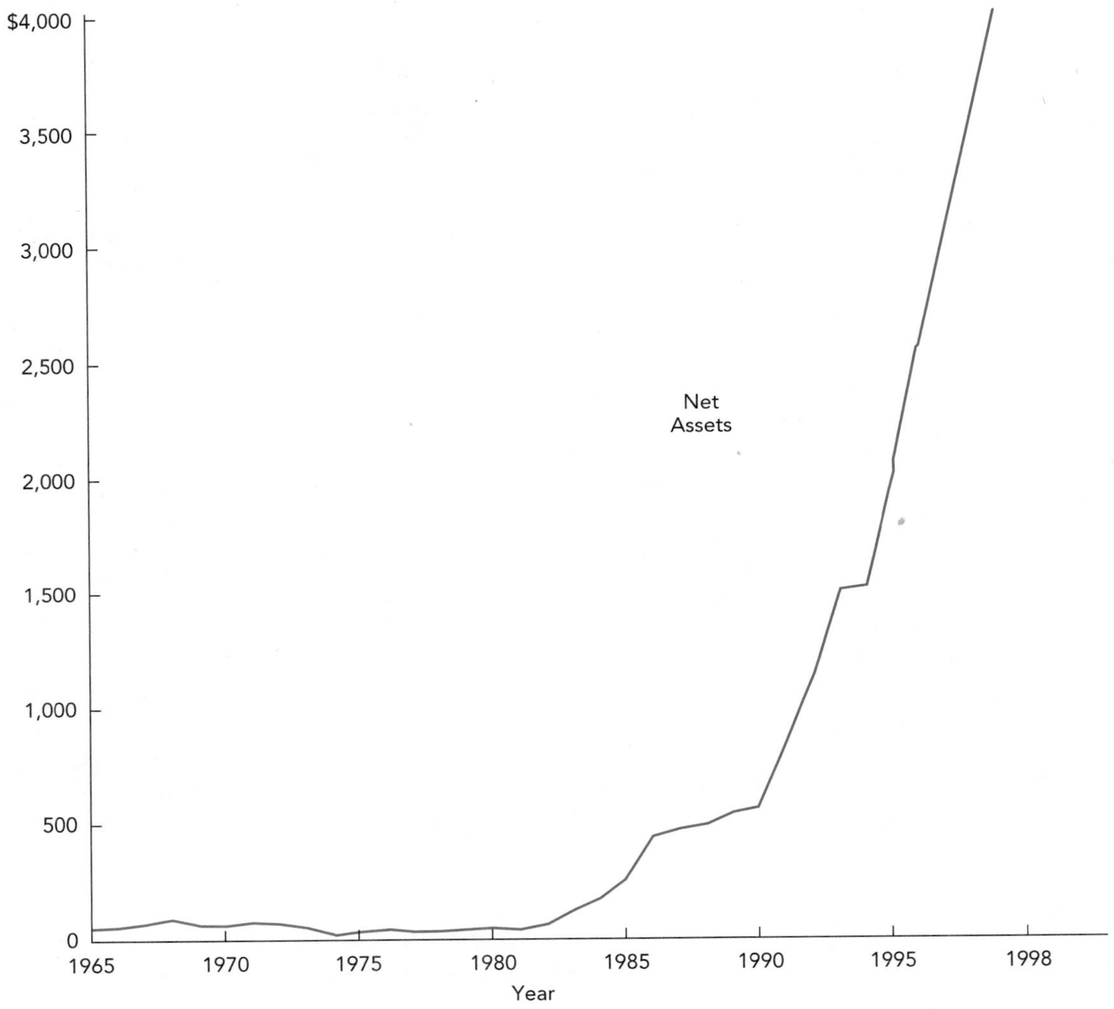

FIGURE 14.1

Mutual Funds' Net Assets, 1965–1998 (in billions)

Source: *Mutual Fund Fact Book, published annually by The Investment Company Institute* (**www.ici.org**). *Reprinted by permission*

individual firms (discussed in Chapter 10) also apply to the dividend reinvestment plans offered by investment companies. Certainly the most important of these advantages is the element of forced savings. Since the stockholder does not receive the money, there is no temptation to spend it. Rather, the funds are immediately channeled back into additional income-earning assets.

One term frequently encountered in a discussion of an investment company is its per share **net asset value.** The per share net asset value of an investment company is the total value of its stocks, bonds, cash, and other assets minus any liabilities (for example, accrued expenses) divided by the number of shares outstanding. Thus, net asset value may be obtained as follows:

NET ASSET VALUE
Asset value of a share in an investment company; investment company's assets minus liabilities divided by the number of shares outstanding

Value of stock owned	$1,000,000
Value of debt owned	+1,500,000
Value of total assets	$2,500,000
Liabilities	−100,000
Net worth	$2,400,000
Number of shares outstanding	1,000,000
Net asset value per share	$2.40

The net asset value is important for the valuation of an investment company, for it gives the value of the shares should the company be liquidated. Changes in the net asset value, then, alter the value of the investment company's shares. Thus, if the value of the firm's assets appreciates, the net asset value will increase, which should cause the price of the investment company's stock to increase.

Based on the number of mutual funds and their total assets, open-end investment companies are more important than closed-end investment companies. This discussion, however, begins with closed-end investment companies, which developed before mutual funds. Closed-end investment companies also have characteristics that are similar to the trading in stocks discussed in Chapter 6.

CLOSED-END INVESTMENT COMPANIES

As was explained in the previous section, the difference between open-end and closed-end investment companies is the nature of their capital structure. The closed-end investment company has a set capital structure that may be composed of all stock or a combination of stock and debt. The number of shares and the dollar amount of debts that the company may issue are specified. In an open-end investment company (in other words, a mutual fund), the number of shares outstanding varies as investors purchase and redeem them. Since the closed-end investment company has a specified number of shares, an individual who wants to invest in a particular company must purchase existing shares from current stockholders. Conversely, any investor who owns shares and wishes to liquidate the position must sell the shares. Thus, the shares in closed-end investment companies are bought and sold just as the stock of IBM is traded. Shares of these companies are traded on the New York and American stock exchanges and through NASDAQ. Sales and prices of these shares are reported in the financial press along with the shares of other firms.

The market price of stock in a closed-end company need not be the net asset value per share: it may be above or below this value, depending on the demand

EXHIBIT 14.1

Net Asset Value and Market Prices of Selected Closed-End Investment Companies as of January 1, 2000

Company	Price	Net Asset Value	Discount or (Premium) as of Percentage of Net Asset Value
Adams Express	$33.563	$40.30	16.7%
Baker, Fentress & Co.	14.125	14.68	3.8
General American Investors	37.188	41.74	10.9
Tri-Continental	27.875	32.82	17.5

Source: The Wall Street Journal, *January 3, 2000, p. C17. Reprinted by permission of The Wall Street Journal.*

DISCOUNT
Extent to which the price of a closed-end investment company's stock is less than the share's net asset value

PREMIUM
Extent to which the price of a closed-end investment company's stock exceeds the share's net asset value

and the supply of stock in the secondary market. If the market price is below the net asset value of the shares, the shares are selling for a **discount.** If the market price is above the net asset value, the shares are selling for a **premium.**

These differences between the investment company's net asset value per share and the stock price are illustrated in Exhibit 14.1, which gives the price, the net asset value, and the discount or the premium as of January 3, 2000, for four closed-end investment companies. All the shares sold for a discount (that is, below their net asset values).[3] The cause of this discount is not known, but one possible explanation is taxation. The potential impact of capital gains taxation on the price of the shares is illustrated in the following example.

A closed-end investment company initially sells stock for $10 per share and uses the proceeds to buy the stock of other companies. If transaction costs are ignored, the net asset value of a share is $10, and the shares may trade in the secondary market for $10. The value of the firm's portfolio subsequently rises to $16 (that is, the net asset value is $16). The firm has a potential capital gain of $6 per share. If it is realized and these profits are distributed, the net asset value will return to $10 and each stockholder will receive $6 in capital gains, for which he or she will pay the appropriate capital gains tax.

Suppose, however, that the capital gains are not realized (the net asset value remains $16). What will be the market price of the stock? This is difficult to

[3]Although many closed-end investment companies sell for a discount, some do sell for a premium. For example, the Malaysia Fund sold for $7.25 when its net asset value was $5.31, a premium of 33.0 percent above the net asset value. Often, closed-end investment companies that sell for a premium have a specialized portfolio that appeals to some investors. For example, some countries, such as Malaysia or India, place severe restrictions on foreign investments. If an individual wants to acquire shares in firms in these countries (perhaps for potential growth or for diversification purposes), a closed-end investment company may be the only means to make the investments. The effect is to bid up the price of the shares so that the closed-end investment company sells for a premium over its net asset value.

determine, but it will probably be below $16. Why? Suppose an investor bought a share for $16 and the firm then realized and distributed the $6 capital gain. After the distribution of the $6, the investor would be responsible for any capital gains tax, but the net asset value of the share would decrease to $10.

Obviously this is not advantageous to the buyer. Individuals may only be willing to purchase the shares at a discount that reduces the potential impact of realized capital gains and the subsequent capital gains taxes. Suppose the share had cost $14 (that is, it sold for a discount of $2 from the net asset value), and the firm realized and distributed the gain. The buyer who paid $14 now owns a share with a net asset value of $10 and receives a capital gain of $6. Although this investor will have to pay the appropriate capital gains tax, the impact is reduced because the investor paid only $14 to purchase the share whose total value is $16 (the $10 net asset value plus the $6 capital gain).

Since the shares may sell for a discount or a premium relative to their net asset value, it is possible for the market price of a closed-end investment company to fluctuate more or less than the net asset value. Since the market price can change relative to the net asset value, an investor is subject to an additional source of risk. The value of the investment may decline not only because the net asset value decreases but also because the shares sell for a larger discount from their net asset value.

Some investors view the market price relative to the net asset value as a guide to buying and selling the shares of a closed-end investment company. If the shares are selling for a sufficient discount, they are considered for purchase. If the shares are selling for a small discount or at a premium, they are considered for sale. Of course, determining the premium that will justify the sale or the discount that will justify the purchase is not simple.

Source of Profit from Investing in Closed-End Investment Companies

Profits are the difference between revenues and costs. Investing in closed-end investment companies involves several costs. First, since the shares are purchased on the secondary market, there is the brokerage commission for the purchase and for any subsequent sale. Second, the investment company charges a fee to manage the assets. This management fee is subtracted from any income that the fund's assets earn and ranges from 0.5 percent to 2 percent of the net asset value. Third, when the investment company purchases or sells securities, it also has to pay brokerage fees, which are passed on to the investor.

The purchase of shares in closed-end investment companies thus involves three costs that the investor must bear. Some alternative investments, such as savings accounts in commercial banks, do not involve these costs. Although commission fees are incurred when an individual stock like IBM is purchased through a broker, the other expenses associated with a closed-end investment company are avoided. However, the investment company does relieve the individual of some of the cost of storing securities and keeping the records necessary for the preparation of tax papers.

Investors in closed-end investment companies may earn profits in a variety of ways. If the investment company collects dividends and interest on its portfolio of

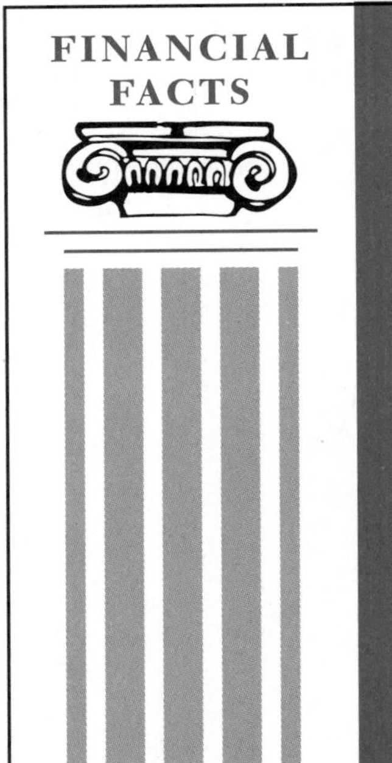

Real Estate Investment Trusts

Real estate investment trusts, commonly referred to as REITs, are specialized, closed-end investment companies that invest in mortgages (a mortgage trust), real properties (an equity trust), or a combination of mortgages and properties. As long as the trust derives 75 percent of its income from real estate and distributes 95 percent of its income as cash dividends, the trust is exempt from federal income taxation. Shares in REITs actively trade on the NYSE and other security exchanges, so the individual may readily add to or liquidate positions in the trusts, which is unlike the often lengthy process of buying or selling properties. ¶ Some REITs specialize in types of properties (for instance, United Dominion REIT invests primarily in apartments), while others specialize in geographical regions. Washington REIT owns properties in the Washington, D.C., metropolitan area. Although REITs offer a real estate investment vehicle to individuals who don't want to own properties, these securities should be considered risky. Even though the shares of REITs permit the investor to obtain more diversification than is possible through directly acquiring properties, fluctuations in interest rates, occupancy rates, and property values mean that the shares of REITs tend to be riskier than the shares of investment companies with more broadly based portfolios. ¶

assets, this income is distributed to the stockholders in the form of dividends. Second, if the value of the firm's assets increases, the company may sell the assets and realize profits. These profits are then distributed as capital gains to the stockholders. Third, the net asset value of the portfolio may increase, which should cause the market price of the fund's stock to rise. In this case the investor may sell the shares in the market and realize a capital gain. Fourth, the market price of the shares may rise relative to the net asset value (that is, the premium may increase or the discount may decrease); the investor may then earn a profit through the sale of the shares.

These sources of profit are illustrated in Exhibit 14.2, which presents the distributions and price changes for Salomon Brothers Fund from December 31, 1993, through December 31, 1998. As may be seen in the exhibit, the investment company distributed cash dividends of \$0.27 and capital gains \$3.19 in 1998. The net asset value rose from \$18.51 to \$18.76, and the price of the stock likewise rose (from \$17.625 to \$18.19). An investor who bought the shares on December 31, 1997, earned a total return of 22.8 percent (before commissions) on the investment.[4]

The potential for loss is also illustrated in the exhibit. If an investor bought the shares on December 31, 1993, he or she suffered a loss during 1994. While

[4]The calculation of the annual return is

$$\frac{\$18.19 + \$0.27 + \$3.19 - \$17.625}{\$17.625} = 22.8\%.$$

EXHIBIT 14.2

Annual Returns on an Investment in Salomon Brothers Fund, a Closed-End Investment Company

Distributions and Price Changes	1998	1997	1996	1995	1994	1993
Per share income distributions	$ 0.27	0.27	0.33	0.35	0.33	0.34
Per share capital gains distributions	$ 3.19	2.63	2.09	1.49	1.39	1.51
Year-end net asset value	$18.76	18.51	17.26	15.43	12.88	14.88
Year-end market price	$18.19	17.625	16.00	13.375	10.50	12.75
Annual return based on prior year's market price						
a. Dividend yield	1.5%	1.7	2.5	3.3	2.6	—
b. Capital gains yield	18.1%	16.4	15.6	14.2	10.9	—
c. Change in price	3.2%	10.2	19.6	27.4	−17.6	—
Total return	22.8%	28.3	37.7	44.9	−4.1	—

Source: *Salomon Brothers Fund annual reports.*

Salomon Brothers distributed $0.33 per share in income and $1.39 in capital gains, the price of the stock declined sufficiently to more than offset the income and capital gains distributions.

Unit Trusts

A variation on the closed-end investment company is the fixed-unit investment trust, commonly referred to as a **unit trust.** These trusts, which are formed by brokerage firms and sold to investors in units of $1,000, hold a fixed portfolio of securities, such as federal government or corporate bonds, municipal bonds, or mortgage loans. An example of such a trust is Merrill Lynch's Government Securities Income Fund, which invested solely in U.S. Treasury securities and other obligations backed by the full faith and credit of the federal government.

UNIT TRUST
Passive investment company with a fixed portfolio of assets that are self-liquidating

A unit trust is a passive investment, as its assets are not traded but are frozen. The trust collects income (for example, interest on U.S. Treasury bonds) and, eventually, the repayment of principal. The trust is also self-liquidating because as the funds are received, they are distributed to stockholders. Since the trust's portfolio is fixed and not altered, operating expenses are low. Such trusts are primarily attractive to investors such as retirees who seek a steady, periodic flow of payments. If the investor needs the funds earlier, the shares may be sold back to the trust at their current net asset value.

MUTUAL FUNDS

Open-end investment companies, which are commonly called mutual funds, are similar to closed-end investment companies. However, there are some important differences. The first concerns how their shares are bought and sold. Shares in mutual funds are not traded like other stocks and bonds. Instead, an investor who wants to buy a particular mutual fund purchases shares directly from the company. After receiving the money, the mutual fund issues new shares and purchases assets with these newly acquired funds. An investor, who owns shares in the fund and wants to liquidate the position, sells the shares back to the fund. The shares are redeemed, and the fund pays the investor from its cash holdings. If the fund lacks sufficient cash, it must sell some of the securities it owns to obtain the money to redeem the shares. The fund cannot suspend this redemption feature except in an emergency, and then it can be done only with the permission of the Securities and Exchange Commission (SEC).

A second important difference between open-end and closed-end investment companies pertains to the cost of investing. Mutual funds continuously offer to sell new shares, and these shares are sold at their net asset value plus a sales fee, which is commonly called a *loading charge.* When the investor liquidates the position, the shares are redeemed at their net asset value. Most funds do not charge for the redemption, but some funds do assess an exit fee (a *back-end load*) if the investor redeems the shares soon after they were purchased (such as six months later). Such fees are designed to discourage quick redemption of the shares.

NO-LOAD FUND
Investment company that does not charge a sales commission when individuals purchase shares from the fund

LOAD FUND
Investment company that charges commissions when individuals purchase shares from the fund

The loading fee may range from zero for **no-load mutual funds** to between 3 percent and 6 percent for **load funds.** The investor should be warned that mutual funds state the loading charge as a percentage of the *offer* price. The effect of the fee being a percentage of the offer price and not a percentage of the net asset value is an increase in the effective percentage charged. If the loading charge is 6 percent and the offer price is \$10, then the loading fee is \$0.60. However, the net asset value is \$9.40 (\$10 minus \$0.60). In this example, the loading charge as a percentage of the net asset value is 6.38 percent (6.0%/[1 − 0.06] = 6.0/0.94 = 6.38%), which is higher than the stated 6 percent loading charge.

In addition to loading charges, investors in mutual funds have to pay management fees, which are deducted from the income earned by the fund's portfolio. The fund also pays brokerage commissions when it buys and sells securities. The total cost of investing in mutual funds may be substantial when all the costs (the loading charge and management and brokerage fees) are considered. Of course, the cost of investing is substantially reduced when the individual buys shares in no-load funds. The investor, however, must still pay the management fees and commission costs. (See the accompanying Financial Facts concerning 12b–1 fees.)

The third difference between closed-end and open-end investment companies is the source of profits to the investor. As with closed-end investment companies, individuals may profit from investments in mutual funds from several sources. Any income is distributed as dividends and realized gains are distributed. If the net asset value of the shares appreciates, the investor may redeem them at the appreciated price. Thus, in general, the open-end mutual fund offers investors the same sources of return as the closed-end investment company does, with one exception. In the case of closed-end investment companies, the price of the stock may rise relative to the net asset value of the shares. The possibility of a decreased discount or an increased premium is a potential source of return that is available only through closed-end investment companies. It does not exist for mutual funds

12b–1 Fees

Whlie no-load mutual funds do not have a sales charge for the purchase of their shares, the funds may levy a fee charged against their income or assets to pay for marketing expenses. These funds have adopted a 12b–1 fee, which is named for the SEC rule that allows the funds to charge this fee. Unlike the loading fee, which is levied only once when the shares are purchased, 12b–1 fees are assessed every year. The fee is levied when the fund does well, and it is levied in years in which the fund experiences losses. These fees reduce the return that the stockholder earns. In addition, since the fee is levied each year, the total amount paid over a period of time may exceed the one-time sales fee charged by the load mutual funds. ¶ One way to determine if a no-load mutual fund has a 12b–1 fee is to read the fund's prospectus. This method, however, requires reading the prospectus of every fund that a person is considering for purchase. An alternate method is to consult *The Individual Investor's Guide to Low-Load Mutual Funds*, which is published annually by the American Association of Individual Investors, 625 North Michigan Avenue, Chicago, Illinois 60611. This publication not only tells you if the fund has a 12b–1 fee but also reports the fund's performance, what services it offers, and other pertinent information that may help determine if this fund should be considered for inclusion in your portfolio. ¶

because their shares never sell at a discount. Load funds are actually sold at a premium (in other words, the loading fee).

Mutual fund net asset values are reported in the financial press. Exhibit 14.3 reproduces mutual fund data from *The Wall Street Journal*. The information is limited to an abbreviated fund name, its net asset value, the change from the previous day, and the percentage return on the fund since the beginning of the calendar year. The figures do not reflect any load charges, redemption fees, or other expenses associated with investing in a mutual fund.

While purchases of shares in investment companies may generate a return, they also subject the investor to risk. Chapter 8 discussed several sources of risk. These included the risk associated with investments in the securities of a particular firm (such as the stock and bonds issued by AT&T). Because many investment companies construct diversified portfolios, the impact of a particular investment on the outcome of the portfolio as a whole is reduced. Thus, the risk associated with an individual firm's securities is small (if not nonexistent).[5]

Other sources of risk, however, cannot be eliminated through the purchases of shares of investment companies. If security prices in general rise (or fall), the value of the investment company's portfolio will probably also rise (or fall). The managements of investment companies cannot consistently predict changes in

[5]The investor still must bear the unsystematic risk associated with the individual investment company's strategy and management. This source of risk is reduced by investing in several investment companies.

EXHIBIT 14.3

Mutual Fund Reporting in the Financial Press

MUTUAL FUND QUOTATIONS

Name	NAV	Net Chg	YTD %ret
UST Int	11.64	+0.04	−0.2
UST Lng	13.97	+0.11	−0.3
USTSh	14.14	+0.01	−0.1
Dreyfus Founders:			
BalF p	10.08	−0.31	−3.7
DiscvF p	38.56	−2.02	−5.6
GovScF	8.93	+0.03	−0.2
GrIncF p	7.20	−0.32	−5.4
GwthF p	22.68	−1.21	−5.0
IntlEqF p	19.45	−0.56	−2.1
MidCapGroF p	8.16	−0.40	−6.0
PassprtF	23.22	−0.28	+1.3
WldGrF p	24.36	−0.90	−3.2
Dreyfus Premier:			
AgGro	11.18	−0.56	−5.9
BalncdA p	15.18	−0.22	−2.0
BalncdB	15.17	−0.22	−2.1
BalncdC	15.22	−0.22	−2.1
BalncdR	15.17	−0.23	−2.1
CAMuA	11.23	...	−0.4
CAMuB t	11.24	+0.01	−0.4
CTMuA	11.12	...	−0.3
CorV A p	29.28	−0.96	−5.0
CorVInst p	29.26	−0.96	−5.0
FLMuA	12.81	...	−0.2
GnmaA	14.19	+0.05	−0.3
GnmaB t	14.20	+0.04	−0.3
GrIncA	20.81	−0.84	−5.1
GrIncB p	20.38	−0.82	−5.1
IntGrA	20.30	−0.69	−2.3
IntGrB t	19.64	−0.67	−2.3
LgCStkA p	24.64	−0.97	−4.6
LgCStkB t	24.38	−0.96	−4.7
LgCStkR	24.65	−0.97	−4.7
LtdHInA p	10.42	−0.02	−0.3
LtdHInB p	10.42	−0.02	−0.3
LtdHInC p	10.42	−0.02	−0.3
LtdInR	10.43	+0.03	−0.2
LtdMuA p	11.78	...	−0.3
LtdMuR	11.78	...	−0.2
MCpStkA p	17.15	−0.69	−4.9
MCpStkB	16.89	−0.68	−4.9
MCpStkR	17.25	−0.69	−4.9
MgdIA p	9.96	+0.02	−0.3
MNMuB t	14.04	+0.01	−0.2
CTMuB t	11.11	...	−0.3
FLMuB	12.81	+0.01	−0.2
LtdMAR r	11.76	...	−0.3
MAMuA	10.59	...	−0.2
MdMuA	11.69	...	−0.3
MdMuB t	11.70	+0.01	−0.3
MIMuA	14.24	...	−0.2
MNMuA	14.01	...	−0.3
MuBdA	12.75	...	−0.3
MuBdB t	12.76	...	−0.2
NYMuA	13.69	+0.01	−0.3
NYMuB t	13.69	+0.01	−0.3
NCMuA	12.63	...	−0.3
NCMuB t	12.62	...	−0.2
OHMuA	11.78	...	−0.3
OHMuB t	11.78	...	−0.3
PAMuA	14.77	...	−0.3
PAMuB t	14.76	...	−0.3
SmCoStA p	17.82	−0.57	−4.1
SmCoStB t	17.15	−0.54	−4.1
SmCoStR	17.97	−0.57	−4.1
TechGroA r	51.87	−2.78	−2.6
TechGroB p	51.60	−2.77	−2.6
TechGroC p	51.55	−2.77	−2.6
ThrdCenZ	13.78	−0.62	−5.3
TxMgdGrA p	17.34	−0.62	−4.6
TxMgdGrB p	17.08	−0.61	−4.6
TxMgdGrC t	17.07	−0.62	−4.6
TXMuA	19.13	+0.01	−0.2
ValueA	19.68	[illegible]	5.3
PerIntA	19.20	−0.26	+0.2
PrecMtlA	11.37	−0.28	−3.0
QualIncA	12.22	+0.03	−0.3
ShIntBdA p	9.48	+0.01	−0.2
ShtDurA	12.09	+0.02	−0.1
SIMunA	9.81	...	−0.1
SmCapValA p	14.22	−0.30	−3.7
SmCoGrA	9.00	−0.48	−5.7
StkSelA p	18.99	−0.80	−5.5
StrGrthA	11.53	−0.56	−4.9
StrIncA	6.43	−0.01	−0.4
TxStraA p	16.20	−0.30	−2.1
USGvtA p	9.09	+0.02	−0.2
UtilityA	13.20	−0.22	−3.2
ValueA p	19.66	−0.55	−5.0
Va MuBdA t	9.65	+0.01	−0.1
Evergreen B:			
AggGroB p	28.14	−1.46	−5.0
BalanB t	10.41	−0.25	−3.1
BluChpB t	33.84	−1.44	−4.8
CapPreB t	9.54	+0.02	+0.1
DivrBdB t	14.37	+0.03	−0.4
EqIncB	15.14	−0.38	−4.4
EvergrnB	25.09	−1.09	−4.9
FLHiB p	10.19	...	−0.3
FLMunB t	9.07	...	−0.2
FoundB	21.83	−0.64	−3.5
GlLeadB t	18.97	−0.64	−4.0
GloOpB t	26.71	−0.93	−3.7
GroIncB	29.96	−1.00	−5.4
HGdMbB t	10.01	...	−0.2
HiYldB t	3.89	−0.02	−1.0
IncGroB	21.39	−0.46	−3.6
IntlGrB t	9.36	−0.26	−2.6
IntmBdB t	8.31	+0.02	−0.2
LatAmB t	10.10	−0.78	−8.1
MastB t	11.71	−0.42	−5.2
MunBdB t	6.78	...	−0.3
NCMuniB t	9.77	+0.01	−0.2
OmegaB t	29.60	−1.49	−4.9
PaMuBdB t	10.68	...	−0.3
PrecMtlB t	11.20	−0.28	−3.0
ShIntBdB	9.50	+0.01	−0.2
SmCapValB p	14.12	−0.30	−3.7
SmCoGrB t	8.86	−0.48	−5.7
StrGrthB t	11.32	−0.56	−5.0
StrIncB t	6.45	−0.01	−0.4
TxStraB p	16.17	−0.29	−2.1
USGvtB t	9.09	+0.02	−0.2
UtilityB t	13.20	−0.23	−3.2
ValueB t	19.62	−0.55	−4.9
Evergreen C:			
CapBalC t	14.69	−0.20	−2.6
CapGroC	22.66	−0.65	−4.6
CapInGrC	17.91	−0.25	−2.7
EqIncC	15.16	−0.38	−4.4
EvergrnC p	25.06	−1.08	−4.9
FoundC p	21.82	−0.64	−3.5
GloOpC t	26.78	−0.93	−3.7
GroIncC p	29.96	−1.00	−5.4
GrowthC	17.94	−0.72	−6.0
HiIncC p	10.21	−0.05	−0.7
MunIncC t	14.15	+0.01	−0.3
OmegaC t	29.67	−1.49	−4.9
PerGlC	21.80	−0.40	−1.2
PerIntC p	18.83	−0.25	+0.2
QualIncC p	12.22	+0.03	−0.3
ShtDurC	12.10	+0.02	−0.1
SmCapValC p	14.11	−0.30	−3.8
StrIncC t	6.44	−0.01	−0.4
TxStraC p	16.14	−0.30	−2.2
Evergreen Y:			
AggGroY	29.73	−1.54	−5.0
BalanY	10.39	−0.25	−3.1
EqIncB	21.19	−0.80	−4.2
EurGroB	18.16	−0.37	−0.7
GISI B t	8.25	+0.02	−0.2
GrStratB	40.24	−2.07	−4.9
IntlGrB p	13.57	−0.14	+0.5
IntlIncB t	9.69	+0.08	+1.3
IntSmCoB	36.49	−0.29	+1.4
LatinAmB	11.11	−0.96	−8.3
LrgCapGr p	15.43	−0.90	−5.7
HiIncBdB t	10.39	−0.04	−0.7
IntlEqB	29.45	−0.36	+0.2
IntlHiB	7.87	−0.02	−0.1
MuniOppB p	9.70	...	−0.2
MuSecB t	9.74	...	−0.3
PAMunB p	10.76	+0.01	−0.2
SmCapStB	21.58	−0.87	−5.2
StkBndB p	17.76	−0.30	−3.1
StrIncB	9.20	−0.02	−0.3
USGvtB t	7.46	+0.01	−0.1
UtilFdB t	11.40	−0.28	−4.1
WldUtlB p	18.21	−0.62	−4.3
Federated C:			
AmLdrC	24.11	−0.70	−4.7
AsiaPacC	15.35	+0.04	+1.2
BondFdC	8.99	+0.02	−0.3
CapAppC p	26.99	−1.13	−4.5
EqIncC t	21.20	−0.80	−4.2
GrStratC r	40.52	−2.08	−4.9
HiIncBdC t	10.39	−0.04	−0.7
IntlEqC t	29.07	−0.36	+0.2
IntSmCoC	36.46	−0.29	+1.4
Com TechC p	18.20	−0.96	−2.4
LatinAmC	11.16	−0.96	−8.2
LrgCapGrC	15.42	−0.90	−5.7
MaxCapC p	28.41	−1.14	−4.8
MiniCapC p	13.56	−0.52	−5.3
MunSecC t	9.74	...	−0.3
SmCapStC	21.55	−0.87	−5.2
StrIncC	9.20	−0.02	−0.3
USGvtC t	7.46	+0.02	−0.1
UtilFdC t	11.39	−0.28	−4.1
Federated F:			
AdjRtF t	9.34	...	0.0
AmLdrF	24.11	−0.70	−4.7
BondFdF r	8.99	+0.02	−0.3
EqIncF t	21.21	−0.79	−4.1
GISI F r	8.25	+0.02	−0.4
LtdMunF t	9.56	...	0.0
MunOppF t	9.71	...	−0.2
OHmunF p	10.72	+0.02	+0.3
StrIncF	9.20	−0.02	−0.2
UtilFdF r	11.39	−0.28	−4.1
Fidelity Advisor A:			
BalancA t	17.57	−0.39	−3.5
DivGrthA	10.31	−0.36	−5.1
EmAsiaA t	19.69	+0.34	+4.8
EqGrA t	67.62	−2.88	−4.3
EqInA	24.46	−0.69	−5.3
GroIncA p	19.45	−0.74	−4.8
GrOppA	43.97	−1.37	−4.7
HiYldA	11.26	−0.04	−0.7
MidCapA p	17.52	−0.86	−5.3
SmllCapA p	21.32	−1.05	−6.8
Fidelity Advisor B:			
BalancB p	17.50	−0.39	−3.5
DivGthB t	10.24	−0.36	−5.1
EqGrB p	66.75	−2.85	−4.3
EqInB t	24.55	−0.71	−5.4
GovInB t	9.12	+0.03	−0.2
GroIncB p	19.21	−0.73	−4.8
GrOppB	43.92	−1.37	−4.7
HiYldB t	11.23	−0.05	−0.8
IntBdB	10.19	+0.02	−0.2
JapanB p	23.48	−0.35	−1.2
NatGas r	13.94	−0.15	−3.4
Paper r	24.47	−0.22	−2.0
PrecMet r	10.16	−0.31	−4.1
Retail r	54.19	−1.98	−6.6
Softwr r	93.61	−5.15	−3.4
Tech r	147.59	−9.61	−3.1
Telecom r	84.91	−4.16	−4.3
Trans r	22.91	−0.59	−4.3
UtilGr r	63.45	−1.94	−4.0
Fidelity Spartan:			
AZMun	10.27	...	−0.4
CAMun	11.43	...	−0.3
CTMun r	10.72	...	−0.3
EqIdx	49.62	−1.97	−4.7
ExtMktIn	32.43	−1.42	−4.5
FL Mu r	10.69	...	−0.3
GovIn	9.89	+0.04	−0.2
IntIn	36.79	−1.07	−2.3
IntMu	9.39	...	−0.2
InvGrBd	9.81	+0.03	−0.3
MAMun	11.09	...	−0.2
MD Mu	9.87	...	−0.3
MIMun	10.84	...	−0.2
MktIn r	96.10	−3.82	−4.7
MNMun	10.60	...	−0.3
MuniInc	11.87	...	−0.3
NJMun r	10.76	+0.01	−0.3
NYMun	11.82	...	−0.3
OHMun	10.83	+0.01	−0.2
PAMun r	10.04	...	−0.2
StIntMu	9.92	...	−0.1
TotMktIn	36.34	−1.48	−4.7
FiduCap	16.06	−0.42	−4.9
Fifth Third A:			
Balanced	15.84	−0.53	−4.1
BondIncA	11.50	+0.03	0.0
CardinalA	17.04	−0.65	−4.2
EqIncA	12.63	−0.39	−6.0
MidCap	15.80	−0.91	−6.5
OhioTF	9.68	...	−0.2
PinacleA	37.07	−1.49	−5.0
QualGr	24.01	−0.97	−4.8
Fifth Third Inst:			
Balanced	15.85	−0.53	−4.1
BondInc	11.50	+0.03	−0.1
Cardinal	17.22	−0.65	NN
EqInc	12.63	−0.40	−6.0
GovtSec	9.53	+0.02	0.0
IntlEq	13.81	−0.25	−1.1
MidCap	15.87	−0.92	−6.5
MuniBd	11.26	...	−0.2
OhioTF	9.69	+0.01	−0.1
Pinacle	37.20	−1.49	−5.0
QualBd	9.36	+0.02	−0.1
QualGr	24.10	−0.97	−4.8
59 Wall St:			
EuroEq	40.23	−0.97	−1.9
IntlEq	15.00	−0.33	−1.2
PacBsn	47.73	−0.57	+1.0
TxEffEq	13.47	−0.52	−5.5
TxFSI	10.21	...	−0.1
US Eq	13.28	−0.51	−4.9
First American Cl A:			
ARMSec p	8.03	...	0.0
Balance p	12.04	−0.17	−2.6
EqIdx	27.10	−1.08	−4.8
FxdInc p	10.42	+0.04	−0.1
IntInc p	9.64	+0.03	−0.1
Intl p	23.69	−0.75	−1.3
LgCpGr p	20.03	−0.93	−4.7
LgCpVal p	20.19	−0.60	−4.7
MdCpGr p	15.15	−0.75	−4.2
MdCpVal p	12.29	−0.39	−5.6
MNTxFr p	10.44	...	−0.2

Source: The Wall Street Journal, *January 5, 2000, p. C25. Reprinted by permission of The Wall Street Journal.*

the market and adjust their portfolios accordingly. The value of investment companies' portfolios and the value of their shares tend to move systematically with the market as a whole. Thus the risk associated with movements in the market is not eliminated through the purchase of shares in investment companies.

Inflation is also another source of risk that cannot be eliminated by acquiring shares in investment companies. If the return these firms earn is below the rate of inflation, their stockholders experience a loss of purchasing power. The value of the investment company's stock may even decline while inflation continues, in which case the investors are worse off then if they had held a regular savings account with a commercial bank.

The Portfolios of Mutual Funds

Mutual funds may be classified by *investment objective*, such as income or growth, or by investment style. Income funds stress assets that produce income: they buy stocks and bonds that pay dividends or interest income. The Value Line Income Fund is an example of a fund whose objective is income. Virtually all of assets are income stocks, such as those of utilities, which pay dividends and periodically increase them as their earnings grow.

Growth funds stress appreciation in the value of the assets, and little emphasis is given to current income. The portfolio of the Value Line Fund is an example of a growth fund. The majority of the assets are the common stocks of companies with potential for growth. These growth stocks include the shares of well-known firms as well as those of smaller firms that may offer superior growth potential. A balanced fund (for example, Fidelity Balanced Fund) combines income and growth. Such funds own a variety of stocks, some of which offer potential growth while others are primarily income producers. A balanced portfolio may also include short-term and long-term debt and preferred stock. Such a portfolio seeks a balance of income from dividends and interest and capital appreciation.

Mutual funds may also be classified according to *investment style*. Investment style refers to a portfolio manager's investment philosophy or investment strategy. Possible styles include the size of firms acquired by the fund or the approach (growth or value) used to select the firms.

Firm size refers to *large cap*, *midsize cap*, or *small cap*. The word *cap* is short for *capitalization*, which refers to the market value of the company. The market value is the number of shares outstanding times the market price. Large-cap stocks are the largest companies, with market value exceeding $1 billion. A small-cap stock is a much smaller firm, with, perhaps, a total value of less than $300 million. Midcap is, of course, between the two extremes. (The difference among a small-cap, a midcap, and a large-cap stock is arbitrary. A small-cap stock could be defined as less than $1,000,000,000 or less than $500,000,000 or less than $300,000,000 total market value. The definition used by the fund is generally specified in the fund's prospectus.)

Two stocks illustrate this difference in firm size. Dexter has 23.0 million shares outstanding; at a price of $36, the total value of the stock is $828.0 million. This is a modest-sized firm, so Dexter could be classified as a midcap stock. Circuit City has over 100 million shares and, at a price of $90, the total value exceeds

$9 billion. Circuit City is a large-cap stock. It is obvious that Dexter is small compared to Circuit City and would not be an acceptable investment for a large-cap portfolio.

An alternative strategy to capitalization-based investing is investing based on *growth* or *value*. A growth fund portfolio manager identifies firms offering exceptional growth by employing techniques that analyze an industry's growth potential and the firm's position within the industry. A value manager acquires stock that is undervalued or "cheap." A value approach stresses fundamental analysis and is based on such investment tools as P/E ratios and comparisons of financial statements explained in Chapter 12. Many technology stocks illustrate the difference between the growth and value approaches. *Amazon.com* may appeal to growth portfolio managers since the company was the first to market books via the Internet and has large growth potential. From a value perspective, the firm had no earnings and was selling substantially above its value based on its accounting statements. Such a stock would appeal to few value investors.

A fund can have more than one style, such as "small cap–value," which suggests that the portfolio manager acquires shares in small companies that appear to be undervalued. A "small cap–growth" fund would stress small companies offering potential growth but not necessarily operating at a profit. Without earnings, a firm's P/E cannot be computed, and comparisons with other firms become more difficult.

The Portfolios of Specialized Mutual Funds

Investment companies initially sought to pool the funds of many savers and to invest these funds in a diversified portfolio of assets. Such diversification spread the risk of investing and reduced the risk of loss to the individual investor. While a particular investment company had a specified goal, such as growth or income, the portfolio was still sufficiently diversified so that the element of unsystematic risk was reduced.

Today, however, a variety of funds have developed that have moved away from this concept of diversification and the reduction of risk. Instead of offering investors a cross section of American business, many funds have been created to offer investors specialized investments. For example, an investment company may be limited to investments in the securities of a particular sector of the economy or particular industry, such as gold with ASA, Limited. There are also funds that specialize in a particular type of security, such as bonds with American General Bond Fund.

In addition to these specialized funds, several investment companies have been established that offer real alternatives to traditional types of mutual funds. For example, money market mutual funds, which were discussed in Chapter 3, provide the individual with a means to invest indirectly in money market instruments, such as Treasury bills and negotiable certificates of deposit. Funds that acquire foreign securities offer the individual a means to invest in stocks of companies located in Europe and Asia. From an American perspective, there are basically three types of mutual funds with international investments. **Global funds** invest in foreign and American securities. Many American mutual funds are

GLOBAL FUND
Mutual fund whose portfolio includes foreign and U.S. firms, especially those with international operations

Families of Funds

Most mutual funds are created by investment management companies that administer money for institutional investors (for example, pension plans, foundations, and endowments) and individuals. These money management firms include commercial banks, insurance companies, or investment counsel firms (for example, Fidelity Investments). After a mutual fund is created, it has its own portfolio managers who select the assets included in the fund's portfolio. The originating investment management company then becomes an investment advisor to the fund. ¶ Many investment management firms offer a wide spectrum of mutual funds often referred to as a "family of funds." Each fund has a separate financial goal and, hence, a different portfolio designed to achieve the fund's objective. For example, Fidelity Investments offers investors the opportunity to choose among over 125 different mutual funds covering a wide spectrum of alternatives. An investor seeking income may acquire shares in an equity income fund, a government bond fund, or a corporate bond fund. These varied investments give the individual a diversified portfolio of income-earning assets. ¶ In addition to offering a variety of funds from which to choose, a family of funds generally permits the individual to shift investments from one fund to another within the family without paying fees. An individual who currently is invested in growth funds may shift to an income fund upon retiring. Such a shift can be achieved by redeeming the shares in the growth fund and buying shares in the bond fund. While the redemption is a taxable event (unless the shares are in a tax-deferred account), the switch may be made without the investor paying commissions (that is, load charges) on the transaction. ¶

global, as they maintain some part of their portfolios in foreign investments. While these funds do not specialize in foreign securities, they do offer the individual investor the advantages associated with foreign investments: returns through global economic growth, diversification from assets whose returns are not positively correlated, and possible excess returns from inefficient foreign financial markets.

In addition to global funds, there are **international funds,** which invest solely in foreign securities and hold no American securities, and **regional funds,** which specialize in a particular geographical area, such as Asia. (There are also mutual funds that specialize in a particular geographical area within the United States.) While the regional funds obviously specialize, the international funds may also specialize in specific countries during particular time periods.

INTERNATIONAL FUND
Mutual fund whose portfolio is limited to non–U.S. securities

REGIONAL FUND
Mutual fund that specializes in the firms in a particular geographical area

The purpose of an **index fund** is almost diametrically opposed to the traditional purpose of a mutual fund. Instead of identifying specific securities for purchase, the managements of these funds seek to duplicate the composition of an index, such as the Standard & Poor's 500 Index. Such funds should then perform in tandem with the market as a whole. Although they cannot generally outperform the market, neither can they underperform the market. Part of the popularity of such funds has been attributed to the poor performance of mutual funds in general in the past. (The returns earned by mutual funds are discussed later in this

INDEX FUND
Mutual fund whose portfolio seeks to duplicate an index of stock prices

chapter.) While these funds cannot overcome any risk associated with price fluctuations in the market as a whole, they do eliminate the risk associated with the selection of specific securities (that is, unsystematic risk).

In addition to erasing asset-specific risk, index funds help investors manage systematic risk. Index funds permit different individuals to tailor their portfolios in accordance with the level of systematic risk they are willing to accept. By altering the proportion of risk-free assets in a diversified portfolio, the individual may establish different levels of risk and return. Thus, conservative investors may invest a large proportion of their wealth in risk-free assets (such as federally insured savings accounts, shares in money market mutual funds, and U.S. Treasury bills) and a small proportion in an index fund. Such portfolios would have a modest expected return but would involve nominal risk. More aggressive investors may commit a larger proportion of their wealth to the index fund. These individuals would expect a higher return because they are bearing more risk.

THE RETURNS EARNED ON INVESTMENTS IN MUTUAL FUNDS

As was previously explained, the securities of investment companies offer individuals several advantages. First, the investor receives the advantages of a diversified portfolio, which reduces risk. Some investors may lack the resources to construct a diversified portfolio, and the purchase of shares in an investment company permits these investors to own a portion of a diversified portfolio. Second, the portfolio is professionally managed and under continuous supervision. Many investors may not have the time and expertise to manage their own portfolios and, except in the case of large portfolios, may lack the funds to obtain professional management. By purchasing shares in an investment company, individuals buy the services of professional management, which may increase the investor's return. Third, the administrative detail and custodial aspects of the portfolio (for example, the physical handling of securities) are taken care of by the management of the company.

Although investment companies offer advantages, there are also disadvantages. The services offered by an investment company are not unique but may be obtained elsewhere. For example, the trust department of a commercial bank offers custodial services, and leaving the securities with the broker and registering them in the broker's name relieves the investor of storing the securities and keeping some of the records. In addition, the investor may acquire a diversified portfolio with only a modest amount of capital. Diversification does not require 100 different stocks. If the investor has $20,000, a reasonable diversified portfolio may be produced by investing in the stock of eight to ten companies in different industries. One does not have to purchase shares in an investment company to obtain the advantage of diversification.

Studies of Returns

Investment companies do offer the advantage of professional management, but this management cannot guarantee to outperform the market. A particular fund

EXHIBIT 14.4

Returns on Various Types of Low- and No-Load Mutual Funds (1994–1998)

Fund Classification	Return	Standard Deviation of Return
Growth	17.6%	17.1%
Growth and income	17.4	14.9
Aggressive growth	15.4	21.9
Balanced	13.2	9.9
International	5.1	16.5
Standard & Poor's 500 Index	24.0	16.2

Source: The Individual Investor's Guide to Low-Load Mutual Funds, *18th ed. (Chicago: American Association of Individual Investors, 1999), p. 30.*

may do well in any given year, but it may do very poorly in subsequent years. Several studies have been undertaken to determine if professional management results in superior performance for mutual funds.

The first study, conducted for the SEC, found that the performance of mutual funds was not significantly different from that of an unmanaged portfolio of similar assets.[6] About half the funds outperformed Standard & Poor's indices, but the other half underperformed these aggregate measures of the market. In addition, there was no evidence of superior performance by a particular fund over a number of years. These initial results were confirmed by later studies.[7] When the loading charges are included in the analysis, the return earned by investors tends to be less than that which would be achieved through a random selection of securities.

More recent but similar information is given in Exhibit 14.4, which provides annualized, five-year returns and their standard deviations for the five classes of funds (as reported by the American Association of Individual Investors). All five groups earned returns that were less than the Standard & Poor's 500 Index. In addition, the variability of the index return (that is, its standard deviation) was less than the variability of the returns for the growth, aggressive growth, and international funds. Perhaps what is most surprising is that the aggressive growth funds earned inferior returns to the growth funds and were riskier. During the time period, additional risk does not appear to have been rewarded.

[6] See Irwin Friend et al., *A Study of Mutual Funds* (Washington, D.C.: U.S. Government Printing Office, 1962).

[7] See, for instance, Patrica Dunn and Rolf D. Theisen, "How Consistently Do Active Managers Win?" *Journal of Portfolio Management* 9 (summer 1983):47–50; Frank J. Fabozzi, Jack C. Francis, and Cheng F. Lee, "Generalized Functional Form for Mutual Fund Performance," *Journal of Financial and Quantitative Analysis* 15 (December 1980): 1107–1120; and Burton G. Malkeil, "Return from Investing in Equity Mutual Funds 1971–1991," *Journal of Finance* (June 1995): 549–572.

Consistency of Returns

The preceding discussion suggests that mutual funds in the aggregate have not consistently outperformed the market. Is it possible that selected funds may outperform the market or at least consistently outperform other funds? If a type of fund consistently outperforms other funds, the implication for investors is obvious: Purchase shares in a fund that has done well on the premise that the best-performing funds will continue to do well (that is, go with the "Hot Hands").

Certainly the popular financial media's coverage of funds that do well during a particular period encourages individuals to invest in those funds. Money flows into funds that have a superior track record, and because fees increase as the funds under management grow, it should not be surprising to learn that mutual funds tout any evidence of superior performance.

Consistency of mutual fund performance is intuitively appealing. Such consistency seems to apply to many areas of life, especially professional sports. The New York Yankees and the Atlanta Braves make the play-offs virtually every year. However, the principle of efficient markets suggests the opposite may apply to mutual funds. Essentially, the question is: If past stock performance has no predictive power, why should historical mutual fund performance have predictive power? The answer, of course, may lie in the superior skills of the funds' managers. If fund managers have superior skills, then the portfolios they manage should consistently outperform the portfolios of less-skilled managers.

Studies have been conducted to determine the consistency of fund returns. Nonacademic studies tend to suggest consistency. For example, a study by the Institute for Economic Research indicated that past performance did predict future performance.[8] The results were consistent over different time horizons; for example, 26-week returns forecasted the next 26-week returns, and one-year returns predicted the next-year returns. Results tended to be best over the longest time horizons. Funds with the highest returns over a period of five years consistently did better during the next two years than the funds with the lowest returns.

The results of academic studies, however, are ambiguous. Although some support consistency, others do not.[9] At least one study explained the observed consistency on the basis of the fund's investment objective or style and not on the basis of the portfolio manager's skill.[10] For example, suppose large-cap stocks do well

[8] Institute for Economic Research, "Mutual Fund Hot Hands: Go with the Winners" (April 1998). Information concerning this study may be obtained from the Institute at 2200 S.W. 10th St., Deerfield Beach, FL 33442.

[9] A sampling of this research includes Ronald N. Kahn and Andrew Rudd, "Does Historical Performance Predict Future Performance?" *Financial Analysts Journal* (November–December 1995): 43–51; William N. Goetzmann and Roger G. Ibbotson, "Do Winners Repeat?" *Journal of Portfolio Management* (winter 1994): 9–18; and W. Scott Bauman and Robert E. Miller, "Can Managed Portfolio Performance Be Predicted?" *Journal of Portfolio Management* (summer 1994): 31–39.

[10] See, for instance, F. Larry Detzel and Robert A. Weigand, "Explaining Persistence in Mutual Fund Performance," *Financial Services Review* 7, no. 1 (1998): 45–55; and Gary E. Porter and Jack W. Trifts, "Performance of Experienced Mutual Fund Managers," *Financial Services Review* 7, no. 1 (1998): 56–68.

while small-cap stocks do poorly. Large-cap mutual funds should consistently outperform small-cap funds. Once the returns are standardized for the investment style, the consistency of the returns disappears. The superior performance of the large-cap mutual funds is the result of market movements and *not the result of the skill of the portfolio managers*. The consistently better performing large-cap stocks give the impression that the large-cap mutual funds are the consistently better performing mutual funds. These findings, of course, support the concept of efficient markets. One set of portfolio managers is not superior to another.

SELECTING A MUTUAL FUND

There are over 8,000 funds from which to choose; the investor cannot buy all of them. Thus, while investment companies relieve you from having to select individual stocks and bonds, they do not relieve you from having to select the specific fund.

A good starting point is to match your financial goals with the fund's objectives. If your goal is primarily long-term growth, a bond fund or money market fund is not appropriate. Such funds would be appropriate for investors who need an increased current flow of income (the bond fund) or a short-term liquid investment (the money market fund). Your need for custodial services, diversification, and tax management may also affect the decision. Additional factors that you want to consider follow.

Fees and Expenses

As explained earlier in this chapter, mutual fund investors pay a variety of fees. These include the loading charge (the sales fee paid to the broker or financial advisor for buying the shares), management fees, 12b–1 fees, and transaction costs incurred by the fund. Whether the load charge is worth the cost is, of course, open to debate, but there is little evidence that load funds earn a higher return than no-load funds. The load must be justified on the basis of services received. The investor must find a broker or financial advisor whose advice and assistance is worth the cost.

By acquiring no-load funds, the load expense is avoided. The investor, however, still pays management fees, operating expenses, and transaction costs, which apply to all funds. While these expenses cannot be avoided, they do differ among the various funds. The investor should consider these costs, because they obviously decrease returns. Higher than average management and operating expenses and frequent portfolio turnover, which generates higher transaction costs, are possible red flags the investor should consider when selecting a particular mutual fund.

The investor may particularly want to analyze 12b–1 fees, which are marketing expenses and are assessed each year by many no-load funds (and even some load funds). Over a period of years, 12b–1 fees can exceed load expenses. A $0.50 annual 12b–1 fee exceeds a $3.00 load fee after six years. If the investor holds the shares for ten years and pays the 12b–1 fee each year, that investor would have been better off buying a load fund without the 12b–1 fee.

The Timing of Distributions and Income Taxation

Taxation is another important consideration when buying the shares of a mutual fund. Tax issues essentially revolve around the timing of distributions from the fund and the fund's ability to minimize its investors' tax obligations. While many U.S. corporations distribute dividends quarterly, most mutual funds make two distributions. The first is a six-month income distribution. A second and year-end distribution consists of both income and capital gains. As a stock's price is adjusted downward for the dividend (see the discussion of the distribution of dividends in Chapter 10), the net asset value of the fund declines by the amount of the dividend. For example, if the NAV is \$34 and the fund distributes \$2.00 (\$0.50 in income and \$1.50 in capital gains), the NAV declines to \$32.

If the investor buys the shares at the NAV (\$34) just prior to the distribution, that individual pays the tax. Even though the appreciation may have occurred prior to the purchase of the shares, the investor must pay the appropriate tax on the distribution. Thus, it may be desirable to defer the purchase until after the fund goes ex-dividend and the NAV declines to \$32.

Tax Efficiency

Differences in mutual funds' portfolio strategies can cause differences in tax obligations, so a fund that generates lower taxes may be preferred. The ability of the fund to earn a return without generating large amounts of tax obligations is often referred to as the fund's tax efficiency. Obviously, if the fund never realizes any capital gains and does not receive any income, there will be no distributions and the investor has no tax obligations. This, however, is unlikely. (Even a passively managed index fund may receive dividend income from its portfolio. This income is distributed and the investor becomes liable for taxes on the distribution.)

At the other extreme are funds that frequently turn over their portfolios. Since each security sale is a taxable event, frequent turnover implies the fund will not generate long-term capital gains. The capital gain distributions will be short-term and subject to tax at the stockholder's marginal federal income tax rate rather than the lower long-term capital gains tax rate.

A "tax efficiency index" permits comparisons based on a fund's ability to reduce stockholder tax obligations. The index expresses after-tax returns as a percentage of before-tax returns. The computation of a tax efficiency index requires assumptions concerning tax rates. In the following example, the income tax rate is 35 percent, and the long-term capital gains tax rate is 20 percent. Fund A's \$2.00 distribution is entirely income, so the tax is \$0.70 (\$0.35 × \$2.00 = \$0.70), and the investor nets, after tax, \$1.30. If the before-tax return is 10 percent, the after-tax return is 6.5 percent (\$1.30/\$2.00). The tax efficiency index is 65 (6.5%/10%). Fund B's \$2.00 distribution consists solely of realized long-term capital gains, which generate \$0.40 in taxes (0.20 × \$2.00). The after-tax return is 8 percent (1.60/\$2.00), so the tax efficiency index is 80. Since the tax efficiency index for each fund is 65 and 80, B is more tax efficient than A.

While this index may seem appealing, it has weaknesses. To construct the tax efficiency index, the investor needs the composition of the returns and the appropriate tax rates in effect when the returns were earned. Tax rates vary with changes in the tax laws, but even without changes in the tax laws, the appropriate income tax rate may differ as the investor moves from one tax bracket to another. The tax efficiency index varies among investors, and published tax efficiency rankings may not be appropriate for an investor whose tax brackets differ from those used to construct the index.[11]

A second weakness is that a high tax efficiency index in a particular year may be achieved when the fund does not realize capital gains. If these gains are subsequently realized, the tax efficiency ratio will decline. For this reason, the index needs to be computed over a period of years so that the impact of differences in the timing of security sales from one year to the next are eliminated.

A third weakness is that high efficiency may not alter performance rankings. Funds with similar objectives and styles (for example, long-term growth through investments in large-cap stocks) may generate similar tax obligations. Suppose one fund's return is 20 percent while another fund generates 16 percent. All gains are distributed and are long-term. The tax efficiency for both funds is the same, so the relative rankings are unchanged. The performance is inferior on both a before- and after-tax basis.[12]

INDEX FUNDS

Few funds outperform the market over an extended period of time. This result should not be surprising in an efficient financial market environment. Over time, most returns should mirror the market unless the portfolio is riskier than the market. Since mutual funds have expenses (for example, operating expenses and management fees), the return after these costs should be lower than the market return, which is not reduced by any expenses.

The inability of many mutual funds to outperform the market has led to an increase in the popularity of index funds, which mirror the market (or a subsection of the market). Their appeal is obvious. They offer (1) portfolio diversification, (2) a passive portfolio whose minimal turnover and minimal supervision result in lower expenses, and (3) lower taxes because the index fund has few realized capital gains.

Support for acquiring index funds may be found in both the popular press and the professional literature.[13] It is, of course, not surprising to learn that strong

[11] *The Individual Investor's Guide to Low-Load Mutual Funds*, published by the American Association of Individual Investors, provides both actual returns and tax-adjusted returns. In the 1998–1999 edition, the returns for 1997 were adjusted using a 39.6 percent income tax rate and a 28 percent long-term capital gains tax rate. For example, Eclipse Equity (a growth fund) reported a return of 33.3 percent but the tax-adjusted return was 25.5 percent. While 39.6 percent and 28 percent tax would not apply to all investors, they were a worst-case scenario in 1997.

[12] That the best before-tax performing funds are often the best after-tax performing funds is discussed in Greg Carlson, "Does Tax Efficiency Count?" *Mutual Funds* (February 1999): 76–78.

[13] See, for instance, James Picerno, "Market Matchers," *Mutual Funds* (April 1995): 57–62.

believers in efficient markets favor index funds.[14] Even with index funds, the investor must still choose: About 50 mutual funds track the S&P 500 Index. Index funds are also not limited to funds that mimic the S&P 500. For example, the Dreyfus S&P MidCap Index fund specializes in moderate-sized equities that match the S&P MidCap 400 Index. The Vanguard Balanced Index fund mimics a combination of stocks and bonds. The Schwab International Index fund tracks the 350 largest non-U.S. firms.

An alternative investment to the index fund is the Standard & Poor's Depository Receipt or SPDRs (commonly pronounced "spiders"). The first SPDR was a closed-end investment company that comprised all the stocks in the S&P 500 Index. This unmanaged closed-end investment company trades on the American Stock Exchange and tracks the S&P 500 Index. During 1998, these SPDRs ranged from $90 29/32 to $124¾, while the index ranged from 928 to 1242, so the movement in the SPDRs was only slightly more volatile than the S&P 500. Since most of the firms in the index pay cash dividends, the portfolio accumulates these payments and subsequently distributes them as cash dividends. (It paid $1.40 per share in 1998.)

While the initial SPDR was based on the S&P 500 Index, the second SPDR was based on the Standard & Poor's MidCap Index. Trading in additional SPDRs based on subsections of the S&P 500 Index began in late 1998. These SPDRs cover basic industries, consumer products, cyclical/transportation, energy, financial, industrial, technology, and utilities issues. Since each SPDR consists of all the stocks in the S&P 500 Index that fall into each category, each is a pure play in the particular subsection of the overall index. If you believe that the large energy companies will do well, you will not have to select the specific companies but can buy the energy SPDRs. Since each SPDR is unmanaged, operating expense should be minimal, and the performance should mirror the return earned on the energy stocks in the S&P 500 Index.

[14] See, for instance, Burton G. Malkiel, *A Random Walk Down Wall Street*, 7th ed. (New York: W.W. Norton, 1999); and John C. Bogle, "Selecting Equity Mutual Funds," *Journal of Portfolio Management* (winter 1992): 94–100. Bogle's arguments, however, may be self-serving—he introduced the first index fund, the Vanguard 500, in 1976.

SUMMARY

Instead of directly investing in securities, individuals may buy shares in investment companies. These firms, in turn, invest the funds in various assets, such as stocks and bonds.

There are two types of investment companies. A closed-end investment company has a specified number of shares that are bought and sold in the same manner as the stock of firms, such as AT&T. An open-end investment company (a mutual fund) has a variable number of shares sold directly to investors. Investors who desire to liquidate their holdings sell them back to the company.

Investment companies offer several advantages, including professional management, diversification, and custodial services. Dividends and the interest earned on the firm's assets are distributed to stockholders. In addition, if the value of the company's assets rises, the stockholders profit as capital gains are realized and distributed.

Mutual funds may be classified by the types of assets they own. Some stress income-producing assets, such as bonds, preferred stock, and common stock of firms that distribute a large proportion of their income. Other mutual funds stress growth in their net asset values through investments in firms with the potential to grow and generate capital gains. There are also investment companies that specialize in special situations, particular sectors of the economy, and tax-exempt securities. There are even mutual funds that seek to duplicate an index of the stock market.

To select an investment company, the individual should match his or her objectives with those of the particular fund. The past performance of the fund may also be used to select funds; however, the historical returns may not indicate future returns. The managements of few mutual funds have outperformed the market over a number of years. Instead, mutual funds tend to achieve about the same results as the market as a whole. This performance is consistent with the efficient market hypothesis, which suggests that few, if any, investors will outperform the market over an extended period of time.

REVIEW QUESTIONS

1. What is the difference between a closed-end and an open-end investment company? Are their shares traded on the stock exchanges?
2. Are mutual funds subject to federal income taxation?
3. What is a loading charge? Do all investment companies charge this fee? What is the difference between a loading fee and a 12b–1 fee?
4. Why may the small investor prefer mutual funds to other investments?

5. What is a specialized mutual fund? How is it different from a special situation fund or an index fund?
6. Should an investor expect a mutual fund to outperform the market? If not, why should the investor buy the shares?
7. Many mutual funds are part of a family of funds under the umbrella of a fund sponsor. From the following list the Web addresses of fund sponsors, select four and answer the following questions.

American Century: **www.americancentury.com**

Dryefus Funds: **www.dreyfus.com**

Fidelity Investments: **www.fidelity.com**

Galaxy Funds: **www.galaxyfunds.com**

Scudder Funds: **www.scudder.com**

T. Rowe Price: **www.troweprice.com**

Vanguard: **www.vanguard.com**

a. Does the sponsor offer a growth fund and an income fund?
b. What are the funds' load fees and 12b-1 fees?
c. What were the income and capital gains distributions made by the funds during the last year?
d. What were each fund's annual expenses and annual return?
e. Do any of the funds offer retirement accounts?
f. What was each fund's portfolio turnover?
g. Would an index fund outperformed the growth funds during the preceding year?

8. The Internet is a major source of information concerning mutual funds. The general sources include:

Bloomberg Financial: **www.bloomberg.com**

Microsoft Investor: **www.investor.msn.com**

MSN MoneyCentral: **www.moneycentral.com**

Quicken: **www.quicken.com**

Quicken Financial Network: **www.qfn.com**

Yahoo Finance: **quote.yahoo.com**.

More specialized sources include:

American Association of Individual Investors: **www.aaii.com**

Brill's Mutual Funds Interactive: **www.funds.interactive.com**

CDA/Wiesenberger: **www.wiesenberger.com**

Moneyclub: **www.moneyclub.com**

Morningstar: **www.morningstar.net** or **www.morningstar.com**

Mutual Fund Investor's Center: **www.mfea.com**

Mutual Funds Magazine Online: **www.mfmag.com**

Value Line Investment Research and Asset Management: **www.valueline.com**.

Select four of the above sources (two from each list) and answer the following questions.

a. Do the sources offer price quotes and links to specific funds?
b. Will the source let you track a stock, a fund, or a portfolio of stocks and funds?
c. Do the sources recommend specific funds?
d. Do the sources offer online brokerage services?
e. Does the source charge for its services or recoup its costs through advertising?
f. Does the source provide non-financial information?

PROBLEMS

1. What is the net asset value of an investment company with $10,000,000 in assets, $600,000 in current liabilities, and 1,200,000 shares outstanding?
2. If a mutual fund's net asset value is $23.40 and the fund sells its shares for $25, what is the load fee as a percentage of the net asset value?
3. An investor buys shares in a mutual fund for $20. At the end of the year the fund distributes a dividend of $0.58, and after the distribution the net asset value of a share is $23.41. What is the investor's percentage return on the investment?
4. If an investor buys shares in a no-load mutual fund for $30 and after five years the shares appreciate to $50, what is (1) the percentage return and (2) the annual compound rate of return using time value of money?
5. Twelve months ago, you purchased the shares of a no-load mutual fund for $22.50 per share. The fund distributed cash dividends of $0.75 and capital gains of $1.25 per share. If the net asset value of the fund is currently $24.45, what was your annual return on the investment? If the value of the shares had been $21.24, what would have been your annual return?
6. The Global Growth Fund is a load fund with a 6 percent front load fee. It started the year with a net asset value (NAV) of $16.50. During the year the fund distributed $1.05, and at the end of the year its NAV was $17.95. What was the fund's return, and what was an investor's return? Why are they different?
7. A closed-end investment company has a net asset value of $12.75. A year ago the shares sold for a 20 percent discount but that discount has narrowed (i.e., declined) to 10 percent. If the company distributed $1.25 a share, what was the return on an investment in the shares before considering commissions on the purchase?

STOCKS
THE WALL STREET
12
1
2
3
4
5
6
7
8
9
10
11

PART III

Corporate Finance

In 1998, Exxon had assets of $92,630,000,000. Imagine managing that many assets!* Versus Technology has assets of $5,543,000. Someone also has to be responsible for the management of Versus Technology's assets, and the financial managers of both Exxon and Versus Technology must find financing to carry their respective firms' assets.

Although managing these firms' assets is important, it may have little impact on you or me (unless we work for either firm). Financing these assets, however, may have an impact on us. It is the savings of individuals, other firms, and governments that form the source of finance that permits Exxon and Versus Technology to acquire their assets. The well-being of our investments may very much be affected by the management of these firms' assets. Even if we don't directly invest in either firm, we may own shares in mutual funds or pension plans that do invest in Exxon or Versus Technology.

Parts 1 and 2 of this text covered areas in finance that touch the lives of everyone: financial institutions and the individual's investments. This last section is devoted to financial management from the business perspective. While few individuals may

become financial managers, they may have contact with specific components of corporate finance (for example, how Exxon finances its assets). And, of course, an individual who becomes an entrepreneur and operates his or her own business will be facing many of the same decisions required of the corporate financial manager but without the specialists available in any large corporation!

The remaining chapters cover a variety of corporate financial decisions: the management of short- and long-term assets, how these assets should be financed, which combination of debt and equity funds is optimal, how to plan when the firm will need finance, how to analyze the firm's performance, and whether the firm should grow through mergers. Financial decisions permeate virtually all business decisions since most business decisions have financial implications. Thus, it is desirable for nonfinance students to be aware of the components of financial decision making. Such knowledge can help individuals to communicate and advance within the business community.

---

*During 1999, Exxon and Mobil merged. Based on their 1998 annual reports, the combined assets will exceed $135 billion.

CHAPTER 15

The Forms of Business and Federal Income Taxation

Learning Objectives

1 Enumerate the differences and similarities among types of businesses.
2 Differentiate among progressive, proportional, and regressive taxes.
3 Explain how the taxation of corporate earnings, dividends, and personal income affects the decision to incorporate.
4 Distinguish between straight-line and accelerated cost recovery systems of depreciation.
5 Explain why accelerated depreciation stimulates investment spending.
6 Illustrate the tax savings from losses.

A former prime minister of Canada, W. L. MacKenzie King, said, "Labor can do nothing without capital, capital can do nothing without labor, and neither labor nor capital can do anything without the guiding genius of management." The preceding chapters have considered (1) how the economy generates and allocates capital through a sophisticated system of financial institutions and (2) the securities available to the individual investor. The remainder of this text will be devoted to the financial manager's tasks. Successful business administration requires the genius of a successful financial manager.

All firms employ someone who performs the role of the financial manager. As the subsequent chapters of this text will discuss, the role of the financial manager is broad, covering financial planning and analysis, management of current assets and liabilities, and long-term investments and financing decisions. This chapter sets the stage for the subsequent discussion by considering the forms of business, the impact of federal taxation, and depreciation. The chapter begins with a discussion of the differences among sole proprietorships, partnerships, and corporations.

A major reason for preferring the corporate form of business over sole proprietorships and partnerships is federal income taxation. One of the important tasks of financial management is to reduce the tax liability of the firm. This chapter discusses differences in personal and corporate income taxes. Special consideration is given to the methods of depreciation that affect both the firm's taxes and the cash flows that are generated by an investment. The chapter ends with a discussion of the carry back and carry forward of corporate tax losses.

FORMS OF BUSINESS

Most businesses can be classified into one of three forms: sole proprietorships, partnerships, and corporations. Other forms include syndications, trusts, and joint stock companies. By far the largest number is sole proprietorships. As of 1995, there were 16,442,000 sole proprietorships to only 1,581,000 partnerships and 4,474,000 corporations. However, corporations generated revenues of $14,539 billion and profits of $881 billion, while sole proprietorships had revenues and profits of $807 billion and $169 billion, respectively.[1] Obviously, corporations own the majority of the nation's productive capacity, generate most of the sales, and earn most of the profits. Sole proprietorships are primarily "ma and pa" operations that are limited to small businesses like the corner store. However, many large corporations had modest beginnings, and American business is filled with stories of a talented person building a small business into an industrial leader.

SOLE PROPRIETORSHIP
Firm with one owner

A **sole proprietorship,** as the name implies, has one owner. The firm may employ other people and may borrow money, but the sole proprietor bears the risk of ownership and reaps the profits if they are earned. These are important elements of a sole proprietorship, for the firm has no existence without its proprietor. The firm is not a legal entity that can be held responsible for its actions. The sole proprietor is responsible for the firm's actions and is legally liable for the firm's debts. Sole proprietors bear the risk of ownership, and this risk is not limited to their personal investments. They can lose more than the money invested in their businesses, because the sole proprietor can be held liable for the debts incurred to operate the business. However, since the sole proprietorship is not a legal entity, the firm pays no income taxes. Any profits are considered to be income for the sole proprietor and are subject only to personal income taxation.

PARTNERSHIP
Firm formed by two or more individuals, each of whom is liable for the firm's debts

A **partnership** is similar to a proprietorship except that there are at least two owners (or partners) of the business. While a partnership may have as few as two owners, there is no limit to the number of partners. A partnership has no life without its partners. The partners are the owners, and they reap the rewards and bear the risks of ownership. Each of the partners contributes something to the firm, and this contribution need not be money. For example, several partners may contribute money while others contribute expertise.

The rights and obligations of the partners are established when the partnership is formed. The most important of these are the partners' shares of profits and the extent of their liability. In the simplest case, each partner contributes some percentage of the money necessary to run the business and receives this percentage of the profits. However, not all partnership agreements are this simple. For example, if one partner contributes cash and the other contributes expertise, the division of profits may not be 50–50. Instead, the distribution will be mutually established by the partners.

[1] *The 1998 Statistical Abstract of the United States* (Washington, D.C.: U.S. Department of Commerce). Available at **www.census.gov**.

When forming a partnership, it is important to have a written agreement that spells out the rights and duties of each partner. In general, all the partners bear the risk of enterprise. Each partner is liable for the total debt of the firm, so the individual partner's liability is not limited to his or her contribution to the business. While creditors initially seek settlement of claims from the firm, they can sue the partners for payment if the firm fails to meet the claims. If one partner is unable to pay the prorated share of these obligations, the other partners are liable for these debts. In addition, a partner's share in the firm may be seized to settle *personal* debts. While the creditors must initially sue the individual for personal obligations, if these cannot be met the creditors then have a claim on the partnership. These claims and counterclaims may be complex, but the general order is that personal creditors have an initial claim on the partners' personal assets, and the firm's creditors have the initial claim on the partnership's assets. If personal assets are insufficient to meet the individual's obligations, creditors may make a claim against that partner's share of the partnership. If the firm's assets are insufficient, the partnership's creditors may make claims against the individual partners.

There is a type of partnership that grants limited liability to certain partners. These partnerships are called **limited partnerships;** in these, the limited partners are liable only for their contributions. While these partners have **limited liability,** they have no control over the operation of the firm. Such control rests with the remaining (or general) partners, who have unlimited liability. This form of partnership is popular for risky types of enterprises, such as oil and gas drilling operations, prospecting and mining, and real estate.[2]

A **corporation** is an artificial, legal economic unit established by a state. Every corporation must be incorporated in a state. There is much variation in the individual state laws that establish corporations, and this variation has caused some states to become more popular than others for forming a corporation. Under the state laws, the firm is issued a certificate of incorporation that gives the name of the corporation, the location of the corporation's principal office, the purpose of the corporation, and the number of shares of stock (shares of ownership) that are authorized (that is, the number of shares that the firm may issue). In addition to the certificate of incorporation, the firm receives a **charter** that specifies the relationship between the corporation and the state. At the initial meeting of stockholders, **bylaws** are established that set the rules by which the firm is governed (for example, the voting rights of the stockholders).

In the eyes of the law, a corporation is a legal entity that is separate from its owners. It may enter contracts and is legally responsible for its obligations. This significantly differentiates corporations from sole proprietorships and partnerships. Once a firm incorporates, the owners of the corporation are liable only for the amount of their investment in the company. Owners of corporations have "limited liability," and this limited liability is a major advantage of incorporating.

LIMITED PARTNERSHIP
Partnership in which some of the partners have limited liability and are not liable for the partnership's debts

LIMITED LIABILITY
Individual's personal liability extending only to his or her investment in the firm

CORPORATION
Economic unit created by a state, having the power to own assets, incur liabilities, and engage in specific activities

CHARTER
Document specifying the relationship between a firm and the state in which the firm is incorporated

BYLAWS
Document specifying the relationship between a corporation and its stockholders

[2]Shares in several limited partnerships (for example, Kinder Morgan) trade on the New York Stock Exchange. These partnerships are analogous to mutual funds, since neither pays income tax. The partnerships distribute any income to the partners, who are responsible for the appropriate tax.

Financial Ethics

Finance courses are generally taught from a positive, rather than a normative, viewpoint. The emphasis is on market forces and the belief that quantitative techniques and the rational application of financial and economic theory lead to correct financial decision making. Such phrases as "the financial manager should take a particular action" suggest that the best financial strategy is the one that will increase both the value of the firm and the decision maker's power or income. ¶ Financial decisions, however, may not be independent of moral decisions. For example, during the 1980s, one moral question was: Should a firm invest in South Africa? Analysis may suggest that such an investment would be profitable and, from a positive perspective, the investment "should" be made. A normative perspective, however, may interject that such an investment suggests implicit support for the segregation policies followed by the South African government. Even though the logic itself may not be correct (that is, the investment need not imply support for segregation), the financial decision maker is still faced with a normative question: Should the investment not be made because it appears to support segregation? Many corporate managers did decide to withdraw from South Africa, but it is impossible to determine whether they left on moral grounds or whether they came to the conclusion that remaining would reduce the value of the firm and decrease their power and income. ¶ Since finance is concerned with the management of money and resources, moral questions frequently lie under the surface. Some are more obvious than others. The use of inside information for personal profit is, of course, both morally and legally wrong. The decision to relocate a plant is neither morally nor legally wrong but will inflict pain on the individuals affected. How that pain may be alleviated is both a moral and a financial problem that management will have to face. ¶

Creditors may sue the corporation for payment if the corporation defaults on its obligations, but the creditors cannot sue the stockholders.

For many small corporations, however, limited liability may not exist. Creditors may ask that the stockholders pledge their personal assets to secure a small corporation's loans. Thus, if the corporation defaults, the creditors may seize assets that the shareholders have pledged. If this occurs, the liability of the shareholders is not limited to their initial investment. Limited liability does apply in substance to large corporations that have assets to pledge or sufficient credit ratings to receive unsecured loans. Thus, an investor knows that on purchasing the stock in a company such as General Motors, the maximum amount that can be lost is the amount of the investment. If the firm goes bankrupt, the creditors cannot seize the assets of the stockholders. Such limited liability is a major advantage of incorporating a firm, for large corporations (for example, Continental Airlines and Macy's) do go bankrupt.

A second advantage of incorporating is permanence. Since the corporation is established by the laws of the state, it is permanent until dissolved by the state. Proprietorships and partnerships cease when one of the owners dies or goes bankrupt. The partnership must be re-formed in order to continue to operate. Corporations, however, continue to exist when one of the owners dies. The stock becomes part of the deceased owner's estate and is transferred to the heirs. The company continues to operate, and a new corporation is not formed. Permanence offers a major advantage for incorporating if the owners envision the firm's growing in size and operating for many years, since the expense of re-forming the relationship among the owners is avoided.

A third potential advantage of incorporation is the ease with which title of ownership may be transferred from one investor to another. All that is necessary for such transfer is for the investor to sell the shares of stock (which are evidence of ownership) and have the name of the new owner recorded on the corporation's record of stockholders. Such transfers occur daily through organized security exchanges like the New York Stock Exchange.

This transfer of ownership, however, may be more difficult for small corporations or corporations that are owned by just a few stockholders. For the ease of transfer to occur, a ready market must exist for the stock. Because no ready market exists for small corporations' stock, the owners may have difficulty finding buyers who will purchase their stock.

In some cases, stockholders may be legally barred from selling their stock. In particular, buyers of shares of a small corporation may be required to sign a letter stating that they plan to hold the shares as a long-term investment. In this context, *long term* generally means a period of at least two years. Once an investor signs such a letter, the stock is called "letter stock" and cannot be sold for the duration of the specified period.

Incorporating may also offer the firm the advantage of being able to raise large amounts of money by issuing bonds and stock. Limited liability for stockholders, the potential for capital gains, and the existence of secondary markets in which the securities can be bought and sold are advantages associated with incorporating that do not exist for unincorporated firms. Firms such as AT&T or IBM can readily issue new bonds or new stock to raise capital. Even corporations with credit ratings that are inferior to AT&T's may be able to raise substantial amounts of money through new issues of stocks and/or bonds. Although these corporations may have to offer higher yields on their securities to induce investors to bear the additional risk, they still may use this source of funds.

This ability of corporations to obtain substantial amounts of money by issuing new securities usually applies only to large firms. The managers of small, privately held corporations may not be able to raise outside financing by selling stocks and bonds. Thus, the advantage of incorporating as a means to raise external funds is limited to a small proportion of the total number of corporations in existence. The remaining corporations encounter the same difficulties obtaining outside funding that the owners of sole proprietorships and partnerships face.

TAXES

Taxes play an important role in financial decision making. Most of the decisions involving taxes stress minimizing the amount of taxes that the firm and its owners have to pay. The diversity and complexities of tax laws that affect financial decision making are staggering and require tax expertise.[3] Few individual business executives can obtain this expertise and still perform their other roles. Hence, some lawyers and accountants have become tax experts and sell their services to individuals and managers of firms.

Taxes are levied by governments at all levels. The financial manger, from the sole proprietor through the manager of the largest corporation, will find a variety of tax laws that affect the business. These taxes include federal and state corporate income taxes, capital gains taxes, and state and local taxes on property, such as real estate, plant and equipment, and inventory.

Progressivity of Taxes

The federal government's personal and corporate income taxes are progressive. Other taxes, such as a municipality's property taxes or a state's sales taxes, are not progressive but are regressive or proportional. What do the terms *progressive*, *regressive*, or *proportional* imply?

Progressivity and regressivity are determined by the taxes paid relative to some tax base, such as an individual's income or a corporation's profits. An income tax is **progressive** if, as the individual's income rises, the tax *rate* increases. It is not sufficient for the absolute amount of taxes paid to increase with the increases in income. For a tax to be **regressive,** the tax rate declines as the tax base increases. If the tax rate remains constant as income increases, then the tax is **proportionate.**

PROGRESSIVE TAX
Tax in which the tax rate increases as the tax base increases

REGRESSIVE TAX
Tax in which the tax rate decreases as the tax base increases

PROPORTIONATE TAX
Tax in which the rate remains unchanged as the tax base increases

The differences in progressive, regressive, and proportionate taxes are illustrated in Exhibit 15.1. The first column gives an individual's income. The second and third columns illustrate a progressive tax, in which the tax rate increases with the increases in income. The fourth and fifth columns illustrate a regressive tax, in which the tax rate declines as income rises. The last two columns illustrate a proportionate tax, in which the rate remains constant as income changes. As may be seen in this table, the absolute amount of tax paid *increases in each case.* However, the effect of the higher tax rates on the total amount of taxes is considerable as the income rises from $10,000 to $50,000. With the regressive tax structure, the tax rises from $1,000 to $3,000. With the progressive tax, the amount paid in taxes rises to $15,000.

Many people believe that taxes should be progressive because individuals with higher income are better able to pay and should bear a larger proportion of the

[3] Some aspect of the federal tax laws is changed every year. In addition, the IRS often issues interpretations and regulations concerning existing laws. Staying current with these laws and regulations is exceedingly time consuming. The following two publications are updated annually, so they are one means by which individuals may obtain recent information on current tax laws: *Federal Tax Course* (Englewood Cliffs, N.J.: Prentice-Hall), and Lasser Institute, *J. K. Lasser's Your Income Tax* (New York: Simon & Schuster.) Specialized books and pamphlets on specific tax topics are published by Commerce Clearing House, Inc., and by The National Underwriter Co. A catalog of their current publications may be obtained by writing them at 4025 W. Peterson Ave., Chicago, Illinois 60646, and 450 East Fourth Street, Cincinnati, Ohio 45202-9960, respectively.

EXHIBIT 15.1

Differences in Taxes Paid under Progressive, Regressive, and Proportionate Tax Rates

Income	Progressive Tax Rate	Total Tax Paid	Regressive Tax Rate	Total Tax Paid	Proportionate Tax Rate	Total Tax Paid
$10,000	10%	$1,000	10%	$1,000	20%	$2,000
20,000	15	3,000	9	1,800	20	4,000
30,000	20	6,000	8	2,400	20	6,000
40,000	25	10,000	7	2,800	20	8,000
50,000	30	15,000	6	3,000	20	10,000

EXHIBIT 15.2

Income Levels and Marginal Tax Rates for a Married Couple Filing a Joint Return for 1999

Taxable Income	Marginal Tax Rate
$0–43,050	15.0%
$43,051–104,050	28.0
$104,051–158,550	31.0
$158,551–283,150	36.0
Over $283,150	39.6

cost of the government. It is on this basis that many regressive and proportional taxes (especially the property tax) are criticized. Regressive taxes place a larger share of the cost of government on those individuals who are the least able to afford the burden. Arguments for progressive taxes, however, are primarily based on ethical or normative beliefs. It is a moral judgment that people with higher income should pay a proportionately higher amount of tax.

The federal personal income tax is progressive; that is, as the individual's taxable income rises, the tax rate increases. As the individual reaches higher income tax brackets, the rate at which additional income is taxed rises. The tax rate on this marginal income is referred to as the individual's **marginal tax rate.** Exhibit 15.2 gives the federal income tax rates for a married couple filing a joint return in 2000 for income earned during 1999. As may be seen in the exhibit, the marginal tax rates increase with income from 15 percent to 39.6 percent, indicating that federal income tax is progressive. (There is one important exception to the rates in the exhibit. The maximum rate on long-term capital gains is 20 percent.)

MARGINAL TAX RATE
Tax rate paid on the last (marginal) dollar of income

For low levels of income, the federal corporate income tax is also progressive, as is illustrated in Exhibit 15.3. The left-hand column gives the corporation's taxable income; the column on the right gives the marginal tax rate. Since the tax rate rises with increases in corporate income, the federal corporate income tax is progressive.

EXHIBIT 15.3

Federal Corporate Income Levels and Marginal Tax Rates

Taxable Income	Marginal Tax Rate
$0–50,000	15%
$50,001–75,000	25
$75,001–100,000	34
$100,001–335,000	39
$335,001–10,000,000	34
$10,000,001–15,000,000	35
$15,000,001–18,300,000	38
Over $18,300,000	35

The 39 percent bracket recaptures the benefits of the 15 percent and 25 percent brackets. The 38 percent bracket recaptures the benefits of the 34 percent bracket. Once corporate income exceeds $18,300,000, all corporate income is taxed at 35 percent.

Differences in Tax Rates and the Decision to Incorporate

The effect of taxes on the decision to incorporate is illustrated in Exhibit 15.4. This table shows the disposable income that an individual will have with a sole proprietorship and with a corporation under two sets of assumptions concerning the retention of earnings. In the first case, there is no reinvestment of funds in the business. In the second example, an equal amount for the proprietorship and the corporation is reinvested in the firm. In both cases, taxes paid reflect the individual's filing a joint return, and, to ease the calculations, personal exemptions, deductions, and social security taxes are not included in the determination of personal taxable income.

Both cases in Exhibit 15.4 start with $50,000 of earnings. Taxes are then subtracted from these earnings to determine the individual's disposable income. Since the proprietorship pays no taxes, the entire $50,000 becomes income of the owner in both cases. In the first case the corporation pays $7,500 in corporate income tax, and the net earnings ($42,500) are distributed as dividends to the owner. The owner then pays personal income tax ($8,404 on the proprietorship's income or $6,375 on the corporation's dividends). The residual is disposable income. As may be seen in the last line of the first case, disposable income is greater for the proprietorship ($41,596) versus $36,125). Why is it larger? The answer lies in the fact that for the corporation the $50,000 was taxed twice, once at the corporate level ($7,500) and once at the personal level ($6,375), for total taxes of $13,875.

The second example in Exhibit 15.4 illustrates a different situation, in which funds are reinvested in the company. Once again, both the sole proprietorship and the corporation earn $50,000. However, in this illustration the corporation pays the owner (and manager) a $20,000 salary, leaving a net profit of $30,000. It then pays $4,500 in corporate income tax and retains $25,500 in earnings, which will be

EXHIBIT 15.4

Comparison of Total Federal Income Tax for a Sole Proprietorship and a Corporation

	Proprietorship	Corporation
Case 1: No Retention of Earnings		
Profits	$50,000	$50,000
Corporate income tax	—	7,500
Net profits	50,000	42,500
Earnings distributed	50,000	42,500
Personal income tax (married, filing a joint return)	8,404	6,375
Disposable income	41,596	36,125
Case 2: Retention of Earnings		
Profits (before salary)	50,000	50,000
Salary	—	20,000
Corporate taxable income	—	30,000
Corporate income taxes	—	4,500
Net available for reinvestment	—	25,500
Personal income	50,000	20,000
Personal income tax (married, filing a joint return)	8,404	3,000
Spendable income	41,596	17,000
Personal reinvestment in firm	25,500	—
Disposable income	16,096	17,000

reinvested in the firm. The proprietorship, however, cannot retain earnings but must distribute its earnings to the owner. Thus, in the case of the proprietorship, the owner receives $50,000, compared with only $20,000 in salary from the corporation. The owner pays personal income tax of $8,404 for the proprietorship and $3,000 for the corporation, leaving net income of $41,596 and $17,000, respectively. If the proprietor now invests $25,500 in the firm (as was done in the case of the corporation), the individual's disposable income is reduced to $16,096, which is smaller than the $17,000 the owner obtained through the corporate form of business. In this example, the corporate form of enterprise resulted in total taxes of $7,500, while the proprietorship resulted in taxes totaling $8,404. Thus, the corporate form saved the individual, who is the owner of the business $904.

This tax saving is the result of the way in which the corporation's funds were distributed. Corporations may pay salaries to managers who are also stockholders and treat these payments as expenses. Salaries to the sole proprietor are not permitted, and all profits are income to the owner. It is the splitting of funds between the corporation and the owners that permits the corporate structure to take advantage of the lower tax rates. If the firm needs additional funds, the ability to pay salaries and retain earnings strongly argues for the corporate form of enterprise.

However, if the firm pays low salaries and distributes earnings as cash dividends, the argument is reversed. Cash dividends are subject to "double taxation" because they are taxed as earnings to the corporation and again as part of the individual recipient's personal income.[4] Such double taxation argues against incorporation. Thus, the decision to incorporate is influenced by (1) the amount of profits earned, (2) the tax rates on the firm's earnings and the owners' income tax bracket, (3) the firm's need to retain earnings, and (4) the owners' need for income. These variables will, of course, differ for various cases; hence, there is no clear-cut answer to the question of whether or not to incorporate. However, if the sole proprietor intends to reinvest earnings and have the firm grow, it will probably be advantageous to incorporate.

S CORPORATIONS

One option that stockholders of small corporations may elect permits them to have the advantages associated with corporations (such as permanence, limited liability, and ease of transfer) without the disadvantage of double taxation (the taxation of corporate income and the subsequent taxation of dividends received by the stockholders). If a corporation has 35 or fewer stockholders, the firm may elect to be taxed as an **S corporation.** If the firm does elect to be taxed as an S corporation, its income is not subject to federal corporate income taxation. Instead, the firm's earnings are taxed as income to its stockholders. Thus, the tax treatment is the same as for partnership or sole proprietorship income.

S CORPORATION
Corporation that is taxed as if it were a partnership

While electing S corporate status circumvents the problem of double taxation, it also means that the individual stockholders are responsible for the appropriate income taxes. This taxation applies even if the corporation does not distribute its earnings as dividends. If the firm retains earnings for reinvestment, the stockholders have to pay taxes on the undistributed earnings. If management desires to retain earnings to finance future growth, the election to be taxed as an S corporation would be the incorrect decision. The firm would be better off having its earnings taxed at the corporate level and retaining (not distributing) its earnings.

LIMITED LIABILITY COMPANIES

An alternative to the S corporation is the limited liability company (LLC), which is a new form of business that has grown in popularity since it received favorable tax treatment from the IRS. Such companies may qualify for tax purposes to be

[4]The possibility of "triple taxation" exists when corporation A buys shares in corporation B. If B generates earnings, it pays federal income taxes. If B then distributes the earnings, A must pay income tax on the dividends (providing that A has taxable income). If A then distributes its earnings, which would include the dividends it received from B, A's stockholders would pay income tax on the distribution. In such a case, there is triple taxation. The earnings are taxed twice at the corporate level and again at the individual level.

However, the impact of triple taxation is reduced by the corporate dividend exclusion, which was discussed in Chapter 10. This exclusion permits A to exclude 70 percent of the dividends it receives from B, so only 30 percent of the dividends received by A from B may be subject to triple taxation.

treated as partnerships; that is, there is no income tax at the firm level. Income (or loss) flows through to the owners who pay the appropriate federal income tax. Although both LLCs and S corporations are not taxed at the firm level, they are different. An S corporation can have no more than 35 stockholders who must be U.S. citizens or resident aliens. LLCs are not subject to this limitation. Foreign investors, corporations, or partnerships may own stock in an LLC.

LLCs also offer the advantage of limited liability. The owners of the LLC are not liable for the debts of the company. While such limited liability applies to limited partnerships, there are important differences between LLCs and limited partnerships. The latter must have at least one general partner who manages the firm and is responsible for its debts. LLCs do not have this constraint. Owners of the firm may actively participate in its management and not be personally liable.

These advantages of the LLC—the pass-through of federal income tax liabilities and limited liability—explain why LLCs have become a popular form of business that will replace many partnerships and S corporations. However, the shares of these companies are not registered with the SEC and are not publicly traded. Thus, the LLC will not replace publicly traded corporations.

OTHER TAX CONSIDERATIONS: FRINGE BENEFITS

Besides differences in the tax treatment given personal and corporate incomes, other tax laws affect financial management. Three areas are particularly important: deductible expenses, depreciation, and losses that generate tax savings.

Business expenses affect taxation because they reduce taxable income. Workers' fringe benefits constitute a particularly important expense. Fringe benefits are expenses to the firm but are not taxed as income. Income tax is levied when income is received, but by using fringe benefits, firms may increase employees' compensation without increasing their taxes. For example, if medical insurance costs $3,000 annually, an individual in the 28 percent federal income tax bracket would have to earn $4,167 before taxes [$4,167 − 0.28(4,167) = $3,000] in order to have $3,000 after taxes to purchase the insurance. However, an employer may participate in a group insurance plan or health maintenance organization that covers the employees. The employees do not receive monetary income but instead receive free medical insurance. The receipt of the benefits is not treated as taxable income, but the firm still has the expense that reduces its taxable income. (There are periodic proposals before Congress to tax fringe benefits.)

Fringe benefits have become a popular means to increase employees' wages and salaries. Corporations may grant fringes instead of increased wages, because the cost of the fringes to the employer is less than the increase in wages that would be necessary for the workers to purchase the goods or services themselves. Employees realize the potential tax savings of fringe benefits, so these benefits become an important reason for working for specific employers. Medical insurance, paid sick leave, life insurance, and pension plans are all illustrative of possible fringe benefits that either escape or defer taxation.

In addition to the previous fringe benefits, many corporations offer retirement plans. Initially, retirement plans defined the amount an employee would receive based on number of years worked and salary or wages received. For example, an individual who worked for the company for 30 years may receive 75 percent of the average earnings for the last five years of employment. This type of plan is referred to as a "defined benefit plan" since the amount of the pension is determined by the plan.

The risk associated with a defined benefit plan rests with the plan sponsor. Assets must be accumulated and if the return on the assets is insufficient to cover the pension liabilities, the sponsor has to make additional contributions. Since the risk associated with funding defined benefit plans rests with the firm (plus the increased complexity of federal pension laws), many companies terminated their defined benefit plans and substituted "defined contribution plans," especially the 401(k) plan.

A defined contribution plan specifies the amount a worker may contribute such as 5 percent of salary. The employer often matches the employee's contribution. The risk associated with a defined contribution plan rests with the employee, who must choose to participate and who decides where to invest the funds from the alternatives provided by the employer's plan. If the employee chooses not to participate, the employer has no matching pension expense and no pension liabilities.

Both defined benefit and defined contribution plans are illustrations of tax shelters to the participants. The money contributed by employers and employees is not taxed until the funds are withdrawn from the plan. From the employer's perspective, the contributions are essentially the same as any other fringe benefit. The costs are deductible business expenses.

One criticism of employer-sponsored pension plans was that they were not available to all workers, since many companies, especially small firms, did not offer the benefit. Congress subsequently passed legislation that enabled all employees and the self-employed to establish their own pension plans. Over time this legislation was expanded to cover more individuals and to permit larger contributions. Currently the deductible individual retirement account (IRA) permits workers not covered by a pension plan to invest up to $2,000 annually ($4,000 for a married couple) and deduct the contribution provided that the worker has earned income of at least $4,000. Workers covered by a pension may also establish a deductible IRA provided their income is below a specified amount.[5]

While self-employed individuals cannot establish corporate pension plans, they may set up Keogh accounts. These accounts essentially work the same as 401(k) plans and deductible IRAs. Contributions are tax deductible in the current

[5]In 1997, enabling legislation created the non-deductible Roth IRA. With the deductible IRA, contributions reduce current income but the withdrawals from the plan are subject to income tax. The Roth IRA's tax advantage occurs when the individual withdraws funds from the account. While the contributions are not tax deductible, the withdrawals are not subject to income tax. Like the deductible IRA, the Roth IRA has a contribution limit of $2,000 annually for an individual's account, and there is also an income restriction for contributing to a Roth IRA. For a summary of pension laws and other tax strategies, see the American Association of Individual Investors, "Personal Tax & Financial Planning Guide," published annually. The Association may be reached at **www.aaii.com**.

year, and income taxes are deferred until funds are withdrawn from the account. In addition, the amount of the annual contribution is the most generous of all the retirement accounts, since the individual may contribute (and deduct) up to 20 percent of earned income or $30,000, whichever is less.

DEPRECIATION

In addition to the deductibility of fringe benefits, the firm may deduct any cost of doing business. Employee wages and salaries, the cost of goods sold, insurance, local property taxes, interest paid, and advertising costs are examples of expenses that are deducted before a business determines its taxable income. These expenses also require the payment of cash. Each is a cash outflow. There is, however, one important expense that does not involve a cash outflow. This expense, depreciation, is exceedingly important. Like any expense, depreciation reduces taxable income and reduces taxes owed, but since depreciation is a noncash expense, it is added back to earnings to help determine cash flow from operations. (See the Statement of Cash Flows in Chapter 12.)

Depreciation is the allocation of the cost of fixed assets, such as plant and equipment, over a period of time. Part of the cost of these assets is written off against the firm's revenues each year. If this allocation of costs is for the same dollar amount each year, the firm is using **straight-line depreciation.** The allocation, however, may be in larger dollar amounts during the initial years and smaller amounts during the later years of the investment's life. This allocation system is called **accelerated depreciation.** As will be illustrated below, the advantage of accelerated depreciation is that it allocates the cost of the asset faster and, therefore, recoups most of the cost of the investment quicker *and* initially reduces the firm's income taxes.

DEPRECIATION
Allocation of the cost of plant and equipment over a period of time.

STRAIGHT-LINE DEPRECIATION
Allocation of the cost of plant and equipment by equal amounts over a period of time

ACCELERATED DEPRECIATION
Allocating the cost of plant and equipment in such a way that a larger proportion of an asset's cost is recovered during the earlier years of the asset's life

Depreciation expense arises in the following way. A firm has the following balance sheet:

Firm X Balance Sheet as of 12/31/XX

Assets		Liabilities and Equity	
Cash	$1,000	Debt	$500
		Equity	$500

It currently has only cash that it acquired from investors (the equity) and from creditors (the debt). In order to produce some product, the firm uses $400 of the cash to acquire equipment. After the purchase, the balance sheet becomes as follows:

Assets		Liabilities and Equity	
Cash	$600	Debt	$500
Equipment	$400	Equity	$500

The $400 cash was spent when the equipment was acquired; thus the firm no longer has these funds.

The firm anticipates that the equipment will operate for several years. For example, the firm may anticipate that the equipment may last four years, after which time it will have to be junked and replaced. If the firm anticipates that the $400 machine will have a useful life of four years, the firm depreciates the machine on a straight-line basis for $100 a year. This is determined by using the following formula:

15.1

$$\text{Annual depreciation} = \frac{\text{Cost}}{\text{Anticipated useful life in years}}.$$

In this case annual depreciation is

$$\frac{\$400}{4} = \$100.$$

In effect the firm is saying that $100 worth of the machine is depreciated or consumed each year and that at the end of four years the machine is totally consumed and valueless.

Depreciation is important for two reasons. First, since it is an expense, it alters the firm's earnings and taxes. Second, since depreciation is a noncash expense, it is treated in finance as a source of cash for the firm. Both these points are discussed below and are illustrated by the depreciation expense on the firm's $400 piece of equipment. To simplify the illustration, straight-line depreciation is used. The annual depreciation expense is thus $100.

The importance of depreciation expense on profit and corporate income tax is illustrated as follows. If the output produced by the firm's machine is sold for $800, and if, after operating and administrative expenses of $500, the firm has earnings of $300, is the $300 a true statement of the earnings? The answer is no, because no allowance has been made for the $100 of the machine's value that has been consumed to produce the output. The true profit is not $300 but $200, which is $300 gross earnings minus the $100 depreciation expense. The firm now pays corporate income tax on its earnings of $200 and not on the earnings before the depreciation expense. If the corporate income tax rate is 25 percent, the firm pays $50 (0.25 × $200) in taxes instead of the $75 (0.25 × $300) it would have to pay if the depreciation expense were omitted. Since the depreciation expense reduces the firm's earnings, it also reduces its income taxes.

Since the firm bought the equipment in the first year, it might seem reasonable to add the entire cost of the equipment to the firm's expenses for that year. In that case would the firm have a true statement of its earnings? It would not, because the firm's costs are incorrectly stated. The firm's expenses would be $900, which includes the $500 operating expense and the $400 cost of the equipment. The firm would be operating at a loss of $100 ($800 revenues minus $900 expenses). This understates the earnings because the equipment's entire value was not consumed during the year. Only one-fourth of its value was consumed during the first year. Hence, only one-fourth of the equipment's value should be charged (or "expensed") against the firm's annual revenues. Overstating depreciation, like understating depreciation, alters the firm's earnings.

The second important feature of depreciation is its impact on cash flow. In the above example, the $100 depreciation expense did not involve an outlay of cash. The operating and administrative expenses required an outlay of money, but the depreciation expense did not involve the expenditure of money. The outlay of cash occurred when the machine was initially purchased and not while it was being used. Depreciation is a noncash expense item that allocates the initial cash outlay (that is, the purchase price of the equipment plus the cost of putting the equipment in place) over a period of time. Because no cash is expended by the firm as a result of the depreciation expense, depreciation is said to be a source of cash flow because it is recouping the original outlay for the machine. Therefore, depreciation increases the flow of cash in the firm.

This seemingly contradictory statement (that an expense will increase the firm's cash flow) may be illustrated by further considering the previous example. A simple income statement for the firm is as follows:

Sales	$800
Operating expenses	500
Income before depreciation	300
Depreciation	100
Taxable income	200
Taxes	50
Net income	$150

Only the operating expenses ($500) and the tax ($50) required a disbursement of cash. The firm has $250 ($800 − $550) left. This is the $150 profit and the $100 depreciation expense that is added back to the profits to obtain the cash flow generated by operations. Thus, cash flow is the earnings (after taxes) plus depreciation expense. The firm has $250 that it may use and $100 of the cash is the result of the depreciation expense. The firm must now decide what to do with the $100 generated by the depreciated asset. For example, it may restore the depreciated asset, purchase a different asset, retire outstanding debt, or make payments to stockholders. Each of these acts is a possible use for the cash generated by the noncash expenditure, depreciation.

Accelerated Depreciation

Conceptually, accelerated depreciation is no different from straight-line depreciation except that a greater proportion of the asset's purchase price is depreciated in the early years of the asset's life. Depreciation charges are larger when the plant and equipment are new and smaller when the plant and equipment are old. This variation in the expense, of course, alters the firm's earnings. When the depreciation charge is larger, the firm's profits and corporate income taxes are smaller. By using accelerated depreciation the firm initially is able to decrease its profits and taxes but increase its cash flow (that is, accelerated depreciation initially increases the sum of earnings plus depreciation expense).

MODIFIED ACCELERATED COST RECOVERY SYSTEM (MACRS)
Type of accelerated depreciation that became law under the tax revision of 1981 and that was revised under the 1986 Tax Reform Act

Plant and equipment are generally depreciated under the **modified accelerated cost recovery system (MACRS),** which uses the schedules given in Exhibit 15.5. The first column presents the year, and the other columns present (for the given classes of depreciable assets) the proportion of the asset's cost that may be depreciated in that year. For example, if an asset is to be depreciated over five years, 32 percent of the cost of that asset is written off in the second year.

The number of years that may be used for depreciating a particular asset is similar to the asset's economic life. For example, cars and light trucks are depreciated over five years, and office equipment is depreciated over seven years. An asset, however, may be used for longer than the period allowed to write off its cost. Prior to the establishment of the accelerated cost recovery system (ACRS) and its subsequent modification (MACRS), depreciation was determined by the asset's useful life. Thus, a piece of equipment that had an expected useful life of ten years would be depreciated over ten years. Under current law, that equipment would be classified as a seven-year asset, and the seven-year schedule would be applied.

Two additional observations should be made. First, a close look at the schedules presented in Exhibit 15.5 reveals that the depreciation schedules are one year longer than the stated number of years. For example, the depreciation of a five-year asset occurs over six years. This is because depreciation is based on the assumption that assets are purchased evenly throughout the year. On the average, assets are only owned for half of the year in which they are acquired. In addition, the depreciation schedules do not consider any residual value that the asset may have. Thus, an asset classified as depreciable under the seven-year schedule will have no value at the end of the eighth year according to the depreciation schedule, even though in reality it may have some residual value.

Methods of Depreciation Compared

All methods of depreciation allocate the cost of plant and equipment over a period of time. The differences relate to their effects on the firm's earnings and thus to their effects on the firm's taxes and the cash flow from the investments. Straight-line depreciation and the accelerated cost recovery system are compared in Exhibit 15.6 for an asset that costs $1,000 and is depreciated over ten years.[6] The first section of this table illustrates straight-line depreciation over the asset's economic life. Notice the half-year convention also applies to straight-line depreciation. Since the average asset is owned for six months, only half of the annual depreciation expense is deducted the first year. To fully depreciate the asset, the final deduction occurs in the 11th year in the exhibit.

The second section illustrates the accelerated cost recovery system, which classifies the asset as a seven-year asset. The first column gives the year and the

[6] Exhibit 15.6 employs a $1,000 asset to facilitate the comparison of straight-line and accelerated depreciation. As of 1999, the firm may immediately deduct ("write-off") up to $19,000 of the cost of equipment. Once the equipment is written off, it has no book value and is excluded from the firm's balance sheet. However, the asset may still have value (that is, it could be sold). This difference between book and market values illustrates that the value carried on the balance sheet (that is, the book value) need not equal the market value (that is, what the asset may be sold for).

EXHIBIT 15.5

Depreciation Schedules under the Modified Accelerated Cost Recovery System

Recovery Year	PERCENTAGE OF COST DEPRECIATED OVER: 3 Years	5 Years	7 Years	10 Years	15 Years	20 Years
1	33.00%	20.00%	14.28%	10.00%	5.00%	3.79%
2	45.00	32.00	24.49	18.00	9.50	7.22
3	15.00	19.20	17.49	14.40	8.55	6.68
4	7.00	11.52	12.49	11.52	7.69	6.18
5		11.52	8.93	9.22	6.93	5.71
6		5.76	8.93	7.37	6.23	5.28
7			8.93	6.55	5.90	4.89
8			4.46	6.55	5.90	4.52
9				6.55	5.90	4.46
10				6.55	5.90	4.46
11				3.29	5.90	4.46
12					5.90	4.46
13					5.90	4.46
14					5.90	4.46
15					5.90	4.46
16					3.00	4.46
17						4.46
18						4.46
19						4.46
20						4.46
21						2.25

second column gives the firm's operating revenues after all expenses except depreciation. The third column gives the depreciation expense for each of the years. The remaining four columns illustrate the effects of depreciation expense. The fourth column presents the firm's taxable income; the fifth column gives the income taxes (assuming a tax rate of 25 percent), and the sixth column gives the net income or profit after the taxes. The seventh column gives the firm's cash flow, which is the sum of its earnings after taxes and its depreciation expenses. As may be seen in the table, the accelerated method of depreciation initially (1) reduces the firm's taxable income, which reduces its taxes, and (2) increases the firm's cash flow.

The table, however, also illustrates that the accelerated method of depreciation increases the firm's income and taxes and reduces its cash flow in the later years of the asset's life. Actually, the total depreciation expense, net income after taxes, taxes, and cash flow over the asset's life are the same for both methods of depreciation. This can be seen by adding the depreciation expense, taxes, net income, and cash flow columns. The sums are equal for both methods.

If accelerated depreciation does not reduce the firm's taxes and increase its cash flow over the life of the asset, what is its advantage? The answer to this

EXHIBIT 15.6 Comparison of Straight-Line and Accelerated Cost Recovery Methods of Depreciation

Year	Income before Depreciation	Depreciation Expense	Income before Taxes	Income Taxes	Net Income after Taxes	Cash Flow
Straight-Line Depreciation						
1	$300	$ 50	$ 250	$ 62.50	$ 187.50	$ 237.50
2	300	100	200	50.00	150.00	250.00
3	300	100	200	50.00	150.00	250.00
4	300	100	200	50.00	150.00	250.00
5	300	100	200	50.00	150.00	250.00
6	300	100	200	50.00	150.00	250.00
7	300	100	200	50.00	150.00	250.00
8	300	100	200	50.00	150.00	250.00
9	300	100	200	50.00	150.00	250.00
10	300	100	200	50.00	150.00	250.00
11	300	50	250	62.50	187.50	237.50
Totals		$ 1,000		$575.00	$1,725.00	$2,725.00
Accelerated Cost Recovery						
1	$300	$ 142.80	$157.20	$ 39.30	$ 117.90	$ 260.70
2	300	244.90	55.10	13.78	41.32	286.22
3	300	174.90	125.10	31.28	93.82	268.72
4	300	124.90	175.10	43.78	131.32	256.22
5	300	89.30	210.70	52.67	158.03	247.33
6	300	89.30	210.70	52.67	158.03	247.33
7	300	89.30	210.70	52.67	158.03	247.33
8	300	44.60	255.40	63.85	191.55	236.15
9	300	—	300.00	75.00	225.00	225.00
10	300	—	300.00	75.00	225.00	225.00
11	300	—	300.00	75.00	225.00	225.00
Totals		$1,000.00		$575.00	$1,725.00	$2,725.00

question is the timing of the taxes and the cash flows. Accelerated depreciation increases the firm's cash flow during the early years of the asset's life and delays the payment of taxes to the later years of the asset's life. Accelerated depreciation increases the cash flow now, so the firm has the cash to invest and increase earnings. By deferring taxes, the firm is receiving a current loan in the form of deferred taxes from the federal government. And equally important, this loan has no interest cost.

In effect, the federal government, by permitting accelerated depreciation, is granting firms interest-free loans that may be used to earn more profits. Accelerated depreciation is another of those devices that the federal government uses to influence behavior. By granting accelerated depreciation, the federal government encourages firms to invest in plant and equipment. By encouraging such investment, the federal government is helping firms to increase both the productive capacity of the nation and the level of employment, for workers must build the plant and equipment and operate it after it has been installed.

LOSSES AND TAX SAVINGS

Not all corporations are profitable. Some operate at a loss, and this loss, like earnings, has tax consequences. All firms must report earnings annually and pay appropriate income taxes. Taxes are paid each fiscal year, but a firm operates for many years, during which the firm may operate at a loss some years and for a profit other years. Firms in cyclical industries especially may have profitable years followed by years of losses. Fortunately, the federal government permits losses from one year to be used to offset income from profitable years, so that over a number of years it is the firm's net earnings after losses that are taxed and not just the earnings in profitable years.

If a corporation operates at a loss in the current fiscal year, the loss may be carried back to offset income earned in the previous three years. (The corporation may elect to carry the loss forward, which may be desirable if management expects to be in a higher tax bracket in the future.) If the loss is carried back, the corporation receives a refund for previously paid taxes. If any loss remains because the total loss exceeded the earnings of the previous three years, the remaining loss is carried forward for up to 15 years to offset future earnings. In this case, the carry forward of the loss erases future taxes.

The impact of the carry back and carry forward of losses may be seen by considering the following illustrations. In each case the corporation has a loss in the current year (that is, year 4). The corporate income tax rate is assumed to be 30 percent. The loss in year 4 of $1,000 is used to offset the total earnings in years 1 and 2, and $200 of the earnings in year 3. Thus, the $120 in taxes paid in each of years 1 and 2 and $60 of the taxes paid for year 3 are refunded in year 4. The $1,000 loss in year 4 recaptures the taxes paid in years 1 and 2 and part of year 3's taxes.

	YEAR					
Case A	**1**	**2**	**3**	**4**	**5**	**6**
Earnings	$400	400	400	(1,000)	400	400
Taxes	$120	120	120	0	120	120
(Tax refund)				($300)		
Net taxes paid (after refund)	0	0	$60	0	120	120

Two important points need to be made. First, notice that the loss is initially used against year 1's income. If that income does not exhaust the loss, the residual is carried to year 2 to offset that year's income. Once again if the earnings do not exhaust the loss, the residual is carried to year 3. The loss is carried forward to years 5, 6, and so on only if it exceeds the sum of the earnings in years 1, 2, and 3. Second, notice that the loss is used first against year 1's and not against year 3's income. The loss is carried back three years and then any remaining loss is moved forward.

				YEAR				
Case B	**1**	**2**	**3**	**4**	**5**	**6**	**7**	**8**
Earnings	$400	400	400	(1,500)	—	—	—	—
Taxes	$120	120	120	0	—	—	—	—
(Tax refund)				(360)				
Net taxes paid (after refund)	0	0	0	0				

In case B, the loss in year 4 exceeds the combined earnings of years 1 through 3 (the $1,500 loss versus the $1,200 combined earnings), so the remaining $300 loss will be carried forward to offset income earnings in subsequent years. The entire $360 previously paid in taxes will be refunded, and the corporation will not have to pay corporate federal income tax on the next $300 of earnings. Of course, this future tax savings depends on the firm's generating future earnings, and in this illustration there are, as of now, no future earnings, so this potential tax saving may be lost.

					YEAR			
Case C	**1**	**2**	**3**	**4**	**5**	**6**	**7**	**8**
Earnings	—	—	—	($1,500)	400	600	800	1,000
Taxes	—	—	—	0	120	180	240	300
(Tax refund)	—	—	—	—	($120)	(180)	(200)	—
Net taxes paid (after refund)	—	—	—	0	0	0	$40	300

In case C, the firm had no earnings or losses in the first three years, so the entire $1,500 loss is carried forward. The order of carry forward is chronological, so the entire $400 profit in year 5 is offset as are the earnings of $600 in year 6. The earnings in years 5 and 6 are offset by only $1,000 of year 4's $1,500 loss. The remaining $500 is used to partially offset the $800 earned in year 7. After year 7, however, the entire loss has been used to offset income, so any income earned in year 8 ($1,000) will be subject to federal corporate income tax.

SUMMARY

Most firms are either sole proprietorships, partnerships, or corporations. The decision to use a particular form of business is often influenced by tax considerations. While both personal and corporate federal income taxes are progressive, the tax rates differ. Hence, individuals may be able to reduce the total taxes paid by using a particular form of business. The tax laws particularly encourage incorporation if the owners desire the firm to grow. The retention and reinvestment of earnings result in lower taxes than the distribution of earnings and their subsequent reinvestment in the firm.

After a firm acquires fixed assets, they are depreciated, which is the allocation of the cost of investment in plant and equipment over a period of time. Under straight-line depreciation, the same dollar amount is subtracted from revenues each year. Under accelerated depreciation, the initial cost of the investment is reduced more rapidly, for larger dollar amounts are subtracted during the early years of an investment's life. Thus, accelerated depreciation permits the cost of the investment to be written off faster, which initially reduces the firm's earnings and taxes. Since depreciation is a noncash expense, accelerated depreciation initially increases the cash flow from the investment. This increased cash flow may be reinvested to increase the profitability of the firm.

Rules for depreciation are established by Congress and the Internal Revenue Service. Since accelerated depreciation writes off an investment more rapidly and increases the cash flow generated by the investment, it encourages capital spending. By altering depreciation schedules, the federal government induces behavior consistent with the economic goals of full employment, stable prices, and economic growth.

If a corporation operates at a loss, the loss may be carried back three years to offset earnings that were previously taxed. This carry back results in the corporation receiving a tax refund. If the previous three years' earnings are offset by the loss, any remaining loss is carried forward and used to offset future earnings. This carry forward may be extended up to 15 years; however, for the loss carry forward to produce tax savings, the corporation must generate earnings in the future.

Review Questions

1. If you purchase the stock of IBM, do you have limited liability? What does limited liability mean, and what is the maximum amount that you can lose on your investment in IBM? If you start your own corporation, why may you not have limited liability?
2. One of the advantages of incorporating is the case of transferring ownership in the corporation. Why is this more true for large, publicly held corporations than for small, privately held corporations?
3. If you saw the following information, what would you conclude about the progressivity of the tax system?

Individual	Income Earned	Taxes Paid
A	$10,000	$ 500
B	20,000	900
C	40,000	1,400

4. It is sometimes suggested that stockholders pay double taxation. What does that mean? Does it apply if a corporation retains all of its earnings? Does double taxation apply to S corporations or limited liability companies?
5. What is the difference between a general and a limited partner? Why do general partners have unlimited liability?
6. If a firm uses accelerated instead of straight-line depreciation, can the firm depreciate an asset by a larger amount? What impact will the use of accelerated depreciation have on the cash flow from an investment in plant and equipment?
7. The right to use accelerated depreciation for tax purposes is granted by the federal government. Why does the federal government permit the use of accelerated depreciation?
8. Can all assets be depreciated? If equipment appreciates in value, does that mean the firm cannot depreciate the equipment?
9. What are the implications if a corporation operates at a loss? What is the potential savings in taxes from operating at a loss?

10. Based on information obtained from the IRS Web site (**www.irs.ustreas.gov** or **www.irs.gov**), what are the federal income tax rates for the current year?

Problems

1. What is the tax owed on the following additions to income if the individual is in the 25 percent income tax bracket?
   a. $1,000 corporate interest
   b. $1,000 overtime pay
   c. $1,000 dividend income
   d. $1,000 municipal interest
   e. $1,000 pension income

2. If a corporation earns $100,000 in pretax income, what is the amount of federal income tax owed?
3. If a corporation earns $270,000 before taxes, how much is owed the federal government? What are the firm's average and marginal tax rates?
4. An asset costs $200,000 and is classified as a ten-year asset? What is the annual depreciation expense for the first three years under the straight-line and the modified accelerated cost recovery systems of depreciation?
5. Assume Lasher's Kitchen has pretax earnings of $75,000 after depreciation expense of $15,000. If the firm's tax rate is 35 percent, what is its cash flow from operations?
6. A firm has earnings of $12,000 before interest, depreciation, and taxes. A new piece of equipment is installed at a cost of $10,000. The equipment will be depreciated over five years, and the firm pays 25 percent of its earnings in taxes. What are the earnings and cash flows for the firm in years 2 and 5, using the two methods of depreciation discussed in the chapter? What is the source of the difference in earnings and cash flow?
7. Barry Breslin's Billboards has been in operation for three years. During the first two years, it earned pretax income of $25,000 and $40,000 but sustained a loss of $30,000 during the third year. If the firm's tax rate is 30 percent, how large a tax refund can management expect, and is there any tax-loss carry forward?
8. A firm had earnings of $100,000 in the prior year and paid taxes of $30,000 (30 percent tax rate). This year it operated at a loss of $120,000. What are the taxes owed or refund it will receive? Is there any tax-loss carry forward? What would be the implication if the firm had lost $100,000 in the prior year instead of earning a profit?
9. Over the last five years, firm A has been consistently profitable. Its earnings before taxes were as follows:

Year	1	2	3	4	5
Earnings	$1,000	3,000	4,300	5,200	4,400

   a. If the corporate tax rate was 25 percent, what were the firm's income taxes for each year?
   b. Unfortunately, in year 6 the firm experienced a major decline in sales, which resulted in a loss of $10,800. What impact will the loss have on the firm's taxes for each of the six years?

CHAPTER 16
Leverage and the Cost of Capital

Learning Objectives

1 Calculate and illustrate the break-even level of output.
2 State the sources of operating leverage and financial leverage and explain their impact on operating income, net income, and risk.
3 Determine the impact of substituting fixed for variable costs and debt for equity.
4 Identify the components of a firm's capital structure.
5 Differentiate among the factors that affect the costs of debt, preferred stock, and common stock.
6 Compute the cost of capital and determine the optimal capital structure.
7 Distinguish between the average cost of funds and the marginal cost of funds.
8 Determine the relationship between the optimal capital structure and the value of a firm's stock.

Disraeli suggested that "what we anticipate seldom occurs; what we least expect generally happens." Perhaps that explains why UAL's (United Airlines) per share earnings declined from $3.97 in 1989 to a loss of $9.94 in 1992 then rebounded to earnings of $4.82 in 1995 and $8.95 in 1997. It is hard to believe that management planned such volatile earnings. The unanticipated happened, and operating and financing decisions magnified the swings in earnings.

One possible source of the volatility is the firm's use of leverage. Operating leverage refers to the use of fixed inputs, such as plant and equipment (planes by UAL), relative to variable factors, such as labor. The substitution of equipment for labor may produce the same level of output but make the firm's operating income (EBIT) more volatile. Financial leverage refers to the use of debt financing. Substituting debt for equity financing (issuing bonds to purchase planes instead of issuing stock) makes net income more volatile. Both operating and financial leverage increase the volatility of earnings and the firm's risk.

The chapter begins with a discussion of break-even analysis, which determines the level of output (sales) necessary to avoid losses. Although this analysis cannot determine whether a particular investment should be made, it can help management decide whether new products should be developed and what markets should be entered. Break-even analysis can also help determine the scale of operations.

The bulk of the chapter is devoted to the determination of the firm's cost of capital, which is the best combination of debt and equity financing. Lenders and stockholders are not altruistic. Creditors demand interest payments, and stockholders want a return through dividends and price appreciation. The question then becomes: What combination of debt and equity financing generates these returns and minimizes the cost of capital? Coca-Cola has traditionally been conservatively managed. In 1980, total debt financed less than 10 percent of Coke's total assets. By 1999, total debt financed 53.9 percent of Coke's assets. Management obviously decided that the firm's capital structure was not optimal and, over time, substituted debt for equity financing.

Ascertaining the cost of capital is important because it is a necessary component of capital budgeting, which is covered in the next chapter. Capital budgeting determines if an investment in plant or equipment should be made, thereby answering a crucial question that break-even analysis cannot answer. Cost of the capital, however, is an involved topic that encompasses the cost of debt and equity and the risk associated with the firm.

Initially, operating and financial leverage are covered to understand their impact on the volatility of the firm's operating and net income. This volatility increases the firm's risk exposure, which affects the cost of debt and equity. After covering the cost of the various components of a firm's capital structure, the weighted-average cost of capital is calculated, and the optimal capital structure is determined. Once this capital structure is determined, it should be maintained because it generates the lowest cost of funds.

Maintaining the optimal capital structure does not mean the cost of capital is fixed. The cost of additional finance may rise even though the optimal capital structure is maintained, so it is necessary to differentiate between the average cost of capital and the cost of additional (marginal) funds. The chapter ends by tying the cost of capital to the value of the firm's stock and showing how the excess use of financing leverage will lead to a higher cost of capital and lower valuation of the stock.

BREAK-EVEN ANALYSIS

Break-even analysis determines the level of sales that generates neither profits nor losses and hence causes the firm to "break even." Break-even analysis also permits management to see the effects on the level of profits of (1) fluctuations in sales, (2) fluctuations in costs, and (3) changes in fixed costs relative to variable costs. Break-even analysis is based on the following three mathematical relationships: the relationship between (1) output and total revenues (sales), (2) output and variable costs of production, and (3) output and fixed costs of production.

BREAK-EVEN ANALYSIS
Technique used to determine that level of output at which total expenses equal total revenues (resulting in neither profits nor losses)

The relationship between output and total revenues (TR) is the number of units sold (Q) times the price (P) for each unit. This may be expressed as a simple equation: Total revenue equals price times quantity sold. In symbolic form this equation is expressed as follows:

$$TR = P \times Q. \qquad (16.1)$$

EXHIBIT 16.1

Relationships between Output and Revenues, Output and Costs, and Output and Profits

1 *P*	2 *Q*	3 *TR*	4 *FC*	5 *V*	6 *VC*	7 *TC*	8 Profits (losses)
$2	0	$ 0	$1,000	$1	$ 0	$1,000	($1,000)
2	200	400	1,000	1	200	1,200	(800)
2	400	800	1,000	1	400	1,400	(600)
2	600	1,200	1,000	1	600	1,600	(400)
2	800	1,600	1,000	1	800	1,800	(200)
2	1,000	2,000	1,000	1	1,000	2,000	0
2	1,200	2,400	1,000	1	1,200	2,200	200
2	1,400	2,800	1,000	1	1,400	2,400	400
2	1,600	3,200	1,000	1	1,600	2,600	600
2	1,800	3,600	1,000	1	1,800	2,800	800
2	2,000	4,000	1,000	1	2,000	3,000	1,000

The larger the number of units that are sold at a given price, the larger the firm's total revenue. This relationship is illustrated in the first three columns of Exhibit 16.1, which presents the costs and revenues of a firm used in break-even analysis. The first column gives the price of the product and the second column the quantity sold. Multiplying these two gives the total revenue in the third column. For example, since the per-unit price is $2.00, the total revenue for a level of sales of 1,000 units is $2,000.

In Figure 16.1, total revenue is illustrated as a straight line that runs through the origin, for at zero units of output there can be no revenues. As output is increased, total revenue increases. The rate at which total revenue increases (the slope of the line) is the price of the output. This rate is constant, for each additional unit of output is assumed to be sold at the given price.

Costs of production are divided into two classes: (1) costs that vary with production, such as labor expense; and (2) costs that do not vary with output, such as administrative expense or interest charges. This classification of costs is arbitrary, for fixed costs may become variable, and variable costs may become fixed. For example, a company may refinance its debt and change its *fixed* interest expense or may change its management personnel and change its *fixed* administrative expense. Union contracts may convert some variable costs into fixed costs. For example, a union contract may require severance pay. The firm may then be reluctant to lay off workers, and thus the labor cost becomes fixed and independent of the level of output. These qualifications make the actual classification of costs into fixed and variable more difficult, but they do not invalidate the concept that some costs are fixed and independent of the level of output, while other costs vary with the level of output.

FIXED COSTS
Those costs that do not vary with the level of output

Fixed costs (*FC*) do not vary with the level of output, which may be expressed by the following simple equation:

16.2

$$\text{Fixed costs} = \text{Constant.}$$

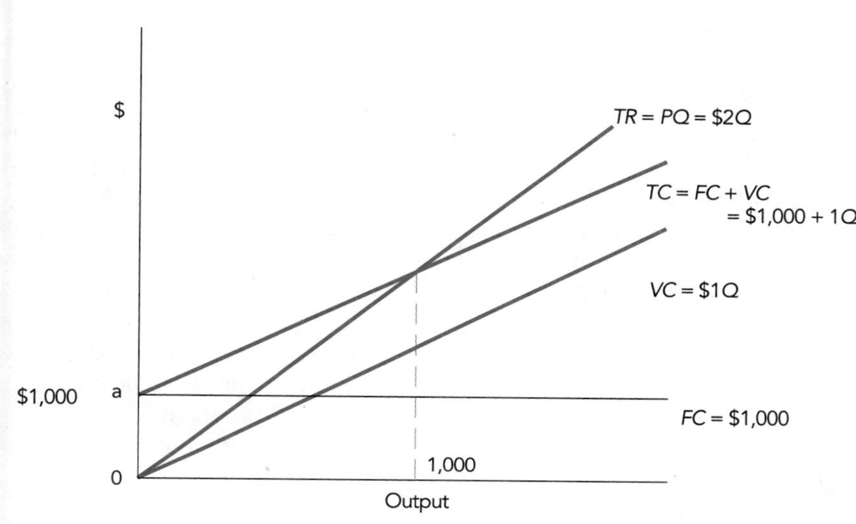

FIGURE 16.1

Relationship among Output and Fixed, Variable, and Total Costs

In Exhibit 16.1, the fourth column gives the fixed costs of operation. these fixed costs are $1,000 whether the firm produces 10 or 100 units of output. The relationship between output and fixed costs is shown in Figure 16.1 as a horizontal line (*FC*) that crosses the *y*-axis at *a*, the fixed dollar amount ($1,000). The line *FC* has no slope, because fixed costs neither rise nor fall with the level of output. They are independent of the level of output.

VARIABLE COSTS
Those costs that vary with the level of output

Variable costs (*VC*) change with the level of output: The more output the firm produces, the larger the total variable costs of production. This relationship may also be expressed by a simple equation:

$$VC = \text{Per-unit variable cost} \times \text{Quantity} = VQ.$$

16.3

The equation states that variable costs are per-unit variable costs times quantity of output, in which *V* is the per-unit variable cost of production. As the level of output rises, variable costs rise in proportion to the increase in output. This relationship is shown in the fifth and sixth columns in Exhibit 16.1, which give the per-unit variable cost ($1) and total variable costs of production. At zero level of output there are no variable costs. Each additional unit of output then adds $1 to the firm's variable costs. Thus, at 200 units of output these costs are $200, and at 1,000 units of output these costs have risen to $1,000.

The total variable costs are represented in Figure 16.1 by the line *VC*. The variable costs line passes through the origin, which indicates that if operations were to cease, the firm would have no variable costs of operation. This is different from fixed costs, which still exist even if the firm ceases production. For example, during a strike variable labor costs cease, but certain costs (such as interest expense) do not disappear just because the firm stops production. A plant that is not operating because of a strike will not be generating output and sales, which puts pressure on management to settle the strike before the fixed costs become an intolerable burden.

TOTAL COSTS
Sum of fixed and variable costs

Total costs (TC) of production are the sum of fixed costs and variable costs ($TC = FC + VC$). In Exhibit 16.1, total costs of operation are shown in the seventh column, which is the sum of columns 4 and 6. In Figure 16.1, the total costs are illustrated by TC, which is the vertical summation of FC and VC.

TOTAL REVENUES
Price times quantity sold

When a firm breaks even, its total costs of production are equal to its **total revenues,** and the firm is neither making profits nor experiencing losses. If the firm were to produce less, it would experience losses. Management knows that it must maintain at least that level of output in order to cover all its costs. If management does not believe that the break-even level of output can be produced and sold, it must make changes. For example, it may decide to produce the output but also seek to find a means to reduce the per-unit costs of production.

At the break-even point, total costs must equal total revenue. In equation form that is

16.4
$$TR = TC.$$

By substituting Equations 16.1, 16.2, and 16.3 into Equation 16.4 and solving for the break-even level of output (Q_B), this level of output is as follows:

$$PQ_B = FC + VQ_B$$

$$PQ_B - VQ_B = FC$$

16.5
$$Q_B(P - V) = FC$$

$$Q_B = \frac{FC}{P - V}.$$

Notice that Equation 16.5 employs a subscript. While Q represents any level of output, the subscript B indicates a particular level of output. In this case, it represents that level of output which equates revenues and costs, so the firm "breaks even."[1]

If this equation is applied to the numerical example in Exhibit 16.1, the break-even level of output is:

$$Q_B = \frac{\$1{,}000}{\$2 - \$1},$$

$$Q_B = 1{,}000.$$

[1] Since FC is the fixed cost of production and V is the per-unit variable cost of output, the formula for the break-even level of output (Q_B) expressed in words is as follows:

$$Q_B = \frac{\text{Fixed costs}}{\text{Price of product} - \text{Per-unit variable cost}}.$$

Breaking Even and Broadway's Angels

Shows are brought to Broadway by producers (general partners) and individual investors (limited partners called "angels"). The angels earn a return only after the show breaks even (that is, meets its operating expenses and recoups the initial financing costs). The financing costs are fixed costs that are spent ("sunk") before the show opens. Once the show premiers, it only has to meet its variable cash costs to continue running. When ticket sales cover the cash operating expenses (when the show breaks even on a cash basis and not on a total cost basis), the producers can continue to run the show. While the angels do not recoup their investment, the producers do continue to collect their management fees. ¶ The majority of Broadway shows open and rapidly close. Even those that have extended runs may cover only the cash operating expenses. Only a handful of shows ever recoup the funds invested in them, and few earn profits. So why invest? There are two obvious answers. Suppose the show is a success. Wouldn't you like to have put money in *Fiddler on the Roof* or *South Pacific*? The backers of those shows will reap the rewards of the investments indefinitely. And, of course, wouldn't you like to attend the cast party and meet ______? Well, you fill in that blank. ¶

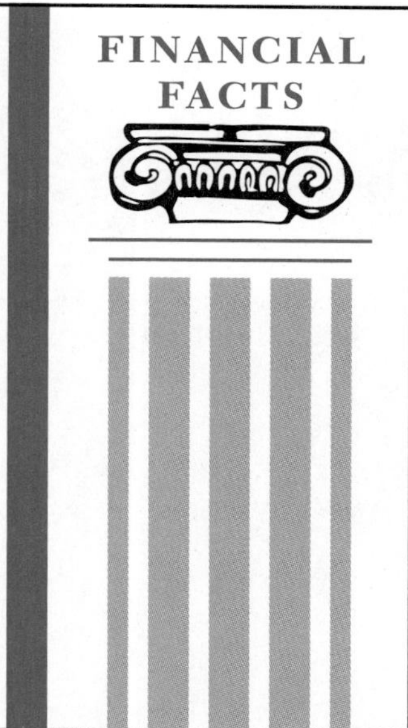

This answer is the same as that obtained in the eighth column of Exhibit 16.1, which gives the profits of the firm. These profits are determined by subtracting column 7 (total costs) from column 3 (total revenues). The break-even point is also illustrated in Figure 16.1. As may be seen in Figure 16.1 and Exhibit 16.1, the firm's total cost exceeds its total revenue for all levels of output below 1,000, and the firm makes a profit at all levels of output greater than 1,000. It breaks even when it produces and sells 1,000 units of output.

Uses for Break-Even Analysis

Besides indicating the level of output that must be achieved to avoid losses, break-even analysis is a means for management to analyze the effects of changes in prices and costs. For example, what would be the effect of a decline in the price of the product in Exhibit 16.1? If, as the result of increased competition, the price of the product were to fall from \$2.00 (column 1 of the exhibit) to \$1.50, break-even analysis indicates that the firm would now have to sell at least 2,000 units of output [\$1,000/(\$1.50 − \$1.00) = 2,000] to meet its total costs. While the decrease in price may produce an increase in sales, can management anticipate increased sales sufficient to absorb 2,000 units of output? An example of a change in costs may be the suggestion of the advertising department for a stepped-up campaign to increase sales. Management may use break-even analysis to ascertain by how much the level of output must be expanded to cover the increased advertising expense. If the advertising campaign adds \$0.25 per unit to the cost of the item, the break-even point becomes

$$\frac{\$1{,}000}{\$2 - \$1.25} = 1{,}333.$$

The advertising campaign will result in losses to the firm unless a level of sales of 1,333 units can be anticipated.

Break-even analysis may also be used to analyze the substitution of fixed for variable costs (for example, the substitution of equipment for labor). Though the equipment may be cost-effective, it may require a higher level of sales in order for the firm to break even. If the higher level of sales cannot be achieved, the substitution may convert a profitable firm into one that operates at a loss. These implications of substituting fixed costs for variable costs are discussed and illustrated in the next section on operating leverage.

OPERATING LEVERAGE

A given level of output may be produced with different combinations of factors of production. One farmer and one tractor may plow a field, but the same result would be achieved by using several workers and hoes. Of course, the latter may seem ridiculous given today's technology, but if the objective is a plowed field, either method achieves the same results.

If a firm uses more fixed factors of production (fixed costs) instead of variable factors (variable costs), it is employing operating leverage. Plowing the field with one farmer plus a tractor instead of several farmers with hoes illustrates using more fixed costs (the cost of the tractor) instead of variable costs (the cost of each farmer). Using several farmers instead of buying the tractor gives you flexibility. You can reduce your costs by reducing your workforce. Or you can increase output by adding another worker, in which case your costs increase. If, however, you have purchased the tractor, your costs are the same whether the tractor is extensively used or spends most of the day sitting idle in the shed.

OPERATING LEVERAGE
Use of fixed factors of production (fixed costs) instead of variable factors of production (variable costs) to produce a level of output

Operating leverage is the use of fixed factors (fixed costs) instead of variable costs. As will be subsequently explained, operating leverage is a major source of risk. However, the current discussion will consider the impact on the break-even level of output.

Consider Exhibit 16.2, which replicates Exhibit 16.1. Management substitutes equipment for labor so that fixed costs are $2,000 instead of $1,000 and variable costs per unit decline to $0.75. Because the firm has more equipment (that is, fixed costs), it is able to produce output with less per-unit variable costs. The changes in costs do not necessarily affect the price of the output, which remains at $2.00 per unit. These changes in costs, however, do have two effects. First, the break-even level of sales is increased from 1,000 units to 1,600 units. Second, once the break-even level of output is passed, earnings rise more rapidly. Previously, an increase in sales of 200 units increased profits by $200 but now profits are increased by $250. The increased use of operating leverage requires a larger level of output to avoid losses, but once that level is reached, earnings rise more rapidly with additional sales.

Fixed Asset Turnover: A Measure of Operating Leverage

As the previous discussion suggests, if a firm has substantial fixed costs, it has a large amount of operating leverage. One means to measure operating leverage is

EXHIBIT 16.2

Relationships between Revenues and Earnings with Higher Fixed Costs and Lower Per-Unit Variable Costs

1 *P*	2 *Q*	3 *TR*	4 *FC*	5 *V*	6 *VC*	7 *TC*	8 Profits (losses)
$2	0	$ 0	$2,000	$0.75	$ 0	$2,000	($2,000)
2	200	400	2,000	0.75	150	2,150	(1,750)
2	400	800	2,000	0.75	300	2,300	(1,500)
2	600	1,200	2,000	0.75	450	2,450	(1,250)
2	800	1,600	2,000	0.75	600	2,600	(1,000)
2	1,000	2,000	2,000	0.75	750	2,750	(750)
2	1,200	2,400	2,000	0.75	900	2,900	(500)
2	1,400	2,800	2,000	0.75	1,050	3,050	(250)
2	1,600	3,200	2,000	0.75	1,200	3,200	0
2	1,800	3,600	2,000	0.75	1,350	3,350	250
2	2,000	4,000	2,000	0.75	1,500	3,500	500

the ratio of sales to fixed assets, which in Chapter 12 was referred to as fixed asset turnover. (Another measure, the degree of operating leverage, is provided in the appendix to this chapter.) Low fixed asset turnover indicates that the firm uses a substantial investment in plant and equipment and that such investments are necessary to generate sales. Fixed assets have costs (such as depreciation) that occur regardless of the amount of sales. Once these fixed costs are covered, earnings tend to rise more rapidly than the earnings of a firm whose costs vary with the amount of sales.

Exhibit 16.3 presents the ratio of revenues to fixed assets (fixed asset turnover) for four firms with revenues in excess of $1 billion. The table ranks the firms from the lowest to highest sales (revenues) to fixed assets and provides each firm's industry. As may be expected, an electric and gas utility, such as Public Service Enterprise, must have substantial investment in plant and equipment to generate revenues. For every $1 in revenues, the firm had over $1.84 in fixed assets. The need for substantial investments also applies to an oil refiner (Phillips). A retailer (The Limited) may not need large investments in plant and equipment to generate sales. The Limited generates almost $7 for every $1 invested in fixed assets.[2]

Although virtually every firm has some fixed assets, companies that generate services may have minimal investments in plant and equipment. For example, firms that create software need few fixed assets. Wind River Systems, which develops operating systems and engineering services, recorded in its 1999 annual report no investment in plant and only a modest amount of equipment. C-Cube, which designs

[2]A retailer's fixed assets may be understated, since it leases space. For example, The Limited obviously does not own the malls in which it locates its stores. It leases (rents) the space. These leased spaces are also a type of fixed asset, and you may want to add the value of these properties to the firm's fixed assets before calculating fixed asset turnover. See the material on capitalizing leases in Chapter 21.

EXHIBIT 16.3

Ratio of Revenues to Fixed Assets of Selected Firms (Revenues and Assets in Billions)

Firm	Industry	Revenues	Fixed Assets	Sales to Fixed Assets
Public Service Enterprise	Gas and electric utility	$ 5.9	10.876	0.54
Phillips Petroleum	Oil refining	11.8	10.585	1.11
Dial	Consumer products	1.5	0.281	5.33
The Limited	Retail clothing	9.3	1.361	6.83

Source: *1998 and 1999 annual reports.*

semiconductors and systems for DVD applications, reported a fixed asset turnover of 11.9 or $11.90 in revenues for every $1 invested in plant and equipment.

Operating Leverage and Risk

The previous discussion suggests that operating income will rise and fall more rapidly for a firm with operating leverage. This section compares the operating leverage for two industries, airlines and retailing, and shows how operating leverage affects the level of risk associated with each industry.

The airline industry is an excellent example of an industry that has a large amount of operating leverage. A large proportion of airlines' costs are fixed (such as depreciation on the planes and equipment). Equally important is that, once the plane is in the air, the cost of the flight is the same whether the plane carries one person or a full load. The difference between break-even and a profitable flight is often a matter of just a few passengers. Once this break-even number of passengers is reached, the profitability of the flight rises rapidly, because the fixed costs are being spread over an increasing number of passengers. Thus, once a profitable level of operation is reached, the level of profits rises rapidly with further increases in passengers carried. A small change in the number of passengers carried produces a much larger change in profits.[3]

Retailing is an entirely different type of operation. A firm may have few fixed costs (such as rent for the building) and many variable costs. As the firm expands output, these variable costs (for instance, wages and costs of goods sold) also expand. Such operations do not have a large amount of operating leverage, for as sales expand there is not a large expansion in profits.

[3]The need to fill planes explains why airlines offer different fares designed to tap various types of travelers and also explains why extremely discounted fares may be available on selected flights just prior to departure. For example, US Airways offers low online discounted fares on Wednesday for travel the following weekend. Such low fares are designed to sell seats on flights that are lightly booked.

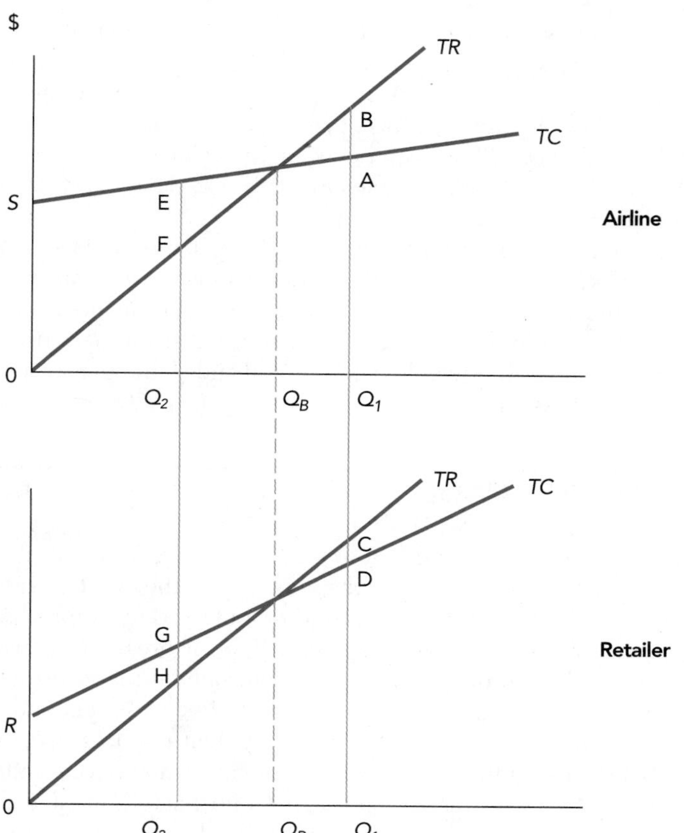

FIGURE 16.2

Break-Even Analysis and Fluctuations in Earnings for an Airline and a Retailer

Figure 16.2 compares an airline with a retailer to illustrate how changes in sales have a larger impact on the earnings of the firm with the higher degree of operating leverage. The top half of the figure is a break-even chart for an airline; the bottom half is a break-even chart for a retailer. For ease of comparison, both the break-even level of output (Q_B) and the total revenue curve (TR) are identical for both firms. The difference between the two firms rests entirely upon their cost curves. The retailer has lower fixed costs ($0R$ versus $0S$), but the total cost curve for the retailer rises more rapidly.

The effect of these differences in costs (that is, the difference in operating leverage) can be seen by moving along the horizontal axis. If output increases from Q_B to Q_1, the earnings are greater for the airline than for the retailer (AB versus CD). If output decreases from Q_B to Q_2, the losses are greater for the airline than for the retailer (EF versus GH). The airline experiences greater fluctuations in earnings and losses for the same change in revenues because it has the higher degree of operating leverage.

These fluctuations in earnings imply that the airline is the riskier firm. In periods of declining sales, it will experience greater losses than the retailer. Firms with more operating leverage are riskier because their earnings are more variable. While firms with less operating leverage may not achieve a rapid increase in earnings as sales expand, they will not experience rapid declines in earnings when sales decline. Most of their costs are variable costs that also decrease with the decline in output and sales.

These differences in operating leverage indicate that some businesses are inherently more risky than others. For the individual firm, risk emanates from two sources: the nature of the business and how the business is financed (*business risk* and *financial risk*). Airlines, then, have a high degree of business risk, while retailers, especially those selling staples such as food and clothing, may not have this high degree of business risk.

FINANCIAL LEVERAGE

Although break-even analysis is one tool available to management, it does have major weaknesses. Break-even analysis does not answer the question should an investment be made. For example, the substitution of fixed costs for variable costs requires investment in additional equipment. Even if break-even analysis indicates the change will be profitable, it cannot determine if the investment should be made. It cannot answer such questions as: Will the investment add to or subtract from the value of the firm? Acquiring equipment requires cash outflows in the present but the cash inflows generated by the investment occur in the future. What is the present value of these cash flows? Unfortunately, break-even analysis does not answer these types of questions. They are, however, answered by using the capital budgeting techniques discussed in the next chapter.

To apply capital budgeting, the financial manager needs to know the firm's cost of capital. The cost of capital, however, is affected by the firm's risk exposure. Business risk and the use of operating leverage were covered in the previous section. This section considers financial leverage and its impact on risk, and the following section considers the cost of capital.

FINANCIAL LEVERAGE
Use of another person's or firm's funds in return for agreeing to pay a fixed return for the funds; the use of debt or preferred stock financing

The previous material demonstrated how the use of operating leverage may increase the firm's operating income as sales expand but also increases the variability of operating income. The use of debt financing instead of equity (**financial leverage**) may increase the return earned by the firm's owners. However, it may also increase the variability of the firm's net income, and more variability implies more risk.

Financial leverage occurs when the firm enters into fixed contracts to obtain funds. When a firm issues debt such as bonds (and preferred stock, which pays a fixed dividend) or borrows from a bank, the firm enters into a contract. This contract requires the firm to meet certain fixed obligations, such as interest payments and principal repayment. The firm, however, may earn more with the funds than it has agreed to pay. In the simplest terms, a firm may borrow funds at 10 percent and earn 12 percent. The additional 2 percent accrues to the owners (that is, the equity) and increases the return earned by the stockholders.

How financial leverage works may be shown by a simple example. Firm A needs $100 capital to operate and may acquire the money from the owners of the firm. Alternatively, it may acquire part of the money from stockholders and part from creditors. If the management acquires the $100 from stockholders, the firm uses no debt financing and is not financially leveraged. The firm would have the following simple balance sheet:

ASSETS		LIABILITIES AND EQUITY	
Cash	$100		
		Equity	$100

Once in business the firm generates the following simplified income statement:

Sales	$100
Expenses	80
Earnings before interest and taxes	$ 20
Taxes (40%)	8
Net earnings	$ 12

What return has the firm earned on the owner's investment (that is, the return on equity)? The answer is 12 percent, for the investors contributed $100 and the firm earned $12 after taxes. The firm may pay the $12 to the investors in cash dividends or may retain the $12 to help finance future growth. Either way, however, the owners' return on their equity is 12 percent.

By using financial leverage, management may be able to increase the owners' return on their investment. What happens to their return if management is able to borrow part of the capital needed to operate the firm? The answer depends on (1) what proportion of the total capital is borrowed, and (2) the interest rate that must be paid to the creditors. If management borrows 40 percent ($40) of the firm's capital at an interest cost of 5 percent, the balance sheet becomes:

ASSETS		LIABILITIES AND EQUITY	
Cash	$100	Debt	$40
		Equity	$60

Because the firm borrowed $40, it is now obligated to pay interest. Thus, the firm has a new expense that must be paid before it has any earnings for the common stockholder. The simple income statement becomes:

EXHIBIT 16.4

Relationship between the Debt Ratio and the Return on Equity

Debt Ratio	0%	20	50	70	90
Amount of debt outstanding	$ 0	20	50	70	90
Equity	$100	80	50	30	10
Sales	$100	100	100	100	100
Expenses	$ 80	80	80	80	80
Earnings before interest and taxes	$ 20	20	20	20	20
Interest expense (5% interest rate)	$ 0	1	2.50	3.50	4.50
Taxable income	$ 20	19	17.50	16.50	15.50
Income taxes (50% tax rate)	$ 10	9.50	8.75	8.25	7.75
Net earnings	$ 10	9.50	8.75	8.25	7.75
Return on equity	10%	11.87	17.50	27.50	77.50

Sales	$100.00
Expenses	80.00
Earnings before interest and taxes	$ 20.00
Interest expense	2.00
Taxable income	$ 18.00
Taxes	7.20
Net earnings	$ 10.80

The use of debt causes the net profit to decline from $12 to $10.80. What effect does this method of financing have on the owners' return? It increases from 12 percent to 18 percent. How does this reduction in the net profit produce an increase in the owners' return? The answer is that the owners invested only $60, and that $60 earned them $10.80. They made 18 percent on their money, whereas previously they had earned only 12 percent.

There are two sources of the additional return. First, the firm borrowed money and agreed to pay a fixed return of 5 percent. The firm, however, was able to earn more than 5 percent with the money, and this additional earning accrued to the owners of the firm. Second, the entire burden of the interest cost was not borne by the firm. The federal tax laws permit the deduction of interest as an expense before determining taxable income; thus this interest expense is shared with the government. The greater the corporate income tax rate, the greater the portion of this interest expense borne by the government. In this case 40 percent, or $0.80, of the interest expense was borne by the government in lost tax revenues. If the corporate income tax rate were 50 percent, the government would lose $1.00 in taxes by permitting the deduction of the interest expense.

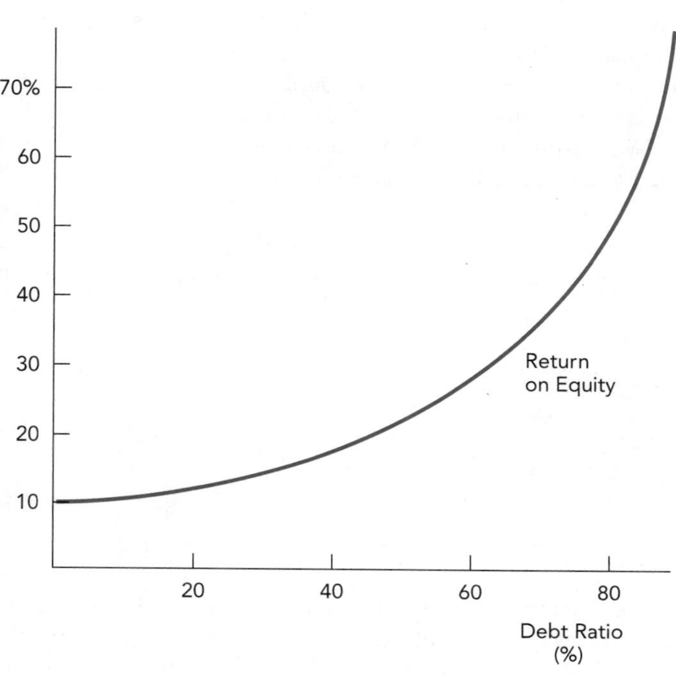

FIGURE 16.3

Use of Financial Leverage and the Return on Equity

As illustrated in the previous example, a firm's management may increase the owners' return by the use of debt (financial leverage). By increasing the proportion of the firm's assets that are financed by debt, management is able to increase the return on the equity. Exhibit 16.4 shows the effect of various levels of debt financing (as measured by the debt ratio) on (1) the net earnings for the firm, and (2) the return on the investors' equity. The table was constructed using a 50 percent tax rate. The rate of interest is assumed to be 5 percent no matter what proportion of the firm's assets are financed by debt. This unrealistic assumption will be dropped later in the chapter. Figure 16.3 plots the return on equity presented in Exhibit 16.4. From both the table and the figure it may be seen that as the debt ratio rises, the return on the owners' equity not only rises but rises at an increasing rate. This dramatically indicates how the use of financial leverage may increase the return on a firm's equity.

FINANCIAL LEVERAGE AND RISK

Because the use of financial leverage increases the owners' return on equity, the question becomes: Why not use ever-increasing amounts of debt financing? The answer is that as the firm becomes more financially leveraged, it becomes riskier.

This increase in risk raises (1) the potential for fluctuations in the owners' returns, and (2) the interest rate that the creditors charge for the use of their money.

That the use of financial leverage increases the potential risk to the owners may be seen by employing the simple example presented in the previous section. What happens to the return on equity if sales decline by 10 percent (from $100 to $90) and expenses remain the same? The income statements for the financially unleveraged and leveraged firms become:

	Unleveraged Firm (0% Debt Ratio)	Leveraged Firm (40% Debt Ratio)
Sales	$90.00	$90.00
Expenses	80.00	80.00
Earnings before interest and taxes	$10.00	$10.00
Interest	—	2.00
Taxable income	$10.00	$ 8.00
Taxes (40% tax rate)	4.00	3.20
Net profit	$ 6.00	$ 4.80

The 10 percent decline in sales produces declines in the earnings and the return on the owners' investment in both cases. For the unleveraged firm the return is now 6 percent ($6/$100); for the financially leveraged firm the return plummets from 18 percent to 8 percent ($4.80/$60).

Why does the return decline more for the leveraged firm than for the unleveraged firm? The answer rests with the *fixed* interest payment. When the firm borrowed the capital, it agreed to make a fixed interest payment. This agreement is a legal obligation stipulating that the firm must pay or default on the loan. The fixed interest payment, which was a source of the increase in the owners' return when sales were $100, causes the larger decline in the owner's return when the firm's sales decline. If the firm had been even more leveraged (if the debt ratio had been greater), the decline in the return on equity would have been even larger. This suggests a general conclusion: The greater the proportion of a firm's assets that are financed by fixed obligations, the greater the potential variability in the owners' return. Small changes in revenues or costs will produce larger fluctuations in the firm's net earnings.

Firms that use large amounts of financial leverage are viewed by creditors as being risky. Creditors may refuse to lend to a highly leveraged firm or do so only at higher rates of interest or more stringent loan conditions. As the interest rate increases, the owners' return on their equity in the firm diminishes. This may be seen in the example presented in Exhibit 16.5, which illustrates what happens to the investors' return as the interest rate rises. The first case (A) illustrates the return if the interest rate is held constant as more debt is employed. The second case (B) assumes that interest rates rise as the debt ratio increases to compensate creditors for the increased risk. The bottom row in each case gives the return on the owners' equity, and, as would be expected, the increased interest expense causes

EXHIBIT 16.5

Relationship between Increased Interest Rates and the Return on Equity (Tax Rate = 40 Percent)

Debt Ratio	0%	20	50	70
A				
Earnings before interest and taxes	$20.00	20.00	20.00	20.00
Interest at 5 percent	NA	$ 1.00	2.50	3.50
Taxable income	$20.00	19.00	17.50	16.50
Taxes (40% rate)	$ 8.00	7.60	7.00	6.60
Net earnings	$12.00	11.40	10.50	9.90
Return on equity	12.00%	14.25	21.00	33.00
B				
Earnings before interest and taxes	$20.00	20.00	20.00	20.00
Interest rate	NA	6.00%	10.00	12.00
Interest	NA	$ 1.20	5.00	8.40
Taxable income	$20.00	18.80	15.00	11.60
Taxes (40% rate)	$ 8.00	7.52	6.00	4.64
Net earnings	$12.00	11.28	9.00	6.96
Return on equity	12.00%	14.10	18.00	23.20

the owners' return to diminish. This may be seen by comparing the bottom lines of both cases. However, even though the return may diminish when the interest rate rises, it might still exceed the return obtained when no debt was used, in which case financial leverage would still be favorable.

As long as the return on the assets financed by debt exceeds the after-tax cost of debt (that is, the interest rate adjusted for the tax savings), financial leverage is favorable and will increase the return on the owners' investment. This after-tax cost of debt is determined by Equation 16.6.

$$k_d = i(1 - t). \quad (16.6)$$

The after-tax cost of debt (k_d) depends on the interest rate (i) and the firm's marginal tax rate (t). The larger the tax rate, the smaller the effective cost of debt, because the tax savings that result from deducting the interest expense from taxable income are larger. This after-tax cost of debt is the true cost of using debt financing. While the interest rate paid for the use of borrowed funds obviously affects the cost of borrowing, it is the after-tax cost of borrowing that determines if financial leverage is favorable.

The use of the effective cost of debt to determine if financial leverage is favorable may be illustrated with the first example presented in this chapter. When the firm did not use debt financing, it earned 12 percent on its assets after taxes. However, the effective cost of debt was only

$$0.05(1 - 0.4) = 0.03 = 3\%,$$

so financial leverage was favorable. As long as the firm could borrow at an effective cost of 3.0 percent and put those funds to work at 12 percent, financial leverage would be favorable.

Actually, in this illustration financial leverage would have been favorable if the interest rate had been 12, 15, or even 18 percent, because the effective cost of debt after adjusting for taxes would have been 7.2, 9, and 10.8 percent, respectively. It is only at 20 percent that financial leverage would have become unfavorable, for then the interest charges would have risen sufficiently to absorb every dollar earned on the borrowed money. If the firm had financed operations with $60 equity and $40 debt at 20 percent, it would have had the following income statement:

Sales	$100.00
Expenses	80.00
Earnings before interest and taxes	$ 20.00
Interest	8.00
Taxable income	$ 12.00
Taxes (40 percent)	4.80
Net earnings	$ 7.20

The return on equity is 12 percent ($7.20/$60), which is exactly the return earned on the equity by the unleveraged firm.

Why can the interest rates be so high and financial leverage still be favorable? A major reason is the ability of the firm to deduct the interest expense before determining taxable income. Only when the after-tax cost of debt exceeds the return earned on the firm's assets acquired by debt financing is financial leverage unfavorable. In the above example, the after-tax cost of debt must rise to 12 percent (20 percent before-tax cost of debt) before financial leverage becomes unfavorable.

The ability to share the interest expense with the government encourages the use of debt financing. Corporations whose federal income tax rate is 35 percent share almost a third of their interest expense with the federal government. From the firm's viewpoint, $1.00 paid in interest to creditors reduces the firm's taxes by $0.35. The true interest cost of $1.00 interest expense is only $0.65, and thus the tax laws become a major incentive to use financial leverage.

FINANCIAL LEVERAGE THROUGH PREFERRED STOCK FINANCING

In the preceding sections financial leverage was achieved through the use of debt. Financial leverage may also be acquired through the use of preferred stock, because preferred stock has a fixed dividend. (The fixed dividend is analogous to the fixed interest payments.) The differences between debt and preferred stock financing are that the dividend on the preferred stock is neither a contractual obligation nor a tax-deductible expense. The fact that the dividend is not a contractual obligation is the primary advantage of preferred stock financing. Preferred stock is less risky for the firm than debt financing. If the firm is unable to meet the dividend payment, the owners of the preferred stock cannot force the firm to make the payment. In the case of debt, if the firm fails to pay the interest, the creditors can take the firm to court to force payment or force bankruptcy.

Although preferred stock financing is a less risky means to acquire financial leverage, the other difference between it and debt financing argues strongly against the use of preferred stock. Since interest is a tax-deductible expense and the preferred dividends are not, the effective cost of debt financing is cheaper. If a firm borrows at 8 percent, the true cost is reduced as a result of the tax laws. If a firm issues preferred stock and pays an 8 percent dividend, the true cost to the firm is 8 percent. Because the cost of debt financing is shared with the government, firms tend to use debt instead of preferred stock as a means to obtain financial leverage.

The inability to deduct preferred dividends reduces the impact of financial leverage. The difference in the return to the common stockholder that results from the use of debt and preferred stock financing is illustrated in the following example. The firm issues $50 worth of common stock and needs an additional $50. It may issue either $50 of debt with a 5 percent interest rate or $50 of preferred stock with a 5 percent dividend. In both cases the firm acquires $50 and pays out $2.50 in either interest or dividends. However, the earnings available to the common stockholder are larger when debt is used instead of preferred stock. This is shown in the following income statements:

	Debt Financing	Preferred Stock Financing
Sales	$100.00	$100.00
Expenses	80.00	80.00
Earnings before interest and taxes	$ 20.00	$ 20.00
Interest	2.50	—
Taxable income	$ 17.50	$ 20.00
Taxes (50 percent)	8.75	10.00
Net earnings	$ 8.75	$ 10.00
Preferred dividends	—	2.50
Earnings available to common stock	$ 8.75	$ 7.50

When debt financing is used, the earnings available to the common stockholders are $8.75, while they are only $7.50 when the preferred stock is used. Thus, the return on the common stockholders' investment is larger (17.5 percent versus 15 percent) when debt financing is used. The ability of the firm to share the interest expense with the federal government encourages the use of debt financing instead of preferred stock financing. The use of preferred stock financing has declined over time, and this decline is partially explained by the unfavorable tax treatment afforded preferred stock.

COMPONENTS OF THE COST OF CAPITAL

OPTIMAL CAPITAL STRUCTURE
Combination of debt and equity financing that minimizes the average cost of capital

Although the use of financial leverage may increase the return on stockholders' equity, it may also increase the risk associated with the firm. This suggests a question: What is the best combination of debt and equity financing? This best combination of the firm's sources of finance is its **optimal capital structure.** The optimal capital structure takes advantage of financial leverage without unduly increasing financial risks. In effect, it minimizes the overall cost of finance to the firm.

To determine the optimal capital structure, the financial manager must first establish the cost of each source of finance and then determine which combination of these sources minimizes the overall cost. This minimum cost of capital is important, because the financial manager must be able to judge investment opportunities. The selection of investments requires knowledge of the firm's cost of capital because an investment must earn a return sufficient to cover the cost of the funds used to acquire the asset. Thus, the determination of the firm's cost of capital is necessary for the correct application of the capital budgeting techniques that are explained in Chapter 17.

This section is devoted to the determination of the costs of the components of the firm's capital structure. After these costs have been determined, the financial manager constructs a weighted average of the various costs. By varying the mix of sources of capital and recomputing the weighted averages, the optimal capital structure is determined.

Cost of Debt

As is explained earlier in this chapter, the effective or true cost of debt (k_d) depends on the interest rate (i), the corporate income tax rate (t), and risk. For a given risk class, the after-tax cost was given in Equation 16.6:

$$k_d = i(1 - t).$$

Notice that the cost of debt is not the interest rate, but the interest rate adjusted for the tax write-off of the interest expense. Also notice that the cost of debt depends on the current rate of interest. It is not the interest rate at which the firm issued debt in the past. If a firm has debt outstanding that was issued ten years ago with a fixed interest rate above or below the current interest rate, it is the current interest rate that is used to determine the firm's current cost of capital. When the older debt was issued, the previous rate was used to determine the firm's cost of capital at that time. Current cost is the interest rate that the firm must presently pay to borrow the money, adjusted for the current tax deduction.

The cost of debt is also affected by any flotation costs associated with issuing new securities and by the term of the debt. Flotation costs paid to investment bankers reduce the proceeds of the sale and increase the interest cost per dollar borrowed. The larger the flotation costs, the greater the effective interest rate will be.

As was previously explained in Chapter 2, short-term debt generally carries a lower yield (lower interest cost) than long-term debt. Thus, if the firm issues

FIGURE 16.4

Cost of Debt

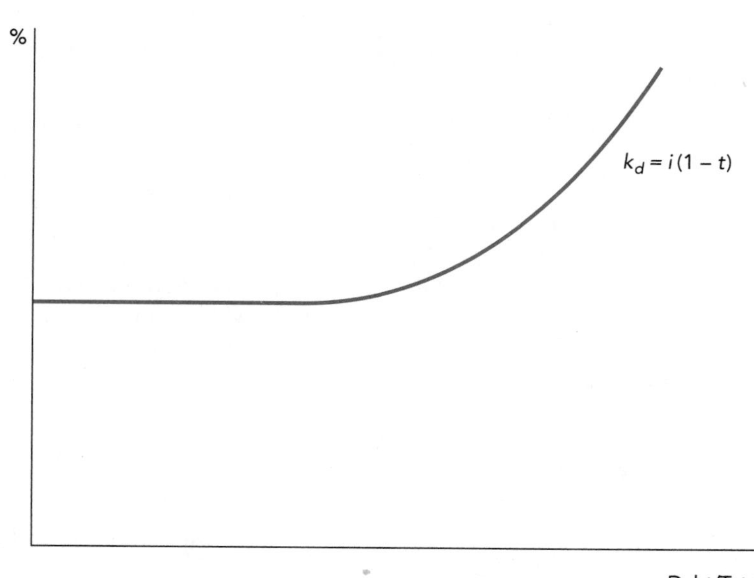

long-term debt, the interest expense will probably be higher than if the firm had used short-term financing. However, by using long-term debt, the firm avoids the problems of retiring or rolling over (refunding) short-term debt, thus avoiding the risk associated with refinancing short-term debt.

The cost of debt also depends on the riskiness of the firm. The risk is related to the nature of the business (business risk) and to the use of financial leverage (financial risk). The more the firm uses debt financing, the greater will be the potential for it to fail to meet its debt obligations. This increase in the risk of default means that as the firm's use of financial leverage increases, the interest rate on borrowed money will increase. This is illustrated by the line k_d in Figure 16.4. Initially, the cost of debt may be stable, as the firm uses more financial leverage without increasing risk for the creditors. As the use of debt increases, the cost of debt starts to rise, because creditors demand more interest to compensate them for the increased risk of loss.

Cost of Preferred Stock

As was explained in Chapter 11, the price or value of preferred stock depends on the dividend and the yield required to induce investors to buy the shares. The equation for the valuation of preferred stock is

$$P_p = \frac{D_p}{k_p}.$$

P_p is the price of the preferred stock, D_p is the dividend paid by the preferred stock, and k_p is the return required by investors necessary to induce them to buy the stock. This equation may be rearranged to isolate the yield or the firm's cost of preferred stock.

$$P_p \times k_p = D_p$$

16.7
$$k_p = \frac{D_p}{P_p}.$$

As may be seen from this equation, the cost to the firm of the preferred stock depends on its dividend and the price that investors are willing to pay for the stock. If the preferred stock pays $1.00 dividend and sells for $12.00, the cost of the preferred stock to the firm is

$$k_p = \frac{\$1.00}{\$12.00} = 0.0833 = 8.33\%.$$

The 8.33 percent is the cost of the funds if the firm currently uses preferred stock financing.

For a new issue of preferred stock, the company should use the net price after selling the stock, which deducts the expense of selling the shares. For example, if this firm issued new preferred shares and had to pay an underwriting fee of 7 percent, it would net only $11.16 [$12.00(1 − 0.07)] per share. Thus, the cost of preferred stock financing would be

$$k_p = \frac{\$1.00}{\$11.16} = 8.96\%.$$

The cost of selling new shares to the public raises the cost of preferred stock. In this case, the cost increased by over half a percentage point.

From the viewpoint of the firm, the cost of preferred stock is higher than the cost of debt. This cost differential results from federal income tax laws; the interest is tax deductible while the preferred dividend payments are not. The increased cost of preferred stock argues for the use of debt. In recent years, there has been relatively little preferred stock financing compared to debt financing. While the preferred stock does not legally bind the firm to pay dividends and meet other indenture agreements, its additional cost overshadows these advantages.

Cost of Common Stock

The cost of common stock is the return required by investors to buy the firm's common stock. This cost of common equity is an opportunity cost: It is the return that investors could earn on comparable, alternative uses for their money. This cost applies both to existing shares and to new shares being issued by the firm.

Since the cost of common stock is an opportunity cost, there is no identifiable expense such as interest that the financial manager may use to determine the cost

The Cost of Debt and Credit Ratings

In the body of the text, the cost of debt depends on the interest rate, the firm's tax rate, and the risk associated with the firm. Risk depends on the nature of the business (business risk) and the firm's use of financial leverage (financial risk). In Figure 16.4, the rate of interest rises as the firm uses more debt. This relationship between the debt ratio and the interest rate essentially applies to all firms. For a given risk class, higher debt ratios are associated with higher interest rates. ¶ The interest rate is also affected by credit ratings assigned by one of the rating services such as Moody's and Standard & Poor's. These ratings assess the risk associated with debt issued by different firms. (Remember: Figure 16.4 gives the interest rate for *one* firm as its become more financially leveraged.) Lower quality debt tends to pay a higher rate of interest. ¶ That lower ratings are associated with higher rates of interest is illustrated by the following table derived from the Standard & Poor's *Bond Guide*, June 1999.

Firm	Coupon	Rating	Yield to Maturity
Bell South	5 7/8	AAA	6.26%
Anheuser-Busch	5 3/4	A+	6.50
Household Finance	6 3/8	A	6.99
Columbia Gas System	7.32	BBB+	7.34
American Standard	7 5/8	BB−	8.37
KinderCare Learning Centers	9 1/2	B−	9.14

The table presents the bond's coupon, the Standard & Poor's rating, and the yield to maturity for several issues due in 2010. While the coupons tend to increase with lower ratings, the yield to maturity is more indicative of the return the investor currently earns over the lifetime of the bond. The return is the interest rate the firm would have to pay to issue comparable debt. The bonds' yields to maturity do increase with lower ratings, which suggests that lower ratings are associated with higher interest rates. ¶

of these funds. However, the financial manager knows that the cost of common stock exceeds the cost of debt. No tax advantage is associated with equity, because dividends are paid in after-tax dollars (that is, dividends are not tax deductible), while interest is paid in before-tax dollars (that is, interest is a tax-deductible expense). In addition, common stock represents ownership and, therefore, is a riskier security than the firm's debt obligations. Although the firm is legally obligated to pay interest and meet the terms of indentures of its debt agreements, there is no legal obligation for the firm to pay dividends.

Since equity is riskier than debt to the investor, one means to estimate the cost of equity is to start with the interest rate paid to the holder of debt and add a risk premium. In this specification the cost of equity is

$$k_e = i + \text{Risk premium}, \tag{16.8}$$

in which k_e is the cost of equity and i is the interest rate being paid on new issues of debt (the current rate of interest unadjusted for the tax advantage). The risk premium associated with the common stock is then added to the interest rate. Although the financial manager knows the interest rate, the amount of the risk premium is not known. Quantifying the amount of this premium could be considered making an educated guess at best or, if you are a cynic, a matter of conjecture.

An alternative approach to the determination of the cost of equity is the capital asset pricing model (CAPM) presented in Chapter 8 and used in Chapter 11 to value common stock. In the CAPM, the required return on equity was expressed in Equation 8.3 as:

$$k_e = r_f + (r_m - r_f)\text{beta}.$$

In this specification, the cost of equity depends on the risk-free rate of interest (r_f) plus a risk premium. The risk premium depends on (1) the difference between the return on the market as a whole (r_m) and the risk-free rate and (2) the firm's beta coefficient, which measures the systematic risk associated with the firm.

Since this required return is the return necessary to induce investors to buy the stock, it may be viewed as the firm's cost of equity. Notice that to make the CAPM operational, the financial manager needs estimates of the risk-free rate, the return on the market, and the beta coefficient. Thus, the financial manager encounters the same general problems making the CAPM operational as the individual investor faces using the model as a tool for the valuation of common stock. However, the approach is theoretically superior to using the interest rate on the firm's bonds and adding on a risk premium, as it more precisely specifies the risk premium associated with investing in the stock.

A third approach defines the cost of equity in terms of investors' expected return on the stock; that is, the expected dividend yield plus expected growth (i.e., capital gains). In Chapter 11, the return on common stock (r) was specified in Equation 11.6 as

$$r = \text{Dividend yield} + \text{Growth rate}$$

$$r = \frac{D_0(1 + g)}{P} + g.$$

As with the CAPM approach, the financial manager has to make this model operational. Although the current dividend and the price of the stock are known, estimates must be made of the future capital gains. This is, of course, the same problem facing the investor who seeks to use the common stock valuation model presented in Equation 11.5 (the dividend-growth model) in Chapter 11.

While the three approaches appear to be different, they are essentially the same. The interest rate plus risk premium method and the CAPM method are very similar. However, the CAPM specifies more clearly the risk premium in terms of the return on a risk-free security, the return on the market, and the systematic risk associated with the individual firm.

The CAPM method and the expected return method are identical if it is assumed that financial markets are in equilibrium. If that assumption holds, the required return found using the CAPM would also be the investors' expected return determined by using the expected dividend yield plus the expected capital gain. For example, if the expected return exceeded the required return, investors would drive up the price of the stock, causing the expected return to fall. If the expected return were less than the required return, the opposite would occur. Investors would seek to sell the shares, which would drive down their price and increase the yield. These changes will cease when the market is in equilibrium and the required return is equal to the expected return.

The same argument may be expressed in terms of a stock's valuation and its price. The CAPM was used in the dividend-growth model to determine the value of the stock. If the price of the stock is less than the valuation, investors bid up the price. If the price exceeds the valuation, investors seek to sell, which drives down the price. The incentive for stock prices to cease changing occurs when the price and the valuation are equal. Thus, if the equity markets are in equilibrium, a stock's price must equal its valuation, and the required return equals the expected return.

If the equity markets are in equilibrium, the stock's price may be substituted for its value in the dividend-growth model ($V = P$):

$$P = \frac{D_0(1 + g)}{k_e - g}.$$

By rearranging terms, the required return is

$$k_e - g = \frac{D_0(1 + g)}{P}$$

$$k_e = \frac{D_0(1 + g)}{P} + g. \qquad \textbf{16.9}$$

In this form, the required return is the sum of the dividend yield plus the capital gain. This is identical to the investor's return and may be used as the cost of common equity.

Equation 16.9 expresses the cost of equity under the assumption that the firm does not have to issue new shares (that is, the cost of equity is the cost of retained earnings). If the firm were to issue additional shares, it would not receive the market price of the stock because it would have to pay the flotation costs associated with selling new stock. To adjust for this expense, the flotation costs (F) must be subtracted from the price of the stock to obtain the net proceeds to the firm. This cost of new shares (k_{ne}) is expressed in Equation 16.10:

$$k_{ne} = \frac{D_0(1 + g)}{P - F} + g. \qquad \textbf{16.10}$$

Obviously, the greater the flotation costs, the smaller will be the amount obtained from the sale of each new share, and the greater will be the cost of the equity.

The following example illustrates how the above model of the cost of common stock is used. A firm's earnings are growing annually at the rate of 7 percent. The common stock is currently paying $0.935 a share, and this dividend will grow annually at 7 percent so that the year's dividends will be $1 [or $D_0(1 + g) = \$1$]. If the common stock is selling for $25, the firm's cost of common stock is

$$k_e = \frac{\$0.935(1 + 0.07)}{\$25} + 0.07$$

$$= 0.04 + 0.07 = 0.11 = 11\%.$$

This tells management that investors currently require an 11 percent return on their investment in the stock. That return consists of a 4 percent dividend yield and the 7 percent growth. Failure on the part of management to achieve this return for the common stockholders will result in a decline in the price of the common stock.

If the firm has exhausted its retained earnings and must issue new stock, the cost of common stock must rise to cover the flotation costs. If these costs are $1 a share (4 percent of the price of the stock), the firm nets $24 per share, and the cost of equity is

$$k_{ne} = \frac{\$0.935(1 + 0.07)}{\$25 - \$1} + 0.07$$

$$= 0.0417 + 0.07 = 11.17\%.$$

The cost of equity is now higher. The firm must earn 11.17 percent in order to cover the flotation costs and investors' required return.[4]

As this discussion indicates, the cost of common equity may be viewed from the standpoint of the investor or of the firm. The investors' required return is the cost of equity to the firm, because this return must be met for investors to commit their funds to the firm. Failure to meet this cost will result in a lower value of the stock as investors seek to move their funds to alternative investments. The lower stock price will increase the difficulty of raising a given amount of money through a new issue of stock. The lower stock price will also hurt the firm's employees, if their compensation is tied to the value of the stock.

In addition to the dividend and the potential for growth, the value of the firm also depends on risk. Increased risk will increase the required return; equity funds

[4]Flotation costs are a cash outflow that occurs when the securities are issued. This expense is capitalized on the balance sheet as an asset that is depreciated or "amortized" over the lifetime of the security (for example, the flotation costs associated with a ten-year bond issue are written off over ten years). The depreciation generates a cash inflow that recaptures the flotation costs. Although writing off the capitalized asset restores the initial cash outflow, the timings of the outflows and of the inflows differ. The outflow occurs first, which raises the cost of a new issue of securities.

FIGURE 16.5

Cost of Equity

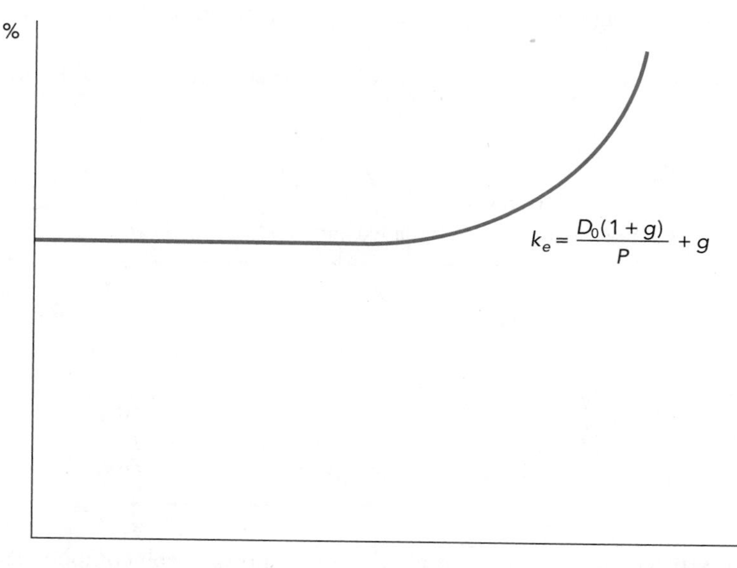

become more expensive, and the firm will have to earn a higher return on its investments to compensate equity investors for the additional risk.

Risk partially depends on the nature of the business (business risk) and partially on how management finances the firm's operations (financial risk). The relationship between financial risk and the cost of equity is illustrated in Figure 16.5, which relates the cost of equity (k_e) to the firm's use of financial leverage. The same relationship between the cost of debt and the firm's use of financial leverage was previously illustrated in Figure 16.4. In both cases, the cost of equity and the cost of debt may be initially stable, but ultimately both of these costs start to rise as the firm becomes more financially leveraged and hence more risky.

COST OF CAPITAL: A WEIGHTED AVERAGE

The **cost of capital** to the firm is a weighted average of the costs of debt, preferred stock, and common stock. The weights depend on the proportion of the firm's assets financed by each source of finance. Management seeks to determine the optimal combination of the various sources that minimizes the weighted-average cost of funds and maximizes the value of the owners' investment in the firm.

COST OF CAPITAL
Weighted average of the costs of a firm's sources of finance

Determining the firm's optimal capital structure requires understanding how the weighted-average cost of funds is derived. This section develops the weighted average and assumes that the best combination (the weights) is known. After the discussion of the weighted cost of capital, the determination of the optimal capital structure will be covered.

Management has calculated that the current cost of each type of financing is as follows:

Cost of debt	5.20%
Cost of preferred stock	8.96
Cost of common stock (retained earnings)	11.00

The proportion (the weights) of the firm's assets financed by each type of financing is

Debt	40%
Preferred stock	10
Common stock (retained earnings)	50

To find the cost of capital, multiply the proportion of each component of the optimal capital structure by its respective costs and add the results. For this firm that yields:

	Cost × Weight = Weighted Cost
Debt	5.20% × 0.40 = 2.080%
Preferred stock	8.96 × 0.10 = 0.896
Common stock	11.00 × 0.50 = 5.500
	Cost of capital = 8.476%

The process of determining the cost of funds is generalized in Equation 16.11.

16.11
$$k = w_1k_d + w_2k_p + w_3k_e.$$

The equation states that the cost of capital (k) is a weighted average in which the costs of debt (k_d), preferred stock (k_p), and equity (k_e) are weighted by the extent to which they are used (that is, w_1, w_2, and w_3, respectively). These weights, along with the cost of each source, then determine the overall cost of funds. In the above illustration, the cost of capital is

$$k = (0.4)5.20 + (0.1)8.96 + (0.5)11.00 = 0.08476 = 8.476\%.$$

For this firm the weighted-average cost of capital is 8.476 percent. The firm must earn at least 8.476 percent on its investments to justify using its sources of finance. It is this cost of capital that will be used in the subsequent chapter to determine whether a firm should make a particular investment in plant and equipment (that is, the cost of capital will be the discount factor used in capital budgeting).

If a firm does earn 8.476 cents after taxes on the investment of a dollar, then the firm has 2.080 cents to pay the interest, 0.896 cent to pay the dividends on the preferred stock, and 5.5 cents to pay dividends on the common stock or to reinvest in the company so that it may grow. The 8.476 cents covers the cost of each individual component of the firm's cost of capital.

If the company earns more than 8.476 percent, it can pay its debt expense and the preferred stock dividends, and it will have more than is necessary to meet the expected return of the common stockholders. For example, if the firm earns 10 percent (10 cents), 2.080 cents are paid to creditors and 0.896 cents goes to the preferred stockholders. That leaves 7.024 cents for the common stockholders, which exceeds the 5.5 cents required as a return on common stock. The firm may increase its dividends or increase its growth rate by reinvesting the earnings. Either way, investors will bid up the price of the stock. Since the return on an investment in the stock exceeded investors' required return, the value of this firm is increased.

THE OPTIMAL CAPITAL STRUCTURE

The previous section illustrated the determination of the firm's weighted cost of capital. In that illustration, the cost of debt was less than the cost of equity because debt is less risky to the investor and the borrower may deduct interest payments before determining taxable income. If debt costs less than equity, couldn't management reduce the firm's cost of capital by substituting cheaper debt for more expensive equity? The answer is both yes and no. As management initially substitutes cheaper debt, the cost of capital does decline. However, as debt finances a larger proportion of the firm's assets and the firm becomes more financially leveraged, the costs of both debt and equity rise. What management needs to determine is the optimal combination of debt and equity financing that minimizes the firm's cost of capital.[5]

The process of determining the optimal capital structure is illustrated in Exhibit 16.6. The first column in the table presents the proportion of debt financing. The second and third columns give the after-tax cost of debt and the cost of equity, respectively. (To ease the calculation, it is assumed that this firm has no preferred stock.) The cost of debt is less than the cost of equity, and both are constant over a considerable range of debt ratios. The costs of both debt and equity start to rise as the firm becomes more financially leveraged. The fourth column presents the weighted-average cost of capital, which incorporates the cost of debt and the cost of equity, weighted by the proportion of assets financed by each.

If the firm is entirely financed by equity, the weighted-average cost of capital is the cost of equity. When the firm begins to use some debt and substitutes the cheaper debt financing for equity financing, the weighted-average cost of capital

[5]This trade off between debt and equity is well understood by many corporate executives and is illustrated by the following statement taken from Coca-Cola's *1998 Annual Report*. "Our company maintains prudent debt levels based on our cash flow, interest coverage, and percentage of debt to capital. We use debt financing to lower our overall cost of capital, which increases our return on shareowners' equity."

EXHIBIT 16.6

Determination of the Optimal Capital Structure

Proportion of Debt Financing	Cost of Debt	Cost of Equity	Weighted Cost
0%	4%	10.0%	10.00%
10	4	10.0	09.40
20	4	10.0	08.80
30	4	10.0	08.20
40	4	10.5	07.90
50	5	11.5	08.25
60	6	13.0	08.80
70	8	15.0	10.10
80	10	18.0	11.60
90	15	22.0	15.70

is reduced. As the use of debt increases, the weighted-average cost of capital initially declines.

However, this decline does not continue indefinitely as the firm substitutes additional cheaper debt. Eventually, both the cost of debt and the cost of equity begin to increase, because creditors and investors believe that more financial leverage increases the riskiness of the firm. At first, the increases in the cost of debt and the cost of equity may be insufficient to stop the decline in the weighted cost of capital. But as the costs of debt and equity continue to increase, the average cost of capital reaches a minimum and then starts to increase. In the table, this optimal capital structure occurs at 40 percent debt (40 percent debt financing to 60 percent equity financing). As additional debt is used, the costs of both debt and equity rise sufficiently that the cost of capital increases.

This determination of the optimal capital structure is also illustrated by Figure 16.6, which plots the cost of debt (k_d), the cost of equity (k_e), and the weighted-average cost of capital (k) given in Exhibit 16.6. As is readily seen in the graph, when the use of debt increases, the weighted-average cost of capital initially declines, reaches a minimum at debt of 40 percent ($D_1 = 40\%$ and $k_1 = 7.9\%$), and then starts to increase.

The optimal capital structure is reached at the minimum point on the weighted-average cost of capital structure. The financial manager should acquire this combination of financing because it involves the lowest cost of funds.

This minimum cost of capital should be used to judge potential investments; it will be employed in the capital budgeting techniques discussed in the next chapter. As the firm expands and makes additional investments in plant and equipment, it must also expand its sources of financing. These additional sources should maintain the firm's optimal capital structure. Additional (or marginal) investments are financed by additional (or marginal) funds. As long as the optimal capital structure is maintained, additional funds should cost the same as the weighted average (that is, the weighted marginal cost of funds is equal to the firm's average cost of capital). Of course, if the additional investments increase the riskiness of the firm or

FIGURE 16.6

Cost of Capital

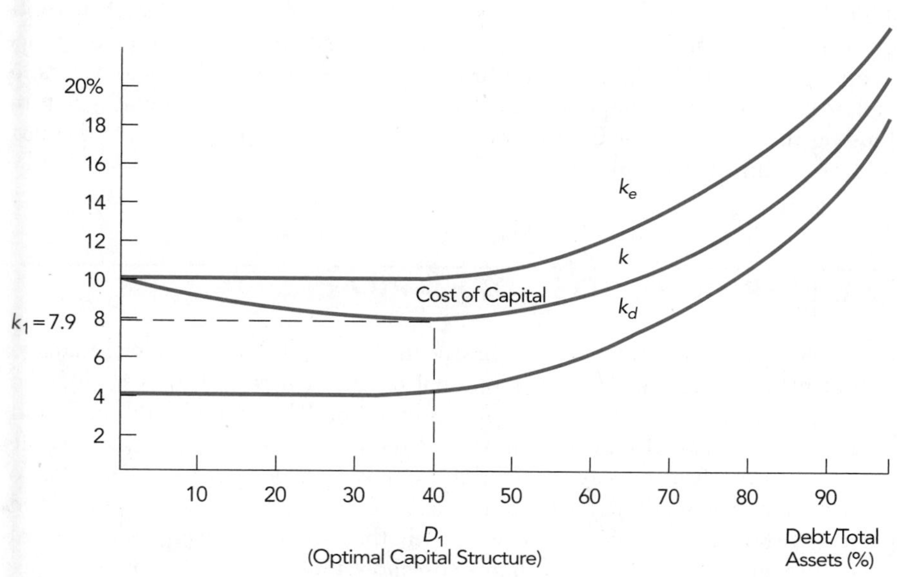

the flotation costs associated with issuing new securities rise, then the cost of the additional funds will increase. In that case, which is discussed in the next section, the cost of the marginal funds will exceed the firm's weighted-average cost of capital.

For many firms, the optimal capital structure is a range of debt financing. In the example presented in Exhibit 16.6 and Figure 16.6, the weighted-average cost of capital evidences little variation for debt financing ranging from 30 percent to 50 percent. This indicates that the effect of debt financing in lowering the firm's cost of capital is achieved when 30 percent of the firm's assets are debt financed. Additional use of debt, however, does not start to increase the cost of capital until more than 50 percent of the assets are debt financed. Thus, the optimal capital structure is a range of debt-to-equity financing and not just a specific combination of debt to equity.

That the optimal capital structure is a range and not a specific combination is important from a practical viewpoint. New issues of debt or common stock are made infrequently, and when debt or stock is issued, the dollar amount of the issue may be substantial. A firm will not sell new securities for a trivial amount of money because of the cost of issuing them. Thus, when new securities are issued, the proportions of debt and equity financing are altered. If the optimal capital structure were not a range, every new issue of securities would alter the firm's cost of capital. Since the optimal debt structure is a range, a firm has flexibility in issuing new securities and may tailor the security issues to market conditions. For example, if management anticipates that interest rates will increase in the future, it may choose to issue debt now and use equity financing at some future date. This flexibility in the type of securities issued is in part the result of the fact that the optimal capital structure is a range of debt-to-equity financing. But even the existence of a range does not mean (1) that a firm can always use the same type of financing, or (2) that it is not important for a firm to seek the optimal capital structure. Finding the optimal capital structure is required if management wants to maximize the value of the firm.

THE MARGINAL COST OF CAPITAL

MARGINAL COST OF CAPITAL
Cost of additional sources of finance

Once the optimal capital structure has been determined, the financial manager should maintain it. Preserving the optimal capital structure, however, does not necessarily mean that the cost of capital is constant. The cost of additional funds (the **marginal cost of capital**) can rise. If the cost of debt or the cost of equity increases as the firm uses more debt and equity financing, the marginal cost of capital will rise, even though the optimal capital structure is preserved. For example, the cost of common stock depends on whether the firm is using retained earnings or issuing new shares. New shares cost more than retained earnings because of flotation costs. The marginal cost of capital will increase when new shares are issued even though the optimal combination of debt and equity financing is preserved.

Consider the illustration in Exhibit 16.6, in which the optimal cost of capital was 7.9 percent with 40 percent debt and 60 percent equity. That cost consisted of the 4 percent after-tax cost of debt and the 10.5 percent cost of equity. This cost of equity is the cost of retained earnings because these equity funds are used before the firm would issue new (and more expensive) common stock.

Suppose, however, the firm has additional investment opportunities that would require more than its retained earnings. It could borrow all the necessary funds, which would increase the firm's use of financial leverage. Such a course of action would be undesirable because the firm would no longer be maintaining its optimal capital structure. To maintain the optimal capital structure, the firm will have to issue additional shares (and pay the associated flotation costs) and simultaneously borrow some additional funds if it wants to make these investments. The firm must borrow 40 percent of the additional funds and issue new shares to cover the remaining 60 percent of the additional financing. The impact of the increase in the cost of equity due to the flotation costs is to increase the cost of capital, even though the proportion of debt to equity is maintained.

To illustrate this increase in the cost of capital, suppose the 10.5 percent cost of equity consisted of the following dividend yield and growth rate:

$$k_e = \frac{\$0.95(1 + 0.055)}{\$20} + 0.055$$

$$k_e = \frac{\$1.00}{\$20} + 0.055 = 0.05 + 0.055 = 10.5\%.$$

Once retained earnings are exhausted, the firm will have to issue new shares with a flotation cost of $1.00 per share, so the firm nets $19 per share. The cost of these new shares (k_{ne}) is

$$k_{ne} = \frac{\$0.95(1 + 0.055)}{\$20 - \$1} + 0.055$$

$$k_{ne} = \frac{\$1.00}{\$19} + 0.055 = 0.0526 + 0.055 = 10.76\%.$$

The cost of the common stock rises from 10.5 percent to 10.76 percent and the firm's cost of capital rises to

$$k = (0.4)(4\%) + (0.6)(10.76\%) = 8.056\%.$$

The cost of capital has risen from 7.9 percent to 8.056 percent even though management is maintaining the optimal capital structure of 40 percent debt and 60 percent equity.

Which of these two costs (7.9 percent and 8.056 percent) does the firm use when making investment decisions? The answer depends on how many investment opportunities the firm has. If the firm has insufficient opportunities to consume its retained earnings, the cost of capital is 7.9 percent. However, after the retained earnings are exhausted and new shares must be sold, the firm's cost of capital rises to 8.056 percent. Then, 8.056 percent should be used to judge additional investment opportunities because that is the firm's cost of capital.

The following example will illustrate this process of making additional investments and maintaining the optimal capital structure as the cost of finance changes. Currently, the firm desires to make six $1,000,000 investments. (Remember, the techniques for selecting investments will be discussed in the subsequent chapter. In reality, the determination of the cost of capital and the decision to make long-term investments are tied together, but only one piece of the puzzle can be discussed at a time!) The firm has $10,000,000 in assets financed 40 percent with debt and 60 percent with equity. This optimal capital structure was determined earlier and has a cost of capital of 10.5 percent. The information used to determine that cost of capital was

1. an after-tax cost of debt of 4 percent,
2. a current dividend of $0.95, which will rise to $1.00 during the year,
3. a stock price of $20,
4. a growth rate of 5.5 percent.

During the period when the desired investments are to be made, the firm will generate retained earnings of $1,200,000. In addition, the firm's creditors have informed management that if the firm borrows more than $2,000,000, the rate of interest will have to be increased, even if the firm maintains its capital structure. The impact of this increase will raise the after-tax cost of debt to 5 percent. What will be the marginal cost of each additional dollar to the firm?

This is the most complicated question posed in this chapter. Management knows the optimal capital structure is 40 percent debt and that this structure should be retained. Thus, for every additional $400,000 of borrowed funds, the firm must have $600,000 in new equity. Thus, the $1,200,000 in new retained earnings will support $800,000 in additional borrowed capital for a total of $2,000,000 in new finance. The cost of these funds is

$$k = (0.4)(4\%) + (0.6)(10.5\%) = 7.9\%.$$

Thus, the cost of the first $2,000,000 in additional funds (that is, the marginal cost) is 7.9 percent. However, $2,000,000 will not cover all the investment opportunities.

Since an additional $4,000,000 is needed to make all the desired investments, the financial manager decides to issue $2,400,000 in additional stock (0.6 × $4,000,000); $2,400,000 in additional stock will support $1,600,000 in additional debt and still maintain the 40 percent debt financing. What will be the cost of the additional funds? If the after-tax cost of debt remains 4 percent and the cost of new shares is 10.76 percent, the firm's cost of capital is

$$k = (0.4)(4\%) + (0.6)(10.76\%) = 8.056\%.$$

However, does the after-tax cost of debt remain at 4 percent? The answer is yes only for the first $2,000,000; above that, additional debt has an after-tax cost of 5 percent. The financial manager anticipated borrowing $800,000 to be used in conjunction with the $1,200,000 in retained earnings and $1,600,000 to be used with the $2,400,000 raised through the issuing of new shares. That is a total of $2,400,000. Only the first $2,000,000 will have an after-tax cost of 4 percent. The last $400,000 will cost 5 percent. Once again, the cost of capital changes even though the optimal combination of debt and equity financing is maintained. The cost of capital now rises to

$$k = (0.4)(5\%) + (0.6)(10.76\%) = 8.456\%.$$

These different costs of capital are illustrated in Figure 16.7, which presents the firm's marginal cost of capital. As additional funds are needed, the marginal cost of capital rises. The first increase occurs at $2,000,000, when the firm runs out of retained earnings. The second increment occurs at $5,000,000, when the firm runs out of borrowing capacity with the lower after-tax cost of debt.

How are these amounts ($2,000,000 and $5,000,000) determined? These breaks in the marginal cost of capital schedule may be determined by the following equation:

16.12 $$\text{Break point} = \frac{\text{Amount of funds available at a given cost}}{\text{Proportion of that component in the capital structure}}.$$

For example, there were $1,200,000 of available retained earnings, and equity constituted 60 percent of the capital structure. Thus, the break point for the retained earnings is

FIGURE 16.7

Marginal Cost of Capital

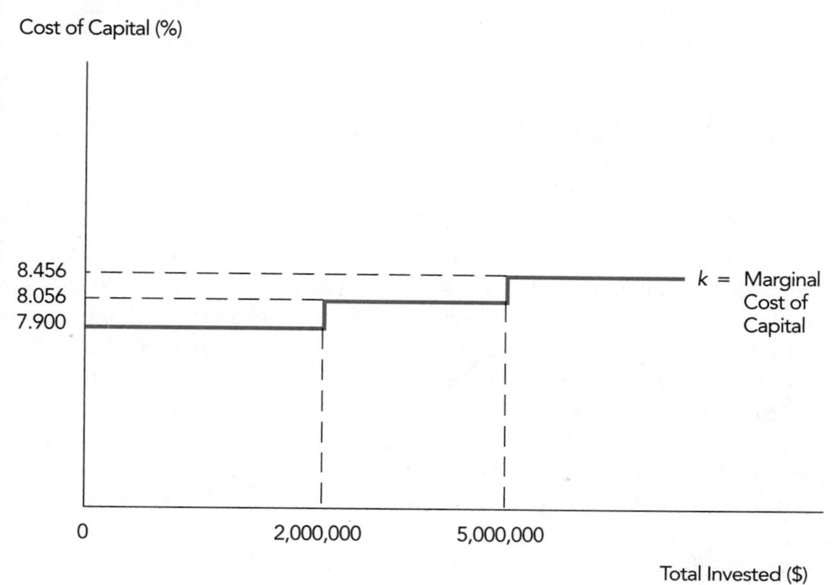

$$\text{Break point (retained earnings)} = \frac{\$1{,}200{,}000}{0.6} = \$2{,}000{,}000.$$

Thus, the cost of capital of the first $2,000,000 uses the lower cost of retained earnings (10.5 percent) in the calculation. Once $2,000,000 is exceeded, the higher cost of new stock (10.76 percent) must be used.

The same logic applies to the cost of debt. The break point for debt is

$$\text{Break point (cheaper debt)} = \frac{\$2{,}000{,}000}{0.4} = \$5{,}000{,}000.$$

As long as the total funds raised are less than $5,000,000, the lower after-tax cost of debt applies (4 percent), but if the total capital exceeds $5,000,000, the higher after-tax cost of debt must be used (5 percent).

When these individual pieces are put together, the cost of capital for different amounts of funds is

$$\$0 - \$2{,}000{,}000\text{: } (0.4)(4\%) + (0.6)(10.5\%) = 7.9\%$$

$$\$2{,}000{,}001 - \$5{,}000{,}000\text{: } (0.4)(4\%) + (0.6)(10.76\%) = 8.056\%$$

$$\text{above } \$5{,}000{,}000\text{: } (0.4)(5\%) + (0.6)(10.76\%) = 8.456\%.$$

This is, of course, the schedule of the marginal costs of funds presented in Figure 16.7, which illustrates the increments in the marginal cost of capital and at what level of total funds these increments occur.

THE OPTIMAL CAPITAL STRUCTURE AND THE VALUE OF THE FIRM'S STOCK

The successful use of financial leverage increases the return on the firm's equity and increases earnings per share. Earnings per share increase because as the firm uses more debt financing and becomes more financially leveraged, it issues fewer shares. Since earnings are spread over fewer shares, per share earnings increase. Does this increased use of debt and higher per share earnings lead to a higher stock price? What is the relationship between the optimal capital structure and the price of the stock?

These are important and difficult questions that are developed more fully in advanced texts on finance. The following discussion can, at best, only indicate the relationship among the components of the cost of capital, the optimal capital structure, and stock valuation.

Since the goal of management is to maximize the value of the firm's stock, the optimal capital structure is that combination of debt and equity financing that maximizes the value of the stock. The financial manager substitutes debt for equity as long as this substitution increases per share earnings without unduly increasing the risk associated with debt financing. The increase in per share earnings, when coupled with only a moderate addition to risk, should increase the value of the stock. However, if the firm continues to substitute debt for equity and use more financial leverage, the element of risk will increase sufficiently to offset the advantage of higher per share earnings. The net effect is to cause the value of the shares to fall.

This trade-off is illustrated in Exhibit 16.7. The firm needs $1,000, so the financial manager considers the impact of borrowing the funds. In part I, the first row presents the amount of debt to be issued in increments of $100. The second line presents the before-tax cost of the debt, and the third line gives the cost of equity. As the firm becomes more financially leveraged, the before-tax cost of debt and the cost of equity rise. The fourth line indicates that as the firm uses more debt financing, the number of shares outstanding is reduced (fewer shares will have to be issued to raise the necessary capital).

Part II presents a simple income statement for the firm as it uses more debt. Operating income ($250) is the same regardless of the choice of financing. As more debt is used (and as the rate of interest charged rises), interest expense rises, reducing taxable earnings and, correspondingly, reducing taxes. The lower taxes do not completely offset the higher interest payments, so net income declines. Earnings per share, however, rise because the smaller earnings are spread over a fewer number of shares.

Parts III and IV present the value of the stock and the cost of capital at the various combinations of debt and equity financing. Initially, the use of financial

Determination of the Optimal Capital Structure Using Market Value of Stock

EXHIBIT 16.7

I.							
Amount of debt	$ 0	$100	$200	$300	$400	$500	$600
Interest rate	10%	10%	10%	11%	12%	14%	16%
Cost of equity	15%	15%	15.5%	16.6%	17.8%	19.4%	21.5%
Number of shares outstanding	10	9	8	7	6	5	4
II.							
Earnings before interest & taxes	$250	$250	$250	$250	$250	$250	$250
Interest	$ —	$ 10	$ 20	$ 33.0	$ 48.0	$ 70	$ 96.0
Earnings before taxes	$250	$240	$230	$217.0	$202.0	$180	$154.0
Tax (at 40%)	$100	$ 96	$ 92	$ 86.8	$ 80.8	$ 72	$ 61.6
Net income	$150	$144	$138.00	$130.20	$121.20	$108.00	$ 92.40
Earnings per share	$ 15	$ 16	$ 17.25	$ 18.60	$ 20.20	$ 21.60	$ 23.10
III.							
Value of a share	$100	$106.67	$111.29	$112.05	$113.48	$111.34	$107.44
IV.							
Cost of capital	15%	14.1%	13.6%	13.6%	13.56% ↑	13.9%	14.36%

leverage increases the value of the stock. These values are derived using the dividend-growth model:

$$V = \frac{D_0(1 + g)}{k_e - g}.$$

To simplify the illustration, it is assumed that all earnings are distributed. Therefore, the value of the stock is

$$V = \frac{D_0(1 + g)}{k_e - g} = \frac{\text{Earnings per share}}{k_e},$$

when $g = 0$. Thus, when per share earnings are $17.25 (at $200 debt), the value of the stock is $17.25/0.155 = $111.29.

As may be seen in part III, the value of the stock initially rises because the firm is successfully employing financial leverage. However, as the firm becomes more financially leveraged, the increased risk starts to offset the advantage of financial leverage. The value of the stock reaches a maximum and then starts to decline.

The combination of debt and equity financing that maximizes the value of the stock also is the firm's optimal capital structure. This is illustrated in part IV, which presents the cost of capital. In this illustration, the minimum cost of capital occurs when the firm seeks to use $400 in debt so that 40 percent of its assets are financed with debt and 60 percent with equity. At that capital structure, the minimum cost of capital is

$$k = w_d(k_d)(1 - t) + w_e(k_e)$$

$$= (0.4)(0.12)(1 - 0.4) + (0.6)(0.178) = 13.56\%.$$

Exhibit 16.7 presents the same concept that was illustrated in Exhibit 16.6 but ties together the maximization of the value of the stock with the minimization of the firm's cost of funds. The combination of debt and equity financing that minimizes the cost of capital will also maximize the value of the stock. This statement has intuitive appeal. If the financial manager is able to minimize the firm's cost of funds, that should benefit the firm's owners. If the financial manager is not minimizing the cost of capital, the firm will not be as attractive to investors, and the value of the equity will be reduced. Thus, maximizing the value of the firm requires minimizing the cost of capital.

COST OF CAPITAL REVIEW AND PROBLEM AREAS

No topic in this text is more important than the determination of a firm's cost of funds and its optimal capital structure. As the previous discussion indicated, this determination is a complex procedure that in reality is difficult to apply. The following discussion reiterates some of the problem areas and reveals others that until now have been swept under the carpet.

First, to determine the cost of capital, the financial manager must know all the component costs. As was previously mentioned, the estimation of the cost of equity requires information (the future growth rate in dividends, the firm's beta coefficient, the appropriate risk-free rate, the expected return on the market, and so on) that is not readily observable. An inaccurate measure of the cost of equity leads to an inaccurate estimate of the cost of capital.

Second, the financial manager needs to know how the market will value the shares after the financing decision is made. This is, of course, impossible to know. Obviously, the financial manager makes the financing decision in anticipation of the market treating the shares in a particular way, but conditions change, and the anticipated correct financial structure in one environment may not be correct in a different environment. The large use of debt financing leverage during the leveraged buyout period of the late 1980s generated lower stock prices for some firms during the early 1990s. Hindsight is perfect, but financial decisions must be made with foresight.

Third, the discussion examined the optimal capital structure in terms of maximizing the value of a firm's stock. That may be acceptable for publicly held firms, but the vast majority of businesses are not publicly held. Even though most privately held firms are small, the determination of their cost of capital remains important. As is explained in the next chapter, this determination is a critical part of the decision to invest in plant and equipment. However, the financial managers of small, private firms cannot know the current value of their firm's equity or the impact their decisions will have on that value.

Fourth, depreciation was excluded from the above discussion. Depreciation expense may generate cash that may be used in a variety of ways, such as restoring the asset that is being depreciated, acquiring an alternative investment, or returning capital to its sources (in other words, retiring debt or equity). Many competing uses exist for the cash generated through depreciation charges, and the financial manager needs an estimate of the cost of depreciation-generated funds in order to help determine the best use of these funds.

Fifth, a notable theory in finance contends a firm's capital structure may be irrelevant. This conclusion is derived from several important assumptions, one of which is that if a firm uses too little financial leverage, investors can substitute their own leverage for the firm's. Consider a firm with no debt financing. Investors can borrow money to buy the stock (that is, buy the stock on margin). In such a case, the stockholders are substituting their own leverage for the firm's use of financial leverage. If the firm uses a large amount of financial leverage, the stockholders can then hold portfolios of cash and the stock, which reduces the impact of the firm's large use of financial leverage. By having stockholders alter their portfolios to offset a firm's use of financial leverage, one can reason that an optimal capital structure is irrelevant. What is important is the operating income the firm generates, and not how that income is divided between creditors in the form of interest payments and owners and in the form of dividends and capital gains.[6]

[6] For a discussion of this proposition and the theory that dividend policy is irrelevant, see the latest edition of an advanced text on corporate finance, such as Eugene Brigham, Louis Gapenski, and Michael Ehrhardt, *Financial Management: Theory and Practice*, 9th ed. (Fort Worth, Tex.: The Dryden Press, 1999), pp. 660–683.

SUMMARY

The break-even level of output occurs when a firm's revenues cover its costs of production. Revenues depend on the number of units sold and their price. Total costs depend on fixed costs, which are independent of the level of production, and variable costs, which rise and fall with changes in the level of production. Although break-even analysis does not identify the most profitable level of output, it is useful when management anticipates introducing a new product or substituting fixed for variable costs of production.

Operating leverage brings to the foreground the importance of fixed costs relative to variable costs. Firms that have large fixed costs have operating leverage. These firms must achieve a higher level of sales to break even. Firms with costs that fluctuate with the level of output do not have operating leverage; they may achieve profits at a lower level of production. However, once profitable levels of output are achieved, the firm with more operating leverage will experience more rapid increases in operating income for given changes in production. This increased variability of operating income increases the business risk associated with the firm.

All assets must be financed. There are two basic sources of finance: debt and equity. If a firm uses debt financing, it is financially leveraged. If the firm is able to earn more with the funds acquired by issuing debt than it must pay in interest, the residual accrues to equity. By successfully using debt financing, the firm increases the owners' return on their investment.

Although the successful use of debt financing increases the return on equity, it also increases financial risk. If the firm experiences a decline in sales or profit margins, it must still pay the interest and retire the principal. Failure to do so may result in bankruptcy. Thus, while the use of debt financing may increase the return on equity during periods of success and growth, the opposite may be true during periods of difficulty. Then the use of debt financing reduces the return on equity, as the firm must meet the fixed obligations of its debt financing.

Management's task is to determine the best combination of debt and equity financing—that is, the firm's optimal capital structure, which takes advantage of financial leverage without unduly increasing risk and produces the lowest cost of capital.

A firm's cost of capital is a weighted average of its various sources of funds. The after-tax cost of debt depends on the interest rate and the firm's marginal income tax rate. The firm's credit rating and the term on the loan also affect the effective cost of debt. The cost of preferred stock depends on the dividend it pays and investors' required

return, which is the yield necessary to induce them to purchase preferred stock. The cost of common stock is an opportunity cost concept in that there are no identifiable costs, such as the interest payment on debt. The cost of common stock, like the cost of preferred stock, is the return necessary to induce investors to buy the stock. This return depends on such factors as the stock's dividend, the firm's expected growth, the expected return on the market, and the volatility of the stock relative to the market.

Once the financial manager has determined the firm's optimal capital structure, the combination of debt and equity financing should be maintained. However, even if the proportions are maintained, the marginal cost of capital may increase as the firm has to pay flotation costs and issue riskier debt with a higher interest rate to raise additional funds.

REVIEW QUESTIONS

1. If the management of a firm is considering introducing a new product, how can break-even analysis be used to help make the decision?
2. Your firm operates in a very stable environment. Sales forecasts can be made with reasonable accuracy. Is that an argument for the use of more or less operating leverage?
3. In some people's minds, financial leverage is the name of the game. If financial leverage is successful, what should happen to the return on equity? As the firm uses more financial leverage, what impact should the increased debt financing have on the variability of the firm's operating income and net earnings?
4. If financial leverage is associated with risk, what can creditors do to protect their investments?
5. Why is preferred stock a source of financial leverage? Since both debt and preferred stock are means to obtain financial leverage, why will a debt issue with an 8 percent interest rate be preferred by management to a preferred stock issue with an 8 percent dividend yield?
6. If a firm has a large amount of operating leverage, should the firm also use a substantial amount of debt financing?
7. What impact does each of the following have on the firm's cost of capital?
   a. an increase in the corporate income tax rate
   b. a decrease in the firm's beta
   c. a decrease in interest rates
   d. an increase in flotation (investment banking) costs
   e. an increase in the firm's use of operating leverage

8. Why would you expect the cost of common stock to exceed the cost of preferred stock and the cost of preferred stock to exceed the cost of debt? What happens to the firm's cost of capital as it initially substitutes debt for equity? Why may the marginal cost of capital exceed the firm's weighted-average cost of capital?
9. If a firm reduced its dividend and retained a large proportion of its earnings, what impact would the change have on its marginal cost of funds?
10. If a firm achieves its optimal capital structure, what does that imply about the value of its common stock?

PROBLEMS

1. Management believes it can sell a new product for \$8.50. The fixed costs of production are estimated to be \$6,000, and the variable costs are \$3.20 a unit.
   a. Complete the following table at the given levels of output and the relationships between quantity and fixed costs, quantity and variable costs, and quantity and total costs.

Quantity	Total Revenue	Variable Costs	Fixed Costs	Total Costs	Profits (Loss)
0					
500					
1,000					
1,500					
2,000					
2,500					
3,000					

   b. Determine the break-even level using the above table and use Equation 16.5 to confirm the break-even level of output.
   c. What would happen to the total revenue schedule, the total cost schedule, and the break-even level of output if management determined that fixed costs would be \$10,000 instead of \$6,000?
2. The management of a successful firm wants to introduce a new product. The product will sell for \$4 a unit and can be produced by either of two scales of operation. In the first, total costs are

$$TC = \$3,000 + \$2.8Q.$$

In the second scale of operation, total costs are

$$TC = \$5,000 + \$2.4Q.$$

   a. What is the break-even level of output for each scale of operation?
   b. What will be the firm's profits for each scale of operation if sales reach 5,000 units?

c. One-half of the fixed costs are noncash (depreciation). All other expenses are for cash. If sales are 2,000 units, will cash receipts cover cash expenses for each scale of operation?

d. The anticipated levels of sales are

Year	Unit Sales
1	3,000
2	4,000
3	5,000
4	6,000

If the firm selects the scale of production with more operating leverage, what can it expect in years 1 and 2? On what grounds can it justify selecting this scale of operation? If sales reach only 5,000 a year, was the correct scale of operation chosen?

3. A firm has the following total revenue and total cost schedules:

$$TR = \$2Q.$$
$$TC = \$4{,}000 + \$1.5Q.$$

a. What is the break-even level of output? What is the level of profits at sales of 9,000 units?

b. As the result of a major technological breakthrough, the total cost schedule is changed to:

$$TC = \$6{,}000 + \$0.5Q.$$

What is the break-even level of output? What is the level of profits at sales of 9,000 units?

4. The manufacturer of a product that has a variable cost of $2.50 per unit and total fixed cost of $125,000 wants to determine the level of output necessary to avoid losses.

a. What level of sales is necessary to break even if the product is sold for $4.25? What will be the manufacturer's profit or loss on the sales of 100,000 units?

b. If fixed costs rise to $175,000, what is the new level of sales necessary to break even?

c. If variable costs decline to $2.25 per unit, what is the new level of sales necessary to break even?

d. If fixed costs were to increase to $175,000, while variable costs declined to $2.25 per unit, what is the new break-even level of sales?

e. If a major proportion of fixed costs were noncash (depreciation), would failure to achieve the break-even level of sales imply that the firm cannot pay its current obligations as they come due? Suppose $100,000 of the above fixed costs of $125,000 were depreciation expense. What level of sales would be the *cash* break-even level of sales?

5. HBM, Inc. has the following capital structure:

Assets	$400,000	Debt	$140,000
		Preferred stock	20,000
		Common stock	240,000

The common stock is currently selling for $15 a share, pays a cash dividend of $0.75 per share, and is growing annually at 6 percent. The preferred stock pays a $9 cash dividend and currently sells for $91 a share. The debt pays interest of 8.5 percent annually, and the firm is in the 30 percent marginal tax bracket.

a. What is the after-tax cost of debt?
b. What is the cost of preferred stock?
c. What is the cost of common stock?
d. What is the firm's weighted-average cost of capital?

6. Sun Instruments expects to issue new stock at $34 a share with estimated flotation costs of 7 percent of the market price. The company currently pays a $2.10 cash dividend and has a 6 percent growth rate. What are the cost of retained earnings and new common stock?

7. A firm's current balance sheet is as follows:

Assets	$100	Debt	$10
		Equity	$90

a. What is the firm's weighted-average cost of capital at various combinations of debt and equity, given the following information?

Debt/Assets	After-Tax Cost of Debt	Cost of Equity	Cost of Capital
0%	8%	12%	?
10	8	12	?
20	8	12	?
30	8	13	?
40	9	14	?
50	10	15	?
60	12	16	?

b. Construct a pro forma balance sheet that indicates the firm's optimal capital structure. Compare this balance sheet with the firm's current balance sheet. What course of action should the firm take?

Assets	$100	Debt	$?
		Equity	$?

c. As a firm initially substitutes debt for equity financing, what happens to the cost of capital, and why?
d. If a firm uses too much debt financing, why does the cost of capital rise?

8. The financial manager of a firm determines the following schedules of cost of debt and cost of equity for various combinations of debt financing:

Debt/Assets	After-Tax Cost of Debt	Cost of Equity
0%	4%	8%
10	4	8
20	4	8
30	5	8
40	6	10
50	8	12
60	10	14
70	12	16

a. Find the optimal capital structure (that is, optimal combination of debt and equity financing).
b. Why does the cost of capital initially decline as the firm substitutes debt for equity financing?
c. Why will the cost of funds eventually rise as the firm becomes more financially leveraged?
d. Why is debt financing more common than financing with preferred stock?
e. If interest were not a tax-deductible expense, what effect would that have on the firm's cost of capital? Why?

9. *a.* Given the following, determine the firm's optimal capital structure:

Debt/Assets	After-Tax Cost of Debt	Cost of Equity
0%	8%	12%
10	8	12
20	8	12
30	9	12
40	9	13
50	10	15
60	12	17

b. If the firm were using 60 percent debt and 40 percent equity, what would that tell you about the firm's use of financial leverage?
c. What two reasons explain why debt is cheaper than equity?
d. If the firm were using 30 percent debt and 70 percent equity and earned a return of 11.7 percent on an investment, would this mean that stockholders will receive less than their required return of 12 percent? What return will stockholders receive?

Using Break-Even Analysis to Justify an Investment

Joseph Galleher, who has produced several successful plays, is considering producing *The Hard Lesson*, a play concerning the adjustment to life after the death of a spouse. The serious nature of the play raised doubts in the backers who previously had financed Galleher's successful plays. Although the individuals with the funds to finance the play were well aware of the risks associated with such investments, they were also aware that the possibility existed for large returns if the play were made into a movie or used as the basis for a TV production. If successful, the backers would receive a residual or royalty that could generate cash flow for years into the future. For this reason, Galleher realized that the backers' primary concern was that the initial production break even. If he could convince them that the show would recoup its initial costs, the possibility of residuals would be sufficient to induce the individual investors to finance the play.

Play production involves certain costs that are fixed and others that are variable. For example, an estimated $250,000 is needed to stage the play. These funds would cover the cost of rehearsals, sets and costumes, initial advertising, and other expenses necessary to mount the production. Once *The Hard Lesson* opens, the actors will receive $20,000 a week, and the producer's fee is $4,000 a week plus 5 percent of gross receipts. The director will also receive a fee of 5 percent of the gross receipts, and the actors will have an incentive contract that pays them an additional 10 percent of the receipts. The author will receive a royalty of $5,000 per week, and it is estimated that weekly advertising expenses will run $12,000.

Galleher is considering two different theaters in which to stage the play. The first, with only 300 seats, has a reputation for housing quality productions of interesting works. It tends to draw an audience that will pay $40 a ticket, and the rent is $10,000 a month. The other theater has 1,300 seats, and since the building is larger, its rent is $16,000 a month. However, the theater management has a policy of charging no more than $15 a ticket. In both cases the play would be performed five times a week.

While Galleher is concerned with making a profit, the fact that he will receive a weekly payment reduces his personal need for the show to earn a profit. In addition, since the backers are primarily concerned with not losing money and secondarily with the possibility of earning large residuals, the greatest financial emphasis is to avoid losses (in other words, to break even).

CASE PROBLEMS

1. Excluding the initial production costs, calculate for each theater how many seats must be sold for each performance in order for the play to cover its weekly operating expenses.
2. If the play ran at 80 percent of capacity in the smaller theater and 70 percent of capacity in the larger theater, how long would it take to recoup the initial $250,000?

CALCULATING THE COST OF CAPITAL WHILE MAINTAINING THE OPTIMAL CAPITAL STRUCTURE

Hector Albeniz was recently promoted to the position of Vice-President of Finance. His first assignment is to determine the firm's cost of finance, which is necessary to judge long-term investments. This is an important assignment since the firm is anticipating substantial growth, which will require considerable investments in additional plant and equipment. Overestimating the cost of funds could lead to the rejection of profitable investments. Even worse, if the cost is underestimated, the firm could acquire assets that are unprofitable.

Over a period of many years, management has adopted a conservative policy of never permitting debt to exceed 30 percent of total financing. Even if the firm could sustain more financial leverage, Albeniz realizes that management would not use additional debt financing if the debt ratio were to exceed 30 percent. If the firm needs equity financing to make desirable long-term investments and simultaneously maintain its conservative capital structure, management is, however, willing to consider reducing the dividend to $1 or issuing additional shares.

Albeniz estimates that the firm will earn $10,000,000 during the year. Forty percent of the earnings will be distributed as cash dividends, and the firm will have retained earnings of $6,000,000 to invest in plant and equipment. Currently, the price of the stock is $50 a share, the dividend is $2, and the expected growth rate is 10 percent. That yields a cost of equity (retained earnings) of

$$k_e = \frac{\$2}{\$50} + 0.10 = 14\%.$$

Management believes that even if the dividend were reduced to $1, the price of the stock would not decline as long as excellent investment choices were made, in which case increased growth would compensate for the lower dividend. Albeniz has ascertained from the firm's investment bankers that additional shares can readily be sold, but that there would be a flotation cost of $2 a share. The firm would net $48 for each share sold, in which case the cost of equity (new shares) becomes:

$$k_{ne} = \frac{\$2}{(\$50 - \$2)} + 0.10 = 14.17\%.$$

Currently, the rate of interest on the firm's long-term debt is 10 percent and the firm's income tax rate is 32 percent. Up to $2,400,000 face amount in new debt can be issued at the going rate. If the firm were to issue more than $2,400,000, the interest would rise to 11 percent.

Albeniz knows that management wants to know the cost of raising additional finance in increments of $3,000,000, consisting of $900,000 in debt and $2,100,000 of equity (30 percent debt and 70 percent equity). Thus, Albeniz must construct a marginal cost of capital schedule, but he decides to present two versions. The first version assumes that the dividend is maintained so that retained earnings will be $6,000,000. In the second version, it is assumed that the dividend is reduced so that retained earnings are increased to $8,000,000. To construct the schedules, Albeniz accepts management's belief that the change in dividend policy will have no impact on the cost of equity.

Case Problems

1. Develop the two marginal cost of capital schedules.
2. What would be the impact on the second schedule if the price of the stock declined as a result of the lower dividend?
3. If the firm's income tax rate rises, what impact would that have on the marginal cost of capital schedule?
4. If the firm needs $12,000,000 in increments of $3,000,000, what is the cost of these funds if it retains $6,000,000?

APPENDIX to Chapter 16

THE DEGREES OF OPERATING AND FINANCIAL LEVERAGE

As is explained in the body of the chapter, operating leverage and financial leverage increase the variability of a firm's operating and net income. Fixed asset turnover and the debt ratios were used as possible measures of a firm's operating and financial leverage. A low fixed asset turnover and a high debt ratio were indicative of high operating and high financial leverage, respectively.

Operating and financial leverage may also be measured by the responsiveness of operating and net income to changes in sales. These measures are the degree of operating leverage and the degree of financial leverage. This appendix illustrates both concepts and shows how a change in net income is affected by both operating and financial leverage.

THE DEGREE OF OPERATING LEVERAGE

DEGREE OF OPERATING LEVERAGE
Measure of the responsiveness of operating income (EBIT) to changes in output or sales

The **degree of operating leverage** quantifies the responsiveness of operating income to changes in the level of output or sales. Specifically, the degree of operating leverage (*DOL*) is defined as the percentage change in operating income divided by the percentage change in the level of output (Q, if expressed in physical units) or sales (S, if expressed in dollars).[1] In symbolic terms this ratio is

16.A1

$$DOL = \frac{\%\Delta EBIT}{\%\Delta S}.$$

This ratio answers the following question: If sales are increased by 10 percent, by what percentage will operating income increase? If the degree of operating leverage for a given level of sales is 2, then a 10 percent increase in sales will increase operating income by 20 percent. A large degree of operating leverage indicates that small fluctuations in revenues will produce large fluctuations in operating income.

[1]Because the degree of operating leverage is the ratio of two percentage changes, it makes no difference if the change in the denominator is in units of output or in dollars.

The degree of operating leverage is not related to how the firm's assets are financed. Operating leverage is independent of the firm's financing decisions. The firm's net income depends not only on its operating leverage but also on its use of financial leverage. Operating leverage is a source of business risk because it relates to the nature of the firm's operations. The use of financial leverage (financial risk) and the degree of financial leverage are discussed later in this appendix.

Equation 16.A2 is an alternative way to express the degree of operating leverage:

$$DOL = \frac{\text{Sales} - \text{Variable costs}}{\text{Sales} - \text{Total operating costs}}.$$

In symbols this is

$$DOL = \frac{Q(P - V)}{Q(P - V) - FC}. \quad \textbf{16.A2}$$

The symbols are as follows:

Q = the initial level of output
P = the price of the product
V = the per-unit variable cost
FC = the fixed operating costs

In this form the degree of operating leverage may be easier to compute, but it is also easy to forget that the degree of operating leverage is the ratio of two percentage changes and that it is a measure of the responsiveness of operating income to changes from one level of sales (or output) to another level of sales.[2] This alternative form masks the definition of the degree of operating leverage and thus may lead to an incorrect interpretation.

[2] Equations 16.A1 and 16.A2 are mathematically equivalent. Operating income is sales ($S = P \times Q$) minus variable costs ($V \times Q$) and fixed operating costs (FC). That is

$$EBIT = P \times Q - V \times Q - FC.$$

The change in operating income is

$$\Delta EBIT = P \times \Delta Q - V \times \Delta Q.$$

Notice that price per unit sold and the variable cost per unit do not change. Only the level of output changes. Also, notice that FC does not change with sales and, hence, is excluded from the second equation.

The degree of operating leverage was defined in Equation 16.A1 as

$$DOL = \frac{\%\Delta EBIT}{\%\Delta S}.$$

The definitions of EBIT and change in EBIT are substituted into Equation 16.A1 and the variables rearranged:

(footnote continued on page 490)

How Equation 16.A2 may be applied is illustrated by the following example. A firm is able to sell a unit of output for \$5.00. Each unit has a variable cost of \$3.00, and the filed costs of operation are \$1,000. What is the degree of operating leverage at 1,000 units? (Notice that the degree of operating leverage is computed at a *given level of sales or output*.) By substituting the numbers into Equation 16.A2, the degree of operating leverage is

$$DOL = \frac{1{,}000(\$5 - \$3)}{1{,}000(\$5 - \$3) - \$1{,}000} = 2.$$

The number 2, then, indicates that if the firm increases output by 10 percent, operating income will rise by 20 percent. This increase is easily verified, for at 1,000 units the level of operating income is \$1,000.

$$\begin{aligned} TR &= \$5{,}000 \\ -TC &= \underline{\$3{,}000 + \$1{,}000}. \\ \text{Operating income} &= \$1{,}000 \end{aligned}$$

If output is increased by 10 percent to 1,100 units, operating income becomes \$1,200, which is 20 percent higher.

$$\begin{aligned} TR &= \$5{,}500 \\ -TC &= \underline{\$3{,}300 + \$1{,}000}. \\ \text{Operating income} &= \$1{,}200 \end{aligned}$$

This alternative method to determine the degree of operating leverage highlights the importance of fixed costs. The greater the fixed costs, the smaller the denominator in the ratio, and hence the larger the degree of operating leverage. Firms

(*footnote continued from page 489*)

$$DOL = \frac{\%\Delta EBIT}{\%\Delta S} = \frac{\dfrac{\Delta EBIT}{EBIT}}{\dfrac{P \times \Delta Q}{P \times Q}}$$

$$= \frac{\dfrac{P \times \Delta Q - V \times \Delta Q}{P \times Q - V \times Q - FC}}{\dfrac{P \times \Delta Q}{P \times Q}}$$

$$= \left(\frac{P \times \Delta Q - V \times \Delta Q}{P \times Q - V \times Q - FC}\right)\left(\frac{P \times Q}{P \times \Delta Q}\right).$$

Both ΔQ and P are in the numerator and denominator and so can be cancelled as shown, which leaves the DOL as:

$$DOL = \left(\frac{\cancel{\Delta Q}(P - V)}{Q(P - V) - FC}\right)\left(\frac{\cancel{P} \times Q}{\cancel{P} \times \cancel{\Delta Q}}\right) = \frac{Q(P - V)}{Q(P - V) - FC}.$$

with small fixed costs will not have large amounts of operating leverage. For such firms the level of sales necessary to generate profits is small, and fluctuations in earnings with changes in sales are modest. Firms with larger amounts of fixed costs have to produce a larger level of output and sales in order to spread out these costs, but once the firms break even, operating income rises more rapidly with further increases in sales. Such firms have higher degrees of operating leverage.

Substitution of Fixed for Variable Costs

As is explained in the body of this chapter, operating leverage is affected when the firm substitutes fixed costs for variable costs (for example, substitutes equipment for labor). There are two implications of such a change. Both the break-even level of output and the degree of operating leverage may be increased, and the increase in operating leverage implies operating earnings are more variable.

These conclusions may be seen by using the previous simple example. The firm's output sold for \$5, and fixed and variable costs were \$1,000 and \$3 per unit, respectively. Suppose the firm increases fixed costs to \$1,500 but is able to reduce variable costs to \$2.50 per unit. The break-even level of output is changed from

$$Q_B = \frac{\$1{,}000}{\$5 - \$3} = 500 \text{ units}$$

to

$$Q_B = \frac{\$1{,}500}{\$5 - \$2.50} = 600 \text{ units.}$$

The degree of operating leverage is also increased. At 1,000 units the degree of operating leverage was

$$DOL = \frac{1{,}000(\$5 - \$3)}{1{,}000(\$5 - \$3) - \$1{,}000} = 2,$$

and now it is

$$DOL = \frac{1{,}000(\$5 - \$2.50)}{1{,}000(\$5 - \$2.50) - \$1{,}500} = 2.5.$$

The higher degree of operating leverage means that if the firm were to increase output by 10 percent, operating income would increase by 25 percent, while previously operating income would have risen by only 20 percent.

These percentage responses in operating income are verified by the following income statements. Case A gives operating income at 1,000 units sold, while B and C present operating income after a 10 percent increase in sales from \$5,000 to \$5,500. Case B assumes no change in operating leverage, but case C assumes fixed costs have been substituted for variable costs.

	A	B	C
Total revenue	$5,000	$5,500	$5,500
Variable costs	3,000	3,300	2,750
Fixed costs	1,000	1,000	1,500
Operating income	$1,000	$1,200	$1,250

Case C shows the effect of substituting fixed for variable costs. When sales rose 10 percent, operating income rose 25 percent from $1,000 to $1,250. The firm used more operating leverage (DOL = 2.5 in C versus 2.0 in B), which produced a larger increase in operating income.

If sales had fallen, the use of more operating leverage would have produced a larger decline in operating income. If sales were to decline to $4,500 (a 10 percent decline), operating income would fall to $800 in B but to $750 in C. This indicates that operating leverage magnifies the swings in earnings in both directions, as sales either rise or fall.

THE DEGREE OF FINANCIAL LEVERAGE

Operating leverage is one means for management to increase the firm's profitability. Regardless of how the firm's assets are financed, the use of fixed costs instead of variable costs increases the firm's potential profitability.

Financial leverage is also a means to increase the return to the firm's owners. By using debt financing instead of equity financing, management may be able to magnify the return on the owners' funds invested in the firm. As with operating leverage, the use of financial leverage increases the variability of the firm's net earnings and increases risk.

DEGREE OF FINANCIAL LEVERAGE
Measure of the responsiveness of net earnings to changes in operating income (EBIT)

Earlier it was shown how the use of debt financing was measured by the debt ratio (debt/total assets). This ratio measures the extent to which the firm uses financial leverage but does not indicate the volatility of the firm's earnings that results from the use of debt financing. This variability may be measured by the **degree of financial leverage.** The degree of financial leverage, like the degree of operating leverage, is a measure of responsiveness. It measures the responsiveness of net earnings to changes in operating income at a given level of output (or revenues). While the degree of operating leverage is defined as the percentage change in operating income divided by the percentage change in output (or sales), the degree of financial leverage (DFL) is the percentage change in net earnings divided by the percentage change in operating income. This relationship is expressed in Equation 16.A3.

16.A3

$$\text{Degree of financial leverage} = \frac{\text{Percentage change in net earnings}}{\text{Percentage change in earnings before interest and taxes}}.$$

The larger the numerical value of the degree of financial leverage, the more responsive are net earnings to changes in operating income. If the numerical value is 2, that means a 10 percent change in the firm's operating income results in a 20 percent change in its net income. If the ratio were only 0.5, a 10 percent change in operating income would produce only a 5 percent change in the firm's net income.

The degree of financial leverage may be computed by using the formula presented in Equation 16.A4.[3]

$$DFL = \frac{\text{Operating income}}{\text{Operating income} - \text{Interest}} = \frac{EBIT}{EBIT - 1}. \tag{16.A4}$$

How this equation works may be illustrated by continuing the example used earlier to demonstrate the degree of operating leverage. The firm had total revenues of \$5,000, variable costs of \$3,000, and fixed costs of \$1,000. The operating income

[3]Equation 16.A4 may be derived as follows:

$$\text{Net earnings} = (\text{Operating income} - \text{Interest})(1 - \text{Tax rate})$$

$$E = (EBIT - I)(1 - t)$$

in which E is net earnings, $EBIT$ is operating income, I is interest, and t is the tax rate. At a given level of output (and the degree of financial leverage, like the degree of operating leverage, is computed at a given level of output), there is no change in interest, so change in earnings is

$$\Delta E = (\Delta EBIT)(1 - t).$$

The degree of financial leverage was defined as:

$$\frac{\text{Percentage change in net earnings}}{\text{Percentage change in } EBIT}.$$

Thus,

$$DFL = \frac{\dfrac{\Delta E}{E}}{\dfrac{\Delta EBIT}{EBIT}}$$

$$= \frac{\dfrac{(\Delta EBIT)(1 - t)}{(EBIT - I)(1 - t)}}{\dfrac{\Delta EBIT}{EBIT}}$$

$$= \left(\frac{(\cancel{\Delta EBIT})(\cancel{1 - t})}{(EBIT - I)(\cancel{1 - t})}\right)\left(\frac{EBIT}{\cancel{\Delta EBIT}}\right)$$

$$= \frac{EBIT}{EBIT - I}$$

was $1,000 and the degree of operating leverage was 2. None of this information, however, considers how the firm financed its assets. It could have used 100 percent equity or a combination of debt and equity, in which case it employed financial leverage.

Consider the following two simple balance sheets. In case A the firm uses no debt financing, but in the second case one-third of its financing comes from borrowed funds.

A

Assets	$6,000	Liabilities	$0
		Equity	$6,000

B

Assets	$6,000	Liabilities	$2,000
		Equity	$4,000

If the interest rate is 10 percent and the income tax rate is 30 percent, the two income statements are as follows:

	A	B
Revenues	$5,000	$5,000
Expenses	4,000	4,000
Operating income	$1,000	$1,000
Interest	0	200
Before-tax income	$1,000	$ 800
Taxes	300	240
Net income	$ 700	$ 560

The degree of financial leverage at revenues of $5,000 in each case is

A

$$\frac{\$1{,}000}{\$1{,}000 - 0} = 1.$$

B

$$\frac{\$1{,}000}{\$1{,}000 - \$200} = 1.25.$$

These numbers imply that if the firm's operating income increases, there will be a larger increase in net income in case B (in which the firm used financial leverage), because a 10 percent increase in its operating income will produce a 12.5 percent increase in net income. For example, suppose operating income did rise by 10 percent, from $1,000 to $1,100. The net incomes of A and B become:

	A	B
Operating income	$1,100	$1,100
Interest	0	200
Before-tax income	$1,100	$ 900
Taxes	330	270
Net income	$ 770	$ 630

In case A the degree of financial leverage was 1, which indicates that a 10 percent increase in operating income would produce a 10 percent increase in net income. That is exactly what happened. Net income rose from $700 to $770 for a 10 percent increase. However, in case B when the degree of financial leverage was 1.25, the 10 percent increase in operating income produced a 12.5 percent increase in net income. That increase in net income occurred because when operating income rose by 10 percent (from $1,000 to $1,100), income rose from $560 to $630, which is a 12.5 percent increase ($70/$560).

COMBINED FINANCIAL AND OPERATING LEVERAGE

Operating leverage refers to the use of fixed costs to alter operating income, and financial leverage refers to the use of borrowed funds to alter net income. A firm's **total leverage** depends on its combined use of operating leverage and financial leverage. Total leverage, then, is the product of the firm's degree of operating leverage and degree of financial leverage. This total leverage is given by Equation 16.A5 as follows:

TOTAL LEVERAGE
Product of the degrees of operating leverage and of financial leverage

$$\text{Total leverage} = \text{Degree of operating leverage} \times \text{Degree of financial leverage}. \quad \text{16.A5}$$

This concept may be illustrated by continuing the example presented above. At total revenues of $5,000 the firm had a degree of operating leverage of 2 and a degree of financial leverage of 1.25. Thus, its combined leverage is

$$2 \times 1.25 = 2.5.$$

This means that a 10 percent increase in its revenues will produce a 25 percent increase in its net income. Consider the following income statements. In A the initial level of revenue ($5,000) is given. In B that level of output and revenue is increased by 10 percent to $5,500. The last line gives the net income.

	A	B
Total revenues ($5 times quantity of 1,000 in A and 1,100 in B)	$5,000	$5,500
Variable costs ($3 times quantity of 1,000 in A and 1,100 in B)	3,000	3,300
Fixed operating costs	1,000	1,000
Operating income	$1,000	$1,200
Interest expense	200	200
Before-tax income	$ 800	$1,000
Taxes	240	300
Net income	$ 560	$ 700

The combined leverage factor is 2.5, which suggests that a 10 percent increase in sales (revenues) will produce a 25 percent increase in net income. Did net income increase by 25 percent after revenues rose 10 percent from \$5,000 to \$5,500? The answer is yes, because net income rose from \$560 to \$700, which is a 25 percent increase (\$140/\$560).

Management may use either operating leverage or financial leverage, or both, to increase the return on stockholders' investment in the firm. However, either form of leverage may increase risk. The use of operating leverage increases business risk because the firm must meet higher fixed costs to be profitable. The use of financial leverage increases financial risk because the firm must meet the interest payments associated with debt financing. Some firms may use a substantial amount of operating leverage but very little financial leverage. For example, IBM has considerable investment in plant and equipment but only a modest amount of debt. Other firms may use a substantial amount of financial leverage but little operating leverage. Most banks (for instance, Citibank) use a large amount of financial leverage, since their deposits represent claims (liabilities), but these firms may have little operating leverage.

It is generally not wise to use a large amount of both financial and operating leverage. Any firm that has a substantial amount of fixed equipment that has been financed with borrowed funds has both operating and financial leverage. The use of both sources of leverage increases the risk exposure of the firm. That is perhaps why airlines are considered among the riskiest of firms. Many airlines have used a substantial amount of debt to buy planes and have both financial and operating leverage. It is not surprising to find many airlines experiencing large swings in earnings from year to year, as their use of both operating and financial leverage increases the fluctuations in their net income (see, for example, the UAL experience that began Chapter 16).

PROBLEMS

1. A firm has the following cost and revenue functions:

$$TR = PQ = \$4Q.$$
$$TC = FC + VC = \$3{,}000 + \$3Q.$$

a. What is the break-even level of output?
b. If the level of output is 5,000 units, what is the degree of operating leverage?
c. If the output increases to 10,000 units, what happens to the degree of operating leverage?
d. If the firm changes its costs so that the new cost schedule is $TC = \$5{,}000 + \$2.5Q$, what happens to (1) the break-even level of output and (2) the degree of operating leverage of 5,000 and 10,000 units of output?

2. The Willie Feed Company sells 30-pound sacks of oats for \$10 each. Variable costs of production are \$4 per sack and annual fixed costs are \$50,000.
a. What is the break-even level of output in units and in dollars?
b. Calculate the firm's operating income (*EBIT*) for 5,000, 10,000 and 15,000 units.
c. What are the level of earnings and the degree of operating income at sales of 12,000 units?

d. If sales rise by 10 percent from 12,000 units to 13,200 units, what is the new level of earnings? Is that consistent with the degree of operating leverage in part c?

e. If fixed costs had been \$25,000, what are earnings and the degree of operating leverage at 12,000 units sold? If sales rise to 13,200 units, what is the firm's profit?

3. A firm in the 30 percent income tax bracket has a capital structure consisting of \$400,000 in 12 percent debt and 5,000 shares of common stock.

a. Calculate the earnings per share (EPS) and the degree of financial leverage for operating income (*EBIT*) of \$75,000. Based on the degree of financial leverage, what would be the percentage increase in earnings per share if *EBIT* rose by 33.3 percent to \$100,000? Confirm your answer by calculating the new EPS.

b. How would the degree of financial leverage differ if the firm had only \$200,000 in 12 percent debt? Why is the degree of financial leverage lower?

4. LisaJ Manufacturing, Inc. reported the following income statement.

Earnings for the Period 1/1/X0 through 12/31/X0	
Sales (50,000 units at \$40)	\$2,000,000
Variable costs (50,000 units at \$22)	1,100,000
Fixed costs	250,000
Operating income	650,000
Interest expense	150,000
Earnings before taxes	500,000
Taxes (35 percent tax rate)	175,000
Net earnings	\$ 325,000

a. Calculate
(1) the break-even level of output in units and sales.
(2) the degree of operating leverage at sales of \$2,000,000.
(3) the degree of financial leverage at sales of \$2,000,000.
(4) total leverage at sales of \$2,000,000.

b. If management expects sales to increase 10 percent to \$2,200,000, what should be the increase in operating income forecasted by the degree of operating income? The increase in net earnings forecasted by total leverage?

c. Confirm the increases in operating income and net earnings by constructing a new income statement for sales of 55,000 units.

5. You are starting a new firm to make pumpkin-seed poppers and anticipate selling these appliances for \$20 each. Fixed costs associated with the operation are \$345,000 and the variable costs are \$13 a unit.

a. What is the level of output necessary to break even?

b. What is the degree of operating leverage at 60,000 units of output?

c. If sales decline from 60,000 units to 54,000 units (a 10 percent decline), by how much should operating income decline?

d. Confirm your answer to part c by calculating operating income for sales of 60,000 and 54,000 units. Did operating income decline by the percentage you expected?

6. Firm A has $10,000 in assets entirely financed with equity. Firm B also has $10,000 in assets, but these assets are financed by $5,000 in debt (with a 10 percent rate of interest) and $5,000 in equity. Both firms sell 10,000 units of output at $2.50 per unit. The variable costs of production are $1, and fixed production costs are $12,000. (To ease the calculation, assume no income tax.)

a. What is the operating income (*EBIT*) for both firms?

b. What are the earnings after interest?

c. What are the degree of operating leverage, degree of financial leverage, and total leverage associated with each firm?

d. If sales increase by 10 percent to 11,000 units, by what percentage will each firm's earnings after interest increase? Verify your answer by determining the earnings before taxes and computing the percentage increase in these earnings from the answers you derived in part b.

CHAPTER 17
Capital Budgeting

Learning Objectives

1. Distinguish between an investment's profit and its cash flows.
2. Determine an investment's payback period, net present value, and internal rate of return.
3. Compare net present value and internal rate of return.
4. Describe the reinvestment assumption employed by the net present value and internal rate of return methods of capital budgeting.
5. Define *mutually exclusive investment* and be able to select among mutually exclusive investments.

According to Henry David Thoreau, "Goodness is the only investment that never fails." Unfortunately, many financial managers know from experience that some investments do fail. In the view of Sir William Gilbert and Sir Arthur Sullivan, however, "Nothing venture, nothing win." This is, of course, the dilemma facing financial managers. They must seek profitable long-term ventures to assure the firm's survival, but they simultaneously run the risk of failure.

In Chapter 16, break-even analysis was used to determine what levels of sales were necessary to avoid losses. While this information can be useful (especially to small businesses), it does not answer the important question: Should a specific long-term investment in plant or equipment be made? And management of virtually every firm, large or small, must answer that question. During 1998, Exxon committed $8.4 billion to additional plant and equipment. Even Clifton Forge–Waynesboro Telephone with revenues of $66 million (less than 1.0 percent of Exxon's sales) increased its investment in plant and equipment by $16.7 million.

The managements of both firms had to decide which long-term investments to make. This selection process is capital budgeting. Capital budgeting answers such questions as: (1) Should an old machine be replaced with a new machine? (2) Should the level of operation of the firm be expanded by purchasing new plant and equipment? or (3) Which of two competing new machines should the firm purchase? These decisions are crucial to the life and profitability of the firm. Since capital budgeting techniques aid in this decision-making process, they are crucial to increasing the wealth of the firm and its stockholders.

This chapter and the next are concerned with the methods of capital budgeting. Chapter 17 presents the basics and Chapter 18 provides applications and extends the analysis by including risk adjustments. Initially the discussion is directed to the determination of the appropriate cash inflows and outflows from an investment. The chapter goes on to describe the payback period, which is a simple method for selecting plant and equipment based on how long it takes to recoup the investment's cost. The bulk of Chapter 17 describes and illustrates the net present value and internal rate of return methods of capital budgeting. All the illustrations use simple numbers. Although few investments cost $1,000 or generate cash inflows from an annuity that provides $400 a year for four years, such examples will facilitate the explanation.

The chapter then explores using net present value and internal rate of return to choose between mutually exclusive investments. Although net present value and internal rate of return often result in the same ranking of competing investments, the possibility of different rankings does exist. The chapter ends with a discussion of what may cause conflicting rankings and how they may be resolved.

VALUATION AND LONG-TERM INVESTMENT DECISIONS

The process for investing in plant and equipment is essentially the same as that for investing in securities. In Chapter 9, the current value of a bond was determined by discounting the future interest payments and principal repayment by the yield on comparable debt instruments. In Chapter 11, future dividend payments and the growth in the firm's dividend were discounted back to the present by the required return to determine the value of a stock. Both models are illustrations of discounted cash flows: Future cash inflows are discounted back to the present and compared with the cost (cash outflows) necessary to make the investment.

An investment in plant and equipment is conceptually no different than an investment in a stock or bond. (Some companies do invest in the stock of other companies in preference to investing in plant and equipment.) Investments in plant and equipment require management to estimate future cash inflows, discount them back to the present at the firm's cost of capital, and compare this present value with the cost of making the investment. This process of determining the value of investment in plant and equipment and selecting among various long-term investments is referred to as **capital budgeting.**

CAPITAL BUDGETING
The process of selecting long-term investments, primarily plant and equipment

Although an investment in plant and equipment may conceptually be the same as an investment in a long-term financial asset, there are important differences. Valuing and buying or selling existing securities transfer existing wealth. The buyer gives cash for the security and the seller receives cash for the security. There is a transfer of assets between the two participants. Many investments in plant and equipment, however, *create new wealth.* The new plant and equipment will be used to create new products and services. If these new products are profitable, they should increase the value of the firm. That is, the creation of new wealth by the firm translates into a higher price for its stock.

Some of these investments are obvious, such as supporting research to develop new products or acquiring new plant and equipment to expand output and enter new markets for existing products. Capital budgeting techniques, however, are also applied to such decisions as whether to replace existing plant and equipment before the end of their useful life or whether to refund a bond issue prior to maturity. (Both of these are illustrated in the next chapter.) In some cases, such as the acquisition of an office building or corporate headquarters, long-term investment decisions must be made even though no specific product may be generated by or identified with the investments.

Occasionally, long-term investment decisions are beyond the control of the financial manager. Installing pollution control equipment required by environmental legislation or meeting new safety standards require mandatory investments by the firm. The choice is not whether to make the investment but which of the competing means to employ. Of course, the firm could cease the operation and thereby avoid making the required investment, but in many cases that is not a realistic option. Car manufacturers are not going to cease building cars to avoid making an investment in equipment that installs a newly required safety improvement.

Some long-term investments rapidly generate returns; others require years to develop and then may never generate a profit. For example, a pharmaceutical company may spend a large amount on research that never succeeds. Merck in its 1998 annual report stated that its long-term growth would come through its commitment to research and that the firm was developing some promising drugs. Such commitment requires current cash outflows. Presumably, Merck's management must determine which of the drugs being developed are potentially the most profitable and will contribute to the growth of the firm and increase the value of Merck's stock.

IMPORTANCE OF CASH FLOW

All investments involve costs. In some cases, these cash outflows may be readily identifiable. When Hertz acquires new cars, their cost is known. Other cash outflows associated with the investment may not be so readily identifiable. Will Hertz have to invest in additional storage and maintenance facilities? Will it have to open additional rental outlets? Will it have to hire more employees and invest in their training? These cash outflows associated with the new cars could be substantial and convert what on the surface appears to be a profitable investment into a money-losing proposition.

In addition to identifying and quantifying cash outflows, the financial manager must estimate the investment's cash inflows. For investments that produce existing products, such estimates may be relatively easy. New products, however, or proposals to enter new markets require estimates of sales and expenses that are not readily available. These estimates are susceptible to built-in biases. If management desires to enter a new field, it may make overly optimistic estimates of future cash flows. The history of business is replete with illustrations of firms entering new markets, taking a beating, and retreating. RCA started to manufacture computers in direct competition with IBM, and Midway Airlines entered the Philadelphia market in direct competition with USAir. Both decisions were probably made after much discussion and analysis of anticipated cash flows. Both failed.

The statement of cash flows was discussed in Chapter 12, and, in Chapter 15, noncash depreciation expense was added back to earnings to determine cash flow from operations. (Depletion, which occurs as natural resources are used, and amortization, which is the process of allocating the cost of an intangible or nonphysical asset, are also noncash expenses that contribute to the firm's cash flow.) Notice that the emphasis is not on accounting earnings. Depreciation (and depletion and amortization expenses), the deferral of income taxes from the current accounting period to another, or a change in current assets, such as an increase in accounts receivable or inventory, affect cash flows. It is the investment's impact on these cash flows that is important for the decision to invest in a long-term asset.

Consider the following situation, in which the financial manager must decide whether to acquire new equipment that costs $50,000 and requires an outlay of $5,000 to install. To make the decision, the financial manager must determine the cash flow generated by the investment. The $5,000 installation charge is a current cash outflow that is recaptured over the same five years that the equipment is depreciated. Estimated annual operating earnings generated by the equipment are $17,200 before the annual depreciation expense. In addition, the firm's investment in inventory rises by $2,000 and its accounts receivable increases by $3,000. These increases in inventory and accounts receivable require additional funds. In the fifth year the inventory and accounts receivable are restored to their current levels (in other words, before the investment in the equipment). At that time the equipment is removed at a cost of $4,500. If the income tax rate is 20 percent, what are (1) the accounting earnings and (2) the cash flow generated by the investment?

The answers to these two questions for years 1, 2 through 4, and 5 are as follows:

	Year 1	Years 2–4	Year 5
Determination of earnings:			
Earnings before depreciation and taxes	$17,200	$17,200	$17,200
Depreciation	10,000	10,000	10,000
Depreciation of installation expense	1,000	1,000	1,000
Removal expense	0	0	4,500
Taxable income	6,200	6,200	1,700
Taxes (20%)	1,240	1,240	340
Net income	$4,960	$4,960	$1,360
Determination of cash flows:			
Net income	$4,960	$4,960	$1,360
Depreciation	10,000	10,000	10,000
Depreciation of installation expense	1,000	1,000	1,000
Change in inventory and accounts receivable	(5,000)	0	5,000
Cash flow	$10,960	$15,960	$17,360

The earnings are $4,960 per year in years 1 through 4 and $1,360 in year 5, but the cash flows are $10,960 in year 1, $15,960 per year in years 2 through 4, and $17,360 in year 5. How can the earnings and cash flows be so different?

In each year, operating income was reduced by the depreciation of both the equipment and installation expense, which had been capitalized.[1] (In reality, the installation expense would be added to the cost of the equipment to determine the depreciable base and that amount would be spread over the time period. This presentation, however, illustrates that depreciation includes other costs associated with putting the equipment into use, such as commissions and installation expenses.) These expenses are noncash expenses that reduce income for tax purposes. Notice also that there is a removal expense in year 5. Since that occurs at the end of the investment's life, it is not depreciated; it is expensed, which reduces taxable income in the fifth year. It is possible for the opposite to occur: The equipment is sold and cash is received. (If the sale is for more than the asset's book value, the sale also increases taxable income and taxes.)

The net income in years 1 through 5 does not represent cash. Cash flow is determined by adding back the noncash expenses and making any other adjustments that generate or consume cash. In each year, the $11,000 in noncash expenses are added back to net income. (Remember that the cash outflow occurred when the equipment was purchased and the installation costs were paid.) Adding back noncash expenses increases the cash flow generated by the investment. Conversely, in year 1, the investment requires an increase in inventory and accounts receivable. These increases are cash outflows that reduce the investment's cash flow in year 1. However, when inventory and accounts receivable are reduced in year 5 to their former levels, cash is released. The reductions in inventory and accounts receivable are sources of funds that contribute to the investment's cash flow in year 5.

The difference between net income and the cash flow is immediately obvious from a comparison of the two bottom lines. An investment of $55,000 ($50,000 to buy the equipment plus $5,000 in installation expense) generates $4,960 in profits in years 1 through 4 and only $1,360 in year 5. That does not appear to be an attractive investment—$55,000 to generate less than $5,000 in profits for each of the five years. However, the same investment generated $10,960 in cash in year 1, $15,960 in years 2 through 4, and $17,360 in year 5. The firm more than earns back the initial $55,000 cash outlay. From this perspective, the investment looks more attractive.

Just because the investment now looks more attractive is not justification to make it. Instead, the financial manager should apply one or more of the following methods of capital budgeting to determine if the investment constitutes a wise use of the firm's scarce resource, its capital.

PAYBACK PERIOD

The **payback period** determines how long it takes for an investment's cash flow to recoup the cost (the cash outflow) of the investment. For example, in the previous illustration, the investment in equipment required an initial cash outlay of

PAYBACK PERIOD
Period of time necessary to recoup the cost of an investment

[1] To simplify the illustration, the requirement that depreciation not start until after six months have passed (the "half-year" convention) is ignored.

$55,000. The cash inflows of $10,960 in year 1 and $15,960 in years 2 through 4 recouped the initial cash outflow in slightly less than four years. If four years are an acceptable period of time to recover the initial cost (and the determination of what is an acceptable time period is subjective), the investment is made.

The payback period may also be used to rank alternative investments. The more rapidly the initial money is returned, the more desirable the investment. If four $1,000 investments have the following cash inflows:

Year	A	B	C	D
1	$250	$334	$400	$100
2	250	333	300	200
3	250	333	200	300
4	250	—	100	400
5	250	—	—	—

investment B would be preferred since it recoups the $1,000 in three years while the other investments take four years.

Obviously, the payback method is a simple means to rank alternatives and select investment projects. There are many flaws in the technique, but it is better to use the payback method than to make long-term investment decisions without using any capital budgeting techniques. The inability to predict accurately the future suggests that emphasizing the near future may be a desirable, or at least pragmatic, means to select among investment alternatives.

The criticisms of the payback method illustrate why other capital budgeting techniques are superior. The weaknesses criticized include the following: (1) the cost of capital (or interest factor) is omitted, (2) the timing of the cash flow is ignored, and (3) cash inflows after the payback period are disregarded. Each of these weaknesses will be discussed briefly. How these limitations may be overcome will be subsequently examined in the sections on the net present value and internal rate of return methods of capital budgeting.

Neglecting to consider the cost of capital means that alternative uses of the money are ignored. The firm must raise funds to acquire an investment, and these funds have a cost, the cost of capital. An investment should be able to earn a return sufficient to compensate investors for the use of their capital. Since the payback period is concerned only with recouping the investment's cost, it says nothing about the investment's return.

This weakness is compounded when the other weaknesses are considered. Consider investments C and D in the table. The payback method's inability to differentiate the timing of the cash flows means that, if strictly applied, the method cannot distinguish between investment C's and investment D's cash flows. Both have payback periods of four years. Of course, C is superior, since the cash inflow in the early years is greater, which provides money that can be reinvested elsewhere.

The third limitation is that payback does not consider cash inflows received after the payback period. The failure to consider cash flows after the payback period results in selecting investments B, C, and D before A. Common sense indicates that A is superior. B, C, and D only recoup the $1,000 cost. They offer no profit. An investment must generate cash flow after the payback period to be profitable, and even then the investment might not be selected when the cost of capital is used in the analysis.

Although the payback method is consistently criticized, it is nevertheless used, because (1) it is readily understood, (2) it is easy to apply, and (3) it avoids making projections into the more distant future. The more uncertain the future, the stronger may be the case for use of the payback method. Thus, while the payback method has little support on theoretical grounds, it has support on pragmatic grounds. It is easy to perform and places the emphasis on the immediate return of the cost of the investment. The small businessperson may simply lack the time, knowledge, or capacity to do more sophisticated types of capital budgeting.

INTRODUCTION TO DISCOUNTED CASH FLOWS METHODS OF CAPITAL BUDGETING

Two alternatives to the payback method are net present value (NPV) and internal rate of return (IRR). Both are discounted cash flows techniques. Future cash flows are brought back to the present; that is, discounted. Both methods overcome the weaknesses associated with the payback method, for both techniques explicitly use the time value of money and all the cash flows generated by an investment. Both techniques recognize that (1) investment decisions are made in the present, (2) the cash inflows are generated in the future, and (3) the cash inflows must be compared to the investment's cash outflows required to make the investment.

Net present value and internal rate of return use the same essential information but process it in different ways. **Net present value (NPV)** discounts future cash inflows at the firm's cost of capital to determine the present value of the investment. This present value is then compared to the present cost (cash outflows) of making the investment. **Internal rate of return (IRR)** determines the return that equates the present value of the cash inflows and the cash outflows of the investment. This return is then compared to the cost of capital necessary to make the investment.

NET PRESENT VALUE (NPV)
Present value of an investment's cash flows minus the cost of the investment

INTERNAL RATE OF RETURN (IRR)
Rate of return that equates the present value of an investment's cash flows with the cost of making the investment

Although the two techniques are similar, there is one essential difference: the treatment of the discount factor that each employs. This difference may be important when the two techniques give conflicting signals as to which investments should be selected. Although this conflict may not occur, the possibility does exist and will be illustrated in the section devoted to selecting between mutually exclusive investments.

The initial discussion, however, will be devoted to explaining and illustrating net present value and internal rate of return. Several symbols will be used:

- C: the investment's cost (cash outflows)
- $CF_1, CF_2, \ldots CF_n$: the cash inflows generated by the investment in years one, two, and on through the last year (n)
- n: the number of years in which the investment generates cash flow

- *PV*: the present value of the investment's cash inflows
- *NPV*: the net present value (*PV* minus *C*)
- *k*: the firm's cost of capital
- *r*: the investment's internal rate of return

The cash inflows and number of years are estimated, so these payments cannot be known with certainty. Initially, the discussion will avoid the question of risk; no adjustment is made for riskier investments. The inclusion of risk is discussed in the next chapter.

NET PRESENT VALUE

The net present value technique of capital budgeting determines the present value of the cash inflows and subtracts from this present value the cost of the investment. The difference is the net present value. This process is illustrated by the following example. A firm is considering an investment that costs $1,000 and has the following estimated cash inflows:

Year	Investment A Cash Inflow
1	$400
2	400
3	400
4	400

Should management make this investment? To answer this question, management needs to know the net present value of the cash flows. To determine the net present value, the firm must know the cost of funds used to acquire the asset (the cost of capital, discussed in Chapter 16). If the cost of capital is 8 percent, the present value of the investment is the sum of the present value of each cash flow. The following illustrates the process of determining the present value of this investment:

CALCULATOR SOLUTION

Function Key		Data Input
FV	=	0
PMT	=	400
I	=	8
N	=	4
PV	=	?
Function Key		*Answer*
PV	=	−1324.85

Year	Cash Inflow	× Interest Factor	= Present Value
1	$400	0.926	$370.40
2	400	0.857	342.80
3	400	0.794	317.60
4	400	0.735	294.00
			Σ = 1,324.80

The individual present values are summed to obtain the present value of the investment. In this case, the present value is $1,324.80. Since the cost of making the investment is $1,000, the net present value (*NPV*) is

$$NPV = \$1{,}324.80 - \$1{,}000 = \$324.80.$$

Since the net present value is positive, the investment is acceptable: It increases the value of the firm and should be made.

This process is applied to all of the firm's investment opportunities to determine their net present values. Suppose the firm is considering the following investments in addition to the one previously discussed:

	Cash Inflows Investment		
Year	B	C	D
1	$295	$250	$357
2	295	150	357
3	295	330	357
4	295	450	357

Management determines the net present value of each investment. The general procedure used for investment A is repeated for each investment. Investments B and D are annuities, and the present value of an annuity table may be used. Investment C, however, is not an annuity; hence, the present value of a dollar table is used.

For investment B the net present value is

$$NPV = \$295(3.312) - \$1{,}000 = \$977 - \$1{,}000 = (\$23).$$

CALCULATOR SOLUTION

Function Key		Data Input
FV	=	0
PMT	=	295
I	=	8
N	=	4
PV	=	?
Function Key		*Answer*
PV	=	−977.08

(3.312 is the interest factor for the present value of an annuity at 8 percent for four years.)

The net present value of Investment B is negative, which means that the firm should not make the investment.

The net present values of investments C and D are ($47) and $182, respectively. (You should verify these results to test your ability to compute an investment's net present value.) These results give the following ranking of all four investments:

Investment	Net Present Value
A	$325
D	182
B	(23)
C	(47)

The firm should make investments A and D (for a total outlay of $2,000) because their net present values are positive. The firm should reject investments B and C because their net present values are negative. Notice that the firm accepts *all* investments whose net present values are positive.

The net present value technique of capital budgeting may be stated in more formal terms. First, determine the present value (PV) by discounting the cash inflow (CF) generated each year by the firm's cost of capital (k). Thus, the present value of an investment is

17.1 $$PV = \frac{CF_1}{(1+k)^1} + \frac{CF_2}{(1+k)^2} + \cdots + \frac{CF_n}{(1+k)^n}.$$

Second, determine the net present value (NPV) of the investment by subtracting the cash outflow (C) of the investment from the present value. That is,

17.2 $$NPV = PV - C.$$

If the net present value is positive, the investment should be made. If the net present value is negative, the firm should not make the investment. The acceptance and rejection criteria for the net present value method of capital budgeting are summarized as follows:

Accept the investment if

$PV - C = NPV > 0.$

Reject the investment if

$PV - C = NPV < 0.$

If the $NPV = 0$, the firm is at the margin. The investment neither contributes to nor detracts from the value of the firm. Management could decide to make or not make the investment.

INTERNAL RATE OF RETURN

The internal rate of return method of capital budgeting determines the rate of return that equates the present value of the cash inflows and the present value of the cash outflows of the investment. This particular rate of return is called the internal rate of return because it is a rate (a percentage) that is unique (internal) to that investment. In effect, the internal rate of return method sets up the following equation:

17.3 $$\text{Present cost} = \text{Present value of the cash inflows.}$$

The method may be illustrated by the same examples used to illustrate the net present value approach. The information for investment A is substituted into the equation for determining present value. That is,

$$\$1{,}000 = \frac{\$400}{(1+r)^1} + \frac{\$400}{(1+r)^2} + \frac{\$400}{(1+r)^3} + \frac{\$400}{(1+r)^4}.$$

Then the equation is solved for the unknown r, the internal rate of return. Since the investment is an annuity, the calculation is easy:

$$\$1{,}000 = \$400 \times \text{interest factor for the present value of an annuity for four years.}$$

Solving for the interest factor (*PVAIF*, ?*I*, 4*N*) gives

$$6400\ (PVAIF,\ ?I,\ 4N) = \$1{,}000$$

$$PVAIF,\ ?I,\ 4N = \$1{,}000/\$400 = 2.50.$$

CALCULATOR SOLUTION

Function Key		Data Input
FV	=	0
PMT	=	400
PV	=	−1000
N	=	4
I	=	?
Function Key		*Answer*
I	=	21.86

Then, 2.50 must be found in the interest table for the present value of an annuity for four years ($n = 4$). This yields an internal rate of return of approximately 20 percent (21.86 using a financial calculator).

Should the firm make this investment? The answer is yes because the internal rate of return exceeds the firm's cost of capital. This investment's internal rate of return exceeds 20 percent, which is greater than the firm's 8 percent cost of capital. Thus, the investment should be made.

As with the net present value, the financial manager computes the internal rate of return for each investment. For investment B, that is

$$\$1{,}000 = \frac{\$295}{(1+r)} + \frac{\$295}{(1+r)^2} + \frac{\$295}{(1+r)^3} + \frac{\$295}{(1+r)^4}$$

$$\$1{,}000 = \$295/PVAIF,\ ?I,\ 4N$$

$$PVAIF,\ ?I,\ 4N = \$1{,}000/\$295 = 3.389.$$

CALCULATOR SOLUTION

Function Key		Data Input
FV	=	0
PMT	=	295
I	=	−1000
N	=	4
PV	=	?
Function Key		*Answer*
I	=	6.97

Locating 3.389 in the interest table for the present value of an annuity for four years, we find the internal rate of return is 7 percent. Since 7 percent is less than the cost of capital, the investment should not be made.

The internal rates of return for investments C and D are computed in the same manner. Since investment D is an annuity, its internal rate of return may be computed in the same manner as those of investments A and B, and its internal rate of return is 16 percent. Investment C, however, is not an annuity. Unless you are using a financial calculator that accepts uneven cash inflows or a computer program that computes internal rates of return, you will have to solve the problem through the use of trial and error. Select a rate such as 10 percent and determine the present value of the cash inflows. If this present value equals \$1,000, you have solved for the internal rate of return. That is,

$$\$1{,}000 = \frac{\$250}{(1+0.1)} + \frac{\$150}{(1+0.1)^2} + \frac{\$330}{(1+0.1)^3} + \frac{\$450}{(1+0.1)^4}$$

$$= \$250(0.909) + \$150(0.826) + \$330(0.751) + \$450(0.683)$$

$$= \$227.25 + \$123.90 + \$247.83 + \$307.35 = \$906.33.$$

Since the present value of the cash inflows is less than \$1,000, 10 percent is too large. A lower rate is selected and the process is repeated until the present values of the cash inflows and outflows are equal. That occurs at approximately 6 percent:

$$\$1{,}000 \approx \$250(0.943) + \$150(0.890) + \$330(0.840) + \$450(0.792)$$
$$\approx \$235.75 + \$133.50 + \$277.20 + \$356.40 = \$1002.85.$$

Given these internal rates of return, the ranking of the four investments is

Investment	Internal Rate of Return
A	20%
D	16
B	7
C	6

The firm should make investments A and D because their internal rates of return exceed the firm's cost of capital but should reject investments B and C because their internal rates of return are less than the firm's cost of capital (less than 8 percent). The total cost of these investments is \$2,000, and once again notice that the firm makes *all* investments whose internal rates of return exceed the firm's cost of capital. Like the net present value method of capital budgeting, the internal rate of return assumes that the firm has the funds or can obtain the funds necessary to make all the acceptable investments.

The internal rate of return method of capital budgeting may be summarized in symbolic terms. The internal rate of return is that value, r, that equates

17.4 $$C = \frac{CF_1}{(1+r)^1} + \cdots + \frac{CF_n}{(1+r)^n} = \sum_{t=1}^{n} \frac{CF_t}{(1+r)^t},$$

and the criteria for accepting an investment are

if $r > k$, accept the investment,
if $r < k$, reject the investment.

If $r = k$, once again the firm is at the margin. The investment neither contributes to nor detracts from the value of the firm. Management could decide to make or not make the investment.

While the above are the acceptance criteria, many firms do not accept all investments with an internal rate of return greater than the cost of capital. Instead, they establish a higher rate of return (or **hurdle rate**) that is used as the acceptance criterion for selecting investments. For example, if the cost of capital is 10 percent, the firm may make all investments with an internal rate of return in excess of 15 percent. Such a hurdle rate helps the firm adjust for risk because it excludes the investments with the lowest anticipated internal rates of return.

HURDLE RATE
Return necessary to justify making an investment; often set higher than the firm's cost of capital

NET PRESENT VALUE AND INTERNAL RATE OF RETURN COMPARED

The internal rate of return and net present value methods of capital budgeting are very similar. Both methods use all the cash flows generated by an investment, and both consider the timing of those cash flows. Both methods explicitly incorporate the time value of money into the analysis. When the two methods are compared,

New present value:

$$NPV = \frac{CF_1}{(1+k)^1} + \cdots + \frac{CF_n}{(1+k)^n} - C$$

Internal rate of return:

$$C = \frac{CF_1}{(1+r)^1} + \cdots + \frac{CF_n}{(1+r)^n}$$

the difference is the discount factor. The net present value approach uses the firm's cost of capital to discount the cash inflows. The internal rate of return method determines the rate of return that equates the present value of the cash inflows and the present cost or outflows. The use of different discount factors results in different statements of the acceptance criteria. For the net present value approach, an investment must yield a net present value equal to or greater than zero to be accepted. For the internal rate of return method, the investment's internal rate of return must be equal to or exceed the firm's cost of capital to be accepted.

While the obvious difference between the two techniques is the discount factor and the resulting difference in the statement of the acceptance criteria, the different discount factors have an important and subtle assumption. That assumption involves the reinvestment rate. The net present value technique assumes that funds earned in years one, two, and so on are *reinvested at the firm's cost of capital*. The internal rate of return assumes that the funds earned in years one, two, and so on are *reinvested at the investment's internal rate of return.*

Consider the investment used earlier in the chapter to illustrate both techniques. It had the following cash flows:

Year	Cash Inflow
1	$400
2	400
3	400
4	400

When the cost of capital was 8 percent, the net present value of the investment was determined to be $324.80. The reinvestment assumption requires that the $400 received in year one be invested for the next three years at 8 percent. The

$400 received in year two will be reinvested for the next two years at 8 percent, and the $400 received in year three will be reinvested for one year at 8 percent. If these funds are not reinvested at 8 percent, the net present value will not be $324.80. If the reinvestment rate is higher, the net present value will exceed $324.80; if the reinvestment rate is lower, the net present value will be lower than $324.80.

When the internal rate of return technique was applied to the above cash inflows, the return was calculated to be approximately 22 percent. The reinvestment assumption requires that all the cash inflows be reinvested at that rate. Thus, the $400 received in the first year must be reinvested at 22 percent for the next three years, and the same reinvestment rate is required for each of the subsequent cash inflows. If these reinvested funds earn less than 22 percent, the true internal rate of return is less than 22 percent. If these reinvested funds earn more than 22 percent, the internal rate of return is greater than 22 percent.

In many investment decisions, the actual reinvestment rate is not important. It would not be important in the above illustration if that were the only investment considered by the financial manager. However, when the financial manager must rank investments and select among competing investments (as will be required later in this chapter), the realized reinvestment rate may be crucial to the decision-making process.

If the financial manager cannot determine the rate at which the funds will be reinvested, then there is a strong argument for preferring the net present value technique over the internal rate of return. The assumption that the cash inflows will be reinvested at the firm's cost of capital is a more conservative assumption. Consider the above illustration. The net present value technique assumed the $400 received in the first year would be reinvested at 8 percent, while the internal rate of return required a reinvestment rate of 22 percent. Certainly, it should be easier to reinvest the funds at the lower rate. Furthermore, if no such investment can be found, the cash may always be used to reduce the firm's capital. The $400 cash generated during the first year, for example, could be used to retire some of the debt and equity issued to make the investment. Since these funds cost 8 percent, their retirement means the financial manager is able to save this cost even if he or she is unable to earn more elsewhere.

RANKING INVESTMENT OPPORTUNITIES

In the preceding section, the firm made all investments in which the net present value was positive or those in which the internal rate of return exceeded the firm's cost of capital. Since the firm made all investments that met these criteria, there was no need to rank investments. However, there are circumstances in which the firm will need to rank investments and choose among the alternatives.

MUTUALLY EXCLUSIVE INVESTMENTS
Two investments for which the acceptance of one automatically excludes the acceptance of the other

The need to rank investments occurs when the investments are mutually exclusive. **Mutually exclusive investments** occur when selecting one alternative automatically excludes another investment. For example, when land is used for one type of building, it cannot be used for a different type of structure. Mutually exclusive investments also occur if a number of investments achieve similar results.

Once one of the alternative investments is selected, the others are excluded. Students are well aware of this type of problem. If you select one class at period A, all other classes at that period are excluded. Or, if you select one section of a finance course, all other sections are excluded. These choices are mutually exclusive.

Once mutually exclusive investments exist, it is necessary to rank investment proposals in order to make the most profitable investments first. In some cases such ranking may pose no problem. Consider the following hypothetical investment proposals. Each costs $1,000 and has a net present value and internal rate of return as listed:

New Investment	Net Present Value	Internal Rate of Return
A	$22	19%
B	43	37
C	5	9
D	6	10

A and B are mutually exclusive, and C and D are mutually exclusive. Therefore, B is selected and A is excluded, and D is selected over C. Both the net present value and internal rate of return techniques select B over A and D over C. Notice also that investment D is made but that A is not, even though A has a higher net present value than D. This occurs because the acceptance of B automatically excludes A. The acceptance of D is immaterial to the acceptance of A, because A's acceptance depends on its net present value relative to B and not to any other investment.

In the above example, both the net present value and internal rate of return techniques selected B over A and D over C. The question becomes: Do the two techniques always produce the same rankings? The answer is no. There are two situations in which the rankings may diverge: The timings of the cash flows differ or the costs of the investments differ. These disparities are, of course, immaterial if the investments are independent. The firm may select (or reject) any of the investments. But these differences may be crucial if the firm must select between investments A and B when net present value favors A while internal rate of return favors B. The financial manager, in effect, must favor one of the two methods of capital budgeting for determining which of the two long-term investments to make.

Differences in the Timing of Cash Flows

Consider the following two mutually exclusive investments. Each investment costs $10,000, but the cash inflows occur in different time periods.

CASH INFLOWS

Year	A	B
1	$12,400	—
2	—	—
3	—	$15,609

CALCULATOR SOLUTION

Function Key		Data Input
PV	=	?
FV	=	12,404
PMT	=	0
N	=	1
I	=	10
Function Key		**Answer**
PV	=	−11,276

The cash inflow of investment A is earned quickly, while investment B has a higher dollar cash inflow but takes longer to earn those funds. Since the two investments are mutually exclusive, the firm must choose between the two alternatives. This requires that the financial manager rank the two investments.

The determination of the net present value and internal rate of return for each investment is easy. If the firm's cost of capital is 10 percent, the net present value of each investment is

CALCULATOR SOLUTION

Function Key		Data Input
PV	=	?
FV	=	15,609
PMT	=	0
N	=	3
I	=	10
Function Key		**Answer**
PV	=	−11,727

$$NPV_A = \frac{\$12{,}400}{(1 + 0.1)} - \$10{,}000 = \$12{,}400(0.909) - \$10{,}000$$

$$= \$11{,}272 - \$10{,}000 = \$1{,}272.$$

$$NPV_B = \frac{\$15{,}609}{(1 + 0.1)^3} - \$10{,}000 = \$15{,}609(0.751) - \$10{,}000$$

$$= \$11{,}722 - \$10{,}000 = \$1{,}722.$$

The internal rate of return for each investment is

CALCULATOR SOLUTION

Function Key		Data Input
PV	=	−10,000
FV	=	12,400
PMT	=	0
N	=	1
I	=	?
Function Key		**Answer**
I	=	24

$$\$10{,}000 = \frac{\$12{,}400}{(1 + r_A)} \text{ and } \$10{,}000 = \frac{\$15{,}609}{(1 + r_B)^3}.$$

Solving for r_A for investment A yields:

$$\$12{,}400\ IF = \$10{,}000$$

$$IF = \frac{10{,}000}{12{,}400} = 0.8065 \text{ and } r_A = 24\%.$$

Solving for r_B for Investment B yields:

CALCULATOR SOLUTION

Function Key		Data Input
PV	=	−10,000
FV	=	15,609
PMT	=	0
N	=	3
I	=	?
Function Key		**Answer**
I	=	16

$$\$15{,}609\ IF = \$10{,}000$$

$$IF = \frac{10{,}000}{15{,}609} = 0.6407 \text{ and } r_B = 16\%.$$

A summary of these results is

	Investment A	Investment B
Net present value	$1,272	$1,722
Internal rate of return	24%	16%

Immediately, the financial manager faces a quandary. Investment A has the higher internal rate of return, while investment B has the higher net present value. Which investment is preferable? If the investments were not mutually exclusive, the firm would make both. However, in this case the investments are mutually exclusive, and management must choose between the two alternatives. The question then becomes how to resolve the conflicting signals.

The reconciliation is built around the answer to a second question: What will the firm do with the cash inflow generated by investment A in year one (that is, what is the reinvestment rate)? Certainly the firm will not let these funds sit but will invest them in year two. If the firm selects investment B, it receives the funds in year three and thus cannot reinvest them in years one and two. The choice between investment A and investment B depends on what the firm can do with the cash generated in year one by investment A. In effect, the firm must consider a third investment that starts in year two and is purchased with the funds generated by investment A.

Suppose the firm could reinvest the \$12,400 at 14 percent for the next two years. What is the terminal value of the investment? That is, what is the future value of investment A if the reinvested funds grow annually at 14 percent for two years? The answer is

$$\$12{,}400(1 + 0.14)^2 = \$12{,}400(1.300) = \$16{,}120,$$

CALCULATOR SOLUTION

Function Key		Data Input
PV	=	−12,400
FV	=	?
PMT	=	0
N	=	2
I	=	14
Function Key		*Answer*
FV	=	16,115

in which 1.300 is the interest factor for the compound value of a dollar at 14 percent for two years. If the \$12,400 is reinvested at 14 percent for two years, the terminal value of investment A is \$16,120, which is greater than the final value of investment B (\$15,609). Thus, the conflicting signals from the net present value and internal rate of return methods are resolved. The firm should make investment A because its terminal value (\$16,120) exceeds the terminal value (\$15,609) of investment B.

In the above illustration, the conflict was resolved in favor of investment A. This, however, need not have been the case. Suppose the firm could have invested the \$12,400 received in year one at only 12 percent instead of 14 percent. Would the firm still have selected investment A? The answer is no, because at 12 percent the \$12,400 would grow to only

$$\$12{,}400(1 + 0.12)^2 = \$12{,}400(1.254) = \$15{,}549.60.$$

CALCULATOR SOLUTION

Function Key		Data Input
PV	=	−12,400
FV	=	?
PMT	=	0
N	=	2
I	=	12
Function Key		*Answer*
PV	=	15,555

If the cash inflow is reinvested at 12 percent, the terminal value of investment A is \$15,549.60, which is smaller than investment B's terminal value (\$15,609). Thus, investment B would be selected.

As these illustrations demonstrate, reconciling the conflict between the net present value and the internal rate of return depends on what the firm can do with the cash inflows that it earns in the early years of an investment's life. If the firm has alternatives that offer high returns, the choice will be the investment with the higher initial cash inflows even though it may have the lower net present value. The lower net present value is offset by the returns earned when the cash is reinvested at profitable rates. The converse is true when the initial cash inflows are reinvested at less profitable rates. Then, the funds earned through reinvesting are not sufficient to justify making the investment with the lower net present value, and thus the conflict is resolved in favor of the investment with the higher net present value but longer time horizon.

This general conclusion is illustrated in Figure 17.1, which presents a profile of the net present value of both investments at various costs of capital. If the discount factor is zero percent, then the net present values of investments A and B are \$2,400 and \$5,609, respectively. As the discount factors rise, the net present values fall. If the discount factors are sufficiently high, the net present values fall to zero. This occurs at 24 percent for investment A and 16 percent for investment B. (These discount factors are each investment's internal rate of return. Since the internal rate of return equates the cost of an investment with the present value of its cash inflows, the net present value must equal zero.)

The net present value of investment B exceeds the net present value of investment A as long as the discount factor is less than 12.2 percent.[2] When the discount factor is less than 12.2 percent, the net present value method selects investment B. However, if the discount factor exceeds 12.2 percent, investment A's net present value is higher; therefore, investment A would be preferred. Thus, as long as the discount factor (the firm's cost of capital) exceeds 12.2 percent, the net present value and the internal rate of return give the same ranking: A is preferred to B. However, if the cost of capital is less than 12.2 percent, the two techniques produce a contradictory ranking that raises the reinvestment question. If the reinvestment rate is less than 12.2 percent, investment B is to be preferred; the funds earned through the reinvestment of investment A's earlier cash inflows do not offset investment B's higher net present value.

Differences in Cost

The previous section showed that differences in the timing of cash flows may lead to conflicting rankings of investments by net present value and internal rate of return. The same problem may arise if there is a difference in the cost of two mutually exclusive investments. Consider the following mutually exclusive investments:

[2] The two discount factors are equal when

$$\frac{\$12{,}400}{(1+r)} = \frac{\$15{,}609}{(1+r)^3}$$

$$\frac{(1+r)^3}{(1+r)} = \frac{\$15{,}609}{\$12{,}400}$$

$$(1+r)^2 = 1.2588$$

$$1+r = \sqrt{1.2588}$$

$$r = 1.122 - 1$$

$$r = 12.2\%.$$

FIGURE 17.1

Net Present Value Profiles for Investments A and B

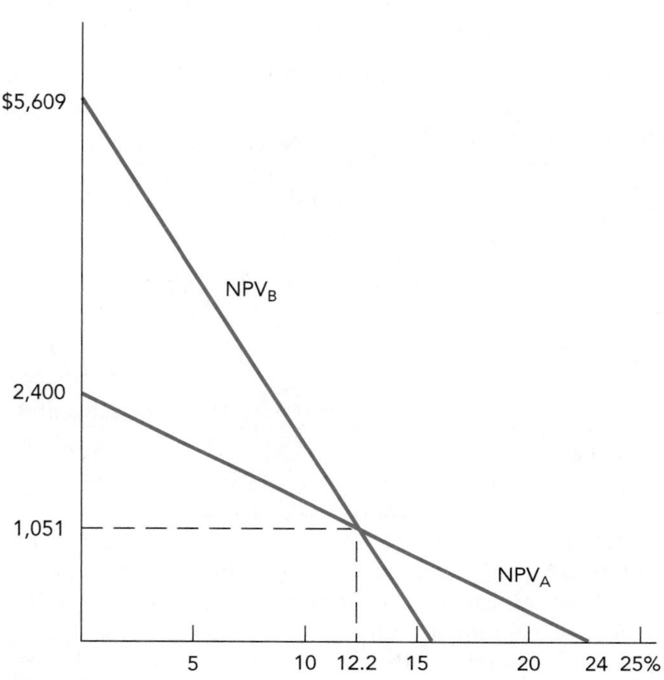

	INVESTMENT	
	A	**B**
Cost	\$1,000	\$600
Cash flow year 1	\$1,150	\$700
Cost of capital: 10 percent		

All the cash inflow occurs in year one but the costs of the investments differ. (In the previous illustration the cash inflows occurred in different years and the costs of the investments were equal.) The net present values of the two investments are

$$NPV_A = \$1{,}150(0.909) - \$1{,}000 = \$45.35.$$

$$NPV_B = \$700(0.909) - \$600 = \$36.30.$$

The internal rate of return for A is

$$\$1{,}000 = \$1{,}150/(1 + r_A)$$

$$1 + r_A = \$1{,}150/\$1{,}000 = 1.15$$

$$r_A = 1.15 - 1 = 0.15 = 15\%.$$

The internal rate of return for B is

$$\$600 = \$700/(1 + r_B)$$

$$1 + r_B = \$700/\$600 = 1.167$$

$$r_B = 1.167 - 1 = 0.167 = 16.7\%.$$

A summary of these results is

	Investment A	**Investment B**
Net present value	$45.35	$36.30
Internal rate of return	15%	16.7%

Once again there is a conflict. The net present value of A exceeds the net present value of B, but their internal rates of return are reversed. B's internal rate of return exceeds A's internal rate of return.

The cause of the conflict is the differences in the amount invested. Investment A costs more, and those additional funds earn 15 percent. These earnings contribute to the investment's net present value, so the *NPV* of A exceeds the net present value of B, even though B earns a higher rate of return on the small amount invested.

The conflict may be resolved by asking what the firm can do with the money it saves by selecting B instead of A. If there were no alternative investment for the $400, the conflict is resolved in favor of A. Even though A's internal rate of return is lower, it is better to invest $1,000 and increase the value of the firm by $45.35 than to invest $600 and increase the value of the firm by $36.30. (Fifteen percent on $1,000 is better than 16.5 percent on $600 and 0 percent on $400.)

Assuming a return of 0 percent is unreasonable, since the firm can always save its cost of capital. (Management can save 10 percent by repurchasing stock and retiring debt.) Therefore, the worst alternative return is not 0 percent but the cost of capital.

If the firm earns 10 percent on $400 and 16.7 percent on $600, the return on $1,000 is a weighted average:

$$(0.4)(10) + (0.6)(16.7) = 14.02\%.$$

Obviously, 14.02 percent is inferior to the 15 percent internal rate of return on investment A, which uses the entire $1,000. If the firm earns 13 percent on $400 and 16.7 percent on $600, the return on $1,000 is

$$(0.4)(13) + (0.6)(16.7) = 15.22\%,$$

in which case combining investment B with the additional investment is superior to investing the entire amount in investment A.

The same conclusion may be seen by using net present value. The net present value of investment B is added to the net present value of the additional investment. For example, if the $400 is invested at 10 percent, the cash inflow at the end of the first year is $440 (the return of the $400 invested plus 10 percent). The net present value of investment B plus the additional $400 investment is

$$NPV = \$700(0.909) + \$440(0.909) - (\$600 + \$400)$$
$$= \$1{,}036 - \$1{,}000 = \$36,$$

which is inferior to the $45 offered by investment A. Earning only 10 percent does not increase the total *NPV* and does not increase the value of the firm. The total is obviously inferior to the $45 offered by investment A.

If, however, the $400 were invested at 13 percent so the cash flow at the end of the year is $452, the net present value of investment B plus the additional $400 is

$$NPV = \$700(0.909) + \$452(0.909) - (\$600 + \$400)$$
$$= \$1{,}047 - \$1{,}000 = \$47.$$

Investment B is now the preferred choice, because its net present value when combined with the net present value of the additional investment is higher than the net present value of all the funds invested in A.

As the previous examples illustrate, the net present value and internal rate of return approaches to capital budgeting are superior to the payback method but are not free from problems. Although in many cases these problems will not arise, they may if the financial manager must select among alternative investments, all of which may be acceptable by themselves. Is there any reason to prefer one technique over the other? The answer is yes. Many individuals prefer the internal rate of return because it may be easier to interpret. Rates of return are frequently used in finance (for example, the yield to maturity on a bond that was discussed in Chapter 9 is an illustration of a rate of return) and many comparisons use percentages (the return on assets or return on equity are expressed as a percentage). This has led many financial managers to be more comfortable with the internal rate of return than with the absolute numbers generated by net present value. However, net present value is the more conservative technique and hence should be preferred.

This conservatism is the result of the reinvestment assumption discussed above. If an investment generates cash flow, the worst case for reinvesting the cash is to return the funds to the firm's sources of finance. The cost of these funds is the firm's cost of capital, so if the financial manager retires some of these sources, he or she is at least meeting the firm's alternative use for the cash. Since net present value assumes that all cash inflows are reinvested at the firm's cost of capital, there is no reason to believe that this assumption will not be met. If the financial manager is able to find even better alternative uses for the cash flow, then such reinvestment should increase the value of the firm.

Such may not be the case when the internal rate of return is used, since that technique assumes that the cash inflows are reinvested at the internal rate of return. Of course, it may be possible to reinvest the cash inflows at a higher rate and realize a higher return, which would, of course, increase the value of the firm. But if the cash flow is invested at a lower rate, the realized return will not be the internal rate of return. If failure to consider the reinvestment rate were to lead to incorrect investment decisions (as was previously illustrated when choosing between mutually exclusive investments), the technique could result in a reduction in the value of the firm.

USING THE INVESTMENT ANALYSIS CALCULATOR

You may use the Investment Analysis Calculator available at **www.harcourt college/finance/mayo** to solve for net present value and internal rate of return. Even though the names "net present value" and "internal rate of return" do not appear in the software, programs under the sections entitled Financial Calculator and Rate of Return (Dollar-Weighted) may be used to determine net present value and internal rate of return.

Since the NPV is the sum of the present value of future cash flows, use the programs that calculate present value. These are Basic Present Value (for the present value of a single payment), Present Value of an Ordinary Annuity, Present Value of an Annuity Due, and Present Value—Unequal Payments. The program that is used depends on the estimated cash inflows. For example, investment A, the first illustration of the calculation of NPV presented in the chapter, is an ordinary annuity of $400 a year. To calculate investment A's present value, use the program for the present value of an ordinary annuity. Enter the nominal rate (the cost of capital of 8 percent), the number of periods per year (1), the number of years (4), and the annuity payment ($400). The program indicates that the present value is $1,324.85. This amount is then subtracted from the $1,000 cost to obtain the net present value ($324.85).

While investments B and D are also ordinary annuities, investment C's cash flows vary each year, which will require using the "Present Value—Unequal Payments." Once again enter the nominal rate (8), the periods per year (1), the number of years (4), and the cash inflows for each period ($250, $150, $330, and $450). The present value is determined ($952.81). This amount is subtracted from $1,000 to obtain ($47.19). Since the net present value is a negative number, the investment should not be made.[3]

To determine an investment's internal rate of return, use the dollar-weighted rate of return programs. (The internal rate of return uses cash inflows and outflows expressed in dollars and the return is weighted by these dollar cash flows.) Investment A (and investments B and D) are ordinary annuities, so the appropriate

[3]Notice that the program also calculates the present value assuming the payments are made at the beginning of each year. If the cash inflows had been received at the beginning instead of the end of the year, the present value would be $1,029.04 and the investment would be made.

program is "Rate of Return, Given PV and a Series of Ordinary Annuity Payments." Enter the present value (the cost of the investment, which is $1,000), the periods per year (1), the number of years (4), and the annuity payment ($400). The program determines the rate of return to be 21.86 percent. This rate is then compared to the firm's cost of capital to determine if the investment should be made. Since the internal rate of return exceeds the cost of capital, the investment should be made.

Investment C's cash flows vary each year, which will require using the "Rate of Return, Given PV and a Series of Unequal Payments at End of Equal Time Periods." Once again enter the present value (the $1,000 initial cash outflow), the periods per year (1), the number of years (4), and the cash inflows for each period ($250, $150, $330, and $450). The program determines that the internal rate is 6.11 percent. This rate is compared to the firm's cost of capital (8 percent) to determine if the investment should be made. Since the internal rate of return is less than the cost of capital, the investment should not be made.

SUMMARY

Capital budgeting is the process for making long-term investment decisions, such as whether to expand plant and equipment. This chapter covered three methods for selecting long-term investments: the payback method, the net present value, and the internal rate of return.

The payback method determines how long it takes the cash inflows to recapture the cost of an investment; those investments with the fastest payback are selected. The net present value (NPV) technique determines the present value of an investment's cash inflows and subtracts the current cash outflows to determine the net present value. If the net present value is positive, the investment is selected. If the financial manager must rank competing investments, those investments with the highest net present value are selected first.

The internal rate of return (IRR) determines the discount factor that equates the present value of an investment's cash inflows and outflows. If this internal rate of return exceeds the firm's cost of capital, the investment should be made. If the financial manager must rank competing investments, those investments with the highest internal rates of return are selected first.

The rankings determined by the net present value and the internal rate of return may conflict. Such conflicts can occur when there are differences in the costs of the investments or differences in the timing of their cash flows. Reconciliation of the conflicts may be achieved by analyzing the reinvestment rates. If the financial manager must choose between the net present value and the internal rate of return techniques, the net present value is to be preferred since it makes the more conservative assumption concerning the reinvestment of cash flow (that is, the cash inflows are reinvested at the firm's cost of capital).

REVIEW QUESTIONS

1. What impact will each of the following have on an investment's net present value?

a. an increase in interest rates
b. an increase in current assets required as part of making the investment
c. an increase in the estimated price at which the equipment may be sold
d. an increase in investors' required return on equity

2. What impact will each of the following have on an investment's internal rate of return?

a. a decrease in the firm's cost of capital
b. an increase in the cost to acquire the investment
c. a switch from straight-line to accelerated depreciation

3. What is the difference between an investment in plant and equipment and an investment in securities? Why does an investment's value rise when interest rates fall?
4. The net present values of two investments are positive, but the investments are mutually exclusive. Should you make both investments? If the investments' internal rates of return were equal, would that affect your previous answer?
5. If an investment's estimated internal rate of return is 16 percent but the firm will not be able to reinvest the investment's cash flow at that rate, what does that imply about the rate of return the firm will earn?
6. Two investments are mutually exclusive and the IRR of investment A exceeds the IRR of B but the NPV of B exceeds the NPV of A. Why does the internal rate of return technique tend to favor the investment with the quicker payback?

PROBLEMS

1. You purchase machinery for $23,958 that generates cash flow of $6,000 for five years. What is the internal rate of return on the investment?
2. The cost of capital for a firm is 10 percent. The firm has two possible investments with the following cash inflows:

	A	B
Year 1	$300	$200
2	200	200
3	100	200

   a. Each investment costs $480. What investment(s) should the firm make according to net present value?
   b. What is the internal rate of return for the two investments? Which investment(s) should the firm make? Is this the same answer you obtained in part a?
   c. If the cost of capital rises to 14 percent, which investment(s) should the firm make?
3. A firm has the following investment alternatives:

CASH INFLOWS

	A	B	C
Year 1	$1,100	$3,600	—
2	1,100	—	—
3	1,100	—	$4,562

Each investment costs $3,000; investments B and C are mutually exclusive, and the firm's cost of capital is 8 percent.

a. What is the net present value of each investment?
b. According to the net present values, which investment(s) should the firm make? Why?
c. What is the internal rate of return on each investment?
d. According to the internal rates of return, which investment(s) should the firm make? Why?
e. According to both the net present values and internal rates of return, which investments should the firm make?
f. If the firm could reinvest the $3,600 earned in year one from investment B at 10 percent, what effect would that information have on your answer to part e? Would the answer be different if the rate were 14 percent?
g. If the firm's cost of capital had been 10 percent, what would be investment A's internal rate of return?
h. The payback method of capital budgeting selects which investment? Why?

4. The chief financial officer has asked you to calculate the net present values and internal rates of return of two $50,000 mutually exclusive investments with the following cash flows:

	Project A Cash Flow	Project B Cash Flow
Year 1	$10,000	$ 0
2	25,000	22,000
3	30,000	48,000

If the firm's cost of capital is 9 percent, which investment(s) would you recommend? Would your answer be different if the cost of capital were 14 percent?

5. A firm's cost of capital is 12 percent. The firm has three investments to choose among; the cash flows of each are as follows:

	Cash Inflows		
	A	B	C
Year 1	$395	—	$1,241
2	395	—	—
3	395	—	—
4	—	$1,749	—

Each investment requires a $1,000 cash outlay, and investments B and C are mutually exclusive.
a. Which investment(s) should the firm make according to the net present values? Why?
b. Which investment(s) should the firm make according to the internal rates of return? Why?
c. If all funds are reinvested at 15 percent, which investment(s) should the firm make? Would your answer be different if the reinvestment rate were 12 percent?

6. Management of Biotech, Inc. is evaluating a new $90,000 investment with the following estimated cash flows:

Year	Cash Flow
1	$10,000
2	25,000
3	40,000
4	50,000

If the firm's cost of capital is 10 percent and the project will require that the firm spend $15,000 to terminate the project, should the firm make the investment?

7. An investment with total costs of $10,000 will generate total revenues of $11,000 for one year. Management thinks that since the investment is profitable, it should be made. Do you agree? What additional information would you want? If funds cost 12 percent, what would be your advice to management? Would your answer be different if the cost of capital is 8 percent?

8. An investor purchases a bond for $949. The bond pays $60 a year for three years and then matures (it is redeemed for $1,000). What is the internal rate of return on that investment? In Chapter 9, what was this return called?

9. Management of a firm with a cost of capital of 12 percent is considering a $100,000 investment with annual cash flow of $44,524 for three years.
   a. What are the investment's net present value and internal rate of return?
   b. The internal rate of return assumes that each cash flow is reinvested at the internal rate of return. If that reinvestment rate is achieved, what is the total value of the cash flows at the end of the third year?
   c. The net present value technique assumes that each cash flow is reinvested at the firm's cost of capital. What would be the total value of the cash flows at the end of the third year, if the funds are reinvested at the firm's cost of capital?
   d. Why does management know that the reinvestment assumption for the net present value method can be achieved but that achieving the reinvestment assumption for the internal rate of return is uncertain?

10. (This problem combines material from Chapters 16 and 17.) The financial manager has determined the following schedules for the cost of funds:

Debt Ratio	Cost of Debt	Cost of Equity
0%	5%	13%
10	5	13
20	5	13
30	5	13
40	5	14
50	6	15
60	8	16

a. Determine the firm's optimal capital structure.
b. Construct a simple pro forma balance sheet that shows the firm's optimal combination of debt and equity for its current level of assets.

Assets	$500	Debt	$
		Equity	—
			$500

c. An investment costs $400 and offers annual cash inflows of $133 for five years. Should the firm make the investment?
d. If the firm makes this additional investment, how should its balance sheet appear?

Assets	Debt	$
	Equity	—

e. If the firm is operating with its optimal capital structure and a $400 asset yields 20.0 percent, what return will the stockholders earn on their investment in the asset?

11. Investments Quick and Slow cost $1,000 each, are mutually exclusive, and have the following cash flows. The firm's cost of capital is 10 percent.

	Cash Inflows	
	Q	S
Year 1	$1,300	$386
2	—	386
3	—	386
4	—	386

a. According to the net present value method of capital budgeting, which investment(s) should the firm make?
b. According to the internal rate of return method of capital budgeting, which investment(s) should the firm make?
c. If Q is chosen, the $1,300 can be reinvested and earn 12 percent. Does this information alter your conclusions concerning investing in Q and S? To answer, assume that S's cash flows can be reinvested at its internal rate of return. Would your answer be different if S's cash flows were reinvested at the cost of capital (10 percent)?

12. A firm has the following investment alternatives. Each one lasts a year.

Investment	A	B	C
Cash inflow	$1,150	560	600
Cash outflow	$1,000	500	500

The firm's cost of capital is 7 percent. A and B are mutually exclusive, and B and C are mutually exclusive.

a. What is the net present value of investment A? Investment B? Investment C?

b. What is the internal rate on investment A? Investment B? Investment C?

c. Which investment(s) should the firm make? Why?

d. If the firm had unlimited sources of funds, which investment(s) should it make? Why?

e. If there were another alternative, investment D, with an internal rate of return of 6 percent, would that alter your answer to part d? Why?

f. If the firm's cost of capital rose to 10 percent, what effect would that have on investment A's internal rate of return?

13. A firm, whose cost of capital is 10 percent, may acquire equipment for $113,479 and rent it to someone for a period of five years.

a. If the firm charges $36,290 annually to rent the equipment, what are the net present value and the internal rate of return on the investment? Should the firm acquire the equipment?

b. If the equipment has no estimated residual value, what must be the minimum annual rental charge for the firm to earn the required 10 percent on the investment?

c. If the firm can sell the equipment at the end of the fifth year for $10,000 and receive annual rent payments of $36,290, what are the net present value and the internal rate of return on the investment? What is the impact of the residual?

d. If the $10,000 residual resulted in the firm charging only $34,290 for the rental payments, what is the impact on the investment's net present value?

14. If the cost of capital is 9 percent and an investment costs $56,000, should you make this investment if the estimated cash flows are $5,000 for years 1 through 3, $10,000 for years 4 through 6, and $15,000 for years 7 through 10?

15. Management of Braden Boats, Inc., is considering an expansion in the firm's product line that requires the purchase of an additional $175,000 in equipment with installation costs of $15,000 and removal expenses of $2,500. The equipment and installation costs will be depreciated over five years using straight-line depreciation. The expansion is expected to increase earnings before depreciation and taxes as follows:

Years 1 and 2	Years 3 and 4	Year 5
$70,000	$80,000	$60,000

The firm's income tax rate is 30 percent and the weighted-average cost of capital is 10 percent. Based on the net present value method of capital budgeting, should management undertake this project?

CASE

Choosing between Long-Term Investment Alternatives

William Still is faced with a dilemma. His firm needs additional storage and production facilities and essentially has two choices. The first is to remodel the existing building and to expand onto vacant land next to the plant. This is the least costly alternative since the building exists and the vacant land is owned. The facility will cost an estimated $25,000,000 and should generate annual cash inflow of approximately $6,500,000 for ten years, after which it will have to be replaced because the current building will need substantial repairs. However, the building may be sold at that time for its book value, $5,000,000.

The second alternative is to build a new facility. This will cost more and require changes in the firm's working capital. In addition, the plant cannot possibly be put into operation for three years while the first alternative could be ready in less than a year. The new plant does, however, offer a major advantage. Its expected life is at least 20 years and perhaps could last 25 years without major repairs. Thus, the decision to build the new plant avoids a major decision after 10 years that will be necessary if the first alternative is chosen.

The estimated cost of the new plant is $64,000,000, plus an increase in current assets of $6,000,000 is expected to result from the larger operation. The estimated cash inflows, starting after three years, are $10,000,000 annually for 20 years at which time the plant may be sold for its book value, $20,000,000. If the plant operates for another five years, the estimated cash inflow drops to $8,000,000 for each of the last five years since repairs will increase. After 25 years it may be sold for its book value, $12,000,000.

Still has to report to the firm's chief operating officer, Vaughan Williams. He knows that Williams has a bias for investments with a short duration, but Still intuitively believes that the new plant is the better alternative. Intuition, however, is insufficient to justify this type of investment; an analysis of each alternative's net present value and internal rate of return is required.

Still decided to determine the net present value for the following alternatives: (1) the expansion of existing facilities, (2a) the new facility assuming cash inflows for 20 years, and (2b) the new facility assuming cash inflows for 25 years. To facilitate the calculations, he assumed that (1) all cash inflows occur at the end of each year, (2) all cash outflows occur immediately, and (3) the increase in working capital is permanent. The firm uses a cost of capital of 9 percent to evaluate typical investments and 10 to 12 percent to judge riskier investments. Still thought the expansion was comparable to the firm's average investment but that the new plant was riskier. He decided to use 10 percent for alternative 2a and 12 percent for alternative 2b.

CASE PROBLEMS

1. What is the net present value of each investment?
2. Would the IRR of alternative 2a exceed the cost of capital?
3. What conclusion may be drawn from this analysis?
4. What is your reaction to Still's using two discount factors to analyze the second alternatives?
5. Are the sale prices for the new plant important to the final decision?

CHAPTER 18
Capital Budgeting: Extensions and Applications

Learning Objectives

1. Differentiate stand-alone and portfolio risk.
2. Explain why cash inflows may be adjusted for the probability of their occurrence.
3. Adjust the firm's cost of capital for the differences in risk associated with long-term investments.
4. Differentiate certainty equivalents from other methods for adjusting an investment's cash flows for risk.
5. Isolate the role that beta coefficients can play in the capital budgeting decision.
6. Isolate the cash flows associated with new and old equipment and determine if the old equipment should be replaced.
7. Resolve if a firm should refinance or refund long-term debt prior to its maturity.

The preceding chapter explained the mechanics of capital budgeting and how discounted cash flow is used to select long-term investments in plant and equipment. This chapter extends the analysis by adding risk and applies the techniques to investment decisions, such as replacing existing equipment before the end of its useful life and refunding existing debt prior to its maturity.

Virtually all investment decisions involve risk. In Exhibit 9.1, differences in risk for bonds were indicated by credit ratings. Lower ratings were associated with higher interest rates as bondholders required a higher return in compensation for additional risk. In Chapters 8 and 11, differences in the volatility of individual stocks were measured by beta coefficients. These betas were used to adjust the returns equity investors required in order to purchase a stock. Individuals who acquired more volatile stock required a higher return to compensate them for the additional risk.

The same concept applies to investments in plant, equipment, and other assets made by the firm. Successful investing in plant and equipment creates wealth and increased the value of the firm. But not all investments are equal with regard to risk. The material on capital budgeting in the previous chapter did not include risk in the analysis. In effect, the discussion assumed that risk was the same for all projects. This is, of course, too restrictive. The cash flows associated with a particular investment may be less certain or more variable than the cash flow associated with an alternative investment.

Integrating the analysis of risk into capital budgeting is the primary thrust of this chapter, which covers means to adjust an investment's cash flows or the cost of capital for risk. Although these adjustments can be difficult to apply, they are a beginning toward the integration of risk into net present value and internal rate of return techniques for selecting investments in plant and equipment.

The chapter ends with two additional applications of net present value. The first is the decision to replace existing equipment before the end of its useful life. The second is the decision to refund a bond issue—that is, to redeem an existing long-term obligation before its maturity date.

THE INTRODUCTION OF RISK INTO CAPITAL BUDGETING

All investments, be they investments in financial assets or in tangible assets, such as plant, equipment, and inventory, are made in anticipation of a return. There are only two sources of return: the income the asset generates or the appreciation that occurs when the asset is sold for more than its cost. When an individual buys a stock and sells it for a capital gain, the investor's wealth is increased. The same concept applies to business. When a firm sells an asset, such as inventory, for more than its cost, the value of the firm is increased. When the firm acquires plant and equipment that generates a positive net present value, the value of the firm is increased.

The return from all investments is earned in the future. But the future is unknown; it is uncertain. In Chapter 8, risk was defined as the possibility of loss, the uncertainty that the expected return will be achieved. This uncertainty permeates financial decisions. An individual purchases a bond with an expected yield to maturity. If the company falls on hard times (for example, Boston Chicken) and defaults on its debt obligations, the investor does not earn the expected return. An individual buys a stock in anticipation of dividend payments and a capital gain. The company is subsequently acquired for a considerable premium over the current price as occurred when Illinois Tool Works bought Premark. Once again the realized return differs from the expected return, but in this case the investor earns a higher return than was originally anticipated when the investment was made.

Concepts concerning risk and return that apply to financial assets also apply to the acquisition of plant and equipment. Investments in plant and equipment are made in the present in anticipation of a return, but the returns are earned in the uncertain future.

In the previous chapter, net present value (NPV) and internal rate of return (IRR) were used to analyze and select long-term investments. In the case of net present value, the future cash flows were discounted back to the present at the firm's cost of capital. The resulting present value was subtracted from the cost of the investment (the initial cash outflow) to determine the NPV. If the NPV was positive, the investment was made because the investment contributed to the value of the firm. In the case of the internal rate of return, the rate that equated future cash inflows to the current cost was compared to the cost of capital. If the IRR exceeded the cost of capital, the investment was made because, once again, the investment increased the value of the firm.

All future cash flows must be projections; they have to be expected values. Although these cash flows are uncertain, the degree of uncertainty differs among alternative investments. In the previous chapter, the applications of net present value and the internal rate of return implicitly assumed that the risk associated with each investment was the same. That is, all cash flows were treated as if they were known; no attempt was made to alter the estimated cash inflows for uncertainty. In addition, the cost of capital was not adjusted for the risk associated with an individual investment.

Some investments, however, are riskier than others, and some investments may be risky by themselves but are not risky when taken in a portfolio context. These investments may actually reduce the firm's risk exposure. Thus the first step for the inclusion of risk into the capital budgeting process is to decide whether a project should be analyzed solely by itself as if it were a stand-alone project that has no impact on the risk associated with the firm or its owners. If an investment is not to be analyzed as a stand-alone project, the financial manager must consider the impact of the investment on the risk exposure of the firm or on the owners. Does the investment reduce the risk associated with the firm? This is, of course, the same consideration an individual makes when adding another security to his or her portfolio: Does the investment diversify the portfolio?

By far it is easier to analyze a project's risk from the stand-alone perspective and avoid asking the question: How does the investment affect the firm's or stockholders' risk? Conceptually, this is incorrect since investments are not made in a vacuum, but in many cases, analysis of the stand-alone risk is sufficient. Many investment projects are small, relative to the firm's total assets, and will have little or no impact on the risk exposure of the firm. For example, if The Limited acquires a centralized warehouse to hold clothing prior to distribution to its stores, this investment may have little, if any, impact on the firm's risk. In addition, new projects are often similar to current operations. These investments offer little potential for diversification and cannot change the firm's or stockholders' risk exposure. For example, if GM builds a new plant for the introduction of a new car (for example, the Saturn), the investment is not different from many existing GM operations. If the specific project is large compared to the firm's typical investment or if the firm is entering a new field, the same observation would not apply, as occurred when GM entered a new field through the acquisition of Electronic Data Systems. In such a case, the financial manager should consider the possible portfolio effects or the impact on the owners' risk.

If the investment is analyzed in portfolio context, the question essentially is this: Does the investment reduce the owners' risk? If investors have constructed well-diversified portfolios, the answer has to be no. The stockholders in many publicly held companies do hold well-diversified portfolios, so the firm's investment in additional plant or equipment in all probability offers little potential for diversification.

If the owners do not hold well-diversified portfolios, the answer could be yes. If the investment reduces the correlation between the return on the company's stock and the return on the other securities held in the individual's portfolio, then the potential for diversification exists. This potential may be especially important for small, closely held (or nonpublic) firms in which the business is the owner's primary asset. A risky investment that reduces the overall risk of the firm could be advantageous because the owner's risk exposure is reduced.

For many firms, the potential for portfolio effects may be ignored simply on pragmatic grounds. Because the financial manager does not know the stockholder's willingness to bear risk or whether they have constructed well-diversified portfolios, it may be impossible to incorporate potential portfolio effects in the analysis of a particular investment. In addition, stockholders may alter their portfolios for changes in risk. If a long-term investment in plant or equipment makes the firm riskier, stockholders may substitute less-risky securities in their portfolios to reduce their risk exposure. Conversely, if the financial manager makes investments that reduce risk and stockholders prefer a riskier strategy, the investors may buy the stock on margin (that is, buy the stock with borrowed funds). Thus, the impact of a firm's particular investment on stockholders may not concern the financial manager since the stockholders can adjust their own portfolios to the level of risk they are willing to accept.

RISK ADJUSTMENTS IN CAPITAL BUDGETING

After deciding to include risk in capital budgeting analysis, the next step is to determine how it may be incorporated into the techniques. Consider the equation for the determination of the new present value:

$$NPV = \frac{CF}{(1+k)^1} + \cdots + \frac{CF_n}{(1+k)^n} - \text{Cost.} \qquad 18.1$$

The investment's cost or cash outflows are known, so the incorporation of risk must either affect the project's estimated cash inflows (the numerator) or affect the cost of capital used to discount the inflows (the denominator). The problem facing the financial manager is how to make the adjustment operational.

If the financial manager is concerned with an investment's stand-alone risk, the emphasis is placed on the variability of the estimated cash inflows. One possible technique, "sensitivity analysis," determines the impact on the cash inflow by altering one variable at a time. The analysis starts with the expected cash inflows and then changes one of the inputs used to determine the cash flows. "What if" the price of the product were increased and all other variables, such as the cost of production, are held constant? What impact would the change have on the investment's estimated cash inflows? The more sensitive the change in the cash inflows to the change in the variable, the greater is the risk associated with the investment. If sales respond to the change in price, then the cash inflows will also respond. Conversely, if revenues are insensitive to changes in price, the estimated cash inflows are more certain and less risky. Similar reasoning is applied to several variables to determine the sensitivity of the net present value to each variable. Sensitivity analysis requires a large number of calculations, but by using a spreadsheet model, the financial manager determines the sensitivity of the net present value to the relevant variables and better understands the risk associated with the investment.

An alternative approach, "scenario analysis," adds the probability of outcomes. It asks not only what will be the impact on the cash inflows and the net present value if variables are changed, but also what is the likelihood of the change. Consider the following investment whose anticipated net present value responds to changes in the economy. The states of the economy, the investment's estimated net present value associated with each state of the economy, and the probability of occurrence are as follows:

State of the Economy	Probability of Occurrence	Net Present Value
Recession	.20	$ 0
No growth	.30	100
Mild growth	.50	300

The expected net present value is an average of each scenario weighted by the probability of occurrence. That is,

$$\text{Net Present Value} = (.20)(\$0) + (.30)(\$100) + (.50)(\$300) = \$180.$$

The variability of the cash inflows is measured by the standard deviation of the cash flows, which is calculated as follows:

(1) Expected *NPV*	(2) Individual *NPV*	(3) Difference (1) − (2)	(4) Difference Squared	(5) Probability of Occurrence	(6) Difference Squared Times the Probability (4) × (5)
$180	$ 0	$180	$32,400	.2	$ 6,480
180	100	80	6,400	.3	1,920
180	300	−120	14,400	.5	7,200
	Sum of the weighted squared differences:				15,600

The standard deviation is the square root of the sum of the weighted squared differences:

$$\sqrt{15{,}600} = 125.$$

The larger the standard deviation, the larger is the variability of the outcome and hence the greater the risk associated with the investment.[1]

[1] The same calculation was illustrated in Chapter 8 on risk measurement.

The standard deviation is an absolute number and should not be compared to the standard deviations of other investments. Comparisons are made by calculating the coefficient of variation, which is the standard deviation divided by the expected value. In this illustration, the standard deviation is 125 and the expected net present value is \$180, so the coefficient of variation is \$125/\$180 = 0.69.

Since the numerical value of the coefficient of variation is a relative number, it may be compared to the same statistic for all investments in order to rank them. Suppose two investments have different net present values (\$100 and \$1,000), and their standard deviations are \$10 and \$20, respectively. The standard deviation of the second investment is larger, but when the standard deviation is expressed relative to the *NPV*, the resulting coefficient is smaller: \$10/\$100 = 0.1 versus \$20/\$1,000 = 0.02. The variability of the second investment is smaller, which indicates more certainty and less risk. An investment's coefficient of variation may also be compared to the coefficient of variation of the firm's typical investment to determine if the specific project is more or less risky than the firm's average investment.

Sensitivity analysis and scenario analysis are means to bring risk into capital budgeting by adjusting an investment's cash inflows. An alternative approach that also adjusts the cash inflow employs "certainty equivalents."

Certainty equivalents attempt to express expected cash inflows as certain cash inflows. For example, suppose a risky \$1,000 investment is expected to pay the following cash flows:

Year	1	2	3
	\$300	\$445	\$568

All the cash inflows are expected and none is certain. An alternative use for the \$1,000 is a three-year \$1,000 U.S. Treasury bond that pays \$100 annually and repays the \$1,000 at maturity. These expected cash flows are as follows:

Year	1	2	3
	\$100	\$100	\$1,100

Because the expected cash inflows are to be paid by the federal government, they are virtually assured and hence are certain.

If the firm's cost of capital is 12 percent and that rate is used to discount the Treasury bond's cash flows, the net present value is

$$\begin{aligned} NPV &= \$100(0.893) + \$100(0.797) + \$1{,}100(0.712) - \$1{,}000 \\ &= \$952.20 - \$1{,}000 = (\$47.80). \end{aligned}$$

The net present value is negative and an investment in the bond will not be made. However, the risky alternative's net present value is

$$\begin{aligned} NPV &= \$300(0.893) + \$445(0.797) + \$568(0.712) - \$1{,}000 \\ &= \$1{,}026.98 - \$1{,}000 = \$26.98. \end{aligned}$$

Because the net present value is positive, the investment would be made.

The decision to make the risky investment and not make the certain investment may not be correct once risk is integrated into the analysis. Because risk has not been considered, the NPVs are not comparable. The question becomes: Can the two sets of cash flows be expressed on a common basis? Certainty equivalents attempt to answer that question.

Suppose the financial manager believes that cash flows from the risky investment are only equivalent to 95 percent of the certain investment and this percentage declines by 5 percent with each subsequent year. From this individual's perspective, the certainty equivalents of the cash flows are

Year	1	2	3
	(0.95)$300	(0.90)$445	(0.85)$568
	$285.00	$400.50	$482.80

After this adjustment to express the cash flows as if they were certain, should the investment be made? Once again the cash flows must be brought back to the present. To determine the present value, a new question arises: What is the appropriate rate to discount the cash flows? The answer cannot be the firm's cost of capital, for that cost encompasses the risk associated with the firm's sources of finance. Instead the appropriate discount rate is the risk-free return, because the cash flows are now considered to be the equivalent of certain cash inflows.

In this illustration, the risk-free, three-year Treasury bond offered 10 percent, so that rate may be applied to the investment's cash inflows that have been expressed in risk-free terms. When 10 percent is applied to the certainty equivalent cash flows, the net present value becomes:

$$\begin{aligned} NPV &= 285.00(0.909) + \$400.50(0.826) + \$482.80(0.751) - \$1{,}000 \\ &= \$952.46 - \$1{,}000 = (\$47.54). \end{aligned}$$

Because the NPV is negative, the investment should not be made.

Although certainty equivalents may be used to adjust the cash flows for risk, it should be obvious that the method has a major problem. How are the certainty equivalents determined? Essentially, the analyst assigns the values. Two financial managers could, and probably would, assign different certainty equivalents and, hence, come to opposite conclusions about the desirability of making the investment. This lack of objectivity is a major weakness in the technique and explains why financial managers may be reluctant to use it.

ADJUSTING THE DISCOUNT RATE

Previously risk was introduced into capital budgeting by adjusting the cash inflows (the numerator in Equation 18.1). Alternative techniques adjust the cost of capital (the denominator) by adding a risk premium to the discount factor for riskier projects and reducing the discount factor for less-risky projects. The problem facing the financial manager is the determination of the risk premium.

One possible method requires a qualitative judgment by the financial manager. The cost of capital is the required return to be used for investments of average risk. If the firm is expanding known products into new markets that are comparable to existing markets, then the use of the cost of capital may be justified. However, if the financial manager is considering new products, then a risk premium is added to the cost of capital. Conversely, if the new products are less risky than the typical investment made by the firm, the cost of capital may be reduced.

Consider the following example. The financial manager has the following risk-adjusted cost of capital schedule:

Project Risk	Risk-adjusted Cost of Capital
Low risk	6.5%
Average risk	8.5
High risk	10.5
Exceedingly high risk	12.5

These risk-adjusted costs of capital act as hurdle rates that are applied to different projects. If the net present value approach is used, the adjusted cost of capital is used to discount the estimated cash inflows. If, after using the adjusted cost of capital, the net present value is positive, the investment is made. If the internal rate of return approach is used, the adjusted cost of capital is used as the criterion for decision making. If an investment's internal rate of return exceeds the appropriate cost of capital, the investment is made.

This approach, like the certainty equivalent approach, presents a problem: How is risk to be measured, and how much of a risk premium should be added? One possibility is to measure risk using the variability of the cash flows. As the variability of the cash inflows increases, the risk premium is increased. This approach, however, still does not tell the financial manager how large a risk premium should be added to the firm's cost of capital. The amount of a risk premium remains a judgment call by the financial manager.

An alternative means to measure risk is to use the beta coefficients discussed in Chapter 8. In that chapter, beta coefficients were used to indicate the volatility of a stock's return relative to the volatility of the market. Beta coefficients were then applied in Chapter 11 as part of the capital asset pricing model's specification of the required return for the valuation of common stock. The same concept may be applied to adjust for risk in capital budgeting. The risk-adjusted required return (the risk-adjusted cost of capital) for an investment (k_a) is

$$k_a = r_f + (k - r_f)\beta, \quad \text{18.2}$$

in which k_a is the firm's cost of capital used for the typical or average investment made by the firm, and r_f is the risk-free rate and β is the beta coefficient associated with the investment being considered. If the risk-free rate is 3 percent and the firm's cost of capital is 9 percent, the general equation for the risk-adjusted required return is

$$k_a = 0.03 + (0.09 - 0.03)\beta.$$

FIGURE 18.1

Relationship between Project Risk and Required Return

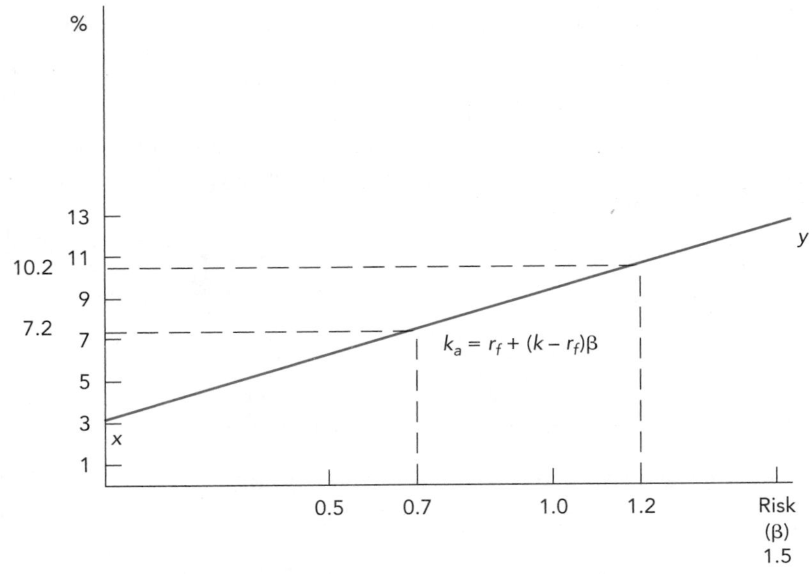

This equation is illustrated by line xy in Figure 18.1, which indicates that as risk increases (the beta increases), the required return increases. If an investment has an estimated beta of 1.2, it is riskier than the typical investment made by the firm. The adjusted required return is

$$k_a = 0.03 + (0.09 - 0.03)1.2 = 0.102 = 10.2\%,$$

which exceeds the firm's cost of capital. If an investment has a beta of 0.7, it is less risky than the firm's typical investment. Its adjusted required return is

$$k_a = 0.03 + (0.09 - 0.03)0.7 = 0.072 = 7.2\%.$$

This return is less than the firm's cost of capital, because this particular investment is less risky than the average investment made by the firm.

If a particular investment offers an internal rate of return that lies above line xy, it is acceptable because the return exceeds the risk-adjusted required return. Any investment with an internal rate of return that lies below line xy is rejected because the return is less than the risk-adjusted cost of capital used to evaluate the specific investment.

Although the above discussion suggests means to incorporate risk into the capital budgeting process, making these propositions operational is difficult. The inclusion of risk increases the accuracy of capital budgeting only if the estimates of risk are accurate. Consider a pharmaceutical firm whose investment in research may take years to develop and to receive government approval to market a new product. How can the firm estimate the beta for such an investment? In Chapter 11, betas were used to value a stock. The estimation of the stock's beta was relatively easy. The historical returns on the stock and the market are known. The biggest problems to estimate the beta and subsequently employ it were (1) determining which measure of the market to use and (2) after estimating the beta, assuming that the historical beta was an accurate measure of the current beta. Although these are important problems, they pale when compared to the problem of estimating a beta for a nonexistent product that may result from a firm's investment in research and development.

Thus, for the financial manager, the problem is not whether to include risk into capital budgeting, but how to accurately measure it. In some cases this measurement is highly subjective, so the selection of investments is also subjective. Accurate data are obviously crucial to capital budgeting decisions. Estimating an investment's future cash flows is no easy task, so it should hardly be any surprise that the measurement of the investment's risk is an exceedingly difficult task.

Before proceeding to the next section and the discussion of replacing existing equipment and refunding existing debt, one important assumption concerning risk adjustments needs to be made explicit. Does management represent and work for the best interests of the firm's owners? The assumption is that management does work for and is responsive to the owners' best interests.[2] Common sense suggests this assumption need not hold. The risks associated with an investment in plant, equipment, research in product development, or any other investment is often different for the firm's owners and the individuals making the decision. This is particularly true for publicly held firms whose stockholders have minimal contact with the firm.

A pharmaceutical firm, such as Merck or Pfizer, must invest in research to develop new products. The period necessary to complete the research, receive approval from the Federal Drug Administration, and market a new drug consumes years. Success may increase the value of the firm so that stockholders benefit as the price of the stock rises. If managers' and employees' benefits are tied to the value of the stock, they also benefit.

Consider, however, the possibility that the research fails to generate new products. The negative impact on stockholders' wealth may be marginal, especially if the research is terminated early. The individuals working on the project, however, may also be terminated. Will these individuals argue to continue a losing project to maintain their jobs? Will management pursue safer and less-risky projects whose probability of success is higher but whose potential payoffs are smaller? The assumption that management operates in the best interests of the stockholders

[2]The same issue was raised in Chapter 10 in the discussion of stock. The questions essentially reduce to: Does management operate in the owners' best interests or their own and how can these objectives be integrated so that management's and owners' interests are the same?

suggests that management's concerns are either the same as those of stockholders or that employees will place stockholders' interests before their own.[3]

ADDITIONAL APPLICATIONS

In the previous illustrations, net present value and internal rate of return were used to aid in the decision to make new investments in plant and equipment. Capital budgeting techniques may also help to determine if equipment should be replaced or if long-term debt (that is, bonds) should be refunded prior to maturity. These decisions are conceptually no different from investing in new plant and hence may be analyzed in terms of their impact on the firm's cash flows.[4]

The Replacement Decision

Equipment has a finite life and must be replaced. This need for replacement is obvious once the equipment is worn out. However, new equipment may be developed that offers the firm savings before the old equipment needs to be replaced. This raises the question of whether the firm should retain the old, less-productive equipment or replace it with the new, cost-saving equipment. This replacement decision, like the decision to invest in new plant and equipment, should be made by using capital budgeting techniques. The new equipment must have a positive net present value to justify replacing the old equipment.

The following factors influence this net present value: (1) the potential savings from the new equipment; (2) the cost of the new equipment; (3) the firm's income tax rate; (4) the residual value of the old equipment; (5) the depreciation on the new and old equipment; and (6) the firm's cost of capital. To make the replacement decision, the firm must determine the net present value of the new equipment in light of these factors. Some of the factors produce cash inflows for the firm, while others result in cash outflows. For example, purchasing the new equipment causes a cash outflow, but the savings from the new equipment increases the firm's cash inflows. The question reduces to: Does the present value of these cash inflows exceed the present value of the cash outflows? If it does, the replacement should be made; if it doesn't, the replacement should not be made.

First, management determines all the cash inflows. The potential savings from the new equipment is a cash inflow. The depreciation on the new equipment is a cash inflow. The residual value, or price at which the old equipment may be sold,

[3] Suppose management acquires a corporate jet. There may be no identifiable cash inflows that justify the investment, and certainly the cost is a cash outflow. Whose interests are served by the investment?

[4] The technique is also useful in deciding to purchase or to lease. For example, after deciding to make an investment in equipment, the financial manager must determine if the equipment should be purchased or leased. The decision requires comparing the present value of the cash outflows associated with purchasing and borrowing to the present value of the cash outflows from leasing. See the discussion in Chapter 21 on leasing.

is a cash inflow. Thus, the primary cash inflows are (1) the potential savings, (2) depreciation charges on the new equipment, and (3) any residual value on the old equipment. Next, the firm must determine the cash outflows, such as the purchase price of the new equipment. The depreciation on the old equipment that will be *lost* when it is replaced is also treated as a cash outflow. Finally, the firm must consider its corporate income tax rate, which affects the cash flows by reducing the firm's profits.

How the replacement decision should be made may be illustrated by a simple example. A firm can replace an old machine with a new machine that costs $1,000 and save $150 a year. The old machine still operates and may be sold for its book value of $500. Both the old and new machines have anticipated lives of five years and are depreciated on a straight-line basis. Thus, the depreciation on the new equipment will be $200 a year ($1,000/5), while the depreciation on the old equipment is $100 a year ($500/5). The firm's income tax rate is 40 percent, and its cost of capital is 9 percent.

The decision to replace the old equipment depends on the net present value of the cash inflows. To determine these inflows, consider the following income statements:

	Present Equipment	New Equipment	Net Change
Sales	$1,000	$1,000	$–
Expenses	700	550	(150)
Depreciation	100	200	100
Earnings before taxes	200	250	50
Taxes (40% tax rate)	80	100	20
Net earnings	$ 120	$ 150	$ 30
Cash flow (profits plus depreciation)	$ 220	$ 350	$130

The first column presents earnings and cash flow generated by the current equipment. The second column gives the earnings and cash flow that would result from selling the old equipment and replacing it with the new equipment. The third column gives the change in columns one and two that results from the replacement of the existing equipment.

Replacing the old equipment results in an increase in earnings and an increase in depreciation expense. Because the depreciation expense is a noncash expense that recoups the cost of the investment, it is added back to earnings to obtain the cash flow generated by the investment. The question now becomes: Is the present value of this cash flow greater than the cost of the investment?

The cost of the investment is the amount that the firm spends to acquire the new equipment. In this case, the new equipment costs $1,000, but the firm is able to sell the old equipment for $500, so the net cash outlay to replace the old equipment is reduced to $500. The decision as to whether to replace the existing equipment depends on the present value of increased cash flows and the present value of the $500 cash outflow required to make the investment. The net present value of the investment is

CALCULATOR SOLUTION

Function Key		Data Input
FV	=	0
PMT	=	130
I	=	9
N	=	4
PV	=	?
Function Key		*Answer*
PV	=	−505.65

$$NPV = \sum_{1}^{5} \frac{\$130}{(1+0.09)^n} - \$500$$
$$= \$130(3.890) - \$500$$
$$= \$505.70 - \$500 = \$5.70.$$

The net present value of the investment is \$5.70, so the replacement should be made. The firm should replace the old equipment, because the present value of the cash inflows exceeds the present value of the cash outflows.

While this example is simple, it illustrates the basic mechanics of the replacement decision. The mechanics become more complex as other factors are considered, such as a tax loss or gain on the old equipment, or differences in the expected lives of the new and old equipment. However, the basic concept and approach are not altered by adding additional factors. The basic approach still remains to determine the net present values of the cash inflows and outflows. As long as the present value of the cash inflows exceeds the present value of the cash outflows, the firm should replace the old equipment. This replacement is profitable and will increase the value of the firm.

The Refunding Decision

The refunding decision is similar to the replacement decision. The firm seeks to replace an existing issue of debt with a new issue. Once again, if the present value of the cash inflows from the refunding exceed the present value of the cash outflows, the investment (the refunding) should be made.

Consider the following situation. A firm has an outstanding ten-year \$1,000,000 bond with a 12 percent coupon with a call penalty of one year's interest. Currently, the firm could issue a new bond with a 10 percent coupon and use the proceeds to retire the existing bond. Should the firm refund the more costly bond? The first impulse may be, of course, to refund the bond. There is an obvious annual savings of \$20,000 in interest.

Unfortunately, the answer is not that simple, because there are other factors to consider. If the existing bond is called prior to maturity, the firm must pay the call penalty, which requires a current cash outflow of \$120,000. This cost is a tax-deductible expense, so part of the burden of the call penalty is shared with the federal government. If the firm's income tax rate is 40 percent, the \$120,000 reduces income taxes by \$48,000, so the net cash outflow is reduced to \$72,000.

In addition to the call penalty, there will be a cost to issue new bonds. While this flotation cost requires a current cash outflow, this cost is capitalized and recaptured over the lifetime of the bond through amortization expense. The impact of amortization is the same as depreciation on the firm's cash flows. Amortization is a noncash expense that recaptures the cost of an intangible asset, such as the capitalized cost of the bond issue. If the flotation cost is \$10,000, this amount is amortized at the rate of \$1,000 each year.

The total cash outflows to retire the bond are \$1,000,000 to retire the bond, \$72,000 (after tax) to pay the call penalty, and \$10,000 to issue the new bond, for a total cash outflow of \$1,082,000. The cash inflows from the refunding include the annual saving in $20,000 interest, but this savings increases taxes by $8,000, so the firm nets only $12,000 annually in interest savings. The other cash inflows are the $1,000 noncash amortization of the flotation costs and the $1,000,000 cash from issuing the new debt.

The cash inflow from the new debt cancels the cash outflow from the old debt, so the analysis is reduced to a comparison of the present value of the annual $13,000 cash inflows (the after-tax interest savings plus the amortization) and the initial $82,000 cash outflow (the call penalty plus the flotation expense). If the firm's cost of capital is 12 percent, the present value of the cash inflow is

$$\$13{,}000(5.650) = \$73{,}450,$$

so the new present value is

$$\$73{,}450 - \$82{,}000 = (\$8{,}550).$$

CALCULATOR SOLUTION

Function Key		Data Input
FV	=	0
PMT	=	13,000
I	=	12
N	=	10
PV	=	?
Function Key		*Answer*
PV	=	−73,452.90

The net present value is negative, so the firm should not refund the bond.

This answer may be surprising, but consider the following alternative. The firm has $82,000 and uses the money to buy an annuity that yields 10 percent each year for the next ten years. How much will the firm receive each year? The answer is

$$\frac{\$82{,}000}{6.145} = \$13{,}344.18,$$

in which 6.145 is the interest factor for the present value of an ordinary annuity. This answer suggests that the financial manager could use the $82,000 necessary to refund the bond to instead purchase the annuity and receive $13,344.18 for the next ten years. That is better than generating $13,000 a year through the refunding, so the implication is obvious. Pay the old higher rate of interest and purchase the annuity. It is the better use of the $82,000.

CALCULATOR SOLUTION

Function Key		Data Input
PV	=	−82,000
FV	=	0
N	=	10
I	=	10
PMT	=	?
Function Key		*Answer*
PMT	=	13,345.12

SUMMARY

As was explained in the previous chapter, capital budgeting is the process for making long-term investment decisions. One technique that is often used is the net present value, which discounts future cash inflows at the firm's cost of capital. The resulting present value is subtracted from the current cost (cash outflow) to determine the net present value. If the net present value is positive, then the investment is made because it increases the value of the firm.

An alternative approach finds the rate of return that equates the present value of the future cash inflows with the cost of the investment. If this internal rate of return exceeds the firm's cost of capital, the investment is made. Because the investment earns more than the cost of funds necessary to make the investment, it contributes to the value of the firm.

Both the net present value and the internal rate of return capital budgeting techniques use forecasted cash inflows. These forecasts are expected values and cannot be known with certainty. An investment's risk may be analyzed on a stand-alone basis in which the financial manager considers only the risk associated with the investment. An investment's risk, however, may also be analyzed in a portfolio context in which the impact on the firm and its owners is considered. If a portfolio approach is used, risky investments whose returns are poorly or even negatively correlated with the returns from other investments may reduce the firm's risk exposure. The lack of correlation has a diversification effect that reduces the firm's risk.

There is also the possibility for a long-term investment in plant or equipment to reduce the owners' risk. If stockholders do not have well-diversified portfolios, investments by the firm that are not positively correlated with the owners' portfolios reduces their risk. This may be especially important for the owners of a small, privately held firm whose portfolios may not be independent of the firm. For large, publicly held companies, however, it is reasonable to assume that the stockholders have well-diversified portfolios and that any portfolio effects on these investors will be minimal or nonexistent.

The analysis of risk may be incorporated into capital budgeting either by adjusting an investment's expected cash inflows or by adjusting the firm's cost of capital. Estimated cash inflows may be restated based on the probability of their occurring or on an estimate of their certainty equivalents. The firm's cost of capital may be adjusted using a risk premium or by applying the capital asset pricing model, which employs beta coefficients. These betas measure the volatility of an investment's return relative to the volatility of the return on the firm's typical or average investment. Although adjusting

either the cash inflows or the cost of capital may be used, the problem facing the financial manager is the measurement of risk and not the application of the risk adjustment.

In addition to determining which new investments in plant and equipment should be made, capital budgeting techniques are used to determine if existing equipment should be replaced before the end of its useful life or if a bond issue should be refunded prior to maturity. In both cases, the future cash inflows from the replacement or refunding are compared with the current cash outflows to determine the net present value. As in the case of a new investment in plant or equipment, if the net present value is positive, the old equipment should be replaced or the existing debt should be refunded prior to its maturity.

REVIEW QUESTIONS

1. What is the difference between analyzing an investment's risk from a stand-alone perspective and analyzing it from a portfolio perspective?
2. Why may a publicly held firm's investment in plant have little, if any, impact on its stockholders' risk?
3. What impact will each of the following have on an investment's risk?
   a. The variability of the cash inflows is increased.
   b. The beta associated with the investment is reduced.
   c. The cost of the investment is increased.
4. What is a major weakness associated with the application of certainty equivalents and risk premiums?
5. An investment has a positive net present value and there is a low correlation between its return and the returns earned by other investments made by the firm. Do these considerations strengthen or weaken the argument for making the investment?
6. What impact will a low beta coefficient have on the following?
   a. an investment's expected cash flows
   b. an investment's internal rate of return
   c. an investment's net present value
7. Why may it be advantageous to replace equipment before it wears out? What factors influence this decision?
8. If interest rates rise, would you expect a firm to refund its existing debt?
9. What impact will each of the following have on a firm's decision to refinance existing debt?
   a. Interest rates decline.
   b. The existing debt has no call penalty.

c. Investment banking fees to issue new bonds are increased.
d. Existing debt has a clause that precludes the firm from using the proceeds from the sale of new debt to retire the old bonds.

PROBLEMS

1. A risky $30,000 investment is expected to generate the following cash flows:

Year	1	2	3
	$14,000	$15,750	$18,000

The probability of receiving each cash inflow is 90, 80, and 70 percent, respectively. If the firm's cost of capital is 12 percent, should the investment be made?

2. A firm has the following investment alternatives. Each costs $13,000 and has the following cash inflows.

	YEAR			
Cash Flow	1	2	3	4
A	$4,300	$4,300	$4,300	$4,300
B	3,500	5,000	4,500	4,000
C	4,800	6,000	3,000	2,000

Investment A is considered to be typical of the firm's investments. Investment B's cash flows increase over time but are considered to be less certain. Investment C's cash flows diminish over time but because most of the cash flows occur early in the investment's life, they are considered to be more certain. The firm's cost of capital is 10 percent, but the financial manager uses a hurdle rate of 8 percent for less-risky projects and 12 percent for riskier projects.

a. Based on the cost of capital, should any of the investments be made?
b. If the financial manager uses a risk-adjusted cost of capital, should any of the investments be made?
c. Would the answers to a and b be different if the three investments were mutually exclusive?

3. A risky $400,000 investment is expected to generate the following cash flows:

Year	1	2	3	4
	$145,300	$175,445	$156,788	$145,000

a. If the firm's cost of capital is 10 percent, should the investment be made?
b. An alternative use for the $400,000 is a four-year U.S. Treasury bond that pays $28,000 annually and repays the $400,000 at maturity. Management believes that the cash inflows from the risky investment are only equivalent

to 75 percent of the certain investment which pays 7 percent. Does this information alter the decision in a?

4. A firm can buy new equipment for $1,000,000. It will last for five years and then can be sold for its book value of $500,000. The new equipment will save the firm $63,000 for each of the five years. The equipment that is to be replaced can be sold for $400,000 which is its book value, so the sale will not generate taxable income. The depreciation on the new equipment will be $100,000 annually and the depreciation to be lost on the old equipment is $80,000. Should the firm replace the old equipment if its cost of capital is 12 percent and the firm is in the 40 percent income tax bracket?

5. The management of Hamilton Squared Products, Inc., may purchase new equipment that costs $250,000. The equipment has an expected life of ten years after which it will have a residual or salvage value of $30,000. If the new equipment increases net income by $25,000 a year, what is the net present value of this investment if (1) the firm's cost of capital or hurdle rate for this type of investment is 12 percent and (2) the equipment is depreciated at $22,000 a year. (Ignore any tax effects associated with the salvage value of the equipment.) Would your answer be different if the cost of capital were 20 percent? If income taxes reduced the realized salvage value to $16,500, would your answers be different at a cost of capital of 12 or 20 percent?

6. Since interest rates have declined to 8 percent, management is considering refinancing a 10 percent bond issue that matures after eight years. The amount of the debt is $10,000,000 but the firm will have to issue $10,500,000 in new debt since selling the new bond involves expenses. The $500,000 in expenses will be amortized over the eight years at the rate of $40,000 annually. The entire bond issue will be retired in one lump payment at the end of the eight years.
   a. What is the cash outflow necessary to refinance the debt?
   b. What is the annual cash savings before considering any tax implications?
   c. If the firm's tax rate is 30 percent, what is the after-tax cash savings?
   d. If management believes the cost of the refunding could be invested elsewhere at 12 percent, is the after-tax savings sufficient to justify the costs of the refunding?

CHAPTER 19
Planning: Forecasting and Budgeting

Learning Objectives

1. Differentiate between forecasting and budgeting.
2. Identify the assets and liabilities that spontaneously vary with the level of sales.
3. Illustrate the percent of sales method of forecasting.
4. Add changes in fixed assets to the percent of sales forecasts.
5. Differentiate between receipts and disbursements and construct a cash budget.
6. Explain the purpose of the cash budget.

In *Don Quixote*, Cervantes suggested that to be "forewarned" is to be "forearmed." To be forearmed is the purpose of planning. By constructing financial plans and budgets, the financial manager is forewarned of future problems. Once problems are identified, the financial manager takes actions to solve (or at least alleviate) the problems before they become unmanageable.

This process of identifying problems and developing plans for adjusting to change is illustrated by two firms concerned with different facets of health care. Owens and Minor is one of the nation's two largest wholesale distributors of medical and surgical supplies. Schering-Plough is one of the nation's premier pharmaceutical firms. The 1995 year was a difficult one for Owens and Minor, as regulators, customers, and health care providers became increasingly cost conscious. Even though sales rose over 20 percent, Owens and Minor operated at a loss and the value of its stock declined. In its 1995 annual report, management detailed several plans and initiatives to improve quality of service, raise performance of underperforming divisions, focus on inventory control, and increase cash flow.

During the same period, the management of Schering-Plough faced the same economic environment, but 1995 was another record year for Schering-Plough. In its 1995 annual report, management reported sales had grown to over $5 billion, new products had been developed, and plans were made for future spending of almost $700 million on research and development. Management realized that the downward pressure on health care costs required they plan for the continual development of new and superior products so that Schering-Plough would be able to continue to compete. Obviously, anticipating change and developing plans for working in the new cost environment is just as important for the continued financial health of Schering-Plough as it is for the restoration of financial health for Owens and Minor.

Although planning applies to all facets of a firm's operations, it is particularly important for financial management. Since all assets must be financed, it is crucial for the health of a firm to forecast the anticipated level of assets in order to plan for their financing. In addition, the financial manager is concerned with the day-to-day timing of cash flows. Cash receipts and disbursements are rarely synchronized. When disbursements precede receipts, the cash must be obtained somewhere, or the firm will be unable to pay its bills. Budgets, especially the cash budget, are constructed to help solve this problem by determining in advance when the firm will need funds to pay its current obligations and when the firm will generate the cash to retire any short-term loans that covered cash deficiencies.

This chapter is concerned with financial planning and forecasting. Two techniques—the percent of sales forecasting method and regression analysis—are illustrated as means to indicate the need for funds to finance the expansion of assets. The chapter concludes with a discussion of budgeting, with emphasis on expected cash receipts and disbursements.

PLANNING

Planning is the process of establishing goals and identifying courses of action (strategies) to meet the goals. Planning is like a road map; it helps point out the roads (or the alternative methods) to reach the destination (or the goal). In finance, the goal of management is often stated as the maximization of the value of the firm. The facets of the financial manager's job, such as the decision to acquire plant and equipment or how to finance the firm's assets, are means to obtain the desired goal of increasing the value of the firm.

The financial manager, however, does not work in a vacuum but must work within the framework of the firm. The management of a firm encompasses marketing, production, and administration as well as finance. The senior executives in charge of a firm's functional areas and operations develop a strategic plan. This plan is a general guide for the management of a firm and encompasses the development of new products through research and development, the expansion of current markets and the identification of new markets for existing products, the controlling of costs and operations, the expansion (or contraction) of plant and equipment required by changes in anticipated sales, and the financing of additional plant and equipment.

Financial management is one part of the strategic plan, as is planning for marketing and production. Financial decisions should not be made without forethought. Financial planning is a process of anticipating future needs and establishing courses of action today to meet financial objectives in the future. Thus, financial management and planning are concerned with when funds will be needed and how much will be available from internally generated sources. The need for external sources raises such questions as: Should the firm use long- or short-term credit? What is the best combination of debt-to-equity financing?

Financial management is not limited to anticipating the future. An integral part of a financial manager's role involves monitoring financial conditions to take advantage of changes in the financial markets. In addition, a financial manager should periodically reevaluate financial plans and decisions to avoid repeating past errors and to improve future financial planning and decision making.

In a sense, virtually every chapter in this text is concerned with financial planning. For example, several earlier chapters considered the variety of debt instruments and stock. Chapter 16 put these pieces together by discussing the optimal combination of debt and equity financing. This information is required before investments in plant and equipment (capital budgeting, discussed in Chapter 17) can be undertaken.

Several specific techniques are used in the planning process. For example, break-even analysis, which determines the level of output and sales necessary to avoid sustaining losses, was covered in a previous chapter. This type of analysis helps establish long-term plans, as the management seeks to reduce costs or increase revenues if it appears that the firm will operate at a loss. Break-even analysis, along with the capital budgeting techniques considered in Chapter 17, is a crucial component of long-term financial planning.

The topics in this chapter are more concerned with short-range planning. In the first section, external financial requirements are determined by projecting assets and liabilities through the use of the percent of sales method of forecasting. Such analysis helps determine if the firm will need external financing as sales expand or contract. An alternative means to determine if the firm will need external funds is the cash budget. While the former techniques stress short-term asset requirements, the cash budget highlights the flow of cash through the firm. It identifies whether the firm will generate cash (when receipts exceed disbursements) or whether the firm will lose cash (when disbursements exceed receipts). Such cash shortages will require short-term external funding.

FLUCTUATIONS IN ASSET REQUIREMENTS

Firms must have assets in order to operate. The amount and type of assets vary with each industry. Airlines and utilities have primarily fixed assets. Retailers must carry current assets, such as inventory. Other firms, especially those providing services, may have few assets. Other than space (which may be rented), the local barbershop or travel agency may operate with few assets.

Just as the amount and type of assets required for operations vary with each industry, the level of a firm's assets within an industry also vary. For example, a firm that sells swimming pools will not want to stock pools during the winter. Sales are obviously seasonal. Firms whose sales are primarily seasonal (or cyclical, such as homes or automobiles) will experience periodic increases and decreases in the level of assets needed for their operations.

These fluctuations are illustrated in Figure 19.1, which presents the levels of various assets over a period of time. Fixed assets (0A) are given and do not vary. Current assets have been divided into two groups: those that remain at a particular level (AB) and those that vary (BC). The firm may carry a minimum amount of inventory and may always have some accounts receivable. In addition, the firm has

FIGURE 19.1

Fluctuations in Assets over Time

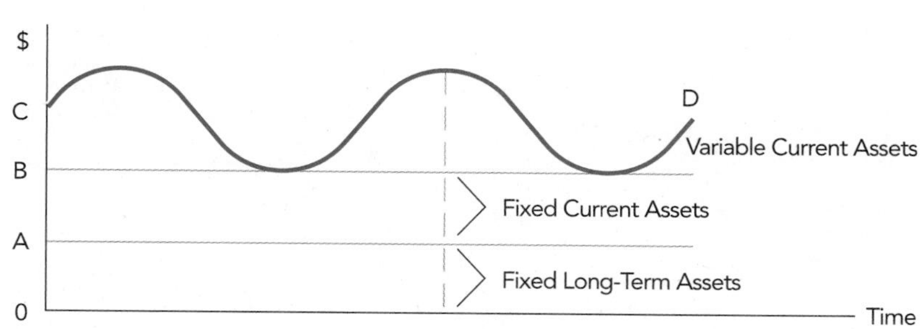

current assets that vary over time. The level of inventory will fluctuate with anticipated changes in demand, which in turn will generate varying amounts of accounts receivable and cash. These fluctuations in the levels of inventory, accounts receivable, and cash are illustrated by CD in Figure 19.1.

The firm may also require additional assets as it expands. As the firm grows, some assets automatically expand with the level of sales. For example, the level of inventory expands to meet the higher volume of sales. Other assets, especially long-term assets such as plant and equipment, will not spontaneously expand with the level of output. Initially, the existing plant and equipment will be used more intensively. The number of shifts will be increased, or employees may work overtime. However, if the expansion of sales continues, management will expand the firm's investment in plant and equipment.

This difference is illustrated in Figure 19.2. The left-hand side illustrates those assets that increase with expanding output. This relationship is shown by the steadily increasing line *AA* that represents the level of these assets at each level of sales. The right-hand side illustrates those assets that are increased only after a higher level of sales has been achieved. From zero sales to sales of S_1, the level of plant and equipment remains constant. After the level of S_1 has been obtained, further increases in the level of output require expansion in the plant and equipment. The level of fixed assets rises from A_1 to A_2. This higher level of assets is maintained until sales rise from S_1 to S_2, when plant and equipment must be further expanded. The level of fixed assets then is increased to A_3.

In the discussion that follows, it is initially assumed that the firm can expand the level of production without having to increase capacity. Thus, only those assets that spontaneously fluctuate with the level of sales will be affected by an increase (or decrease) in sales. After explaining how the percent of sales may be used to forecast assets and liabilities, the assumption that the firm has excess capacity is relaxed, so that expanding the level of sales requires more investment in plant and equipment. Since all assets must be financed, the forecasted expansion in assets forewarns the financial manager of the firm's future need for funds.

FIGURE 19.2

Relationships between Sales and Various Assets

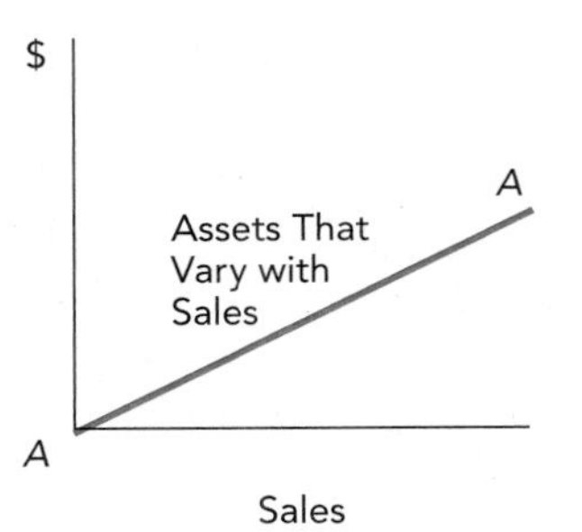

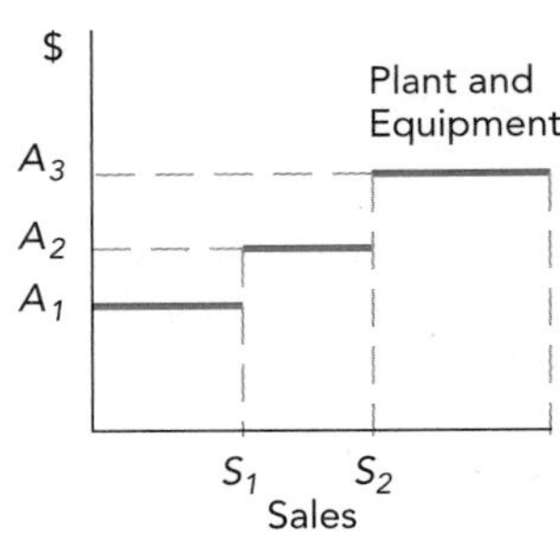

FORECASTING EXTERNAL FINANCIAL REQUIREMENTS: PERCENT OF SALES

PERCENT OF SALES
Forecasting technique that assumes specific assets and liabilities will vary directly with the level of sales

The **percent of sales** technique for forecasting financial requirements isolates the assets and liabilities that *spontaneously change with the level of sales* and expresses each as a percent of sales. These percentages are then used to forecast the level of each asset and liability. The forecasted increase in the level of assets must be financed and the increased level of liabilities will automatically finance some of the increase in assets. The difference between the increase in the assets and the liabilities must be financed by other means.

What assets vary with the level of sales? Consider a firm with the following balance sheet:

ASSETS		LIABILITIES AND EQUITY	
Cash	$ 100	Accounts payable	$ 200
Accounts receivable	300	Bank note	200
Inventory	300	Other current liabilities	100
Plant and equipment	500	Long-term debt	300
	$1,200	Equity	400
			$1,200

Several of the assets will vary with the firm's level of sales. A higher level of sales will require that the firm carry more inventory and will also increase the accounts receivable, as credit sales should expand if all sales increase. The level of cash may also rise with increased cash sales, and management may want to increase its level of cash holdings to meet the expanded liquidity needs, such as the payroll associated with higher sales volume.

While cash, inventory, and accounts receivable increase as sales rise, other assets do not automatically expand. For example, plant and equipment may not be increased but will be used at a higher level of capacity. If the level of sales rises sufficiently, more plant and equipment will need to be acquired, but no automatic increase in these fixed assets must occur as sales volume increases.

All the assets that increase with the higher level of sales must be financed. The funds to finance these assets must come from somewhere, and one source is any liability that also spontaneously expands with the level of sales. If liabilities increase sufficiently, they will cover the expansion in assets, but if they do not, the firm will have to find additional financing to operate at the higher level of sales.

Accounts payable are the primary liabilities that increase with expanded sales, because the firm's suppliers increase goods sold to the firm on credit. Other liabilities, such as accrued wages and salaries, also automatically expand. The other short-term liabilities, such as notes payable and the current portion of long-term debt due this fiscal year, do not spontaneously expand with the level of sales and thus are not automatic sources of financing.

The previous balance sheet may illustrate how the percent of sales technique of forecasting works. After those assets and liabilities that spontaneously vary with the level of sales are identified, they are expressed as a percent of sales. Thus, if the firm has inventory of $300 and sales of $2,000, inventory is 15 percent of sales ($300/$2,000). The following exhibit expresses as a percentage of sales all the assets and liabilities in the previous balance sheet that vary with the level of sales (assuming a level of sales of $2,000):

ASSETS		LIABILITIES	
Cash	5%	Accounts payable	10%
Accounts receivable	15%		
Inventory	15%		

(The percent of sales for the assets and liabilities that do not automatically increase with the level of sales is not calculated.) Thus, as may be seen from the exhibit, the ratio of all assets that vary with sales is 35 percent, and the ratio of liabilities is 10 percent.

Once the percentages have been determined, the anticipated level of sales is multiplied by each percentage to determine the anticipated level of each asset and liability necessary to sustain that level of sales. For example, if management anticipates that the level of sales will rise to $2,400 (a 20 percent increase), the percent of sales technique will forecast the following level of assets and liabilities for each asset and liability that varies with sales:

ASSETS		LIABILITIES	
Cash	$120	Accounts payable	$240
Accounts receivable	360		
Inventory	360		

In this case the percent of sales forecasting method states that the level of inventory ($300) will rise to $360 ($2,400 × 0.15), the level of accounts receivable

($300) will be $360 ($2,400 × 0.15), and the level of cash ($100) will be $120 ($2,400 × 0.05). The automatic expansion in assets is $140, which may be found by multiplying the increase in sales ($400) by 35 percent, which is the sum of the ratios of all assets that vary with the level of sales.

Concurrently with the increase in assets, accounts payable will rise to $240 ($2,400 × 0.10). The total increase in assets is $140, while the increase in liabilities is $40. This $40 increase in liabilities will finance only part of the increase in assets. Thus, $100 ($140 − $40) of assets will require other sources of financing. Management may expect that the firm will operate at a profit, and these profits could be retained to finance the additional assets. But profits after taxes would have to be $100 to finance the expansion in assets. If management cannot anticipate after-tax profits of $100, an outside source of finance (such as a bank loan) will have to be found to finance the anticipated increase in assets necessitated by the increase in sales.

If management anticipates earning 5 percent on the total sales and retaining 60 percent of the earnings, the forecasted increase in equity is

$$(0.05)(\$2{,}400)(0.6) = \$72.$$

Given this increase in equity and the forecasted levels of the current assets and current liabilities, management may construct the following pro forma balance sheet:

ASSETS		LIABILITIES AND EQUITY	
Cash	$ 120	Accounts payable	$ 240
Accounts receivable	360	Bank note	200
Inventory	360	Other current liabilities	100
Plant and equipment	500	Long-term debt	300
	$1,340	Equity	472
			$1,312

The balance sheet entries include the forecasted entries (the assets and liabilities that spontaneously changed with the level of sales); the entries that did not change, such as the long-term debt; and the new equity, which is the old equity plus the earnings that are to be retained.

Immediately it is obvious that the balance sheet does not balance. The forecasted increase in the assets exceeds the forecasted increase in the liabilities and equity. Total assets exceed total liabilities and equity by $28. To achieve the forecasted increase in assets, the firm will have to find $28 in *additional* funding. Without these additional sources, the expansion in assets cannot occur. However, this is a forecasted and not an actual balance sheet, so management now has the task (and presumably the time) to obtain the additional sources of finance.

Management has several options. Any increase in equity, any increases in liabilities, or any decrease in assets will help provide the needed financing. For example, the dividend policy may be changed to reduce dividends and increase the retention of earnings. Another possibility may be to seek an additional bank loan. A third option is to reduce the holdings of cash. In the above analysis, it was assumed that cash increased. If the firm can avoid the increase in cash and perhaps decrease its holdings of cash, the effect will be to reduce the firm's need for additional finance.

If management decides not to reduce dividends, not to reduce the firm's cash, but instead to increase borrowing from the bank by $28, the pro forma balance sheet becomes

Assets		**Liabilities and Equity**	
Cash	$ 120	Accounts payable	$ 240
Accounts receivable	360	Bank note	228
Inventory	360	Other current liabilities	100
Plant and equipment	500	Long-term debt	300
	$1,340	Equity	472
			$1,340

The balance sheet now balances; the sum of the projected assets equals the sum of the projected liabilities plus equity.

The Percent of Sales Summarized as an Equation

The previous example illustrates the percent of sales technique of forecasting, which asserts that if an asset or liability is some percent of sales and sales expand by some percentage, then the assets and liabilities will also expand by the same percentage. This relationship is illustrated in Figure 19.3. The horizontal axis represents the level of sales, and the vertical axis shows the level of inventory. (A similar graph may be drawn for any asset or liability that varies with sales.)

The relationship between inventory and sales is summarized by the following equation:

$$I = bS. \quad (19.1)$$

I is inventory; S is the level of sales; and b is the percent of sales, which is also the slope of the line. Once this percentage is known, it is easy to predict the level of inventory associated with any level of sales. Thus, if sales are $1,000, inventory will be $150 ($1,000 × 0.15). If sales expand to $20,000, inventory must expand to $3,000 ($20,000 × 0.15). By this method, all that is necessary to forecast the level of the asset is (1) the ratio of the current level of that asset to current sales and (2) the anticipated level of sales.

The financial manager may use a simple equation that summarizes (1) the assets and liabilities that vary with sales, (2) the profits the firm earns on its projected sales, and (3) the distribution of those earnings. The equation, summarizing the percent of sales forecasting method, is

FIGURE 19.3

Relationship between Inventory and Sales

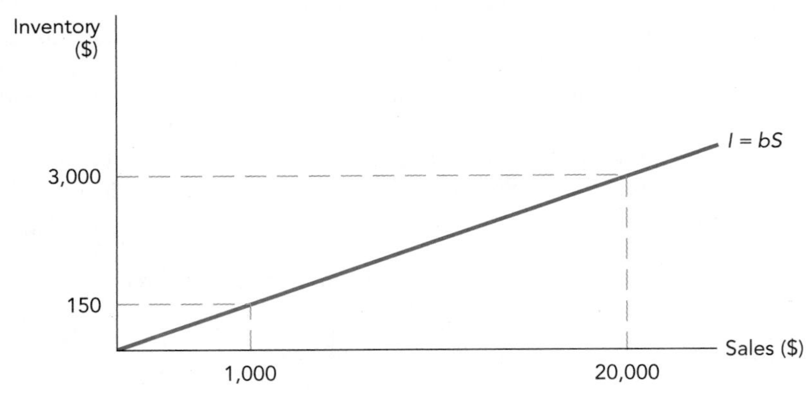

External funding requirements =

$$\left[\left(\frac{\text{Assets that vary with sales}}{\text{Sales}}\right) \times \begin{matrix}\text{Change}\\ \text{in}\\ \text{sales}\end{matrix} - \left(\frac{\text{Liabilities that vary with sales}}{\text{Sales}}\right) \times \begin{matrix}\text{Change}\\ \text{in}\\ \text{sales}\end{matrix}\right] - \begin{matrix}\text{Increase in}\\ \text{retained}\\ \text{earnings.}\end{matrix}$$

In symbolic form this equation for external funding requirements (EFR) is

19.2 $$EFR = \left[\frac{A}{S}(\Delta S) - \frac{L}{S}(\Delta S)\right] - (PS_1)R.$$

Although this equation may look formidable, it is not. The equation states that the firm's requirements for outside financing equal the funds needed to finance those assets generated by the projected change (Δ) in sales (S) minus the funds generated by the change in sales and the increase in retained earnings. Both the assets and liabilities that vary with the level of sales are expressed as a percent of current sales (A/S and L/S, respectively). The *additional* retained earnings depend on the profit margin of the firm's *projected sales* (PS_1) and the proportion of the earnings that are retained (R).

Suppose that a firm with sales of $10,000 has the following balance sheet:

Assets		**Liabilities and Equity**	
Accounts receivable	$ 3,000	Accounts payable	$ 2,500
Inventory	2,000	Long-term debt	4,000
Plant and equipment	8,000	Equity	6,500
	$13,000		$13,000

Accounts receivable, inventory, and accounts payable all vary with sales; the other entries do not. If the firm expands sales from \$10,000 to \$12,000, these assets and liabilities will spontaneously increase. Accounts receivable and inventory are 50 percent of sales, while accounts payable are 25 percent of sales. Thus, the first part of the equation is

$$EFR = (0.5)(\$2{,}000) - (0.25)(\$2{,}000) = \$1{,}000 - \$500.$$

If the firm earns 5 percent on its total sales and distributes 30 percent of its earnings as dividends, it retains the remaining 70 percent. Thus, the additional retained earnings are

$$\text{Additional retained earnings} = (0.05)(\$12{,}000)(0.7) = \$420.$$

The firm's need for external financing, then, is

$$\begin{aligned} EFR &= (0.5)(\$2{,}000) - (0.25)(\$2{,}000) - (0.05)(\$12{,}000)(0.70) \\ &= \$1{,}000 - \$500 - \$420 \\ &= \$80. \end{aligned}$$

The spontaneous increase in current assets will require \$1,000. The spontaneous increase in liabilities generates only \$500, and the firm retains only \$420 of its earnings generated on its projected sales. Thus, the firm will need \$80 of external financing to cover the anticipated increase in assets.

By this analysis the financial manager now knows that the firm will need more funds. If the financial manager is reluctant to obtain this money outside of the firm, one possible internal source is to distribute fewer dividends (retain more earnings). If the firm retains a larger percentage of its earnings, those retained earnings can finance more assets. In this case, if the firm retained all its earnings, its need for outside funding would be

$$\begin{aligned} EFR &= (0.5)(\$2{,}000) - (0.25)(\$2{,}000) - (0.05)(\$12{,}000)(1) \\ &= \$1{,}000 - \$500 - \$600 \\ &= (\$100). \end{aligned}$$

The firm would have no need for outside finance to cover the expansion in assets spontaneously generated by the increase in sales. The negative number indicates that the firm would have excess funds that could be invested elsewhere or be distributed as dividends.

The percent of sales forecasting method is one technique for predicting the firm's need for outside finance. Unfortunately, the method may produce biased and inaccurate estimates. If such estimates understate financial needs, finding additional credit rapidly may be difficult. If the technique overpredicts the financial needs, it may cause the firm to borrow more than is necessary and cause the firm to pay unnecessary interest expense.

The percent of sales method assumes that the current percentage will hold for all levels of sales. This assumption need not be true and is a potential source of bias. For example, the firm may be able to economize on inventory as it becomes larger. Thus, inventory as a percent of sales may decline as the level of sales rises. The converse may also be true as sales decline. The firm may continue to carry items even though sales have diminished, or there may be a lag after the decline in sales before the firm recognizes which items are moving slowly and ceases to carry them. Thus, inventory as a percent of sales may rise when the level of sales declines.

Although the percent of sales technique of forecasting may produce biased estimates, it is still employed as a forecasting tool for two reasons. First, it is very simple and may be computed with ease. Second, if the change in sales is relatively small, the estimate may not be significantly biased. The larger the increase in sales, the greater the bias will be; but if management is concerned with only a small change in the level of sales, the percent of sales method of forecasting financial needs may be sufficient.

FORECASTING EXTERNAL FINANCIAL REQUIREMENTS: REGRESSION ANALYSIS

One method by which to overcome the bias of the percent of sales technique is to consider the relationship between the asset or liability and sales over several years. For example, Exhibit 19.1 depicts a firm's level of inventory and sales for the last five years. This information indicates that there is a positive relationship between the level of inventory and sales, but inventory as a percent of sales has declined. If this decline continues, the use of a percentage determined from only one year's observations will overpredict the necessary level of inventory.

This relationship between sales and inventory is plotted in Figure 19.4, which also indicates a positive trend, since the points are rising. Using the graph in this form, however, may be difficult. For example, it would be difficult to project the level of inventory if the level of sales were to rise to $2,500. This problem can be overcome if the points are expressed as an equation. The technique that summarizes the points in equation form is called **regression.**

REGRESSION
Statistical technique that estimates an equation summarizing a set of data

Figure 19.5 reproduces the points in Figure 19.4 but in addition passes a line through the points so that the relationship between inventory and sales is expressed by the following simple linear equation:

19.3

$$I = a + bS.$$

The vertical intercept, a, gives the level of inventory the firm carries even when it has only the minimal amount of sales. The rate at which the line rises is the slope, $\Delta I/\Delta S$, and this is represented by the symbol b. Regression analysis estimates numerical values for a and b, the intercept and the slope.

For this firm, regression analysis indicates that the equation for the relationship between inventory and sales is

$$I = \$234.28 + 0.1825$$

EXHIBIT 19.1

Five-Year Level of Inventory and Sales

Year	Sales	Inventory	Inventory as a Percent of Sales
X5	$2,000	$600	30%
X4	1,700	530	31
X3	1,400	500	36
X2	1,200	470	39
X1	1,000	400	40

The $234.28 is the y-intercept and indicates the level of inventory if there were no sales. The 0.182 is the slope of the line and indicates that for every increase in sales of $1,000, the level of inventory will rise by $182.[1]

Once the equation has been formulated, it can then be used to forecast the level of inventory for any level of sales. For example, if sales are $3,000, the equation

[1]Although regression is generally done through a computer program (for example, Excel), it may be performed manually, in which case the slope and intercept are computed as follows:

X	Y	X²	Y²	XY
2,000	600	4,000,000	360,000	1,200,000
1,700	530	2,890,000	280,900	901,000
1,400	500	1,960,000	250,000	700,000
1,200	470	1,440,000	220,900	564,000
1,000	400	1,000,000	160,000	400,000
$\Sigma X = 7{,}300$	$\Sigma Y = 2{,}500$	$\Sigma X^2 = 11{,}290{,}000$	$\Sigma Y^2 = 1{,}271{,}800$	$\Sigma XY^2 = 3{,}765{,}000$

n = number of observations (5).

$$\text{slope} = b = \frac{n\Sigma XY - (\Sigma X)(\Sigma Y)}{n\Sigma X^2 - (\Sigma X)^2}$$

$$= \frac{(5)(3{,}765{,}000) - (7{,}300)(2{,}500)}{(5)(11{,}290{,}000) - (7{,}300)(7{,}300)} = 0.182.$$

$$\text{intercept} = a = \frac{\Sigma Y}{n} - b\,\frac{\Sigma X}{n}$$

$$= \frac{2{,}500}{5} - (0.182)\,\frac{7{,}300}{5} = 234.28.$$

The Investment Analysis Calculator (**www.harcourtcollege.com/finance/mayo**) may also be used to calculate the equation. Use the submenu "Simple Linear Regression" under the section "Statistical Calculator." Enter the data from Exhibit 19.1. The number of observations is 5, the independent variable is Sales (X), and the dependent variable is Inventory (Y). Enter the data, and click on enter. The software indicates that the y-intercept is 234.28 and the slope of the line is 0.182.

FIGURE 19.4

Trend in Inventory and Sales

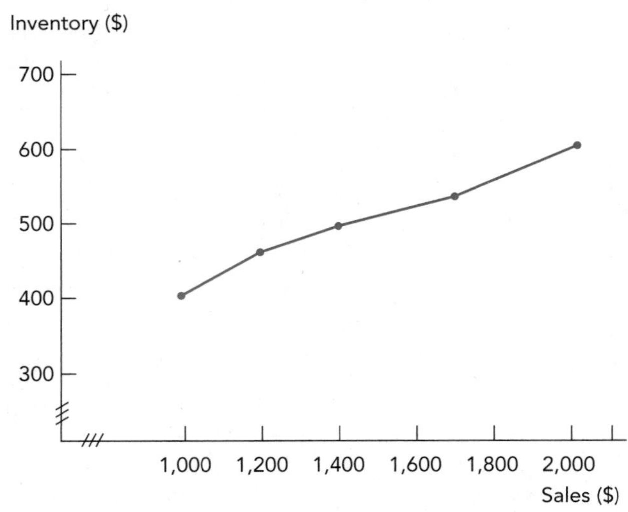

FIGURE 19.5

Trend in Inventory and Sales (Using Linear Regression Analysis)

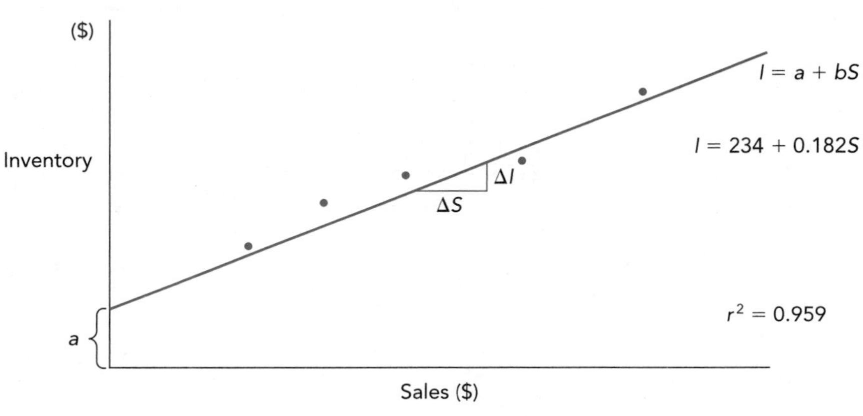

estimates that the level of inventory will be $780. This number is obtained from the equation by substituting $3,000 for sales and solving for inventory:

$$\begin{aligned}\text{Inventory} &= \$234.28 + 0.182(\$3{,}000)\\ &= \$780.28.\end{aligned}$$

Figure 19.5 indicates that the relationship between sales and inventory is close, since the individual observations (that is, the individual points) lie very close to the regression line. Such closeness indicates a high correlation between the independent variable (sales) and the dependent variable (inventory).

This correlation may be measured by the "correlation coefficient" or the "coefficient of determination." In statistics these are often symbolized as r or r^2, respectively. As was explained in Chapter 8, in which regression analysis was used to estimate a stock's beta coefficient, the numerical value of the correlation coefficient ranges from +1.0 to −1.0. If the two variables move exactly together (if there is a perfect positive correlation between the independent and dependent variables), the numerical value of the correlation coefficient is 1.0. If the two variables move exactly opposite of each other, the correlation coefficient equals −1.0. All other possible values lie between these two extremes. Numerical values near zero, such as −0.12 or +0.19, indicate little relationship between the two variables.

The coefficient of determination is the square of the correlation coefficient and measures the proportion of the variation in the dependent variable explained by movement in the independent variable. Thus, if the correlation coefficient is 0.1, the coefficient of determination is 0.01 (0.1^2), which indicates that the movement in the independent variable explains very little of the movement in the dependent variable.

Computation of these two coefficients is part of statistics and need not concern us in this text.[2] The computer programs that estimate the regression equation routinely give the numerical values of the correlation coefficient and the coefficient of determination. The interpretation of the coefficients is potentially useful to the financial manager who is concerned with the accuracy of the estimated equation. The coefficient of determination (the r^2) gives the proportion of the variability in inventory that is explained by the variability in sales. In this illustration the r^2 is 0.959, which indicates a very close relationship between sales and inventory.[3] The high r^2 should increase the financial manager's confidence in using the regression equation to forecast inventory as sales change.

Such a close correspondence between the variables need not occur, but regression analysis will still summarize the relationship. For example, consider the relationships between sales and inventory presented in Exhibit 19.2 and Figure 19.6. In case A, the individual observations relating sales and inventory are scattered throughout the graph, but the regression technique still estimates an equation summarizing the individual observations. The correlation is low, with an r^2 of only 0.216, so the quality of the equation as a forecasting tool is questionable.

The same conclusion concerning the forecasting ability of the estimated equation applies to case B. In this case, the individual observations for all levels of sales between \$1,000 and \$2,000 lie above the line. However, regression analysis still

[2] How the correlation coefficient is determined may be found in an elementary text on statistics. See, for instance, Robert D. Mason and Douglas A. Lind, *Statistical Techniques in Business and Economics*, 9th ed. (Chicago, Ill.: Irwin, 1996).

[3] The Investment Analysis software also provides the correlation coefficient ($r = 0.98$) and the coefficient of determination ($r^2 = 0.96$). These results suggest that only 4 percent of the variability in inventory is explained by something other than fluctuations in sales.

EXHIBIT 19.2

Relationships between Sales and Inventory

Sales	Case A Inventory	Case B Inventory
$1,000	$400	$400
1,200	380	550
1,400	600	600
1,700	500	700
2,000	450	750

estimates an equation that summarizes the relationship between sales and inventory. While the quality of the equation is rather high ($r^2 = 0.813$), the forecasting ability of the estimated equation is suspect.

This example points out a possible problem with simple linear regression analysis. First, the actual relationship between the variables may not be a straight line. Case B in Figure 19.6 implies that the relationship between inventory and sales is curvilinear. The dots rise but appear to taper off as the level of sales increases. By visual inspection the true relationship between sales and inventory appears to be the curved line AB drawn through the points. An equation for this curved line should give more reliable forecasts than the simple straight line (linear) equation that was previously estimated.

Another potential source of difficulty with simple linear regression is the possibility of several variables affecting the dependent variable. For example, the level of inventory may be affected not only by sales but also by the availability of the goods, the season of the year, or the cost of credit. That appears to be the situation in case A in Figure 19.6 because the relationship between inventory and sales is weak. Something other than sales must explain the level of inventory.

These problems with simple linear regression may be solved by using nonlinear regression analysis or multiple regression, which includes more than one independent variable. Both of these statistical techniques are covered in more advanced texts.

Although nonlinear and multiple regression analysis will not be developed here, it is desirable to compare simple linear regression with the percent of sales technique for forecasting. The percent of sales is the simple case of regression analysis in which there is no intercept and the slope is determined by the origin and one observation. The percent of sales technique assumes that the present ratio of inventory to sales will remain constant, and it takes that ratio as the slope of the equation. On the basis of that assumption, the technique then projects the level of inventory. Regression analysis, however, does not make that assumption and formulates an equation using several observations that relate inventory and sales.

The differences in the predictive power of the two techniques are illustrated in Exhibit 19.3, which is based on the previous example. The first column gives the level of sales, and the second and third columns give the estimated levels of inventory. The second column uses the percent of sales method, which assumes that the ratio of inventory to sales is constant (30 percent). The third column uses the

FIGURE 19.6

Relationships between Sales and Inventory

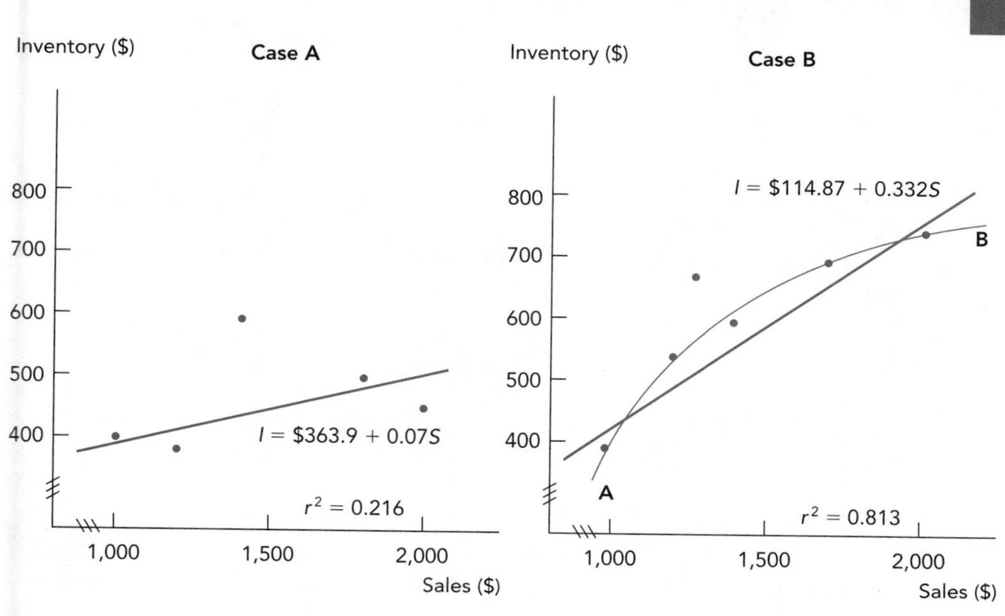

EXHIBIT 19.3

Comparison of Percent of Sales and Regression Techniques of Forecasting

Sales	Percent of Sales Forecast	Regression Analysis Forecast
	(Inventory = \$0.30 Sales)	(Inventory = \$234.28 + 0.182 Sales)
\$1,500	\$450	\$507.28
2,000	600	598.28
2,500	750	689.28
3,000	900	780.28

regression equation ($I = \$234.28 + 0.182S$), which was formulated on the basis of data for past levels of inventory and sales.

As may be seen in the exhibit, the higher the anticipated level of sales, the larger the estimated level of inventory. But the estimated level of inventory is larger for the percent of sales method than for the regression technique. The percent of sales technique may be overestimating the desired level of inventory. For example, if as the firm grows there are economies in inventory management, the level of inventory need not continue to grow at the same rate. Thus, the ratio of inventory to sales will decline. Under these circumstances, regression analysis gives a better estimate of the desired level of inventory and is the more accurate predictor.

FORECASTING EXTERNAL FINANCIAL REQUIREMENTS: CHANGES IN FIXED ASSETS

In the previous sections it was assumed that as the firm expanded sales, only those assets that spontaneously changed with the level of sales varied. Such expansion of sales can only occur if the firm has excess capacity. In this section, it is assumed that the firm must expand its fixed assets, as well as those assets that spontaneously change with the level of sales.

To ease the explanation, the example that was used for the percent of sales will be employed here. The firm in that illustration had the following balance sheet:

ASSETS		LIABILITIES AND EQUITY	
Cash	$ 100	Accounts payable	$ 200
Accounts receivable	300	Bank note	200
Inventory	300	Other current liabilities	100
Plant and equipment	500	Long-term debt	300
	$1,200	Equity	400
			$1,200

Sales were $2,000, which increased to $2,400. If the net profit margin on sales is 10 percent and the firm retains 40 percent of its earnings, the percent of sales method would forecast the following projected balance sheet entries:

ASSETS		LIABILITIES AND EQUITY	
Cash	$ 120	Accounts payable	$ 240
Accounts receivable	360	Bank note	200
Inventory	360	Other current liabilities	100
Plant and equipment	500	Long-term debt	300
	$1,340	Equity	496
			$1,336

Cash, accounts receivable, inventory, and accounts payable all increased because they spontaneously changed with the level of sales. Equity increased by $96 since the firm earned $240 on its sales ($2,400 × 0.1 = $240) and retained 40 percent of its earnings ($240 × 0.4). The other entries remained constant because it was assumed that they did not change with the level of sales.

In the example, assets increased by $140 while liabilities and equity increased by $136. The projected balance sheet, of course, does not balance; the difference of $4 equals the projected shortage of funds. The financial manager would have to plan for this $4 in additional finance to cover the projected expansion in assets. Because the required amount is so modest, it is safe to assume that finding the additional finance would not be a major problem.

Suppose, however, the expansion in sales also required an increase of $200 in fixed assets. The projected balance sheet would become:

ASSETS		LIABILITIES AND EQUITY	
Cash	$ 120	Accounts payable	$ 240
Accounts receivable	360	Bank note	200
Inventory	360	Other current liabilities	100
Plant and equipment	700	Long-term debt	300
	$1,540	Equity	496
			$1,336

The firm's need for finance is larger (that is, $204), since the expansion in sales cannot be achieved in this example without an expansion in plant and equipment.

What choices are available to the financial manager to raise the required $204? Actually, the financial manager has several options. First, the holdings of cash could be reduced to acquire another asset. Second, a larger proportion of the earnings could be retained instead of being distributed. Earnings that are retained, of course, could help finance the projected expansion in assets. Third, the firm could issue additional debt, such as bonds, or issue additional stock to raise the cash to acquire other assets.

Obviously, the financial manager has several possible courses of action. As was discussed in Chapter 16, one of the questions that he or she will have to face is what combination of debt and equity financing is the most desirable to finance the expansion. The use of debt financing may increase the return earned by the owners, but the additional use of financial leverage also increases the risk associated with the firm. For the purposes of this discussion, assume that the financial manager decides to (1) reduce the holdings of cash to $80, which releases $40, (2) distribute only 40 percent of earnings and thus retain $144 instead of $96, and (3) float additional debt to cover the remaining deficiency. After these changes occur, the projected balance sheet becomes:

ASSETS		LIABILITIES AND EQUITY	
Cash	$ 80	Accounts payable	$ 240
Accounts receivable	360	Bank note	200
Inventory	360	Other current liabilities	100
Plant and equipment	700	Long-term debt	416
	$1,500	Equity	544
			$1,500

Thus, the financial manager has provided for the expansion in accounts receivable, inventory, and plant and equipment through the spontaneous increase in accounts payable, a reduction in cash, the issuing of new long-term debt, and the retention of earnings.

THE CASH BUDGET

In the previous sections, forecasts of short-term assets and liabilities were used to determine the firm's need for finance resulting from an expansion in the firm's sales. The firm may also require cash to cover periods when receipts are insufficient to cover disbursements. Cash receipts are seldom synchronized with cash disbursements, and if disbursements temporarily exceed receipts, the shortage will have to be financed.

To help determine when the firm will need external funds (for example, a commercial bank loan) to cover cash disbursements, the financial manager may construct a **cash budget.** This is simply a table that enumerates all the firm's cash outlays and cash receipts. A cash budget is not synonymous with an income statement, which enumerates revenues and expenses. Some revenues may not be cash. For example, a credit sale generates revenues but the cash will not immediately be collected. The same applies to a purchase on credit. While such purchases may be expenses, the actual cash outlay occurs in the future. In addition, the firm may make some cash payments that are not expenses. For example, principal repayment requires an outlay of cash but is not an expense.

CASH BUDGET
Projected financial statement that enumerates cash receipts and disbursements for a period of time

The term *budget* is often encountered in conjunction with financial planning and decision making. All budgets are estimates of anticipated receipts and disbursements for a period of time. Individual households as well as firms may construct such plans, and certainly the budget of the federal government is one of the most discussed documents that emanate from Washington, D.C. In each case these budgets are planning devices, as their construction requires that financial managers anticipate when outlays will be made and receipts collected.

In addition to being planning devices, budgets can be used as tools of control. Individual departments within the firm can have budgets that constrain their ability to spend or require that excess spending decisions be made by higher management. The budgets then act as a constraint on the firm's divisions and give management more internal control of the firm's operations. The budget may also be used as a tool to judge performance. Was the budget maintained? Which divisions within the firm overextended their budgets? By comparing the actual performance with the anticipated performance, management may be able to identify sources of financial problems.

The period of time for a budget is variable and depends on the nature of the firm and the purpose of the budget. Some budgets may be for short periods, such as six months. A firm with seasonal or fluctuating sales may develop a budget that covers the season. Other budgets may cover many years. A public utility may have a budget for capital spending on plant and equipment that covers planned receipts and disbursements for five to ten years.

Budgets are particularly useful planning tools for short time periods. A cash budget may be constructed for three or six months and then used to predict the short-term needs of the firm for cash. The cash budget helps the financial manager to determine not only that cash is needed but also *when* it is needed. This element of time is crucial, for the financial manager can contact sources of short-term credit before the funds are needed. Such early contact indicates that management is aware of its financial needs, and this should increase the confidence of lenders in the firm's management. Such confidence may result in more favorable terms, which reduce the cost of the funds.

The cash budget is basically a table relating time, disbursements, and receipts. The units of time may be months, weeks, or even days. For purposes of exposition, a monthly cash budget will be developed. The cash items are grouped into inflows (receipts) and outflows (disbursements). The difference between the inflows and outflows is the summary that indicates to the financial manager whether to expect excess cash that needs to be invested or cash deficiencies that must be financed.

The construction of a simple cash budget for the fall season may be illustrated by the following example. The financial manager has determined the following anticipated levels of sales for the next seven months:

May	$15,500	August	50,000	November	10,000
June	20,000	September	40,000		
July	30,000	October	20,000		

Thirty percent of the sales are for cash, and 70 percent are on credit. Of the credit sales, 90 percent are paid after one month, and 10 percent are paid after two months. Thus, the financial manager expects that of the anticipated sales of $15,000 in May, $4,500 will be for cash ($15,000 × 0.3) and $10,500 will be on credit ($15,000 × 0.7). Of these credit sales, $9,450 will be collected after one month ($10,500 × 0.9), and $1,050 will be collected after two months ($10,500 × 0.1).

If the firm owns any other assets that will become cash during the time period, those assets must also be included in the cash budget. For example, if the firm owns a short-term asset, such as a U.S. Treasury bill valued at $10,000 that will be due on June 1, it must be included in the cash budget. Since the purpose of the cash budget is to determine the excess or shortage of cash that the firm will experience, all cash items must be included in the budget. Noncash expenses like depreciation are excluded.

In this case, the firm's sales are seasonal, so it will seek to build up inventory in anticipation of the seasonal business. As the inventory is produced, the firm must pay for labor and materials. The estimated disbursements for wages and materials for the season are

May	$ 3,000	August	30,000	November	3,000
June	25,000	September	10,000		
July	38,000	October	5,000		

These estimated disbursements indicate that the buildup in inventory occurs in June, July, and August. The sales, however, occur primarily in July, August, and September. There is a lag in sales after the buildup of inventory; thus there will be a drain on the firm's cash.

Besides the cash outlays that vary with the level of output, the firm has fixed disbursements that do not vary with the level of operations. These include interest

EXHIBIT 19.4

Monthly Cash Budget (for a Firm's Fall Season)

	May	June	July
Part 1			
1 Anticipated sales	$15,000	$20,000	$30,000
2 Cash sales	4,500	6,000	9,000
3 Accounts collected (one-month lag)		9,450	12,600
4 Accounts collected (two-month lag)			1,050
5 Other cash receipts		10,000	
6 Total cash receipts	4,500	25,450	22,650
Part 2			
7 Variable cash disbursements	3,000	25,000	38,000
8 Fixed cash disbursements	3,000	3,000	3,000
9 Other cash disbursements			
10 Total cash disbursements	6,000	28,000	41,000
Part 3			
11 Cash gain (or loss) during the month (line 6 minus line 10)	(1,500)	(2,550)	(18,350)
12 Cash position at beginning of month	12,000	10,500	7,950
13 Cash position at end of month (line 12 plus line 11)	10,500	7,950	(10,400)
14 Less desired level of cash	(10,000)	(10,000)	(10,000)
15 Cumulative excess (or shortage) of cash (line 13 minus line 14)	500	(2,050)	(20,400)

and rent of $1,000 a month and administrative expenses of $2,000 a month for a total of $3,000 a month. The firm also has to make an estimated quarterly income tax payment in September of $2,500 and a payment of $1,000 on August 1 to retire part of a debt issue. Management likes to maintain a minimum cash balance of $10,000 as a safety valve in case of emergency. The firm's cash position at the beginning of May is $12,000, which exceeds the desired minimum level for the cash balance.

The financial manager now uses this information to obtain estimates of the monthly net increase or decrease in the firm's cash position. (The budget may be constructed on a weekly, monthly, or quarterly basis depending on the time available for its construction, the need for extreme accuracy, and the volatility of the entries.) The monthly cash budget is illustrated in Exhibit 19.4. The first part of the table presents the estimated cash that the firm receives monthly. The first line of the table gives the estimated sales, and the next three lines give the estimated cash generated by the sales: line 2 enumerates the cash sales; line 3 gives the collections that occur on the credit sales after one month; and line 4 gives the credit

August	September	October	November	December	January
$50,000	$40,000	$20,000	$10,000		
15,000	12,000	6,000	3,000		
18,900	31,500	25,200	12,600	6,300	
1,400	2,100	3,500	2,800	1,400	700
35,300	45,600	34,700	18,400		
30,000	10,000	5,000	3,000		
3,000	3,000	3,000	3,000		
1,000	2,500				
34,000	15,500	8,000	6,000		
1,300	30,100	26,700	12,400		
(10,400)	(9,100)	21,000	47,700		
(9,100)	21,000	47,700	60,100		
(10,000)	(10,000)	(10,000)	(10,000)		
(19,100)	11,000	37,700	50,100		

collection that occurs two months after the sales. The arrows show when May's credit sales yield cash receipts. Line 5 gives other sources of cash receipts (for instance, the $10,000 Treasury bill that matures). The sum of lines 2 through 5 is the monthly cash receipts of the firm and is given in line 6.

The second part of the table enumerates the firm's monthly cash disbursements. Line 7 gives the monthly disbursements that vary with the level of sales, while line 8 gives the disbursements that do not vary with the level of sales (such as the interest, rent, and administrative disbursements). Line 9 gives other cash disbursements (for instance, the $2,500 tax payment and the $1,000 debt retirement payment). The sum of all the monthly cash payments is given in line 10.

The third part of the table summarizes the first two parts and indicates whether the firm has a net inflow or outflow of cash during the month. Thus, the cash budget establishes whether the firm has excess cash that it can use to purchase short-term income-earning assets (such as a certificate of deposit) or has insufficient cash, which requires that the firm find short-term financing. Line 11 is the difference between lines 6 and 10; it gives the net inflow or outflow of cash during the month. Line 12 gives the firm's cash position at the beginning of the month. The sum of lines 11 and 12 equals the firm's cash position at the end of the month, which is given in line 13. Notice that the cash position can be negative (see July, for example), which indicates the cash outflow exceeded the cash inflow plus the cash from the preceding time period. The minimum desired level of cash is given in line 14. The difference between cash position at the end of the month and the desired minimum level of cash is given in line 15 of the table. This is the most important line, for it indicates either that the firm will have excess cash generated by operations during the month or that it will have a cash deficiency.

How is the information contained in the cash budget interpreted? The process of interpretation may be illustrated by considering several months. For example, during the month of May, the firm has a net cash outflow of $1,500 (line 11), but since the firm began the month with $12,000 in cash, it has enough to cover the anticipated cash drain and still maintain its desired level of cash holdings. This is indicated in line 15, which shows that there is excess cash of $500 over the desired cash balance level. In the month of June, cash disbursements once again exceed receipts (by $2,550). The extent to which the cash expenditures exceed the receipts, however, is reduced by the receipt of the $10,000 payment from the Treasury bills. Thus, it appears that the financial manager was previously aware of the firm's cash needs in June and July and purchased a short-term asset that matured in June. Even with this extra inflow of cash, the cash position at the end of the month drops to $7,950 (line 13), which is less than the desired level of cash balances by $2,050 (line 15). The financial manager would then have to decide either to let the cash position fall below the desired minimum or to borrow the $2,050 to maintain the desired minimum level of cash.[4]

In July the difference between the cash outflows and cash receipts grows even larger. Anticipated cash payments exceed cash receipts by $18,350, before allowance is made for the desired minimum level of cash. When the actual cash outflow and the desired level of cash are added, the cumulative shortage is $20,400 (line 15). Thus, the financial manager can anticipate that the firm will need $20,400 of short-term financing to cover the firm's cash needs for June and July. In August, cash receipts slightly exceed disbursements, so the cumulative shortage falls to $19,100. After August the firm's cash position improves dramatically as the cash from its credit sales flows into the firm. In September the firm will have generated a cash gain of $30,100. After September the firm's cash position continues to improve, and the cumulative excess cash grows to $50,100 by the end of November. Thus, the financial manager can anticipate having excess cash that can be used to purchase a short-term income-earning asset that matures when the cycle begins again.

If the financial manager decides to maintain the minimum cash balance and to borrow from the bank the funds necessary to cover the cash shortages, the firm

[4]The cash gain (or loss) for a given month is equal to the difference between the cumulative excess (or shortage) between that month and the preceding month. Thus in June, the cash loss of $2,550 is equal to the change in cumulative cash from May to June. During the month, cash fell from a positive $500 to a negative $2,050 for a total decline in cash of $2,550.

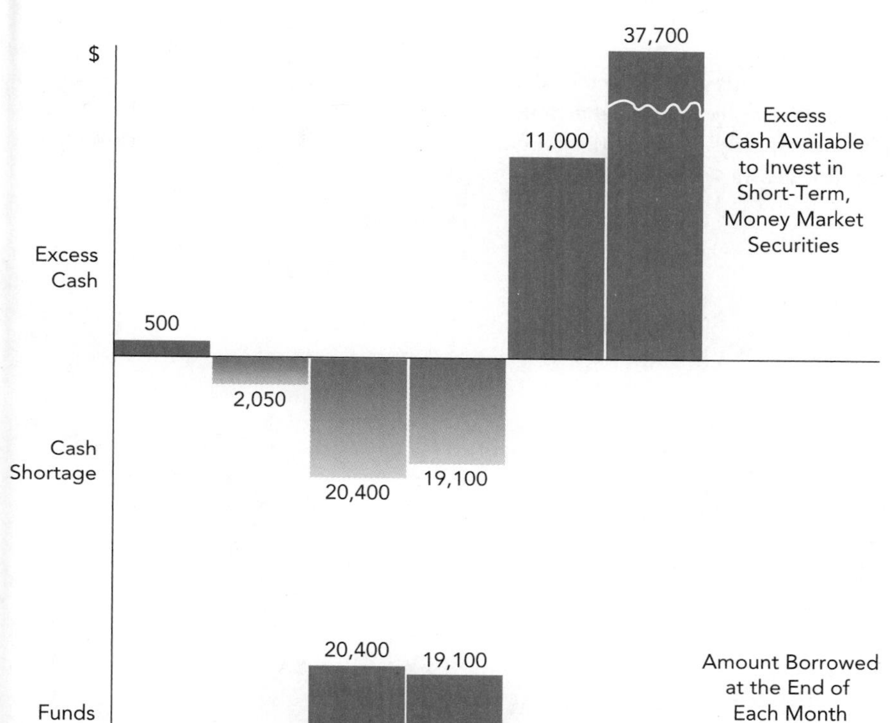

FIGURE 19.7

Excess and Shortage of Cash and Borrowings to Cover the Cash Shortages (May–October)

will have a short-term bank loan outstanding in June, July, and August. The excess cash, cash shortage, and bank loan outstanding are illustrated in Figure 19.7. The top half shows the firm's excess cash or shortage of cash. The bottom half gives the amount of the outstanding loan. This loan, of course, balances the cash shortages in June through August. Once the cash flows into the firm in September, the loan is repaid and no longer is outstanding.

The cash budget helps the financial manager to establish when the firm will need external financing. In the example, the financial manager can anticipate how much cash the firm will need in June, July, and August, and he or she also knows when the firm will generate sufficient cash to retire the short-term loan. Thus, the financial manager can approach the lender with estimates of (1) the firm's cash needs and (2) when the firm will be able to repay the loan. This information is important for the lender, who is concerned with earning interest and being repaid the principal. From the lender's viewpoint, a cash budget is more important than the firm's income statement, since it shows how the cash will be used and when repayments will be made.

Preparing the cash budget also permits the financial manager to shop around for terms. Since the financial manager is able to anticipate the firm's financial needs, he or she is able to arrange for the necessary financing in advance. Such planning should increase the bargaining position of the borrower and may result in more favorable credit terms.

SUMMARY

Management constructs strategic plans that establish general goals for a firm. The strategies designed to meet the goals are executed by the various executives responsible for a firm's operations, marketing, and finance. The plans and their execution need to be periodically evaluated to determine if the general goals are being achieved.

Financial plans must fit within the general strategic plan of a firm. These plans require forecasts of when a firm will need outside sources of finance. These forecasts can have a short- or long-term time horizon, but this chapter emphasizes forecasting a firm's short-term needs for finance. Such requirements arise when a firm must acquire assets for operations or cover shortages resulting from the nonsynchronization of receipts and disbursements.

Some assets, such as accounts receivable and inventory, automatically expand with increases in a firm's sales. Other assets, such as plant and equipment, have to be increased after a firm reaches a certain level of sales. Once capacity is reached, further expansion will require additional investment in plant and equipment.

All assets have to be financed, so projecting a firm's level of assets is crucial to the financial health of a firm. One forecasting technique uses the percent of sales. It expresses all assets and liabilities that spontaneously change with the level of sales as a percent of sales. That percentage is then used to forecast the future level of these assets and liabilities as sales increase. A more sophisticated forecasting technique uses estimated equations (regression analysis) to estimate the level of assets and liabilities associated with various levels of sales.

Either technique may be used to construct a projected balance sheet that indicates a firm's estimated future assets, future liabilities, and future equity. If the estimated assets exceed the estimated liabilities plus equity, the financial manager must plan today to find the finance required by the forecast of the firm's future assets.

Budgeting is another tool for financial planning and control. The cash budget, which enumerates cash inflows and outflows, enables management to plan its short-term cash needs. By constructing such a budget, management is better able to plan its financial strategy, for the cash budget indicates both the timing and the amount of a firm's need for short-term financing.

REVIEW QUESTIONS

1. Budgeting is a means by which management in a large firm may control operations. Is such budgeting also necessary in a small firm? What role can a cash budget play in a firm of any size?
2. A firm uses the percent of sales method of forecasting. Its inventory is 12 percent of sales, while accounts receivable are only 6 percent of sales. If sales double, what happens to the levels of inventory and accounts receivable according to the percent of sales? What assumption has been made by this technique of forecasting?
3. What differentiates a cash budget from an income statement?
4. If a firm collects its receivables quickly, but delays paying its payables, what impact will that have on the cash budget?
5. If a firm's cumulative cash rises, what can be concluded about its receipts and disbursements?

PROBLEMS

1. ABC, Inc., with sales of $1,000, has the following balance sheet:

ABC, Incorporated Balance Sheet as of 12/31/X0

ASSETS		LIABILITIES AND EQUITY	
Accounts receivable	$ 200	Trade accounts payable	$ 200
Inventory	400	Long-term debt	600
Plant	800	Equity	600
	$1,400		$1,400

It earns 10 percent on sales (after taxes) and pays no dividends.

a. Determine the balance sheet entries for sales of $1,500 using the percent of sales method of forecasting.
b. Will the firm need external financing to grow to sales of $1,500?
c. Construct the new balance sheet and use newly issued long-term debt to cover any financial deficiency.

2. A firm has the following balance sheet:

CDE, Incorporated Balance Sheet as of 12/31/X0

ASSETS		LIABILITIES AND EQUITY	
Cash	$ 1,000	Accounts payable	$ 5,300
Accounts receivable	7,200	Bank note	3,200
Inventory	6,100		
Long-term assets	4,200	Equity	10,000
	$18,500		$18,500

a. If the firm expects sales to rise from $20,000 to $25,000, what are the forecasted levels of accounts receivable, accounts payable, and inventory?
b. Will the expansion in accounts payable cover the expansion in inventory and accounts receivable?
c. If the firm earns 12 percent on sales after taxes and retains all of these earnings, will it cover its estimated needs for short-term financing?
d. Construct a new balance sheet that incorporates the issuing of additional short-term debt to cover any needs for additional finance. (Assume cash remains $1,000.) If cash also increases proportionately with sales, what impact will the increase in cash have on the firm's need for funds?

3. CDE, Inc. has the following balance sheet:

CDE, Incorporated Balance Sheet as of 12/31/X0

ASSETS		LIABILITIES AND EQUITY	
Cash	$ 1,000	Accounts payable	$ 5,300
Accounts receivable	7,200	Bank note	3,200
Inventory	6,100		
Long-term assets	4,200	Equity	10,000
	$18,500		$18,500

It has estimated the following relationships between sales and the various assets and liabilities that vary with the level of sales:

Accounts receivable = $3,310 + 0.35 Sales,

Inventory = $2,264 + 0.28 Sales,

Accounts payable = $1,329 + 0.22 Sales.

a. If the firm expects sales of $25,000, what are the forecasted levels of the balance sheet items above?
b. Will the expansion in accounts payable cover the expansion in inventory and accounts receivable?
c. If the firm earns 12 percent on sales after taxes and retains all of these earnings, will it cover its estimated needs for short-term financing?
d. Construct a new balance sheet that incorporates the issuing of additional short-term debt to cover any needs for additional finance. (Assume cash remains $1,000.)
e. Compare your answers in parts a–d with your answers to parts a–d in Problem 2.

4. EFG, Inc., with sales of $500,000, has the following balance sheet:

Assets		Liabilities and Equity	
Cash	$ 25,000	Accounts payable	$ 15,000
Accounts receivable	50,000	Accruals	20,000
Inventory	75,000	Notes payable	50,000
Current assets	150,000	Current liabilities	85,000
Fixed assets	200,000	Common stock	100,000
		Retained earnings	165,000
Total assets	$350,000	Total liabilities and equity	$350,000

The firm earns 15 percent on sales and distributes 25 percent of its earnings. Using the percent of sales, forecast the new balance sheet for sales of $600,000 assuming that cash changes with sales and that the firm is not operating at capacity. Will the firm need external funds? Would your answer be different if the firm distributed all of its earnings?

5. A firm has the following monthly pattern of sales:

January	$ 100
February	300
March	500
April	1,000
May	500
June	300

(Sixty percent of the sales are on credit and are collected after a month.) The company pays wages each month that are 60 percent of sales and has fixed disbursements (for example, rent) of $100 a month. In March it receives $200 from a bond that matures; in April and June it makes a tax payment of $200. The firm seeks to maintain a cash balance of $150 at all times. Construct a cash budget that indicates the firm's monthly needs for short-term financing. Its beginning cash position is $150.

6. Management wants to know if there will be a need for short-term financing in February. Essential information is as follows:

a. Estimated sales for January and February are $1 million and $800,000, respectively.
b. Sixty percent of sales are for cash and 40 percent are credit sales that are collected the next month.
c. Cash disbursements that vary with sales are 40 percent of sales.
d. Fixed operating disbursements are $300,000 a month.
e. Depreciation expense is $50,000 a month.
f. A tax payment of $100,000 is due in January.
g. A bond payment of $300,000 is owed and will be due in February.
h. The cash balance at the beginning of January is $12,000.

i. Management seeks a minimum cash balance of $10,000.
j. December credit sales were $100,000.

7. With sales of $350,000, United Electronics and Illuminating is operating at capacity but management anticipates that sales will grow 25 percent during the coming year. The company earns 10 percent on sales and distributes 50 percent of earnings to stockholders. Its current balance is as follows:

Assets		**Liabilities and Equity**	
Cash	$ 7,500	Accounts payable	$ 38,000
Accounts receivable	30,000	Accruals	45,000
Inventory	65,000	Notes payable	0
Current assets	102,000	Current liabilities	83,000
Plant and equipment	100,000	Common stock	70,000
		Retained earnings	49,500
Total assets	$202,500	Total liabilities and equity	$202,500

a. In addition to cash, which assets and liabilities will increase with the increase in sales and by how much if the percent of sales is used to forecast the increases?
b. How much external finance will the firm need?
c. If cash did not increase but could be maintained at $7,500, what impact would the lower cash have on the firm's need for external finance?
d. If the firm distributed 25 percent instead of 50 percent of its earnings, would it need external finance?
e. Construct a new balance sheet assuming that cash increases with the increase in sales and the firm distributes 50 percent of its earnings to stockholders. If the firm needs external finance, acquire the funds by issuing a short-term note to a commercial bank. Compare this financing strategy to the strategies implied by the answers to parts c and d.

8. A firm with sales of $10 million and a net profit margin of 7 percent in 20X0 is expecting sales to grow to $12 million and $14 million in 20X1 and 20X2, respectively. Management wants to know if additional funds will be necessary to finance this anticipated growth. Currently, the firm is not operating at full capacity and should be able to sustain a 25 percent increase in sales. However, further increases in sales will require $2 million in plant and equipment for every $5 million increase in sales. The firm's balance sheet is as follows:

ABD Corporation Balance Sheet as of 12/31/X0

ASSETS		LIABILITIES AND EQUITY	
Cash	$1,500,000	Accruals	$1,500,000
Accounts receivable	2,000,000	Accounts payable	1,000,000
Inventory	1,500,000	Notes payable	500,000
Plant and equipment	3,000,000	Long-term debt	3,000,000
		Equity	2,000,000
	$8,000,000		$8,000,000

Management has followed a policy of distributing at least 70 percent of earnings as dividends. Management believes that the percent of sales method of forecasting is sufficient to answer the question, "Will outside funding be necessary?" In order to use this technique, management has assumed that accounts receivable, inventory, accruals, and accounts payable will vary with the level of sales.

a. Prepare projected balance sheets for 2001 and 2002 that incorporate any necessary outside financing. Any short-term funds that are required should be obtained through a loan from the bank, and any excess short-term funds should be appropriately invested. Any long-term financing that is needed should be obtained through long-term debt and/or appropriate reductions in short-term assets.

b. If the firm did not distribute 70 percent of its earnings, could it sustain the expansion without issuing additional long-term debt?

c. If the firm's creditors in part a require a current ratio of 2:1, would that affect the firm's financing in 2001 and 2002? If so, what additional actions could the firm take?

d. If the percent of sales forecasts are replaced with the following regression equations:

$$\text{Accounts receivable} = \$100{,}000 + 0.12\ \text{Sales},$$

$$\text{Inventory} = \$250{,}000 + 0.15\ \text{Sales},$$

$$\text{Accruals} = \$100{,}000 + 0.07\ \text{Sales},$$

$$\text{Accounts payable} = \$250{,}000 + 0.08\ \text{Sales},$$

what is the firm's need for outside funding (if any) in 2001 and 2002?

e. If the firm's creditors in part d required a current ratio of 2:1, would that affect the firm's financing in 2001 and 2002? If so, what additional actions could the firm take?

9. Given the information below, complete the cash budget:

a. Collections occur one month after the sale.

b. January's credit sales were $80,000.

c. The firm has a certificate of deposit for $40,000 that matures in April.

d. Salaries are $145,000 a month.

e. The monthly mortgage payment is $25,000.
f. Monthly depreciation is $20,000.
g. Property tax of $35,000 is due in February.

	February	March	April
Sales	$150,000	$200,000	$250,000
Cash sales	30,000	20,000	60,000
Collections	—	—	—
Other receipts	—	—	—
Total cash receipts	—	—	—
Salaries	—	—	—
Other disbursements	—	—	—
Total cash disbursements	—	—	—
Net change during the month	—	—	—
Beginning cash	30,000	—	—
Ending cash	—	—	—
Required level of cash	10,000	10,000	10,000
Excess cash or (shortage)	—	—	—

10. A firm has the following balance sheet:

Assets		Liabilities and Equity	
Cash	$ 3,200	Accruals	$ 4,900
Marketable securities	2,000	Accounts payable	17,050
Accounts receivable	17,130	Notes payable	7,000
Inventory	19,180		
		Long-term debt	22,000
		Common stock	20,000
Plant and equipment	41,000	Retained earnings	11,560
	$82,510		$82,510

Sales are currently $160,000, but management expects sales to rise to $200,000. The net profit margin is expected to be 10 percent, and the firm distributes 60 percent of its earnings as dividends.

Management is concerned about the firm's need for external funding to cover the expansion in assets required by the expansion in sales. To achieve sales of $200,000, management will have to *expand plant by $10,000* and expects to *increase its holdings of cash by $1,000.* However, the holding of marketable securities may be reduced to zero.

a. According to the percent of sales and the additional information, will the firm need external finance, and, if so, how much?

b. Construct a pro forma balance sheet indicating the forecasted new entries for sales of $200,000. If the firm has excess funds, they should be invested in marketable securities. If the firm needs funds, these should be covered by issuing new long-term debt.

CASE

FORECASTING THE IMPACT OF A DECLINE IN SALES

Leonard Copland is the financial manager for a firm with the following balance sheet:

ASSETS		LIABILITIES AND EQUITY	
Cash	$ 1,000	Accounts payable	$16,000
Marketable securities	2,000	Accruals	4,100
Accounts receivable	14,130	Bank loan	5,000
Inventory	17,180	Long-term debt	12,000
Plant and equipment	31,000	Common stock	10,000
		Retained earnings	18,210
	$65,310		$65,310

Sales are currently $80,000, but Copland expects them to fall to $60,000, which will require a contraction of assets. Copland uses the percent of sales technique to forecast those assets and liabilities that vary directly with sales (in other words, accounts receivable, inventory, accounts payable, and accruals). Since the firm is contracting, Copland would like to retire the long-term debt; however, the terms of the issue do not permit a partial repayment. Copland would like to retain the short-term bank loan, but the bank will not renew the loan if the renewal results in the firm having a current ratio of less than 2:1. Since the firm is contracting, management would like to increase the marketable securities by $1,500 to meet emergencies. However, if the firm needs funds to retire debt, Copland is willing to liquidate all the marketable securities. Copland anticipates that the firm's historic profit margin on sales of 10 percent and the firm's policy of distributing 30 percent of earnings will be maintained.

To help forecast the firm's future financial position, fill in all the anticipated entries in the following balance sheet *prior to* any change in the firm's debt structure:

ASSETS		LIABILITIES AND EQUITY	
Cash	$1,000	Accounts payable	$1,000
Marketable securities		Accruals	
Accounts receivable		Bank loan	
Inventory		Long-term debt	
Plant and equipment		Common stock	
		Retained earnings	
	$		$

Then, construct a new pro forma balance sheet that incorporates all the anticipated changes with the assumption that the firm pays the dividend. If the firm has funds after the change in the debt structure, add them to cash.

ASSETS		LIABILITIES AND EQUITY	
Cash	$	Accounts payable	$
Marketable securities		Accruals	
Accounts receivable		Bank loan	
Inventory		Long-term debt	
Plant and equipment		Common stock	
		Retained earnings	
	$		$

CASE PROBLEMS

1. Can the firm retain the short-term bank loan?
2. Can the firm retire the long-term debt?
3. If the firm distributed no dividends and retained all of its earnings, could the firm retire the long-term debt?

CHAPTER 20
Management of Short-Term Assets

Learning Objectives

1. Define working capital, net working capital, and working capital policy.
2. Isolate the risks and advantages of an aggressive working capital policy.
3. Explain how the operating cycle leads to fluctuations in a firm's need for current assets.
4. Calculate the economic order quantity (EOQ).
5. Differentiate between LIFO and FIFO and their impact on a firm's taxes.
6. Enumerate the components of credit policy.
7. Explain the advantage offered by lockbox systems and electronic funds transfers.
8. List several alternative money market instruments and distinguish their features.
9. Calculate the annual yield on a discounted, short-term security.

"Yesterday is a cancelled check; tomorrow is a promissory note; today is ready cash." This quote from Hubert Tinley expressed working capital management. The management of current assets seeks to increase the speed with which inventory and accounts receivable flow into cash. If the cash is not immediately needed, it is invested in short-term income-earning securities, such as corporate commercial paper or U.S. Treasury bills, to earn interest income.

The amount of the short-term investments can be substantial. VF Corporation, maker of Vanity Fair intimate apparel, Lee and Wrangler jeans, and Jantzen sportswear, held at the end of 1998 $63,208,000 in cash and short-term investments. The Coca-Cola Company, one of the nation's leaders in soft drinks and juice-based beverages, had over $1,807,000,000 in cash and marketable securities, which accounted for 28.3 percent of the firm's total current assets. Other firms, however, may have little cash. Columbia Sportswear reported cash of $6,777,000. This modest amount was less than 3.0 percent of the firm's total current assets.

The next two chapters consider the management of current assets and current liabilities. This chapter is devoted to the management of the firm's cash and other current assets; the subsequent chapter covers the sources of short-term funds. Current assets flow through the firm. Inventory is acquired and subsequently sold for cash or on credit. Accounts receivable are collected, and the cash is used to acquire other income-producing assets or to retire debt. The cycle is then repeated as the firm acquires new inventory for sale.

Since all assets must be financed—and the sources of finance are not free—the financial manager must establish the firm's optimal level of inventory and the firm's credit policy. Any excess cash must not be left idle but should be invested to earn interest. The management of short-term assets is a dynamic job that requires keeping current with day-to-day changes in the economic environment and the demand for the firm's products.

This chapter begins with a discussion of the firm's working capital policy, its operating cycle, and the choice between long-run and short-term financing. This is followed by a discussion of inventory management: the inventory cycle, the optimal order quantity, and inventory valuation. The next section considers the management of accounts receivable: the establishment of credit policy and the analysis of accounts receivable. Once these accounts are collected, the firm receives cash, so the chapter concludes with a discussion of cash management. This discussion includes policies for collecting cash more rapidly and the various short-term securities that may be acquired by the financial manager as temporary parking places for the firm's cash.

WORKING CAPITAL AND ITS MANAGEMENT

A firm's day-to-day operations center around generating sales and managing current assets and current liabilities. Although the determination whether to invest in new plant and equipment or refund a bond issue is obviously important, such decisions may be made intermittently. Management, however, is continuously concerned with current assets and how they are financed. Managing inventory, selling the inventory, collecting accounts receivable, investing temporary excess cash, raising short-term funds, and meeting current obligations as they come due require decisions on a daily basis.

A firm's current assets are often referred to as its **working capital.** The difference between its current assets and current liabilities is its **net working capital.** The way a firm manages its short-term assets and short-term liabilities is its **working capital policy.** Management of working capital is important to a firm's well-being because most business failures can be related to the mismanagement of current assets and their financing. Excess investment in inventory, inability to collect accounts receivable or retire its own accounts payable, or excessive use of short-term finance can rapidly destroy a firm that previously generated earnings and appeared to be profitable.

WORKING CAPITAL
Short-term assets; cash, cash-equivalents, accounts receivable, and inventory

NET WORKING CAPITAL
Difference between current assets and current liabilities

WORKING CAPITAL POLICY
Management of short-term assets and liabilities

The two essential questions regarding working capital are: What should be the level of the various current assets? and, How should these assets be financed? The second question divides into two additional questions: Should management use sources of short-term or long-term finance? and, What specific sources should be used? The answers to these questions vary among industries and among firms within a given industry.

EXHIBIT 20.1

The Operating Cycle

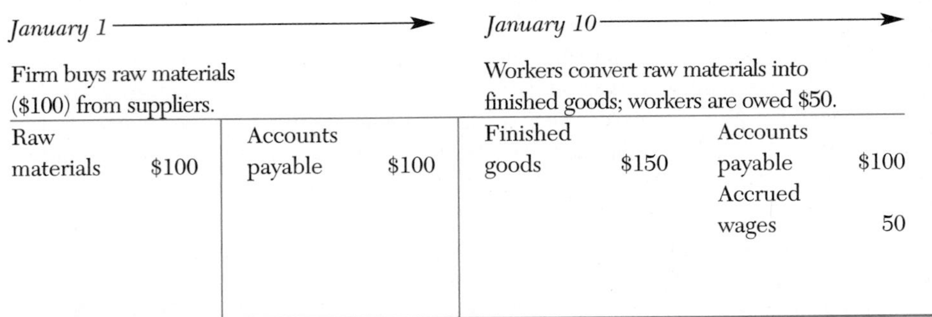

January 1
Firm buys raw materials ($100) from suppliers.
Raw materials $100
Accounts payable $100
January 10
Workers convert raw materials into finished goods; workers are owed $50.
Finished goods $150
Accounts payable $100
Accrued wages 50

THE IMPACT OF THE OPERATING CYCLE ON WORKING CAPITAL POLICY

Working capital policy is affected by the firm's operating cycle and by the fact that cash receipts and disbursements are rarely synchronized. The longer the operating cycle, the greater will be the firm's investment in current assets. Also, the less synchronization of receipts and disbursements, the greater will be the need for working capital.

In order to have product to sell, the firm needs inventory. Some firms (Macy's and The Limited) purchase inventory that may be immediately sold. Other companies, such as VF Corporation, manufacture the goods (Wrangler and Lee jeans, Jantzen swimwear, and Healthtex children's clothes) bought by Macy's and The Limited. These manufacturing companies acquire raw materials and employ labor to transform the raw materials into finished goods. The carrying of raw materials, work-in-process, and finished goods requires a source of funds. Paying the firm's suppliers and the labor that processes the goods also requires funds. However, the finished goods generate funds only after they are sold, and if the sales are on credit, funds are obtained only when the accounts receivable are collected.

This operating cycle is illustrated in Exhibit 20.1, which presents a time line in which a firm acquires raw materials, processes them, sells its inventory, collects its credit sales, and pays its creditors. The whole process is compressed into a month, and the firm's balance sheet is given as each step in the operating cycle occurs. On January 1, the firm buys $100 worth of raw materials on credit from its suppliers. At that point in time, the firm has $100 in assets financed by $100 in accounts payable. On January 10, the firm's workers convert the raw materials into finished goods. This adds $50 to the value of the raw materials, and the firm owes accrued wages of $50. The firm now has $150 in assets financed by the accounts payable ($100) and the accrued wages ($50).

On January 20, the goods are sold on credit for $190. The firm's assets become the $190 accounts receivable, which are financed by the $100 in accounts payable, $50 in accrued wages, and $40 in retained earnings. On January 30, the accounts receivable are collected, so the firm now has $190 in cash. On January 31, all the liabilities are paid off, so the firm's cash declines to $40. The accounts payable and

January 20 →		*January 30* →		*January 31* →	
Goods are sold on credit for $190.		Accounts receivable are collected.		All liabilities are paid off.	
Accounts receivable $190	Accounts payable $100 Accrued wages 50 Retained earnings 40	Cash $190	Accounts payable $100 Accrued wages 50 Retained earnings 40	Cash $40	Accounts payable $ 0 Accrued wages 0 Retained earnings 40

accrued wages cease, and the firm retains the $40 in earnings, which finances the $40 in cash. The operating cycle is complete. The goods have been produced and sold, and the accounts receivable have been collected. The firm now has cash and is ready to repeat the cycle.

For some firms, this process may occur over an extended period of time. Consider a building contractor. A house takes several months to complete, during which time raw materials are converted into the finished product. The contractor needs short-term financing during the construction process. However, once the house is sold, the builder may rapidly collect payment, as a commercial bank or savings and loan association issues a mortgage loan to the buyer, who in turn immediately pays the builder. For homebuilders, the need for working capital and short-term funds is primarily a need to finance construction—not to carry accounts receivable generated by the sale.[1]

Firms in other industries may not have as great a need for working capital because their operating cycle differs or is shorter. Consider a public utility, such as Tucson Electric and Power, that generates electric power. This firm's primary assets are plant and equipment. It has little inventory, and its primary short-term assets are accounts receivable, which are continually being collected as customers pay their utility bills. An electric utility does not experience the same buildup of short-term assets as the building contractor. Instead, the utility bills some of its customers each day and receives payment each day. It needs fewer short-term sources of funds than many other firms because there is a virtual synchronization of payments and receipts.

A firm's working capital policy is also affected by the nature of its sales (especially if the sales are cyclical or seasonal), the firm's credit policy (its willingness to sell on credit), and management's willingness to bear risk. With cyclical or seasonal sales, sales are not evenly spread over a period of time. Management may increase the firm's investment in inventory in preparation for the period of increased sales (for example, the winter season at Macy's). The firm will need funds to carry the

[1]A construction company may reduce its operating cycle by requiring payment as segments of the structure are completed. Such percentage of completion contracts are common in construction.

inventory. Once the inventory is sold, there may still be a need for financing if the sales are for credit. After these accounts receivable are collected, the firm uses the cash to retire the liabilities that financed the initial increase in inventory and the subsequent accounts receivable.

A firm's credit policy may also affect working capital. A lenient credit policy is designed to increase sales, so the firm sells its inventory more rapidly. However, a lenient credit policy generates more accounts receivable that the firm must carry, and may retard its collection of cash. Such a policy requires the firm to have sufficient sources of funds to carry the additional receivables.

Management's willingness to bear risk also affects working capital policy. A conservative management may carry more inventory to be certain that sales are not lost from lack of goods in stock or to protect against work stoppages. The increased inventory requires financing. Willingness to bear risk also affects management's choice of funding for the firm's short-term assets. As is explained in the next section, the use of short-term instead of long-term funds to finance short-term assets increases the element of risk, because additional risks are associated with refunding the debt and changes in the cost of credit (in other words, changes in the rate of interest).

FINANCING AND WORKING CAPITAL POLICY

All assets must be financed. One of the most important tasks facing a financial manager is the choice of financing. Various sources of long-term financing were previously discussed (from the investor's perspective) in Chapter 9 (bonds), Chapters 10 and 11 (preferred and common stock), and Chapter 13 (convertible bonds and convertible preferred stock). The next chapter will consider specific sources of short-term finance, while this section covers the trade-off between sources of short-term and long-term finance and how that trade-off affects the risk associated with a firm's working capital policy.

Exhibit 20.1 illustrated that a firm's current assets vary through the operating cycle. As a firm's current assets rise, its sources of finance also must increase. In the illustration, the increase in assets was covered by increases in accounts payable and accrued wages. These are, of course, not the only possible sources, but a major principle of finance suggests that a financial manager should match the sources of finance with their use.

Short-term sources of finance, such as a loan from a commercial bank, require frequent refunding; long-term debt and equity do not require frequent refunding, which makes them appropriate for financing long-term assets. The firm should not use short-term sources to finance long-term assets. It may be years before the long-term assets generate funds; the short-term loans, however, must be repaid during the fiscal year. Unless this credit can be refunded (for instance, the funds borrowed from one source can be used to retire the debt from another source) or renewed, management will face a substantial problem meeting its short-term obligations as they come due.

While the firm should not use short-term finance to acquire long-term assets (rather, it should use long-term sources), the firm may use either short- or long-term sources to acquire short-term assets. Short-term sources may be used to finance inventory and accounts receivable because as these assets are converted into cash, the funds may be used to repay the short-term loans. Long-term sources may be used to finance current assets since these sources do not have the problem of frequent refunding.

Since long-term sources may be used to finance both short-term and long-term assets, why does the financial manager use short-term sources? The answer revolves around the cost and the risks associated with each source. The choice of long- versus short-term sources of funds is ultimately a question of the funds' impact on earnings and the risk associated with management's choices of finance. Generally, short-term sources are riskier because these obligations have to be refinanced. The firm is not pressed with the continual need to refinance or retire long-term sources. Hence, long-term sources are not as risky as short-term sources.

If the use of short-term sources increases risk, the question again arises, "Why do firms use this source?" There are both specific and general answers to that question. The specific answers will be developed in the next chapter, which covers short-term sources of finance. The general answer is that short-term sources are often less expensive than long-term sources. (This relationship between the yield or cost and the term of a debt instrument was illustrated in Figure 2.1 in Chapter 2.) Short-term lenders accept lower interest rates for rapid repayment of principal. They trade some return for increased liquidity. This lower interest cost results in increased earnings for the firm using short-term rather than long-term debt financing.

The possible impact on the firm's earnings may be shown by the following illustration. Firm A has a balance sheet as follows:

Balance Sheet as of 12/31/XO			
Assets		**Liabilities and Equity**	
Assets	$10,000	Debt	$6,000
		Equity	$4,000

The balance sheet does not specify the term of the debt. For illustrative purposes, we shall assume three cases: (1) one year at 8 percent, (2) five years at 10 percent, and (3) fifteen years at 12 percent. If sales are $4,000 and other expenses are $2,500, the profits earned by the firm in each case are

	1	2	3
Sales	$4,000	$4,000	$4,000
Expenses	2,500	2,500	2,500
Earnings before interest expense	1,500	1,500	1,500
Interest expense	480	600	720
Earnings after interest expense	$1,020	$ 900	$ 780

As one would expect, the higher interest cost associated with the long-term debt produces the lowest earnings. The lower interest cost associated with the short-term debt produces the highest earnings.

Now consider what happens to the firm's earnings if after a year the short-term interest rate rises to 13 percent. The income statements now become:

	1	2	3
Sales	$4,000	$4,000	$4,000
Expenses	2,500	2,500	2,500
Earnings before interest expense	1,500	1,500	1,500
Interest expense	780	600	720
Earnings after interest expense	$ 720	$ 900	$ 780

If the firm initially uses short-term debt, its earnings are reduced because short-term debt is more expensive. The earnings that resulted from the use of intermediate-term and long-term debt (for instance, five and fifteen years, respectively) are not changed. Even if the cost of long-term debt is *currently* higher (for example, 15 percent), the earnings of the firm are unaffected. Why? Because the firm borrowed in the past at 12 percent, and this rate is fixed for the term of the debt. The current cost of long-term debt only matters if the firm is issuing more long-term debt.

This example illustrates that the use of short-term instead of long-term debt may increase the firm's earnings now but reduce them in the future if short-term interest rates rise. The fact that short-term interest can rise above long-term rates was previously illustrated in Figure 2.2, in Chapter 2. In that illustration the yields on short-term Treasury bills exceeded the yields on long-term Treasury bonds.

Large and rapid changes in the cost of short-term credit imply that the choice of short-term finance can affect both the earnings and the risk exposure of the firm by increasing the variability of the earnings. Managements of companies in cyclical industries, such as construction, may follow conservative working capital policy and use more long-term sources of finance. Managements of firms with stable revenues, such as electric utilities, may have a less conservative working capital policy. They can afford the risk associated with having a larger proportion of current assets financed by current liabilities.

Differences in working capital policy are illustrated in Exhibit 20.2, which gives the current assets, current liabilities, current ratio, and net working capital for four firms in different industries. A high current ratio and large amount of net working capital suggest a conservative working capital policy.[2] As may be seen in

[2]Another ratio that indicates a conservative working capital policy is net working capital divided by current liabilities. This ratio offers the advantage of standardizing for size so that large firms like Coke may be compared to smaller firms like C-Cube and Mylan Labs. For C-Cube and Mylan Labs, net working capital divided by current liabilities ratios are 3.1 and 5.1, respectively, which essentially suggests the same working capital policy as the current ratios and net working capital.

EXHIBIT 20.2

Working Capital Policies

Firm	Industry	Current Assets*	Current Liabilities*	Current Ratio	Net Working Capital*
Coca-Cola	Beverages	$6,380	$8,640	0.74	$(2,260)
C-Cube Microsystems	Semiconductors	292	71	4.12	221
Maytag	Appliances	969	791	1.23	178
Mylan Laboratories	Pharmaceuticals	583	96	6.07	487

**Current assets, current liabilities, and net working capital in millions.*

Source: 1998 annual reports.

this exhibit, Mylan Labs has a current ratio that exceeds 6:1 and net working capital of $487 million, which suggests a very conservative use of short-term financing. Coca-Cola, however, has negative net working capital and a current ratio of less than 1:1. Coke appears to have a very aggressive working capital policy. Coke, however, also has about $2 billion in marketable securities, which management has not classified as current assets. These securities may be sold so there is no question of Coke's ability to meet its current obligations as they come due.

THE INVENTORY CYCLE

A firm produces output to sell, or it buys items wholesale and retails the product. In either case the firm acquires inventory. This inventory must be paid for; it must be financed by either borrowed funds or equity. The more rapidly the firm turns over the inventory, the less finance is necessary to carry the inventory. (In Chapter 12, one of the ratios used to analyze a firm was inventory turnover.) Rapid turnover indicates that the firm is able to sell the inventory quickly, and hence the firm ties up fewer of its funds. Rapid turnover, however, is not in itself desirable, for such turnover may result in the firm's not having inventory available when there are buyers. Being out of stock may result in the loss of sales and profits. While rapid inventory turnover decreases the firm's financial needs, it may also result in lower earnings.

The inventory cycle is illustrated by Figure 20.1. The firm initially purchases inventory (AB). As time passes, some inventory is sold, and the stock of inventory is drawn down, and at T_1 the inventory is sold and the stock is depleted. The firm then purchases new inventory (AB), and the cycle is repeated (T_1 to T_2).

In reality a firm would not let its inventory fall to zero before it restocked its shelves. Instead, it would maintain a minimum level of inventory (a **safety stock**) to assure that some stock is always available for sale. Such a safety stock is illustrated in Figure 20.2. The minimum level of inventory (the safety stock) is CA.

SAFETY STOCK
Desired minimum level of inventory designed to protect against loss of sales due to being out of stock

FIGURE 20.1

Simple Inventory Cycle

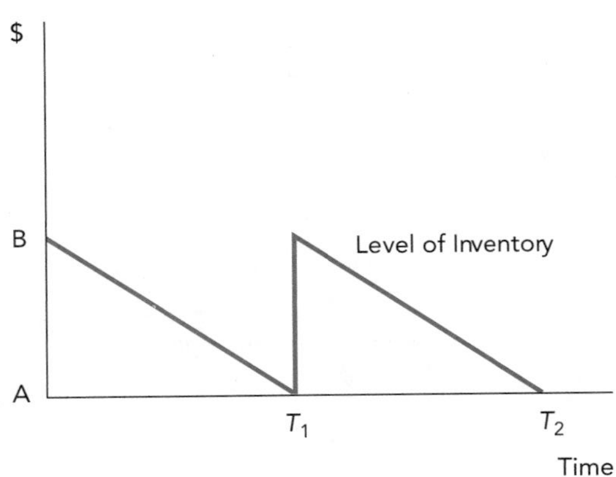

FIGURE 20.2

Simple Inventory Cycle Including a Safety Stock

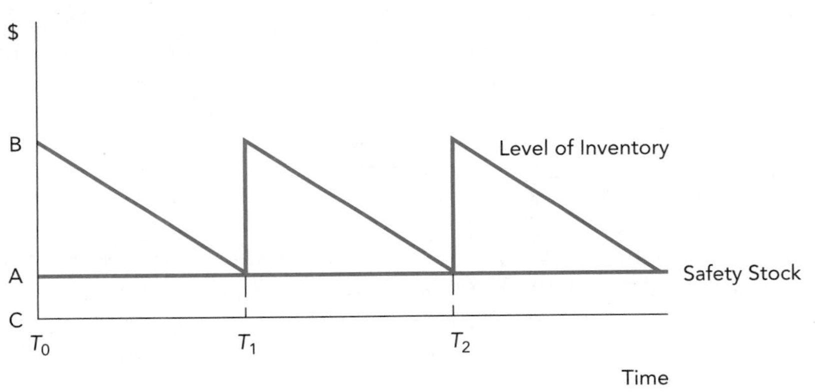

The inventory order is added to the safety stock, so that the firm has a maximum inventory of CB, which consists of the safety stock CA and the order AB. This total inventory is drawn down as sales are made. As the level of inventory approaches the safety stock, the firm reorders.

The firm could avoid reordering the inventory by increasing its initial purchase. By doubling its initial purchase, the firm can double the time before it has to reorder. Of course, the firm could avoid all inventory cycles if it had sufficient inventory. However, it costs money to carry inventory; hence, management determines the best level of inventory to purchase to reduce the carrying costs. One possible model that determines this level is the economic order quantity (EOQ) covered in the next section.

THE ECONOMIC ORDER QUANTITY

The optimal size of an order of inventory, the **economic order quantity (EOQ),** is the order size that minimizes the total cost of carrying and processing inventory. This cost has several components, and minimizing one component increases another component. What are these components? First, there is the cost of placing the order, which includes shipping, brokerage, and processing costs. These costs decline (are lower per unit) as inventory increases.

ECONOMIC ORDER QUANTITY (EOQ)
Optimal size of an order of inventory

A second set of costs consists of those associated with carrying the inventory. These costs include insurance, storage, and the cost of financing the inventory. These carrying costs increase as the size of the inventory increases and offset the lower per-unit costs of larger orders. The job of management, then, is to balance the savings from larger orders with the increased carrying costs.

The total annual cost associated with inventory is the sum of ordering costs and carrying costs. Ordering cost (OC) is the product of (1) the number of orders and (2) the cost per order (F). The number of orders depends on the number of units sold (S) and the size of each order (Q). The number of orders equals units sold divided by the size of each order. Thus, total ordering costs are

$$OC = \left(\frac{S}{Q}\right)F. \tag{20.1}$$

If annual sales are 10,000 units and the size of each inventory order is 1,000 units, the firm places 10 orders a year. If the cost of placing an order is \$50,[3] then total ordering costs are \$500.

$$OC = \left(\frac{10{,}000}{1{,}000}\right)\$50 = \$500.$$

Annual carrying costs (CC) are the product of average inventory ($Q/2$) and per-unit carrying costs (C). Total carrying costs are

$$CC = \left(\frac{Q}{2}\right)C. \tag{20.2}$$

[3] In this illustration, the shipping and ordering costs are fixed at \$50. The cost of each order is independent of the size of the order, and as the number of orders is reduced, total costs decline. It is possible, however, that the cost of ordering may increase with the size of the order but per-unit costs still decline. For example, suppose it costs \$2 to ship one book but \$3 to ship two books. Even though the ordering cost of a larger shipment rises, the per-unit cost of shipping one book is lower, and fewer but larger shipments reduce total ordering costs.

EXHIBIT 20.3 Relationships between Inventory and Ordering Costs and between Inventory and Carrying Costs

Total Sales (S = 10,000 units)	Size of Inventory Order	Number of Orders	Cost per Order (F = $50)	Total Order Costs	Average Inventory	Per-Unit Carrying Cost (C = $10)	Total Carrying Costs	Total Costs
10,000	50	200	$50	$10,000	25	$10	$ 250	$10,250
10,000	100	100	50	5,000	50	10	500	5,500
10,000	200	50	50	2,500	100	10	1,000	3,500
10,000	300	34	50	1,700	150	10	1,500	3,200
→ 10,000	316	32	50	1,600	158	10	1,580	3,180 ←
10,000	400	25	50	1,250	200	10	2,000	3,250
10,000	500	20	50	1,000	250	10	2,500	3,500
10,000	600	17	50	850	300	10	3,000	3,850
10,000	800	13	50	650	400	10	4,000	4,650
10,000	1,000	10	50	500	500	10	5,000	5,500

If the firm orders 1,000 units of inventory and sells them evenly over the year, its average inventory is 500 units (1,000/2). If the per-unit carrying cost is $10, the annual carrying cost is $5,000.

$$CC = \left(\frac{1{,}000}{2}\right)\$10 = \$5{,}000.$$

Total inventory costs (TC) are the sum of the two components:

20.3
$$TC = OC + CC = \left(\frac{S}{Q}\right)F + \left(\frac{Q}{2}\right)C.$$

In this example, total inventory costs are

$$TC = \left(\frac{10{,}000}{1{,}000}\right)(\$50) + \left(\frac{1{,}000}{2}\right)(\$10) = \$5{,}500.$$

The relationships between inventory and ordering costs and between inventory and carrying costs are presented in Exhibit 20.3. The first column presents the given level of sales, while the second and third columns give various possible order sizes and the number of inventory orders for the given level of sales. As the size of each order is increased, the number of orders is reduced. The fourth column specifies the cost of placing an order. Column 5, which is the product of the number of orders and the cost per order (the product of columns 3 and 4), presents the total order costs associated with various levels of inventory. Notice how the total ordering costs decline with larger orders (higher levels of inventory) because the firm is placing fewer orders and thus is incurring fewer ordering costs.

FIGURE 20.3

Determination of EOQ

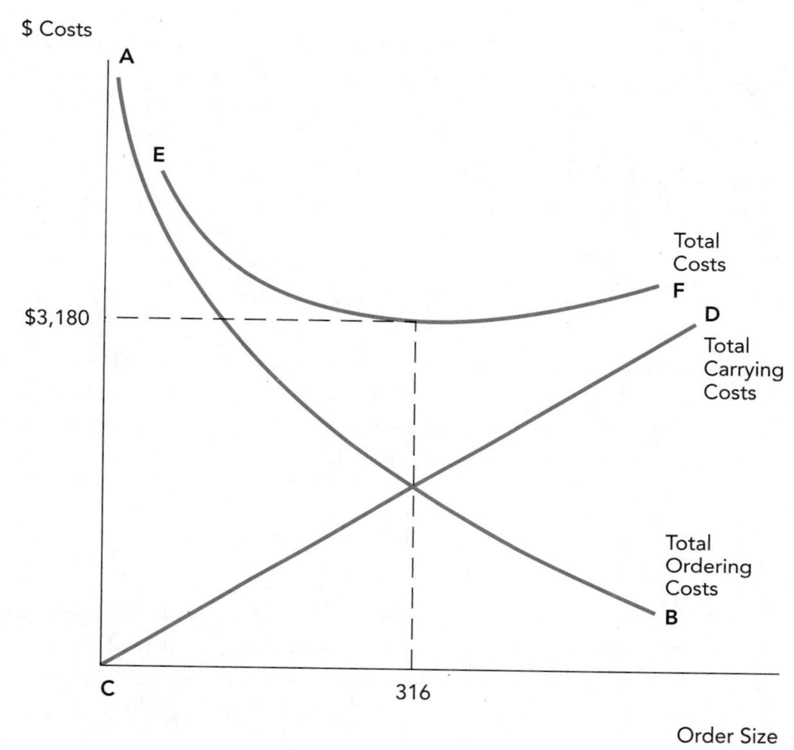

The second part of Exhibit 20.3 presents in column 6 the average level of inventory (column 2 divided by two) and the per-unit carrying costs (column 7). The total carrying costs (column 8) are the product of columns 6 and 7. Notice how total carrying costs rise with the level of inventory. Higher levels of inventory inflict more costs on the firm to carry the inventory.

The sum of the total ordering costs (column 5) and the carrying costs (column 8) is the total cost associated with each level of inventory. That cost is presented in column 9. As may be seen in this column, total costs initially decline as the level of inventory is increased. However, the decline moderates, reaches a minimum point at 316 units, and then starts to increase. The level of inventory that minimizes the total cost of the inventory is the best quantity for the firm to order. That quantity is the "economic order quantity" or EOQ.

The trade-off between ordering costs and carrying costs demonstrated in Exhibit 20.3 is illustrated in Figure 20.3. The horizontal axis measures the size of the inventory order while the vertical axis shows the total costs associated with those orders. Line AB shows total ordering costs, which decline as the size of each order increases. This decline occurs because the total number of orders is reduced. Line

CD shows total carrying costs, which rise with increased order size. These increased costs are the result of the firm having more inventory. Line EF combines these two costs and illustrates the total costs associated with each level of inventory. It clearly demonstrates the initial decline in total costs, their minimum value ($3,180 at 316 units), and their subsequent increase as the size of the inventory order increases beyond 316 units.

Mathematical models have been developed to help determine this economic order quantity. Perhaps the simplest model starts with Equation 20.3:

20.4
$$TC = OC + CC = \left(\frac{S}{Q}\right)F + \left(\frac{Q}{2}\right)C,$$

and then determines the order size that minimizes total costs. This is a calculus problem in which the first derivative with respect to ordering quantity is set equal to zero and solved. The resulting solution is referred to as the economic order quantity (EOQ) and is given in Equation 20.4.[4]

$$EOQ = \sqrt{\frac{2SF}{C}}.$$

The example in Exhibit 20.2 may be used to illustrate how the formula works. A firm uses 10,000 units of an item each year, and it costs the firm $10 to carry each unit.[5] The cost of an order is $50. When these values are substituted into Equation 20.4, the economic order quantity is determined on the following page:

[4]Calculus is used to determine the EOQ. The calculation is as follows:

$$TC = (S)(F)(Q)^{-1} + (Q)(C)/2.$$

Take the first derivative with respect to Q:

$$\frac{d(TC)}{d(Q)} = -(S)(F)(Q^{-2}) + C/2.$$

Set the first derivative equal to zero and solve for Q:

$$(S)(F)(Q^{-2}) = C/2$$

$$C = \frac{2(S)(F)}{Q^2}$$

$$Q^2 = \frac{2(S)(F)}{C}$$

$$Q = \sqrt{\frac{2(S)(F)}{C}}.$$

[5]The cost to carry may also be expressed as the percentage of carrying costs times the cost of a unit of inventory. If inventory costs $100 per unit, and the percent cost of carry is 10 percent, then the cost of carrying is $100 × 0.10 = $10.

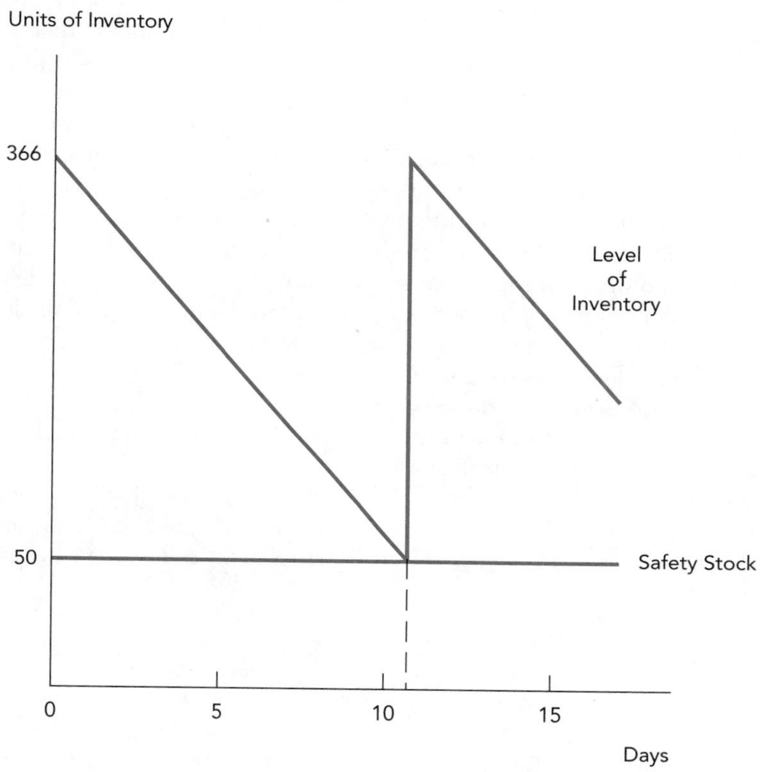

FIGURE 20.4

Inventory Cycle with EOQ

$$EOQ = \sqrt{\frac{2(10{,}000)(\$50)}{\$10}} = 316.$$

Thus, the most economical order size for this item is 316 units.

How this information is related to the inventory cycle is illustrated in Figure 20.4. In this illustration a safety stock of 50 units has been assumed. The initial order is 366 units, which is the sum of the safety stock (50) and the economic order quantity (316). Since annual sales are 10,000 units, sales per day are

$$\text{Sales per day} = 10{,}000/365 = 27.4.$$

If sales per day are approximately 28 units, the economic order quantity is sold in approximately 11 days.

$$\text{Duration of the EOQ} = \text{EOQ/Daily sales}$$

$$316/28 = 11.3.$$

This passage of time is shown in Figure 20.4 from day 0 to day 11, at which time the level of inventory has declined to the safety stock and must be replenished. Then the cycle is repeated. The amount of inventory the firm should reorder once again is the EOQ, which remains 316 units unless the carrying costs or the ordering costs have changed.

When will management place an order for the 316 units? The answer depends on how long it takes to receive delivery. For example, if the firm expects shipment to take 5 days and the EOQ to last 11 days, then management must place an order 6 days after taking possession of the inventory to be certain to receive the next order. Of course, if the order is late, the firm will start to use its safety stock, so the possibility of late shipments is one reason for carrying a safety stock. If delivery is slow, the reorder point may be several weeks before the inventory is needed. For example, if delivery requires 14 days, the firm will have to place a second order before the first order is received, since the duration of the EOQ is 11 days. If delivery is rapid, however, the reorder may occur close to when shipment is needed. If the firm could receive shipment within a day, the reorder point would be only one day before the inventory is needed.

A change in any of the variables used to calculate the EOQ will, of course, affect the desired amount of each order. For example, if the cost of placing an order in the previous illustration increases from \$50 to \$100, the economic order quantity becomes:

$$EOQ = \sqrt{\frac{2(10{,}000)(\$100)}{\$10}} = 447.$$

The increase in the cost of processing the order raises the best reorder size from 316 to 447 units. If the carrying costs were to rise from \$10 to \$20, the EOQ would decline from 316 to 224:

$$EOQ = \sqrt{\frac{2(10{,}000)(\$50)}{\$20}} = 224.$$

These changes in costs do not produce proportionate changes in the economic order quantity. The doubling of the order cost does not double the economic order quantity and a doubling of the carrying cost does not result in halving the optimal order. There is more than one variable affecting the optimal order quantity. If one variable changes and the others are unaffected, there is no reason to assume that there will be a proportionate change in the economic order quantity. Hence, there is no simple proportionate relationship between one component of the costs and the EOQ.

Weaknesses in the EOQ

The EOQ model is a simple model for the determination of the optimal order quantity. It is based on simplifying assumptions that rarely apply to all firms at all times. Of course, this criticism may apply to other models explained in this text.

Each model has a set of assumptions. However, of all the models presented in this text, the simple EOQ may have the least realistic assumptions.

A major assumption is that sales occur smoothly during the time period. This assumption permits the line representing the level of inventory in Figure 20.4 to decline at the same rate of 11.3 units a day. Sales, however, generally do vary over a period of time. Some sales are seasonal, and even nonseasonal sales may occur at different rates throughout the year. There are periods when sales are sluggish, and inventory is drawn down at a slower rate. Even stable sales do not imply that the same amount is sold daily as suggested by the simple EOQ model.

In addition, the simple EOQ model does not consider quantity discounts and delays in processing orders. Of course, discounts for large purchases and delays in shipping can affect the level of inventory carried by the firm. There is also a problem applying the model if the firm carries many products. A retailer like Home Depot carries thousands of items and applying the EOQ model may be impossible. For example, how would you allocate the shipping costs for the various items received in one shipment? The ordering costs of each item cannot be known, so the model could not be applied to each item but to batches.

Even if the model could be expanded and made more sophisticated, the basic concept that it illustrates remains unaltered. The EOQ seeks to determine the size of the order that minimizes the total costs of carrying and processing inventory. As such it brings to the foreground the trade-off between carrying and ordering costs. These costs move in opposite directions, so decreasing one tends to increase the other. If management underestimates ordering costs (or overestimates carrying costs), the firm may lose sales from lack of inventory. In the opposite situation in which management overestimates the cost of ordering (or underestimates carrying costs), the effect will be to order too much inventory. Carrying excess inventory is costly. One of the quickest means to place a firm in financial difficulty is to have excess inventory, especially during a period of rising short-term interest rates. Under that scenario, the firm has unsold inventory being financed with increasingly expensive short-term credit.

A firm could reduce these problems if it could better coordinate the receiving of inventory with its sale. Raw materials would arrive "just in time" for the production process, and the production process would be completed "just in time" for delivery. Inventory would consist only of work-in-process for a manufacturer and would be virtually nonexistent for a retailer.

A "just-in-time" inventory system seeks to achieve just that. Raw materials arrive only as needed and finished goods are immediately shipped. Just-in-time inventory management requires (1) very accurate sales forecasts that are updated often, (2) a flexible production schedule with tight deadlines, (3) reliable equipment and preventive maintenance programs (a breakdown in part of the process throws the tight schedules off), and (4) frequent communication with and cooperation from suppliers.

When successful, just-in-time inventory management erases the need for determining the economic order quantity. Just-in-time reduces the need for safety stocks and for capacity since facilities and labor are used more intensely, and increases the firm's ability to respond to changes in customers' demands. The system manufactures exactly what customers need when they need it, permitting customers to also institute just-in-time inventory management. Shipping costs tend to increase because the firm must make more (and smaller) shipments; however, increased supplier and buyer loyalty, the savings in inventory carrying costs, and the reduced need for plant and equipment result in increased earnings when just-in-time inventory management is successfully employed.

One advantage of e-commerce is the ability to better control inventory and practice "just-in-time" inventory management. Firms such as Amazon.com or eToys do not rent retail stores and carry large quantities of inventory. Instead they lease inexpensive centralized warehouse space. While Amazon.com and eToys do carry inventory, they avoid display expense and reduce carrying costs by ordering replacement inventory as they make shipments. The firms can also reduce or in some cases even avoid shipping expense by charging customers for the service.

Maximum, Minimum, and Average Inventory

The EOQ gives the optimal order quantity for inventory; that, however, is not the same as the maximum inventory to be carried by a firm. Consider the firm in Figure 20.4 at the beginning of day 1. Its maximum inventory is the EOQ (316) plus the safety stock (50). The minimum inventory at the end of day 11 is the safety stock, if sales occur as anticipated. Of course, the minimum possible inventory is 0 if the entire safety stock is sold before new inventory is received.

The average inventory depends on the EOQ and the safety stock. If sales occur evenly throughout the time period (approximately 28 units per day), the average inventory associated with the EOQ has to be the EOQ/2. The inventory at the beginning of day 1 is 316 units and at the end of day 11 is 0. The average of these two numbers is 158 ([316 + 0]/2). At the beginning of the second day, inventory is 288 units because 28 were sold during the first day. At the end of the tenth day, inventory is 28 units. The average of these two numbers is 158 ([288 + 28]/2). By similar reasoning, it may be shown that the average inventory associated with the EOQ is always the EOQ/2, as long as sales occur evenly throughout the period.

The average inventory associated with the safety stock is the amount of safety stock. Consider the safety stock in Figure 20.4. At the beginning of day 1, the safety stock is 50 units. At the end of day 11, the safety stock is still 50 units. The average of these two numbers is obviously 50. As long as the safety stock is not drawn down, the average safety stock is 50 units.

Of course, the firm's average inventory is the sum of the two averages. Thus,

$$\text{Average inventory} = \text{EOQ}/2 + \text{Safety stock}.$$

The average inventory for the firm in Figure 20.4 is 208 units ([316/2] + 50), while the maximum and minimum levels of inventory are 366 and 50 units, respectively.

INVENTORY VALUATION

The preceding section considered the determination of the optimal order quantity, which was expressed in units of inventory. This section considers the valuation of that inventory. A firm purchases inventory at different times and the cost of the inventory may vary. The firm subsequently sells the inventory, and a question arises. Which units of the inventory were sold? Were the first units of inventory purchased the first to be sold, or were the last units of inventory purchased the first units to be sold? During periods of fluctuating prices, the answer to this question affects the firm's earnings and income taxes.

There are two prevalent means to value inventory. According to one method, the first units of inventory purchased are the first units sold—that is, **first in, first out (FIFO).** In the second method, the last units of inventory purchased are the first units sold. Under this system the newest inventory is sold first—that is, **last in, first out (LIFO).** If the firm sells all its inventory and carries none over from one year to another, or if prices do not fluctuate, the difference between the two methods is immaterial. However, firms do carry inventory from one fiscal year to another; hence, it is important to establish which items of inventory are actually sold. This determination becomes even more important during periods of fluctuating prices because the cost of the inventory fluctuates. For example, during a period of inflation, the cost of the inventory increases, and the selection of the method of inventory valuation affects the firm's earnings and income taxes.

FIRST IN, FIRST OUT (FIFO)
Method of inventory valuation in which the first inventory received is the first inventory sold

LAST IN, FIRST OUT (LIFO)
Method of inventory valuation in which the last inventory received is the first inventory sold

How this effect occurs may be illustrated by the following example. A firm purchases 100 units of inventory every two months. As a result of inflation the cost of the inventory increases during the year. The following schedule gives the dates of purchase and the cost of the inventory:

	Price per Unit	Total Cost of Inventory
January	$1.00	$100
March	1.04	104
May	1.06	106
July	1.08	108
September	1.11	111
November	1.15	115
		$644

During the year the firm purchased 600 units of inventory for a total cost of $644. The inventory was sold for $1.30 a unit. Total sales were 500 units, for total revenues of $650. The firm ended the year with 100 units of inventory to sell during the next year. How much profit did the firm earn during this year? The answer will be influenced by the method of inventory valuation that is selected, because the cost of the inventory rose during the year.

If FIFO is used, the first inventory is sold first. The firm sold the 500 units of inventory acquired from January to September, and this inventory cost $529. If LIFO is used, the last inventory was sold first. The firm sold the 500 units acquired during March through November, and this inventory cost $544.

The effect on the firm's earnings of the choice of LIFO or FIFO is illustrated by the following simple income statements. The first statement is constructed using FIFO, and the second statement is constructed using LIFO.

	FIFO Income Statement	LIFO Income Statement
Sales	$650	$650
Cost of Goods Sold	529	544
Income	$121	$106

The firm's earnings are higher in the FIFO income statement because the cost of the goods sold is less. The use of the lower inventory valuation produces higher earnings, and these higher earnings will result in higher income taxes. In effect, the cost of the inventory acquired during the year has been understated, which creates the illusion of higher profits. If the firm had used LIFO, profits would be less, and the taxes on its income would be less. During a period of inflation the use of LIFO may give a better indication of the firm's true profitability, because LIFO uses the higher costs of goods sold to determine earnings.

The impact of the choice of LIFO over FIFO during a period of inflation is not limited to the effect on taxable income; the choice also affects the analysis of the firm's financial statements. Since a firm sells its most expensive inventory first with LIFO, its year-end inventory (and thus its average inventory) is lower. Inventory turnover (that is, sales divided by average inventory) is increased because the fraction's denominator is decreased.

Inventory valuation also affects profitability ratios. The choice of LIFO during a period of rising prices reduces any ratio that uses net income. For example, the return on sales and return on equity ratios both use net income. Since the choice of LIFO reduces profits during inflation, both of these ratios are reduced. Lower earnings also suggest that retained earnings will rise less (unless the firm reduces its dividend). This implies that the debt ratio or the ratio of debt to equity is also affected. The firm will appear to be using more financial leverage.

The financial analyst needs to be aware of the firm's choice of LIFO or FIFO in order to make consistent comparisons of a firm's financial statements over time or to compare a firm's financial statements with those of other firms. Obviously, if one set of financial statements is constructed using LIFO while another is constructed using FIFO, any comparisons may be misleading unless the analyst restates the financial statements to put them on a common footing.

MANAGEMENT OF ACCOUNTS RECEIVABLE

Accounts receivable arise through credit sales. Sales may be for cash or for credit. If the firm accepts credit, it is accepting a promise of future payment. To determine credit policy, management should consider several factors. As in all financial decisions, these factors involve the potential benefits versus the costs associated with the policy. The potential benefit of offering credit is increased sales, for many consumers use credit extensively and many firms, especially retailers, also buy on credit.

But credit involves costs. There are the obvious processing fees, for the firm must bill its credit customers and keep records. These processing costs have encouraged many retail firms to accept such credit cards as MasterCard or VISA. The retailer accepts the card and lets the issuing agent process and collect the accounts receivable. The retailer, however, only collects some percentage of the credit sales, such as $0.98 on every $1.00, with the $0.02 going to the collecting agent. While this arrangement reduces the proceeds of the sale, it virtually eliminates the processing costs of credit.

Offering credit also involves the possibility of loss; not all credit sales are collected. Some purchasers will default. Of course, many accounts are of excellent quality, as is illustrated by the accounts receivable of utilities. These accounts are generally of high quality because the company can force payment by threatening to discontinue service. One method of increasing the safety of accounts receivable is to require the buyer to pledge the merchandise against the loan. In case of default the seller repossesses the goods, which may then be resold. The seller, however, may be unable to obtain the full value of the account receivable. In such a case the seller still has a claim on the original buyer for the balance but may never be able to collect that claim.

Credit Policy

Credit policy has three components: the selection of those customers who will be granted credit, the terms of credit, and the collection policy. While all three components are important, the firm faces legal constraints with regard to the granting of credit and the terms. For example, the firm may not discriminate in granting credit; it must be given to all who meet the standards. Furthermore, the firm may not discriminate in terms offered. Once the firm establishes the terms, they apply to all.

To determine who will be granted credit, the firm establishes credit standards. These standards consider such factors as the capacity of the borrower to pay, the collateral the borrower may have to secure the loan, and the borrower's record of payment. The capacity to pay primarily depends on the borrower's income and other sources of cash. Individuals with higher levels of income have more capacity to meet credit payments and are better credit risks. However, income level is not the only consideration because an individual (or firm) may have other debt obligations. Thus, the lender also considers the amount of debt the borrower already has outstanding. While it may seem that such information is unobtainable, such is not the case. The lender may ask for the information directly and not grant credit if such information is withheld. Even if the information is supplied by the borrower, it is wise to verify the information through various credit bureaus. These firms maintain financial information that may be purchased by firms who desire financial information concerning potential borrowers.

Collateral refers to specific assets that may be pledged to secure a loan and reduce the risk of loss to the lender.[6] However, not all assets make good collateral. For an asset to be good collateral, it must be saleable. For this reason, marketable securities, such as stocks and bonds, make excellent collateral, for they may be

[6]The use of collateral to secure a loan was considered earlier with mortgage loans in Chapter 7 and equipment trust certificates in Chapter 9.

readily sold. Real estate may also serve as collateral. However, it may take an extended period to sell real estate, during which time the lender's funds are tied up in the bad loan. Since the marketability of assets differs, their usefulness as collateral varies. The variation in marketability and quality explains why creditors lend varying amounts against specific assets. The more readily the asset may be sold near its assessed value, the more it can be used to secure the loan.

As is discussed in more detail in the next chapter, lenders do not want the collateral that is used to secure the loan. For example, a bank makes its profits through lending; it is not in the business of selling assets seized for the nonpayment of debt. Thus, part of the role of collateral is psychological. The purpose is to encourage the borrower to meet the required payments. Failure to meet the payments may result in the borrower losing the pledged asset. Since the pledged asset is worth more than the amount of the loan, the borrower may suffer a loss if the asset is sold. This threat of loss gives the use of collateral teeth and increases the likelihood that the borrower will meet the required payments.

In addition to the borrower's capacity to meet its debt obligations and the assets that are available to secure the loans, the lender considers the borrower's past credit history. Does the borrower have a history of slow payment? Has the borrower ever declared bankruptcy? A good track record implies that the borrower is a safer risk. Once again this information may be obtained through credit-rating agencies and credit bureaus that maintain credit histories on individuals for the previous 7 years (10 years in case of a previous bankruptcy). While such past histories do not assure the creditor will continue to be a good risk, they do differentiate borrowers with a good credit history from those who have been slow payers or who have defaulted in the past.

After establishing who will be granted credit, the firm must establish the terms. The terms of the loan include the time period for the loan, the discount (if any) for early payment, and the penalty for late payment. In the next chapter, the terms of trade credit are illustrated by phrases like 2/10, n30. In that case, the term is 30 days with a 2 percent discount for payment by the tenth day. (These terms do not specify any penalty for failure to apply by the thirtieth day.) Often terms are n30 (or n60) with interest on the unpaid balance at 1.5 percent monthly (18 percent annually) after the initial 30 days have elapsed. Such terms let the borrower have the "free" use of credit for 30 days (60 days if the terms are n60). The lender is carrying the loan for the specified term and has built this cost of credit into the price of the goods sold to the borrower. Since the credit is already paid for, such terms encourage the borrower not to pay until the term of the loan has elapsed.

Actually, the lender may have little flexibility in the terms that are offered, since competition forces firms to offer similar terms. (If a major retailer in the mall accepts VISA, virtually all other retailers are forced to accept VISA.) However, while competition may determine the terms and legal constraints restrict the selection of potential borrowers, the firm has more flexibility with regard to its collection policy. Such policy can range from sending a second billing or an overdue statement to harsher measures, such as threats of legal action. Failure to collect forces the lender to (1) write off the loan as uncollectible, (2) take more drastic action, such as initiate legal action designed to force payment, or (3) sell the account to a collection agency. While drastic action may force payment, it may also result in the loss of goodwill. Buyers may feel threatened if the firm follows a rigorous collection policy.

Like all assets, accounts receivable are a use of funds that must be financed. All accounts receivable must offer an implied return or benefit (for example, increased profitable sales) to justify their use of funds. If credit sales do not yield this return, they decrease the profitability of the firm. Credit policy, then, is ultimately designed to assure that the extension of credit increases the profitability of the firm.

Analzying Accounts Receivable

Having granted credit, management needs to supervise and analyze the firm's accounts receivable. One technique for monitoring accounts receivable is to analyze their turnover. Turnover ratios, such as annual sales/accounts receivable or the average collection period (days that sales are outstanding), were discussed in Chapter 12. The faster the accounts receivable turn over, the faster they are collected and converted into cash. This cash may then be used to acquire other income-earning assets or to retire debt.

RECEIVABLES TURNOVER The potential for savings from increasing turnover of accounts receivable may be seen in the following example. The industry average turnover ratio is 6 (that is, every two months). This particular firm has credit sales of \$100,000,000 and accounts receivable of \$25,000,000. Thus, its accounts receivable turn over four times a year (Credit sales/Accounts receivable = \$100,000,000/\$25,000,000 = 4). If this firm were able to match the industry average, what would be the amount of its accounts receivable? The answer is

$$\frac{\text{Credit sales}}{\text{Accounts receivable}} = 6$$

$$6 = \frac{\$100{,}000{,}000}{X}$$

$$X = \$100{,}000{,}000/6 = \$16{,}666{,}667.$$

If the firm achieved a receivables turnover that was comparable to the industry average, its accounts receivable would decline from \$25,000,000 to \$16,666,667. That is a net reduction of \$8,333,333 in accounts receivable. If funds cost 10 percent annually, the reduction in the accounts receivable would save the firm \$833,333 a year in finance charges (\$8,333,333 × 0.10 = \$833,333). Obviously, increasing the turnover of the accounts receivable increases the profitability of the firm.

AGING SCHEDULES Another tool used to analyze credit sales is to age the accounts. This simple technique constructs a table showing the length of time each account has been outstanding (unpaid). How this technique works is illustrated by the following example. A firm has total accounts receivable of \$1,100, which are composed of five customers. The amount of each account and the number of days outstanding are as follows:

Customer	Amount of the Account	Number of Days Outstanding
A	$300	45
B	100	70
C	200	20
D	200	35
E	300	15

From this information, the following table can be constructed:

AGING SCHEDULE (IN DAYS)

Accounts	0–30	31–60	61–90	More Than 90
A	–	$300	–	–
B	–	–	$100	–
C	$200	–	–	–
D	–	200	–	–
E	300	–	–	–
	$500	$500	$100	$0
Percentage of total accounts receivable	45.5%	45.5%	9.1%	0%

This table shows that $600 (or 54.6%) of the accounts receivable has been outstanding for more than a month and that one account has not been paid for more than two months.

By aging the receivables, a pattern, or norm, is established. Then, if the percentage of slow accounts increases, the financial manager has identified a problem and can take action either to force collection or to acknowledge the accounts to be bad and discontinue carrying them at the stated value on the firm's books. However, slow accounts are not necessarily bad and may eventually be collected. In many cases a firm's best or most important customers may be slow payers. This may be especially true if the buyer is larger than the seller and accounts for a major portion of the smaller firm's sales. Such a buyer has the power to ride the credit, and the small supplier may not press for payment because it fears loss of future sales.

The Decision to Grant Credit

The decision to grant credit compares the benefits from an increase in sales and presumably earnings with the additional costs associated with granting the credit. These include (1) the cost of the additional goods sold, (2) the cost of credit checks, (3) collection and bad debt expenses, and (4) the cost of carrying the accounts receivable. Suppose a firm has sales of $100,000 without offering credit, but management believes that it can increase sales by 50 percent (from $100,000 to $150,000) if the firm offers customers 30 days to pay. Should the firm make the offer?

The answer depends on the costs associated with the additional sales. To ease the illustration, make the following assumptions:

1. The cost of the additional goods sold is 60 percent of sales.
2. Credit checks and collection costs are $7,000.
3. Five percent of the *new* sales will be uncollectible.
4. In addition to new customers, all existing customers will take 30 days to pay, while previously they paid immediately.
5. The cost of borrowing the funds to carry the receivables is 10 percent.

Consider the following projected income statement that will result from offering customers credit for 30 days:

Additional sales		$50,000
Costs		
Cost of additional goods sold ($50,000 × 0.6)	$30,000	
Credit/collection costs	7,000	
Bad debt expense ($50,000 × 0.05)	2,500	
Carrying costs (interest)	1,250	
Total costs		40,750
Net increase in earnings		$ 9,250

The carrying costs are figured as follows. Annual sales will be $150,000; all sales will be on credit; and all accounts receivable will be collected at the end of 30 days. Thus, accounts receivable will be $150,000/12 = $12,500. Since the cost of carrying the receivables is 10 percent, the interest expense is $1,250.

The analysis indicates a net increase in earnings of $9,250, which argues for granting the credit. However, several crucial assumptions were made. First, and most important, offering the credit increases sales. If the firm's competitors offer similar credit terms, the projected sales increase may not materialize. Second, the costs were known. However, an increase in any of the costs obviously reduces the projected increase in earnings. Thus, increased collection expense, an increase in defaults (bad debt), or an increase in the rate of interest will reduce earnings. Third, the analysis assumed that payments are made on the thirtieth day. If customers pay late, the accounts receivable will remain outstanding for a longer period of time and increase the carrying costs even if the rate of interest remains unchanged.

In summary, a firm's credit policy, like all economic decisions, involves a balancing of offsetting variables. By offering credit, a firm may increase sales, but with these increased sales come increased costs, including the cost of processing collections, the cost of financing the accounts, and the risk of loss. Like any investment decision, a firm's credit policy considers the potential benefits of offering credit (increased cash inflows) versus the increased expenses (increased cash outflows). If these benefits exceed their present costs, the firm extends credit, for such a credit policy enhances the value of the firm.

CASH MANAGEMENT

After inventory flows through the firm into sales and after accounts receivable have been collected, the financial manager must decide what to do with the cash. Cash management is important, because the firm must have sufficient liquidity to meet its obligations as they come due. However, liquidity reduces profitability because cash itself earns nothing. The cash must be used to purchase an income-earning asset in order to increase profitability.

Cash Management Policies

Cash management policies revolve around (1) hastening collections and retarding disbursements and (2) investing excess short-term funds into income-earning assets, especially money market securities that offer yield plus safety of principal. Increasing the speed of collections is not to be confused with increased turnover of inventory or accounts receivable. The turnover of these assets depends on inventory control and credit policy. Cash management is concerned with the speed with which cash is processed, especially the speed with which checks clear.

The more rapidly checks payable to the firm clear, the sooner the firm has the use of the funds. Correspondingly, the slower the checks that the firm has distributed clear, the longer the firm has the use of the funds. If the firm can increase the time that it has the use of the funds, it increases its profitability. An extension of just one day can generate thousands of dollars in earned interest. For example, suppose a firm were to increase its cash holdings by $1 million a day. At 5 percent, such a holding generates $136.98 in interest daily ($1,000,000 × 0.05/365) and $50,000 annually.

LOCKBOX
System of collections designed to decrease the float (increase the speed of collecting checks) to obtain the use of the funds more quickly

To generate this additional cash, the firm may establish a **lockbox** system of collections. When a firm bills a customer, the customer sends a check for payment. Checks take time to clear (this is the "float" discussed in Chapter 4 on the Federal Reserve System). The firm does not have the use of the funds until the check clears; thus, a system for decreasing the float (speeding up collections) will increase the cash that the firm has to use. A lockbox system is designed to do just that—increase the speed of collections.

Instead of having a central billing location to which all payments are sent, the firm establishes several collection points throughout the country (the lockbox). A local bank then removes the checks and immediately processes them for payment. Notice that the bank processes the checks; the firm does not use its own staff, which would increase the time necessary to process the checks. At the end of each day, the bank sends by wire (electronically) the funds that have cleared and are available for use to a central location, which is usually another bank in a financial center (or the firm's corporate headquarters). The funds are now available for the

FIGURE 20.5

Flows of Checks and Funds through a Lockbox or a Centralized Collection System

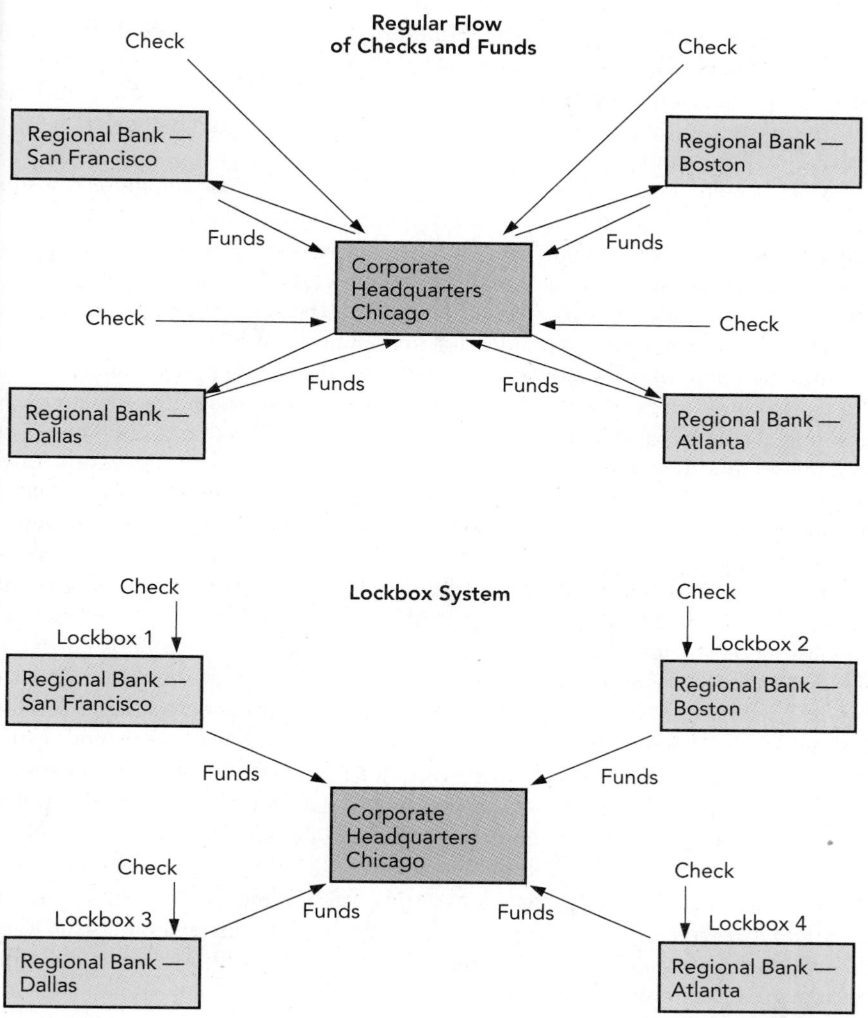

Regular Flow of Checks and Funds

Check
Check
Regional Bank — San Francisco
Regional Bank — Boston
Funds
Funds
Corporate Headquarters Chicago
Check
Check
Funds
Funds
Regional Bank — Dallas
Regional Bank — Atlanta

Lockbox System

Check
Check
Lockbox 1
Lockbox 2
Regional Bank — San Francisco
Regional Bank — Boston
Funds
Funds
Corporate Headquarters Chicago
Check
Check
Lockbox 3
Funds
Funds
Lockbox 4
Regional Bank — Dallas
Regional Bank — Atlanta

firm to use either to reduce its outstanding short-term debt (and thus reduce interest expense) or to invest in short-term securities.

Figure 20.5 illustrates how a lockbox system works. The top half shows the process by which a check clears through a centralized system. As may be seen in the figure, the check may spend several days in the mail arriving at its destination and several days being cleared as it works its way through the Federal Reserve's clearing mechanism. However, in the second half of the exhibit, the firm uses a lockbox system. The check is sent to a location that requires less time in the mail.

The location of the lockbox facilitates the collection of the funds, which are then sent to the centralized bank for the firm to use.

For such a lockbox system to be profitable, the firm must have a sufficient volume of business. The banks that operate the lockboxes, process the checks, and wire the funds charge for this service. The firm obviously must earn a sufficient return on the additional funds generated by the system to justify the expenses associated with the lockboxes.

Cash receipts may also be speeded up by the use of electronic funds transfers. Under such a system, funds are transferred electronically from one account to another through the use of computer terminals instead of checks. For example, an individual may make a purchase and use a debit card. This produces an immediate transfer of funds from the buyer's account to the seller's account. (The bank, however, may charge the seller a fee for providing the service.)

Management of disbursements is, of course, the exact opposite of collections. Except in those cases in which immediate payment reduces interest charges (for example, a commercial bank loan in which interest owed is determined daily), the intent is to retard payment so the firm may have the use of the money for a longer period of time. This may be achieved by making payments on Friday so the checks cannot clear until the next week or by remitting funds drawn on banks in another geographic location. The recipients of the checks will consider the funds received, even though the checks may take several days to clear. In such cases, the firm disbursing the funds drawn on a distant bank is increasing its use of the cash at the expense of the recipient of the check.

An analysis of when checks clear may offer a means to increase the firm's funds. For example, suppose a firm distributes dividend checks totaling $1 million throughout the country. The financial manager knows that not all of those checks will immediately clear. Exhibit 20.4 presents an analysis of when the checks do clear. The first column presents the number of days the checks are outstanding, and the second and third columns present the daily amount and the cumulative amounts that have cleared. As may be seen in this exhibit, the firm needs only $700,000 to meet the checks that clear during the first four days. Thus, there is no need to have the entire $1 million in the bank when the disbursement is made. If $1 million were available now, the financial manager could invest this cash for a few days to earn interest as long as there will be sufficient money available to cover the checks as they clear.[7]

The financial manager's capacity to execute such a strategy is enhanced by two facts. First, since firms obtain lines of credit from commercial banks, these lines may be used to meet the checks should they clear more rapidly than anticipated. Second, the market for short-term investments is so sophisticated that the financial

[7] One of the reasons for an investor to leave stock registered in the street name instead of taking delivery is to obtain the use of funds faster. The dividends are electronically transferred to the brokerage firm, which in turn credits the funds to the individual's account. The money is immediately available and, in some cases, is automatically swept into an income-earning money market account.

EXHIBIT 20.4

Speed with which Dividend Checks Clear

Number of Business Days for Checks to Clear	Amount	Cumulative Total
1	$250,000	$250,000
2	250,000	500,000
3	120,000	620,000
4	80,000	700,000
5	70,000	770,000
6	60,000	830,000
7	60,000	890,000
8	40,000	930,000
9	25,000	955,000
10	15,000	970,000
Checks still outstanding:	$ 30,000	

manager may invest excess funds for as short a period as one day. If the financial manager can determine that the cash will be available for an additional day, it may be invested for that short a time period and need not lie idle.

MONEY MARKET INSTRUMENTS AND YIELDS

In Chapter 3, various money market instruments were described. These short-term, liquid securities are bought and sold in what is called the *money market.* This term differentiates short-term financial assets from long-term securities, such as stocks and bonds, which are traded in what is sometimes referred to as the *capital market.*

Although there are many money market instruments (and each instrument has its own specific name), they have common characteristics. All money market instruments offer short-term yields, liquidity, and safety of principal. They may be readily converted into cash with little risk of loss. Thus, these instruments are a safe haven for funds that would otherwise sit idle. They are a means for individual investors and financial managers of firms (and governments and nonprofit operations, such as churches) to earn interest for brief periods of time.

Yields on money market instruments are similar but do vary with the term and small differences in risk. These differences in yields are illustrated in Exhibit 20.5, which gives the term and yield on various money market instruments. (This information is readily available in *The Wall Street Journal* in a column called "Money Rates.") As may be seen in the exhibit, Treasury bills are considered the safest of the instruments and offer the lowest yields.

Most money market instruments are illustrations of discounted securities. They pay no set rate of interest; instead, they are sold at a discount. Although the

EXHIBIT 20.5

Yields on Money Market Instruments (as of January 4, 2000)

Instrument	Term to Maturity	Yield
Treasury bills	3 months	5.360%
	6 months	5.585%
Commercial paper	2 to 5 months	5.75%
	5 to 9 months	5.85%
Negotiable CDs	3 months	5.95%
	6 months	6.15%
Bankers acceptances	3 months	6.06%
	6 months	6.09%

denomination for many money market instruments is $1,000,000, the determination of yields may be illustrated with a $10,000 Treasury bill.[8]

The Treasury auctions T-bills, and potential investors bid for them, with the highest bidders obtaining the bills. For example, a buyer may bid $9,700 for a six-month $10,000 bill and earn $300 when the bill matures. This is a six-month simple rate of 3.09 percent ($300/$9,700) and an annual noncompounded rate of 6.18 percent. If the bid price were higher, the interest cost to the Treasury (and the yield to the buyer) would be lower. If the discounted price were lower, the yield would be higher.

Once Treasury bills have been auctioned, there is a secondary market for them (that is, they may be readily sold). Bills are quoted daily in the financial press. For example, the quotes for January 4, 2000, given in *The Wall Street Journal,* are provided in Exhibit 20.6. These quotes indicate that for the bill maturing on April 6, 2000, buyers were willing to bid a price that yielded 5.26 percent. Sellers, however, were willing to offer the bills at a smaller discount (higher price) that yielded 5.25 percent. The 5.4 percent in the yield column gives the annualized yield on the bill based on the asking price.

The yields on Treasury bills, commercial paper, and other money market instruments change daily with changes in the conditions in the money market. These fluctuations are illustrated in Figure 20.6, which shows the yields on six-month Treasury bills and six-month commercial paper. As would be expected, the figure indicates that the yield on the commercial paper exceeded the yield on the Treasury bills and that both rates moved together (were highly correlated). The figure also illustrates that the yields do fluctuate over time, ranging from almost 10 percent on commercial paper in the late 1980s to much lower rates only a few years later in 1992 and 1993.

[8]Treasury bills are one of the few money market instruments issued in units as small as $10,000. Thus Treasury bills are one of the few short-term securities available to the typical investor. These investors are essentially limited to money market mutual funds that pool the funds of many investors and acquire commercial paper, negotiable certificates of deposit, and other money market instruments, whose large denominations exclude most investors.

EXHIBIT 20.6

Yields on U.S. Treasury Bills (January 2000)

	39
	.45
	6.51
	6.34
	6.52
	6.45
	6.46
	6.46
	6.58
	6.61
	6.50
	6.61
	6.53
0	6.61
0	6.63
0	6.52
0	6.63
0	6.65
11	6.54
11	6.61
10	6.51
10	6.66
10	6.61
10	6.51
10	6.67
10	6.67
10	6.66
11	6.70
11	6.56
11	6.71
11	6.57
11	6.72
11	6.56
11	6.69
11	6.76
11	6.77
11	6.78
12	6.76
12	6.81
	6.81
	6.82

Feb 29 bp 16:02 16:06 + 10 6.35

TREASURY BILLS

Maturity	Days to Mat.	Bid	Asked	Chg.	Ask Yld.
Jan 06 '00	1	4.21	4.13	+0.19	4.19
Jan 13 '00	8	5.31	5.23	+0.05	5.31
Jan 20 '00	15	5.22	5.14	+0.02	5.22
Jan 27 '00	22	4.82	4.74	−0.13	4.82
Feb 03 '00	29	4.88	4.80	−0.24	4.89
Feb 10 '00	36	5.00	4.96	−0.12	5.05
Feb 17 '00	43	5.00	4.96	−0.12	5.06
Feb 24 '00	50	5.01	4.97	−0.11	5.07
Mar 02 '00	57	5.16	5.12	−0.07	5.23
Mar 09 '00	64	5.16	5.14	−0.08	5.26
Mar 16 '00	71	5.17	5.15	−0.08	5.28
Mar 23 '00	78	5.18	5.16	−0.07	5.29
Mar 30 '00	85	5.22	5.20	−0.06	5.34
Apr 06 '00	**92**	**5.26**	**5.25**	**−0.09**	**5.40**
Apr 13 '00	99	5.25	5.23	−0.08	5.38
Apr 20 '00	106	5.28	5.26	−0.07	5.42
Apr 27 '00	113	5.30	5.28	−0.06	5.44
May 04 '00	120	5.35	5.33	−0.07	5.50
May 11 '00	127	5.36	5.34	−0.07	5.52
May 18 '00	134	5.39	5.37	−0.07	5.56
May 25 '00	141	5.41	5.39	−0.09	5.58
Jun 01 '00	148	5.43	5.41	−0.06	5.61
Jun 08 '00	155	5.47	5.45	−0.04	5.66
Jun 15 '00	162	5.44	5.42	−0.05	5.63
Jun 22 '00	169	5.51	5.49	−0.04	5.71
Jun 29 '00	176	5.50	5.48	−0.05	5.71
Jul 06 '00	**183**	**5.50**	**5.49**	....	**5.73**
Jul 20 '00	197	5.55	5.53	−0.03	5.77
Aug 17 '00	225	5.61	5.59	−0.04	5.84
Sep 14 '00	253	5.67	5.65	−0.03	5.92
Oct 12 '00	281	5.70	5.68	−0.02	5.96
Nov 09 '00	309	5.70	5.68	−0.02	5.98
Dec 07 '00	337	5.68	5.67	−0.03	5.99
Jan 04 '01	365	5.65	5.64	−0.06	5.98

INFLATION-INDEXED

Source: The Wall Street Journal, *January 5, 2000, C19. Reprinted by permission of The Wall Street Journal.*

FIGURE 20.6 **Yields on Six-Month Treasury Bills and Six-Month Commercial Paper**

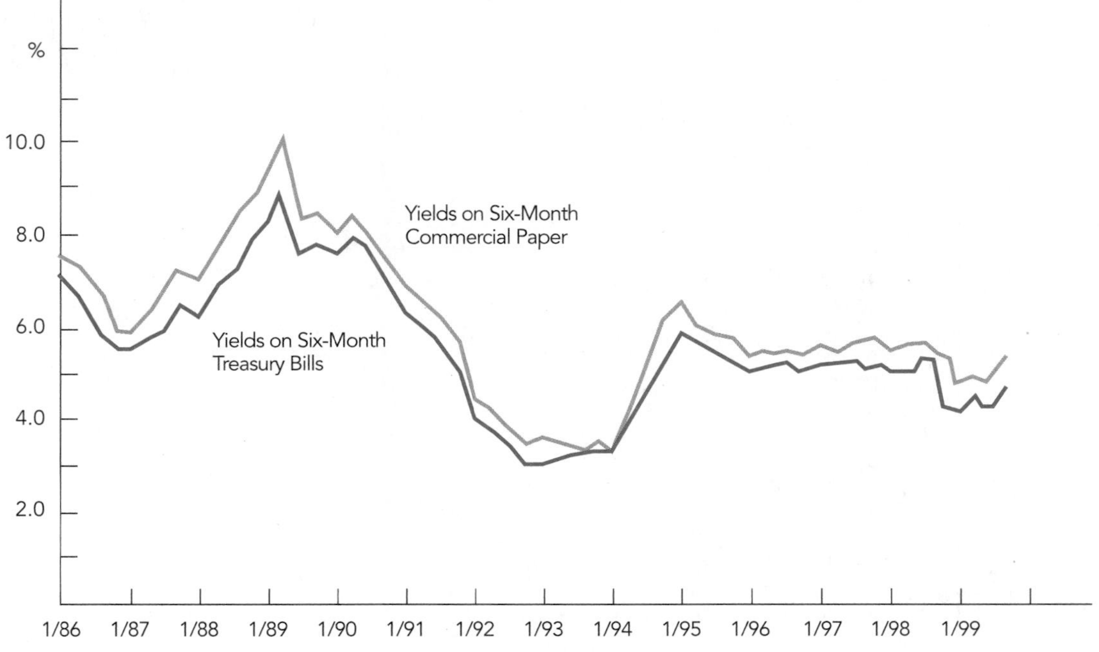

Source: Derived from Federal Reserve Bulletin, *various issues.*

THE CALCULATION OF YIELDS

Because most short-term money market instruments are discounted securities, the difference between the discounted price and the face value is the interest the investor earns (and the issuer pays). This interest is the source of the investor's return, but the actual yield also depends on the amount invested and how long the security is held. For example, an investor such as a corporate cash manager may buy a Treasury bill for \$9,791 with 180 days to maturity and hold the bill until it is redeemed for \$10,000. What is the yield on the investment? Although that seems like a simple question, the answer is not simple because the yield may be calculated in different ways. The word *yield* is ambiguous, because there is more than one yield.

The "discount" yield (y_d) is calculated as follows:

$$y_d = \frac{\text{Par value} - \text{Price}}{\text{Par value}} \times \frac{360}{\text{Number of days to maturity}}.$$

Thus, in the above illustration employing the Treasury bill, the discount yield is

$$y_d = \frac{\$10{,}000 - \$9{,}791}{\$10{,}000} \times \frac{360}{180} = 4.18\%.$$

The discount yield understates the true yield because it uses (1) the par value and not the amount the individual must invest and (2) a 360-day year.

An alternative method corrects these two problems. The calculation for the "simple" yield (y_s) is

$$y_s = \frac{\text{Interest earned}}{\text{Amount invested}} \times \frac{365}{\text{Number of days to maturity}}.$$

In this illustration, the simple yield is

$$\frac{\$209}{\$9{,}791} \times \frac{365}{180} = 4.33\%.$$

This rate is higher than the discount rate because it uses the amount invested (\$9,791) instead of the principal amount (\$10,000) in the denominator and 365 days instead of 360 days.

The simple yield, however, is not the true annualized rate when compounding is considered. In the previous example, the term of the investment is 180 days, so the investor can repeat the process twice a year. The annualized "compound" yield (i) is determined by the following equation:

$$\$9{,}791(1 + i)^n = \$10{,}000,$$

in which n is 180/365 or 0.49315. Rephrased, the question is: At what rate does \$9,791 grow to \$10,000 in 0.49315 of a year? The solution for the compound interest rate the borrower is paying and the investor is earning is

$$\$9{,}791(1 + i)^{0.49315} = \$10{,}000$$

$$(1 + i)^{0.49315} = \$10{,}000/\$9{,}791 = 1.02135$$

$$i = (1.02135)^{2.0278} - 1 = 4.38\%.$$

CALCULATOR SOLUTION

Function Key		Data Input
PV	=	−9791
PMT	=	0
FV	=	10,000
N	=	0.49315
I	=	?
Function Key		*Answer*
FV	=	4.38

Thus, the true, annualized compound yield is 4.38 percent.[9]

In this illustration, the difference between the true annualized rate and the simple rate is small (4.38 percent versus 4.33 percent). However, as the time period shortens (so the frequency of compounding increases) and the amount of the discount increases (so more interest is earned), the difference between the two

[9] $(1.02135)^{2.0278}$ may be determined by using an electronic calculator with a y^x key. Enter 1.02135; press the y^x key; enter 2.0278, and press =.

calculations increases. Suppose the investor purchases a Treasury bill for \$9,560 and sells it for \$9,630 after 30 days. The simple rate is

$$\frac{\$70}{\$9{,}560} \times \frac{365}{30} = 8.91\%.$$

CALCULATOR SOLUTION

Function Key		Data Input
PV	=	−9560
PMT	=	0
FV	=	9630
N	=	0.8219
I	=	?
Function Key		*Answer*
FV	=	9.28

The true, annualized compounded interest rate is

$$\$9{,}560(1 + i)^{30/365} = \$9{,}630$$

$$\$9{,}560(1 + i)^{0.08219} = \$9{,}630$$

$$(1 + i)^{0.08219} = \$9{,}630/\$9{,}560 = 1.007322$$

$$i = 1.007322^{12.1669} - 1 = 9.28\%.$$

The difference between the simple rate and the true compounded rate is greater than in the previous example.

The discount rate and the simple rate give a less accurate indication of the true annual yield being earned. Selecting among the various money market instruments with differences in prices, interest earned, and time horizons (and hence differences in compounding) requires that the cash manager determine the true yield on each security. Reliance on the discount rate or the simple rate may lead to the selection of a security with a lower yield. The financial manager may select an alternative with a lower yield for a valid reason, such as selecting a Treasury bill over commercial paper because it is the less risky of the two alternatives. But that is different than selecting one security over another based on inaccurate estimates of their respective yields.

SUMMARY

This chapter has been devoted to a firm's current assets. How these assets are managed and financed is a firm's working capital policy. In general, the cost of short-term funds is less than the cost of long-term funds. Thus, the use of short-term credit tends to increase a firm's profitability. However, sources of short-term finance are riskier because they must be retired or renewed within a year. The terms may become more onerous or the costs may increase when the firm seeks to refinance these short-term obligations.

Inventory is acquired and sold, generating accounts receivable or cash. To facilitate the flow of current assets through the firm, the financial manager analyzes the speed with which inventory and accounts receivable turn over, determines how much inventory to order and carry through use of the economic order quantity (EOQ) model, and selects LIFO or FIFO to determine the valuation and allocation of the cost of inventory when it is sold.

Inventory is sold either for cash or on credit. Increased sales may be generated by a more lenient credit policy. However, more credit sales will require that the firm carry more accounts receivable, which must be financed. The firm's credit policy is a crucial component of working capital management, as the credit policy determines who will be granted credit, the terms of the credit, and the enforcement of the terms. The financial manager faces a typical economic trade-off: additional sales through easier credit versus the increased cost of carrying the receivables. Once the credit policy has been established, the financial manager monitors the collection of accounts receivable through turnover ratios and aging schedules, which identify slow-paying accounts.

Increasing the turnover of inventory or accounts receivable will generate more cash, which may be used to acquire other income-earning assets or to retire debt. If there is a temporary lag between the receipt of the cash and its subsequent disbursement, the funds may be invested in money market securities, including U.S. Treasury bills, corporate commercial paper, repurchase agreements, negotiable certificates of deposit, bankers' acceptances, money market mutual funds, and tax anticipation notes. Money market securities are safe havens for funds that are invested for short periods of time. These securities offer the financial manager a means to increase profitability by earning money market rates of interest instead of holding non-interest-bearing cash.

REVIEW QUESTIONS

1. What is working capital? What is the impact on net working capital of each of the following?
   a. The firm issues stock and holds the cash.
   b. Cash is used to retire an account payable.
   c. A firm borrows short-term from a bank to acquire inventory.
   d. Cash is used to retire an issue of bonds (long-term debt).
   e. Cash is used to acquire inventory.
   f. Equipment is sold for cash.
   g. The firm pays a stock dividend.
   h. Bonds are converted into stock.
2. How will the following affect the amount of cash a firm has?
   a. an increase in the turnover of accounts receivable
   b. an increase in administrative expenses
   c. an increase in cash dividends
   d. an increase in the turnover of accounts payable
   e. an increase in depreciation expense
3. Why may an aggressive working capital policy increase a firm's profitability but also increase its risk exposure?
4. What are the costs associated with carrying inventory? Why might a firm have a safety stock? If inventory turns over rapidly, does that increase cash and earnings?
5. What does the EOQ model seek to establish? Is the EOQ a realistic model for firms with seasonal sales?
6. What are the inventory turnover ratios for Amazon.com (AMZN), Barnes & Noble (BKS), eToys (ETYS), and Toys "R" Us (TOY)? What are the implications of any differences in these ratios? (You may find financial information for each firm by using its ticker symbol given in parenthesis. Sources of stock price data such as **www.quote.yahoo.com** or **www.bloomberg.com** generally provide an analysis of financial statements or links to sites that do provide ratios based on financial statements.)

7. During a period of inflation, why may the use of FIFO instead of LIFO result in higher taxes? Why, during a period of falling prices, will the use of FIFO instead of LIFO result in lower profits?
8. If a firm has a slow turnover of its accounts receivable, why may that reduce its profitability?
9. If a firm offers credit, why may collateral reduce the risk of loss? What features should this collateral have?
10. If a firm has excess liquidity, what are several possible short-term assets that it could acquire?
11. Both Treasury bills and commercial paper are sold at a discount. What does this mean? Can one suffer a loss by buying these debt instruments?
12. Exhibit 20.5 provided the yields on several money market instruments as of January 2000. Have these yields changed from the date in the exhibit?

PROBLEMS

1. A firm needs \$1 million in additional funds. These can be borrowed from a commercial bank with a loan at 6 percent for one year or from an insurance company at 9 percent for five years. The tax rate is 30 percent.
   a. What will be the firm's earnings under each alternative if earnings before interest and taxes (EBIT) are \$430,000?
   b. If EBIT will remain \$430,000 next year, what will be the firm's earnings under each alternative if short-term interest rates are 4 percent? If short-term interest rates are 14 percent?
   c. Why do earnings tend to fluctuate more with the use of short-term debt than with long-term debt? If long-term debt had a variable interest rate that fluctuated with changes in interest rates, would the use of short-term debt still be riskier than long-term debt?
2. The following structure of interest rates is given:

Term of Loan	Interest Rate
1 year	3%
2 years	4%
5 years	6%
10 years	8%

Your firm needs \$2,000 to finance its assets. Three possible combinations of sources of finance are listed below:

(1)

Assets	\$2,000	Liabilities	\$ 0
		Equity	2,000

(2)

Assets	\$2,000	Liabilities (a one-year loan)	\$800
		Equity	1,200

(3)

Assets	\$2,000	Liabilities (a ten-year loan)	\$800
		Equity	1,200

a. The firm expects to generate revenues of \$2,400 and have operating expenses of \$2,080. If the firm's tax rate is 40 percent, what is the return on equity under each choice?
b. During the second year, sales decline to \$2,100 while operating expenses decline to \$1,900. The structure of interest rates becomes:

Term of Loan	Interest Rate
1 year	6%
2 years	7%
5 years	8%
10 years	10%

Given the three choices in the previous year, what is the return on equity for the firm during the second year?

c. What is the implication of using short-term instead of long-term debt during the two years?

3. *a.* What is the EOQ for a firm that sells 5,000 units when the cost of placing an order is $5 and the carrying costs are $3.50 per unit?

b. How long will the EOQ last? How many orders are placed annually?

c. As a result of lower interest rates, the financial manager determines the carrying costs are now $1.80 per unit. What are the new EOQ and annual number of objects?

4. Given the following information:

Annual sales in units	30,000
Cost of placing an order	$60.00
Per-unit carrying costs	$ 1.50
Existing units of safety stock	300

a. What is the EOQ?

b. What is the average inventory based on the EOQ and the existing safety stock?

c. What is the maximum level of inventory?

d. How many orders are placed each year?

5. Lasher Glass has annual sales of $1,750,000. Although it extends credit for 30 days (n30), the receivables are 20 days overdue. What is the average accounts receivable outstanding, and how much could the company save in interest expense if customers paid on time and if it costs Lasher Glass 10 percent to carry its receivables?

6. To increase sales, management is considering reducing its credit standards. This action is expected to increase sales by $125,000. Unfortunately, it is anticipated that 7 percent of the sales will be uncollectible. Accounts receivable turnover is expected to be 6 times a year, and it costs the firm 10 percent to carry its receivables. Collection costs will be 4 percent of sales, and the cost of the additional goods sold is $64,000. Will earnings increase?

7. If a firm's sales are $1,500,000 and it costs 9 percent to carry current assets, what is the potential savings if management can increase inventory turnover from 3 to 4 times a year and increase receivables turnover from 4.5 to 6 times a year?

8. As of January 1, a firm has the following accounts receivable:

Receivable	Amount Due	Days Outstanding
A	$1,000	35
B	2,500	42
C	1,500	57
D	3,500	29
E	1,200	48
F	3,100	52
G	1,700	39

As of March 1, the firm's receivables are:

Receivable	Amount Due	Days Outstanding
A	$2,000	28
B	1,500	51
C	1,800	47
D	2,500	63
E	3,500	42
F	1,200	40
G	2,700	56

The firm offers credit terms of net 30 days. Construct aging schedules that show the amount and percentage of total accounts receivable that are 0, 10, 20, and 30 days overdue. Has there been any change in the firm's collections?

9. A firm sells 100,000 units of inventory for $10 a unit. Inventory purchases and their costs were

Date	Inventory Purchased	Cost per Unit
1/2	30,000 units	$7.70
4/7	30,000	8.20
8/1	30,000	8.40
12/1	30,000	8.90

If the firm's income tax rate is 40 percent, how much will the firm save in taxes if it uses LIFO instead of FIFO for inventory valuation?

10. Management of a firm with annual sales of 5,000 units decides to establish the EOQ model for inventory management. The firm has two possible suppliers. Data concerning these suppliers are as follows:

Supplier A	Shipping costs $1,000
	Per-unit carrying costs $74
Supplier B	Shipping costs $800
	Per-unit carrying costs $80

a. What is the EOQ for each supplier?
b. If the firm establishes a safety stock of 100 units, what is the firm's average inventory for both suppliers?
c. What will be the firm's expected maximum and minimum inventory with each supplier?
d. If delivery takes eight days, what should be the firm's level of inventory when it places an order with supplier A?

11. Big Toy, Inc. annually sells 100,000 units of Big Blobs. Currently, inventory is financed through the use of commercial bank loans. Big Toy pays $12.20 per Big Blob. The cost of carrying this inventory is $3.20 per unit while the cost

of placing an order involves expenses of $400 per order. Since Big Blobs are imported, delivery is generally 20 days but may be as long as 30 days. In order to manage inventory more efficiently, the management of Big Toy, Inc. has decided to use the EOQ model plus a safety stock to determine inventory levels.

a. What is the economic order quantity?
b. Today is January 1 and the current level of inventory is 10,000 units; when should the first order be placed based on the economic order quantity?
c. Management always wants sufficient Big Blobs so that they never are out of stock. If management considers late deliveries to be the prime reason for being out of stock, what should be the safety stock?
d. According to the above analysis, what are the maximum inventory, the minimum inventory, and the average inventory?
e. If sales of Big Blobs double, will the average inventory also double?

12. Firm X has sales of $5,000,000; $3,000,000 are for cash, but two customers who generate sales of $2,000,000 pay after 30 days. Management believes that sales will increase by 20 percent if all customers have 30 days to pay. Should the firm change its credit policy given the following information?
a. The cost of the additional goods sold is 70 percent of sales.
b. Credit checks and collection costs will be $5,000.
c. Three percent of the new sales will be uncollectible.
d. The cost of borrowing the funds to carry the receivables is 12 percent.

13. What is the effective, compound rate of interest you earn if you enter into a repurchase agreement in which you buy a Treasury bill for $76,789 and agree to sell it after a month (30 days) for $77,345? What is the compound rate of interest you pay if you sell a Treasury bill for $76,789 and repurchase it after 30 days for $77,345?

CASE

USING THE ECONOMIC ORDER QUANTITY TO MINIMIZE INVENTORY COSTS

Alexander and Charlene Weber operate a small retail store that serves a small, but wealthy, community. Most of the items carried tend to be high-markup but slow-moving goods. Since many of the goods are imported, there is often a substantial time lapse between when the goods are ordered and when they are received. No analysis is used to determine what is the best quantity to order. The Webers know that carrying excess inventory is expensive, because their commercial bank charges a substantial interest rate for the funds the Webers use to buy their inventory. Thus, they believe that better inventory management may increase profitability by reducing the amount of inventory they carry.

Sales are generally spread evenly throughout the year with a small increase during the Christmas season. The Webers recently read that a computer program would help them determine the best or optimal level of each order, so they purchased the program (a computerized model to calculate the economic order quantity). Since applying the model to all of the firm's inventory items seemed excessive, the Webers decided to first determine the economic order quantity (EOQ) of only three items. They would then use the EOQ of each item to determine what the average inventory should be, and use that information to determine how much could be saved in carrying costs. If there were a savings, then they could apply the model to more items carried in the store.

The annual sales of the three items (A, B, and C) are 120, 420, and 720 units, respectively. On the average, the Webers maintain four months' supply. The wholesale prices are $300, $128, and $85, for items A, B, and C, respectively. The Webers invest $36,000 in item A each year, and the average amount of inventory is 40 units ($12,000 invested). At an interest rate of 15 percent, the annual carrying cost of item A is $1,800, and the per-unit carrying cost is $15. The cost of placing an order, including shipping, is $150, $70, and $80 for items A, B, and C, respectively.

Case Problems

1. What is the annual amount invested in items B and C, and what are their per-unit carrying costs?
2. Based on the economic order quantity, what should be the average inventory of each item?
3. What is the potential savings in carrying costs if the firm adopts the average inventory associated with the EOQ?
4. If there is no potential savings in carrying costs, what does that imply about the ordering costs paid by the Webers?
5. Since the economic order quantity assumes no safety stock and the Webers want to carry inventory to cover five days' sales, what is the additional carrying cost (interest charges) necessary to sustain the safety stocks?

CHAPTER 21

Sources of Short- and Intermediate-Term Funds

Learning Objectives

1. Distinguish among commercial bank loans, commercial paper, and trade credit as sources of funds.
2. Be able to determine the cost of a commercial bank loan, commercial paper, and trade credit.
3. Explain why commercial paper is a major source of credit for a small number of firms while trade credit is a major source for many firms.
4. Explain how pledging or factoring accounts receivable can provide short-term finance.
5. Differentiate the features of intermediate-term notes from short-term sources and long-term bonds.
6. Determine if a firm should lease or buy a piece of equipment.
7. Differentiate operating and financial leases, explain the accounting for leases and its impact on the firm's debt ratio and use of financial leverage.
8. Determine the order of payment in a bankruptcy liquidation and explain why creditors may prefer reorganization to liquidation.

Ralph Waldo Emerson said, "Pay every debt as if God wrote the bill." While short-term creditors are not God, they do possess a substantial amount of power over the firm. When a firm has financial difficulties, its problems generally arise when it is unable to meet its short-term obligations. Even if the firm has quality long-term assets, the inability to meet current obligations can cause the firm to fail. Such failure is not limited to firms. Governments and charitable organizations can also be forced into bankruptcy if they are unable to meet their short-term obligations. (Bankruptcy and corporate reorganizations are briefly discussed at the end of this chapter.)

Few firms can exist without short-term funds. Even IRT Property, a real estate firm that owns properties and leases them to others, has a few short-term obligations. (In 1999, about $61.5 million of its $291.7 million in liabilities was short-term.) Virtually all the obligations of some firms are short-term. Salomon Inc., a large investment banker and securities dealer, reported assets of $188.4 billion, of which 53.7 percent was financed by a variety of short-term debt obligations. That amounts of $101.2 billion in short-term debt.

Commercial banks are a major source of short-term financing for large and small firms, especially manufacturers, wholesalers, and retailers. Unless the firm is exceptionally risky, commercial banks may individually be the most important source of short-term funds. The first section of this chapter is devoted to the short-term loans made by commercial banks.

Many firms use their suppliers as a source of funds. Such trade credit is spontaneous and a major source of short-term finance for small firms, especially retailers. Large, creditworthy firms have alternative sources of trade credit, such as commercial paper which is an unsecured promissory note issued by a corporation with an excellent credit rating. Since commercial paper is unsecured, its use is limited primarily to large firms. Although bank loans, trade credit, and commercial paper are the primary sources of short-term finance, other sources include secured loans, warehouse financing, and factoring.

Chapter 9 covered the variety of corporate bonds, which are sources of long-term funds. Most of this chapter considers short-term debt obligations but also includes two alternatives to short- and long-term debt: intermediate-term debt and leasing. These sources have a longer time dimension than short-term debt but have a shorter term than long-term bonds. Intermediate-term debt extends for 5 to 10 years and is obtained through commercial banks and insurance companies and selling intermediate-term notes to the general public.

Some firms own properties in order to lease them to others. Washington Real Estate Trust owns office buildings, industrial distribution centers, apartments, and shopping centers and rents space to stores, such as Williams-Sonoma and Laura Ashley. These retail establishments want the use of the asset but not ownership. They prefer not to borrow and buy, but to lease the properties. Leasing is an especially important means for retailers to acquire the use of assets.

While some firms succeed, others are failures. The event that often precipitates failure is the inability to make current payments. Management's inability to meet payments required by the various sources of short-term funds results in the firm's being declared bankrupt. While a bankrupt firm may be liquidated and cease to operate, many are reorganized with the creditors becoming the new owners of the surviving firm. Creditors are often willing to accept such reorganizations because they believe they will receive more from the firm's continuing to operate than from the liquidation of the firm's assets.

FREE SOURCES: ACCRUALS

In the previous chapter, the operating cycle illustrated how the normal course of business generates accruals. Wages, taxes, and other short-term obligations accrue with the passage of time. The accruals then are paid as of a particular date. As is also explained (in Chapter 12 on financial statements), any increase in a liability is a source of funds. Thus, increases in accruals are sources of funds.

Because the amount paid to employees (or accrued taxes owed the government or any other accrual) is not affected by when payments are made, accruals are often thought of as free sources of funds. If management can convince employees to accept payment every month instead of every two weeks, accruals increase. The increase is a source of finance because the firm has the use of the funds longer. In effect, the firm receives an interest-free loan from the employees, who are not compensated for waiting longer to receive payment.

Although firms (and governments and nonprofit organizations) have free use of the funds, there are limits to expanding accruals as a source of funds. While employees realize that payments will not be made daily, they will not wait several months for payment. Thus, increases in accruals as a source of additional short-term finance are unrealistic. The firm in need of additional short-term finance will have to use the short-term sources that comprise the body of this chapter.

COMMERCIAL BANK LOANS

Commercial banks are concerned with liquidity and safety of principal. They prefer to make loans that are of short duration and, hence, are a primary source of short-term financing.[1] Although bank loans are obtained by virtually all types of firms, the primary borrowers are retailers and wholesalers. Firms that have large investments in fixed assets do not use short-term bank financing to purchase the fixed assets, for such financing is inappropriate. Such long-term assets should be financed by long-term financing, such as bonds or equity. Retailers and wholesalers, however, are concerned with short-term assets, and bank loans are an appropriate means to finance these assets. The primary users of bank credit are small firms. While this does not mean that large firms do not use bank financing, the proportion of a firm's financing that is obtained from commercial banks declines as the size of the firm increases. Larger firms have a wider range of financing alternatives and thus do not have to rely so heavily on commercial banks.

A loan from a commercial bank is a package that is individually negotiated between the borrower and the bank. The negotiated package includes the size of the loan, the maturity date, the amount of the interest, any security requirements (that is, the pledging of specific assets), the subordination of other debt, and other limitations on the financial activity of the firm. Since the bank is lending its funds, it is generally in a position to demand financial constraints. For example, the bank may demand that the firm maintain a minimum current ratio (such as 2 to 1), or the bank may place limitations on dividend payments.

Besides lending money, the bank may provide other services for a fee. For example, the bank may be a source of information on the financial condition of the borrower's credit customers. If the firm has foreign transactions, the bank can handle foreign exchange (foreign currency). These services may be advantageous to the firm and help justify borrowing from one bank rather than another.

PROMISSORY NOTE
Document specifying the amount owed, the interest rate, the maturity date, and other features of a loan

The firm may borrow a specific amount of money or it may arrange for the right to borrow up to a specified amount. The former creates a promissory note while the latter is called a line of credit. A **promissory note** is an agreement between the borrower and the commercial bank for a specific amount of money for a specified time period. When the note is signed ("executed"), the bank credits the

[1] In Exhibit 3.2, loans constituted over half of Sovereign Bancorp's assets. Other assets included securities, such as Treasury bills, which are the short-term obligations of the federal government.

funds to the borrower's account with the bank. The note specifies the rate of interest, collateral requirements (if any), and the repayment schedule. Repayment either may be made in one lump payment or may be spread over time through a series of installment payments.

A **line of credit** is an informal (noncontractual) agreement that grants the firm an option to borrow up to a specified amount whenever the firm needs the funds. For example, the financial manager may arrange a line of credit for $500,000. If the firm requires $100,000 to finance inventory, the financial manager draws $100,000 from the line of credit. The firm now has a $100,000 loan outstanding but still can borrow an additional $400,000 if the funds are needed. The credit line offers the borrower the flexibility to use the credit only when it is needed. Under this type of agreement, the firm has a source of short-term financing but does not have to use the funds. Interest is paid only on the funds the firm actually borrows.

LINE OF CREDIT
Informal agreement in which a bank extends the right to borrow (at the option of the borrower) up to a specified amount

An alternative to the credit line is the **revolving credit agreement**. Revolving credit is similar to the line of credit in that the bank agrees to extend the firm credit up to a specified limit whenever the firm needs the funds. However, while the line of credit is an informal agreement, revolving credit is a formal, contractual obligation of the bank. The agreement has a time limit (generally a year to 15 months), after which the terms are renegotiated. The bank charges a commitment fee ("origination" fee) for establishing revolving credit, which tends to be ¼ of a percent of the amount of credit granted by the bank. Thus, a revolving credit agreement for $10 million requires a payment of $25,000.

REVOLVING CREDIT AGREEMENT
Formal agreement in which the bank extends the right to borrow up to a specified amount within a specified time period

Fees charged by commercial banks for establishing revolving lines of credit may be paid either at the beginning or at the end of the loan period. If the fee is solely for establishing the credit, it is paid up front. If the fee is on the unused balance, the bank will not know the amount of the fee until after the period of the loan has elapsed. These differences may be seen by the following illustration of terms:

Bank A: $1,000,000 revolving credit for one year at 10 percent with a fee of 1/2 percent of the amount of the loan

Bank B: $1,000,000 revolving credit for one year at 10 percent with a fee of 1/2 percent on the unused balance of the loan

Bank C: $1,000,000 revolving credit for one year at 10 percent with a fee of 1/4 percent of the amount of the loan and 1/4 percent on the unused balance of the loan.

Bank A requires a payment of $5,000 when the credit is granted whether the revolving credit is or is not used. If the creditor lacks the $5,000, the borrower may have to use the credit to cover this fee. Bank B requires a payment of $5,000 only if the credit is not used. Obviously, this payment cannot be made when the loan is granted. (The bank may prorate this fee monthly instead of waiting until the end of the year.) Bank C initially charges $2,500, with the balance dependent upon the use of the revolving credit.

Revolving credit agreements are used primarily by large firms, and the amount of the loans can be substantial. Fort James, the manufacturer of Northern bathroom tissue, Brawny paper towels, and Dixie cups and disposable plates, reported in its 1998 annual report that it had an unsecured revolving credit loan of up to $2.1 billion, of which $1.2 billion was unused. Because revolving credit loans can be substantial, the bank usually parcels out some of the loans so that a group of banks participate in the revolving credit agreement.

Revolving credit, like the line of credit, is used to finance short-term assets. However, the firm may also use revolving credit to finance the development of long-term assets. For example, the firm may draw on its revolving credit to pay for the construction of plant and equipment. After the plant is completed, the revolving credit is converted into an intermediate-term loan, or the firm may retire the outstanding balance on the revolving credit loan. This can be done through an issue of long-term bonds, new equity, or any other source of funds available to the borrower.

Cost of Commercial Bank Credit

The costs of the line of credit and revolving credit and their effective interest rates depend on the commitment fees charged, the interest paid, the amount borrowed, and how long the firm has the use of the funds. For example, a firm obtains revolving credit for $1,000,000 at 6 percent annually (0.5 percent monthly) plus a commitment fee of $^3/_4$ percent on the *unused* balance. If the firm borrows the entire $1,000,000, the annual interest is $60,000. If the firm uses only $600,000 for the year, the interest cost will be $36,000 ($600,000 × 0.06) *plus* $^3/_4$ percent of the unused balance of $400,000 ($3,000). The total amount paid is $39,000 ($36,000 + $3,000) for the use of $600,000. If the firm does not use the credit, it still must pay the $7,500 commitment fee, which is the cost of obtaining, but not using, the credit.

PRIME RATE
Interest rate charged by commercial banks on loans to their best customers

In addition to the terms, the cost of a bank loan varies with the quality of the borrower. The bank's best customers (the best credit risks) are charged the **prime rate**. Other customers may be charged the prime plus a percentage, such as 2 percent. Thus, if the prime rate is 6.5 percent, the rate to other customers might be 8.5 percent. If the prime rate rises, the cost of other loans will also rise, so any interest rate that is tied to the prime will vary as the prime rate varies.

During periods of tight money, the prime rate can rise very rapidly. For example, the prime rate was 11.5 percent in July 1979, 15.5 percent in December 1979, and 20 percent in April 1980. The increase from 11.5 percent to 20 percent in less than a year illustrates the potential volatility of short-term rates. These fluctuations are related to the demand for short-term funds and the supply of short-term credit. While the period July 1979 to April 1980 is unique, it does illustrate that short-term interest rates can fluctuate during a limited period of time.

While commercial banks often quote a prime rate, some large corporate borrowers are able to negotiate loans at interest rates below the prime. Many commercial business loans made by the nation's largest banks are at a discount from the prime. This means that in effect there are two prime rates: the announced rate and the discounted rate, which is available to large corporate borrowers.

As stated earlier, the cost of a commercial bank loan (or any loan) may not be the stated rate of interest. The cost is related to the interest paid, the amount of funds that the borrower can use, and the term of the loan. The commercial bank can increase the cost of the loan by altering the amount that the borrower can use or by altering the length of time the loan is outstanding.

Equation 21.1 may be used to calculate the cost (the interest rate) of a commercial bank loan (i_{CB}) that is paid off *with interest at maturity*.

$$i_{CB} = \frac{\text{Interest paid}}{\text{Proceeds of the loan that the borrower may use}} \times \frac{12}{\text{Number of months that the firm has use of the proceeds}} \qquad \textbf{21.1}$$

This equation is appropriate only if interest is paid at the end of the period and the loan is not renewed, so there is no compounding (that is, it is simple and not compound interest).

How commercial banks increase the interest cost of a loan may be illustrated by several examples that use Equation 21.1. All the subsequent examples will be based on the following simple loan: $1,000 at 6 percent for one year. The borrower has $1,000, and if the loan is retired at the end of the year and the borrower pays the $60 interest at that time, the cost of the loan is

$$\frac{\$60}{\$1{,}000} \times \frac{12}{12} = 6\%.$$

CALCULATOR SOLUTION

Function Key		Data Input
PV	=	−1000
FV	=	1060
PMT	=	0
N	=	1
I	=	?
Function Key		*Answer*
I	=	6

The borrower has the use of the $1,000 for the entire year and pays $60 for the use of the proceeds: thus the true rate of interest is 6 percent.[2]

The bank may require that the borrower pay the interest in advance; that is, the bank requires that the loan be discounted. The borrower receives not $1,000 but $940 ($1,000 − $60). In effect, the borrower is paying $60 for the use of $940, which increases the cost of the loan. Instead of an interest rate of 6 percent, the interest rate is

$$\frac{\$60}{\$940} \times \frac{12}{12} = 6.38\%.$$

CALCULATOR SOLUTION

Function Key		Data Input
PV	=	−940
FV	=	1000
PMT	=	0
N	=	1
I	=	?
Function Key		*Answer*
I	=	6.38

By discounting the loan in advance the bank has caused the true cost of interest to rise from 6 percent to 6.38 percent.[3]

[2] An alternative way to calculate the interest rate is to use time value calculations:

$$\$1{,}000\,(1+i)^1 = \$1{,}060$$
$$1+i = 1.06$$
$$i = 1.06 - 1 = 0.06 = 6\%.$$

[3] The alternative calculation is

$$\$940\,(1+i) = \$1{,}000$$
$$1+i = \$1{,}000 \div \$940 = 1.0638$$
$$i = 1.0638 - 1 = 6.38\%.$$

The borrower has the use of $940 and repays $1,000 at the end of the year.

In a second method for affecting the cost of the loan, the bank can require the borrower to pay a fee. These fees may be to originate the loan. For example, if an origination fee is 5 percent, a $1,000 loan will require an immediate payment of $50. If the previous illustration is continued and the terms of the $1,000 loan are 6 percent interest with a 5 percent origination fee, the borrower pays $60 for the use of $950 ($1,000 − $50). The cost of the loan now becomes

CALCULATOR SOLUTION

Function Key		Data Input
PV	=	−950
FV	=	1000
PMT	=	0
N	=	1
I	=	?
Function Key		*Answer*
I	=	6.32

$$\frac{\$60}{\$950} \times \frac{12}{12} = 6.32\%.$$

The origination fee has the effect of reducing the amount the borrower may use (the denominator), which increases the cost of the loan.

If the firm needs the entire $1,000, it will have to borrow more than $1,000 to have that amount and cover the origination fee. The amount of the loan necessary to cover the needed funds plus the origination fee is

21.2
$$\text{The amount of the loan} = \frac{\text{Funds needed}}{1.0 - \text{Origination fee (as a decimal)}}.$$

Thus, the amount of the loan with a 5 percent origination fee is $1,000/(1.0 − 0.05) = $1,052.63. The financial manager will have to borrow $1,052.63 for the firm to have the use of $1,000 and pay the origination fee. This may be confirmed as follows:

Amount borrowed	$1,052.63
Origination fee ($1,052.63 × 0.05)	52.63
Amount available	$1,000.00

Since the interest paid is $63.16 ($1,052.63 × 0.06), the cost of the loan is

$$\frac{\$63.16}{\$1{,}000} \times \frac{12}{12} = 6.32\%.$$

Notice that the interest is figured on the total amount borrowed ($1,052.63), but the true rate of interest is based on the amount that the borrower actually gets to use.

In addition to origination fees, commercial banks may charge a fee on the unused balance of a loan. For example, the borrower may arrange for a revolving line of credit for $1,000 with a fee on any unused balance. If the borrower only uses $600, the bank charges a fee on the unused balance of $400. In effect, the borrower has an option to borrow the money but does not exercise the option. The bank is compensated for granting the option through the origination fee and any fee on the unused balance.

While origination fees are paid up front, the fee on the unused balance can only be assessed at the end of the loan (or at the end of some specified period, such as a month). While the origination fee is subtracted from the amount the borrower may use, the fee on the unused balance is added to the interest paid to determine the true cost of a loan. For example, if the fee on the unused balance is 1 percent and the firm arranges a credit agreement for $1,000 at 6 percent but only borrows $600 for the year, the annual interest cost is $600(0.06) + $400(0.01) = $40. The annual rate of interest is

$$\frac{\$40}{\$600} \times \frac{12}{12} = 6.67\%.$$

Once again, the effective, true rate of interest (6.67 percent) exceeds the stated rate (6 percent).

TRADE CREDIT

TRADE CREDIT
Credit extended by suppliers to their customers

Trade credit, which is credit granted by a firm's suppliers, is individually the most important source of short-term finance for small firms, especially retail establishments. It can be, however, a very expensive source, and the financial manager should be aware of the cost of the credit. Trade credit arises when a supplier sells goods but does not demand immediate payment. Instead, the purchaser is permitted to choose between immediate payment or payment in the future. For immediate payment, or for payment within a short time period such as 10 days, the buyer may receive a discount, such as 2 percent off the purchase price. If the buyer does not remit during the first 10 days, payment in full must be made within a specified time period, such as 30 days. These terms are written 2/10, net 30, which means a 2 percent discount for payment within the first 10 days or the net (full) price within 30 days.

The impact of trade credit on the supplier's and the retailer's balance sheets is as follows:

Supplier		Retailer	
Assets	**Liabilities**	**Assets**	**Liabilities**
Accounts receivable ↑ Inventory ↓		Inventory ↑	Accounts payable ↑

The supplier trades an account receivable for its inventory. The retailer's inventory is increased, which is a use of funds. This use must be balanced by a source. This source is the increase in accounts payable. The increase in liabilities finances the increase in inventory.

Trade credit may be very beneficial to a firm that must carry a large amount of inventory. As the firm expands its inventory, its suppliers expand their credit. The expansion of trade credit, then, is a *spontaneous* response to the expansion in inventory and comes automatically without the need for the firm to seek credit elsewhere. If the firm is able to turn over the inventory rapidly, it may obtain cash quickly enough to pay the suppliers without having to use other sources of credit. For example, if the terms of trade credit are 2/10, net 30, the firm has the use of the goods for a month before payment is due. If the inventory turns over once a month, trade credit may be sufficient to cover the entire inventory. Of course, the firm is still paying the cost of the trade credit. If the firm is able to turn over the inventory only six times a year (every two months), trade credit will carry only one-half of the firm's inventory. Since the terms of trade are for one month and the inventory turns over every two months, the firm must find other sources of financing to cover the cost of maintaining the inventory for the second month.

The important question that the financial manager must consider is whether trade credit is the best source of finance for carrying the inventory. This is the question of the cost of trade credit versus the cost and availability of other sources of finance. The cost of trade credit depends on the terms of the credit. If the terms are net 30 days (n30), the cost of the credit is nil. The supplier has built the cost of offering the credit into the price of the goods. Unless the financial manager can negotiate a discount for prompt payment, the firm should use the credit as extensively as possible, for there is no advantage to paying before the thirtieth day.

Cost of Trade Credit

If the terms are 2/10, net 30, trade credit is not free. It may appear that trade credit is free, for the supplier is permitting the buyer to use the goods for no explicit interest charge. That, however, is a misconception of what constitutes the *price* of the goods and the *interest charge*. In finance, the price of the product is considered to be the discounted price. The discounted price is the price that the buyer pays if cash is available and the buyer promptly pays for the goods. The net price, then, includes the purchase price plus a penalty for not paying the bill promptly. This penalty should be treated as the interest charge for the use of the goods. Thus, if an item costs $100 and is supplied under the terms 2/10, net 30, the price of the goods is $98, and the firm has 10 days in which to pay. If the firm does not or cannot meet that price within 10 days, it pays a finance charge (interest) of $2 for the use of the goods for the next 20 days. When expressed in those terms, the interest charge becomes evident.

How expensive trade credit really is may be seen when the interest rate (i_{TC}) is expressed in annual terms. This calculation of the simple interest rate is given by Equation 21.3.

21.3

$$i_{TC} = \left(\frac{\text{Percentage discount}}{\begin{array}{c}\text{100\% minus}\\\text{percentage discount}\end{array}}\right) \text{times} \left(\frac{360}{\begin{array}{c}\text{Payment period minus}\\\text{discount period}\end{array}}\right)$$

The component parts of the equation are the percentage discount, the number of days for which the credit is extended (that is, the payment period minus the discount period), and 360, which is the term that converts the cost to an annualized basis.[4] When the terms are substituted into this equation, the cost of trade credit is determined. For 2/10, net 30, the cost of credit is

$$i_{TC} = \left(\frac{0.02}{1 - 0.02}\right)\left(\frac{360}{30 - 10}\right) = 36.7\%.$$

On an annual basis 2/10, n30 costs 36.7 percent, which is quite expensive compared with other sources of credit.[5]

Equation 21.3 may be used to illustrate the factors that affect the cost of trade credit. As may be seen from the question, the interest rate for trade credit is related to (1) the amount of the discount and (2) the length of time for which the buyer has the use of the goods. An increase in the amount of the discount increases the cost of trade credit. An increase in the payment period reduces the cost of trade credit. Both of these statements may be explained with the aid of Equation 21.3.

An increase in the discount in effect reduces the price of the goods and increases the interest cost of carrying the goods on credit. If the discount were 3 percent instead of 2 percent (3/10, net 30), then the firm would pay $97 for the goods during the first ten days and a $3 penalty for the use of the goods after the discount period. Using Equation 21.3, the interest rate is

$$i_{TC} = \left(\frac{0.03}{1 - 0.03}\right)\left(\frac{360}{30 - 10}\right) = 55.7\%.$$

The cost of trade credit is now 55.7 percent. The increase in the discount then increases the cost of trade credit, for the penalty is larger (the interest charge is greater). Thus, if a supplier wants to induce prompt payment, one method is to increase the discount. This tells the buyer that credit is more expensive and should encourage the buyer to find credit elsewhere and pay the supplier promptly.

An increase in the payment period means that the buyer has the use of the goods longer, and thus the cost of trade credit is less. If the payment period is increased from 30 days to 60 days (2/10, net 60), the interest rate becomes

$$i_{TC} = \left(\frac{0.02}{1 - 0.02}\right)\left(\frac{360}{60 - 10}\right) = 14.7\%.$$

By lengthening the payment period from 30 to 60 days, the supplier has reduced the interest rate from 36.7 percent to 14.7 percent. The cause of this reduction in cost is, of course, the fact that the buyer has the use of the goods for 30 additional days. If a supplier wishes buyers to use trade credit, increasing the length of the payment period reduces the cost and encourages the increased use of trade credit.

[4]The use of 360 is a common convenience that has the effect of understating the interest rate.

[5]The 36.7 percent is a simple, noncompound rate of interest. As will be subsequently illustrated, the compound rate of interest is higher.

Actually, the above calculations understate the true annualized rates of interest, because they fail to consider the impact of compounding. If a supplier grants credit such as 2/10, n30 and collects the receivable after 20 days, the process may be repeated every 20 days. The supplier compounds the interest more than eighteen times annually.

To determine the compound interest rate, treat the credit as a discounted note and rephrase 2/10, n30 into the following question: $98 at the beginning of the period (P_0) grows to $100 at the end of the time period (P_n) of 20 days *at what rate* (i)? That is,

21.4

$$P_0(1 + i)^{n/365} = P_n$$

$$\$98(1 + i)^{n/365} = \$100,$$

in which n is the number of days in the credit period and i the compound interest rate. If the terms of credit are 2/10, n30, then n is 20, and the equation to be solved is

$$98(1 + i)^{20/365} = \$100.$$

CALCULATOR SOLUTION

Function Key		Data Input
PV	=	−98
FV	=	100
PMT	=	0
IV	=	.05479
I	=	?
Function Key		*Answer*
I	=	44.56

The solution is

$$(1 + i)^{0.05479} = \$100/\$98 = 1.0204$$

$$i = (1.0204)^{18.25} - 1 = 1.4456 - 1 = 44.56\%.$$

The effective rate of interest is 44.56 percent when the interest is compounded 18.25 times a year.[6]

This calculation for the determination of the compound rate of interest when an amount (P_0) is borrowed for n days and the terminal value (P_n) includes the repayment of the principal plus the interest is stated in Equation 21.5:

21.5

$$i = (P_n/P_0)^{365/n} - 1.$$

Equation 21.5 may be used to determine the interest rate on any discounted loan in which the entire interest payment and principal repayment occur at the end of the term of the loan.

If a firm uses trade credit, when should it make payments? If a firm intends to pay the discount price and thereby not accept trade credit, the payment should be made as late as possible during the discount period. The price that the seller is charging includes the cost of supplying the goods during the discount period. Thus, the purchaser should take advantage of this "free" use of the goods during the entire discount period. If the buyer is unable to make the payment by the end

[6]The amount $(1.0204)^{18.25}$ may also be determined by using an electronic calculator with a y^x key. Enter 1.0204; press the y^x key; enter 18.25; press =, and 1.4456 is derived. Then subtract: 1.4456 − 1 = 44.56%.

of the discount period, payment should be made at the end of the payment period. Once the discount period has passed, the buyer has to pay the cost of the trade credit. There is nothing to be gained by paying early. If early payment is made, the cost of trade credit is increased, for the buyer does not have the use of the credit for the entire period.

While the terms of trade credit set the cost of the credit, what affects these terms? Trade credit is very competitive, and suppliers are aware that the terms they offer affect the sale of their products. By offering more generous terms, the supplier may be able to execute a sale. The terms of credit then become a means to differentiate one supplier from another. As each supplier tries to encourage sales by offering trade credit, the terms of the various offers should be similar, for competition will force the suppliers to offer comparable terms.

If trade credit tends to be expensive, why is it used? There are several explanations. First, it is convenient. By deferring payment until the end of the payment period, the buyer automatically receives the trade credit. Second, trade credit avoids sources of financial interrogation. A public offering of securities is subject to the security laws, and a bank scrutinizes the financial condition of the borrower before a bank loan is granted. Trade credit, however, may come from suppliers who do not require the buyer to be subjected to this financial analysis. Third, the buyer may lack an alternative source of credit. While bank credit is almost inevitably cheaper, it may not be available. Suppliers, however, need outlets for their goods, and offering trade credit may be a way to assure themselves of buyers for their goods. These suppliers are usually larger firms with established sources of credit. They are able to borrow at cheaper rates from their sources and in turn pass on the credit to small retail firms.

This section has covered the mechanics and cost of trade credit. In reality, however, trade credit may work differently. Buyers may stretch the terms of credit by either (1) remitting the discounted price after the payment period instead of the net price, or (2) "riding the credit" and paying after the payment period. This latter situation may occur if the buyer has not sold the inventory and does not have the funds to pay the supplier. Such practices, of course, reduce the cost of credit. When such practices occur, the suppliers then must decide whether to enforce the terms of the credit or be lenient and let the credit ride. In many cases the suppliers may not enforce the terms, for they need the retailers to purchase their goods. Such extensions of credit, however, cannot be indefinite. Eventually the supplier must decide how rapidly it wants to collect its accounts receivable. While suppliers may initially be lenient and not enforce the terms of trade, their cost of carrying the receivable eventually forces them to seek payment.

COMMERCIAL PAPER

As is explained in Chapter 3, commercial paper is an unsecured short-term promissory note issued by a corporation. The debt is issued in denominations or \$100,000 or greater and usually matures in two to six months. It may have a maturity date of only one day, but it rarely has a maturity date beyond nine months (270 days). Maturities of longer than 270 days must be registered with the SEC.

By limiting commercial paper issues to less than 270 days, corporations avoid the expense of registering the issue with the SEC.

Since there are no specific assets backing commercial paper, only companies with good credit ratings are able to issue this type of debt. Many firms are unable to sell commercial paper, and thus for them it cannot be a source of funds. Even though the paper is issued by large corporations with excellent credit ratings, there still is an occasional default. Perhaps the most celebrated example was the Penn Central Railroad. The firm had issued commercial paper and was thrown into bankruptcy when it was unable to retire the paper at maturity. This failure inflicted large losses upon the buyers of the paper. And these losses then made it more difficult for other firms to sell their commercial paper.

Evidence of the quality of a firm's credit rating may be obtained through one of the credit rating services. These services and their respective ratings for commercial paper are

Moody's Investor Service: Prime 1 (P-1), Prime 2 (P-2), and Prime 3 (P-3);

Standard & Poor's Corporation: A1, A2, and A3;

Fitch Investors Service: F-1, F-2, and F-3.

P-1, A-1, and F-1 are the highest ratings, and these are obtained only by the best and safest firms.

Commercial paper is issued by a variety of firms, but the primary users are finance companies and large bank holding companies, which account for about three-fourths of all commercial paper sold. The rest is issued by manufacturers and utilities. Manufacturers may use it as a source of funds to meet seasonal needs, and utilities may issue commercial paper to help finance construction of plant and equipment. After the construction is completed, the firm sells new debt or equity, and the proceeds of the sale are used to retire the commercial paper. Thus, the commercial paper is often used as a temporary source of funds prior to the firm's obtaining more permanent financing.

Firms may issue commercial paper and sell it directly to buyers (*direct paper*). Direct sales require a sales staff or the service of an investment banker to place the paper. Such direct sales require sufficient volume of commercial paper to justify the sales expense and constitute the bulk of commercial paper issued. The remaining sales are made through dealers (*dealer paper*). These dealers generally charge 1/8 of 1 percent of the face amount for selling the paper (for example, $1,250 for $1 million principal amount).

Commercial paper is purchased by banks, insurance companies, financial institutions, pension funds, trust departments, and companies that have excess liquidity and need a safe short-term investment. Individual investors rarely have a sufficient amount of money to participate in the market for commercial paper, since it is issued in large denominations, such as $100,000 or $1,000,000. Of course, individuals indirectly participate by purchasing shares of money market mutual funds, which in turn buy commercial paper.

For large corporations, commercial paper is a substitute for other types of short-term debt. It is usually cheaper than bank loans, for the interest cost is generally about 0.5 percent less than the prime rate. Unlike bank loans, commercial paper does not have restrictive convenants. This is particularly true for paper with the highest credit ratings. However, the investment community frequently requires that the issuing firm have unused credit lines at a bank to support the paper. To get these credit lines, the firm may have to pay a commitment fee. Thus, to sell commercial paper the firm must still bear the cost of obtaining the credit line, but other restrictions often required by banks are not placed on the firm.

Commercial paper does not pay a stated amount of interest. Instead the paper is another example of a discounted note. A $1 million 180-day note may be sold for $970,000. When the paper matures, the firm retires $1 million of debt and thus pays $30,000 for the use of $970,000 for six months (180 days). To figure the interest rate, Equation 21.1, which was used earlier to calculate the cost of a bank loan, may be rephrased and used to calculate the cost of commercial paper. In this example, the simple, annual interest rate on commercial paper (i_{CP}) is

$$i_{CP} = \frac{\text{Interest}}{\text{Proceeds used}} \times \frac{12}{\text{Number of months paper is outstanding}}$$

$$= \frac{\$30{,}000}{\$970{,}000} \times \frac{12}{6} = 6.19\%. \qquad \textbf{21.6}$$

If the paper had been sold for $940,000, the simple interest rate rises to

$$i_{CP} = \frac{\$60{,}000}{\$940{,}000} \times \frac{12}{6} = 12.77\%,$$

because the firm now pays $60,000 for the use of $940,000, while in the previous example it paid $30,000 for the use of $970,000.

As with the cost of trade credit, this simple calculation is an oversimplification, because it does not consider the impact of compounding. This omission is corrected by rephrasing the problem as follows:

$$\$970{,}000(1 + i)^{n/365} = \$1{,}000{,}000,$$

in which n is 180 days. So, the compound interest rate is

$$(1 + i)^{180/365} = \$1{,}000{,}000/\$970{,}000 = 1.03093$$

$$i = (1.03093)^{2.0278} - 1 = 1.0637 - 1 = 6.37\%$$

when the 180-day paper was sold for $940,000, and

$$(1 + i)^{180/365} = \$1{,}000{,}000/\$940{,}000 = 1.0638$$

$$i = (1.0638)^{2.0278} - 1 = 1.1336 - 1 = 13.36\%$$

when the paper was sold for $940,000.

CALCULATOR SOLUTION

Function Key		Data Input
PV	=	−970,000
FV	=	1,000,000
N	=	.49
PMT	=	0
I	=	?
Function Key		*Answer*
I	=	6.37

CALCULATOR SOLUTION

Function Key		Data Input
PV	=	−940,000
FV	=	1,000,000
N	=	.49
PMT	=	0
I	=	?
Function Key		*Answer*
I	=	13.37

In these illustrations, the compound rates of interest are slightly higher than the simple rates (6.37 percent versus 6.19 percent and 13.36 percent versus 12.77 percent). Compounding makes a difference, but the discrepancy is not as large as when comparing the simple and compound cost of trade credit. Commercial paper with a term of 180 days compounds only twice a year while trade credit with a 20-day credit period compounds 18 times a year. Obviously, commercial paper with a shorter maturity (30 days or less) compounds more frequently, and the impact of such compounding should be considered when determining the compound interest rate paid for the use of the funds.

Even after adjusting for compounding, the rate may still understate the true cost of the paper. If the firm pays a dealer a fee to sell the paper, the proceeds of the sale are reduced, which raises the cost. If the issuer must maintain a credit line with a commercial bank in order to sell the paper, the costs associated with the credit line also reduce the amount of cash the issuer can use from the sale of the paper. Once again, these expenses raise the cost of borrowing through the issuance of commercial paper.

SECURED LOANS

An alternative to trade credit and unsecured commercial paper is the secured loan. Inventory, accounts receivable, or any other sound short-term asset (for example, a government security) may be used to secure a short-term loan. This collateral serves to protect the lender who has a lien against the asset. This security should increase the availability of credit and reduce the interest cost of the loan to the borrower.

Secured loans are made by commercial banks and insurance companies. These lenders make their profits through the lending process; they do not want to take title to the pledged assets. If they are forced to take the pledged asset, they can choose either to hold the asset or to liquidate it. Liquidation may not bring the face value of the asset; thus, the lender will not grant a loan for the entire value of the pledged asset. Instead, the bank or finance company may lend some proportion, such as 70 percent of the asset's stated value. The borrower must have some equity in the asset that will be lost in case of default and seizures of the asset.

The amount that the creditor will lend against the pledged asset depends on the quality of the pledged asset, the ease with which the asset can be liquidated should the debtor default, the anticipated sale value, and the transaction costs of liquidation. A firm's short-term assets are not equally desirable for pledging against short-term loans. Inventory is less liquid than accounts receivable (especially raw materials and work-in-process). Hence, creditors may be less willing to accept inventory than accounts receivable as collateral to secure short-term loans.

When inventory is pledged to secure a loan, one of three general types of agreement is used. In the first type of agreement, the lender receives a lien against all of the borrower's inventory. Such an agreement is a blanket inventory loan because it covers all of the inventory. The second type of inventory loan is a trust receipt. The borrower holds specified inventory in trust for the lender. As these goods are sold, the borrower remits the proceeds to the lender to retire the loan.

The third type of loan secured by inventory involves a third party (in addition to the borrower and the lender). The pledged inventory is placed in a warehouse controlled by the third party, who is usually in the business of warehousing. When purchase orders for the merchandise are received, the borrower informs the lender of the pending sales. The lender instructs the warehouse to deliver the goods, and the proceeds of the sale are then used to repay the loan. Such warehouse financing obviously reduces the risk of loss to the creditor, because the creditor has effective control over the goods. The warehouse will release the inventory only on the instructions of the lender.

Just as warehouse financing is advantageous to lenders, it can also have advantages for borrowers. Manufacturers know that finished goods may not be sold as soon as they are available for sale. (If finished goods were sold that quickly, the need to finance them would be limited to the time required to convert the raw materials into finished goods.) Obviously, the goods have to be stored until they are sold and delivered. Unless the firm uses its own facilities, it will store the inventory at a warehouse and pay for the space. Thus, the warehouse may offer the manufacturer both space and the custodial service that facilitate financing the inventory.

When accounts receivable are used to help obtain short-term financing, the firm may either pledge the accounts to secure the loan or sell them outright for cash. When the accounts are pledged, the borrower retains them and, of course, must collect them. If an account cannot be collected, the firm still owes the bank or finance company the amount of the loan that was secured by the account.

The lender is aware that not all accounts receivable may be collected. If an account does not meet the lender's standards, it is not accepted as collateral for a loan. The lender realizes that if a buyer were to default on the receivable, the seller (the borrower and owner of the account receivable) might not be able to pay off the loans. By refusing to accept riskier accounts receivable as collateral, lenders protect themselves from the risk of loss.

Pledging short-term assets offers the firm a cost advantage over other sources of finance. The security for the loan reduces the cost of obtaining short-term financing from finance companies, and secured loans are much cheaper than trade credit. Secured credit from finance companies is generally more expensive than credit from commercial banks, but it has the advantage of avoiding the restrictions placed on the firm by commercial banks. While these restrictions may not have stated costs, the management of the firm may feel that there are implicit costs in the restrictions and thus may avoid bank credit when other sources of short-term financing exist. Bank credit can always be used in addition to this secured credit should the need arise.

FACTORING

If the firm does not want to retain and collect its accounts receivable, it may sell them. This process is called **factoring**. The sale of the accounts receivable is a source of funds, because a reduction in any asset is a cash inflow. Thus, factoring the accounts receivable is similar to pledging the accounts and borrowing from a

FACTORING
Selling accounts receivable

commercial bank. In both cases, the firm receives cash. The question then becomes: What is the advantage offered by factoring?

Factoring offers one major advantage: The seller is no longer concerned with collecting the accounts receivable. The risk of collecting is transferred to the buyer (that is, the factor).[7] However, there are two means by which the factor can control this transfer of risks. First, when the seller receives an order on credit, he or she may be required to have the sale approved by the factor. If the factor believes that the credit sale is a bad risk, approval may be denied (the factor may refuse to accept the account receivable). Thus, the seller will have to choose between carrying the account or refusing the credit sale. Second, the factor may either accept the receivable at a substantial discount or establish a large reserve that is not remitted until the account is collected. The larger the discount or the larger the reserve, the greater is the incentive not to factor the account receivable. The firm must then decide if its cash needs are sufficient to accept the discount or the reserve.

Factoring is often an expensive source of funds. This need not be the case if the financial manager compares the cost of factoring to 2/10, n30 from suppliers. The cost of factoring depends on (1) the factor's commission, (2) the interest cost on the outstanding balance owed the factor, and (3) any reserve held by the factor. The commission cost is generally 2.5 percent of the price and covers the cost of credit checks and collections. The interest rate is generally related to other short-term interest rates. The reserve is similar to any reserve set up for the collection of loans. Since the factor does not remit the amount of the reserve to the seller until the account is collected, the reserve both increases the cost of the source of funds to the seller and gives the factor a means to control his or her risk exposure.

How these elements affect the cost of factoring may be seen in the following illustration in which a firm makes a \$10,000 credit sale for n30 and the resulting account receivable is sold to a factor. The factor (1) charges a 2.5 percent commission, (2) charges the seller 10 percent interest on the balance owed the factor, paid in advance, and (3) establishes a \$1,000 reserve. What does the firm receive from the sale of the account? First, the factor takes out the \$250 commission (\$10,000 × 0.025). Second, since the account will be outstanding for a month, the factor takes out \$83.33 in interest (\$10,000 × 0.1 × 1/12). Third, the factor holds the \$1,000 reserve. So, the firm receives \$10,000 − (\$250 + \$83.33 + \$1,000), or \$8,666.67. If it is assumed that the \$1,000 reserve is returned at the end of the month, the firm has paid \$333.33 for the use of \$8,666.67 for one month, which is an interest cost (before considering compounding) of:

$$\frac{\$333.33}{\$8{,}666.67} \times \frac{12}{1} = 46.1\%.$$

[7] The factor can demand and may receive recourse if there is a default, in which case the risk is not transferred from the seller to the factor.

If the reserve had been only $200, the firm would have received $9,466.67, and the interest cost would have been

$$\frac{\$333.33}{\$9{,}466.67} \times \frac{12}{1} = 42.3\%.$$

Thus, the smaller the reserve, the lower is the interest rate.

These interest costs are substantial, but they overstate the cost of factoring. Since the firm has passed the costs of credit checks and collections to the factor, it avoids these expenses. These credit checks and collection costs are included in the above calculations. (They are part of the factor's commission.) If the seller can obtain the same services for less than the $250 commission fee, then the factor is expensive. However, many sellers may not be able to perform these tasks as cheaply as the factor. In this case, the *combined* costs of credit checks, collection expenses, and the carrying of the accounts may be more expensive than selling the accounts to the factor.

INTERMEDIATE-TERM DEBT

While accountants classify all liabilities as either short-term (due in less than one year) or long-term (due in more than one year), debt can also be classified as short-term, intermediate-term, or long-term. **Intermediate-term debt** is outstanding for more than a year (and hence appears as long-term debt on the firm's balance sheet), but it matures quicker than long-term debt. While long-term bonds may mature 20, 25, or 30 years after being issued, most intermediate-term debt will mature in 5 to 10 years. Based on the positive yield curve illustrated in Figure 2.1, the interest rate on intermediate-term debt is less than the rate on long-term debt. Conversely, intermediate-term debt tends to be more expensive than short-term debt.

INTERMEDIATE-TERM DEBT
Debt instrument with 5 to 10 years to maturity

Intermediate-term debt issued by corporations and sold to the general public may be referred to as "notes" to differentiate it from the bonds of the corporation, which are long-term debt. For example, in October 1999, Tenneco issued $500 million of 11.625 percent notes due in 2009 (10 years to maturity). Different terminology may be used when intermediate-term debt is obtained from a commercial bank or an insurance company. Such debt is often referred to as a **term loan.**

TERM LOAN
Loan obtained from a bank or insurance company for a period of 5 to 10 years

These loans are usually secured by equipment or real estate. Commercial banks, which make term loans of 1 to 5 years' duration, generally require that the loan be secured by equipment. Insurance companies, which tend to make term loans of from 5 to 15 years, generally use real estate as collateral for the loan.

In addition to the collateral, term loans have restrictive covenants that are negotiated between the debtor and the creditor. Common restrictions include a minimum current ratio such as 2.0:1, or a minimum amount of net working capital (that is, the difference between current assets and current liabilities must exceed some specified dollar amount). The creditors will also require periodic financial statements from the borrower and may require prior approval before the debtor can issue additional debt. While these restrictive covenants are common in term loan agreements, they do not exhaust all the possibilities, as each loan is individually negotiated. Conditions in the credit markets and the relative strengths of the parties also affect the terms. Based on the positive yield curve illustrated in Figure 2.1, the interest rate on intermediate-term debt is less than the rate on long-term debt. Conversely, intermediate-term debt tends to be more expensive than short-term debt.

Term loans are generally paid back in periodic payments and hence are like mortgage loans. The repayment schedules call for the payment of interest and the retirement of the principal. The way in which the payment is determined and the schedule of the reduction in a term loan are illustrated by the following example.

A firm wants equipment that costs $12,000 and has an expected life of 5 years. The firm arranges a term loan with a commercial bank. The following conditions apply:

1. a down payment of 20 percent of the cost of the equipment
2. five equal annual payments to pay the interest and retire the loan
3. 9 percent interest rate on the declining balance
4. the loan to be secured by the equipment.

The first condition establishes the amount that the bank is willing to loan. Notice that the bank is not willing to lend the entire amount and instead requires that the borrower have some funds invested in the equipment. The borrower must put up $2,400 (0.20 × $12,000) and the bank finances the balance, $9,600. Terms 2 and 3 establish the rate of interest and the payment schedule. The fourth term designates the equipment as collateral against the loan and gives the bank the right to take the equipment and sell it should the debtor default.

The repayment schedule is determined as follows. The borrower must make equal payments so that the bank earns 9 percent annually and the loan is retired in 5 years. This is another illustration of the time value of money. The equation necessary to solve this problem (that is, to determine the annual payments) is

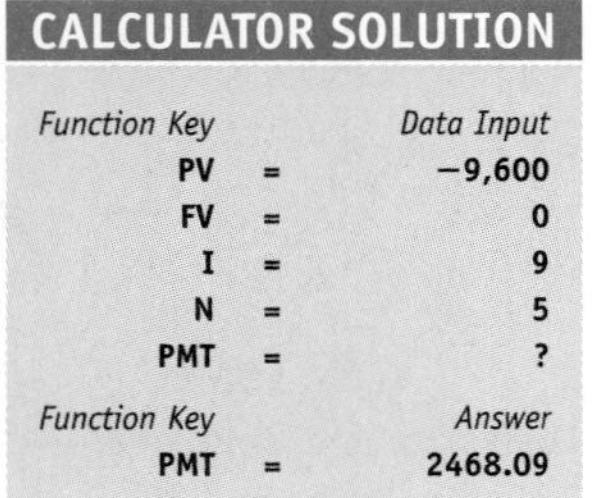

$$\$9{,}600 = \frac{PMT}{(1+0.09)^1} + \frac{PMT}{(1+0.09)^2} + \frac{PMT}{(1+0.09)^3} + \frac{PMT}{(1+0.09)^4} + \frac{PMT}{(1+0.09)^5}.$$

This is an example of an annuity, so the problem collapses to:

$$PMT(\text{PVAIF 9I, 5N}) = \$9{,}600$$

$$PMT(3.890) = \$9{,}600$$

$$PMT = \$9{,}600/3.890 = \$2{,}467.87.$$

CALCULATOR SOLUTION
Function Key Data Input
PV = −9,600
FV = 0
I = 9
N = 5
PMT = ?
Function Key Answer
PMT = 2468.09

Thus, $2,467.87 is the annual payment that retires this loan and pays 9 percent of the declining balance.

The actual payment schedule and the division of the payment into interest payment and principal reduction are given in Exhibit 21.1. This table is essentially the same as the mortgage loan amortization schedule illustrated in Exhibit 7.3 in Chapter 7. In both examples, the amount of the interest declines with each payment as the outstanding balance on the loan is reduced. Conversely, the amount

EXHIBIT 21.1

Repayment Schedule for a $9,600 Term Loan at 9 Percent for Five Years

Year	Payment	Interest	Principal Retirement	Balance Owed on Loan
1	$2,467.87	$864.00	$1,603.87	$7,996.13
2	2,467.87	719.65	1,748.22	6,247.91
3	2,467.87	562.31	1,905.56	4,342.35
4	2,467.87	390.81	2,077.06	2,265.29
5	2,467.87	203.87	2,264.00	1.29*

**The $1.29 results from rounding off. The payment determined by the financial calculator avoids this error.*

of the principal repayment rises with each payment as the interest required by the lower principal is reduced.

Generally, the depreciation of the equipment and the resulting cash flow cover the required loan payments. In this case, the annual straight-line depreciation expense would be $2,400 ($12,000/5). The cash flow generated by this $2,400 depreciation expense is approximately equal to the $2,467.87 payment required by the loan. (In many cases accelerated depreciation is used so that the initial depreciation expense is increased.) By matching the repayment schedule with the cash flow, the firm enhances its capacity to service the debt.

Since each loan is individually negotiated between the borrower and the lender, a variety of possible terms exist. One possibility is for the lender to require equal principal repayments with interest being computed on the remaining balance for each period. The repayment schedule under these terms for the $9,600 term loan is presented in Exhibit 21.2. In this case, the principal is retired in five equal installments of $1,920 ($9,600/5 = $1,920 in the second column). The amount of interest (column 3) depends on the balance owed (column 4). Thus, the payment in the second year is the sum of the principal repayment ($1,920) plus the interest on the balance owed at the end of the first year ($691.20), for a total payment of $2,611.20 (column 5).

Other possible terms include no principal repayment until the loan is due at the end of the fifth year. In this case, the firm would annually remit the $864 interest payment, and at the end of the fifth year make the last interest payment plus the principal repayment ($864 + $9,600 + $10,464). The lender could combine the two previous illustrations and annually require a partial principal repayment (for example, $1,000 annually) with the balance of $4,600 ($9,600 − $5,000) paid at the end of the term of the loan. Such a lump repayment at the end of a loan is referred to as a **balloon payment**.

BALLOON PAYMENT
Large, single payment to retire a debt obligation at maturity

Although firms obtain intermediate-term credit from banks and insurance companies, intermediate-term securities may also be sold to the general public. Notes sold to the general public are not collateralized while term loans usually are, and generally the notes do not have a compulsory repayment schedule. Such notes

EXHIBIT 21.2

Repayment Schedule for a $9,600 Term Loan at 9 Percent with Equal Principal Repayments

Year	Principal Repayment	Interest	Balance of Loan	Total Payment
1	$1,920	$864.00	$7,680	$2,784.00
2	1,920	691.20	5,760	2,611.20
3	1,920	518.40	3,840	2,438.40
4	1,920	345.60	1,920	2,265.60
5	1,920	172.80	0	2,092.80

are really more similar to long-term bonds than to term loans. However, these notes may have specific features that make them attractive to investors. The intermediate term (for example, 7 years) may make these notes attractive to investors who do not want to make investments for a longer term (such as 20 years). In addition, intermediate-term notes frequently cannot be called and refunded before maturity. Since the notes lack a call feature, the investor knows that the firm cannot force the buyer to give up the security should interest rates fall. Since many long-term bonds can be called and refunded if long-term interest rates fall, this non-callability of intermediate-term notes assures investors of their interest income (if no default) for the term of the notes.

LESSEE
Firm that rents (leases) property or equipment for its own use

LESSOR
Firm that owns property or equipment and rents it (leases the equipment) to other firms or individuals (the lessees)

LEASE
Renting (as opposed to owning) property or equipment; the contract between the lessee and the lessor

OPERATING LEASE
Lease for the use and maintenance of equipment in which the term is less than the expected life of the asset

FINANCIAL (CAPITAL) LEASE
Lease in which the term is equal to the expected life of the asset

LEASING

Leasing is essentially renting, and the two terms are often interchanged. Since lease contracts may cover any time period, lease financing may be an alternative to short- or long-term debt.

A lease contract is for the use of an asset such as plant or equipment. Firms want the use of the asset. They perform the capital budgeting techniques discussed in Chapter 17 to determine which investments are profitable. After deciding which investments to make, they must decide how to finance the asset. Notice that it is the use of the asset that the firm desires and not necessarily title to the asset. Leasing permits the firm (**lessee**) to use the asset without acquiring title, which is retained by the owner (the **lessor**). In return, the lessee enters into a contract (the **lease**) to make specified payments for the use of the asset.

Leases take one of two forms. An **operating lease** provides the lessee with both the use of the asset and a maintenance contract. The cost of servicing the equipment is built into the lease. The contract may be canceled after proper notice if the lessee should desire to change equipment. This type of lease is primarily used for renting equipment, especially computers, cars, and trucks. The length of the lease is less than the expected life of the asset but the lease may be renewed. Since the lease is not for the life of the asset, the lessor anticipates either having the lease renewed or selling the asset at the lease's expiration.

A **financial lease**, which may also be referred to as a **capital** lease, differs from an operating lease in several significant ways. These contracts are not cancelable and do not include a service clause. The duration of a financial lease is the expected life of the asset. The lease payments cover the cost of the asset and earn a set return for the lessor. Thus, a financial lease is similar to debt financing. If the firm had issued bonds to obtain the funds to acquire the asset, the payments to the bondholders would cover the cost of the equipment plus their return (the rate of interest). Of course, if debt had been used, the firm would own the asset, while with leasing it does not acquire title. This difference is important if at the end of the asset's life there is residual value that accrues to the asset's owner.

While there are two classes of leases, there are three types of lease agreements. From the viewpoint of the lessee, the type of lease agreement is immaterial; the firm still acquires the use of the asset. The type of lease has an impact only on the lessor. The first type of lease agreement is the **direct lease**. The lessor owns the asset and directly leases it to the lessee. Direct leases are offered by manufacturers who build the asset, such as IBM, as well as by finance companies and leasing companies that acquire assets with the intent to lease them to prospective users.

DIRECT LEASE
Lease agreement in which the owner (the lessor) directly leases the asset to the user (the lessee)

The second type of lease is a **sale and leaseback**. Under this type of agreement, the firm that owns the asset sells it to the lessor and then leases it back. The selling firm receives cash from the sale to the lessor that can be put to other uses but still retains the use of the asset. The lessee, however, relinquishes title to the asset and thus loses any residual value that the asset might have. And, of course, the firm must now make the lease payments.

SALE AND LEASEBACK
Financial agreement in which a firm sells an asset such as a building for cash and subsequently rents (leases) that asset

The third type of lease is a **leveraged lease**. Since the lessor owns the asset, that firm must have the funds to acquire it. In a leveraged lease the lessor borrows part of the funds necessary to acquire the asset. For example, a finance company may borrow from a commercial bank so that it may acquire an asset that it in turn leases to the ultimate users. If financial leverage is favorable, the lessor will increase the return on its funds invested in the asset.

LEVERAGED LEASE
Lease agreement in which the lessor acquires an asset (which it subsequently leases) through the use of debt financing

Lease or Purchase

The question of whether it is better to buy or to lease depends on several crucial variables. These include the firm's tax bracket, the terms of the lease, the asset's anticipated residual value, and the cost of obtaining funds to buy the asset. While this introductory text cannot fully develop this topic, the following example will provide some of the essential information necessary to make the choice.

A firm decides to acquire equipment that costs $5,000. The equipment has an expected life of five years, after which the equipment will be sold for an expected salvage value of $500. Depreciation will be straight-line (to lease the calculation; normally the firm would use accelerated depreciation if possible).[8] Maintenance is expected to be $200 annually, and the firm's marginal tax rate is 40 percent. The annual cash outflows and inflows ( ) from buying are shown on the following page:

[8]As was explained in Chapter 15, depreciation expense starts after six months have elapsed. This half-year convention is ignored to simplify the illustration.

Year	0	1	2	3	4	5
Purchase price	$5,000					
Maintenance		$200	200	200	200	200
Depreciation		$1,000	1,000	1,000	1,000	1,000
Tax deductible expenses		$1,200	1,200	1,200	1,200	1,200
Tax savings		($480)	(480)	(480)	(480)	(480)
Sale of asset after tax						(300)
Cash outflows (inflows)	$5,000	(280)	(280)	(280)	(280)	(580)

Initially (Year 0) there is the $5,000 outflow to acquire the equipment. In each year there is a $200 cash outflow for maintenance. The $200 plus the $1,000 non-cash depreciation expense produces $1,200 in tax-deductible expenses, which annually saves $480. The tax saving more than offsets the $200 maintenance, so in this simple example, the net is a cash inflow of $280, which is expressed in parentheses.

While depreciation, maintenance, and the tax savings are the same each year, the cash inflow is the same each year except for the last year in which the equipment is sold for $500. The sale is a cash inflow, but if an asset is sold for more than its book value, the cash inflow is reduced by the taxes generated by the sale. (If the asset were sold for less than its book value, the sale would reduce taxes.) In this illustration, the asset is completely depreciated so its book value is $0. All of the sale is taxable income, so the firm nets only $300 after paying taxes of $200 on the $500 sale.

Alternatively, the firm could lease the equipment from a lessor who wants a 10 percent return. To determine the annual lease payments, the lessor answers the following question: How much must I charge each year so that my $5,000 invested in the equipment yields 10 percent? That is,

$$\frac{PMT}{(1+0.1)^1} + \ldots + \frac{PMT}{(1+0.1)^5} = \$5{,}000$$

$$PMT(\text{PVAIF } 10I,\ 5N) = \$5{,}000.$$

CALCULATOR SOLUTION

Function Key		Data Input
PV	=	−5,000
FV	=	0
I	=	10
N	=	5
PMT	=	?
Function Key		*Answer*
PMT	=	1,318.99

The interest factor is 3.791, so the equation becomes

$$PMT(3.791) = \$1{,}319$$

$$PMT = \$5{,}000/3.791 = \$1{,}319.$$

For the lessor to earn 10 percent, the annual lease payment should be $1,319.

If the lessor charges $1,319 annually, the lessee's annual cash outflows are

Year	1	2	3	4	5
Lease payment	$1,319.00	1,319.00	1,319.00	1,319.00	1,319.00
Tax savings	($527.60)	(527.60)	(527.60)	(527.60)	(527.60)
Cash outflow	$791.40	791.40	791.40	791.40	791.40

As may be seen by comparing the two projections, the cash flows differ under leasing and owning. Leasing produces a constant $791.40 outflow each year, while owning results in varying cash inflows and outflows.

Which alternative is better? That depends on the time value of money. Which alternative produces the *lower* present value of the *cash outflows*? If the financial manager can borrow the funds for 12 percent, the two cash outflows are discounted back at 12 percent. The present value of the cost of owning (that is, the present value of the cash outflows associated with owning) is

Present value of cost of owning

$$= \$5{,}000 + \frac{\$280}{(1+0.12)^1} + \frac{-280}{(1+0.12)^2} + \frac{-280}{(1+0.12)^3} + \frac{-280}{(1+0.12)^4} + \frac{-580}{(1+0.12)^5}$$

$$= \$5{,}000 + (-280)(0.893)(-280)(0.797) + (-280)(0.712) + (-280)(0.636) + (-580)(0.567)$$

$$= \$5{,}000 - 250 - 223 - 199 - 178 - 329$$

$$= 3{,}821.$$

The present value of the cost of leasing (that is, the present value of the cash outflows associated with leasing) is

$$\text{Present value of cost of leasing} = \frac{\$791.40}{(1+0.12)^1} + \ldots + \frac{\$791.40}{(1+0.12)^5}$$

$$= \$791.40(3.605)$$

$$= \$2{,}853.$$

Since the present value of the cash outflows associated with leasing is less than the present value of the cash outflows associated with borrowing and owning, leasing is preferred.[9]

While this illustration argues for leasing, there are several critical variables in the illustration. The first is the expected residual value. If the anticipated residual value were higher, that would argue against leasing. The owner of the equipment

[9]These present values may be found by using a financial calculator. For the present value of the cost of leasing, enter PMT = −791.40, I = 12, N = 5, FV = 0, and solve for PV. For the payment as a cash outflow, I = 12, N = 5, FV = 0, and solve for PV. Subtract this amount from $5,000.

receives the residual, and this present value is lost if the firm leases. The smaller the expected residual, the stronger is the argument for leasing. Second, the owner pays the maintenance and the lessee does not. However, if the lease contract does not include maintenance, the lessee will also have to pay that expense, and maintenance is a cash outflow. Third, the present value of the cash outflows depends in part on the choice of the discount rate. If a lower discount rate had been used in the illustration, the present value of the cash outflows generated by borrowing and buying may have been less than the present value of the cash outflows generated by leasing. This may occur because the lower rate would increase the present value of the residual value in year 5.[10]

Accounting for Leases

Prior to changes in accounting standards, one reason for using leasing was that the lease would not appear on the firm's balance sheet. While the lease would be mentioned in the footnotes, the fact that it did not appear on the balance sheet understated the firm's use of financial leverage. This important distinction between the use of debt, which must appear on the balance sheet, and leasing, which would not appear on the balance sheet, is illustrated by the following example. Both firms initially have the same assets, liabilities, and equity:

Firm A Balance Sheet As Of 12/31/X0				Firm B Balance Sheet As Of 12/31/X0			
Assets	$10,000	Debt	$5,000	Assets	$10,000	Debt	$5,000
		Equity	5,000			Equity	5,000

Both firms acquire a $5,000 piece of equipment. Firm A purchases the equipment and sells bonds to acquire the funds to pay for it. Firm B leases the equipment. After these transactions, their respective balance sheets become:

Firm A Balance Sheet As Of 1/31/X1				Firm B Balance Sheet As Of 1/31/X1			
Assets	$10,000	Debt	$5,000	Assets	$10,000	Debt	$5,000
Equipment	5,000	Bonds	5,000			Equity	5,000
		Equity	5,000				

Both firms have the use of the equipment, but firm A has more debt outstanding. Firm A appears to be riskier because its debt ratio is now higher. In reality, however, it is no riskier than firm B, for firm B also has a new contractual obligation,

[10] For a discussion of the impact of different discount rates, see the discussion of mutually exclusive investments in Chapter 17.

the lease payment. Since the lease does not appear on the balance sheet, firm B appears to be less risky.

The use of leases to obtain such "off the balance sheet" financing is in many cases no longer possible. The Financial Accounting Standards Board ruled that if the lease gives the lessee substantially all the benefits and risks of ownership, the lease must be "capitalized" and included on the firm's balance sheet. This means that the present value of the asset is listed as an asset, and the present value of the lease payments is listed as a liability. The value of the asset then diminishes over time as it is depreciated, and the liability is reduced as the lease payments are made.

The lease must be included on the balance sheet if it meets *any* of the following four conditions:

1. The lease transfers ownership of the asset at the end of the lease.
2. The lease permits the lessee to buy the asset below its value at the expiration of the lease.
3. The length of the lease is more than 75 percent of the asset's estimated life.
4. The present value of the lease payments exceeds 90 percent of the fair market value of the property to the lessor.

The first two conditions obviously give the lessee the benefits and risks of ownership. In the first condition, ownership is transferred and in the second condition the lessee has the option to buy the asset at a bargain price. While the lessee does not have to exercise the option and buy the asset, the important consideration is the existence of the option.

The third and fourth conditions require some explanation. Consider the illustration presented earlier in which the financial manager had to choose between either the lease or borrowing and buying. In the illustration, the analysis indicated that leasing is the better alternative. Will the lease have to be capitalized? The answer is yes because it meets the third condition. The life of the asset is five years and the lease is for five years, so the length of the lease exceeds 75 percent of the estimated life of the asset.

The fourth condition requires calculating the present value of the lease payments. In the illustration, that is the present value of the $1,319 lease payments. Of course, the present value of the lease payments depends upon the discount rate. This rate has to be the lower of (1) the rate used by the lessor to establish the lease payments or (2) the interest rate the lessee would pay to borrow the funds to purchase the assets. In the illustration, the lessor used 10 percent and the lessee used 12 percent, so 10 percent must be the discount rate. When the lease payments are discounted at 10 percent, the present value is

$$\$1{,}319(3.791) = \$5{,}000.$$

The present value of the lease payment is greater than 90 percent of the cost of the investment; hence, the lease must be capitalized.

Many leases do not meet any of the preceding criteria for capitalizing a lease. If an employee rents a car for a week, that is certainly an operating lease, and it will not be capitalized. But if the car is rented for several years, the terms of the lease may meet one of the criteria and hence must be capitalized. If management wants to avoid having to capitalize the lease, then the terms must be structured in such a way as to avoid all the criteria.

The inclusion of the lease would have the following impact on the balance sheet of firm B if the lease were capitalized:

Firm B
Balance Sheet
As Of 1/31/X1

Assets	$10,000	Debt	$5,000
Assets under capital lease	5,000	Capital leases	5,000
		Equity	5,000

This revised balance sheet for firm B brings to the foreground the fact that a financial lease is an alternative to debt financing. Both firms A and B have $15,000 in assets and $5,000 in equity. The remaining sources of funds are either debt or the capitalized lease. The debt ratio for both firms then is $10,000/$15,000 = 67 percent. Now the balance sheets indicate that firm A and firm B are equally financially leveraged.

While capital leases must be capitalized, leases often avoid being capitalized. For example, many firms lease equipment and rent space. These agreements are usually operating leases that are not capitalized and do not appear on the balance sheet. The firm, however, must report future lease payments. Payments for the next four years and for all subsequent years are provided in a footnote to the balance sheet, so the information is not hidden. In some cases, these lease payments are substantial. For example, The Limited leases space in malls and shopping centers but has no capitalized leases on its balance sheet. The Limited stated in a footnote in its 1998 Annual Report that the company had minimum rent commitments under noncancelable leases of:

1999	$643,828,000
2000	632,785,000
2001	563,468,000
2002	502,880,000
Thereafter	1,427,862,000

These rental payments are obviously a sizable commitment!

Arguments for Leasing

Since many leases can no longer be hidden, the advantages of leasing are hard to isolate. For example, it may be argued that the use of lease financing avoids the restrictive covenants associated with debt financing, which are designed to protect the lender. However, lessors will also take steps to protect themselves. If they believe that the lessee is a poor credit risk, they will not grant the lease or will charge higher rentals to protect themselves.

A second argument offered in favor of leasing is that the firm obtains the use of the asset without using any of its own funds. The lessor puts up 100 percent of the funds to acquire the asset. But certainly the lessor would not lease the asset to the lessee if the latter did not have an equity base, and the use of the lease should reduce the borrowing capacity of the lessee.

A third argument in favor of leasing is that the lessee avoids the risk of obsolescence. The gist of this argument is that if a firm buys equipment that becomes obsolete through technological change, that firm is left with outmoded equipment, which puts it at a competitive disadvantage. If this firm had leased the equipment, it could choose to cancel the lease (if that option were available) or not renew the lease when it expired. Obtaining the use of the asset through leasing instead of purchasing makes replacing the obsolete equipment easier.

This line of reasoning has led some advocates of leasing to assert that leasing shifts the risk of loss from the lessee to the lessor. However, the lessor will certainly charge a rental fee that compensates for this risk. In effect, the lessee pays the lessor to bear the risks. Of course, if the lessor does not anticipate the obsolescence, the lessee may be able to shift the risk. However, many firms that are lessors are also manufacturers of or specialists in a particular type of equipment (for example, computers or trucks). Presumably, they should know the risk of obsolescence and charge accordingly. Failure on their part to protect themselves from this risk of loss would soon result in their being out of business.

While leasing may not be a means to (1) hide the use of debt financing, (2) avoid having equity in an investment, or (3) shift the risk of obsolescence, it is still a viable means to obtain the use of an asset. The primary argument for leasing revolves around the tax positions of the lessor and the lessee. The terms of the lease may be structured to generate savings for both parties. For example, if a firm is in the highest income tax bracket, it may prefer to own rather than lease. Accelerated depreciation of the asset generates a tax shelter, which is not possible through leasing.

Besides tax issues, leasing offers flexibility. Many firms, such as IBM and Xerox, lease their computers and copiers to users in addition to selling them. Lease terms are structured to the benefit of both parties. This may be particularly true if the lessee needs the use of the asset for a period less than the life of the asset. For example, virtually all retail space is leased. Sears, The Limited, and Kmart do not own the shopping malls in which they locate their stores. If such retailers want to move, they don't have to sell the buildings. Although they have to meet the terms of the leases and they run the risk of higher payments when the leases are renewed, retailers find flexibility in leasing that would not be possible if they owned the buildings.

BANKRUPTCY AND REORGANIZATION

Some firms grow, expand, and prosper. Others are not so fortunate. Many firms fail every year, but most of these are relatively small firms. Although failure by large firms are rare, these failures affect more people and receive more publicity.

There may be many causes of failure. While management may have used too much financial leverage or did insufficient financial planning, the precipitating act is usually the failure to meet a current liability as it comes due. If the firm fails to meet these financial claims, it is insolvent, and the debt goes into default. An insolvement firm need not be bankrupt. **Bankruptcy** is a legal procedure for the reorganization or liquidation of a firm that cannot meet its obligations.

BANKRUPTCY
Legal proceeding for the liquidation or reorganization of an insolvent firm

If a firm cannot meet its obligations, creditors must decide on a course of action. Creditors will act in the manner that they believe is in their own best interest and may not press for payment or liquidation. Forcing payment through bankruptcy court proceedings is expensive and perhaps futile. Thus, the creditors of many financially troubled firms have accepted a restructuring of debt instead of pressing for payment through court action.

In many cases, the insolvent firm solicits a voluntary reorganization with its creditors. Such voluntary reorganizations restructure the firm's obligations. For example, creditors may extend the maturity of the debt or waive some of the restrictive covenants. Long-term debt obligations may be converted into equity in a new, reorganized firm. Why could creditors be willing to agree voluntarily to such changes? The question really is: Are the creditors better off with the firm operating or liquidated? If the creditors push to have the firm liquidated, they probably will not receive the full value of their claims but may instead receive a mere fraction of what they are owed. If they permit the firm to continue to operate, profitable operations may be restored and the creditors may receive the full value of what they are owed. Since these profits cannot occur until some time in the future, creditors are faced with a typical financial question: Which is greater, the present liquidation value of their claims or the present value of the future claims if the firm continues to operate?

How individual creditors answer this question depends in part on their positions in the pecking order in which claims are met. Not all claims are equal. Some are subordinated to others and the superior claims are paid first. If the firm is liquidated, the strict order of payment is

1. the cost of the liquidation (court expenses)
2. unpaid labor expenses
3. taxes
4. secured debt
5. unsecured debt
6. preferred stock
7. common stock

This list points out the tenuous position of the unsecured debt, preferred stock, and common stock. Even the secured creditors may prefer reorganization if the firm's assets have deteriorated in value. If the assets are sold at bargain basement prices through a forced liquidation, secured creditors may receive only a fraction of their claims. Creditors realize that they may profit through a voluntary reorganization that avoids formal bankruptcy proceedings, and thus they agree to accept reorganization.

If the firm is unable to work out a voluntary arrangement with its creditors, it may be forced into bankruptcy. Bankruptcy is as much a legal as a financial question. The firm may seek bankruptcy voluntarily to obtain protection from its creditors while the firm and the creditors work out a reorganization. The firm may be involuntarily thrown into bankruptcy by a creditor seeking payment. The bankruptcy court appoints a trustee for the debtor's property who continues to operate the business, examines the debtor's books for fraud, and initiates a plan for reorganization. The emphasis is usually on reorganization and not on liquidation, but liquidation may be the final result. The final plan for reorganization must be acceptable to two-thirds of the creditors. The court will accept the plan if it believes that the plan meets the statutory requirements of being feasible, fair, and equitable. Once the plan has been accepted, the firm is released from bankruptcy.

Some creditors fare very well in reorganizations. For example, Interstate Stores went bankrupt and creditors received stock in a subsidiary that was spun off from Interstate. The terms were one share for every $10 of principal plus one share for every $10 of accrued and unpaid interest. The subsidiary was Toys R Us. An Interstate creditor received 100 shares of Toys R Us for every $1,000 of claims on Interstate. Within six years, that stock in Toys R Us was worth over $17,000! While Toys R Us is obviously an exception, it does illustrate why creditors may accept reorganization instead of liquidation. Some firms do successfully bounce back from bankruptcy and generate substantial profits for those investors and creditors willing to accept the risk associated with the reorganization.

Prepackaged Bankruptcy

Obtaining concessions from creditors is a formidable task, especially if the firm has publicly held bonds. The indentures of these issues often specify that a large proportion of the bondholders (80 to 90 percent) must agree to accept the change in the terms for it to be effective. Thus, a small proportion of the bondholders may refuse to agree in an effort to obtain a better settlement. Southland (7-Eleven) tried unsuccessfully to reach an agreement with its bondholders in an effort to avoid bankruptcy. Although a majority of the bondholders did accept the terms of the reorganization, a minority was able to block the proposed reorganization.

Failure to win approval often means that the firm defaults and is forced into bankruptcy. Since bankruptcy proceedings can take years to work out a reorganization plan and win court approval, the managements of several firms have used a strategy called the **prepackaged bankruptcy**. The idea is deceptively simple: Devise a reorganization plan and obtain approval of at least 50 percent of the creditors holding at least two-thirds of the debt. File this plan with the bankruptcy court, and if the court accepts the plan, it can impose the terms on the dissenting minority of creditors. Once the plan has been imposed, the firm emerges from bankruptcy. The whole process can take six months, while a normal bankruptcy proceeding can last for years.

PREPACKAGED BANKRUPTCY
Reorganization plan accepted by the firm and a majority of its creditors prior to the firm filing for bankruptcy

While a prepackaged bankruptcy sounds simple, there are risks. Militant creditors may seek to fight the plan in court. The disclosure of information may be insufficient or some detail of the agreement may not meet a facet of the bankruptcy standards, either of which results in the plan being voided. If the plan is thrown out, then management and creditors must start again, and all the expenses associated with developing and filing the prepackaged plan are lost.

The initial prepackaged bankruptcy filing by Republic Health was successful and several firms, including Southland, Trump's Taj Mahal, and Vestron (producer of several movies and distributor of movie videos), quickly filed prepackaged bankruptcies designed to reorganize the companies without extended bankruptcy proceedings. Since each filing is judged on its own merits, it is impossible to anticipate how each plan will be received. However, the Southland reorganization plan was confirmed by the bankruptcy court in less than five months. The speed with which this reorganization was achieved should encourage the future use of the prepackaged bankruptcy strategy.

SUMMARY

The management of a firm's current assets and liabilities is one of the most important facets of the financial manager's job. The firm must meet its current obligations as they come due or face bankruptcy. Short-term debt (current liabilities) is a major source of finance for current operations, but it is also a potential problem since it must be frequently retired or rolled over.

The major sources of short-term funds are loans from commercial banks, trade credit, commercial paper, secured loans, and factoring. Commercial banks grant short-term loans (promissory notes), lines of credit, and revolving term credit agreements. These short-term loans may be converted into intermediate-term or mortgage loans upon maturity. Banks increase the interest cost to the borrower by discounting loans in advance and by charging origination fees and fees on a credit line's unused balance.

Many firms use trade credit, which is spontaneously generated through purchases of inventory. The seller grants the credit (an account receivable to the seller and an account payable for the borrower) to encourage the sale. Trade credit is a particularly important source of credit for small retailers who lack other sources of short-term finance. The terms of credit (such as 2/10, net 30) establish the cost of this credit, but many firms attempt to ride their accounts payable, which reduces the cost of trade credit.

Large, creditworthy firms are able to issue commercial paper, which consists of unsecured promissory notes sold in large denominations through dealers or directly placed with buyers. Commercial paper is sold for a discount. At maturity the issuing firms pay the principal, so the cost of the paper to the issuing firm depends upon how long the security is outstanding and the difference between the discounted price and the principal amount.

Firms may also factor (sell) accounts receivable to raise cash, and they may pledge current assets, such as inventory or accounts receivable, as collateral for loans. These secured loans are for less than the value of the collateral, because the creditors do not want to take title to the collateral, and liquidation will rarely bring the face value of the asset. Without this reduction in risk, it is doubtful that the lenders would be willing to grant the short-term credit.

Intermediate-term debt and leasing are alternatives to short- and long-term debt. Intermediate-term debt is generally outstanding 5 to 10 years. While it may be similar to other forms of long-term debt, its shorter maturity and the fact that it is often secured differentiate it from long-term bonds. The repayment schedule for intermediate-term debt is generally paired with the anticipated cash flow that is generated by the acquired asset.

Leasing is similar to renting. The firm (the lessee) acquires the use of the asset without actually owning it. In return, it must make periodic payments to the owner (the lessor) for the use of the asset. Leases may be classified as operating leases or financial leases. The latter type of lease is very similar to purchasing the asset with debt financing; the present value of the lease payments (and the value of the asset) must be capitalized and included on the lessee's balance sheet.

The cash inflows and outflows generated by leasing may differ from the cash flows generated through borrowing and purchasing the asset. The financial manager needs to determine and compare the present value of the cost of owning and the cost of leasing to determine which is cheaper. Taxation, the timing of interest payments or lease payments, depreciation schedules, and estimates of the asset's salvage value will affect these present values and affect the decision to either lease or purchase.

Failure to make payments on current obligations results in the firm being insolvent and often leads to bankruptcy. Bankruptcy is a court proceeding that leads either to the reorganization of the firm and its obligations or to the firm's liquidation. Management may enter bankruptcy voluntarily to seek court protection from creditors. Creditors, who want to enforce the firm's financial obligations, may involuntarily place the firm in bankruptcy.

In a reorganization, the claims are restructured. Since unsecured creditors have inferior claims, these individuals often accept reorganization in preference to liquidation. In some cases the reorganization is agreed to prior to the bankruptcy filing. In this prepackaged bankruptcy all that is necessary is for the court to accept the reorganization and recognize the new claims.

Review Questions

1. Why is a line of credit or a revolving credit agreement a flexible source of short-term funds? Why does discounting a loan in advance or charging an origination fee increase the cost of the loan? What is the cost to a firm that obtains a revolving credit agreement but does not use the credit line?
2. Why is trade credit a spontaneous source of funds? Who uses trade credit? Is such credit appropriate for financing equipment?
3. If you were a supplier and your customers had a high rate of failure, would you increase or decrease the cash discount when stating the terms of trade credit? Would you lengthen or shorten the discount period or the pay period?

4. If the terms of credit are n30, what is the cost of the credit? If a firm uses trade credit, who is supplying the credit? On what does the cost of this credit depend?

5. What is commercial paper, and who issues it? If you had $5,000 to invest, could you buy commercial paper? Why is commercial paper a relatively safe short-term investment alternative?

6. How does a factor earn a return when purchasing accounts receivable? What is the impact on the implied interest rate when the factor increases the amount of the reserves? If the reserves are returned by the factor after the receivables are collected, does that suggest the reserve had no impact on the cost of the funds?

7. How may the repayment schedule for an intermediate-term loan be determined? What impact will each of the following have on the periodic payment required by an intermediate-term loan?
   a. an increase in the rate of interest
   b. an increase in the term from five to seven years
   c. an increase in the balloon payment

8. What is the difference between an operating lease and a financial lease? If an employee takes a business trip and rents a car at the airport, is that an example of an operating or a financial lease?

9. Why is a financial lease similar to a long-term bond? What is the implication of a financial lease on the firm's use of financial leverage? Does the lease have to be capitalized and expressed on the lessee's balance sheet?

10. Many manufacturers retain ownership and lease their products instead of selling them. Such leases often include maintenance contracts. Are these contracts financial or operating leases? Does the lessee avoid the risk of obsolescence?

11. The lease versus purchase analysis stresses cash inflows and outflows. What impact does each of the following have on estimated cash flows, and do they argue for leasing or owning?
   a. Depreciation is spread over more years.
   b. The estimated residual value is increased.
   c. The lease payment occurs at the beginning instead of at the end of the year.
   d. Estimated maintenance expense is increased.

12. An asset's estimated life is 10 years and the firm enters into a lease agreement that covers 6 years. Based on this information, does the lease have to be capitalized?

13. What is the difference between a voluntary and an involuntary bankruptcy?

14. Why may the strict order of claims that could be upheld in a bankruptcy court proceeding encourage voluntary reorganizations and prepackaged bankruptcy reorganizations?

PROBLEMS

1. Firm A borrows $1 million from a commercial bank. The bank charges an annual rate of 10 percent and requires a 3 percent origination fee. What is the interest cost of the loan? (Assume the loan is outstanding for one year.)
2. SSC, Inc. finances its seasonal working capital need with short-term bank loans. Management plans to borrow $65,000 for four months. The bank has offered the company a 10 percent discounted loan with a 5 percent origination fee. What are the interest payment and the origination fee required by the loan? What is the rate of interest charged by the bank?
3. You can borrow $5,000 for 60 days with an interest payment of $125. What is the simple rate of interest? What is the compound rate of interest?
4. XYZ, Inc. needs to borrow $2,000,000 for 6 months. It can sell 180-day commercial paper with a face value of $2,000,000 for $1,900,000 or borrow the money from a commercial bank at 10 percent. In both cases the interest is $100,000. Which loan is more expensive and why?
5. An individual wishes to borrow $10,000 and is offered the following alternatives:
   a. a 10 percent loan discounted in advance
   b. an 11 percent straight loan (i.e., interest paid at maturity).
   Which loan is more expensive?
6. Which of the following terms of trade credit is the more expensive?
   a. A 3 percent cash discount if paid on the 15th day with bill due on the 45th day (3/15, net 45)
   b. A 2 percent cash discount if paid on the 10th day with the bill due on the 30th day (2/10, net 30)
7. Trade credit may be stated as n60 plus 18 percent on the balance outstanding after two months. What is the cost of this credit?
8. Clare Construction needs to borrow $200,000 for 45 days in order to take advantage of the cash discount of 3/10, n55 offered by a supplier. Clare Construction can borrow the funds from a bank with an interest payment of $5,000 at the maturity of the loan. Should management borrow the funds from the bank to take advantage of the discount?
9. If $1 million face amount of commercial paper (270-day paper) is sold for $982,500, what is the simple rate of interest being paid? What is the compound annual rate?
10. A financial manager may sell $1 million of six-month commercial paper for $950,000 or borrow $1 million for six months from a commercial bank for 10 percent annually and a 2 percent origination fee. Which set of terms is more expensive?
11. Bank A offers the following terms for a $10 million loan:
    - interest rate: 8 percent for one year on funds borrowed
    - fees: 0.5 percent of the unused balance for the unused term of the loan

Bank B offers the following terms for a $10 million loan:

- interest rate: 6.6 percent for one year on funds borrowed
- fees: 2 percent origination fee

a. Which terms are better if the firm intends to borrow the $10 million for the entire year?
b. If the firm plans to use the funds for only three months, which terms are better?

12. A commercial bank offers you a $200,000 annual line of credit with the following terms:

- origination fee: $2,000 paid when the line is accepted
- fee on unused balance of 1 percent paid at the end of the year
- interest rate of 9 percent

What is the effective cost of the loan
a. if you expect to borrow the entire $200,000 for the year?
b. if you expect to borrow the $200,000 for only three months?

13. Little Store buys inventory using trade credit. The terms are stated as 2/10, n30, but Little Store rides the credit and generally pays on the 40th day. Occasionally, payment is made as late as the 50th day. What is the approximate cost of the credit (a) if paid on time, (b) if paid on the 40th day, and (c) if paid on the 50th day? What is the compound cost of credit in each case? Why does the cost change?

14. High Time's suppliers tend to offer generous terms of trade credit (2/30, n90), but High Time can also issue commercial paper, receive $0.978 and repay $1.00 at the end of 60 days. What are the compound interest rates offered by the two alternatives? What would be the impact if High Time's suppliers changed the terms to n30?

15. A five-year $100,000 term loan has an interest rate of 7 percent on the declining balance. What are the equal annual payments required to pay interest and principal on the loan? Construct a table showing the declining balance owed after each payment.

16. What are the repayment schedules for each of the following five-year, 10 percent $10,000 term loans?
a. equal annual payments that amortize (retire) the principal and pay the interest owed on the declining balance
b. equal annual principal repayment, with interest calculated on the remaining balance owned
c. no principal repayment until after 5 years, with interest paid annually on the balance owned
d. $1,000 annual principal repayment, with the balance paid at the end of 5 years and annual interest paid on the balance owed

17. Photo, Inc. plans to update its equipment at a total cost of $90,000. Management anticipates making a $15,000 downpayment and the remainder from a local commercial bank at 12 percent interest. The first option provides for five equal, annual payments to be made at the end of the year. The second option requires five equal, annual payments plus a balloon payment of $15,000 at the end of the fifth year. What are the annual payments required by each option?

18. Northwest Bank has been asked to purchase and lease to Clare Construction equipment that costs $1,200,000. The lease will run for 6 years. If Northwest seeks a minimum return of 12 percent, what will be the required lease payment?

19. A lessor acquired equipment for $83,250 and plans to lease it for a period of 5 years. If the equipment has no estimated residual value, what must be the annual lease charge for the lessor to earn 12 percent on the investment? What would be the annual lease charge if the lessor sought to earn 8 percent? If the equipment will have a residual value of $10,000, what lease payment will earn the lessor 12 percent?

20. A firm wants the use of a machine that costs $100,000. If the firm purchases the equipment, it will depreciate the equipment at the rate of $20,000 a year for 4 years, at which time the equipment will have a residual value of $20,000. Maintenance will be $2,500 a year. The firm could lease the equipment for 4 years for an annual lease payment of $26,342. Currently, the firm is in the 40 percent income tax bracket.

a. Determine the firm's cash inflows and outflows under borrowing and purchasing the equipment and under leasing.

b. If the firm uses a 14 percent cost of funds to analyze decisions that involve payments over more than a year, should management lease the equipment or borrow and purchase it?

c. Would your answer differ if the cost of funds were 8 percent?

CASE

DETERMINING THE COST OF SHORT-TERM FUNDS

Alaine Scarlatti is the financial manager of a moderately sized manufacturer of women's apparel. The firm has been exceptionally successful in the market for young women ages 25 to 40. It has seasonal needs for working capital, and its excellent credit rating has given it the enviable position of being able to consider a variety of possible sources. Ms. Scarlatti is planning the firm's short-term financing strategy for the next six months. She anticipates either one of two situations arising:

1. The firm will need $40,000,000 for six months.
2. The firm will need $40,000,000 for only three months.

Ms. Scarlatti, however, must plan for either situation since there is an equal likelihood that either will occur.

One possible source of short-term funds is commercial paper. She has been informed that the firm may issue $42,190,000 worth of commercial paper and receive $40,000,000. The paper will be due at the end of six months (180 days). A second possibility is to borrow from the First Bank of Town, which offers a line of credit with an annual interest rate of 9.5 percent and an origination fee of 2 percent. A competing bank, the First Bank of City, offers revolving credit of $50,000,000 at 9 percent but with a fee on the unused balance of 0.5 percent paid at the end of the six months.

In order to help Ms. Scarlatti determine which of the three alternatives is the most attractive, answer the following questions.

Case Problems

1. How much will the firm have to borrow from each bank?
2. What is the interest rate on each of the alternatives if the money is borrowed for six months? (To ease the comparison, compute simple, noncompound rates of interest.)
3. If the firm generates $40,000,000 after three months and thus can pay off the loan, what is the rate of interest under each alternative?
4. If Ms. Scarlatti does select the commercial paper and the firm generates the $40,000,000 at the end of three months, she expects to be able to invest the money in a three-month Treasury bill that will earn $700,000. What impact will that have on the interest rate paid for the commercial paper?
5. Is the difference between a line of credit and a revolving credit agreement important to Ms. Scarlatti's decision?
6. Which alternative source of finance do you believe Ms. Scarlatti should accept?

CHAPTER 22
Mergers, Divestitures, and Overview of Finance

Learning Objectives

1. Identify the types of and reasons for mergers.
2. Enumerate the terms of a merger agreement and the means of payment.
3. Explain how management may fight a hostile takeover attempt.
4. Differentiate divestitures, carve outs, and spin-offs.
5. Reexamine the role of the financial manager, and restate the criterion for judging performance.
6. Explain the possible impact that monetary and fiscal policy may have on a firm.
7. Ask yourself the following questions:
   a. Was my conception of financial management too narrow?
   b. Do I understand why financial management is crucial for the successful management of a firm?
   c. Do I realize how the study of finance will help me make personal financial decisions?

The twentieth-century novelist John Phillips Marquand suggested in *The Late George Apley* that "marriage . . . is a damnably serious business." Mergers are also a damnably serious business. Hardly a day passes without reference in the financial press to a merger or takeover. As of January 2000, Exxon and Mobil had just completed their merger. ARCO and BP (British Petroleum) were still in the process of obtaining approvals necessary for them to merge. Chesapeake Corporation was attempting to purchase Shorewood Packaging Corporation, which had earlier offered to purchase Chesapeake. Bell Atlantic and GTE were continuing the consolidation in telecommunications, and MCI WorldCom had agreed to acquire Sprint.

While some firms are merging, other firms are doing the opposite. Dial split into two companies, and The Limited sold off part of Intimate Apparel but retained a controlling interest in the company. Although such divestitures may not be as common as mergers, they are occurring with increasing frequency. This chapter briefly describes the reasons for mergers and acquisitions and their opposites—divestitures.

The text ends with an overview of corporate financial management. That famous saying, "They cannot see the forest for the trees," applies to this (and many) textbooks. Topics are individually discussed and developed in each chapter, but these concepts are not independent of one another. Each is a part of a larger picture. A textbook is like a mural. You study one facet of a discipline at a time, but the pieces fit together. The text ends with a reminder of this integration by reviewing the components of finance: institutions, investments, and corporate financial management and how they are interrelated.

MERGERS

Firms may expand by external as well as by internal growth. Firms grow internally by retaining earnings and using their cash flow to replace and expand plant and equipment. Firms expand externally by purchasing or merging with another existing firm. This section covers mergers—the combining of two firms into a single firm—and will briefly consider the causes of external growth and different types of **mergers.**[1] The subsequent sections will discuss how the combination of two firms may be accomplished, hostile takeovers, and leveraged buyouts.

MERGER
Combining of two or more firms into a single firm

Reasons for Mergers

There are several reasons for external growth. First, if a firm seeks to enter an industry, there are start-up costs. The firm must plan for the entry and contract for the plant and equipment. This process may be both expensive and time consuming. The span of time from the decision to enter a new field to the actual production and sales of the output may be many years. Purchasing an existing firm can reduce the time necessary to enter the industry and may reduce the cost of entry. Second, entry into a new industry has risk and is uncertain of success. While management will not enter a new line of business unless it anticipates earning profits, success is not assured. For example, RCA entered the computer industry to compete with IBM and Digital Equipment. Even though RCA had previously been a leader in electronics, it failed to compete successfully with the established computer firms and suffered one of the largest losses ever incurred by a corporation. By purchasing or merging with an existing, profitable firm, this uncertainty is reduced. Third, when a firm enters a new industry, it increases the number of firms within the industry. This increases the element of competition and may reduce the level of profits for all firms in the industry. Such an increase in competition might not occur if the entering firm purchases or merges with an existing firm.

Possible Impact on Earnings

Mergers may be a means for a firm to increase its per share earnings. Consider the information on the following page concerning two firms:

[1]The term *merger* is often used to imply two firms mutually agreeing to join together into one firm. The term *acquisition* is often used to imply one firm taking over another firm.

	Firm A	Firm B
Net income	$1,000,000	$2,000,000
Number of shares outstanding	500,000	500,000
Earnings per share (EPS)	$2	$4
Price per share	$14	$40
Price/earnings ratio (price divided by EPS)	7.0	10.0

Firm B offers to exchange its stock for the stock of firm A at the rate of one share of A for 0.45 share of B. These terms may be attractive to the stockholders of A since 0.45 of B is worth $18 (0.45 × $40), which exceeds the current market price of $14 for a share of A.

If the stockholders accept the offer, firm B issues 225,000 of its shares (0.45 × 500,000) for the 500,000 shares of A. The effect of this transaction on the per share earnings of B is

Net income	$3,000,000
Number of shares outstanding	725,000
Earnings per share	$4.14

As a result of this merger, B's per-share earnings are increased from $4 to $4.14.

What effect will this increase have on the stock's price? This question is impossible to answer before the merger, because no one knows how the market will value the new, larger firm. If B's price/earnings ratio remains 10, the price of the stock will rise to $41.40. If the market views the combination of A and B to be a stronger firm than B by itself, the price should rise above $41.40. However, if the market believes that the acquisition of A by B will be detrimental to B, the price of B's stock will fall.

Presumably, management follows the course of action that maximizes the value of the shares.[2] The takeover of A by B does increase the value of A's stock. Unless management can arrange better terms elsewhere, accepting the offer may be in the stockholders' best interests (but not necessarily the best interests of management). The decision of B's management to make the offer need not result in a higher value for B's stock. As with all investment decisions, the realized results will not be known until after the investment (in this case the merger) is completed.

Not all mergers lead to an immediate increase in earnings per share. Instead, there may be a decrease in per-share earnings as the firm that takes over another firm issues new stock, which dilutes the existing stockholders' position. Earnings per share may also be reduced if the firm has to issue substantial debt to finance the takeover, because this debt will require interest payments that may reduce the firm's net earnings. If the additional interest expense is substantial, the increase in operating income from the merger may be insufficient to offset the interest

[2] When the managements of Monsanto and Phamacia & Upjohn announced an agreement to merge the two firms, the prices of both stocks declined!

expense. Thus, net income could decline even though the firm issues no additional stock to finance a takeover.

Such a decline in earnings was forecasted by the management of GTE Corporation when it purchased Contel. The increase in GTE shares issued in exchange for the Contel shares resulted in lower earnings per share. Management, however, anticipated that the rate of growth in earnings would increase. Thus, although there would be an initial decline in per share earnings, future earnings would rise as a result of the merger. Management's expectations were realized, for GTE earned $1.6 billion one year prior to the merger and $1.8 billion one year after the merger. By 1998, earnings had grown to $2.8 billion.

Synergy

In addition to increased potential for growth and higher per share earnings, mergers may be justified on the grounds that the combined firm is stronger than the two individual firms. This is called **synergy.** Synergy may occur when two firms with different but complementary strengths are merged so that the resulting firm is stronger than the sum of its parts. For example, the management of Illinois Tool Works implied synergy when it wrote in the proxy statement concerning the acquisition of Premark that ITW "can increase Premark's operating margin by introducing ITW's proven engineering and manufacturing expertise at Premark."

SYNERGY
Combining of two firms so that the combined firm is stronger than both firms were individually

Synergy has been frequently used to justify mergers. Firms with low profitability have been taken over on the grounds that the management of the company doing the takeover could "turn around" the unprofitable firm. While it may be impossible to verify that such synergy existed, it is an intuitively appealing explanation (or perhaps rationalization) for such takeovers.

Types of Mergers

Mergers may be classified into three types: horizontal, vertical, and conglomerate. Mergers of two firms within the same industry (those which produce the same products) are **horizontal mergers.** Thus, the merger of Exxon and Mobil is an example of a horizontal merger. **Vertical mergers** involve the merging of two firms in different aspects of the same industry, especially when one of the firms is a supplier for the other firm. If an automobile manufacturer merged with a producer of automobile parts, that would be a vertical merger. Another example is the merger of a steel mill with an ore producer. Because steel mills buy iron ore to produce steel, the producer of the ore is one of the steel mill's suppliers. If a steel mill merged with a metal fabricator, that also would be a vertical merger because the steel mill sells its products to the fabricator. Many mergers are vertical mergers, since firms seek to assure themselves of supplies of raw materials by merging with firms that are suppliers of these materials.

HORIZONTAL MERGER
Merger of two firms in the same industry

VERTICAL MERGER
Combination of a firm with a supplier or distributor

There are also mergers between firms with diverse product lines. These conglomerations are called **conglomerate mergers,** and in some cases there is no apparent relationship between the two firms. Many firms that currently have diverse product lines grew through such mergers.

CONGLOMERATE MERGER
Merger between two firms in different industries

In the 1990s, some managements reversed the process and many conglomerate firms were dismantled. During the 1970s, Paramount (then called Gulf &

Western) grew into a large and diverse industrial firm with operations in financial services (Associates Corp.), publishing (Simon and Schuster, Prentice-Hall), film and television production (Paramount), natural resources (New Jersey Zinc), and consumer products. In addition Gulf & Western held a large portfolio of common stocks of other firms, so that by 1980 it was one of the best illustrations of a conglomerate firm.

With the death of its founder and the resulting new management, the firm changed directions. Management sold the stock portfolio, divested entire divisions and streamlined operations into a firm primarily concerned with entertainment. Gulf & Western's name was changed to Paramount Communications, which, ironically, was one of the firms Gulf & Western bought during its period of merger activity. Paramount became one of the most successful producers of television shows ("Cheers") and movies (the *Indiana Jones, Star Trek,* and *Godfather* series). Subsequently, Paramount Communications sold out to Viacom who then beat out QVC in one of the most protracted takeover battles of the 1990s.

Tenneco pursued an objective similar to that of Gulf & Western but executed it in a completely different way. Management determined that the conglomeration of products did not strategically fit and started to break up the company. Unlike Gulf & Western, most divisions were not sold off. The farm equipment (Case) was sold to the general public in an initial public offering. Newport News Shipbuilding was spun off to stockholders, and the energy-related business was merged with El Paso Natural Gas Company. Shares in El Paso Natural Gas were distributed to Tenneco's stockholders. The company then split into two companies. Tenneco stockholders received stock in Pactiv, which manufactures specialty packaging (Hefty trash bags and One Zip freezer bags), and Tenneco Automotive, which manufactures Monroe shocks and struts. Unlike the stockholders of Gulf & Western, who received cash when the firm was ultimately sold to Viacom, the original Tenneco stockholders ended with shares in four companies: Newport News Shipbuilding, El Paso Natural Gas, Pactiv, and Tenneco Automotive.

EXECUTING THE MERGER

External growth through a merger is an investment and should be treated in the same way as other investment decisions. The capital budgeting techniques discussed in Chapter 17 should be applied to prospective mergers. These techniques will help identify possible merger candidates and establish the terms of a merger that are acceptable to the acquiring firm.

The terms of a merger are extremely important. They include the following: (1) the price paid for the acquired firm; (2) the relationship between the acquired firm's previous management and the acquiring firm's management; (3) relationships among divisions of the two firms; and (4) the relationship between the new management and labor unions affected by the merger. In some cases, the managements of the acquiring firm and the firm to be acquired are compatible and able to establish mutually acceptable terms. However, if the two firms are not on friendly terms, the acquiring firm may seek to gain control from the other firm's management. This may be done through a cash offer for the firm's stock at a price sufficiently high to induce the current stockholders to sell their shares. Once the acquiring firm gains control, it may replace the old management and merge the two companies.

After the price has been established, the means of payment must be determined. The acquiring firm has basically the following three choices: (1) pay in cash; (2) issue a specified amount of debt in trade for the acquired firm's stock; or (3) issue a specified amount of stock in trade for the acquired firm's stock. These three choices are significantly different from each other from the viewpoints of both the buyer and the seller.

If the firm pays cash (the Viacom purchase of Paramount), it is trading one asset for the acquired firm's stock. It receives the firm's assets and liabilities, but no new shares are issued, and its current stockholders' ownership is not diluted. Payment with cash means that the firm must either have the cash or a ready source of funds. From the viewpoint of the sellers the prime advantage is the receipt of money, which the sellers may use as they desire. However, since this is a cash sale of their stock, the sale is subject to capital gains tax if the stockholders sell their shares for a profit.

If the firm issues debt to pay for the acquisition, it conserves its cash but increases its use of financial leverage. This obliges the firm to meet the terms of the indenture, to pay the interest, and to retire the debt. There is no dilution of its current stockholders' position, however, for no new shares are issued (unless the debt is convertible into the firm's stock). From the viewpoint of the sellers, the flow of interest income and the obligation of the acquiring firm to meet the terms of the indenture may be important advantages. Since the sellers have agreed to accept debt instead of cash, they may be able to negotiate a higher price for the shares to compensate them for accepting payment that is spread over several years.[3] There is, however, a major disadvantage in accepting debt instead of cash. The Internal Revenue Service treats the acceptance of debt as being no different from a cash sale. For tax purposes capital gains are realized, and the sellers must pay capital gains taxes if they have made a profit on the transaction.

If the acquiring firm issues stock as payment (The Illinois Tool Works acquisition of Premark),[4] its current stockholders' position may be diluted. This dilution depends on the earnings of the acquired company and the number of shares issued. However, no additional debt is issued that requires interest payments and eventual retirement. The sellers who receive the stock of the acquiring firm can sell these shares or retain them. The shares may appreciate in value if the firm flourishes and grows, but there is no assurance that the firm will prosper, and the firm is not obligated to pay dividends. Should the value of the stock decline, the sellers might not realize the purchase price of the shares.

[3]Another possibility would be a higher interest rate on the debt the stockholders receive for their stock.

[4]Illinois Tool Works (ITW) issued 0.8081 of its shares for every share of Premark. Based on the price of Illinois Tool Works' stock, the price paid for Premark was $55 a share. This price represented a considerable premium over Premark's price of $34.25 prior to the merger announcement.

There is a major tax advantage in accepting stock as payment instead of cash or debt. The Internal Revenue Service does not treat the swapping of stock in a merger as a realized sale. The seller has the cost basis of the old shares transferred to the new shares and does not recognize any gains or losses for the purpose of capital gains taxes. Those investors who want cash or who do not want to invest in the combined firm may sell their stock and pay any applicable capital gains taxes. Other investors, however, may continue to hold the new stock and not pay any capital gains taxes until the stock is sold. This tax advantage argues for accomplishing mergers through stock swaps, for stockholders may more readily accept the terms of the merger since profits are not subject to capital gains tax unless the stock is sold.

The firm taking over a second firm may offer to swap convertible preferred stock instead of common stock or debt. Since the preferred is convertible into the common stock of the company doing the takeover, such a transaction is considered a swap of "like" securities and is not subject to capital gains taxation. In addition, the value of the convertible security will rise if the surviving firm prospers and its stock price increases. The dividend on this preferred may also be higher than would be paid to the holders of the firm's common stock. Thus, the preferred stockholders can receive a larger flow of income that is more comparable to the flow of interest paid by a bond but does not have the tax consequences associated with swapping their stock for a debt instrument. This tax advantage is probably the primary reason that convertible preferred stock is issued in a merger. The stockholders can earn more income, have potential for capital gains through the conversion feature, and defer any applicable capital gains taxes until the shares are sold.

THE HOSTILE TAKEOVER

Not all business combinations are the result of the managements of two firms willingly merging their operations. In many cases, one firm seeks to acquire another whose management prefers to remain independent. This leads to a hostile takeover attempt. The managements of the two firms square off in a fight for control: The acquiring firm fights to gain control, while the other firm battles to retain control.

Often the scenario of such battles follows a distinct pattern. In this discussion, the firm initiating the takeover is called Suitor, and the target firm is called Takeover. Suitor may initially take a position in Takeover's stock. Although this purchase is unannounced, an increase in the volume of trading in a given stock is often an indication that someone is accumulating a position in the shares. Once Suitor has accumulated 5 percent of Takeover's stock, Suitor is required to file with the SEC Form 13-D, which discloses the position. For this reason, Suitor may cease accumulating the stock prior to acquiring 5 percent. On the other hand, Suitor may file the required document and continue to accumulate the shares.

If Suitor desires to pursue the acquisition, it may announce an offer to buy the remaining shares at a specified price. That is, Suitor makes a "tender offer" for the shares that it does not already own. The price is almost inevitably above the current market price to induce current stockholders to sell. This immediately puts the stock "in play" as the market awaits the reaction from Takeover's management.

The reaction is almost always negative. Takeover's board of directors meets to consider the offer to buy the firm, but the answer is generally that the price is "inadequate."[5] Suitor may respond by threatening to take the offer to Takeover's stockholders and seek their approval for the sale of the company. Since most stockholders vote by proxy and not in person, this scenario produces the "proxy fight," in which current management and Suitor each fight for the votes (the proxies) of Takeover's stockholders. The procedure can be costly to both sides, so some alternative course of action usually develops.

For example, Suitor may fight the claim that the price is inadequate by raising the offer. This puts immense pressure on Takeover's management and the board of directors to accept the sweetened offer. If they refuse and the offer is withdrawn, the price of the stock will probably return to its pre-takeover level. Stockholders will sustain a loss and may sue management and the board of directors for failure to perform their financial responsibilities to stockholders.

Another possibility is that Takeover will find a different buyer. Once Suitor makes the offer and the stock is in play, an alternative buyer may surface, which could lead to a bidding war. The alternative buyer, White Knight, may strike a deal with Takeover's management, which accepts the offer to sell the company to White Knight. Although the price may not exceed Suitor's sweetened offer, it should be comparable. A higher price, of course, ends the possibility of legal action against management since the firm is sold to the highest bidder (assuming that Suitor does not further increase its offer).

If this scenario occurs, Takeover's management positions are often retained. Suitor also fares well. Since it initially took a position prior to making its offer, it has stock acquired for a price that may be below the price paid by White Knight. Even if White Knight does not emerge or eventually withdraws, Suitor's initial purchases usually cost less than its subsequent purchase of the remainder of Takeover's shares.

In the previous illustration, White Knight "saved" Takeover's management; however, if White Knight does not emerge, there is still the possibility that Takeover will fend off the unsolicited and unwanted offer to buy the firm. Takeover's management may offer to repurchase the shares already acquired by Suitor. This offer may even exceed the going market price, in which case Takeover pays "greenmail" to induce Suitor to cease the hostile offer. The terms of the sale may include a stipulation in which Suitor agrees not to purchase stock in the company for a period of time (five or ten years). In other cases, the terms may permit Suitor to hold a position for "investment purposes" but forbid the purchase of additional shares (a "stand still agreement"). Suitor's management then may hold the

[5] There is an obvious potential conflict of interest. Takeover's board of directors and management have fiduciary responsibility to the firm's stockholders. Fighting the takeover attempt, however, may be motivated by a desire to protect the board's position and the managers' salaries, perks, and other benefits—not to benefit stockholders.

Fending Off Hostile Takeovers

How can management reduce the likelihood of a takeover? One means that many publicly held firms have adopted is the rights offering. Such a strategy is designed to make the takeover more expensive, which reduces the firm's attractiveness to possible buyers. The strategy cannot be used to erase the possibility of a takeover. That would obviously be beneficial to existing management at the expense of the firm's stockholders. ¶ How the strategy works may be illustrated by the plan established by El Paso Electric. A right was attached to each share of El Paso common stock that grants the shareholder the right to buy an additional share for $25. These rights trade with the stock and may be exercised only if (1) 15 percent or more of the stock is acquired by an individual or another firm or (2) an offer to buy the company is made. ¶ These terms will certainly increase the cost of a takeover if the price of El Paso stock exceeds $25 a share. For example, suppose El Paso stock is trading for $29 and another firm offers to buy the stock for $33. Immediately the rights may be exercised. Each current stockholder may buy an additional share at $25 for each share held. The firm seeking control of El Paso would have to purchase two shares instead of one. Although this will not preclude a takeover attempt, it obviously raises the cost. ¶ Since this additional cost generates cash for the existing stockholders, it can be argued that they are the beneficiaries of the rights offering. But the strategy does reduce the probability of an outsider seeking to buy the firm. Thus, the rights also protect existing management from a hostile takeover that would, in all probability, result in management's losing its job. ¶

shares, a strategy it will find acceptable if the managers believe that Takeover's stock is undervalued and the price will rise in the future.

To discourage an unwanted offer, Takeover's management may take actions in anticipation of and prior to an attempted hostile takeover. (See, for example, Financial Facts: "Fending Off Hostile Takeovers.") Management may break up the firm and spin off pieces to its stockholders. For example, Ethyl Corporation distributed First Colony Corp. and Tredegar Industries to its stockholders. As is discussed in the section on divestitures, this course of action could be motivated by several reasons. First, the parent desires to rid itself of a division that is not doing well and hence is hurting the parent's financial position. Second, the parent desires to divest itself of a profitable division that no longer fits into its long-term goals. Third, the parent desires to remove a division that other firms may want. The other firms will no longer consider taking over the parent as a separate entity. When the last possibility is the motivating factor, the spin-off (or any sale of a division) may be referred to as a "scorched earth" policy designed to protect the parent from a hostile takeover attempt.

Other strategies used to fend off takeovers include the recapitalization and the leveraged buyout. Leveraged buyouts may be motivated by other considerations and are covered in the next section. In a recapitalization, management borrows a substantial amount of money and uses it to repurchase stock or pay a large cash dividend. For example, GenCorp borrowed $1.3 billion and used the money plus other internally generated funds to repurchase 54 percent of its outstanding stock at $130 a share. The effect of this repurchase was to completely change GenCorp's financial structure. Long-term debt rose from $200 million to over $1.4 billion and equity declined from $1.1 billion to a *negative* $360 million.

A variation of this strategy was employed by Harcourt Brace Jovanovich, which borrowed $2.5 billion and used the money to distribute a one-time cash dividend of $40 a share. While this action did not reduce the number of shares, it certainly changed the firm's capital structure. In effect, Harcourt substituted a substantial amount of debt for equity, as the dividend distribution wiped out its earnings.

These actions were taken by GenCorp and Harcourt in response to hostile takeover offers. In both cases, the large reduction in equity coupled with the large amount of new debt thwarted the takeover. In a sense, the recapitalization is a variation on the scorched earth strategy because incurring the new debt thwarts the takeover by destroying at least part of the firm. While both managements obviously anticipated that the surviving firm would be viable, this is not a certainty. After these recapitalizations, managements of both GenCorp and Harcourt Brace Jovanovich were forced to sell off divisions and streamline operations in an attempt to restore the financial viability of their respective firms. As of the end of its 1998 fiscal year, GenCorp had reduced debt and increased equity, but total debt still constituted over 80 percent of total financing. Harcourt, however, never regained financially and was purchased by General Cinema. (General Cinema subsequently spun off its movie operations and renamed the surviving company Harcourt General.)

LEVERAGED BUYOUTS

Although may firms are sold to other companies, firms can also be sold to their managers and/or other private investors. In some cases, these sales are in response to hostile takeover offers. Instead of accepting an offer to sell the company, management itself buys the company (that is, buys out the existing stockholders). After the purchase is completed, the firm is no longer publicly held but becomes a private corporation owned by a few individuals.

Few investors have sufficient funds to buy all the firm's publicly held shares. To finance these purchases, the buyers borrow the funds from commercial banks and pledge the assets of the firm to secure the loans. In effect, the investors are using the firm's borrowing capacity (and not their own) to buy the company. The buyers have to invest only a small amount of the total purchase price, since the bank finances the balance. The loans are subsequently repaid with funds generated by the firm's assets.

Such **leveraged buyouts** have become an important strategy for avoiding an unwanted takeover. For example, Cone Mills, a major manufacturer of denim, received an unwanted offer to purchase the firm from Western Pacific Industries.

LEVERAGED BUYOUT
Acquisition (purchase) of a firm through the use of debt financing

E-II Holdings and Pac-Man

The takeover of Beatrice Companies was one of the largest leveraged buyouts: $6.2 billion. Soon after completing the purchase, management started to restructure the firm. Several divisions were sold in order to raise funds to retire some of the large debt issued to finance the purchase of Beatrice. Then, a hodgepodge of consumer products, such as Samsonite luggage, Stiffel lamps, and Louver drapes and blinds, were put together and sold back to the general public. The new company's name: E-II Holdings. ¶ E-II Holdings illustrates the new financial restructuring/takeover game. The sale of E-II to the public not only raised funds to help pay off debt but also raised a substantial amount of money to continue the process—that is, to acquire additional companies. However, when E-II Holdings sought to make a major acquisition, the unexpected happened. E-II offered to purchase American Brands, but the firm resisted by using the "Pac-Man" defense. This defense is named after the video game in which the character seeks to gobble up its opponents before it is eaten. American Brands counteroffered to buy the shares of E-II Holdings. While this defense is rarely used to fend off an unwanted takeover attempt, it succeeded in this case. E-II Holdings did not acquire American Brands but was itself acquired by its target, and American Brands maintained its independence. ¶

Instead of seeking a merger partner to buy Cone Mills as a means of avoiding the takeover, management chose a leveraged buyout. It offered the stockholders $70 a share, which was higher than the offer by Western Pacific Industries. The total cost was $465.3 million. The majority of funds to finance this purchase came from ten commercial banks that put up $420 million. These loans, which accounted for more than 90 percent of the total purchase price, were secured by the company's assets. By such a leveraged buyout, Cone Mills's management avoided the takeover and maintained its control of the firm.

Not all leveraged buyouts are the results of hostile takeover attempts. Some firms use the leveraged buyout as a means to dispose of unwanted divisions. For example, Mobil sold its Montgomery Ward division to its managers in a leveraged buyout. Mobil received cash for the sale. The managers of Montgomery Ward retained their positions and became the owners of the firm. If they successfully manage the independent company, they could earn a substantial return on their investment in the firm.

Many leveraged buyouts result in the creation of substantial amounts of debt, virtually all of which would be classified as high-yield "junk bonds." Occasionally, firms (Macy's, for example) default on their junk bonds, and investors who financed the leveraged buyouts sustain large losses. However, not all leveraged buyouts fail, and managements of several successful leveraged buyouts have taken the firms public. For example, Cone Mills had an initial public offering and sold shares to the general public. Management had successfully fought off the Western Pacific hostile takeover, sustained the company during the period when it was privately held, and restored Cone Mills as a publicly held firm.

DIVESTITURES

While mergers have frequently been a means to grow, a reverse pattern has emerged in which firms divest operations by selling subsidiaries or spinning them off to stockholders. For example, Dial was a conglomerate with diverse operations. (At one time it owned Greyhound, the intercity bus line.) Dial split into two companies: Dial, a consumer products company that manufactures Dial soaps and Purex bleach, and Viad, a service company with such operations as Premier Cruise Lines and Dobbs International, which caters airline food. The rationale for the split was that the two firms had more potential as separate companies. Management could focus on each firm's core business and have more incentives to perform. If successful, the separation would then increase stockholder wealth.

Divestitures may be achieved in a variety of ways. A company may sell off the subsidiary to another firm. For example, RJR Nabisco sold its candy operations to Nestlé. Such sales often occur if the subsidiary is not performing up to management's expectation or if it no longer fits in with the parent company's strategic objectives. Another reason for the sale may be the parent company's need for cash.

Although the sale of a subsidiary to another firm still occurs, the divestitures of the 1990s are differentiated by the use of alternative strategies—the equity carve out and the spin-off. In an equity carve out, the parent company sells a preexisting subsidiary through an initial public offering. In some cases, the parent maintains a controlling interest. For example, The Limited sold a minority interest in its Intimate Apparel to the general public. The sale was an initial public offering in which the services of an investment banker were used to underwrite the new shares. The parent could sell the entire subsidiary, in which case it would no longer hold a majority (or minority) interest in the new firm.

The alternative strategy is the spin-off, in which the parent company distributes ("spins off") the subsidiary to its stockholders. In 1999, The Limited spun off Too, Inc. to its stockholders. After the divestiture, The Limited no longer maintained any interest in Too, Inc., which became a separate, publicly owned company. In some cases the spin-off is simply a breaking up of one firm. The Dial example cited earlier resulted in the creation of two virtually equal firms.

Although both the carve out and the spin-off result in the divestiture of operations, their impacts on the parent firm differ. In the carve out, the parent sells the stock and receives cash from the sale. (It may also have to pay taxes if the sale generates taxable income.) The stockholders of the new company are the buyers of the stock and are not necessarily the owners of the parent. In the case of the spin-off, the parent company distributes the stock in a tax-free distribution to existing stockholders. Since a spin-off is a distribution and not a sale, the parent does not receive any funds (nor will it have any tax liabilities). The initial stockholders of the new company are the same as the owners of the parent. These stockholders do not have any tax liabilities unless they sell the new shares. If they do sell the shares, the cost basis is prorated between the parent company's stock and the new stock.

Whether divestitures increase the wealth of stockholders is open to debate. If the parent company maintains a controlling interest in the carve out, the new company may not attract investors, which could depress the stock's price. In the case of a spin-off, stockholders who do not want the new shares may sell their interest, which also may drive down the price of the stock. Such price declines could create buying opportunities. Whether such buying opportunities do exist or whether acquiring these shares leads to superior investment results is not the purpose of this discussion. Such divestitures will certainly continue as managements streamline operations and seek means to increase stockholder wealth.

In summary, mergers may be justified on the grounds of increased earnings or increased potential for growth. Mergers may be executed through a stock swap or a purchase. Stock swaps off the advantage of deferring capital gains taxes until the newly acquired shares are sold. An increase in hostile takeovers had led to leveraged buyouts, in which a firm's management uses the firm's borrowing capacity to buy out the shares held by the general public. The leveraged buyout, then, becomes a means to avoid the takeover.

Just as firms may merge operations, they may also divest operations. Management may sell subsidiaries to other firms or to the general public through an initial public offering that employs the services of an underwriter. Subsidiaries may also be spun off to existing stockholders. As with mergers, there are tax implications if firms or stockholders sell their positions. Both mergers and divestitures are strategies used by managements to pursue strategic goals that presumably increase the value of their firm's stock.

AN OVERVIEW OF FINANCE

The parts of this text (financial institutions, investments, and corporate finance) are not independent of each other. The financial manager constructs financial plans and budgets, makes long-term investment decisions, determines how the firm's current assets will be managed, and obtains the financing necessary to acquire the assets. None of these decisions can be made in a vacuum. The firm can obtain assets only if savers (be they individuals, governments, or other firms) are willing to invest the funds in the firm. Certainly one of the primary purposes of financial institutions is to facilitate the transfer of money from those with excess funds to those in need of the funds.

Just as corporate finance is not an independent world unto itself, a firm's financial decision making is not independent of other business decisions, such as marketing, location, or management structure. While the financial manager integrates the facets of finance, the firm's management must integrate financial decision making with the other functional areas of business administration. Finance is obviously a crucial component of any firm's decision-making process, but financial decisions must fit into the firm's overall strategy.

Ultimately, management's (and the financial manager's) performance must be judged. In finance, the criterion used to judge performance is the value of the firm. Management should take those actions that increase this value. Even decisions involving nonfinancial aspects of a firm's operations are judged by their impact on the value of the firm. A course of action should not be taken if it is not in the best interest of the owners of the firm (that is, if the action reduces the value of the firm).

Many firms are owned by investors (stockholders) who do not participate in management decisions. Instead corporate managers are employed by these stockholders to operate the firm. It is the value of the owners' investment that management should seek to maximize. There is, however, an obvious potential conflict, since an action by management could be in its best interest (for example, higher salaries or job security) but not in the best interests of the stockholders. Thus, stockholders and managers must find means to integrate the interests and objectives of management and owners. One means for achieving this end is to tie management compensation to the value of the firm so all actions that increase the value of the firm benefit management, employees, and stockholders.

The Role of the Financial Manager

The complex role of the financial manager has been described in the preceding chapters. For sole proprietorships, the job will probably fall into the hands of the owner. Along with other roles, such as manager, salesperson, purchaser, and bookkeeper, the owner will have to perform the many roles of the financial manager. With so many varied duties that must be performed, is it any wonder that many small firms fail? Large corporations have staffs reporting to a vice-president in charge of finance to perform the financial manager's job, but even the existence of these staffs does not guarantee that the job will be adequately performed.

What is a restatement of the financial manager's job? First, the financial manager must assure that the firm has sufficient liquidity to meet its financial obligations as they come due. Perhaps this is individually the most important facet of the financial manager's job, for the firm must survive day to day. If the firm cannot meet these current cash needs, it will have no future. Thus, it is crucial that the financial manager ensure that the firm has cash coming in to meet its bills as they come due. Of course, increased liquidity costs the firm profits, for liquid assets (cash and demand deposits) do not earn any income. The financial manager must obtain a balance between sufficient liquidity and the investment of short-term funds in income-earning assets. Successful cash management requires knowledge of the firm's liquidity needs and knowledge of the money market and the various short-term money market instruments in which excess cash may be invested.

The financial management has several techniques to help forecast the level of sales and the assets necessary to achieve the anticipated level of sales. The percent of sales method of forecasting, regression analysis, and the cash budget may be used to plan the firm's cash needs by permitting the financial manager to anticipate the firm's receipts and disbursements and its level of assets and liabilities. Such planning permits the financial manager to know when cash will be coming in and when the firm will have to seek outside sources of financing.

Besides planning tools, the financial manager may use ratios to analyze the firm's performance and financial condition. These ratios help to identify trends and to compare the firm with other firms in the industry. Liquidity ratios given an indication of the firm's ability to meet its obligations as they come due. Activity ratios show how rapidly assets flow through the firm. Leverage ratios indicate the extent to which debt is used to finance the firm, and profitability ratios rate the firm's

Financial Theory and the Nobel Memorial Prize in Economic Science

In 1990, the Nobel Prize in economics was awarded to Harry Markowitz, William Sharpe, and Merton Miller for their contributions to the theory of finance. Markowitz developed the concepts of diversification and efficient portfolios. Sharpe's contributions grew from the work of Markowitz and led to the development of the capital asset pricing model and beta as the crucial measure of risk. While today it may seem intuitively obvious that investors will make riskier investments only if they anticipate a higher return, the specification of the relationship between risk and return and making the model operational were major contributions that currently permeate both the theory and practice of finance. ¶ Merton Miller, along with Franco Modigliani who won the Nobel Price in economics in 1985, advanced the theory of the cost of capital. Modigliani and Miller demonstrated that in perfect capital markets, the earnings capacity of a firm's assets and not how the assets are financed determines the value of a firm. Taken to its logical conclusion, their theory indicates there is no optimal capital structure. If there is an optimal capital structure, it depends on such factors as taxes (for example, the deductibility of interest expense), rigidities in the capital markets (for instance, firms and investors cannot borrow at the same rate of interest), and certain costs (that is, costs associated with bankruptcy). If these real world considerations did not exist, then no optimal capital structure would exist. This startling conclusion became the theoretical underpinning that justified the junk bonds, leveraged buyouts, and takeovers of the 1980s. ¶

performance. Coverage ratios indicate ability to meet, or "cover," specific expenses, such as interest or lease payments.

Besides assuring that the firm has sufficient liquidity and that excess cash is invested in income-earning assets, the financial manager helps select long-term investments from the many alternative uses of the firm's resources. The firm cannot make every possible investment but must select among the alternatives. Methods of capital budgeting, ranging from the simple payback method to net present value and internal rate of return approaches, help determine profitable long-term investments in plant and equipment.

Investments are made in the present, but the returns accrue in the future. The future is not certain; the financial manager works in a world of uncertainty and risk. There is the risk associated with the nature of the business. Some industries require substantial amounts of fixed assets (that is, they have a high degree of operating leverage). These firms experience a greater effect from fluctuations in the industry's sales and are inherently more risky than firms in industries that require fewer fixed assets.

A second source of risk pertains to a firm's financing. All assets must be financed, and there are two sources of financing: the owners' funds or creditors' funds. A firm (or anyone) that uses creditors' funds is financially leveraged. The advantage to the firm of borrowing funds is the potential to make the creditors' funds generate sufficient revenue not only to pay the interest but also to generate additional funds that accrue to the owner. By borrowing funds and successfully using financial leverage, management increases the return on equity. The use of borrowed funds commits the firm to legal obligations that vary with such factors as the amount of the loan, the length of time the loan is outstanding, and the creditworthiness of the borrower. If the firm fails to meet the terms, the creditors can take the firm to court to enforce the obligations. Since legal obligations increase the element of risk, the financing of a firm affects both the potential return to the owner and risk.

One important role of the financial manager is to determine the firm's optimal combination of debt and equity financing. This optimal capital structure takes advantage of debt financing but does not unduly increase financial risk. By determining the optimal capital structure, the financial manager minimizes the cost of capital, the criterion by which all potential investments must be judged. A firm's cost of capital is a measure of what the funds could earn if placed in alternative investments; hence, the firm must earn at least its cost of capital to justify using these funds.

To determine the optimal capital structure, the financial manager must know the varied sources of financing and their respective costs. A firm may borrow from many sources, including commercial banks, insurance companies, trade creditors, and the general public. Securities may be privately placed with financial institutions, sold to the general public through investment bankers, or sold to current owners. The financial manager must be aware of the potential sources of finance and know when the utilization of a particular source is the best alternative for raising funds.

The Impact of Competition

No firm operates in a vacuum. All firms compete among each other for markets for their products. In many cases this competition is obvious. Exxon-Mobil and Texaco, large oil refiners, compete for the sale of gasoline and other petroleum products. Book publishers, such as Harcourt, produce textbooks such as this one that must compete against texts published by McGraw-Hill and Prentice-Hall. As competition intensifies, profit margins are squeezed and firms become less profitable.

Competition is not limited to markets for products but extends to sources of finance. Since all firms must have funds, they must compete for the available supply of debt and equity capital. As this competition intensifies, interest rates and the cost of equity rise to ration the available supply. This higher cost of capital reduces the attractiveness of some of the firm's possible investments, and the profitability of the investments that the firm does make is reduced by the higher cost of finance.

Although competition has always played a major role in a free market economy, today it is even more intense since many markets are not national, but global, in scope. Competition is not limited to domestic firms but extends to firms from many nations. GM and Ford compete with Japanese, German, and other European automobile manufacturers, such as Honda, Nissan, Toyota, Volkswagen, BMW, and Volvo.

Domestic and foreign firms also compete for financing. Securities issued by such firms as Honda or Toyota trade in the U.S. security markets in competition with the securities issued by Ford and GM. Capital will flow where returns are greatest for a given level of risk. If potential returns from foreign securities rise, individuals in the United States will not invest in domestic firms but will invest in foreign firms. In the past, foreign investors have purchased securities issued in the United States. The reverse will certainly occur if domestic investors perceive opportunities to be greater in Europe or Asia.

This flow of funds interlocks the economies of virtually all nations. A nation's supply of money and credit, domestic interest rates, and the value of its currency cannot be independent of investment opportunities and events in other countries. Without artificial barriers, isolation in today's global markets for goods and services and for financing is virtually impossible.

The Impact of Fiscal and Monetary Policy on Financial Decision Making

Besides the forces of competition, the firm is affected by national economic policy. This policy emanates from two sources: the fiscal policy of the federal government, and the monetary policy of the Federal Reserve. Fiscal policy concerns federal expenditures and taxation, and management of the national debt. Federal government expenditures may affect the firm directly if it is a government supplier. A firm may be indirectly affected by the effects of the federal government's actions on other firms and households. Federal taxation at both the corporate and individual levels impacts virtually every firm. Because all taxes are a transfer of resources from the private sector to the public sector, changes in taxation alter the resources that firms and households have to use.

Monetary policy is concerned with changes in the supply of money and the capacity of banks to lend. It affects firms by altering the cost of funds (interest rates) and the availability of credit. To the extent that monetary policy affects aggregate spending, it also alters the demand for a particular firm's output. This policy is implemented by the Federal Reserve, the nation's central bank. To carry out its goals of price stability and economic growth, the Federal Reserve has several tools of monetary policy. Of the various tools, the three most important are the reserve requirement, the discount rate, and open market operations. These tools are used to affect the reserves of banks, which alters their ability to lend.

By far the most important of these tools is open market operations. By buying government securities, the Federal Reserve expands the money supply and the lending capacity of banks, thereby increasing the supply of money in the nation. The opposite effect occurs when the Federal Reserve sells government securities; this absorbs the banks' reserves and decreases the supply of money.

Fiscal and monetary policies can have a major impact on a firm's financial health by altering both the cash flow from investments and the cost of funds. To some extent the financial manager may be able to anticipate particular actions by the federal government and the Federal Reserve and take steps to insulate the firm from effects. The firm may obtain funds during periods of lower interest rates by issuing long-term debt securities and investing the money in short-term assets, such as Treasury bills. The bills can then be converted into cash as funds are needed. If the financial manager anticipates future increases in the cost of credit, it may be desirable to issue long-term securities now, for such an action locks in the current interest rate.

Even if financial managers are unable to anticipate national economic policy, they certainly will react to it. Of course, much of this policy is designed to induce particular behavior. For example, accelerated depreciation is designed to induce spending on capital equipment by increasing the cash flow from the investment. High interest rates are designed to discourage investment spending by increasing the cost of capital. Financial managers incorporate these policy changes into the analyses they perform and respond accordingly. If a financial manager fails to react to changes in national economic policy, this may hurt the firm and reduce its value.

THE PURPOSE OF THIS TEXT REVISITED

A large proportion of finance is concerned with the creation of wealth. Investment in plant and equipment generates new facilities, which are used to manufacture new products. Investment in developing services, such as computer programs, also leads to new output. In either case, goods or services, the result of the investment is the creation of new wealth.

The process of creating new wealth also leads to the creation of financial claims. Claims are issued by firms (and governments and individuals) to raise funds to finance the production of goods and services. Savers acquire these debt and equity obligations (that is, bonds and stocks). Without the creation of financial claims, the creation of wealth would not occur. If savers did not buy stocks, bonds, and other debt obligations, savings would not be channeled into productive uses.

For investors, financial claims are assets. Many financial assets, such as corporate stocks and bonds, are easily transferred through secondary markets, such as the New York Stock Exchange. Although finance is obviously concerned with the creation of wealth, it is also concerned with the transfer of securities. Without secondary markets and the ability to buy and sell securities (that is, to transfer wealth), many individuals would not invest their savings. Without that investment, the economy's ability to create wealth would be diminished.

This ability to approach finance either from a business perspective (the creation of wealth) or from an investor's perspective (the valuation of assets, portfolio construction, and the transfer of wealth) differentiates the study of finance from other business disciplines. Business disciplines such as management and marketing are approached solely from a business perspective. Finance, however, has a business perspective and an individual's perspective. It has relevance to individuals who may not pursue careers in business or who may not continue the study of business.

Since an initial course may be a student's only exposure to a discipline, this text serves as an introduction to the three facets of finance: financial institutions, investments, and business finance. The text lays the foundation for further study in each. Students who specialize in finance will encounter the material at greater depth and at a higher level of sophistication in more advanced courses.

Many students, who do not continue their study of finance, will encounter finance as part of their private lives. Individuals use financial leverage when they borrow funds to finance purchases ranging from consumer goods to homes. Households manage cash to have funds to meet bills as they come due. Individuals save for various purposes, such as financing a child's education or providing for retirement. They must decide where to invest these savings and construct a portfolio of assets.

As these illustrations suggest, the content and analytical techniques used in finance permeate life. While the study of managerial finance should contribute to a successful business career, the study of financial institutions and investments should also contribute to an increased ability to manage personal resources. This increased knowledge and understanding of finance should help all individuals better meet their financial needs and goals.

Review Questions

1. How would each of the following mergers be classified?
   a. Ford and Honda
   b. The Limited and VF Corp (a manufacturer of clothing)
   c. Viacom and U.S. Steel

2. What is the tax implication of accepting stock instead of cash when you tender (sell) your stock in a merger?

3. How may management fight an unsolicited or hostile takeover?

4. What differentiates a carve out from a spin-off?

5. In finance, what is the specific goal of management?

6. Why should the financial manager be concerned with determining the firm's optimal capital structure?

7. Day-to-day financial decisions are concerned with the management of short-term assets and short-term liabilities. Why is this management of working capital so important? Why may liquidity reduce profitability?

8. How may economic policy affect financial decision making? Why may anticipating changes in economic policy be crucial to a firm's success?

9. Many firms fail because of poor financial management. Now that you have completed this text, could you explain why this statement is true?

APPENDIX A

Interest Factors for the Future Value of One Dollar: $FVIF = (1 + i)^n$

Time period (e.g., year)	1%	2%	3%	4%	5%	6%	7%	8%	9%	10%	12%	14%	15%	16%	18%	20%
1	1.010	1.020	1.030	1.040	1.050	1.060	1.070	1.080	1.090	1.100	1.120	1.140	1.150	1.160	1.180	1.200
2	1.020	1.040	1.061	1.082	1.102	1.124	1.145	1.166	1.188	1.210	1.254	1.300	1.322	1.346	1.392	1.440
3	1.030	1.061	1.093	1.125	1.158	1.191	1.225	1.260	1.295	1.331	1.405	1.482	1.521	1.561	1.643	1.728
4	1.041	1.082	1.126	1.170	1.216	1.262	1.311	1.360	1.412	1.464	1.574	1.689	1.749	1.811	1.939	2.074
5	1.051	1.104	1.159	1.217	1.276	1.338	1.403	1.469	1.539	1.611	1.762	1.925	2.011	2.100	2.288	2.488
6	1.062	1.126	1.194	1.265	1.340	1.419	1.501	1.587	1.677	1.772	1.974	2.195	2.313	2.436	2.697	2.986
7	1.072	1.149	1.230	1.316	1.407	1.504	1.606	1.714	1.828	1.949	2.211	2.502	2.660	2.826	3.186	3.583
8	1.083	1.172	1.267	1.369	1.477	1.594	1.718	1.851	1.993	2.144	2.476	2.853	3.059	3.278	3.759	4.300
9	1.094	1.195	1.305	1.423	1.551	1.689	1.838	1.999	2.172	2.358	2.773	3.252	3.518	3.803	4.436	5.160
10	1.105	1.219	1.344	1.480	1.629	1.791	1.967	2.159	2.367	2.594	3.106	3.707	4.046	4.411	5.234	6.192
11	1.116	1.243	1.384	1.539	1.710	1.898	2.105	2.332	2.580	2.853	3.479	4.226	4.652	5.117	6.176	7.430
12	1.127	1.268	1.426	1.601	1.796	2.012	2.252	2.518	2.813	3.138	3.896	4.818	5.350	5.936	7.287	8.916
13	1.138	1.294	1.469	1.665	1.886	2.133	2.410	2.720	3.066	3.452	4.363	5.492	6.153	6.886	8.599	10.699
14	1.149	1.319	1.513	1.732	1.980	2.261	2.579	2.937	3.342	3.797	4.887	6.261	7.076	7.988	10.147	12.839
15	1.161	1.346	1.558	1.801	2.079	2.397	2.759	3.172	3.642	4.177	5.474	7.138	8.137	9.266	11.973	15.407
16	1.173	1.373	1.605	1.873	2.183	2.540	2.952	3.426	3.970	4.595	6.130	8.137	9.358	10.748	14.129	18.488
17	1.184	1.400	1.653	1.948	2.292	2.693	3.159	3.700	4.328	5.054	6.866	9.276	10.761	12.468	16.672	22.186
18	1.196	1.428	1.702	2.026	2.407	2.854	3.380	3.996	4.717	5.560	7.690	10.575	12.375	14.463	19.673	26.623
19	1.208	1.457	1.754	2.107	2.527	3.026	3.617	4.316	5.142	6.116	8.613	12.056	14.232	16.777	23.214	31.948
20	1.220	1.486	1.806	2.191	2.653	3.207	3.870	4.661	5.604	6.728	9.646	13.743	16.367	19.461	27.393	38.337
25	1.282	1.641	2.094	2.666	3.386	4.292	5.427	6.848	8.623	10.835	17.000	26.462	32.919	40.874	62.688	95.396
30	1.348	1.811	2.427	3.243	4.322	5.743	7.612	10.063	13.268	17.449	29.960	50.950	66.212	85.850	143.370	237.370

APPENDIX B

Interest Factors for the Present Value of One Dollar: $PVIF = 1/(1 + i)^n$

Time period (e.g., year)	1%	2%	3%	4%	5%	6%	7%	8%	9%	10%	12%	14%	15%	16%	18%	20%	24%	28%
1	.990	.980	.971	.962	.952	.943	.935	.926	.917	.909	.893	.877	.870	.862	.847	.833	.806	.781
2	.980	.961	.943	.925	.907	.890	.873	.857	.842	.826	.797	.769	.756	.743	.718	.694	.650	.610
3	.971	.942	.915	.889	.864	.840	.816	.794	.772	.751	.712	.675	.658	.641	.609	.579	.524	.477
4	.961	.924	.889	.855	.823	.792	.763	.735	.708	.683	.636	.592	.572	.552	.516	.482	.423	.373
5	.951	.906	.863	.822	.784	.747	.713	.681	.650	.621	.567	.519	.497	.476	.437	.402	.341	.291
6	.942	.888	.838	.790	.746	.705	.666	.630	.596	.564	.507	.456	.432	.410	.370	.335	.275	.227
7	.933	.871	.813	.760	.711	.665	.623	.583	.547	.513	.452	.400	.376	.354	.314	.279	.222	.178
8	.923	.853	.789	.731	.677	.627	.582	.540	.502	.467	.404	.351	.327	.305	.266	.233	.179	.139
9	.914	.837	.766	.703	.645	.592	.544	.500	.460	.424	.361	.308	.284	.263	.226	.194	.144	.108
10	.905	.820	.744	.676	.614	.558	.508	.463	.422	.386	.322	.270	.247	.227	.191	.162	.116	.085
11	.896	.804	.722	.650	.585	.527	.475	.429	.388	.350	.287	.237	.215	.195	.162	.135	.094	.066
12	.887	.788	.701	.625	.557	.497	.444	.397	.356	.319	.257	.208	.187	.168	.137	.112	.076	.052
13	.879	.773	.681	.601	.530	.469	.415	.368	.326	.290	.229	.182	.163	.145	.116	.093	.061	.040
14	.870	.758	.661	.577	.505	.442	.388	.340	.299	.263	.205	.160	.141	.125	.099	.078	.049	.032
15	.861	.743	.642	.555	.481	.417	.362	.315	.275	.239	.183	.140	.123	.108	.084	.065	.040	.025
16	.853	.728	.623	.534	.458	.394	.339	.292	.252	.218	.163	.123	.107	.093	.071	.054	.032	.019
17	.844	.714	.605	.513	.436	.371	.317	.270	.231	.198	.146	.108	.093	.080	.060	.045	.026	.015
18	.836	.700	.587	.494	.416	.350	.296	.250	.212	.180	.130	.095	.081	.069	.051	.038	.021	.012
19	.828	.686	.570	.475	.396	.331	.276	.232	.194	.164	.116	.083	.070	.060	.043	.031	.017	.009
20	.820	.673	.554	.456	.377	.312	.258	.215	.178	.149	.104	.073	.061	.051	.037	.026	.014	.007
25	.780	.610	.478	.375	.295	.233	.184	.146	.116	.092	.059	.038	.030	.024	.016	.010	.005	.002
30	.742	.552	.412	.308	.231	.174	.131	.099	.075	.057	.033	.020	.015	.012	.007	.004	.002	.001

APPENDIX C

Interest Factors for the Future Value of an Annuity of One Dollar:

$$FVAIF = \frac{(1 + i)^n - 1}{i}$$

Time period (e.g., year)	1%	2%	3%	4%	5%	6%	7%	8%	9%	10%	12%	14%	16%	20%
1	1.000	1.000	1.000	1.000	1.000	1.000	1.000	1.000	1.000	1.000	1.000	1.000	1.000	1.000
2	2.010	2.020	2.030	2.040	2.050	2.060	2.070	2.080	2.090	2.100	2.120	2.140	2.160	2.200
3	3.030	3.060	3.091	3.122	3.152	3.184	3.215	3.246	3.278	3.310	3.374	3.440	3.506	3.640
4	4.060	4.122	4.184	4.246	4.310	4.375	4.440	4.506	4.573	4.641	4.770	4.921	5.067	5.368
5	5.101	5.204	5.309	5.416	5.526	5.637	5.751	5.867	5.985	6.105	6.353	6.610	6.877	7.442
6	6.152	6.308	6.468	6.633	6.802	6.975	7.153	7.336	7.523	7.716	8.115	8.536	8.978	9.930
7	7.214	7.434	7.662	7.898	8.142	8.394	8.654	8.923	9.200	9.487	10.089	10.730	11.413	12.915
8	8.286	8.583	8.892	9.214	9.549	9.897	10.260	10.637	11.028	11.436	12.300	13.233	14.240	16.499
9	9.369	9.755	10.159	10.583	11.027	11.491	11.978	12.488	13.021	13.579	14.776	16.085	17.518	20.798
10	10.462	10.950	11.464	12.006	12.578	13.181	13.816	14.487	15.193	15.937	17.549	19.337	21.321	25.958
11	11.567	12.169	12.808	13.486	14.207	14.972	15.784	16.645	17.560	18.531	20.655	23.044	25.732	32.150
12	12.683	13.412	14.192	15.026	15.917	16.870	17.888	18.977	20.141	21.384	24.138	27.271	30.850	39.580
13	13.809	14.680	15.618	16.627	17.713	18.882	20.141	21.495	22.953	24.523	28.029	32.089	36.786	48.496
14	14.947	15.974	17.086	18.292	19.599	21.051	22.550	24.215	26.019	27.975	32.393	37.581	43.672	59.195
15	16.097	17.293	18.599	20.024	21.579	23.276	25.129	27.152	29.361	31.772	37.280	43.842	51.659	72.035
16	17.258	18.639	20.157	21.825	23.657	25.673	27.888	30.324	33.003	35.950	42.753	50.980	60.925	87.442
17	18.430	20.012	21.762	23.698	25.840	28.213	30.840	33.750	36.974	40.545	48.884	59.118	71.673	105.93
18	19.615	21.412	23.414	25.645	28.132	30.906	33.999	37.450	41.301	45.599	55.750	68.934	84.140	128.11
19	20.811	22.841	25.117	27.671	30.539	33.760	37.379	41.446	46.018	51.159	63.440	78.969	98.603	154.74
20	22.019	24.297	26.870	29.778	33.066	36.786	40.995	45.762	51.160	57.275	72.052	91.025	115.37	186.68
25	28.243	32.030	36.459	41.646	47.727	54.865	63.249	73.106	84.701	98.347	133.33	181.87	249.21	471.98
30	34.785	40.568	47.575	56.085	66.439	79.058	94.461	113.283	136.308	164.494	241.333	356.878	530.310	1181.8

APPENDIX D

Interest Factors for the Present Value of an Annuity of One Dollar:

$$\text{PVAIF} = \frac{1 - \frac{1}{(1+i)^n}}{i} = \frac{1-(1+i)^{-n}}{i}$$

Time period (e.g., year)	1%	2%	3%	4%	5%	6%	7%	8%	9%	10%	12%	14%	16%	18%	20%	24%	28%	32%	36%
1	0.990	0.980	0.971	0.962	0.952	0.943	0.935	0.926	0.917	0.909	0.893	0.877	0.862	0.847	0.833	0.806	0.781	0.758	0.735
2	1.970	1.942	1.913	1.886	1.859	1.833	1.808	1.783	1.759	1.736	1.690	1.647	1.605	1.566	1.528	1.457	1.392	1.332	1.276
3	2.941	2.884	2.829	2.775	2.723	2.673	2.624	2.577	2.531	2.487	2.402	2.322	2.246	2.174	2.106	1.981	1.868	1.766	1.674
4	3.902	3.808	3.717	3.630	3.546	3.465	3.387	3.312	3.240	3.170	3.037	2.914	2.798	2.690	2.589	2.404	2.241	2.096	1.966
5	4.853	4.713	4.580	4.452	4.329	4.212	4.100	3.993	3.890	3.791	3.605	3.433	3.274	3.127	2.991	2.745	2.532	2.345	2.181
6	5.795	5.601	5.417	5.242	5.076	4.917	4.766	4.623	4.486	4.355	4.111	3.889	3.685	3.498	3.326	3.020	2.759	2.534	2.399
7	6.728	6.472	6.230	6.002	5.786	5.582	5.389	5.206	5.033	4.868	4.574	4.288	4.039	3.812	3.605	3.242	2.937	2.678	2.455
8	7.652	7.325	7.020	6.733	6.463	6.210	5.971	5.747	5.535	5.335	4.968	4.639	4.344	4.078	3.837	3.421	3.076	2.786	2.540
9	8.566	8.162	7.786	7.435	7.108	6.802	6.515	6.247	5.985	5.759	5.328	4.946	4.607	4.303	4.031	3.566	3.184	2.868	2.603
10	9.471	8.983	8.530	8.111	7.722	7.360	7.024	6.710	6.418	6.145	5.650	5.216	4.833	4.494	4.193	3.682	3.269	2.930	2.650
11	10.368	9.787	9.253	8.760	8.306	7.887	7.499	7.139	6.805	6.495	5.988	5.453	5.029	4.656	4.327	3.776	3.335	2.978	2.683
12	11.255	10.575	9.954	9.385	8.863	8.384	7.943	7.536	7.161	6.814	6.194	5.660	5.197	4.793	4.439	3.851	3.387	3.013	2.708
13	12.134	11.348	10.635	9.986	9.394	8.534	8.358	7.904	7.487	7.103	6.424	5.842	5.342	4.910	4.533	3.912	3.427	3.040	2.727
14	13.004	12.106	11.296	10.563	9.899	9.295	8.745	8.244	7.786	7.367	6.628	6.002	5.468	5.008	4.611	3.962	3.459	3.061	2.740
15	13.865	12.849	11.938	11.118	10.380	9.712	9.108	8.559	8.060	7.606	6.811	6.142	5.575	5.092	4.675	4.001	3.483	3.076	2.750
16	14.718	13.578	12.561	11.652	10.838	10.106	9.447	8.851	8.312	7.824	6.974	6.265	5.669	5.162	4.730	4.003	3.503	3.088	2.758
17	15.562	14.292	13.166	12.166	11.274	10.477	9.763	9.122	8.544	8.002	7.120	6.373	5.749	5.222	4.775	4.059	3.518	3.097	2.763
18	16.398	14.992	13.754	12.659	11.690	10.828	10.059	9.372	8.756	8.201	7.250	6.467	5.818	5.273	4.812	4.080	3.529	3.104	2.767
19	17.226	15.678	14.324	13.134	12.085	11.158	10.336	9.604	8.950	8.365	7.366	6.550	5.877	5.316	4.844	4.097	3.539	3.109	2.770
20	18.046	16.351	14.877	13.590	12.462	11.470	10.594	9.818	9.128	8.514	7.469	6.623	5.929	5.353	4.870	4.110	3.546	3.113	2.772
25	22.023	19.523	17.413	15.622	14.094	12.783	11.654	10.675	9.823	9.077	7.843	6.873	6.097	5.467	4.948	4.147	3.564	3.122	2.776
30	25.808	22.937	19.600	17.292	15.373	13.765	12.409	11.258	10.274	9.427	8.055	7.003	6.177	5.517	4.979	4.160	3.569	3.124	2.778

APPENDIX E
Answers to Selected Problems

Chapter 5

1. 0.667 pounds
2. $75,000 gain
3. 6.2% premium
4. balance on the current account ($1.7)
   balance on the capital account ($16.5)
6. *a.* payment in terms of the current price: $1,600,000
   b. payment in terms of the futures price: $1,560,000
   c. loss =.($250,000)
   d. $40,000

Chapter 6

1. margin = 25%: amount invested: $1,250; return: 80%
2. margin = 75%: amount invested: $3,750; return: (26.7%)
3. *a.* loss: $3.50
   b. gain: $3.50
4. at $49 a share, loss = 500 × $7 = $3,500
5. interest expense: $275.40
   return: 69.8%
6. *a.* required investment: $11,500 × .55 = $6,325
   b. interest paid: $517.50
7. $2 loss
8. initial investment: $3,600
   necessary increase: $2.25 a share

Chapter 7

Answers to time value of money problems may be derived using interest tables, financial calculators, or computer software. Since interest tables are rounded off, answers derived using the tables may differ from answers derived by using calculators or computers. Use common sense. If the answer is $13,467 using the tables and $13,487 using a financial calculator, the difference is probably the result of rounding, and either answered may be considered "correct."

1. *a.* interest: $629
b. interest: $500

2. *a.* 3 years

3. a. $219,318
b. $120,531
c. $17,671

4. total accumulated: $102,320; annual withdrawal: $11,210

5. Your account: $157,751

6. $2,421

7. No; she can withdraw $14,491.

8. Overvalued ($90,770)

9. PVA: $4,262; Yes
PVB: $3,936; No

10. *b.* $216,100

11. *a.* $29.38
b. $42.00

12. 9%

13. 15%

14. $10,000

15. at 6%, select the $900; at 14%, select the $150 for 5 years

16. annual payment: $8,312.65

17. $45,695 (using interest tables)

18. approximately 12 percent (12.25%)

19. 13+ years

20. $14,238

21. total value: $42,935

22. select A

23. $990,450; 6%

24. 6.4% (between 6 and 7 percent)

25. mortgage payment: $10,180
principal repayment (first year): $1,180

26. approximately 7 percent (6.9%)

27. annuity payments are preferred
28. 16.5%
29. return: 10% (9.84%)
30. your withdrawals: $60,792
your twin's withdrawals: $51,984

Chapter 7 Appendix

1. Bob: $91,524
Betty: $98,846
2. B: $6,253; select B
3. annuity due: $16,560
ordinary annuity: $15,193
4. at 5%: present value of the ordinary annuity: $7,723
present value of the annuity due: $7,623
at 10%: present value of the ordinary annuity: $6,145
present value of the annuity due: $6,354

Chapter 8

1. 4.4%
3. *a.* 12.5%
4. 10.3%
5. *a.* average return investment Y: 18%
b. standard deviation investment Y: 2.55
6. realized return: 3.25%
8. Stock A: 4%
9. 1.5
10. 13.1%

Chapter 9

1. *a.* coupon: 6%
b. current yield: 6.7%
c. yield to maturity: 8.8%
2. current yield: 8%; yield to maturity: 8%
3. *a.* $864
b. $919
e. current yield in (a): 6.94% and 6.53%
yield to maturity in (a): 8% in both cases

4. *a.* 7.25%
   b. 10%
   c. \$810 (if semiannual payments: \$807)
5. *b.* \$919
   d. \$1,112
8. *a.* Bond A: \$1,000
   Bond B: \$729
   b. Bond A: \$1,000
   Bond B: \$873
10. *a.* \$313
    d. 12%
    f. 75%
    h. \$39,795
11. 4.67%
12. Tax rate of 25%: select the corporate bond (5.175% versus 5.1%)

Chapter 10

1. EPS: \$1.38 before the split
   Price of stock: \$20 after the split
2. cumulative voting: 4,000 votes
3. *a.* new price of the stock: \$45
   b. payout ratio before the split: 52.6%
4. *a.* cash: \$26,000,000
   retained earnings: \$60,000,000
   paid-in capital: no change
   common stock: no change
   b. cash: \$28,000,000
   common stock: (2,100,000 shares; \$50 par) \$105,000,000
   paid-in capital: \$15,000,000
   retained earnings: \$52,000,000
   c. cash: \$28,000,000
   common stock: (1,000,000 shares; \$100 par) \$100,000,000
   paid-in capital: \$10,000,000
   retained earnings: \$62,000,000
7. earnings per share: \$2.10
   total equity: no change
   long-term debt: no change
   paid-in capital: no change
   shares outstanding: 2,000,000
   earnings: \$4,200,000 (no change)
8. times-dividend-earned for X 1: 5.0
9. *a.* new price: \$18
   retained earnings: \$200,000

b. new price: $49.09
retained earnings: $178,400

Chapter 11

1. at 13%: $69.23

2. a. $114.29
b. $110.55

3. *b.* $83

4. loss: preferred stock: $333
bond: $193

5. *a.* $53
b. $79.50
c. $141.33
d. $34.76
e. $39.87

6. $77

7. *a.* stock A: $15.29 < $23
b. 11.65%
c. stock A: $14

8. 17.6%

9. *a.* 12.2%
c. $80 > $76.94

10. *a.* $45.65
c. $35
e. $63.93

11. *a.* stock A: 12.56%
f. neither

12. stock A: $55.26
stock B: $30.98

13. $22

Chapter 12

1. Income statement:

Sales	$1,000,000
Cost of goods sold	600,000
Other expenses	100,000
EBIT	300,000
Interest	80,000
EBT	220,000
Taxes	100,000
Net earnings	$ 120,000
Earnings per share	$1.20

Balance Sheet:

Assets	
cash	$ 50,000
accounts receivable	250,000
inventory	300,000
plant and equipment	400,000
Total assets	$1,000,000
Liabilities	
accounts payable	$ 200,000
other current liabilities	50,000
long-term debt	300,000
Equity	450,000
Liabilities & equity	$1,000,000

2. earnings per share: $2.48

4. Accounts receivable before allowance: $1,340,000
Total current assets: $2,980,000
Accumulated depreciation: $690,000
Long-term debt: $0
Retained earnings: $2,440,000

5. current ratio: 1.8:1.0
quick ratio: 0.9:1.0

6. Return on assets: 26%
a. sales: $1,666,667
c. total asset turnover: 1.53

7. *b.* total assets: $1,086,957
d. total debt: $489,131
e. return on equity: 42%

8. $3,167,137

9. *a.* receivables turnover: 7
c. overdue by twenty-two days

10. reduction in inventory: $75,000

11. $48,333 saved

12. return on equity: 38.6%

13. operating profit margin A: 15%
net profit margin A: 8%
return on assets A: 8%
return on equity A: 13.3%

14. return on total equity: 11.7%
return on common equity: 12.2%

15. times-interest-earned issue C: 0.7

16. inventory turnovers: 3.25 and 2.7

17. inventory turnover: 10 times a year

18. Summary for 20X0

current ratio	3.9:1
quick ratio	0.5:1
average collection period	1 day
inventory turnover (Sales/Inventory)	4.0
operating profit margin	9.9%
net profit margin	5.1%
return on assets	14.7%
return on equity	20.9%
debt ratio	29.8%
times-interest-earned	10.3X

Chapter 13

1. *b.* $3
c. $2

2. *a.* at the price of the stock = $35, the buy makes $2
b. at the price of the stock = $40, the seller makes $3

3. *a.* $4
b. $4
c. increases
d. $8
e. $8
f. ($8)
g. $8
h. $3
i. $3

4. *a.* $1
b. $4
c. declines
d. $5
e. unlimited
f. $1
g. ($1)
h. ($5)
i. $5

5. *a.* intrinsic value: $1
time premium: $3
b. value of the warrant if stock is $20: $0
value of the warrant if stock is $40: $15
c. return on the warrant: 400%

6. *a.* $2,500
b. $29,400
c. 11.8%
d. (12%)
e. (100%)

7. *a.* 4.8%
   b. $864
   c. $38.52
   d. $176
   e. $817
   f. $223
   g. nil
8. *a.* $726
   b. 40 shares
   c. $1,200
   d. $1,200
   f. $1,040

Chapter 14

1. $7.83
2. 6.8%
3. 19.95%
4. compound return: 10.8%
5. 17.6% and 11.0%
6. individual's return: 8.6%
   fund's return: 15%
7. 24.8%

Chapter 15

1. *a.* $250
   b. $250
   c. $250
   d. $0
   e. $250
2. $22,500
3. average tax rate: 32.9%
4. straightline depreciation: $10,000
   accelerated depreciation year two: $18,000
5. $63,750
6. cash flow year 2 straight-line: $9,500
7. $9,000 refund
8. Tax refund: $30,000
9. *a.* tax in year 4: $1,300
   b. tax in year 1: $250 refunded

Chapter 16

1. *a.* profit at 2,000: $4,600
   b. 1,132 units
   c. 1,887 units
2. *a.* 2,500 and 3,125
   b. $3,000
3. *a.* 8,000 units
   $500 earnings
4. *a.* earnings: $50,000
   b. 100,000
   c. 62,500
   e. 14,286
5. *a.* 5.95%
   b. 9.9%
   c. 11.3%
   d. 9.3575%
6. cost of retained earnings: 12.55%
   cost of new stock: 13.04%
7. *a.* cost of capital at 40% debt; 12.0%
   b. debt $20; equity $80
8. cost of capital at 20% debt: 7.2%
   cost of capital at 40% debt: 8.4%
9. *a.* 30% debt; 70% equity
   b. excessive
   d. stockholders earn 12.86%

Chapter 16 Appendix

1. *a.* 3,000 units
   b. degree of operating leverage at 5,000 units: 2.5
   d. 3,333 units
   degree of operating leverage at 5,000 units: 3.0
2. *a.* $83,330
   b. operating income at 10,000 units: $10,000
   c. degree of operating leverage: 3.27
3. *a.* EPS: $3.78
   degree of financial leverage: 2.78
   new EPS: $7.28
4. degree of operating leverage: 1.39
   degree of financial leverage: 1.30
   total leverage: 1.81

5. *c.* 56% decrease
6. *b.* earnings A: $3,000
   earnings B: $2,500
   d. firm A: 50%
   firm b: 60%

Chapter 17

1. 8%
2. *a.* NPVA: $33
   NPVB: $17
   b. IRRA: approximately 14% (14.7%)
   IRRB: 12%
3. *a.* NPVA: ($165)
   NPVB: $333
   c. IRRA: 5%
   IRRB: 20%
   f. at 10%: $4,356
   at 14%: $4,669
4. at 9%: select B
   at 14%: select neither
5. *a.* NPVA: ($51)
   NPVC: $108
   b. IRRA: 9%
   IRRC: 24%
   c. at 15%: $1,887
6. NPV: ($6,315)
7. when cost of capital = 12%, NPV = ($177)
8. 8%
9. *a.* IRR: 16%
   b. at 16%: terminal value : $156,101
10. *a.* debt: 40%
    b. equity: $300
    c. 20%
    d. liabilities: $360
    e. 30%
11. a. select S
    b. select Q
    c. at 20%: $2,072.25
    at 10%: $1,791.42
12. *a.* NPVA: $75.25
    b. IRRB: 12%
    d. no

13. *a.* NPV: $24,096
IRR: 18%
b. $29,939
$30,306

14. NPV: $5,160

15. cash inflow: years 1 and 2: $60,400
year 5: $51,650
cash outflow: $190,000

Chapter 18

1. PV: $30,265

2. *a.* NPVA: $631
b. NPVA: $631
NPVB: ($141.50)
NPVC: $438.80

3. *a.* NPV: $93,778
b. NPV: ($4,305)

4. cash inflows years 1–4: $45,800
cash inflow year 5: $545,800

5. cash inflows years 1–9: $47,000
cash inflow year 10: $77,000

6. *a.* $500,000
b. interest savings: $160,000
savings after amoritization: $120,000
c. increase in cash flow: $124,000
d. NPV: $116,032

Chapter 19

1. *a.*

accounts receivable	$300
inventory	600
trade accounts payable	300

b. external funds needed: $50

c.

accounts receivable	$ 300
inventory	600
plant	800
total assets	1,700
trade accounts	300
long-term debt	650
equity	750
total liabilities and equity	1,700

2. *a.*

accounts receivable	$9,000
inventory	$7,625
accounts payable	$6,625

b. expansion in accounts payable: $1,325
c. increase in retained earnings: $3,000

d. cash ($1,000 + excess funds of $1,000)	$ 2,000
accounts receivable	9,000
inventory	7,625
accounts payable	6,625

3.

a. accounts receivable	$12,060
inventory	9,264
accounts payable	6,829

b. increase in accounts payable: $1,529
c. increase in retained earnings: $3,000
d. cash: $1,000
total assets: $26,524

4.

cash	$30,000
accounts receivable	60,000
inventory	90,000
accounts payable	18,000
accruals	24,000
increase in retained earnings	67,500

5. excess cash (shortage):

January	($120)
February	($220)
March	($ 40)
April	($240)
May	$160
June	$100

6. Total receipts January: $700,000
February: $880,000
Ending cash position January: ($88,000)
February: ($128,000)

7. *b.* external funds needed: $8,027
c. $1,875 reduction
d. retained earnings increase by $32,813
e. total assets: $253,125
(answer may be different as result of rounding)

8. *a.* external funds needed 20X1: ($52,000)
20X2: $1,906,000
b. maximum increase in retained earnings: $1,820,000
c. current ratio < 2:1
d. external funds needed 20X1: $188,000
20X2: $1,946,000
e. current ratio < 2:1

9. cash shortage February: $75,000
March: $105,000
ending cash position April: $15,000
excess cash April: $5,000

10. cash $ 4,200
    marketable securities 0
    accounts receivable 21,420
    inventory 23,980
    plant & equipment 51,000

cash	$ 4,200
marketable securities	0
accounts receivable	21,420
inventory	23,980
plant & equipment	51,000

Chapter 20

1. *a.* earnings with bank loan: $259,000
   earnings with insurance company loan: $238,000
   b. earnings year 2 with bank loan at 4 percent: $273,000
   earnings year 2 with insurance company loan: $238,000
2. *a.* return on equity—alternative a: 9.6%
   return on equity—alternative b: 14.8%
   return on equity—alternative c: 12.8%
   b. return on equity—alternative a: 6.0%
   return on equity—alternative b: 7.6%
   return on equity—alternative c: 6.8%
3. *a.* 120 units
   b. 9 days (42 orders per year)
   c. 167 units
4. *a.* 1,549 units
   b. 1,074.5 units
   c. 1,849 units
   d. 19
5. interest saved: $9,722
6. collection expense: $5,000
   bad debt expense: $8,750
   carrying costs: $2,083
7. $18,720
8. As of January 1: accounts not overdue: 24.1%
   20–30 days overdue: 31.7%
9. tax savings: $9,600
10. *a.* supplier A: 368 units
    supplier B: 316 units
    b. average inventory supplier A: 284
    c. maximum inventory supplier A: 468
    minimum inventory supplier A: 100 (or 0 if safety stock is completely used)
    d. 212 units
11. *a.* 5,000 units
    b. approximately January 16
    c. maximum safety stock: 2,740 units

d. maximum inventory: 7,740
minimum inventory: 2,740
average inventory: 5,240
e. EOQ: 7,071 units

12. additional sales: $1,000,000
total costs: $775,000

13. 9.17%

Chapter 21

1. 10.3%

2. interest payment: $65,000(.1)(4/12) = $2,167
origination fee: $3,250
amount received after the discount: $59,583
simple interest rate: 10.9%

3. simple interest rate: 15%
compound rate: 15.96%

4. commercial paper: 10.5%

6. *a.* 37.1% (compounded: 44.9%)
b. 36.7% (compounded: 44.6%)

7. 0%

9. 2.37% (compounded: 2.42%)

10. commercial paper: 10.53%
commercial bank: 10.20%

11. *a.* Bank A: 8%
Bank B: 6.73%
b. Bank A: 9.5%
Bank B: 6.73%

12. *a.* 9.09%
b. 12.12%

13. payment on day 50: 18.4% (compounded: 20.2%)

15. Annual payment: $24,390.24 ($24,389.07 using a financial calculator)
year 1 principal repayment: $24,390 − $7,000 = $17,390

16. *a.* annual payment: $2,637.83
answers for year 3:
interest payment: $656.06
principal repayment: $1,981.77
balance owed: $4,578.79
c. answers for year 3:
interest payment: $600
principal repayment: $0
balance owed: $10,000

19. $23,093

INDEX

The **bold** entries refer to the page on which the term is defined in the margin notes. While the definition usually occurs the first time the word is used, there are instances in which a term cross-references prior to the marginal definition.

D

S

T